Intellectual Property Law
for Engineers and Scientists

Intellectual Property Law for Engineers and Scientists

Howard B. Rockman
Adjunct Professor of Engineering
University of Illinois at Chicago

Adjunct Professor of Intellectual Property Law
John Marshall Law School, Chicago

Intellectual Property Attorney
Barnes & Thornburg, Chicago

A UIC/Novellus Systems Endeavor

IEEE Antennas and Propagation Society, *Sponsor*

IEEE PRESS

A JOHN WILEY & SONS, INC., PUBLICATION

Published by John Wiley & Sons, Inc., Hoboken, New Jersey.
Published simultaneously in Canada.

For general information on our other products and services please contact our Customer Care Department within the U.S. at 877-762-2974, outside the U.S. at 317-572-3993 or fax 317-572-4002.

Wiley also publishes its books in a variety of electronic formats. Some content that appears in print, however, may not be available in electronic format.

Library of Congress Cataloging-in-Publication Data is available.

ISBN 0-471-44998-9

Printed in the United States of America.

10 9 8 7 6 5 4 3

"Ingenuity should receive a liberal encouragement."

"The first thing we do, let's kill all the lawyers."

William Shakespeare
2 Henry VI, Act IV, Scene II

Contents

Foreword

A few years ago, I contacted Mr. Howard B. Rockman, a patent attorney, and asked him to develop a graduate-level course in Engineering Law to be offered on the Internet to all students enrolled in our Master of Engineering web-based degree program, as well as to senior undergraduates in all fields of engineering. That course was very successful, and a follow-up course in Intellectual Property Law quickly followed. It soon became clear that no satisfactory textbook existed for this second course, hence I convinced Mr. Rockman to write such a textbook and put him in touch with the publications office of the Institute of Electrical and Electronics Engineers, Inc. (IEEE).

The IEEE Press and John Wiley & Sons decided to publish Mr. Rockman's manuscript, whose first edition is here presented to all practicing and student engineers and scientists who have an interest in intellectual property. I am convinced that this timely book will be very well received and will be very useful to both technical and legal personnel not only in the United States, but worldwide.

Piergiorgio L. E. Uslenghi, Ph.D.
Professor and Associate Dean
College of Engineering
University of Illinois at Chicago

Preface

THE PROPER PERSPECTIVE—A FABLE

After a long and productive life on earth, an engineer arrived at the gates of heaven. The gatekeeper scanned through the book of expected arrivals, and then advised the engineer that there was a mistake and that he was supposed to go to the "other place." The engineer was directed by the gatekeeper to a long escalator, and told to take the escalator all the way down, where he would be greeted by someone in a red suit. The engineer did what he was told, and ended up in Hades.

After being in Hades for a short while, the engineer noticed that it was uncomfortably hot. Being that he had been a heating, ventilating and airconditioning (HVAC) engineer on earth, he began assembling various parts of scrap materials lying around, and in a matter of three weeks, had constructed and was operating an air conditioning system throughout Hades. A week later, he had completed a cold water delivery system. Shortly thereafter, God and the devil were on the phone for their monthly status conference call, and the devil stated: "You wouldn't believe! We have an engineer down here, of all people. He's installed air conditioning and cold water down here; he's done great things. It's almost livable down here now." God replied: "You have an engineer down there? That's a horrible mistake! You have to send him up here right away!"

"No!" said the devil. "He's doing wonderful things down here, and I love him a lot!"

God said: "You send him up here right away!"

"No!" retorted the devil.

"You send him up here immediately, or I'll sue you," responded God.

The devil said: "You're bluffing."

"What do you mean, I'm bluffing!" said God.

The devil replied: "Where are you going to get a lawyer?"

OVERTURE

Having thus established the appropriate relationship between technology and the law, the material in this book pertains to protection afforded by the law to ideas, creations and inventions of engineers, scientists and others covered by the umbrella term "technology professionals." With technological advancements moving forward today at what appears to be an exponential rate, the need to transform intangible novel ideas into tangible, protectable assets has increased. Where in the past, the word "patent" or "copyright" only rarely appeared in the daily newspapers, today the popular press is repeatedly relating news items regarding the effect of intellectual property protection in our everyday lives. For example, pharmaceuticals and patents have become a global issue. Also, each time you install a new program on your computer, or open the shrink wrap on a package containing software, you must "agree" to respect the intellectual property rights of the creator of the software.

The fields of science and engineering have, and always have had, a direct correlation to the work of intellectual property attorneys and agents throughout the world. In case you're wondering, the term "intellectual property attorney" encompasses all of us who practice in the areas of patent, copyright, trade secret, trademark and unfair competition law, and their related fields, as included in this text. For example, I have been counseling and dealing with engineers, scientists and other creative types for over 40 years, and throughout this period, I have constantly worked with the interface between technology and the law that, for the most part, defines "intellectual property creation and protection."

The one thing that has been evident to me throughout my practice is that the engineers and scientists I have worked with have wonderful educations and experience in the technology field in which they toil. However, practically each time I have advised an inventor or creator of the steps to be taken to protect their new invention or novel creation, I found myself describing the law to them from the beginning. Since an inventor or creator may actually lose rights in their intellectual property before deciding whether to obtain protection or not, I came to an understanding that technology professionals should at least have a handy resource available to obtain general knowledge about intellectual property law before they complete their inventions and creations, so as to avoid taking steps that would cause the loss of all or mostly all intellectual property rights before they have the opportunity to reap the rewards of their creative work.

As an adjunct faculty professor at the College of Engineering of the University of Illinois at Chicago, I prepared a course entitled "Intellectual Property Law for Engineers and Scientists," which was and is taught as part of the Master of Engineering degree program offered totally over the Internet. I prepared fifteen weekly lectures of one-half to one-hour duration. The lectures are delivered orally to students who enroll in the course as a voice-over to a slide presentation depicting highlights of each lecture. In addition, the entirety of each lecture is posted on our web site, on a week-by-week basis, and can be downloaded, printed and used to follow the audio presentation. My ad libs, some anecdotes, and poor attempts at humor forming the audio broadcast are not included in the written text. From the assignment answers submitted by the students, I can perceive a keen interest in the subjects covered in our course, and enrollment in the course keeps increasing.

Professor George Uslenghi, Associate Dean of the College of Engineering at UIC suggested that the series of lectures that I prepared, with augmentation, be prepared as a draft manuscript and submitted for publication. Professor Uslenghi determined that a proper background in intellectual property modalities was becoming increasingly important for an engineer and scientist to have an awareness of. To make a long story into a saga, the result of the Professor's suggestion is this text.

I don't expect that this text will be read from cover to cover. The table of contents and index have been carefully crafted to allow you, the reader, to go directly to the information you need regarding a specific project you are involved in. For example, I expect the electrical and mechanical engineers to avoid the chapter on Biotechnology.

A major purpose of this text is to enable you, as an inventor or creator, to efficiently interface with an intellectual property attorney, for example, and provide him or her with information enabling you to obtain the maximum protection for your invention or creation. On the other side of the coin, the text material will aid you and the intellectual property attorney to take steps to ensure that your invention or creation does not infringe upon the intellectual property rights of others. The last thing in the world you want is to invite a lawsuit when you introduce your new product or process to the world.

Included in this text are patent, copyright, trade secret, mask work, trademark and cybersquatting legal and procedural principles, as well as how to properly use new vehicles of intellectual property protection for novel software, biotech, and business method inventions. Also, this text covers trademark protection for domain names, and other ancillary matters that fall within the genre of intellectual property protection.

The material in the pages that follow also provides you with information regarding employment contracts as they relate to an assignment of intellectual property rights to an employer, the concepts of confidentiality of proprietary information, and covenants not to compete following a change in employment.

By no means is this text intended to transform you into an intellectual property attorney, or to do the work of one. The purpose is to provide you with knowledge of a very arcane, but important, adjunct to the technology professions, that of the protection of the technology you develop, and the steps necessary to prevent stepping on the intellectual property "toes" of others.

Between each of the chapters of this work devoted to intellectual property subjects, I have placed essays on famous and noteworthy inventors and their inventions, followed by a copy of the first page of patents resulting from these inventors' efforts. A complete copy of each patent may be obtained from the United States Patent & Trademark Office website, http://patft.uspto.gov/netahtml/srchnum.htm. I found the research devoted to these historical incidents to be fascinating, particularly the differences between those who developed their inventions through diligent periods of trial and error, and others whose inventions resulted from an act of serendipity.

The content of this text does not provide everything there is to know about intellectual property protection. Such a text would be too thick to be mobile. In covering each of the subjects, I have taken you, the reader, to the point where your next step will be to consult with a competent intellectual property law professional to provide you with the detailed information necessary to protect the results of your intellectual endeavors. Keep in mind that the publisher of this text is not in the business of offering or rendering legal advice, or other professional services to the reader.

HOWARD B. ROCKMAN
Chicago, Illinois
hrockman@btlaw.com

Acknowledgments

I am greatly indebted to many people and organizations that assisted me in the preparation and production of this work. My thanks go out to each, and the order in which their names appear is not indicative of the degree of my appreciation. You were all wonderful.

The publishers, IEEE Press and John Wiley & Sons are to be commended for allowing me to present the intellectual property information in this work to the engineering and scientific community. It is my fervent desire that by bringing this material to those who generate inventions and creative works, a greater awareness of how the worldwide intellectual property laws work to advance technology, science and the creative arts will lead to more developments reaching the light of day. To Catherine Faduska and Anthony VenGraitis of IEEE Press, and Melissa Yanuzzi of John Wiley & Sons, thank you for your guidance through the publication process.

A large measure of my appreciation goes to George Uslenghi, PhD, Professor and Associate Dean, College of Engineering, University of Illinois at Chicago (UIC), for creating the on-line Master of Engineering program at UIC, where my two courses, "Engineering Law" and "Intellectual Property Law for Engineers and Scientists" are taught to students world-wide over the Internet. It is the latter of these two courses which provided the foundation for this work, and it was Prof. Uslenghi who shepherded this project through the IEEE Publications Committee. My thanks also extend to Carolyn C. Williams, the administrator of the Masters of Engineering program at UIC who has been of extraordinary assistance in my interface with academia, and who seeks only chocolates as a reward.

Davide Negri, PhD has assisted me in developing, digitizing and maintaining my course materials from the start several years ago, and who single-handedly composed the LATEX compilation of this book and the editorial suggestions. As I am a certified digital dinosaur, having completed my undergraduate engineering coursework in 1959 using only a sliderule, I would have been cast onto the off-road of the digital highway had it not been for Davide's uncompromising assistance and encouragement.

My thanks also go out to two fine patent attorneys who assisted me in the preparation of the biotechnology patent portions of this text. They are David Rosenbaum, of David Rosenbaum & Assoc., and Alice Martin, PhD of Barnes & Thornburg, both in Chicago.

I also received valuable assistance from Frederick R. Ball, a labor attorney with the firm of Duane Morris LLC of Chicago, who with Michael Silverman and Peggy Daley, prepared and furnished me with information on non-competition and trade secret legal issues that impact upon the engineer and scientist employee and employer.

My thanks also go out to William T. McGrath, an excellent copyright law attorney with the Chicago law firm of Davis, Mannix and McGrath, who provided guidance to me in the intricacies of copyright law, including the new Digital Millennium Copyright Act (DMCA). Bill has taught Copyright Law at John Marshall Law School for many years, and I have the utmost respect for his wisdom in the mysterious ways of copyright law.

This text would not have been able to be produced without the able assistance of my secretarial assistants Debbie Dudek and Paula Perez. Without them, the pages of this work may have been chiseled on stone tablets.

A hearty thanks also are due to the National Inventors Hall of Fame, whose website provided the starting point for my idea to include brief biographies of Inventors and Inventions between the chapters of this text. I also want to thank all of the authors of the many research texts given attribution in my Bibliographies. The hardest part of preparing the Inventors and Inventions essays was deciding upon which fascinating facts about these enlightened individuals had to be omitted for the sake of brevity. My thanks also extend to Anthony Loder, the son of famed actress/inventor Hedy Lamarr, for furnishing me with first-hand knowledge about his mother's invention of what is known today as spread spectrum technology.

For assistance in researching the history of the Wright Brothers, my appreciation is extended to Ronald C. Young, a local historian from Blue Island, Illinois. My essay on Nikola Tesla would not have been possible without the kind cooperation of the wonderful people at the Nikola Tesla Museum, Belgrade, Serbia, and the Antique Wireless Association of the United States. Also, my hand is extended to Paul Schatzkin for furnishing me with invaluable documentation on the Farnsworth-Zworykin patent battle.

Maxwell Rockman deserves a well-earned thank you for conducting the preliminary research for the Inventors and Inventions essays, while I struggled to keep up with my day-time vocation as an intellectual property attorney. Maxwell, your service was well above and beyond the call of duty.

JoAnn Rockman, my wife of many years, deserves more expressions of appreciation than I am capable of giving. First, she had to tolerate my "lack of attention" while the underlying UIC course materials were developed. Then, she had to stand by alone and watch while her spouse poured over the papers and research material to transform fifteen course lectures into twenty-seven chapters of text and a like amount of Inventors and Inventions essays. As a consolation, I now have turned control of the dining room table back to her and the family.

HOWARD B. ROCKMAN

Top Ten List of Intellectual Property Protection

There are several important points regarding the potential loss of intellectual property rights by the actions of an inventor or creator, and other matters, that warrant special and advanced mention. Adherence to these points will help you avoid the unintended loss of rights to your novel technology. Each of these matters is discussed in detail in this text, but I want to prevent the potential loss of intellectual property rights until you get to the appropriate page.

1. Do not publicly disclose your patentable invention to anyone outside your development team until a patent application covering your invention has been filed with the U.S. Patent & Trademark Office, or your respective home Patent Office. In the United States, in broad terms, an inventor has one year following the public disclosure of an invention to file a patent application. However, public knowledge of your invention anywhere will destroy all patent rights in most countries outside the United States. These countries adhere to the "absolute novelty" rule, that requires a patent application to be filed covering an invention in the inventor's home country before any public disclosure of the invention. Thus, by filing your patent application in your home country before any public disclosure of the invention, you have saved all of your international patent rights. If you must disclose your invention to another before a patent application can be filed, have the recipient of the disclosure sign a confidential non-disclosure agreement before receiving the information. This makes the disclosure "non-public," and saves your patent rights.

2. Even though you obtain a patent on your invention, products incorporating your invention may still infringe the patent rights of someone else. Therefore, my advice is to have an infringement search conducted before you bring your new, and patentable, product to market.

3. Be sure you advise your patent attorney of all prior art relating to your invention that you are aware of before the patent application covering your invention is filed, and during the pendency of your application. It is a strict requirement that all material prior art of which you are aware must be submitted to the U.S. patent examiner.

4. When beginning new employment, carefully read and fully understand the agreements you sign, particularly the language regarding ownership of inventions made prior to your employment, and those inventions made during your employment. Also make sure you understand any language that may affect your ability to work for a competitor if and when your new employment terminates.

5. If you are adopting a name, trademark, logo, etc. for use in your business, have a search conducted to ensure that someone else in the same line of business is not already using a similar name or symbol.

6. When asking a vendor or supplier to provide input to a development project, have the vendor first sign an agreement that any contribution they make toward the development of protectable intellectual property will belong to you or your company, and not to the vendor.

7. If you intend to maintain certain information as trade secrets, fully inform yourself of the steps you legally have to take to prove later that you have in place a strict policy and safeguards for maintaining the secrecy of all confidential information.

8. Keep adequate document records of all development work. It may be important years later in proving the earliest date of conception of your invention.

9. The copyright law prevents copying. You may set forth a previously written-about concept or development in your own words, but do not copy the same expression of that concept used by someone else.

10. Consider initially that any new development you produce may be patentable, or may be covered by one or more of the other intellectual property vehicles. Just as science and technology changes, the Intellectual Property Laws also change to protect new forms of innovation.

◆ INVENTORS AND INVENTIONS ◆

Eli Whitney

THE COTTON GIN

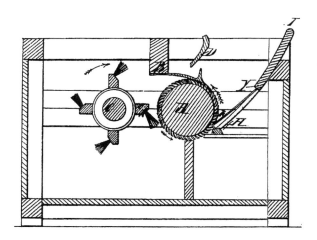

The first patent of major importance to be issued by the United States government after it was formed was Eli Whitney's patent for the cotton gin (gin is short for "engine"), which was issued on March 14, 1794. The patent description is in longhand, for reasons I cannot explain.

Upon graduating Yale as an engineer in 1792, Whitney, like many college graduates of today, found himself in debt and in need of a job. He left his home in Massachusetts and took a job as a teacher in South Carolina. That job fell through and Katherine Greene, the war widow of General Nathanial Greene, invited Whitney to stay at her Georgia cotton plantation in early 1793. He noticed that long-staple cotton, which was readily separated from its seed, could only be grown along the coast. The inland-grown variety of cotton had sticky green seeds that were difficult to cull from the fluffy white cotton bolls, and thus was less profitable to grow and harvest. It took ten hours of hand labor to sift out a single point of cotton lint from its seeds.

Whitney, after observing the manual process being used for separating the sticky seeds from the cotton bolls, built his first machine, which did not work. The bulk cotton was pushed against a wire mesh screen, which held back the seeds while wooden teeth extending from a rotating drum pulled the cotton fibers through the mesh screen. However, this machine jammed. His next version incorporated thin wire hooks to replace the wooden teeth, and the collected fibers were cleared away by a moving brush. This second machine was successful.

According to some accounts, a question remains to this day whether Whitney or his employer, Mrs. Greene, was the "inventor" of the key element of the successful cotton

Intellectual Property Law for Engineers and Scientists, by Howard B. Rockman
ISBN 0-471-44998-9 © 2004 The Institute of Electrical and Electronics Engineers

gin—the wire hooks. Some say the plantation foreman suggested to Greene that the wooden teeth be replaced by wires, and that Greene then told Whitney. Whitney supporters, on the other hand, cite a letter to the editor of *Southern Agriculturist* magazine, admittedly based on shaky sources, that Whitney specifically asked Mrs. Greene for a pin to use at the start of his experimentation. A factor tending to swing the pendulum toward Whitney was that before he left Massachusetts, he was the new country's only hatpin manufacturer.

In 1794, Whitney filed a patent application for his (or Greene's) cotton gin. He also gave a demonstration of his model to a few friends, producing in one hour a full day's output of several workers. The witnesses to this demonstration immediately had whole fields planted in green seed cotton. Word spread, and the farmers grew excited and impatient. Whitney's shop was broken into, and examinations made of his new cotton gin. Then, more fields were planted with cotton.

Before Whitney had a chance to prepare a patent model of his invention (required in those days), or to secure patent protection, the cotton crops were ready for harvest, and the planters did not have time to work within ethical or legal parameters. Whitney's cotton gin was simply pirated. Whitney and his partner, Phineas Miller, decided to build cotton gins and lease, not sell, them to the planters in exchange for one pound of every three pounds of cotton put through their machines. The planters revolted at this arrangement, as a virtual flood of white cotton was erupting from the Southern soil.

The partners, heavily in debt, were forced to approach the Southern courts to enforce their patent rights, which resulted in disaster. In 1801, they opted for grants from several Southern states, and in return, the cotton gin would become public property. One state accepted, offered $50,000, made a down payment of $20,000, and never paid the remainder. Eventually, Whitney and Miller received about $90,000 from the states, which was used up immediately to pay legal costs and other expenses. In 1803, the states repudiated their agreements, and sued Whitney for the return of the money they paid previously. In 1804, Whitney petitioned the U.S. Congress for relief, and by one vote avoided financial ruin. At that point, he felt the past ten years were wasted. Whitney became discouraged with cotton, and left the South forever.

Upon returning to New Haven, Connecticut, he started manufacturing goods and developing mass production techniques and factories. In time, his manufacturing process developments changed the industrial capabilities of the North, just as his cotton gin had changed the face of the South.

72X

E. Whitney,

Cotton Gin.

Patented Mar. 14, 1794.

2 Sheets—Sheet 1.

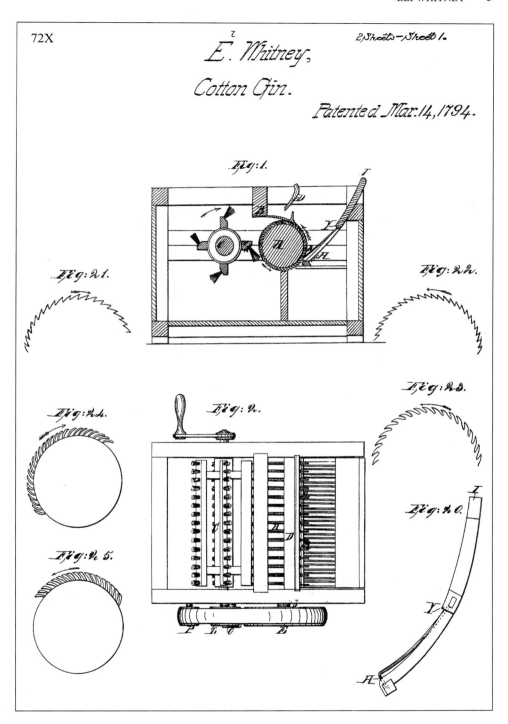

Fig: 1.

Fig: 21.

Fig: 22.

Fig: 23.

Fig: 24.

Fig: 2.

Fig: 20.

Fig: 2. 5.

1 Overview of Intellectual Property Law

1.1 DEFINING "INTELLECTUAL PROPERTY"

First, we need to define the core term of our subject: "Intellectual Property." The term Intellectual Property generically describes those intangible property rights—those you usually cannot see or touch—which are initially created by one's intellectual creative efforts. The results of those intellectual efforts, in most cases, are then anointed with these intangible property rights which give their creator or owner the exclusive ability to control, and profit from, the results of this creativity. "Intellectual Property Law" is that field of law which defines those intellectual creations that are entitled to protection as intellectual property, how to obtain (or lose) those intellectual property rights, how to properly use and benefit from those rights, and how to obtain enforcement and compensation when those intellectual property rights are infringed upon by a competitor or other evil person. Intellectual property law also provides guidance to a competitor who desires to produce a new product or use a new process by designing around, and thus avoiding, the proprietary territory defined by your intellectual property rights.

Winning or losing out in business and financial opportunities sometimes heavily depends upon whether your creative output, inventions, products and business ideas and services are protected by patents, trademarks, copyrights, trade secret rights, mask work rights, and others. Commercially useful ideas, inventions, products and business services are the foundation of many highly successful businesses. As a result, successful business owners and entrepreneurs typically place a high value on the exclusive rights granted to intellectual property developed by their employees.

Businesses have succeeded or failed because of their owner's efforts to protect their intellectual property, or their failure to do so. The value of many publicly traded companies has taken huge swings based principally upon whether the company has been successful in obtaining and enforcing its patent rights, for example. There are many common myths and understandings surrounding the need for and the difficulty in obtaining patent, trademark or copyright protection. Understanding the protection process and appreciating the valuable rights which can be acquired ensures that your intellectual property is protected, as well as that of your employer.

"Tangible" property includes things such as land, houses, jewelry, communication system terminals and networks, and even animals—things you can see and feel and physically possess. Intellectual property rights, on the other hand, are "intangible" rights which cannot be seen or touched, but they still exist, or can exist, if the rules laid down by centuries of intellectual property law are understood and followed. Intangible property, to be protectable, must ultimately be described or depicted in some tangible form, such as a description in a patent grant, or a work of art or manuscript of a book covered by a copyright

Intellectual Property Law for Engineers and Scientists, by Howard B. Rockman
ISBN 0-471-44998-9 © 2004 The Institute of Electrical and Electronics Engineers

certificate. In each of these two examples, the law describes the intangible rights possessed by the owner and/or creator of a patentable or copyrightable work.

The building blocks of intellectual property law are patents, copyrights, trademarks and service marks, as well as anti-cybersquatting laws, trade secret protection laws, and mask work protection laws. These are all concepts that were created by legal systems in mostly all of the countries of the world, and although they are merely legal devices, they provide powerful instruments of protection for your intellectual creations. These systems of rights were developed to document the existence of intellectual property rights, how they can be protected, and to give the creator the right to exclusively use, own, transfer ownership, or license their rights of intellectual property.

In general terms, each intellectual property law system throughout the world provides a system devised to document enforceable protection for specific types of creative output, and to allow someone to own and transfer ownership in their intellectual property. For example, patents cover novel, useful and non-obvious machines; articles of manufacture; compositions of matter; ornamental designs; plants; manufacturing, electrical and chemical processes; and other methods, including software algorithms and methods of doing business. Patents also cover any improvement made to an article or process falling in any of the above categories. Copyrights cover the creative works of authors, composers, software developers, artists and the like. Trademark and service mark registration laws, as well as the common law, which I shall explain, protect the source identity of a product or service, such as the name and/or logo, and sometimes product configuration, under which one advertises and markets their goods or services to the trade or public. Trade secret protection laws prevent a competitor or another from misappropriation of valuable and confidential information which is not generally known or available to a competitor or to the public, such as a secret chemical formula or a secret process. Mask work protection is a recent intellectual property structural block, which provides exclusive rights in creative mask works used in the manufacture of semiconductors. In all, the specific nature and content of the results of your creative endeavors determines which vehicle or vehicles of the various intellectual property laws are best suited to protect the ultimate output of your efforts.

1.2   SPECIFIC INTELLECTUAL PROPERTY VEHICLES

1.2.1   Patents

A U.S. patent grant covering your invention can only be obtained from the United States government, namely, the United States Patent and Trademark Office, currently located across the river from Washington, D.C. in Arlington, Virginia. In foreign nations, patents are also granted only by the nation's government. Each country's patents are enforceable only in the issuing country and its territories. In the United States, the patent laws are found at Title 35 of the United States Code, a body of laws passed by the U.S. Congress, as mandated by Article 1, Section 8 of the United States Constitution. These U.S. laws define what can and cannot be patented, the conditions and requirements for obtaining a patent grant on patentable subject matter, the rights granted by a patent, the ability of a patent owner to enforce the exclusive rights embedded in the patent grant, and the ability of a patent owner to license or transfer ownership of the intangible rights embedded in the invention and patent grant for monetary consideration.

As mentioned briefly above, patents are granted on "new and useful processes, machines, manufactures or compositions of matter, or any new and useful improvement thereof". (35 U.S.C. §101). Designs of utilitarian articles of manufacture may also be protected by a Design Patent. Recent court decisions in the field of intellectual property law have held that anything "new" falling within the definition of 35 U.S.C. §101, quoted above, can be the subject of a patent. This includes new forms of animal life, for example, the Harvard Mouse, which is particularly susceptible to cancer and therefore valuable in research, and the modified *E. coli* bacterium, which produces insulin. More recently, novel and unobvious methods of conducting business have also been pronounced to be the subject of patents, as well as software under certain circumstances. By way of comparison, any material which appears naturally in nature cannot be the subject of a patent, since it was not "invented" by the alleged inventor. Pure ideas and concepts that have no "physical" embodiment are not protectable under the patent laws. However, as discussed later, a novel concept embodied in a new and useful device or procedure may come close to being fully protected by effective and creative patent application and claim drafting.

An issued patent grant describes and illustrates the covered invention, and its advantages over the "prior art," and also includes specifically worded "claims" which define the metes and bounds of the protection afforded by the patent grant. If a competing device or process falls within the definition set forth in a patent's claim or claims, or comprises equivalent structure, the competing device infringes the patent. But, I'm getting ahead of myself—the topic of patent infringement will be covered later.

1.2.2 Trademarks and Service Marks

Trademarks, services marks, collective membership marks, trade dress or product configuration, trade names and the like are directed toward the protection of the reputation and goodwill of the manufacturer of a product or a provider of services who uses a mark or symbol distinguishing the source of origin of its products or services from those of another manufacturer or service provider. These marks comprise a name, logo, symbol, product shape, container shape, or other distinctive and non-functional feature of a product or service which indicates that a certain supplier or group is the sole source for that particular brand of product of service, and the supplier or group stands behind the quality and reputation of the particular product or service. Rights in the mark are protected to avoid the likelihood of consumer confusion in the marketplace as to the source of the goods or services they purchase, thereby protecting the public against fraud by the second user of a mark.

A trademark or service mark registration application must be submitted to the government for Federal Registration, and sets forth both the identifying mark and those goods or services with which the mark is, or is intended to be, used. A trademark never stands alone. A trademark or service mark is always considered as an adjective, modifying the goods or services to which it pertains. Thus, Scotch tape is proper usage, as long as the Scotch is followed by the identifying word "tape." When used, a trademark or service mark should always be followed by the descriptive term of the associated goods or services.

Trademarks and service marks may also be protected in the U.S. and certain other common law countries without registration, if long usage and advertising of the mark has advised the public that the name or symbol has been adopted as a distinctive mark by its owner.

1.2.3 Copyrights

A copyright protects the expression of the authorship or artistic rendition of the author or creator, but does not protect the idea or concept upon which the expression is based. A concept for doing something cannot be protected by copyright, but the fixation or expression of that concept can be protected. For example, the concept of writing a book about tornado hunters is not protectable. However, a book or film about tornado hunters is a "fixation" of the author's expression, and is protectable under the copyright statutes.

Copyright protection is normally easier and less expensive to obtain than either patent or trademark protection. Under existing law, the creator of a copyrightable work obtains an intangible copyright in the work upon the fixation of the work in a tangible medium of expression. To obtain a registration of that copyright, which provides tangible evidence of the existence of the copyright, a form setting forth among other things, the author's name, the identity of the work to be protected, and its date of creation are submitted on an appropriate form to the Register of Copyrights, along with a deposit sample of the work. The Register of Copyrights works under the aegis of the U.S. Library of Congress. The application is subjected to an examination procedure, which is much quicker than the examination of patent or trademark applications, because there is no examination for novelty or likelihood of confusion compared to existing copyrighted works. The copyright application must indicate which portions of the work are original and which are not. This permits the public to ascertain which portions are protected and which remain in the public domain. Copyrights are used to protect books, films, videos, works of art, sculptures, and more recently choreography and software.

It is possible to overlap protection between the copyright and patent laws. For example, a novel, useful and non-obvious computer program may be protectable under both the patent laws and the copyright laws. The expression of an algorithm or formula can be protected as a literary work under copyrightable law. In addition, a novel method for controlling a machine by use of an algorithm may qualify for patent protection.

1.2.4 Trade Secrets

As discussed later in this text, patents and copyrights expire after a term of years, while trade secrets do not. As long as the information covered by a trade secret umbrella remains secret, that information is protected from improper discovery or use by others, unless it is independently discovered, as by reverse engineering, or otherwise made public by someone else. Where the secret is very difficult to discover and the owner is willing to maintain security to ensure it's secrecy, trade secret protection is a valuable option and has no endpoint.

However, once the trade secret becomes known, there is no way to restore secret status. If the secret is discoverable upon reviewing the articles in which the secret is used, trade secret protection is useless. In such case, patent or copyright protection should be considered instead. Unlike patents and copyrights and trademarks, there is no Federal law regulating trade secret protection in the United States. Each state has its own trade secret protection law, and if it is determined that the best way to protect your intellectual property is through the trade secret law, an attorney familiar with this area of your state law should be consulted in the state or states in which you are operating. In the State of Illinois, where I practice, the State Legislature has enacted the Illinois Trade Secrets Act, which is currently in effect. This Act sets forth what types of subject matter are considered as trade secrets, such as secret processes, formulas, customer lists, etc., and how they are protected. Even if a particular state has not enacted a statute granting trade secret protection, the common law may be available in that state to enforce trade secret rights once they are created against misappropriation.

1.2.5 Mask Works for Semiconductors

In 1984, the Federal Congress created a law to protect mask works used in creating semiconductor microprocessor chips. This law became part of the Federal Copyright Statute. In one of the later chapters of this text, I describe in detail how mask work protection can be obtained for semiconductor chips.

1.3 WHICH FORM OF INTELLECTUAL PROPERTY PROTECTION TO USE?

Depending on the nature of the technological project you are engaged in, one or several of the vehicles of intellectual property may be advisable to use. In some situations, you may not have any choice. If the subject matter of protection is a book or manuscript, patent or trademark protection cannot be obtained. For example, book titles other than periodical titles cannot be the subject of trademark registration, since each book title is descriptive of the precise book sold under that title. In some situations, multiple forms of protection will be available. For example, in the case of a novel form of packaging, both article and design patent protection may be available, covering a novel construction embedded in the packaging, as well as the aesthetic outward design of the package. Also, the name of the packaging would be susceptible to trademark protection, while the graphics used on the packaging label could be protected under the copyright laws.

Which protection to be used is a business decision that has to be arrived at by the creator or the owner of the invention or creative work. This decision should be made with the assistance of an attorney with experience in the intellectual property law field, and after the creator or owner has a full understanding as to the best vehicle or vehicles to be used for protection.

◆ INVENTORS AND INVENTIONS ◆

Cyrus McCormick

CROP REAPER

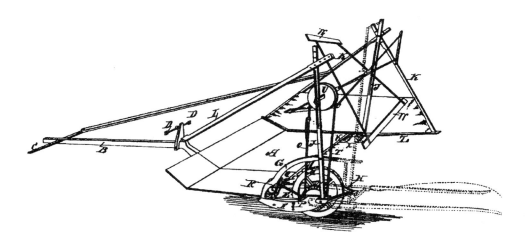

We have all heard about the inventors Eli Whitney and Cyrus McCormick, and the latter's invention, the reaper, in grade school when we studied the Industrial Revolution.

Cyrus Hall McCormick was born in Rockbridge County, Virginia in 1809. He developed an interest in inventing from his father, Robert McCormick, a Virginia landowner who had several patents of his own on improved farming implements. Around the time of Cyrus' birth, his father started designing and experimenting with a design for a mechanical reaper. He worked on this idea for 22 unsuccessful years before turning the idea over to his son Cyrus in 1831. In only six weeks, in July of 1831, Cyrus had fixed the design, tested it, and remodeled it for public trial. This was not the first time Cyrus had built something; in fact, at the age of fifteen he invented a lightweight cradle for harvesting grain. After more refining of his new reaper, he obtained a patent in 1834.

Until 1846, McCormick had sold fewer than 100 machines, but then they started selling much more rapidly. Too rapidly, in fact; the blacksmith shop that McCormick was selling his reapers out of couldn't produce enough. So, in 1847, McCormick moved from his farm in Virginia to Chicago, Illinois to manufacture his reaper closer to the immense fields of the Midwest. He also changed the name of his company to McCormick Harvesting Machine Company. McCormick's brothers, William and Leander, came to Chicago to become partners with Cyrus. The Chicago operation was a huge success partly due to the fact that Chicago was a major industrial and rail center, and partly because of the McCormicks' business techniques: door-to-door sales, easy credit, written performance guarantees, and advertising techniques.

By 1856, Cyrus and his invention were world famous. His "Virginia Reaper" hastened the westward development of the United States, thus creating new markets for the reaper. By 1858, his company was the largest manufacturer of farm equipment in the United States.

In 1871, the entire factory was destroyed by the great Chicago fire, but this turned out to benefit the company. McCormick built a new factory with expanded production capacity, which allowed him to start selling more reapers overseas, and by the early 1880s his company's products had reached as far as Russia and New Zealand. In 1902, McCormick's company merged with Deering Harvester Company to form the International Harvester Company.

C. H. McCORMICK.
>   REAPER.
>
>> Patented June 21, 1834.
>> No. X8277

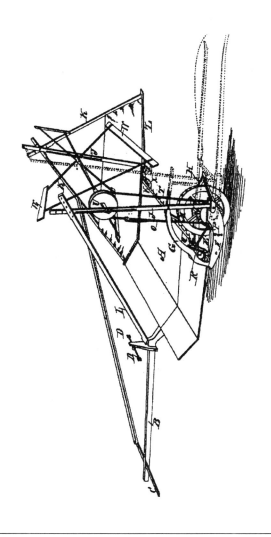

2 The Use of Intellectual Property in Business

2.1 INTRODUCTION TO INTELLECTUAL PROPERTY STRATEGIES

In today's and tomorrow's "technology-driven" economy, the proper development of intellectual property assets is seen as crucial to business survival and advancement. Just look around you and see how many items were not available just 50 years ago. Lately, many organizations have included intellectual property strategies in their business plans early on, rather than merely wait for a new development to emerge from their R&D Department, and then try to figure out how to best use and protect that new development. Also, in the past several years, different types of inventions have been added to the list of patentable subject matter that was not so considered before. These include computer software, methods of doing business, and biotechnology innovations. Along with the increase in patentable subject matter, many businesses have developed creative thinking in strategizing the development and use of their intellectual property. Today, intellectual property is on the radar scope of upper management, where patents, copyrights, trademarks, trade secrets, know-how, etc. are now part of strategic thinking, planning and implementation.

Without the systems for granting limited exclusive rights in innovation described in the previous chapter, technology would be submerged by their creators and kept from public use. Therefore, the intellectual property systems throughout the world serve the purpose of providing full public access and use of innovative ideas (which promotes innovation), and providing a foundation for economic wealth for the innovator during the period of exclusivity.

Although each country has its own procedures for obtaining intellectual property protection, the substance of the requirements for protectable subject matter are somewhat universal on this planet. To obtain a patent, for example, practically every country requires that an invention be useful in a real-world environment, be novel or new (not previously publically known), and be non-obvious, or comprise an inventive step, over the relevant preceeding "prior art." The trademark laws of each country normally require that a mark you use in commerce cannot be overly descriptive, and does not confusingly conflict with a mark used on similar goods or services by another. Copyrights are broader in scope of enforceability, where the owner of a copyright in one country can normally enforce that copyright in another country, and copyrights are enforceable in most countries (except the United States) without seeking or obtaining government registration of the copyright.

2.2 OBJECTIVES OF INTELLECTUAL PROPERTY MANAGEMENT

This chapter is dedicated to the economic and business factors involved in the generation and effective use of your entire intellectual property portfolio to maximum advantage.

Intellectual Property Law for Engineers and Scientists, by Howard B. Rockman
ISBN 0-471-44998-9 © 2004 The Institute of Electrical and Electronics Engineers

These principles apply not only to the management of an established business, but also to the entrepreneur who is using the strength of one or several patents or other intellectual property vehicles to launch a new venture by creating an organization that will continue to develop new ideas and technology based upon an initial innovative concept. Many entrepreneurs recognize that a patent or a copyright may be the primary vehicle for intellectual property protection, which is the lifeblood of high-tech start-ups and other small companies created upon research, innovation and creativity. Patents and other intellectual property also attract capital to these new technology-based ventures. Several primary objectives of a business strategy crafted to achieve optimum development, use and protection of intellectual property are:

1. To create procedures that will encourage early and full disclosure of all potentially patentable and otherwise protectable technology from your research and development teams (i.e., bringing the ideas to the surface);

2. To establish criteria for evaluating invention and other innovation disclosures, and determining which new technology warrants consideration for patenting or copyright protection (i.e., what do we want to protect);

3. To establish additional criteria for deciding in which countries patent protection should be obtained, as contrasted to where patent or trademark protection may not be cost beneficial, or where patents and trademarks may not be readily enforceable (i.e., where do we want protection);

4. To create an awareness among all technical personnel of patent, trademark and copyright infringement avoidance, and from whom to seek guidance in avoiding infringement of another's intellectual property rights;

5. To create a patent and intellectual property portfolio that has both offensive and defensive capabilities vis-à-vis your competitors and potential competitors, and which portfolio increases the value of your and your company's intangible assets; and

6. If your company is primarily driven by technology, it is highly recommended that an Intellectual Property Audit be conducted, and periodically updated. This audit is for the purpose of providing an inventory of your company's intellectual property assets so that information is readily available when it becomes necessary to enforce, license or sell any of those assets. A proper audit, in broad terms:

   (a) identifies all intellectual property in your portfolio, including patents, trademarks, copyrights, trade secrets, know-how, license agreements, technology transfer agreements, and anything else your company considers as intellectual property;

   (b) analyzes the categories of subject matter your company desires to protect, and includes a plan for identifying the categories of technology you desire to protect in the future; and

   (c) includes a policy statement or manual setting forth internal procedures for the protection of your company's intellectual property, and for maintaining the confidentiality of your company's proprietary and trade secret information.

In today's large business environment many companies with extensive patent and intellectual property assets have no idea what the totality of these assets are. Therefore, it is wise to create a searchable database with important information on all intellectual property assets. The database should, for example, record all important data from your patents, and a scanned image of the patent drawings. This helps you and the engineers readily identify the innovation that pertains to the database information. This database will also allow you to identify obsolete technology that can be dropped rather than expend money on patent maintenance fees.

2.3   SOLE INVENTOR IN AN ALIEN FIELD

Many inventors and creators are those who have developed an idea or concept into a workable embodiment, which idea or concept falls into a technology arena totally alien to the field of their everyday work or activities. I am referring to the homemaker who conceives of a new childproof safe-lock for a food jar, or the insurance salesman who jots down on paper a new lubricating system for the two-cycle engine on his lawnmower, by way of example. These are the inventors and creators who can easily obtain exclusive protection for their novel and creative ideas through copyrights, patents, trade secret agreements and the like. However, during my practice, I have noted that many, if not most, of these sole inventors encounter great diffculty in overcoming the hurdles in bringing their idea to the marketplace.

The primary reason for tripping over the hurdles is that many of these inventors and creators want to start their own businesses to develop, market and sell the products or services incorporating their ideas. This requires financing, and in most cases much more than our homemaker or insurance salesman can come up with. For example, if the novel product can be injection molded out of plastic, an initial expenditure of $40,000–$60,000 (at the time of writing this book) will be required to design and manufacture a mold which will produce the first prototype. Then, the costs of finalizing and testing the design, manufacturing production versions, marketing the product, and creating a sales distribution network for the product can require financing of a million dollars or more. This is before a single dollar in income has been produced by the product. A few of my clients have attempted to profit on their ideas in this way, but found it diffcult, if not impossible to obtain the necessary financing for a new, but yet unknown, marketable product. As a result, I have seen several potentially good ideas literally die on the vine.

To those of you who fall into the category of innovators who are unable to fully fund the development, marketing and sales of your new product, my advice is to explore the licensing path with the assistance of your patent professional. By granting an exclusive (or non-exclusive) license to a company or other entity which is already in the marketplace selling products which are similar to, but not as good as, yours, you will achieve the goals of:

1. Successfully having your new product produced and into the hands of consumers;
2. Receiving royalty income from the sale of products embodying your idea without lifting a finger; and
3. Avoiding the agony of raising funds, or using your own limited resources, to launch your new product into the marketplace.

I have recommended to many individual inventor and creator clients that they pursue the licensing route, rather than start their own business, as the least expensive, quickest, least frustrating, and most profitable way to commercialize their novel idea or concept.

For information on patent licensing, see Chapter 19, Section 19.2 of this text. Also, I strongly recommend that the sole entrepreneurs who are reading this text seek advice from both a patent professional and a financial advisor to assist you in deciding how best to bring your idea to the consumers, and how to make money at the same time without risking your own resources beyond your reasonable capability.

If you have no desire to license your invention or creation, venture capital can be sought after you have begun the pursuit of your intellectual property rights. Your banker should be able to connect you with a venture capital group that may seek investors for a business founded upon the intellectual property rights in your new invention or creation. In such cases, the investors may demand a controlling interest in your business venture in exchange for their providing the finances to get you started.

Besides licensing your invention, you also have the right to sell all of your rights in your invention or creation to a company that is already marketing a similar product. You will then "assign" your intellectual property rights to that company, and receive a lump sum payment for the assignment, or be compensated on a percentage of sales of products or services comprising your invention or creation. Assignments of patent rights are discussed at Chapter 19, Section 19.1 of this text.

2.4 STRATEGIC DEVELOPMENT OF INTELLECTUAL PROPERTY

It is important in conducting a successful business that a potent intellectual property development and protection strategy be developed covering the entire business. I recommend that at least the following steps be taken.

- First, the marketing focus of the company's products is identified, including the needs of potential customers and how competitive products or services presently fail to adequately meet these needs.

- Second, the new technology and efforts to develop the technology required to meet the demands of customers is calculated. This includes identifying current technologies and products and services having strategic importance over the next three to five years, and identifying emerging technologies of your company, universities and other companies that are likely to be used by you or by competitors.

- Third, research and development resources and personnel are allocated to create the new technology.

- Fourth, a strategy is put in place to identify those innovations which should and can be protected with the proper intellectual property vehicles (i.e., patents, trade secrets, copyrights, etc.), and how unpatented technology can also be protected.

- Fifth, patent and other filings are put in place before any public disclosure of the technology.

- Sixth, continual monitoring of the technology development process takes place to ensure that adequate protection is timely obtained on all improvements to, and new uses of, the basic technology.

This strategy is better achieved at a high management level, and on a company-wide basis. Combining all, or most, of these strategies should lead to achieving a competitive advantage through new technology.

Thus, consideration should be given to generating an entire program of innovation protection from the start, rather than just filing for patents or other intellectual property protection on new technology without considering how that technology fits into your overall business opportunities. The goal is to achieve a higher value for the entire new technology area. For example, when reviewing the claims of a patent application on your invention to ensure that the claims adequately cover your invention, extend your thoughts "outside the box" and think how a competitor might use alternate devices, materials, steps, etc. to achieve the same result as your invention. Also, think how your invention can be used in other, non-competing products or processes that are not within the scope of your company's business sphere. In each of these cases, suggest to your patent professional how the patent claims can be broadened to encompass your thoughts "outside the box."

If broad patent protection is not possible due to close prior art, strategic efforts can be directed to obtaining several limited, but soundly based, patents that can be just as effcient as having one broad patent. These several patents should be crafted to close all the possible avenues open to competitors to encroach upon your technology. This strategy could be combined with securing maximum market position through coordinated advertising and using your established, well-known trademarks for your products.

One possibility of managing your business' intellectual property is to establish a unit with specific responsibility for carrying out this mission. This unit should report directly to management to function properly. If a licensing program is established by this unit, the unit could become its own profit center. Most importantly, the members of this unit should be in direct and frequent contact with product managers to ensure that all intellectual property developments are brought to the attention of management.

2.5   DISGORGING PATENTABLE INVENTIONS

Based on my experience, waiting for your scientists and engineers to bring their innovations to the intellectual property department is a bad idea. Instead, recommend that the intellectual property department include an engineering team that swoops down on the R&D and product development people, for the purpose of inquiring (or pestering), identifying and documenting patentable and otherwise protectable technology. This process should be accomplished early and often, and on a regular basis. The sooner new technology is ferretted out and protection is sought, the better.

Your technology development personnel should be aware of the benefits to them and to the company in submitting invention and new technology disclosures for possible patenting or other protection. These personnel should understand that they are part of the innovation process, and what the intellectual property program is. This will let each innovator know the value of intellectual property to him/herself and to the company, and will encourage the disclosure of quality inventions and other innovations. To provide this awareness to the engineering and scientific personnel, it is recommended that guidelines be established and disseminated identifying the primary and secondary product lines or services of the business unit, and identifying how the business unit plans to utilize its patent and technology assets to maximum advantage.

After new technology has been placed in an understandable format or embodiment, such as a prototype or drawings, a disclosure of the invention should be furnished to the intellectual property department. Also, the developer of the technology should be asked to define what additional technology areas (both inside and outside the company's core business) the innovation may have use. The developer should also provide information on ways that someone else could "design around" the innovation, since it would be wise to cover such design around in an eventually filed patent application.

A proven way to insure that innovative technology bubbles to the surface is to create an invention or innovation incentive or reward program. This involves recognizing the submittal of patentable technology through monetary or non-monetary incentives. Here are some ideas that may be adopted.

- The innovator shares in a percentage of the profits or sales of the product or service embodying the new technology.
- The innovator is paid a monetary "reward" upon the filing and/or patenting of an invention. If the reward is paid upon filing only, the inventor may not be motivated to assist during prosecution of the patent, and may be less inclined to remain employed during the patent prosecution cycle. I recommend that the monetary reward be given upon both the filing and issuance of the patent. This program nullifies the two disadvantages mentioned above by providing the inventor with an incentive to help in obtaining issuance of the patent, and to stay with the company. The monetary reward could consist of cash or stock. On the negative side, the potential inventors must be forewarned that not all of their invention disclosures will be accepted for patenting, and they should not be dissuaded from submitting additional new technology disclosures after a previous disclosure has been turned down or consideration has been deferred.
- The innovator may be recognized with a non-monetary gesture, such as a plaque, luncheon or dinner, extra vacation time, or payment of tuition for advanced education courses.

No matter which system above is adopted or if no reward system is adopted, the key thing to remember is that promotions and advancements within the company, as well as compensation, are normally a direct result of the innovations brought to the attention of management by the R&D, engineering, scientific, and other technology personnel.

2.6   DETERMINING WHAT AND WHAT NOT TO PATENT

Since most new engineering and scientific technology developments are protectable through patents, rather than copyrights and trademarks, this section presents the factors for considering what should and should not be patented in a typical technology business environment. Also covered are several suggestions for implementing intellectual property protection strategies into an overall business plan. Your intellectual property can be used in several basic ways:

- Defensively, to protect and enhance your market position in the protected product or service by preventing competitors from copying your new products. This could include developing protectable technology that would build a wall around other patents or technology your company owns, or to build a fence around your competitor's technology.

- The generation of income revenues through the strategic licensing, or possible sale, of intellectual property assets.
- As an effective wedge in entering a new product market or geographic area, and gaining market share from a competitor.
- Assisting you in making trade-offs to acquire needed technology from a competitor.
- Convincing a competitor to establish a strategic business partnership with you to complete a business deal that you could not accomplish on your own.
- The merger with or acquisition of a competitor.

The discussion of what to patent and, in fact, any other intellectual property matters, should include personnel involved in R&D, engineering, product development, licensing, intellectual property development and enforcement, and of equal importance, finance. This group should be embedded with managements' policies and goals to guide the decision making process.

2.6.1 Search Results

The results of the novelty search of your invention, described in detail in Chapter 9, Section 9.1, will allow you to determine whether broad or more limited patent protection is available. If your invention is truly unique, and broad patent protection is available, the patent you obtain on your invention should allow you to market your new product without serious competition during the introductory offering period, until and if a competitor figures out how to design around your patent, or develops an improvement on your patented technology. If you recall, the Polaroid instant image photography patents were broad enough to knock Kodak out of the market entirely several years ago.

However, your novelty search results may disclose that something less than broad claims, or possibly quite limited claims, may be all that is available to cover your invention. With these results, it is possible that a competitor may be able to readily design around your patent claims soon after your new product introduction, thus reducing the ability of the patent protection you obtain to insulate you from effective competition. In such cases, where only limited patent protection appears to be available, it may not be worth the expense to pursue patents. Also, consider whether the required disclosure of your invention is worth obtaining only limited patent claim coverage.

By "limited patent protection," we are faced with those situations where the search results show that you may obtain patent protection covering, for example, only a small, new element forming part of the overall invention, or covering only a slight improvement over the prior art that may not be significant in marketing your new product. In the latter case, competitors may be able to keep your market share low by selling their present products at a cheaper price without your improvement. For example, does everyone need a car equipped with a heater and air-conditioner system that responds to the sound of your voice?

Thus, where the search results suggest that only limited patent protection may be available for your invention, further business considerations of a practical rather than emotional nature come into the equation. The cost of obtaining a patent or patents in the various markets where the invention has value must be weighed against the degree and nature of exclusivity a limited patent will provide. If a cost–benefit analysis shows that competitors will probably not be kept at bay by a limited patent, the decision may be to avoid the cost of patenting a particular invention, and to proceed with an aggressive advertising, marketing and sales campaign to launch and promote your new product.

2.6.2 Business Factors Determining Whether to Obtain Patent Protection

A proper intellectual property evaluation system should:

- Determine those individuals, and where they are in your company or organization, who are responsible for, or are likely to, develop or create innovations related to new products or existing products;
- Establish a procedure where those individuals periodically advise management of all innovations they are working toward and/or have developed; and
- Create a protocol for review of each innovation to determine whether intellectual property protection should be sought, based on the criteria set forth below.

In determining whether patent protection should be sought covering an invention, the following criteria are considered, usually by a team made up of design/technical, new product marketing, management and, all important, financial personnel from your organization. Also, a patent attorney or patent agent may sit in on such discussions to offer guidance, when needed, when patenting procedure issues arise:

Importance of the Technology If the technology embodied in the invention under consideration relates to one or more of the important product lines of your company, or to an important new product, strong consideration should be given to obtaining patent protection covering the invention. If the technology relates only to a small portion of the company's business, and the marketing people indicate that the potential for gaining new market share based on this invention is minor or non-existent, the importance factor may be minimal, leaning toward a decision not to obtain patent protection.

In determining the value of an invention or new technology, consideration should be given to the following:

- To what use will you or your company put the invention or technology?
- Would a patent be effective in preventing a competitor from copying or using the invention or technology? Or would a competitor or another be interested in obtaining a license to practice the invention or technology?
- Is the invention or technology capable of effective protection through trade secret and/or confidentiality processes and, if so, is this preferable to patenting?
- How much time and money will it take to develop the invention or technology into a profitable product? Does the company have the personnel and equipment required to develop and produce products incorporating the invention or technology?
- Would the development of this technology interfere with the intellectual property rights of a competitor, or of a non-competitor, whose rights may be purchased or licensed?
- Could the subject invention be submitted as a new industry standard?

After the invention has been discussed with those having the authority to make decisions on whether patents should be filed or not, an analysis should be made of the importance of the invention to the company's product lines prior to making the decision whether or not a patent should be obtained. This analysis should be presented to the decision makers so that they have all the facts in front of them when making their determination.

Competitive Advantage Another factor in determining whether or not patent protection should be sought is the competitive advantage to be gained by obtaining patent protection on the subject invention, which will provide your company with the right to exclude others from making, using, selling or importing products containing similar technology. For example, determine which technology will provide an advantage over competitors, and what competitors' features provide marketability to their products.

The marketing experts should compare the product embodying the invention to other products on the market, and make a determination whether the invention will provide the product, or product line, with a distinct advantage in gaining consumer acceptance and desire for the product.

Also, if the state of the prior art indicates that only limited patent protection may be available, the marketing department may determine, such as through focus groups, that the competitive advantage to be gained by patent protection is minimal. The ability of competitors to design around the patent and avoid its claims, if the claims are limited, must also be given consideration in determining whether or not to obtain patent protection for a particular invention. Also, keep in mind that if your competitors are increasingly obtaining patents on their innovations, you should have a policy of building your intellectual property portfolio to avoid being left behind in the possession of enforcable innovation protection rights.

Enforceability Based upon the above factors, you may have determined that patent protection should be sought. The next question to consider is whether or not the patent that you obtain will be readily enforceable. For example, if your patent is directed to a process that is used internally of a manufacturing facility, or in a chemical processing plant, a question arises whether or not you will be able to determine whether your competitor is using the particular patented process or not. Your competitor will probably be producing products similar to yours, and then it becomes necessary for you to determine whether or not the competitor is using the patented process to produce such products, which may or may not be evident from an examination of the final product.

In certain cases where significant sales and profits are involved, companies have actually resorted to industrial espionage to obtain valuable trade secret information from their competitors, including information regarding the processes used to manufacture the competitor's products. Of course, such industrial espionage is illegal if one gets caught. However, it is my experience and understanding that such espionage continues even today.

If it becomes necessary to resort to underhanded tactics to police your patent rights, it may not be worthwhile to file for a patent in the first place. However, if your process patent is such that the final product will indicate whether or not the patented process has been used, then obtaining patent protection may be valuable since the enforceability of the patent will not involve extra expense or underhanded practices.

The enforceability of the patent will also be a factor in determining in what countries the patent application should be filed, which subject is discussed at Section 2.9.

Commercial Value An additional factor to be considered in determining whether or not patent protection should be sought is the commercial or cost–benefit value of the invention, and of the product in which the invention is used. If the invention itself will be costly to implement in the new product, but at the same time the product is in such a market that you will not be able to increase its price to cover the cost of implementing the new technology, then patent protection may not be worth the expenditure of resources. Also, if the project in which the invention is used is one that has a terminal date, that is, when the product will be taken off the market to be replaced by new products that are also in development, again the patent may not be worth the anticipated cost.

On the other hand, if your new technology can be readily implemented into the product without much additional cost, and even though you cannot increase the cost of the product, but you determine that sales of the product will be greatly enhanced by implementation of the new invention, the filing of a patent application is quite worthwhile. Also, if the new technology will lengthen the sales life of the product in which the invention is used, again this will be a factor leaning toward filing the patent application.

An intangible commercial value of obtaining patents is the creation of a positive image of your company, both inside and outside the organization. A visible patent program shows the employees that innovation is the expected norm, and will be rewarded. In this regard, many large companies provide financial incentives to their employees upon the filing of patent applications and/or issuance of patents. The patent program also advises outsiders, such as competitors, investors, and the general public, of the technology advances your company has made, and will be expected to make in the future, thus providing intangible value to your enterprise.

Licensing Value   The licensing value of the subject invention, and the establishment of a licensing program for your company, are important considerations in determining whether to file a patent application. The subject technology may not be immensely important to your particular industry. However, the new technology may have value to someone else, who is not a competitor, who may be willing to license your technology. Eventually, if you or your company develop a significant patent portfolio, you may be able to establish a profitable licensing program involving many of your patents. By way of anecdotal information, several years ago a major technology-driven company earned $500 million from licensing its patents in one year.

If you or your company establishes a licensing program, it is important to keep the patent professionals who are preparing your intellectual property documents aware of your program. For example, if you desire to license your patented technology outside the areas of your core business, it is necessary that your patent application include claims, and supporting descriptive material to support a license of products and processes outside of your primary business. For example, if you produce steam irons, and your R&D department has developed the combination of a new iron with a new switch which automatically turns the iron off when the iron is moved to a vertical orientation, make sure your patent application includes claims directed to both the combination of the iron plus switch, and claims directed to just the new switch alone. This will enable you to offer licenses to others to produce the switch alone on non-competing products, and provide you with income from their sales of non-competing products.

After your company has established a patent portfolio, a program can be established to offer licenses to those non-competing companies that may find value in the technology embodied in your patents. Since those entities are not directly competing with the core business of your company, they can freely use your inventions in a way that will not affect your market position.

Another strategy involves offering licenses under your technology to those who are competitors of your primary business. Factors which may make it feasible to offer such licenses include:

- Would you market position be harmed, or even helped, if alternate sources for your new product were available, such as in areas where you do not have a strong marketing position?
- Does technology in your industry become obsolete so rapidly that you will have "newer" technology developed by the time a competitor can come on line with your "new" technology?
- In comparison to your profit margin, would it be to your advantage to have a competitor sell your new technology to the market, and you share in the profits of those sales?
- Is there an advantageous possibility that you may have to become a partner with a competitor or an emerging company to make a bid on a large project that could benefit from your new technology?

After you have developed a patent portfolio, your licensing program should begin by seeking out potential licensees for the technology not only covered by your patents, but also embodied in confidential proprietary information and know-how which has not been subject to patent protection. As such, a licensing program can be administered by marketing personnel, or by a licensing coordinator if your company is of suffcient size. Potential purchasers of licenses under your technology are identified on a case by case basis after an investigation and analysis of companies that may be interested in your technology. An aggressive patent licensing program can generate substantial additional revenues for you and/or your company from the technology covered by your patents, and other proprietary technology in the possession of your company.

Foreign Markets   It is quite possible that the technology embodied in your latest invention may not have an impact on the U.S. market, but for other reasons may have a significant impact on foreign markets where your company operates. In such cases, in order to obtain patents in the foreign countries, it is required that you first file a patent application in the United States, or your home country, and then file corresponding patents in those foreign countries of interest. Therefore, all of the above factors must also be applied to each foreign country in which your company is marketing its products. This analysis, when the above considerations are applied to a foreign market, may lead to a different conclusion then arrived at when analyzing your home country market position.

Defensive Patenting   By defensive patenting, consider the situation where you or your company, once you develop and market your new products, may be accused of infringing someone else's patent or patents. Let's assume that when such accusations are made, you have a large portfolio of patents that cover the technology you have developed over the last 20 or so years. Thus, immediately upon receiving a charge of infringement, usually in the form of a letter from a competitor's attorney, you search your patent portfolio and compare the claims of those patents to the products sold by the competitor who is charging you with infringement. In many instances, it is possible to find certain patents that you own that are or may be infringed by your competitor. If this is the case, you write your competitor indicating that you are counter-charging them with infringement of your patents, and possibly the whole situation can be resolved by both parties retreating back to their own baselines, and continuing to market each party's products without expensive patent litigation.

This reminds me of the bumper sticker I once saw that said "My lawyer can beat up your lawyer." If you have a meaningful and substantial patent portfolio, you can withstand the charges of infringement lodged by your competitors by throwing your legal department and your patents in the direction of the competitor.

Timing of Public Disclosure of the Invention   A further consideration determinative of obtaining patent protection is the timing of the public disclosure of the subject invention and the possibility that competitors will become aware of the invention and may incorporate your technology into their own development projects. One way of warning competitors to keep away from your technology is to use the statement "Patent Pending" on your products, or advertising or packaging, when introducing your product. You cannot legally use the term "Patent Pending" unless you actually have a patent application on file and pending in the U.S. Patent & Trademark Offce. To do otherwise will give your competitor cause to file a false advertising claim against you. Therefore, if your new technology is such that you believe your competitors will immediately incorporate your technology once they see your new product on the market, filing a patent application and using "Patent Pending" in your advertising and product literature will give such competitors second thought when attempting to incorporate your technology to their own use.

I have recently gone through such an analysis where a client sent me a competitor's product bearing the statement "Patent Pending." I conducted an analysis to determine whether or not our client could make a similar product even though I could not determine what patents the other party had on their product, since the patents we did uncover did not bear any relation to the competitor's product, and we were not able to uncover pending patent applications. However, I did determine that the device my client wanted to make could be produced from technology existing in the prior art, and I concluded that the competitor could not obtain a patent on its product broad enough to cover the product that my client was manufacturing due to the volume of related prior art, for example expired patents.

In addition to those factors discussed in the previous section, consider also the development of several related inventions in a particular technology or product area, that when combined, provide a major potential for a new and profitable business foundation. In this scenario, several patents will be developed, each fitting with the other like the teeth on a group of mating gears. This strategy protects the technology by developing patents that cover alternate devices or processes for accomplishing the same objectives as your technology. Also, as research on this new technology moves forward, this business strategy calls for obtaining additional "improvement" patents to maintain the exclusive market position of the technology for an extended period of time.

This strategy also includes considering how your business should be extended into related areas based on your successful technology patenting program, and protecting extended product lines with patents covering specific new products incorporating your technology. For example, envision the development of heat resistant ceramics for aircraft and space vehicles, and how that technology was adapted to cookware. This strategy calls for the coordination of efforts between the technology team, the marketing and business development team, and the intellectual property team.

Therefore, consider the relative market positions of you and your competitors, and whether or not the initial launch of your product will cause your competitors to incorporate your technology into their development efforts. The designation "Patent Pending" may be a decided marketing advantage.

2.7 DETERMINING WHO WOULD BE AN APPROPRIATE LICENSEE TO EXPLOIT YOUR INVENTION

We previously discussed the possibility of establishing a program to license your patented technology, as well as your unpatented trade secrets, know-how and other proprietary information, to non-competitors. Consider also that it may be beneficial to license a portion of your technology to your competitors, under carefully devised conditions where the competitors will not gain an advantage over you and your products in the marketplace.

The first way of determining who might be approached with an offer of a license under your technology is to compile a list of all the competitors in the industry related to your products. Your marketing staff could readily come up with such a list. Also, your marketing people can identify non-competitor companies which may be interested in using the technology embodied in your patent applications and your patents. It is my understanding that certain databases exist that can identify entities and companies that are involved in specified technological areas. It would then be incumbent upon you or someone under your direction to review the list of companies, and their products, to determine which of these companies could be approached for consideration of a license arrangement.

The above licensing factors are particularly relevant in the field of software, where your software can be used by different competitors and non-competitors to operate certain programs that analyze different data or produce different results, that are not competitive or damaging to your business.

Another way to determine who would be a potential licensee for your technology is to review the patents developed by the novelty searches directed toward your inventions that were conducted by your patent attorney, and look at the names of the owners of the patents that were uncovered by the searches. As discussed previously, the searches should have uncovered those patents that are most closely related to your technology. By definition, the owners of these patents are involved in the development of the same technology as your company, and therefore would most likely be good prospects for a potential license, if competitive factors do not bar such an arrangement.

Also, it may be advantageous to review the prior art patents that are cited in the patent applications and patents in your portfolio that relate to the same or similar technology. These patents will reveal the names of owners of similar technology, who may also be considered as potential licensees.

Another recommended procedure to obtain potential licensees is through the trade associations in which you are members.

2.8 DRAFTING STRATEGIC PATENT CLAIMS

After your or your company's strategic goals for intellectual property have been established, guidelines should be created to direct the patent professional in the preparation of patent application claims which dovetail with these goals. The claims of your patents should be able to encompass the products and/or processes of a broad gamut of infringing conduct by present and future competitors at the manufacturing, distribution and user levels. This is most important in the electronic and computer hardware and software industries. You should discuss the scope of the claims in all patent applications with your patent professional before the patent application is filed, to ensure that the guidelines have been satisfied. By way of example, in a computer-related patent application, different types of claim structures should be included, where applicable. This may include apparatus claims, method claims, computer-readable medium claims, data structure claims and/or signal claims. These types of patent claims are discussed in more detail at Chapter 14 of this text.

2.9   DETERMINING WHERE TO OBTAIN PATENTS

If your product will be or is being offered in the global market, your technology should be protected in those countries where: (1) your products are being sold, (2) the company reasonably expects to be marketing its products, and (3) your competitors can be expected to begin manufacturing competing and potentially infringing products. The process of determining where corresponding foreign patents should be filed should begin six months after your United States or home country patent application has been filed, since the foreign patent treaties and conventions require that action be taken within one year of the filing of the United States or home country application to protect your ability to file foreign patent applications in those countries in which you have selected to do so.

Careful consideration must be given to the question of international patent filings, primarily due to the cost factors involved. Filing, prosecution and maintenance (annuity) costs could, if not thought out, far outweigh the benefits of having a patent position in a foreign country.

My recommendation is that the following criteria be used to determine if and where foreign counterpart patent applications should be filed. In specific industries, other more tailored considerations will also be important:

- In which foreign countries will your technology be manufactured and marketed, or reasonably expected to be marketed by you and your company?
- What is the possibility and probability of enforcement of the patent in the respective foreign countries? As you have undoubtedly read in the press, there are certain countries in the world today where piracy is rampant and the enforceability of intellectual property laws in those countries seems very diffcult if not impossible to obtain. Consider, however, that most countries are currently expressing a desire to be members of the World Trade Organization (WTO), which requires a member country to establish a system for the enforcement of intellectual property rights, including patents. Therefore, if you determine that a country today does not have a strong system for enforcing intellectual property rights, consider what may change in the near future.
- Where can your competitors be expected to manufacture and/or import or export competing and potentially infringing products? Those countries should definitely be included in your list of foreign patent filings.
- What is the cost benefit of the expenses anticipated to be incurred in filing and

prosecuting foreign counterpart patent applications versus the commercial value of that technology to the company? If your company generates only small sales in one particular country, and does not foresee those sales increasing, the advantage of obtaining patent protection in that country may not be worth the expense.

- Consider also that there may be secondary or smaller foreign markets in which patent protection should be obtained. These could be countries where you currently may not have a marketing position, however your foreign sales personnel are now discussing potential marketing or manufacturing arrangements with potential licensees or distributors in those countries.

- Are there countries where you or your company can potentially license your technology to a manufacturer, distributor, competitor or to an entity in a totally different industry? If such possibilities exist, it may be within you and your company's best interests to obtain patent protection in those countries.

2.10   DETERMINING OTHER INDUSTRIES WHICH MAY BENEFIT FROM A LICENSE

This requires a determination of those other industries and related technologies that can find value in the technology you are now considering for patent protection. If, for example, you developed a new heating element for use in the engine block of your company's tractors, can that heating element also be used by the automotive industry, in oil well drilling equipment in cold environments, and other equipment used in colder weather such as air compressors, etc? Once you have selected other products that can benefit from your technology, your marketing people should be able to furnish you with the names of potential licensees in those particular industries. You should then approach these companies with the prospect of a license.

2.11   ENSURING YOUR PRODUCT DOES NOT VIOLATE THE PATENT RIGHTS OF OTHERS

It is important that before you introduce your new product to the market, a patent infringement search and analysis is conducted to uncover any potential unexpired patents that may be infringed by the marketing of your new product. Recall also that your product can infringe the patent of another even though your product is covered by its own patent. This infringement analysis should be conducted just before your new product is released for introduction to the marketplace. If you discover that your product may have potential infringement problems, it may be wise to either redesign the product, or have your patent attorney determine whether or not the potentially infringed patent can be invalidated.

However, I do want to emphasize that it is quite important that your new patented product does not violate the patent rights of others upon its market introduction. Patent infringement can lead to unnecessary and very costly patent litigation, and can ultimately result in your product being removed from the market. One glaring example, mentioned briefly before, is the expense that Kodak went to several years ago to introduce its instant imaging photography to the market, only to have Polaroid attack them in patent litigation, and force Kodak to make the decision to entirely leave the market. Thus the importance of this type of infringement analysis cannot be overstated.

2.12   POLICING THE MARKET FOR POTENTIAL INFRINGEMENTS OF YOUR PATENTS

Your sales force should be made aware of the protection afforded your products by the issued patents and pending patent applications which comprise your patent portfolio. Then, when your salespeople go into a customer's facility, if they determine that the customer has been approached by one of your competitors to sell a similar product, and usually at a lower price, your sales person can report back to you the existence of those competing products, and you can then initiate an analysis to determine whether or not those competing products are covered by any of the patents or pending patent applications in your portfolio. Today, in industries that use computer chips to operate their equipment, for example, it may not be easy for the salesperson to determine that a competing product is infringing, and competing product literature and website information may have to be reviewed.

The market should also be surveyed for potential infringing importations. Today, a vast amount of products are manufactured overseas, and then brought into this or another country by importers, where the importers never bothered to determine whether or not a patent may be infringed by the imported product. Therefore, it is up to you to police the importation and introduction of these foreign made products into the marketplace to determine whether or not any of the patents in your portfolio may be infringed.

2.13   THE ENFORCEMENT OF PROCESS PATENT CLAIMS AGAINST AN IMPORTER OF A PRODUCT MADE ABROAD

The U.S. Process Patent Act of 1988 introduced a new element into the enforcement of United States process or method patents. Under that act, if a foreign manufacturer uses a process outside the United States, which process is covered and claimed in a United States process patent, the importation into the United States of the product made by that patented process constitutes an infringement of the United States process patent. This is new in our law, since prior to 1988 if an infringing process were used overseas, that process did not infringe a U.S. patent and the product manufactured by that process could be freely imported into the United States. However, this 1988 act of the U.S. Congress now provides that such importation is an infringement of the U.S. process patent. This is one reason why it is important to include method claims in your patent applications where feasible. The 1988 act covers the importation of products that may or may not be covered by a U.S. article patent, but where the product is manufactured overseas by a process that violates a United States method patent, the importation of that product into the United States may be halted.

2.14   TRIMMING THE INTELLECTUAL PROPERTY TREE

As with anything else, the costs of developing and maintaining an effective intellectual property portfolio must be kept under control. One way to accomplish this is to periodically trim the fat (unnecessary patents and technology) from your program. This will prevent the unnecessary payment of maintenance (U.S.) and annuity (elsewhere) fees on patents covering obsolete technology, for example. Therefore, at regular intervals, the individual technology elements making up your intellectual property portfolio should be reviewed for:

- You or your company's present and future interest in the technology;
- Any current business requirement involving the technology;
- The technical importance of the technology to competitors or others; and
- The intended or future use, if any, by you or your company of the technology.

2.15 ESSAY ON INNOVATION MANAGEMENT

I recently attended a lecture on Innovation Management, where the speaker said: "Each technology push needs a market pull." I interpret this to mean that the need for new and better products in the marketplace is the pull that provides the push behind innovations in technology. If a need or desire exists, technologists will provide the means to satisfy that need or desire.

He also defined "innovation" as the successful implementation of a new idea. Thus the acts of technology implementation track the ideas that are born in an effort to solve problems. If you are able to recognize the existence of a problem, you will be led to the solution of that problem through innovation and creativity.

The beginning of problem solving may be the work of a single thought, or more likely the result of a "brainstorming" or information gathering session among the members of a research or development team. In the latter situation, you have a broad skill base in which to generate ideas, and no idea is considered a bad idea. In a good brainstorming session, everyone must speak, and everything mentioned is written down for later analysis. In these sessions, the newer members of the team gain the benefit of the knowledge of the more experienced engineers and scientists, each member gets to know the other members, and each participant gains an awareness of the analytical approach to problem solving used by other team members.

The implementation of a new idea begins with the work of the inventor or inventors. Management can construct a framework for this process by advising inventors how to find a patentable invention or otherwise unique feature in their work. The patent attorney can assist management in this educational aspect of the invention process. The patent attorney can also use the problem solving process to define a search profile of each technology project, and then conduct a search to determine if unexpired patents exist which stand in the way of the current direction of your research.

Once an innovative idea has been reduced to feasibility of implementation, the idea must be sold to the decision makers, usually management. Remember, since the idea is unique, it must be sold to those who may be skeptical about changing the current technology. Therefore, the innovative idea must be presented with all the technical benefits of making the change, along with marketing, sales and financial (e.g., cost, profit, time saving) benefits. Hopefully, your presentation will be made to a receptor who will leave the presentation with a full understanding of the innovative technology, and who is now encouraged with the prospect of adopting the new technology as a result of the receptor's recognition of the economic opportunity in the innovation.

The purpose of this presentation is to convince management that they should buy into the innovative idea. Expect that management will initially respond with questions, and you should be prepared to promptly respond to those questions. Some of these questions may require comparisons of your recommended new approach to other ideas that were brainstormed and discarded. It is helpful if the R&D organization maintains a systemization of stored ideas that can easily be retrieved. This allows the innovation team to provide important assistance in the decision-making process.

◆ INVENTORS AND INVENTIONS ◆

Charles Goodyear

VULCANIZATION OF RUBBER

Charles Goodyear was born in New Haven, Connecticut in December 1800, and eventually entered the hardware business with his father. However, their hardware business failed in 1830, forcing father and son into bankruptcy. At that time, natural or "India" rubber had little usefulness to industry. Rubber products melted in hot weather, froze and cracked after becoming brittle in cold weather, and stuck to virtually everything they came in contact with.

After the failure of the hardware business, Goodyear tried selling a valve for rubber life preservers, but the rubber market was going down because of rubber's aforementioned drawbacks. So Goodyear decided he should try to revive the failing market. He began his research in jail, where he was serving time because of debt. In jail, Goodyear worked with rubber and a rolling pin for hours at a time.

Rubber, being a natural adhesive, was very sticky, so after being freed from jail, Goodyear decided to use a powder to dry out the rubber. He started with magnesia powder that he purchased at drugstores. The added magnesia made the rubber less sticky, and armed with this improvement he received some backing from a friend to make rubber overshoes. Before he could market them though, summer arrived and the shoes melted.

Goodyear started adding quicklime to his mix, and at a trade show in New York he was awarded a medal for his work.

One day in 1836, while working with the rubber, he began to run low on samples, so he decided to melt down and reuse old rubber. By this time, Goodyear had started painting his samples, so he used nitric acid to remove the old paint, but the rubber turned black and he decided he could not use it. A day or so later, Goodyear noticed the sample was smooth and dry, so he retrieved it from the trash and started working with this new improved smooth rubber. He obtained more money based on this new rubber, but after a vacation with his family he returned to his nitric acid treated rubber and found it was still the soft glue that it always was. By 1839, Goodyear was still experimenting, now using sulfur. One day, while showing off his new rubber formulation and getting nothing but laughs, he became furious and the rubber slipped out of his hands, landing on a sizzling-hot potbellied stove. Instead of melting the rubber, it charred into a leather-like substance and around the burnt area was a springy brown part or "gum elastic." Goodyear observed that heat was required to cure or strengthen a rubber–sulfur compound. This change made the rubber into an almost completely new substance. Goodyear had invented waterproof rubber, through what he called the "vulcanization" process.

Goodyear still needed to know how long to cook his rubber. This was the hardest time for Goodyear and his family as he spent even more time trying out the heating techniques. He was forced to sell most of his family's possessions, but then he finally found that

Intellectual Property Law for Engineers and Scientists, by Howard B. Rockman
ISBN 0-471-44998-9 © 2004 The Institute of Electrical and Electronics Engineers

steam under pressure, applied for four to six hours at approximately 270 degrees Fahrenheit, gave him the most uniform results. In 1844, Goodyear obtained a patent on his vulcanization process after spending five years developing his process. Vulcanization is a process in which sulfur reacts with carbon–carbon double bonds in the rubber to form "bridges" of sulfur atoms that cross-link the molecules.

As you might expect, the principal use of Goodyear's process is in the manufacture of tires, hoses, and footwear. Goodyear's unique process strengthened rubber, made it resistant to heat and cold, and ultimately revolutionized the rubber industry. However, Goodyear was unable to profit financially from his discovery, although he did license his process. His numerous patents were continually infringed upon, and he spent large sums of money on unsuccessful businesses, costly experiments, and attempts to promote his process. The company that bears his name today was founded many years after Charles Goodyear's death. He was able to establish his rights legally, but died in 1860 a poor man.

UNITED STATES PATENT OFFICE.

CHARLES GOODYEAR, OF NEW YORK, N.Y.

IMPROVEMENT IN INDIA-RUBBER FABRICS.

Specification forming part of Letters Patent No. 3,633, dated June 15, 1844.

To all whom it may concern:

Be it known that I, CHARLES GOODYEAR, of the city of New York, in the State of New York, have invented certain new and useful Improvements in the Manner of Preparing Fabrics of Caoutchouc or India-Rubber; and I do hereby declare that the following is a full and exact description thereof.

My principal improvement consists in the combining of sulphur and white lead with the india-rubber, and in the submitting of the compound thus formed to the action of heat at a regulated temperature, by which combination and exposure to heat it will be so far altered in its qualities as not to become softened by the action of the solar ray or of artificial heat at a temperature below that to which it was submitted in its preparation—say to a heat of 270° of Fahrenheit's scale—nor will it be injuriously affected by exposure to cold. It will also resist the action of the expressed oils, and that likewise of spirits of turpentine, or of the other essential oils at common temperatures, which oils are its usual solvents.

The articles which I combine with the india-rubber in forming my improved fabric are sulphur and white lead, which materials may be employed in varying proportions; but that which I have found to answer best, and to which it is desirable to approximate in forming the compound, is the following: I take twenty-five parts of india-rubber, five parts of sulphur, and seven parts of white lead. The india-rubber I usually dissolve in spirits of turpentine or other essential oil, and the white lead and sulphur also I grind in spirits of turpentine in the ordinary way of grinding paint. These three articles thus prepared may, when it is intended to form a sheet by itself, be evenly spread upon any smooth surface or upon glazed cloth, from which it may be readily separated; but I prefer to use for this purpose the cloth made according to the present specification, as the compound spread upon this article separates therefrom more cleanly than from any other.

Instead of dissolving the india-rubber in the manner above set forth, the sulphur and white lead, prepared by grinding as above directed, may be incorporated with the substance of the india-rubber by the aid of heated cylinders or calender-rollers, by which it may be brought into sheets of any required thickness; or it may be applied so as to adhere to the surface of cloth or of leather of various kinds. This mode of producing and of applying the sheet caoutchouc by means of rollers is well known to manufacturers. To destroy the odor of the sulphur in fabrics thus prepared, I wash the surface with a solution of potash, or with vinegar, or with a small portion of essential oil or other solvent of sulphur.

When the india-rubber is spread upon the firmer kinds of cloth or of leather it is subject to peel therefrom by a moderate degree of force, the gum letting go the fiber by which the two are held together. I have therefore devised another improvement in this manufacture by which this tendency is in a great measure corrected, and by which, also, the sheet-gum, when not attached to cloth or leather, is better adapted to a variety of purposes than when not prepared by this improved mode, which is as follows: After laying a coat of the gum, compounded as above set forth, on any suitable fabric I cover it with a bat of cotton-wool as it is delivered from the doffer of a carding-machine, and this bat I cover with another coat of the gum—a process which may be repeated two or three times, according to the required thickness of the goods. A very thin and strong fabric may be thus produced, which may be used in lieu of paper for the covering of boxes, books, or other articles.

When this compound of india-rubber, sulphur, and white lead, whether to be used alone in the state of sheets or applied to the surface of any other fabric has been fully dried, either in a heated room or by exposure to the sun and air, the goods are to be subjected to the action of a high degree of temperature, which will admit of considerable variation—say from 212° to 350° of Fahrenheit's thermometer, but for the best effect approaching as nearly as may be to 270°. This heating may be effected by running the fabrics over a heated cylinder; but I prefer to expose them to an atmosphere of the proper temperature, which may be best done by the aid of an oven properly constructed with openings through which the sheet or web may be passed by means of suitable rollers. When this process is performed upon a fabric consisting of the above-named compound it must be allowed to remain upon the cloth on which it is made, in order to sustain it, as it is so far softened during the operation as not to be capable of supporting its own weight without such aid. If the exposure be to a temperature exceeding 270°, it must continue for a very brief period.

Having thus fully described the nature of the process by which I prepare my improved india-rubber fabric, I do hereby declare that I do not now claim the combining of sulphur with caoutchouc, either in the proportion named or in any other, this combination having been the subject of a patent granted to me on the 24th of February, 1839; but

I do claim—

1. The combining of the said gum with sulphur and with white lead, so as to form a triple compound, either in the proportions herein named or in any other within such limits as will produce a like result; and I will here remark that although I have obtained the best results from the carbonate of lead, other salts of lead or the oxides of that metal may be substituted therefor, and will produce a good effect. I therefore under this head claim the employment of either of the oxides or salts of lead in the place of the white lead in the above-named compound.

2. The formation of a fabric of the india-rubber by interposing layers of cotton-batting between those of the gum, in the manner and for the purpose above described.

3. In combination with the foregoing, the process of exposing the india-rubber fabric to the action of a high degree of heat, such as is herein specified, by means of which my improved compound is effectually changed in its properties so as to protect it from decomposition or deterioration by the action of those agents which have heretofore been found to produce that effect upon india-rubber goods.

CHARLES GOODYEAR.

Witnesses:
    THOS. P. JONES,
    B. R. MORSELL.

3 How to Read and Obtain Information From a Modern U.S. Patent

Beginning on the next page is a copy of a randomly selected patent that was issued on June 17, 1975, and is therefore expired. The purpose of this chapter is to describe what information is set forth in the pages of that patent, or any modern patent, to enable you to read a patent and gain information about the disclosed and claimed invention with ease.

3.1 INFORMATION PAGE

The first page of patents printed today is known as the information page, and at the top identifies the document as a "United States Patent." The patent number, currently a seven-digit number, appears in the upper-right-hand corner. Your patent attorney, in correspondence, may refer to a patent by the last three numerals of the patent number, such as "the '710 patent." The last name of the first named inventor appears on the left side of the page on the second line beneath the identification of the document as a U.S. patent. This patent was issued to an inventor named Brost.

Beneath the patent number at the top of the information page is the date of issuance of the patent, which also determines the beginning of the enforcement period of the patent. As of June 7, 1995, the term of patent enforcement was changed from 17 years from the date of issue, to 20 years from the filing date of the parent application from which the patent issued, for patent applications filed subsequent to June 8, 1995. Additional time may be added to the enforceability term due to specied delays occurring in the U.S. Patent & Trademark Office, such as the time spent appealing, and reversing, a final rejection of the patent examiner.

For patents issuing from patent applications pending on June 8, 1995, or were in force as of that date, the patent enforcement term is the greater of (1) seventeen years from the date of issue, or (2) twenty years from the date of filing of the earliest related patent application.

Beneath the above-described identifying nomenclature, the next line on the left side of the information page sets forth the title of the invention, in this case "CHECK VALVE WITH ELASTOMERIC VALVE ELEMENT." The title is required to be placed on the application, and should be descriptive of a structural or result aspect of the invention.

The numbers in brackets throughout the information page are INID Codes, which stands for "Internationally Agreed Numbers for the Identification of Bibliographic Data." These code numbers identify the category of information set forth on the issued patent's information page.

Intellectual Property Law for Engineers and Scientists, by Howard B. Rockman
ISBN 0-471-44998-9 © 2004 The Institute of Electrical and Electronics Engineers

United States Patent [19]

Brost

BEST AVAILABLE COPY

[11]   **3,889,710**

[45] **June 17, 1975**

[54] **CHECK VALVE WITH ELASTOMERIC VALVE ELEMENT**

[76]   Inventor: **Julien H. Brost,** 56 Sauganash Dr., Fontana, Wis. 53125

[22]   Filed: **Jan. 11, 1974**

[21]   Appl. No.: **432,610**

Related U.S. Application Data

[63]   Continuation of Ser. No. 307,352, Nov. 7, 1972, abandoned.

[52]   **U.S. Cl.**.............................. **137/512.15;** 137/525
[51]   **Int. Cl.**.. **F16k 15/00**
[58]   **Field of Search** 137/102, 525, 525.1, 525.3, 137/525.5, 512.15, 533, 516.15

[56]   **References Cited**

UNITED STATES PATENTS

797,739	8/1905	Meer	137/516.15
1,412,473	4/1922	Lane	137/102
1,506,012	8/1924	Lewis	137/102
2,547,377	4/1951	Juhasz	137/525.3
3,247,866	4/1966	Sanz	137/533
3,664,371	5/1972	Schneider	137/525

Primary Examiner—Martin P. Schwadron
Assistant Examiner—George L. Walton
Attorney, Agent, or Firm—Larson, Taylor and Hinds

[57]   **ABSTRACT**

The invention relates to a check valve comprising two rigid body members which cooperate to provide a valve chamber with generally opposed inlet and outlet passageways. One of the body members defines a concave seating surface surrounding the inlet passageway and the other member defines the outlet passageway and an abutment structure confronting but spaced from the center of the concave seating surface. A normally flat elastomeric valve disk, smaller than the seating surface, is located between that surface and the abutment structure, which flexes or dishes the disk to maintain its periphery in sealing contact with the seating surface. Fluid pressure against the face of the disk engaged by the abutment structure increases its sealing engagement with the seating surface, but pressure on the opposite disc face overcomes the resiliency of the disk and allows fluid to flow around its periphery to the outlet passageway.

21 Claims, 6 Drawing Figures

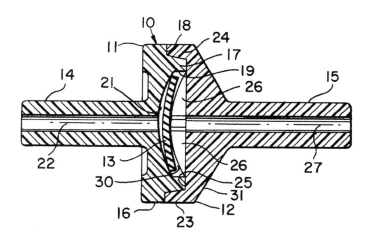

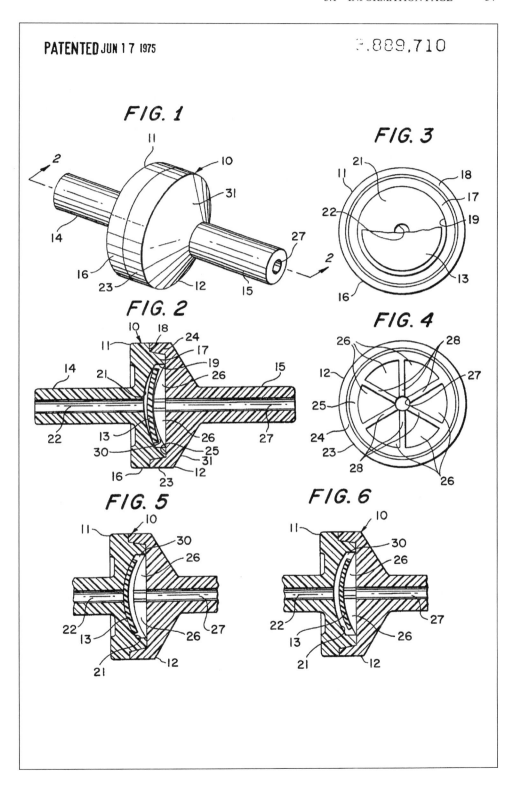

PATENTED JUN 1 7 1975   3.889,710

FIG. 1

FIG. 3

FIG. 2

FIG. 4

FIG. 5

FIG. 6

3,889,710

1

CHECK VALVE WITH ELASTOMERIC VALVE ELEMENT

This is a continuation of application Scr. No. 307,352, filed Nov. 7, 1972, now abandoned.

BACKGROUND OF THE INVENTION

FIELD OF THE INVENTION

The present invention relates to check valves, i.e. valves adapted to allow the passage or pressurized fluid in only one direction, and more particularly to an improved check valve employing an elastomeric disk as the valve element.

DESCRIPTION OF THE PRIOR ART

Many types of check valves have been developed which use an elastomeric valve element retained against a valve seat by its own resiliency so that fluid can pass through the valve in the direction in which it deflects the valve element away from the seat but cannot flow in the opposite direction in which the seating pressure is increased by the fluid. In previously known check valves of this type, however, the configuration of the valve element generally has been such as to require it to be either a relatively expensive molded component or an undesirably fragile element cut from sheet material. Furthermore, the production of such valves has heretofore been complicated by the need to align the valve element accurately with other valve components and/or to physically attach it to one or more of such other components during the assembly operation. Additionally, because prior art check valves of this type have required the valve element to always engage the same area of the valve seat, a piece of grit or the like that may become accidentally imbedded in the sealing face of the resilient element repeatedly scratches the same region of the seat and rapidly destroys the effectiveness of the valve.

SUMMARY OF THE INVENTION

The principle object of the present invention is to provide a simple and reliable check valve comprising only three basic components including an elastomeric valve disk adapted to be cut from sheet material.

Another object of the invention is to simplify the assembly of such valves without complicating the structure thereof.

Still another object of the invention is to provide a check valve particularly suited to embody simple molded plastic body members.

A further object of the invention is to provide such a check valve with a valve element that is capable of repositioning itself with respect to the seat surface engaged thereby.

Another object of the invention is to provide a simple and inexpensive check valve capable of responding to relatively low pressure differentials.

Yet another object of the invention is to provide an improved elastomeric disk check valve particularly suitable for miniature applications.

Briefly, these and other related objectives are realized in accordance with the present invention by means of a check valve comprising two rigid body members which cooperate to provide a valve chamber with generally opposed inlet and outlet passageways. One of the body members defines a concave seating surface surrounding the input passageway and the other body

2

member includes an abutment structure confronting but spaced from the center of the concave seating surface. A normally flat elastomeric valve disk, smaller than the seating surface, is located between that surface and the abutment structure, which flexes or dishes the disk to maintain its periphery in sealing contact with the seating surface. Fluid pressure against the face of the disk engaged by the abutment structure increases its sealing engagement with the seating surface, but pressure on the opposite disk face overcomes the resiliency of the disk and allows fluid to flow around its periphery to the outlet passageway.

Various means for practicing the invention and other advantages and novel features thereof will be apparent from the following detailed description of an illustrative preferred embodiment of the invention, reference being made to the accompanying drawings in which like reference numerals denote like elements.

IN THE DRAWINGS

FIG. 1 is a perspective view of a check valve according to a preferred illustrative embodiment of the invention;

FIG. 2 is a longitudinal cross sectional view of the illustrative valve taken along line 2—2 of FIG. 1;

FIG. 3 is an end elevation view of the inlet member of the illustrative valve, depicting the elastomeric valve disk in its operative position but partially broken away to show the concave seating surface;

FIG. 4 is an end elevation view of the outlet member of the illustrative valve showing the abutment structure embodied therein;

FIG. 5 corresponds to a portion of FIG. 2 and illustrates the closed position of the valve disk in which it prevents fluid from flowing through the valve from the outlet passageway to the inlet passageway; and

FIG. 6 is similar to FIG. 5 but shows the open position of the valve disk when fluid is passing through the valve from its inlet passageway to its outlet passageway.

DESCRIPTION OF THE ILLUSTRATIVE PREFERRED EMBODIMENT

The illustrative valve shown in the accompanying drawings is particularly suited to be of relatively small size for use in low or moderate pressure applications such as fluidic logic circuits, carburetor control systems, vacuum operated windshield devices, etc. As previously mentioned, the valve 10 is made up of only three basic components; mainly an inlet body member 11, and outlet body member 12 and an elastomeric valve disk 13. The two body members are preferably injection molded components made of nylon or any other suitable plastic material and the valve disk is preferably die cut out of a flat smooth sheet of elastomeric material such as natural or synthetic rubber. Alternatively, the valve disk can be an injection molded elastomeric member, in which case its seating face is either smooth or provided with concentric seating ridges. When the valve is assembled, as best shown in FIGS. 1 and 2, the two body members 11 and 12 are joined in coaxial relation to each other with their respective inlet and outlet tubes 14 and 15 extending in opposite directions along the central valve axis to permit the valve to connect two pieces of a flexible hose or tube slid over the corresponding valve tubes.

The inlet body member 11 includes a cylindrical head 16 provided with an annular rib 17 that defines a

3,889,710

3

peripheral notch 18 and an internal cylindrical wall 19 encircling a concave seating surface 21 that surrounds an inlet passageway 22 extending along the axis of the inlet tube 14. The outlet body member likewise includes a cylindrical head 23 provided with a peripheral axial lip 24 that encircles a flat annular face surface 25 surrounding a convex abutment structure comprising six radially disposed abutment members 26. As best illustrated in FIG. 4, these abutment members are symmetrically disposed about axial outlet passageway 27 continuing through outlet tube 15 and are separated by radial slots 28 extending from that passageway to the periphery of the abutment structure. The sector shaped faces of the abutment members preferably are coincident with an imagnary spherical or conical surface coaxial with the valve, but different forms of either single or plural abutment members could be substituted for this preferred structure.

To assemble the valve, the inlet body member is supported with its head facing upwardly and the elastomeric valve disk 13 is placed on the concave seating surface 21 as shown in FIG. 3, which is very easily accomplished inasmuch as the outer diameter of the valve disk is substantially smaller than the inner diameter of wall 19 surrounding the seating surface. The outlet body member is then mated with the inlet member and those two members are permanently sealed together in fluid-tight relation to each other. Preferably, the peripheral surface of the inlet body member rib 17 and the mating surface of outlet body member lip 24 are tapered and adapted to provide an interference fit with each other to facilitate sealing the two body members together by ultrasonic welding. Alternatively, the two body members can be joined by heat sealing, solvent welding, spin welding, cementing or any other other appropriate technique. Regardless of the sealing process employed, however, it will be seen that rib 17 isolates the sealed area from the internal valve chamber 30 to prevent excess sealing material from reaching that chamber.

Referring now particularly to FIG. 2, when the valve is assembled, the apexes of the abutment members 26 adjacent outlet passageway 27 centrally engage the confronting face of valve disk 13 so that the latter is dished toward but not into engagement with the central region of the seating surface 21 while the periphery of the disk is pressed against that surface by the resilient tendency of the disk to assume its normal flat condition. Because a circular disk engages any portion of a spherical surface along a flat plane, the preferred valve construction employs a normally flat circular valve disk and a substantially spherical seating surface; but the resiliency of the disk allows both it and the concave seating surface to deviate substantially from those ideal shapes without detracting significantly from the operation of the valve. In all cases, however, it is essential that the abutment means engageable with the central portion of the disk is spaced from the concave or female seating surface by more than the thickness of the disk but is close enough to the seating surface to resiliently distort the disk when the latter is in peripheral engagement with that surface.

When the fluid pressure in the outlet passageway 27 exceeds the pressure in the inlet passageway 22, the valve disk is thereby further distorted into contact with substantially all of the corresponding area of the seating surface, as shown in FIG. 5, thus insuring tight seal-

4

ing of the inlet passageway without imposing destructively high unit pressures on either the valve disk or the seating surface. When the inlet passage pressure exceeds the outlet passage pressure, however, the periphery of the valve disk is flexed partially or wholly out of contact with the seating surface as shown in FIG. 6; whereby fluid can pass around the edge of the disk and through slots 28 into the outlet passageway. As shown at numeral 31 in FIGS. 1 and 2, the external axial face of the outlet body member 12 is tapered to provide an arrow-like representation of the direction in which fluid can pass through the valve; thereby simplifying the proper installation of the valve.

Although the drawings illustrate the valve disk in a central or coaxial position relative to the body members, it should be recognized that the disk can shift edgewise in any direction against internal cylindrical wall 19, but that such movement does not detract from the proper performance of the valve inasmuch as the valve disk cannot move beyond confronting alignment with passageway 22. In addition to simplifying the assembly of the valve, such lateral freedom of the disk is also advantageous in that it allows the latter continuously to seek different positions and thereby uniformly distributes any wear that may occur between the disk and the seating surface. Furthermore, it should be apparent that the sensitivity of the valve to pressure differentials between its inlet and outlet passageways can be easily modified by altering the thickness or elastomeric resiliency of the valve disk or by changing the relation of the seating surface to the abutment structure.

The invention has been described in detail with particular reference to an illustrative preferred embodiment thereof, but it will be understood that variations and modifications can be effected within the spirit and scope of the invention as described hereinabove and as defined in the appended claims.

I claim:

1. A check valve comprising:

a housing defining a chamber having first and second opposing ends,

an inlet passage having an opening entering the chamber through one of said opposing ends and an outlet passage having an opening entering the chamber through the other of said opposing ends,

an annular portion of said one end of the chamber immediately surrounding the inlet passage opening forming an annular concave valve seat,

an abutment means in the chamber, fluid openings being provided through the abutment means to permit fluid to flow from the inlet passage therethrough to the outlet passage, one end of the abutment means projecting towards the inlet opening,

a resilient disc which is essentially flat in its relaxed condition extending transversely across the chamber between the said one end of the abutment means and the annular valve seat, said disc being of a sufficiently large cross-section, taken in the direction transverse to the flow direction, that in its normal closed condition in the chamber, the said one end of the abutment means engages the central portion of the disc on the side thereof facing the outlet opening and flexes the disc convexly toward the inlet opening as the outer periphery of the disc sealingly engages the annular valve seat,

said fluid openings in the abutment means positioned to remain open for fluid flow from the inlet opening

3,889,710

5

around the outer periphery of the disc and through the fluid openings to the outlet opening when the resilient disc has flexed toward the outlet opening as far as its outer dimensions and resilience allow when subjected to the largest possible pressure differential from the inlet opening toward the outlet opening,

said resilient disc having sufficient resiliency and arranged to increase the area of its sealing contact with the annular concave valve seat from said initial sealingly engaging outer periphery, radially inwardly, as the fluid forces from the outlet toward the inlet increase beyond the flexing force exerted by the abutment means on the disc,

and the outer periphery of the disc, when in the said normal closed position, being spaced radially inwardly from the outer periphery of the concave valve seat, permitting at least slight transverse movement of the disc within the chamber when sealingly engaging the annular valve seat.

2. A check valve according to claim 1, said abutment means including a central portion which includes said one end engaging the disc, and portions extending transversely from the central portion including said fluid openings.

3. A check valve according to claim 2, in which the abutment means are integral with the said other end of the chamber and comprise a plurality of abutment protrusions spaced from each other and surrounding the said outlet opening within said chamber.

4. A check valve according to claim 2, said abutment means comprising sector shaped elements separated by a plurality of radial grooves extending radially outwardly from said outlet opening a greater radial distance than the radius of the disc.

5. A check valve according to claim 4, in which said sector shaped elements define a portion of a spherical surface concentric with the axis of the outlet passage.

6. A check valve according to claim 1, including an inlet body member including said inlet opening and said annular valve seat, and an outlet body member forming the other end of the chamber and said outlet opening.

7. A check valve according to claim 6, said inlet and outlet body members being generally cylindrical and constructed to mate together coaxially, said inlet and outlet passages being located along the common central axis of said mated body members.

8. A check valve according to claim 7, in which one of said body members comprises an internal cylindrical annular rib and the other body member includes an annular lip adapted to mate with the external surface of the said annular rib to enclose said chamber.

9. A check valve according to claim 1, said annular valve seat defining a portion of a sphere.

10. A check valve according to claim 9, said abutment means defining a portion of a sphere concentric with the spherical portion of the valve seat.

11. A check valve having means including opposed spaced apart first and second walls defining a chamber, an inlet passage opening into the first wall and an outlet passage opening into the second wall, the direction from the first wall to the second wall being defined as the longitudinal direction of the valve,

said first wall including an essentially annular portion which is continuously concave, the said inlet pas-

6

sage opening into the center of this annular concave portion,

said second wall including raised abutments located about the opening to the outlet passage to form airflow passageways between the abutments in a direction transverse to the longitudinal direction from the transverse outer limits of the abutments inwardly to the outlet passage,

and a resilient disc which is essentially flat in its relaxed condition located in the chamber and extending transversely across the space between the first and second walls, the transverse outer periphery of the disc engaging the annular concave portion, the disc being of smaller cross-section in the transverse direction than the outer limits of the annular concave portion but larger than the inner limits of the annular concave portion, the disc thus being movable transversely within the space such that its sealing peripheral edge can sealingly engage different parts of the annular concave portion,

the said abutments engaging the central part of the side of the disc facing the second wall and resiliently flexing the central part of the disc towards the first wall beyond any plane at which the peripheral edge of the disc can sealingly engage the annular concave portion, such that, in the rest condition of the valve, the disc is convex towards the first wall to form said sealing engagement of the disc edge with the annular portion,

the disc being sufficiently resilient such that when fluid forces from the outlet toward the inlet exceed the flexing force of the abutment on the disc, the surface of the disc facing the first wall moves against the annular portion to enlarge the sealing area between the disc and the first wall,

and said abutments extending transversely a greater distance than the outer periphery of the disc such that when the disc is urged by fluid forces from the inlet to the outlet as far as possible against the second wall, a fluid flow path is provided from the inlet opening around the outer periphery of the disc and between the abutments to the outlet openings.

12. A check valve according to claim 11, said valve being formed of a one-piece inlet body member including said inlet passage and said first wall and a one-piece outlet body member including said second wall and said outlet passage.

13. A check valve according to claim 12, in which said inlet and outlet body members include respective generally cylindrical heads adapted to mate together in coaxial confronting alignment with each other, said inlet and outlet passages being located along the common central axis of said mated body members.

14. A check valve according to claim 12, in which said valve disc is substantially circular and is cut from a flat sheet of resilient material.

15. A check valve according to claim 12, in which one of said body members comprises an internal cylindrical annular rib and the other body member includes an annular lip adapted to mate with the external surface of said annular rib to enclose the said chamber.

16. A check valve according to claim 12, in which said abutments are integral with said outlet body member and comprise a plurality of abutment protrusions spaced from each other and surrounding said outlet passage within said valve chamber.

3,889,710

7

17. A check valve according to claim **12,** in which said annular concave portion of the first wall defines a portion of a sphere.

18. A check valve according to claim **13,** in which said inlet and outlet body members include respective inlet and outlet tubes extending beyond said heads along said common axis.

19. A check valve according to claim **16,** in which said abutments comprise sector shaped elements separated by a plurality of radial grooves extending radially

8

outwardly from said outlet passage and terminating beyond the outer radial periphery of the disc.

20. A check valve according to claim **19,** in which said sector shaped elements define a portion of a spherical surface concentric with the axis of said outlet body member.

21. A check valve according to claim **19,** in which said sector shaped elements define a conical surface coaxial with the axis of said outlet body member.

* * * * *

5

10

15

20

25

30

35

40

45

50

55

60

65

Just beneath the title of the invention, the name and complete addresses of the inventor or inventors are listed, and these are the home addresses, not the work addresses of the inventors. Under U.S. Patent Law, the inventor(s) must always be identified, and these must be the inventor or inventors actually responsible for creating the disclosed invention. Corporations in the U.S. cannot be inventors.

Where a patent application was assigned by the individual inventor(s) to a corporation or other entity during the prosecution of the patent, such as the inventor's employer, and that assignment document was submitted to the U.S. Patent & Trademark Office for recording, the name and location of the assignee corporation or other entity will appear on the information page below the inventor(s) name and location. The '710 patent was not so assigned, because no assignee name appears. It is possible, however, that the patent was assigned prior to issuance by an unrecorded assignment document, or by an assignment document executed after the patent issued. In the latter case, if the assignment document is recorded after issue with the U.S. Patent & Trademark Office, the true owner of the patent may be found through a search of the publicly available assignment records of the U.S. Patent & Trademark Office. If an assignee is listed on the information page of a patent, the patent is issued to the owner/assignee.

Beneath the names and addresses of the inventors and the assignee is the date that the patent application was filed with the U.S. Patent & Trademark Office, and that is followed by the application Serial Number assigned to the application upon its filing. The Serial Number and the Patent Number have no relation to each other. Beneath the filing date and Serial Number is a statement of related U.S. applications or patent information, or foreign application or patent information, as the case may be. In the present case, the Brost '710 patent issued on an application that was a continuation of an earlier filed application, Serial No. 307,352, filed November 7, 1972, which earlier application went abandoned upon the filing of the continuation application.

Next, the information page sets forth the United States and International search classification in which the technical subject matter of the particular patent is classified, showing the class and subclass of classification. In this particular instance, the patent is classified in class 137, subclass 512.15. Also, the field of search through which the examiner looked during the examination process is indicated beneath the classification information.

Next, in the left column and sometimes following over to the right column, is a list of all prior art patents either applied and/or cited by the patent examiner during the prosecution of the patent application which led to the issuance of the Brost patent, or which were submitted by Brost's attorneys via an Information Disclosure Statement. These patents are listed by patent number, issue date, name of first named inventor, and search class and subclass where copies of these patents are classified and may be found. Since the patents are identified by number, the references cited can also be obtained from the U.S. Patent & Trademark Office's website (www.uspto.gov).

Next, and in the Brost '710 patent shown on the top of the right-hand side of the information page, is set forth the name of the Primary Patent Examiner, the Assistant Patent Examiner, and the attorney, agent or law firm that prosecuted the patent application on behalf of the inventor. This is followed by a paragraph constituting the Abstract of the Invention, which is a statement being less than 250 words which describes the environment and nature of the invention in concise terms to enable the reader to determine quickly the substance of the invention covered by the patent. Beneath the abstract is a brief statement setting forth the number of claims and drawing figures in the patent.

At the bottom of the information page, one of the figures of the patent drawings, as selected by the applicant, is illustrated. If you look at the second page of the Brost patent, which contains Figures 1-6 of the patent, you will note that the applicant selected Figure 2 to be reprinted on the information page.

3.2   DRAWINGS

The second page of the Brost '710 patent contains Figures 1–6, showing various views of the invention covered by the patent. Note, for example, that in Figure 5 the illustrated check valve is shown closed, while in Figure 6 the check valve is shown in an open position. Note also that there is one perspective view, three section views, and Figures 3 and 4 are end-elevation views of the illustrated check valve. The drawing Figures 1–6 of the Brost '710 patent contain numerals and lead lines identifying various parts of the check valve. These numerals are keyed to the description of the invention found in the specification portion of the issued patent.

The Patent Statute, at 35 U.S.C. §113 requires that drawings of the invention must be submitted "where necessary for the understanding of the subject matter sought to be patented." Where required, the drawings must illustrate each of the elements of the claimed invention. The patent drawings are normally a special type of mechanical drawing, and are usually prepared by patent draftspersons who are specialists in their field. In patent applications where no drawing is required for explanation of the invention, such as in certain chemical and composition of matter inventions, no drawings are submitted. Since a patent can be obtained based upon drawings or illustrations of the invention, it is not necessary that the inventor actually construct the invention before being granted a patent. The need to submit models of one's invention was abolished long ago.

3.3   SPECIFICATION

The almost three-and-a-half pages which follow the drawings in the Brost '710 patent constitute the specification of the patent, ending with the claims which are technically considered part of the specification. The text of the patent specification begins at column 1 with a repetition of the title of the invention, and a statement of the related parent patent application, which is now abandoned.

The specification continues with the background of the invention comprising a statement of the field of the invention, i.e., check valves, and a description of the content of the prior art and the problems associated with the prior art. This is followed by a summary of the invention which begins at column 1, line 40 of the Brost '710 patent. The summary may set forth objects or results achieved by the invention, followed by a brief statement of the elements and function of the invention which provide the objectives and results set forth.

A brief statement of the drawings appears in the middle of column 2 on the first page of the specification, followed by a lengthy description of the illustrative preferred embodiment of the invention. This is the portion of the specification which describes the structure and one cycle of operation of the check valve, and keys the numerals and lead lines of the drawings to the description of the invention.

Section 112 of the Patent Statue requires that the specification:

". . . contain a written description of the invention, and the manner and process of making and using it, in such full, clear, concise and exact terms as to enable any person skilled in the art to which it pertains, or with which is most nearly connected, to make and use the same, and shall set forth the best mode contemplated by the inventor of carrying out the invention."

This section of the statute comprises the "written description" requirement, the "enablement" requirement, and the "best mode" requirement. Therefore, when you read a patent, the specification should provide you with a complete description of the invention, and how it operates. The specification description must also enable one skilled in the art to make and use the invention. Lastly, from reading the specification, you can be assured that the best mode of carrying out the invention, as known by the inventor on the patent application filing date, has been disclosed. If these requirements do not come through upon a reading of the patent by one of ordinary skill in the art, the entire patent may be declared by a court to be invalid.

3.4 CLAIMS

Beginning at column 4, line 39, the claims of the Brost '710 patent are set forth and continue until the end of the patent at column 8. You will note that this patent has 21 claims, with Claims 1 and 11 being independent and the rest of the claims depending from either Claim 1, Claim 11 or claims intermediately dependent upon one of these two independent claims. The description of the invention is set forth in the "Description of the Illustrative Preferred Embodiment," while the claims define the scope of protection afforded by this particular patent grant.

3.5 WARNING

When reading a patent issued to or owned by someone else, an engineer or scientist should NEVER come to a conclusion that a product you or your employer is making, or is about to introduce to the market, infringes a claim in that patent. Further, the engineer or scientist should NEVER put in a memo, letter, e-mail or voice mail his or her opinion that a product infringes, possibly infringes or may infringe another's patent. For the reasons stated in the next paragraph, if you do form the impression that the disclosure of a third party patent is of interest to your research and development direction, or to a product you or your company is making, personally and informally bring that patent to the attention of your patent attorney or agent, and orally explain to the attorney or agent why you feel the patent is worth investigating.

There are two primary reasons for rigidly adhering to this policy. The first may sound elitist, and if it is, it is still an important reason. A claim in an issued patent has been written by a trained patent attorney or agent, and has gone through rigid examination, and most likely amendment, as a result of the examination by a patent examiner. The correct meaning and scope of coverage of that claim cannot be fully understood without a) a full understanding of the examination history of the patent, and b) knowledge of the principle of determining literal infringement and the correct application of the Doctrine of Equivalents. This is an evaluation that should be conducted by a trained patent attorney or agent. With all due respect, your "conclusion" of infringement of a patent claim has a good chance of being incorrect.

The second reason is that it is important that no paper, electronic or voice trail is created with your "concern" that a claim in a patent is or may be infringed by your or your company's product or process. If a patent infringement lawsuit is lodged against your or your company's product or process, during the discovery process in that litigation the opposing lawyer will obtain discovery of every non-privileged document, e-mail, voice mail, notation, etc. that relates to the allegedly infringing product or process. This would include any message of any kind you sent expressing your opinion or conclusion about infringement of the patent asserted against you. Your message could fly in the face of your own attorney's arguments that the patent in question is not infringed.

The problem arises when the lawyer for the patent owner shows your message to the jury, "admitting" that there is infringement. In addition to giving the jury fuel to conclude that there is infringement, you or your company may be held liable for willful infringement because you had "prior knowledge" of a possible infringement problem. A finding of willful infringement could lead to a trebling of damages if there is a finding of infringement by the court or jury.

If you have communicated your concern about a potential problem with a third party patent orally, there is no message trail that can be used against you or your company. In most situations, your conversation bringing the "patent of concern" to the attention of your attorney is a privileged communication. In addition, your patent attorney will later orally give you the results of his or her investigation, while preparing a privileged written or electronic opinion letter to you or your management team with advice on how to avoid any potential infringement problem.

Therefore, it is very important that you not make any discernable record of any conclusion you come to about potential infringement problems when reading a patent issued to another individual or company. Talk to your patent attorney directly, giving him or her the patent number, and asking him or her to investigate the coverage of that patent. Your patent attorney or agent will do the rest.

In addition, when presented with your "patent of interest," your patent attorney or agent will decide whether the patent is material to the examination of any pending patent applications he or she has filed recently, or are about to be filed. If necessary, your patent attorney will furnish the patent to the appropriate patent examiner under the duty of full disclosure of known, material prior art.

Remember, read a patent of another party from the standpoint of its relevance as prior art in relation to a research or development project in which you are involved. DO NOT make statements in any tangible medium regarding potential infringement issues. Leave that problem to the attorneys—that's their job!

◆ INVENTORS AND INVENTIONS ◆

George Westinghouse

STEAM POWER BRAKE DEVICES AND ALTERNATING CURRENT

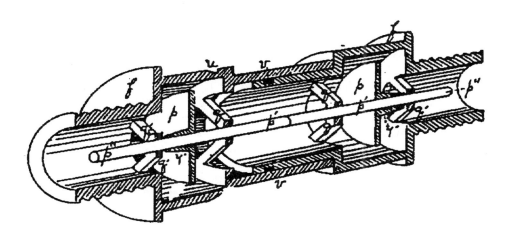

George Westinghouse is considered by some as one of the most productive inventors of his era, who perpetuated the Industrial Revolution through his ambition to resolve technical, commercial, and social obstacles. For example, in 1871, his employees were given a half day off on Saturday, the initial step toward the five-day work week. He created an employee pension fund in 1908, and his workers were given paid vacations in 1913. The first radio station in the world was Westinghouse KDKA in Pittsburgh.

George Westinghouse was born in Central Bridge, New York on October 6, 1846. He worked in his father's farm machinery shop in Schenectady, New York until the age of 15, when he joined the Union Army as a cavalry scout, and then the Union Navy as a naval engineer where he served throughout the Civil War. He briefly attended Union College, and upon returning to his father's shop in 1865, he developed and patented a rotary steam engine, a device for replacing derailed freight cars, and a railroad frog.

In 1866, after the war was over, Westinghouse, while working for his father, was a passenger in a train that stopped suddenly to avoid colliding with a wrecked train ahead. He got out, looked over the site, talked to the trainmen, and determined that there must be a better way to brake a heavy train. At that time, the railroads were heavily prone to accidents because each railroad car had its own brakes that were applied separately and manually by brakemen, leaping from car to car upon a signal from the engineer. The danger inherent in this system is obvious.

Meanwhile, in 1867, Westinghouse married Margaret Erskine Walker and moved to Pittsburgh where he had met others who shared his interest in inventing and manufacturing products for the railroad industry. Westinghouse continued to seek a solution to the train braking problem. He first considered using a chain to couple all of the train's brake controls, but this did not work. His next idea of using the steam generated by the locomotive to operate steam brakes on each car became impractical when the steam condensed to water and froze in cold weather before reaching the brake systems.

He then learned that engineers drilling dynamite holes in an Alpine tunnel used a steam engine to produce compressed air that was piped 3000 feet into the tunnel to run the air drills. He applied this technology to an air brake system for trains, and obtained a patent for his air brake on April 13, 1869.

Westinghouse wanted to install a test air brake system on a full sized steam-driven train and approached Cornelius Vanderbilt, president of the New York Central Railroad with a request to "borrow" a locomotive and several cars. When Westinghouse told Vanderbilt that he wanted to stop a train with just air, Vanderbilt had Westinghouse removed from his office.

In 1869, however, Westinghouse convinced the Panhandle Railroad to provide him with a locomotive and four cars on which he installed his air brake system. A test was arranged over the Pittsburgh–Steubenville stretch of the Panhandle's right of way. Panhandle officials and Westinghouse boarded the train and it started out. At the first and second stations, the train stopped as promised. Before reaching the third station, the engineer saw a horse and carriage stuck at a crossing. The brakes were applied by the engineer hard and fast. The train came to a screeching halt, with most passengers being hurled to the floor. This convinced the Panhandle officials, and Westinghouse, that the engineer-operated air brake was a vast improvement over the prior manual braking system.

As the Westinghouse Air Brake Company, which was organized in July 1869, began to receive orders, Westinghouse built his first factory in Pittsburgh. His brake system gave railroad passengers greater confidence in the safety of their ride, and provided increased efficiency to the owners of the railroads. The Railroad Safety Appliance Act of 1893 made air brakes required equipment on all United States trains. The use of air brakes also took hold in Europe, and is today the industry standard.

Business expanded and Westinghouse bought land east of the city where he erected a larger plant, and in 1890 built a town around the plant. The town was named "Wilmerding," the name of the family from whom he bought the land. Unlike other U.S. factory towns of the late 19th century, the stores were privately operated, not by the Westinghouse Company. Workers were not bound by a scrip system, and houses were either rented from the company or could be purchased at a modest cost. In addition to the benefits mentioned in the first paragraph of this essay, Westinghouse also provided pensions covering wives and orphans of retirees, sickness and accident benefits, student training courses in the company's shop, employee incentive plans, and the basic principles of collective bargaining.

In 1879, Westinghouse invented a pneumatic interlocking railroad signal system to control the increased speed and flexibility railroads gained by the invention of the air brake. In 1881, he organized the Union Switch and Signal Company to develop and sell his railroad safety and traffic control inventions.

In the mid-1880s, Westinghouse became interested in electricity and, in particular, the disadvantages of DC power systems fostered by Thomas Edison. He pursued AC power generating technology, bought the United States rights to Gaulard and Gibbs' AC distribution system in 1885, and hired William Stanley to improve on the Gaulard–Gibbs "transformer." In 1886, Westinghouse organized the Westinghouse Electric Company to advance the introduction and use of AC power systems in direct competition with Edison's DC power systems, as described in more detail in the essay "Current Events" following Chapter 27, supra. In 1887–1888, Westinghouse also acquired rights under Nikola Tesla's AC polyphase system patents, and hired Telsa to work for Westinghouse Electric and develop the AC motor with the rotating magnetic field that Tesla had conceived and had been working on. In 1892, Westinghouse, using Tesla's AC polyphase system, was awarded the contract to light the "White City," the 1893 Colombian Exposition in Chicago. Westinghouse's company also installed the electrical generators to turn the kinetic energy of Niagara Falls into hydroelectric energy. Commercial service of these huge generators began in the fall of 1896. Due to financial problems, Westinghouse lost control of his electric company in 1907, but retained control of his other companies.

George Westinghouse was issued 361 patents in all, and died on March 12, 1914 in New York City. He and his wife are buried in Arlington National Cemetery. In my judgment, George Westinghouse appears to be a successful industrialist who was driven more by the desire that his efforts would benefit mankind than by the drive for money for money's sake.

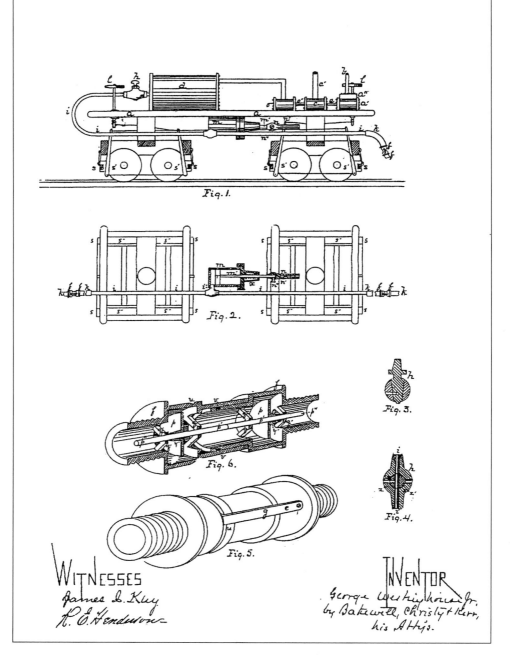

G. WESTINGHOUSE, Jr.

Steam-Power Brake Devices.

No. 5,504.

Reissued July 29, 1873.

Fig. 1.

Fig. 2.

Fig. 3.

Fig. 6.

Fig. 4.

Fig. 5.

WITNESSES

James G. Key

R. E. Henderson

INVENTOR

George Westinghouse Jr.
by Bakewell, Christy & Kerr,
his Att'ys.

4 Introduction to Patents

4.1 BRIEF HISTORY OF PATENT PROTECTION

4.1.1 Early European Patent Custom

It is commonly recognized that the history of patents is wrapped in obscurity and uncertainty. Prior to any patent system, there was a "patent custom" in many countries throughout Europe. Before the creation of the United States Constitution, the governments of several European countries granted exclusive rights in patentable and sometimes unpatentable subject matter as a privilege, rather than a property right. At the time the United States transitioned to a Federal form of government under its Constitution, the patenting of inventions had been known and practiced in several countries for centuries. The "patent custom" which was already known to the framers of the U.S. Constitution, and which was embodied in the first United States Patent Act of 1790, simply put, was the practice of the state granting some form of limited term exclusive right to engage in a new trade or craft, sometimes denominated an industry, to that person or persons responsible for introducing that industry into the state, either by creation or importation. The privilege consisted of a temporary and exclusive right to exploit the new subject matter, covered by the grant, whether it be called a patent, letters patent, or something else.

This patent custom involved grants of privileges rather than property rights. The distinction between a patent privilege and a patent property right is an important one and one not always recognized in the early literature of the patent law. Nonetheless, inventors, who had the most practical interest in obtaining exclusive rights to exploit their inventions, were increasingly aware of the distinction, and in the 18th Century the inventors began to argue that they had a natural, inherent property right in their inventions, which it was the obligation of the state to protect, thus arguing that the state had no right to refuse them an exclusive position in their inventions.

In an effort to encourage individuals who contributed to the advance of a culture, earlier governments recognized the "natural" right of a person to his own ideas and inventions, and strengthened that right by granting early governmental proclamations and regulations restraining the opposing "natural" right to copy. For the most part, this protection was limited in terms of time by those early governments. Since these early forms of government were of an authoritarian nature ruled by monarchs, sovereigns, kings and emperors, the practice that was most prevalent in the early monarchies was to grant royal favors to certain individuals, giving exclusive rights to sell certain commodities which had previously been available to all. Needless to say, this type of monopoly did not find favor with the general public. These so-called city or state monopolies were outlawed in the Roman Empire in a proclamation by Emperor Zeno in 480 A.D. His proclamation read:

> "We order that no one will dare exercise a monopoly upon any garment or fish or . . . any kind of thing in that respect, or any material, whether it is already ascertained in a sacred way,

Intellectual Property Law for Engineers and Scientists, by Howard B. Rockman
ISBN 0-471-44998-9 © 2004 The Institute of Electrical and Electronics Engineers

or by a later rescript which ascertains it, or by empirical decree, or by a sacred notation of a kindness. . . ."

Similar state or royal monopolies were outlawed in medieval Europe and Great Britain at a much later date.

Despite this general prohibition on state monopolies, various practices developed to reward individuals for certain unique ideas. The archives of Venice indicate that protection was granted from about the year 1200 to dredges, wells, flour mills and other water-controlling or water-utilizing facilities. The Guilds of Venice, unlike those of most medieval Europe, encouraged the granting of protection to new devices and arts. Thus, between 1400 and 1432, the Senate of Venice enacted a statute providing a ten year exclusive privilege to use any machine or process that a person invents to speed up silk making or to improve the process. This grant was given by the Guild Welfare Board of the Republic, and was soon extended to other devices and arts such as flour mills, cook stoves for die shops, a device for raising water, the art of printing, and mills for grinding grain products. All this protection was granted in the 15th century. Such exclusive grants were made not only to encourage the citizens of Venice to invent unique materials and methods, but also to attract ingenious persons into the republic.

Before granting a patent, the Guild Welfare Board of Venice usually examined the invention to be certain it was new and indeed, useful. The disclosure of the invention was made by public use, not by filing a written document such as a patent application, and examination of the invention took place by interview, observation and the explanations of experts. The grant of exclusivity was often based on a showing that the invention had to be truly useful and could achieve the advantages asserted by the inventor. What is believed to be the world's first general patent statutes evolved from these practices, and in 1474 the Senate of the Republic of Venice reorganized its patent system by enacting a statute with the clear intent of encouraging both native ingenuity and the importation of new ideas. The preamble to the statute is noteworthy, and is dated March 19, 1474:

> "We have among us men of great genius, apt to invent and discover ingenious devices; and in view of the grandeur and virtue of our city, more such men come to us every day from diverse parts. Now, if provision were made for the works and devices discovered by such persons, so that others who may see them could not build them and take the inventor's honor away, more men would then apply their genius, will discover, and will build devices of great utility and benefit to our commonwealth."

This was followed in the Venice law by a grant of a ten-year exclusive right to anyone who constructed any new and ingenious device in Venice, which was not previously made. Notice had to be given of the invention to the Guild Welfare Board of Venice. The penalty for infringement was one hundred ducats, and the infringing device would be destroyed immediately. It should be noted from the vantage point of modern patent statutes, that this Act of 1474 by the fathers of Venice included concepts that the device be actually constructed, that it be useful, and that it be novel. Also, the further test of innovation apparently is referred to by the term "ingenious devices" in the Venice statute. It is interesting to note that most of these concepts are embedded in modern patent laws worldwide. Today, you may obtain a patent on a new, useful and unobvious device, but you need not construct your invention to obtain an enforceable patent.

Modern patent law systems developed out of a realization by the state that there was indeed a societal need to both recognize and protect a "property right" with respect to inventions, as opposed to making such grants a privilege, although for reasons having very little to do with any perceived "natural law" right. At the time of the creation of the United States, this "property right" theory and its realization was beginning to come into full flower in England. As Great Britain was the mother country, its laws were most familiar to those in the new nation. Thus the United States embodied a property right in inventions as part of the Constitution in 1787.

The term "property right" involves the limited term exclusive right with regard to the invention, as opposed to a property right in the invention itself, or the device embodying the invention. This distinction is important because it is almost embarrassing how often the controversial idea of a property right in an invention is confused with the non-controversial idea of property rights in a patent. You must have the patent to acquire the exclusive property right.

While most of the history of the U.S. patent system relies upon English law, it is now clearly established that the custom of granting limited term exclusive privileges to inventors or importers for introducing new trade or industry into a state began in the Italian city-states, and particularly in Venice late in the 14th and early in the 15th centuries. From there the patent custom spread to Germany, France, The Netherlands, England and to the United States.

The term "patent custom" describes the practice in each country of granting inventors limited exclusive rights in inventions, but without a fully developed uniform system or administrative practice, nor consistent legal principles applicable under rules of law which properly define a true patent system. The first attempts to develop such a patent system occurred in England, and subsequently the United States, which will be discussed shortly in detail. Prior to the U.S. Constitution, certain of the colonial states were granting patents, while other states had in their Constitutions provisions declaring that the granting of monopolies was abhorrent. Certain states were enacting individual private laws granting exclusive patent rights. Under the English patent custom, as it had been in Europe for almost four centuries at the time of the creation of the American Republic, patents were granted not only to those who made new inventions, but also those who brought inventions known or used elsewhere and introduced them into the country. The patent custom had developed and spread throughout Europe primarily as a means of encouraging importation of new trade or industry, and only secondarily as a means of encouraging the creation of new inventions. The United States Congress in its deliberation of the Patent Act of 1790, the first U.S. patent law, specifically removed provisions that would have expressly authorized patents of importation.

At the time the U.S. Constitution was ratified, a patent custom existed in a number of states which granted exclusive rights in inventions by private legislative enactment. There was nothing in the Constitution which precluded states from continuing to issue patents, but the advent of a Federal patent system was viewed by almost everyone as removing any need for state patents. A few states, most notably New York, would continue to issue state patents for several decades after the Constitution.

4.1.2 British Patent System

The transition from a patent custom to a patent system came about in Great Britain through the recognition of patents as a form of property rather than merely a privilege. As was typical in Venice, Great Britain had a long history of royal grants prior to the first formal statute establishing patents.

As an island nation, the importation of skills from abroad was encouraged by the British in an effort to compete with the progress of other European countries. In the 14th century, the arts of weaving, ship making, glass making and iron making were stimulated in England by special grants to foreign artisans. During the reign of Queen Elizabeth I, which began in the year 1558, the first elements of a modern patent system appeared. Patents for a dredging machine, the making of soap, alum, and saltpeter were granted. However, in England as well as in other countries, there was abuse of the royal prerogative in granting patents, and public opinion in opposition was reflected in complaints to the House of Commons, and in the ultimate enactment of legislation to halt the practice of royal patent grants. In the year 1602, the case of *Darcy v. Allin,* 11 Coke 846 (King's Bench 1602) came before the court of England, called the King's Bench, challenging the right of the Crown to grant monopolies to items, in this case playing cards, which the citizens of London claimed a free right to trade in. Apparently this case decided that the monopoly was not valid.

In another case before the English courts in 1614 which involved the weaving art, entitled "The Cloth Workers of Ipswich," it was held that the King could not create a monopoly that would take away free trade which is the birthright of every subject. But the court held that if one brings a new invention and a new trade within the Kingdom, or has made "a new discovery," in such cases the King, of his grace and favor, may grant by charter that only he the inventor shall use such a trade or traffc for a certain time, because at first the people of the Kingdom are ignorant and do not have the knowledge or use of the new invention or trade." The Court went on to hold that when the patent right is expired, the King cannot make a new grant, for when the trade has become common and others have bound apprentices to the same trade, there is no reason that such use should be forbidden.

Ten years after the Cloth Workers decision, the English Statute of Monopolies was passed in 1623 during the reign of James I. This law invalidated the prior grants of patent rights given by the Crown, and declared that "any patent granted shall be maintained for a fourteen-year period or under, if the patents were directed to new manufactures within the realm, to the true and first inventor and inventors of such manufactures, which others, at the time of making such Letters Patent and grant, shall not use so as also they be not contrary to the law." The key point of this statute was that the granting of an exclusive right by way of Letters Patent was taken away as a prerogative of the Crown, and given as an inherent right to any inventor, and at that time, one who brought new inventions into the realm, as a right that could not be deprived by the Crown. This subtle but important difference is embodied in all of the patent laws of the world today. Note also that the Statue of Monopolies, as did the early Venetian statute, referred to "new" manufactures within the realm, setting up the requirement of novelty as a prerequisite to the grant of patent protection.

Although the patent custom originated in other European countries prior to adoption in Britain, the patent custom began to flourish in Britain during the reign of Elizabeth I. But it was not until the Statute of Monopolies was enacted in 1623 that the custom was given a statutory foothold in England. This law arose from a particular exemption to the general ban on monopolies, and Letters Patent were granted for a limited term of 14 years. This statutory language, together with the few common law judicial opinions that interpreted patent law in England, provided the legal basis for the English patent law that existed in 1787 when the American Constitution was being drafted.

However, there was a virtual dearth of reported common law cases in England relating to patents. For example, during the 17th Century there were only three reported common law cases on patents, and two of those had occurred prior to 1623. By the time of the American Constitution, there was considerable uncertainty in England as to the nature of what the patent law was because of the lack of court decisions interpreting the statutory provision. That uncertainty was compounded in the United States.

The framers of the U.S. Constitution also based their provision regarding patents and copyrights on the patent custom that was practiced during the colonial period, and later by the states right after the Revolutionary War.

The early English patent custom arose out of a desire to create new industry in the realm, primarily by importation and only secondarily by what would now be termed invention by entrepreneurs. As a consequence, novelty, which is the *sine qua non* for patentability throughout the world today, was predicated on whether the subject matter of the grant was presently being worked in England. It mattered not whether the art or manufacture was known and practiced elsewhere or even whether it had previously been practiced or worked in England. Originality was only peripherally involved, and the inventive subject matter was considered new if it had not been worked in England within recent memory. The seminal belief was that the Statute of Monopolies of 1623 did not change this.

4.1.3   The U.S. Constitution and the Development of the Present U.S. Patent Examination System

Origin and Early Development of Patent Law in the United States   The development of the United States patent law extends from 1787 at the Constitutional Convention, to the enactment of the Patent Act of 1836 which is the basis for the modern patent system in use today. During this time frame, the United States system changed from a patent custom to an established patent system.

Prior to the Constitutional Convention of 1787, many of the American colonies had enacted legislation forbidding monopolies, except as for such new inventions that were profitable to the colony, and those grants would only be for a short time. Massachusetts had such a law in 1641, and Connecticut in 1672. By the time of the Declaration of Independence in 1776, many colonies had been issuing patents, and they continued to do so between the time of the Declaration of Independence and the Constitutional Convention in 1787. The granting of patents by individual states even continued to some degree after the adoption of the Federal Constitution in 1789 and the passage of the first patent act of 1790. However, the granting of individual state patents eventually ceased.

The members of the Constitutional Convention were aware of the activities of inventors and authors, and of the efforts to aid them in the individual state legislatures and in the Continental Congress which preceeded the Constitutional Convention. James Madison and Charles Pinckney, the latter of South Carolina, each submitted proposed clauses to the Constitutional Convention in August of 1787 which stated as follows:

> "The Congress shall have power ... to promote the progress of science and useful arts, by securing for limited times to authors and inventors the exclusive right to their respective writings and discoveries."

The Constitutional Convention which gave rise to the United States Constitution in effect today, took place in hot and humid Philadelphia from May until September of 1787. Little is written on how the patent and copyright clause was placed into the Constitution.

What is known is that after discussing and debating the more important issues in the Constitution, on August 31, 1787, the delegates to the convention agreed to refer portions of the Constitution that had been postponed up to that time to a committee made up of a member from each state. Since Rhode Island had never been asked to attend the constitutional convention, and the New York delegation had left the convention in the middle to go back to their farming, this became the Committee of Eleven. On September 5th, 1787, the Committee of Eleven reported out five unresolved matters pertaining to the powers to be granted to Congress, the fifth of these was what became the Intellectual Property Clause of the U.S. Constitution, "to promote the progress of science and useful arts by securing for limited times to authors and inventors, exclusive right to their respective writings and discoveries." On September 12th, 1787, a committee of the convention reported a draft of the entire Constitution which left the Intellectual Property Clause intact. The final draft of the Constitution was approved on September 17th, 1787, including the Intellectual Property Clause.

Apparently the provision was uncontroversial, as there is no record of any debate on this matter. James Madison, writing in the *Federalist,* No. 43, stated that an author's copyright has long been adjudged in Great Britain to be a right held by the author at common law. The right to useful inventions seems with equal reason to belong to inventors. Thus, this statement by one of the leading founders of our nation, indicates the right of inventors to exclusive rights in their inventions, as distinguished from prerogative writs granted at will and fiat by the government.

It should be noted that an inventor does not have an exclusive right to his invention at common law, as that statement is strictly read. In 1850, the U.S. Supreme Court held in the case of *Gayler et al. v. Wilder,* 51 U.S. (10 How.) 477 (1850) that the inventor of a new and useful improvement has no exclusive right to the invention until he obtains a patent grant. This right is created by the patent and no action can be maintained by the inventor against an infringer before the patent is issued. The Court went on to hold that this exclusive right did not exist at common law, but was created by the Act of Congress in enacting the patent statutes. Again, in 1913 the U.S. Supreme Court stated in the case of *Bawer & Cie. v. O'-Donnell,* 229 U.S. 1 (1913), that the right to make, use and sell an invented article is not derived from the patent law. The patent law secures to the inventor the exclusive right to make, use and sell the patented item, and to prevent others from exercising like privileges without the consent of the patentee. The Court stated that the patent law was passed for the purpose of encouraging useful inventions and promoting new and useful improvements by the stimulation of exclusive rights give to inventive genius, and was intended to secure to the public, after the lapse of the exclusive privileges granted, the full benefit of such inventions and improvements.

Initial U.S. Patent Laws   The first patent law established by the Congress of the United States was the Patent Act of 1790, which created an examination system that was way ahead of its time. This examination system and law lasted only three years, and was repealed by the Patent Act of 1793, which, in turn, established a registration system rather than the prior short-lived examination system, which registration system was somewhat similar to the English system at that time. Apparently, the time and expense of running a patent examination system in 1790 was too much for the young government, and delays and frustration occurred. In the next forty-three years, five additional patent acts were passed, but all for the purpose of correcting some perceived deficiency in the existing legislation.

Under the Act of 1793, inventors would be required merely to submit written statements describing their invention, and the government would register those statements. The flaw in this system was that the courts were left to interpret what exactly was covered by the statements submitted by inventors and developers in view of infringements that may or may not have exactly corresponded to the material submitted and covered by the letters patent. It was also difficult to determine from the inventor's statement what was new about an invention in comparison to what was previously known and in the public domain.

After many years of having courts wrestle with trying to determine what the actual invention was based upon the inventor's description of the invention covered by the certificate of registration, with no examination by the government to define the limits of the grant, the modern Patent Act was enacted in 1836, which set up a Patent Office charged with the responsibility for the examination of the novelty, utility and importance of an invention, and established the office of the Commissioner of Patents to oversee the new examination system. This law also embodied the prior court-established rules for submitting specifications setting forth the invention, and stating precisely what it was that the inventor saw as the "novelty" or "invention" covered by the patent grant. The requirements of a written specification, and a statement or statements defining the scope of the invention, and its novel features were created from the previous court decisions and enacted into the Patent Act of 1836. In a subsequently enacted patent statute, a patent application was required to specifically "claim" or state the subject matter of the invention in separate claims forming part of the patent application. The difference between the former registration system and the new examination system of 1836 was that under the registration system, the courts developed the entire body of patent law in the United States, without any assistance or guidance from Congress. Beginning in 1836, with the enactment of a comprehensive legislative act, Congress set forth the standards of patentability and patentable subject matter to guide the courts, as well as inventors. It is this examination system, with the established law guiding the courts, that is in existence today and comprises the United States patent system.

Inventions, not Discoveries   It is important to note that although the Constitutional mandate uses the word "discoveries," there is a strong distinction in patent law as to whether patents can be obtained on inventions and discoveries. An invention, or creation of a work of art under the copyright law, is a creation by a human of something new, and something that is not found before, either manmade or in nature. This is the substance of what can be covered under the intellectual property laws. To the contrary, if someone "discovers" something that already exists in nature, or exists because of someone else's creation, such "discovery" is not rewarded by exclusive rights under the Intellectual Property Laws. It is possible that early use of the term "discovery" referred to inventions or novel things that were novel to a particular country, and when someone discovered them overseas and then brought them into the realm, they were awarded exclusive rights under the patent laws. However, that provision has been written out of every patent law in the world, and today, universally, a patent can only be granted on something developed by an inventor. You cannot obtain exclusive rights on something found overseas and then brought into your home country.

This, in my mind, raises interesting issues involving the patenting of genomes and DNA strains, where most of the public is of the understanding that scientists are discovering something that is in all of our bodies, and therefore, how can someone obtain a patent on something that already exists? The quick answer is that patents today may be granted on new living organisms, such as recombinant DNA, which is modified from its form found in nature. For a more thorough discussion of DNA patent protection, see Chapter 15.

Importance of Disclosure of the Invention   Disclosure of one's invention to the public is the primary object of patent systems everywhere, with exclusive rights granted to those inventors to exploit the invention for a limited period being their reward for disclosing their invention to the public. Prior to the existence of patent laws, inventors were operating their inventions in secret, trying to maintain such secrecy as long as possible so as not to have their invention stolen from them. As early as 1623 in England, it was decided that to urge these inventors to disclose their inventions to the public and make such inventions available for the public good, a limited exclusive right should be granted to those inventors for the exploitation of their inventions. In exchange for that limited exclusive right, the law required that the inventors make full disclosure of their inventions to the public so that once the patent grant expired, the public would have the full benefit of using that particular invention. Today's patent law requires, for example, that the specification in a patent contain a full, clear, exact, concise description of the invention so as to enable one skilled in the art to practice the invention upon the expiration of the patent without undue experimentation. The United States patent law also requires that the inventor must place in the specification the "best mode" of practicing the invention as of date of filing the patent application. This prevents an inventor from setting forth in any patent specification a less than perfect embodiment of the invention, while exploiting a more perfect version of the invention. Such conduct under American law invalidates the issued patent.

Therefore, the laws of the United States and many countries are quite specific as to the depth of description that must be placed in the patent application, including drawings where necessary to inform one skilled in the related art of the structure and operation of the invention. In the case of software inventions, many inventors place the source code in the patent specification. Others do not, and use flow diagrams to fully describe the invention. I have been looking for court decisions that may indicate that if a patent issues without a source code on software, the invention has not been fully disclosed. So far, I have not seen such a decision. It is my understanding, being a mechanical engineer, that possibly one can duplicate an algorithm or a computer program without information supplied from the source code. See Chapter 14 for the proper way to obtain patent protection for computer-related inventions.

Present Patent Law, Rules and Guides   In 1952, the Patent Act as it primarily exists today was enacted by Congress as part of 35 United States Code, (35 U.S.C. §100 et. seq.) as part of the federal statutory scheme. The 1952 Patent Act has been modified frequently over the past fifty plus years to bring some of its requirements into harmonization with international treaties, and to clarify or change details in the law.

The Patent Act authorizes the U.S. Patent & Trademark Office (USPTO) to issue its own Rules of Practice, which set forth in further detail the particulars of how the USPTO operates, procedurally, substantially, and financially. These Rules, which are found at Volume 37 of the Code of Federal Regulations (37 C.F.R.), have been enacted under the Administrative Procedures Act, and have the authority of law.

The U.S. Patent & Trademark Office has also issued a rather lengthy tome entitled "The Manual of Patent Examining Procedure" (MPEP) that comprises the set of guidelines the patent examiners and other personnel of the USPTO adhere to when examining or otherwise processing U.S. patent applications. Those of us, patent attorneys and agents alike, also refer to the MPEP as a reference in preparing, amending and prosecuting U.S. patent applications. The MPEP is a set of guidelines issued by the USPTO, and does not have the effect of law, as do the Patent Act (35 U.S.C.) and the Rules of Practice (37 C.F.R.).

The Patent Act, the Rules of Practice, and the MPEP are all available on the web site of the U.S. Patent & Trademark Office (`www.uspto.gov`), as well as a wealth of other information relating to patents.

4.2 TYPES OF PATENT COVERAGE

4.2.1 What Is a Patent?

A patent is far more than simply a legal document. It is a technical publication, a sales brochure, and a precise definition of the fence around the technology protected by the exclusive right encompassed by the patent grant. As a technical document, the patent contains a written description of the patented invention sufficient to permit anyone interested in the field of technology to which the patent relates to make and use the invention by reading the information in the patent. It follows therefore, that the United States Patent and Trademark Office provides a wealth of technical information available to the public, that may be unavailable elsewhere. As a sales brochure, the patent describes the prior art that was known before the invention set forth in the patent, and then describes how the invention improves, advances, and provides advantages over the known state of the art. As a complete description of the invention, along with claims setting forth the metes and bounds of the inventor's exclusive rights, the patent also acts as an advisory to those who would be infringers as to the limits of the inventor's exclusive technological territory.

Original patents comprise a set of printed pages, and drawings where required, bound together with a red ribbon under a gold seal. Duplicate copies of each patent are available from the U.S. Patent and Trademark Office, or from the internet at `www.uspto.gov`. All issued patents are available to any member of the public either in the public search room of the U.S. Patent and Trademark Office, or in collections of U.S. Patents bound numerically in several libraries across the country. In the U.S. Patent and Trademark Office, the patents are arranged by subject matter, in excruciating detail by class and sub-class for ease of searching, which will be discussed in Chapter 9.

As a bottom line, a patent is a grant by the government of intellectual property rights that permits the patent owner to stop others from exploiting the patented invention covered by the claims, and supported by the specification of the patent. The components of a patent are the drawings, where required, the specification which describes and explains the patented invention, and the claims which define that which the patent right covers. These documents are called "patents" because the word means "open, exposed or evident." Letters patent have always been open to public inspection once granted setting forth the knowledge contained in the grants. Under existing U.S. law, U.S. patent applications are published electronically 18 months after filing, unless the applicant states that he or she will not file corresponding patent applications in countries outside the United States.

"Letters Patent" and "Patent" mean the same thing. The U.S. Patent and Trademark Office issues several types of patents, namely, utility patents including article or apparatus patents, method or process patents, design patents and plant patents. Upon expiration of a patent, it cannot be renewed, and its subject matter enters the public domain. If an improvement is made to an originally covered invention by either the original inventor, or someone totally different, an entirely new patent on that improvement can be obtained. However, it is important to remember that once a patent reaches its expiration date, its contents fall into the public domain and there is no renewal provision.

4.2.2   Article or Apparatus Patents

Article, or apparatus, patents protect new machines, items or articles of manufacture, and compositions of matter. Article patents can also be written to cover improvements in any of the above categories. These patents are granted for a term beginning on the date the patent issues, and normally ending 20 years from the date the application for the patent was first filed in the United States. If the patent claims priority from an earlier filed U.S. patent application directed to the same invention, 20 years from the date of the earliest such U.S. application, other than a provisional application, would be the date of expiration. The term of patenting in the U.S. previously was 17 years from the date of issue, however that was changed recently by law. But if a patent was granted on an application filed before June 8, 1995, the term of that patent is either 17 years from date of issue or 20 years from date of application, which ever is later.

4.2.3   Method or Process Patents

Method, or process, patents cover the novel process or steps which transform material from one state to another. They can also cover a novel process or method of manufacturing or using a machine performing an operation on an item of manufacture or a composition of matter. In method or process patents, (the names are synonymous), it is the process used, and not the end result, which must be novel to support patentability. The term of method or process patents is the same as article or apparatus patents described above.

4.2.4   Design Patents

Design patents are granted for any new, original, ornamental and non-functional design of, or placed on, an article of manufacture. Design patents are granted for a term of 14 years from the date of issue and cannot be renewed. These patents cover the esthetic features of the article shown in the patent illustrations, however, functional features of the design are specifically excluded from protection under the design patent. If a functional feature of the article is novel, that particular feature should be covered by an article patent. Design patents are covered in more detail in Chapter 13.

4.2.5   Plant Patents

Plant patents are granted to one who invents or asexually reproduces any distinct and new variety of plant, including cultivated spores, mutants, hybrids, and newly found seedlings, other than a tuber, propagated plant or a plant found in an uncultivated state. The term of a plant patent is the same as that of an apparatus patent. These patents are quite important to the agricultural industry in the United States, as well as the flower industry. At present, there is a controversy growing between the manufacturers of patented seed corn, and the farmers who raise seed corn using the patented seeds, and then taking the results of that crop and planting the seeds themselves for their new crop.

4.2.6   New Technologies

As touched on previously, process patents have been extended recently to cover methods of doing of business, which were not considered as protected under the patent laws until 1998. Also, algorithms used in computer programs are now subject to patent protection under certain conditions, as well as biotechnology creations, such as genomes and DNA strains. As science has progressed and created totally new categories of subject matter, initially the patent law has been seen to be a bulwark against the protection of such new technology. However, once the importance of such new technology to the economy and to the welfare of society as a whole is realized, then the patent laws are interpreted by the courts to allow patent protection for such new technologies.

4.3   HOW TO DETERMINE WHAT TO PATENT AND WHAT NOT TO PATENT

4.3.1   Broadly, What Can and Cannot Be Patented Under the Law

To be eligible for a patent, an invention must fall within one of the categories of patentable subject matter. Thus not all inventions are patentable. Normally the U.S. Patent & Trademark Office is liberal in applying the limitations of the invention categories, providing that an invention is presented for examination in a suitable fashion.

To understand what may be patentable, it is helpful to indicate items that are not patentable. Unpatentable subject matter includes business forms, perpetual motion machines because they are not useful under the Constitutional mandate, promotional advertising schemes, intended results of desired goals, functions without any apparatus to perform that function, nebulous concepts or ideas, items appearing in nature, and laws of nature. However, the useful and novel application of a law of nature could be subject to patentability. Therefore, while desired functions are not patentable, the item or method that provides that function can be patented, while not the mere result.

In general terms, to be patentable an invention must be useful, novel and unobvious. This presumes, of course, that the invention first falls into one of the above mentioned patentable categories. "New" and "useful" are requirements that are easy to ascertain and understand. The unobviousness requirement has provided more difficulty over the years.

A process or method patent can be obtained to cover a new use for a known apparatus or composition, for example a known pharmaceutical or an existing machine. Using a known asthma drug to suppress pre-term labor contractions would be an existing new use for a known composition, and would be patentable as a new method.

4.3.2   From a Business Standpoint, What Should Be Patented

There are many reasons that go into deciding whether a patent should be obtained for a particular invention. The first criterion, of course, is whether or not the invention is patentable, based on the previously mentioned criteria. Another consideration is the importance the invention has to the profitability of the company for whom the inventor works. Also, an independent inventor can determine what importance the invention will have to that inventor's future economic situation. A further consideration is whether or not there exists a market for the product or process which will include the invention, or whether a market could be created from scratch for the particular product or process where there is no other item on the market quite like the subject invention.

After an invention is made, consider the importance of protecting against competition by others when you create your market introduction plans for that invention. Is there a large competitor that can copy your product and put you out of business if your product is not covered by a patent? Consideration must also be given to the potential for foreign markets for the product or process, and whether foreign patent protection should be sought for your invention. Also, consider whether a competitor would have the capability of manufacturing a product in a foreign country to compete with you on a global scale, and whether or not you should obtain patent protection in that foreign country to deny the competitor of the ability to manufacture in that country, thereby choking off potential infringement at the source.

There are additional factors that impact the decision whether or not to spend resources to obtain a patent, and these additional factors pertain to the individual characteristics of the given company and the industry in which the company operates. When decisions of a business nature have to be made, it is important to seek the advice of a competent patent professional so that all of the options regarding intellectual property protection for your intellectual assets may be provided to those responsible for making the business decision. Obtaining worldwide patent protection on an important invention is an expensive proposition, and careful consideration should be given to making such decisions.

Careful study should likewise be given to the required investment for creating a new product, and bringing that product to market. Consideration should be given to the possibility of making necessary changes in existing production facilities to produce and launch a new product. Consideration of the advertising budget required to advise the public of the reasons they should buy a new product, and to change their buying habits to accept the new product, is important. The size of the market for the new product and profitability studies are also important factors.

While the commercial importance of an invention is probably the most important consideration as to whether to obtain a patent, the credibility granted the inventor(s) associated with an invention is a primary factor in assisting the inventor to convince his/her employer to exploit the invention. A successful inventor requires credibility in the same way that a successful artist or author does. If the inventor has no prior successes to advertise, the inventor must establish credibility by proving that the product embodying the invention is worthy of the investment of resources. A favorable sales history for a patented product also builds credibility. All of these factors make it easier for the inventor to span the gap between a conceived idea and actual commercial exploitation of the embodiment of that idea.

The inventor must also determine whether the public is ready for the invention. For example, a variety of economic, production and management factors may come into play to shift the period of patent protection away from the period when the invention is commercially important. Several of my clients have attempted to interest companies in exploiting their inventions, and a frequent response was that the company had no further funds available that year to introduce new products. This can be disappointing for the inventor, and not because the invention did not have a high profitability forecast. An example are heavy industries, where actual production methods may lag behind current available technology by a period that is much longer than the life of a patent. Thus, the value of a patent can be greatly influenced by the patterns for change that exist for specific products in given industries. Anecdotal information shows that many inventors often underestimate the cost and difficulty of exploiting and commercializing their inventions, and overestimate the market size and expectations of purchaser acceptance. The inventor must be prepared to face and overcome numerous difficulties before an invention returns a monetary award, and the inventor must be willing to work hard and not be dissuaded in the face of negative responses to move the invention to market before he/she realizes any reward. In other words, keep pushing your idea, and be patient.

4.4 BROADLY, WHAT DATA GOES INTO A PATENT

4.4.1 Describing the Background and Essential Elements of the Invention

An article or process patent begins with a title generally describing the invention, followed by a short paragraph comprising a broad statement of the field of technology to which the invention relates. This is immediately followed by a more specific statement as to the subject matter of the invention.

The specification next sets forth a statement of the background of the invention, including an explanation of the problems in the existing art to which the present invention is directed at solving, and the known relevant prior art which can be shown to have failed to specifically solve these problems. The prior art is that which the inventor is aware of, or obtained from a pre-examination novelty search (see Chapter 9 for searches). The patent at this point may also state briefly what the various prior art patents disclose, followed by one or two statements indicating what the reference patents lack, compared to the details of the subject invention.

The background of the invention section may also include a statement of the objects of the invention. These are usually broad statements setting forth the results achieved by the invention which are different from and superior to the results obtained by using the devices shown in the prior art, without setting forth the details concerning the structure and functioning of the invention's elements to achieve these results. This latter information appears later in the patent.

Next, the patent includes a summary of the covered invention, which is a short statement of the elements of the invention, how they relate to each other, a statement of the function of those elements, and a statement setting forth how the invention will meet the objects or results set forth in the previous paragraph.

The background of the invention is followed by a brief description of the drawings or illustrations, where present, describing the view depicted of the device in each drawing figure.

After the brief description of the drawings is the all important detailed description of the illustrated embodiment of the invention, which sets forth a complete explanation of the invention's structure, the relationship between all structural elements, and the operation/function of the structural elements of the invention shown in the drawings. This description includes only the essential features of the invention, eliminating descriptions of features that are non-essential. In this portion of the patent specification, each essential element of the inventive structure is named, numbered, and the numbers coordinated with the illustrations in the drawing. The accuracy of this particular section of the application is important since it must enable a person skilled in the art to replicate the invention once the patent expires without undue experimentation. The description must be a full, clear, concise and exact description of the invention. Common terminology in the industry or trade is used to describe the invention, with the patent attorney having some latitude in using broader language than that normally used to describe an element or function of the invention. Where a process or method is described and no illustration is necessary to understand the invention, a detailed description of the process used, including examples, is set forth.

4.4.2 Claiming the Invention

The patent concludes with one or more numbered statements, or "claims," which particularly point out and distinctly claim the subject matter which the applicant regards as the invention. These claims form the "heart" of the patent, and are normally written in "non-prose" terms that the average reader may find cumbersome to read. The claims define a specific point or points of novelty embodied in the invention. The claims must also recite the specific non-novel structure necessary to properly "locate" or support the elements of novel structure of the invention. As will be discussed in Chapter 11, the objective of a patent's claims is to define the elements of the invention in terms such that the claims cover any related device developed in the future falling within the same product category, and at the same time each claim must not cover or "read on" the vast body of relevant prior art, or prior technology, that preceded the invention. Therefore, the claims define the narrow point of "invention" that is fenced off to define the exclusive rights of the inventor.

4.5 WHAT A PATENT IS NOT

As discussed previously, a patent is not a trademark or copyright or trade secret, these being distinct additional elements of intellectual property protection ostensibly having little to do with one another. Whether goods are patented or not has nothing to do with rights afforded by trademark law, and the same can be said of the interface between copyright and patent law.

A copyright permits the copyright owner to exclude others from copying the copyrighted material, such as books, plays, music, statues, motion pictures, television programs, computer programs, etc. Copyright protection does not extend to an underlying invention which, for example, might be described in the copyrighted material. Thus, a copyright could be used to prevent others from copying a book describing an invention, but the copyright could not be used to prevent someone from using the knowledge set forth in the book and then making, using or selling the invention. That restriction would have to be found in a patent.

It is also very important to understand that owning a patent on an invention does not confer a right to make, use, sell, offer to sell or import the invention. What is granted is strictly the legal right to exclude others from doing so. For example, a patent may be obtained on an invention, the manufacture and sale of which can infringe a different patent owned by someone else. This is an important concept. You may obtain a patent on your invention, however your invention may also infringe a broader patent of a prior inventor. The classic illustration I use is where you have a patent on a chair, without arms, and I decide to improve your chair by adding arms to the chair. You have your patent on your chair; I now have a patent on the chair plus the arms. However, every time I manufacture a chair with arms under my patent, I am infringing your patent on the chair per se. Another example of a patent not assuring the inventor that the invention can be introduced is a new drug that is patented, but the Food and Drug Administration requires approval before the drug is marketed to the public.

A patent is not self-enforcing. The government issues the patent, but will not take any positive action on behalf of the patent owner to enforce the inventor's rights established by the patent. The government simply grants the owner of the patent the right to exclude others from practicing the invention, and leaves it to the patent owner to enforce the patent in the courts. The government of the U.S. provides the Federal Judicial System through which patent enforcement is obtained.

Since a patent simply grants the intangible right to exclude, its value rests entirely upon the utility and importance of the invention, and the desire of others to use it or to be in possession of the right to exclude. For example, someone may desire to buy the patent from its owner. The patent is simply a document, and not an invention. The invention is that which is described and claimed in the patent.

A patent, and the information it discloses, cannot be kept secret. An essential aspect of obtaining a patent is that a full and complete disclosure of the invention is made so that others may practice the invention upon expiration of the patent without having to go through undue experimentation. United States patent applications are published 18 months after filing, unless no foreign corresponding patent applications will be filed. Patent applications are held secret in the Patent Office until publication, if published, and if not published, until issued. However, issued patents are freely available to the public, with certain limited exceptions where national security is involved. The patent grant does give the right of the inventor to not commercialize the invention, or refuse to allow others to commercialize the invention by a refusal to grant licenses. However, the patent itself issues as a public document available to all. Thus, inventions themselves may be suppressed by keeping the technology out of the public eye, but patents can neither be kept secret nor suppressed.

A U.S. patent is limited in enforcement to the 50 states of the U.S. and its territories and possessions. A U.S. patent cannot be enforced in Canada, Japan, Europe or any other foreign country. However, a U.S. patent may be used to stop the importation of products from abroad into the United States which infringe the patent. Also, if a U.S. patented method is used to manufacture a product overseas, the product made by that method may be stopped from entering the United States by enforcement of the U.S. method patent against the importer of the product, even though the infringing method was not used in the United States.

The United States has ratified several treaties which provide significant advantages for those seeking foreign patent protection, based on a patent application initially filed in the United States. Remember, there is no such thing as an international patent; patents must be obtained in each of the countries in which patent protection is sought. At present, there is a single European patent, which ultimately must be registered in those member countries in which enforcement will be a consideration.

4.6   INVENTIONS RELATING TO ATOMIC WEAPONS

As part of the Atomic Energy Act of 1954, Congress enacted a separate law covering inventions that have utility solely relating to nuclear material or atomic weapons. This statue appears at 42 U.S.C. §2181, and is entitled "Inventions Relating to Atomic Weapons." Section 2181(a) states: "No patent shall hereafter be granted for any invention or discovery which is useful solely in the utilization of special nuclear material or atomic energy in an atomic weapon. Any patent granted for any such invention or discovery is revoked, and just compensation shall be made therefore." Section (b) of the statute states that: "No patent hereafter granted shall confer any rights with respect to any invention or discovery to the extent that such invention or discovery is used in the utilization of special nuclear material or atomic energy in atomic weapons. Any rights conferred by any patent heretofore granted for any invention or discovery are revoked to the extent that such invention or discovery is so used, and just compensation shall be made therefore."

The statute also provides a definition of an "atomic weapon." Note that if an invention can be used in an atomic weapon, but it also has non-weapon utility, a patent may issue. However, the patent may be held up in the secrecy division of the United States Patent and Trademark Office, preventing the inventor from exploiting the invention.

4.7   THE U.S. GOVERNMENT'S RIGHT TO PRACTICE YOUR PATENTED INVENTION

During the First World War, the United States Government mobilized the nation's industries to provide munitions and other materials to support the war effort. This program ran into several barriers when patent owners filed patent infringement lawsuits against government contractors, and obtained injunctions stopping the production of needed weaponry, among other military necessities. To correct this situation, the Congress, circa 1918, passed a law which is now codified at 28 U.S.C. §1498. This law provides that whenever a manufacturer is using or manufacturing an invention described in a U.S. patent, for the Government and with the authorization and consent of the Government, the patent owner cannot bring a patent infringement suit against the infringing user or manufacturer. The patent owner's only remedy is to file a patent infringement action against the Government in the Court of Federal Claims, and the patent owner can only recover "reasonable and entire compensation for such use and manufacture." 28 U.S.C. §1498(a). The patent owner cannot obtain an injunction stopping the use or production of the patented invention when the Government is the ultimate customer.

Under this law, which is still in effect today, the Government, by authorizing and consenting to have a patented process used, or a product manufactured, on its behalf, is effectively taking a license under the patent under the powers of eminent domain, whether or not the patent owner wants to grant the Government a license or not. This procedure is akin to the Government's ability to condemn and take private property to construct a highway, for example. When such "taking" occurs, the one whose property, or patent right has been taken is entitled to be reasonably and entirely compensated, with money, for such taking.

If you discover that the U.S. Government has awarded a contract to a competitor who underbid you, and you hold a patent on the subject of the contract, you cannot sue your competitor for patent infringement. You must file your lawsuit against the Government in the Court of Federal Claims, and the Government lawyers of the U.S. Department of Justice will respond to your lawsuit, usually raising defenses of non-infringement, patent invalidity, unenforceability of the patent, plus any other of the many defenses to patent infringement that are available. If your competitor, who is the Government contractor, has agreed in the contract to indemnify or hold the Government harmless from patent infringement, the Justice Department attorneys may be accompanied by your competitor's attorneys in defending against your lawsuit. At the end of the lawsuit, if you prevail, you are awarded your "reasonable and entire compensation" as determined by the court, which usually is based on a reasonable royalty payment for the infringing sales. However, you will not be awarded an injunction stopping the Government from obtaining infringing products from your competitor.

If you discover that the U.S. Government has awarded your competitor a contract for the use or manufacture of an invention on which you hold a U.S. patent, my advice is that you contact your patent professional to make a determination regarding the viability of asserting your patent against the Government. Remember, that since the U.S. Government can obtain a license under any U.S. patent, the contract award can be made to the lowest bidder, regardless of who owns the patent on the subject invention.

Additionally, the same or similar provisions apply to the U.S. Government taking a copyrighted work (28 U.S.C. §1498(b)), a patented plant variety (28 U.S.C. §1498(d)), or a mask work or vessel hull design (28 U.S.C. §1498(e)).

John Deere

HORSE-DRAWN PLOW

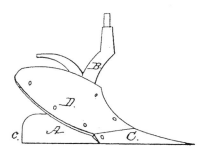

If you have ever been to the country, you have undoubtedly either seen a hat with his name on it or been stuck driving behind one of the behemoth tractors named after him. John Deere is his name and the self-polishing cast steel plow is his invention.

John Deere was born in Rutland, Vermont on February 7, 1804. He lived in Middlebury, Vermont for a good portion of his life. In 1825, after serving a four-year apprenticeship, Deere started working as a blacksmith, producing hay forks and shovels, among other implements. He was so good that he soon gained significant fame in the area for his careful workmanship and ingenuity. During the Great Depression of the 1830s, things were not good for Deere or the people of Vermont. Many people decided to move out west, and they sent back stories of "golden opportunities." After hearing these stories, Deere decided to abandon his business in Vermont and he moved to Grand Detour, Illinois, which was settled by other natives of Vermont. He brought with him a small amount of cash and his tools, which was fortunate because the town needed a blacksmith. Two days after his arrival he had already set up a shop, built a forge, and was busy working. His family then followed him to Grand Detour.

Deere became busy working in his new shop shoeing horses and oxen, and making and repairing farm equipment. From repairing farm equipment, Deere discovered that the rich, fertile soil of the Midwest prairie would stick to the plow bottoms. Plows designed for the light, sandy New England soil could not handle cutting and turning the Midwest soil. Farming in the Midwest became a slow, labor-intensive task, and many farmers considered moving further west or back east.

Deere thought about this problem, and decided if he made a plow that was highly polished and shaped in the right way, it would scour itself and the prairie soil would not stick to the plow. Deere, with help from his partner, Major Leonard Andrus, made a plow to these specifications in 1837. The cutting part of this plow was constructed of steel, cut from an old sawmill blade and shaped by bending the blade over a log. The moldboard, used for lifting and turning the soil, was made of wrought iron and polished on the upper surface to prevent clogging. The plows were successfully tested on a farm near Grand Detour.

His new plow was very successful and Deere, instead of making them as they were ordered, would produce a supply of plows and go out into the country and sell them. This approach was completely different from previous farm implement sales methods, and word quickly spread of Deere's "self-polishers."

The Deere plow was so successful that by 1846, Deere and his partner were selling one thousand plows a year. Deere decided to sell his interest in the Grand Detour business to his partner, Leonard Andrus. He then organized a plow company in Moline, Illinois in 1848, taking advantage of the water energy and transportation provided by the Mississippi River. He began experimenting with imported English steel, and had a cast steel plow made for him in Pittsburgh. By 1855, he was selling more than 13,000 such plows a year. He obtained his first patent for a walk-behind, horse-drawn plow in 1865, Patent No. 46,454.

Deere encountered a few problems, however. Living in the frontier, there were few banks, poor transportation, and a scarcity of steel. Deere's first plows were made out of any steel he could find. In 1843, Deere ordered a shipment of specially rolled steel from England. This shipment had to cross the Atlantic Ocean, go up the Mississippi and Illinois Rivers, and go forty miles in a wagon to reach Deere's shop in Grand Detour. In 1846, the cast steel plow rolled in Pittsburgh and shipped to Moline, Illinois solved this problem.

J. DEERE.

Plow.

No. 46,454.   Patented Feb. 21, 1865.

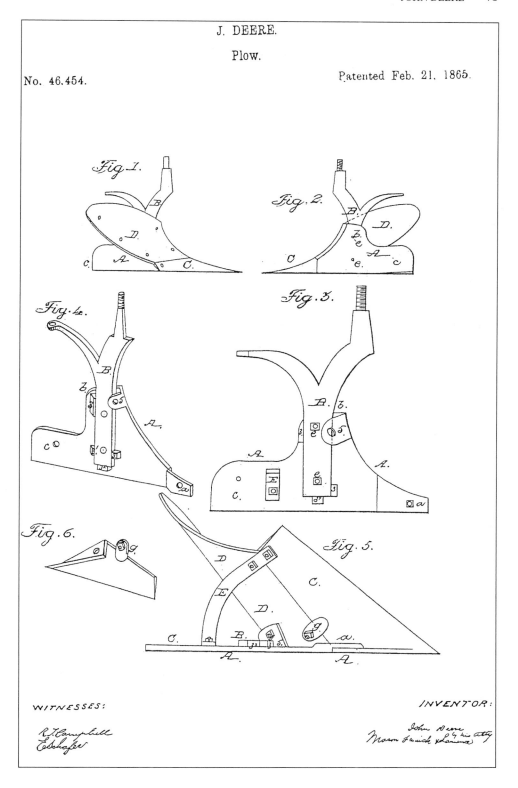

Fig. 1.

Fig. 2.

Fig. 4.

Fig. 3.

Fig. 6.

Fig. 5.

WITNESSES:

R. T. Campbell
E. Schafer

INVENTOR:

John Deere
by his atty
Mason Fenwick & Lawrence

5 Patentable Subject Matter and Utility

5.1 WHAT CONSTITUTES PATENTABLE SUBJECT MATTER

5.1.1 Categories of Patentable Subject Matter

The first threshold that must be reached in determining whether your invention constitutes patentable subject matter is to establish that the invention itself is in the form of an embodiment, such as a prototype, or has been described or illustrated in terms sufficiently concrete, and not merely conceptual, to qualify for patent protection. Once this concrete embodiment of your invention has been created, it must be determined whether the invention falls within one of the statutory classes of patentable invention covered by 35 U.S.C. Section 101, which means that the invention must be a process, a machine, an article of manufacture, or a composition of matter, or any new and useful improvement thereof. At this point, it must also be determined whether an article patent, method patent, design patent or a combination of any of these would best serve the interests of protecting the invention.

More specifically defining the categories of patentable subject matter, a process or method may involve treating a material to produce a particular result or product, or may involve manipulating tangible matter to produce a desired end result. One example would be a process to temper glass to make it break resistant. Processes can also comprise a new use for a known composition, such as a new use for a chemical compound.

A machine is a device which performs a useful operation, usually having mechanical or electrical elements such as for example, springs, hinges, transistors, resistors, sensors, etc. A composition of matter is a combination of two or more substances, and includes chemical elements or compositions, such as a soft drink formulation or a drug compound. A manufacture is a catch-all category for the remaining statutory subject matter which comprises anything not a process, machine or composition of matter.

A manufacture may be a man-made genetically engineered bacterium, for example, which is capable of breaking down crude oil. Included among "things" that are not patentable subject matter are mental processes, naturally occurring articles, or scientific principles.

5.1.2 The Invention Must Be Useful and Work for Its Intended Purpose

To be patentable, an invention must be shown to work for its intended purpose. Under the Constitutional mandate of Article 1, Section 8, patents can only be granted for advances in the "useful" arts. A patent cannot be granted for an inoperative device or method, and is subject to post-grant cancellation if the covered device is proven to be inoperative. This is the reason why patents on perpetual motion machines are not granted.

Intellectual Property Law for Engineers and Scientists, by Howard B. Rockman
ISBN 0-471-44998-9 © 2004 The Institute of Electrical and Electronics Engineers

5.1.3   The Invention Must Be Novel Compared to the Prior Art

Throughout the globe, patents are granted only on inventions that are novel, as measured against the vast body of relevant prior art existing in the world. Different countries have different definitions of what constitutes prior art. For example, a public use or sale of, or an offer to sell, a product in the United States by someone else prior to your invention, which product embodies your "new" technology, is considered prior art and would bar you from obtaining a patent. However, the actual existence of that product in a foreign country would not bar patentability. These limitations on novelty will be covered in more detail in Chapter 6.

5.1.4   The Invention Must Be Non-Obvious Compared to the Prior Art

The United States patent statutes, and most patent statutes throughout the world, state that even though there are differences between the invention attempted to be patented and the prior art, if those differences would be mere obvious manifestations by one skilled in the art to which the subject matter of the patent relates, patent protection may not be obtained. The determination of obviousness is rather difficult to those uninitiated in dealing with patents, and Chapter 7 is dedicated solely to the history and technical determinations involved in showing how the standard of unobviousness plays an important part in the granting and upholding of patents.

5.1.5   Brief Commentary on Recent Developments in Categories of Patentable Subject Matter

Initially upon the development of mathematical algorithms for use in computer software, the U.S. Patent and Trademark Office refused to grant patents on such algorithms, since they were considered to be merely mathematical expressions of relationships that existed before. However, as the importance of protection for such embedded software became important to business and society, the patent laws were changed by the courts and the U.S. Patent and Trademark Office to include such algorithms, and the machines which use these algorithms, within the scope of patentable subject matter, upon the satisfaction of certain requirements, including novelty and unobviousness. Therefore, today it is possible to obtain patent protection, as well as copyright protection, for computer-related inventions. This subject is covered in excrutiating detail in Chapters 14, 22, and 23.

Secondly, it was previously held that living organisms could not be the subject of a patent. However, at present, modified living organisms which are the product of genetic engineering can be patented, except that people cannot be patented. The products of genetic engineering that are patentable must satisfy all the other conditions for patentability. Two examples are first the Harvard Mouse, which has been genetically engineered to be more susceptible to certain strains of cancer for purposes of medical research, and second, certain genetically modified organisms which can absorb oil have to clean up oil spills that occur when a tanker or pipeline accidentally splits open.

Today, the whole subject of genetics falls within the scope of patentable subject matter, and discussions are continually ongoing about the patentability of the results of the Genome Project, which was recently completed. It is my prediction that, in the future, additional patent laws or court decisions will be required to determine which newly developed subject matter may be patented and which may be available for public use without restraint as medical procedures are today. The subject matter of biotechnology patents is discussed in Chapter 15.

Thirdly, prior to a few years ago, methods of doing business did not fall within the category of patentable subject matter. However, the *State Street* decision by the Court of Appeals for the Federal Circuit in 1998, discussed at Chapter 16, Section 16.1, determined that methods of doing business, whether or not implemented using a computer or software, may also be patented, provided all of the other conditions for patentability are met. One such example of a patent which embodies a business method and which has been litigated in court is a patent covering the method of ordering a product online using a single click of the pointer rather than a double click. This subject matter is covered in Chapter 16. The law relating to patentability of inventions in each of the above three genres of subject matter has been expanding. Therefore, you and your patent attorney may find it worthwhile to file a patent application covering an invention that does not, or may only marginally, meet the current criteria for patentable subject matter, with an eye towards the future that your patent claims may be found to cover a new, or existing, category of patentable subject matter.

5.2 UTILITY—THE INVENTION MUST BE USEFUL

As briefly touched upon previously, under the Constitutional mandate of Article 1, Section 8, patents can only be granted for advances in the "useful" arts. Following this directive, the U.S. Patent and Trademark Office and the courts have determined that a patent cannot be granted for an inoperative device or method, and is even subject to post-grant cancellation if the covered device is proven to be inoperative.

It is also required that the invention disclosed in a patent or patent application must define an invention and a device that will work for its intended purpose. If the device will not work for the purpose set forth in the specification, the patent, if granted, will become unenforceable and invalid.

The requirement of usefulness also mandates that inventions which have not been developed to the point where a working embodiment can be disclosed in concrete form cannot be supported by a patent application. This requirement that the invention must be useful is especially significant for a new chemical compound (including pharmaceuticals) because there may be no known use for the new compound. Often much work must be performed to experimentally verify the utility of a new compound before a patent application can be filed.

Upon development of any invention, the inventors should ask themselves the question, "What is my idea useful for and why?" Once this question has been answered, the patent application can be drafted around a showing that the invention will solve problems in the area in which your idea has been determined by you to be useful.

By way of anecdotal information, many years ago when I was a U.S. patent examiner, some of the other examiners in the chemical arts, over lunch, would tell me stories about patent applications that were filed on chemical compounds, and the usefulness for the chemical compound was described as "for filling sandbags". These were patent applications that were filed before the inventor really knew what the chemical could be useful for. Today, the requirement is that the invention must have some stated use before the patent application is filed. I don't think filling sandbags today will carry much weight.

Alfred Nobel

DYNAMITE

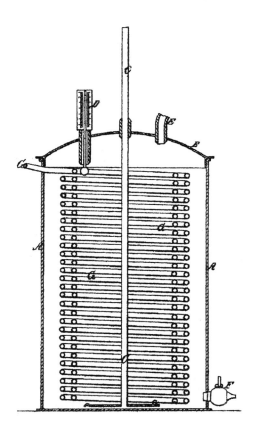

Recall all those cartoons from your childhood where the bad guy would always think of an elaborate plot to beat the good guy, and time after time the bad guy would pick up a box of Acme TNT and get blown up. If it were not for Alfred Nobel and his invention, we probably would not have those wonderful memories of dynamite blowing up the bad guy.

Alfred B. Nobel was born in Stockholm, Sweden on October 21, 1833. His father left his family in Sweden in 1837 and moved to St. Petersburg, Russia to start a new business producing submarine mines and torpedoes he designed for the Russian government. In 1842, the family, including Alfred, his mother, and three brothers, moved to St. Petersburg. The mines made by Alfred's father were submerged wooden caches filled with gunpowder, and were successfully used in the Crimean War (1853–1856).

Alfred Nobel and his brothers were all educated by private teachers, and they also traveled extensively. At the age of 17, Alfred was fluent in five languages, and had taken an early interest in chemistry, as well as physics, English literature, and poetry. During his travels, he visited Paris, where he met Ascanio Sobrero, an Italian chemist who had previously invented nitroglycerine, a highly explosive liquid. Nitroglycerine was a powerfully explosive but unstable mixture of glycerin and sulfuric and nitric acids. It would explode unpredictably when subjected to heat and pressure, and was considered too dangerous for practical use. Alfred Nobel became interested in solving the safety problems inherent with nitroglycerine and finding a method for its controlled detonation.

In 1852, Alfred Nobel returned to St. Petersburg to work in the family business, where he and his father experimented in reducing nitroglycerine to a useful explosive for construction purposes. After the Crimean War, in 1863, Alfred's parents and one of his brothers, Emil, returned to Stockholm, where they worked on developing a useful form of nitroglycerine. Several explosions in their shop, including one in 1864 which killed Emil and several others, led the Stockholm city government to forbid nitroglycerine experiments within the city limits. Alfred moved his experiments to a barge on Lake Mälaren, where he began to mass produce nitroglycerine.

Through further experimentation, he found that mixing nitroglycerine with silica would form a paste that could be molded into rods that would fit into construction drilling holes, and did not react to minor changes in temperature and pressure. He obtained a patent on this invention in 1867 (1868 in the United States), and called his product "dynamite." He also invented and patented a detonator, or blasting cap, for the dynamite rods. Fortuitously, at the same time, the diamond drilling crown and the pneumatic drill began being used in the construction and excavating industries. The market for dynamite and detonating caps rapidly grew. His factories also developed a gelatin form of dynamite that was safe to handle.

Alfred Nobel also was a skillful entrepreneur and businessman, and eventually established factories and research facilities in 90 different locations in more than 20 countries. He made his home in Paris, though he traveled constantly. At the age of 43, he advertised for a woman to take employment as secretary and supervisor of his bachelor household. An Austrian woman, Countess Bertha Kinsky, was hired, but worked for Nobel for a very short time; she returned to Austria to marry Count Arthur von Suttner. Alfred and Bertha remained friends, and corresponded for many years. Bertha von Suttner became a leader of the antiarmament race proliferating throughout Europe at that time, and authored a famous book, *Lay Down Your Arms*. Sources indicate that she influenced Alfred Nobel when he included prizes for persons or organizations promoting peace in his final will, which was signed on November 27, 1895.

In point of fact, the 1905 Nobel Peace Prize was awarded to Bertha von Suttner by the Norwegian Parliament.

Alfred Nobel died at his home in San Remo, Italy, on December 10, 1896, but that was not the end of his influence on humanity. When his will was opened, those who knew him, and particularly his relatives, were surprised to learn he had left the bulk of his sizeable fortune to establish an invested fund. The interest of the fund was to be distributed in the form of prizes in the categories of physics, chemistry, physiology or medicine, literature, and peace "to those who, during the preceding year, shall have conferred the greatest benefit on mankind." The paragraph from his will establishing the Nobel Prizes is reprinted on the following page.

The executors of his will, two young engineers, Rudolf Lilljequist and Rognar

Sohlman, formed the Nobel Foundation to accomplish Nobel's lofty purposes. These young men successfully battled the relatives and authorities in several countries who challenged and questioned the will. Upon successfully battling the opposition, the first Nobel Prizes were awarded in 1901.

"The whole of my remaining realizable estate shall be dealt with in the following way: the capital, invested in safe securities by my executors, shall constitute a fund, the interest on which shall be annually distributed in the form of prizes to those who, during the preceding year, shall have conferred the greatest benefit on mankind. The said interest shall be divided into five equal parts, which shall be apportioned as follows: one part to the person who shall have made the most important discovery or invention within the field of physics; one part to the person who shall have made the most important chemical discovery or improvement; one part to the person who shall have made the most important discovery within the domain of physiology or medicine; one part to the person who shall have produced in the field of literature the most outstanding work in an ideal direction; and one part to the person who shall have done the most or the best work for fraternity between nations, for the abolition or reduction of standing armies and for the holding and promotion of peace congresses. The prizes for physics and chemistry shall be awarded by the Swedish Academy of Sciences; that for physiology or medical works by the Karolinska Institute in Stockholm; that for literature by the Academy in Stockholm, and that for champions of peace by a committee of five persons to be elected by the Norwegian Storting. It is my express wish that in awarding the prizes no consideration be given to the nationality of the candidates, but that the most worthy shall receive the prize, whether he be Scandinavian or not."

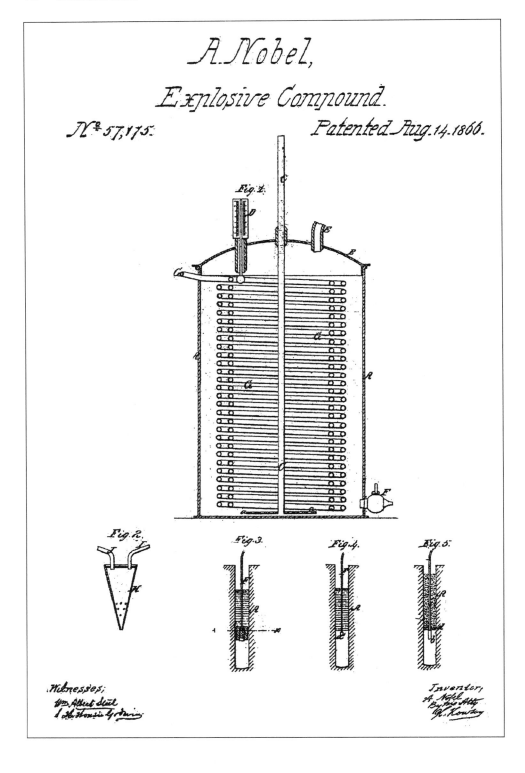

United States Patent Office.

ALFRED NOBEL, OF HAMBURG, GERMANY, ASSIGNOR TO JULIUS BAND-MANN, OF SAN FRANCISCO, CALIFORNIA.

Letters Patent No. 78,317, dated May 26, 1868.

IMPROVED EXPLOSIVE COMPOUND.

The Schedule referred to in these Letters Patent and making part of the same.

TO ALL WHOM IT MAY CONCERN:

Be it known that I, ALFRED NOBEL, of the city of Hamburg, Germany, have invented a new and useful Composition of Matter, to wit, an Explosive Powder.

The nature of the invention consists in forming out of two ingredients long known, viz, the explosive substance nitro-glycerine, and an inexplosive porous substance, hereafter specified, a composition which, without losing the great explosive power of nitro-glycerine, is very much altered as to its explosive and other properties, being far more safe and convenient for transportation, storage, and use, than nitro-glycerine.

In general terms, my invention consists in mixing with nitro-glycerine a substance which possesses a very great absorbent capacity, and which, at the same time, is free from any quality which will decompose, destroy, or injure the nitro-glycerine, or its explosiveness.

It is undoubtedly true, as a general rule, that nitro-glycerine, when mixed with another substance, possesses less concentration of power than when used alone; but while the safety of the miner (to prevent leakage into seams in the rock) prohibits the use of nitro-glycerine without cartridges, which latter must of course be somewhat less in diameter than the bore-holes which are to contain them, the powder herein described can be made to form a semi-pasty mass, which yields to the slightest pressure, and thus can be made to fill up the borehole entirely. Practically, therefore, the miner will have as much nitro-glycerine in the same height of borehole with this powder as with nitro-glycerine in its pure state.

This is the real character and purpose of my invention; and in order to enable others skilled in the art to which it appertains (or with which it is most nearly connected) to make, compound, and use the same, I will proceed to describe the same, and also the manner and process of making, compounding, and using it, in full, clear, and exact terms.

The substance which most fully meets the requirements above mentioned, so far as I know or have been able to ascertain from numerous experiments, is a certain kind of silicious earth or silicic acid, found in various parts of the globe, and known under the several names of silicious marl, tripoli, rotten-stone, &c. The particular variety of this material which is best for my compound is homogeneous, has a low specific gravity, great absorbent capacity, and is generally composed of the remains of *infusoria*.

So great is the absorbent capacity of this earth, that it will take up about three times its own weight of nitro-glycerine and still retain its powder-form, thus leaving the nitro-glycerine so compact and concentrated as to have very nearly its original explosive power; whereas, if another substance, having a less absorbent capacity, is used, a correspondingly less proportion of nitro-glycerine will be absorbed, and the powder be correspondingly weak or wholly inexplosive.

For example, most chalk will take but about fifteen per cent. of nitro-glycerine and retain its powder-form. Twenty per cent. will reduce it to a paste.

Porous charcoal has also a considerable absorbent capacity, but it has the defect of being itself a combustible material, and also of less elasticity of its particles, which renders it easy to squeeze out a part of its nitro-glycerine.

The two materials are combined in the following manner:

The earth, thoroughly dried and pulverized, is placed in a wooden vessel. To it is introduced the nitro-glycerine in a steady stream so small that the two ingredients can be kept thoroughly mixed.

The mixing may be effected by the naked hand, or by any proper wooden instrument used in the hand, or by wooden machinery

Sufficient of nitro-glycerine should be used to render the compound explosive, but not so much as to change its form of powder to a liquid or pasty consistency.

Practically, about sixty parts, by weight, of nitro-glycerine to forty of earth, forms the useful minimum, and seventy-eight parts, by weight, of nitro-glycerine to twenty-two of earth, the useful maximum of explosive power. The former has a perfectly dry appearance, the latter is pasty.

Between these two extremes the composition will be explosive powder, and it will be more easily exploded, and its explosive power greater, as the relative proportion of the nitro-glycerine is greater.

The proportions, by weight, of seventy-five of nitro-glycerine to twenty-five of earth, gives a powder as well adapted to ordinary practical purposes as that from any proportions I am now able to name, and can be easily compressed to a specific gravity nearly equal to that of pure nitro-glycerine.

When the mass has been intimately mixed and thoroughly incorporated by stirring and kneading, it is rubbed through a hair, silk, or brass-wire sieve, (iron corrodes,) and any lumps which may remain are rubbed with a stiff-bristle brush till they are reduced and made to pass through the sieve.

The powder is then finished and ready for use.

The fineness desired for the powder will determine the fineness of the sieve to be used.

The chief characteristic of this powder is its nearly perfect exemption from liability to accidental or involuntary explosion.

It is far less sensitive than nitro-glycerine to concussion or percussion, and contained in its usual packing, (a wooden cask or box,) the latter may be smashed completely to pieces without any danger of an explosion.

Unlike gunpowder, in the open air or in ordinary packing, (a wooden cask or box,) it burns up, when set fire to, without exploding. It can, therefore, be handled, stored, and transported with less danger than ordinary gunpowder.

When confined in a tight and strong enclosure it explodes by heat applied in any form when above the temperature of 360° Fahrenheit. Under all other circumstances it may be exploded by some other explosion in it or into it.

The most simple and certain method known to me of exploding it is as follows:

The end of a common blasting-fuse is inserted into a percussion-cap, and the rim of the cap crimped tightly and firmly about the fuse by nippers, or other means, so as to leave the fulminating-powder of the cap and the end of the fuse tightly and firmly enclosed together. The end of the fuse, with the cap attached, is then embedded in the powder—the more firmly, the more certain the explosion.

In blasting, the powder is pressed tightly about the cap and fuse, and tamping, of sand or other proper material, added, and pressed but not pounded in. A tamping firmly pressed is as good as if rammed in the most solid manner.

The fuse explodes the cap, and this explosion explodes the powder.

I will add here that by carefully packing the end of a good fuse amidst the powder of a charge enclosed, like a blasting charge, in a tight place, the fuse alone will explode the powder, especially if the powder is strongly charged with nitro-glycerine. But this method of explosion requires too much care, and is too uncertain to be depended upon or generally used.

As before stated, the more strongly the powder is charged with nitro-glycerine the more easily it explodes. If, therefore, the powder contains a low proportion of nitro-glycerine, it is necessary to employ in its explosion a correspondingly long, strong, and heavily-charged percussion-cap, made especially for the purpose. For the sake of certainty of explosion it is better to use such a cap in all cases.

If the fire from the fuse comes in contact with the powder before the cap is exploded, which is liable to occur if the fuse is leaky and the cap extends too far into the powder, a portion of the powder will be burned before the explosion takes place. To guard against this, the cap should only be fairly inserted into the powder, and poor fuses wound next to the cap firmly with strong glued paper or hemp, or otherwise secured.

The bore-holes, as a practical but not absolute rule, should be about one-half the size, and the charge should be from one-fifth to one-tenth the quantity ordinarily used in gunpowder-blasting.

A very convenient form in which to use the powder is to pack it firmly in cartridges of strong paper.

Having thus described my invention, what I claim as new, and desire to secure by Letters Patent, is—

The composition of matter, made substantially of the ingredients and in the manner and for the purposes set forth.

ALFRED NOBEL.

Witnesses:

FR. T. PROHME,

HEINR. BARTELTSSEN

6 Novelty—The Invention Must Be New

6.1 STATUTORY REQUIREMENTS

Starting a development project, the engineer or scientist has at hand the full wealth of known prior technology related to the goals of the project. This is what is defined as the "prior art." The developer knows, however, that the amassed knowledge of the prior art cannot solve the current problem; the prior art must be advanced to reach the current goals of this new development project. Thus the inventor toils until an advance over the prior art allows the new goal to be reached. At project's end, the inventor's advanced structure, and its function or method are measured against the state of the prior art to establish the novelty of the advance, and to ensure that such advance would not be obvious, given the teachings of the prior art. When the advance satisfies these criteria, patentable invention is made out, and a meaningful patent can be obtained to provide exclusive rights to the owner of the invention, as long as the other criteria for patentability are satisfied.

6.1.1 Time Limits for Filing a Patent Application

The time at which a patent application is filed is important as providing a benchmark applicable to the activities of the inventor and as to the inventions of others. By way of example, consider a modified version of history regarding the discovery of the wheel as a way of explaining some of the time limits for patentability.

Suppose the first inventor of the wheel merely recognized the problems associated with moving large loads on rolling logs, which comprises the prior art. At this point, the inventor has only recognized the need for a better structure, and a patent application would not yet be timely since a patentable invention has not yet been fully thought through. A patent application is not proper until a working form of an invention has been fully conceived. At the time when a complete invention is mentally pictured, that is conceived in operating form, the inventor may properly pursue patent protection.

In continuing with the example, quite independently of the effort to obtain patent protection on the wheel, the same inventor might have published a description of his or her wheel, or may have built a wagon and gone into the moving business prior to seeking patent protection. Such activities raise another question of timing under the patent laws. A patent application must be filed within one year after the invention is first described in any publication anywhere in the world, or placed on sale, sold or used publicly in the United States. This is known as the one-year "grace period," and is based on the philosophy that the inventor abandons his/her patent rights if a proper patent application is not filed within one year from public disclosure or commercial activity in the United States with

Intellectual Property Law for Engineers and Scientists, by Howard B. Rockman
ISBN 0-471-44998-9 © 2004 The Institute of Electrical and Electronics Engineers

respect to the invention. Note that under this law, a non-published or non-patented public disclosure of a similar invention in a foreign country is not grounds for non-patentability in the United States.

A major exception to the rule that public disclosure of the invention by the inventor more than a year before filing for a patent may destroy patent rights, is the case of the disclosure constituting legitimate experimental use to perfect or develop the invention. For example, in a famous case dating back to the late 1800's, an inventor filed a patent application directed to asphalt paving material that was used for six years on a highway before the patent application was filed. The Supreme Court held that the patent was still valid since six years of experimentation were required to determine whether the highway material would hold up under long and continued use.

A further timing consideration involves the protection of foreign patent rights. It is important to know that any publication or public use of an invention that takes place before the filing date of a patent application in the United States may prevent the inventor from obtaining valid patents in many foreign countries that rely upon the "absolute novelty" standard, which are those countries that do not allow the one-year grace period. In those countries, a patent application must be on file in the inventor's home country prior to any public use or disclosure of the invention anywhere in the world. Chapter 17 covers in more detail how to adequately protect your foreign patent rights. An inventor may keep his/her invention secret for a period of time, and still obtain a patent. However, a long delay in applying for a patent may result in the loss of all patent rights, which may end up going to a second independent inventor of the same subject matter who acts more promptly to file a patent application. The better route to follow is to file a patent application at the earliest practical time, and most importantly before any public description or disclosure or commercial development of the invention has been made.

6.1.2   Prior Art Activities of the Inventor and Others That Can Defeat Patent Rights

One of the provisions of the patent law states that an inventor shall be entitled to a patent unless the invention (1) was known or used by others in the United States, or (2) patented or described in a printed publication in the United States or a foreign country, before the invention by the applicant for the patent. Therefore, if the same invention was made public by someone else prior to your invention date, according to these rules, you cannot obtain a patent. The time consideration here is the date of your invention, which equates to the date of your initial conception, followed by diligent efforts toward reducing the invention to practice. If someone else were found to have conceived the invention prior to you, but took a longer time to reduce the invention to practice, but still remained diligent, that someone else may be entitled to the patent in lieu of you.

Consider also that when you file a patent application, the patent examiner knows only the filing date of your application, and does not know the dates of your conception and reduction to practice. The conception date and reduction to practice date are not required to be furnished to the patent examiner during the process of examination. However, if the examiner finds a prior art patent or other reference that describes your invention in a publication that is dated before your filing date, the examiner makes the assumption that the prior art invention date was prior to yours and then reject your patent application based upon this prior art reference.

This provision of the patent law also prevents a person who merely recognizes the commercial merits of an existing product, or who discovers the product in an ancient document, in a foreign country or from other existing source, from properly obtaining a U.S. patent, for patents in the United States are granted only to the first to invent. The activities of others who may have publicly disclosed the same invention as yours, without necessarily obtaining any patent protection for that invention may also defeat your right to a patent if those activities occurred prior to your conception and reduction to practice of the same invention.

A further provision of the patent law, which was touched upon previously, prohibits an inventor from obtaining a patent if the invention (1) was patented or described in a printed publication in this or a foreign country, or (2) was in public use or on sale in the United States, more than one year prior to the date of the filing of the application for patent in the United States. This is a very important provision, and controls the time in which patent protection must be applied for, or patent protection is lost. This is the provision that includes the "grace period" requiring that a patent application be filed within one year from the date of first public disclosure in the United States or publication anywhere of the invention. The purpose of this provision is to require inventors to make a prompt decision regarding filing a patent application, so that the public will obtain the benefit of the inventor's work upon expiration of the patent that much earlier. One who suppresses, abandons or conceals their invention is not entitled to patent protection.

Under this provision of the Patent Statute, the activities of the inventor or inventors themselves, as well as the activities of others may defeat rights to patents. For example, if one completes an invention, and then publishes a paper or delivers a speech regarding that invention to a professional or a trade group, that inventor then has one year from the time of that publication or disclosure to file a U.S. patent application. Therefore, it is imperative that inventors discuss the patentability of their inventions during that first year period, or face the loss of all patent protection.

It is also important to note what was briefly discussed previously about avoiding the loss of foreign patent rights. If at all possible, it is highly recommended to seek the advice of a patent attorney prior to any public disclosure of any invention, so that foreign patent rights will not be lost. In today's global economy, I cannot think of one invention that would have use solely in the United States, and not be marketable in other countries throughout the world.

If during the development of your invention, it becomes necessary to disclose the invention outside your company, or outside the group of inventors working on the invention, such disclosure should be made only after a confidential non-disclosure agreement has been signed by the recipient party to whom the disclosure is being made. The non-disclosure agreement should state, among other things, that the recipient party will not use the disclosed information for its own benefit, nor disclose the subject matter of your invention to anyone else, without your prior written consent. In addition, all information and physical devices given to the recipient party relating to the invention should be clearly and boldly marked CONFIDENTIAL. This will establish later, if necessary, that the disclosure of the invention to the recipient party was confidential, and was not a "public" disclosure under the patent laws. Taking these steps, therefore, allows you to privately disclose your invention to another, without starting the one year clock from running under the U.S. patent law, and will also save a majority of your foreign patent rights from extinction.

For more information on the provisions in a typical Confidential Non- Disclosure Agreement, see Chapter 20, Section 20.3 of this text.

Public use of an invention that can be proven to be an experimental use is not considered a prior public use when applying the requirement that an application must be filed within one year from public use in the United States. However, it is important to realize that in litigation, against an adversary party, any disclosure which you may have considered experimental may ultimately be held by a court or a jury to be proven as a public use. In one instance I can recall, a conversation on a bus traveling between a hotel and a convention center during a trade show, where the inventor disclosed some of the ideas of his invention to someone on the bus, constituted a public disclosure. Therefore, it is important to note that if any public comments or disclosures are made about an invention, the inventor should be aware of what can and cannot be done with regard to protecting patent rights in the United States and throughout the world.

6.1.3   Prior Publications, U.S. and Foreign, as Prior Art

In the U.S. Patent and Trademark Office, and in the courts, the novelty and thus the validity of a patent application or of an issued patent is tested against the body of prior patents, public inventions and published material known as "prior art," which basically encompasses everything known throughout the world that took place prior to your invention and/or filing of your patent application. Under the United States patent examination and legal system, (1) any publication that shows all or part of your invention prior to your invention date is prior art, and (2) any prior publication or patent that was made public or issued more than one year before your patent application filing date is also "prior art" under the patent laws. In addition, any foreign patents, foreign publications, information in text books or data bases, and any other publicly available knowledge about work that was performed relating to your invention becomes prior art for use by the patent examiner and the courts in determining the novelty and thus the validity of your patent application or patent.

An inventor is charged with "constructive knowledge" of all public prior art that was generated from the beginning of time up until the date of his/her invention, regarding the subject matter of his/her invention. Although it is impossible for any single inventor to know all of this subject matter, without such constructive knowledge the patent system would not work. As will be explained in Chapter 9, it is possible to obtain a search of literature, patents, and other materials prior to filing a patent application to substantially determine the state of the prior art regarding the subject matter of any invention. Thus, it is possible before the filing of a patent application for an inventor and the inventor's attorney to obtain a fairly large and detailed amount of information regarding the state of the prior art to which an invention pertains upon which to base a decision regarding the novelty of your invention.

Upon examination by a patent examiner, and later in litigation before the courts, such prior publications, uses and knowledge are used to limit the scope of the claims of a patent application or issued patent to define only that which is new, and to eliminate those claims which cover the prior art. The claims of a patent are supposed to cover everything related to the invention which may be devised by others in the future, and yet the same claims cannot cover any material that has been shown or disclosed in the prior art. Thus, determining the content of the prior art is very important in the patenting process.

6.2   PROTECTING FOREIGN PATENT RIGHTS

As alluded to previously, a significant amount of foreign countries throughout the world utilize what is called the "absolute novelty" rule, which requires that a patent application be on file in that country before any public disclosure of the invention. In other words, there is no one year grace period as offered by U.S. law. However, based upon a series of treaties adhered to by the United States and most countries throughout the world, developed and undeveloped, procedures have been established to protect the patentability of inventions throughout the world.

Pursuant to these treaties, if an inventor files a patent application in the inventor's home country, and a corresponding patent application is filed in a foreign country within one year of the date of the home country application filing date, the constructive filing date of the foreign patent application is the home country application filing date, or the "priority date." By way of example as to how this system works, if you were to file an application for a patent on an invention on January 1 in the United States Patent & Trademark Office, and then publicly disclose that invention at a trade show, sales meeting or otherwise on January 2, and then filed patent applications in the United Kingdom, Germany, France and Italy on December 1 of the same year, the filing date of your European patent applications would be the same as your United States filing date, and therefore your patent application in those foreign countries would not be barred based upon your public exposure of the invention on January 2. There is a further treaty called the Patent Cooperation Treaty (PCT) which allows you to file a document within that one-year period with the U.S. Patent & Trademark Office, which extends the time that you have to file foreign patent applications for a total of up to 31 months from your initial U.S. patent application filing date. PCT applications are covered in Chapter 17, Section 17.3.

Therefore, if you determine that your invention has potential worldwide acceptance and value, it is extremely important to ensure that there is no public disclosure of your invention before your United States or home country patent application filing date. After that, you are free to publicly show and exploit your invention. There are provisions in the United States patent law, such as Provisional Patent Application filings, which allow the patent attorney to make a rapid and proper filing in the United States Patent & Trademark Office, and obtain an official filing date before you make any public disclosure of your invention. If necessary, the patent attorney can work to one or two day requirements in preparing a provisional patent application. However it is not recommended that you wait until such a late date to inform your patent attorney about the subject matter of your invention, and your desire to obtain protection.

6.3 EXPERIMENTAL USE VERSUS ACTUAL USE OF THE INVENTION

If for reasons that are beyond your control, such as a lack of financing or the fact that a budget for introduction for new products for a given year has already been expended, you find yourself in a situation where your invention, or certain aspects of your invention, may have been exposed to third parties more than a year before your patent application filing date without being covered by a Confidential Disclosure Agreement, consideration must be given to inquire whether such use was experimental use and not public use. One major consideration is whether or not the disclosure to third parties involved a disclosure of a complete, workable invention, or whether or not development work was still being conducted on the invention, and additional work on the invention took place after such disclosure. A disclosure that will defeat the validity of a patent must be a disclosure of the complete invention. Disclosures to third parties such as vendors or potential marketing partners more than a year before the patent application was filed may be held to be "experimental uses" if it can be shown that development work continued from the point of that disclosure forward to perfect and modify the invention, and the invention was not complete and should not be considered an "invention" upon the date of disclosure. Any significant changes to your invention made after such disclosure tend to prove that the disclosure was made only of the experimental model, and not the completed invention. Also, public uses of the invention for technical test purposes are usually considered as experimental uses, while on the other hand, market testing of the complete or near complete invention are considered as public uses, and not experimental uses.

Again, to avoid any possibility of creating "public information" that may affect the validity of the patent adversely, I suggest that as soon as you have determined that the project you are working on may lead to a patentable invention, and before there is any public disclosure of the invention outside the realm of the inventors or the company for or with whom you may be working, consideration be given to patenting of your invention, and that you gain information from a patent professional as to what disclosure of the invention can or cannot be made, and how "confidential" disclosures can be made that will not affect patent rights. This will avoid issues adverse to patentability from arising in the first place, and eliminate all doubt as to the validity of your patent.

Louis Pasteur

PASTEURIZATION PROCESS

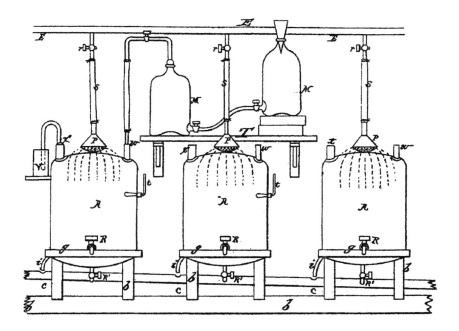

Throughout human history, physicians have struggled with the problem of determining what cause diseases. In the mid 19th century, many people believed in Miasma, the concept that disease was caused by polluted air. However, the milestone work leading to understanding the causes of diseases was not made by a doctor, but by a chemist, Louis Pasteur. Pasteur destroyed the widely held myth of spontaneous generation as the cause of diseases, thus setting the direction for modern biochemistry and biology.

Louis Pasteur was born on December 27, 1822 in Dole, Jura, France, and grew up in the nearby town of Arbois. As a child, Pasteur showed an interest in chemistry, and the headmaster of the local college convinced Louis and his father that Louis should try to enter the École Normale Suprieure in Paris, a highly regarded French university specifically created to train students for university careers in science and the arts. Pasteur began his successful journey as a scientist in the École Normale.

When Pasteur was 26 years old, crystallography was a new branch of chemistry. One of his first projects while working at the École Normale was attempting the crystallization of tartaric acid, an organic acid that exists in the sediments of fermenting wine. A second acid, paratartaric acid or racemic acid, was also found in the sediment in wine barrels. At

Intellectual Property Law for Engineers and Scientists, by Howard B. Rockman
ISBN 0-471-44998-9 © 2004 The Institute of Electrical and Electronics Engineers

the time of the beginning of his studies, science had already determined that tartaric and paratartaric acids had the identical chemical composition; however tartaric acid rotated a beam of polarized light passing through it to the right, and paratartaric acid did not rotate the light at all. Pasteur was determined to find out what caused this difference. Upon microscopic examination, Pasteur discovered that the paratartrate crystals were comprised of two types of optically asymmetric crystals, one being the mirror image of the other.

Pasteur then performed one of the more elegant procedures in the anals of chemistry experimentation. He separated the left and right paratartrate crystal shapes from each other with a dissecting needle to form two collections of crystals. When placed in solution, one form of the crystal rotated light to the left, the other to the right. This showed that organic molecules having the same chemical composition can have two different stereospecific forms. He concluded that this molecular asymmetry was one of the mechanisms of life, in that living organisms only produce molecules of one specific orientation, and these molecules are always optically active. He also found that fermenting solutions contained optically active compounds, which led him to surmise that fermentation was a biological process performed by microorganisms, or germs. This hypothesis, designated the germ theory, was used by Pasteur as a foundation for many experiments that showed positively the existence of microorganisms and their effect in the fermentation process. The germ theory was the basis of his work in the large-scale brewing of beer and wine, the pasteurization of milk, antiseptic operations on humans, and in curing contagious diseases since he also discovered that the blood of diseased humans contained increased amounts of germs. He, and later other scientists, discovered that manipulation of infection agents in test tubes could be used to immunize humans and animals against diseases caused by germs.

Pasteur later began teaching at Strasbourg University, where his studies on molecular asymmetry continued. While at Strasbourg, Pasteur married the university rector's daughter, Marie Laurent, with whom he spent the rest of his life. In 1854, Pasteur became Dean and Professor of Chemistry at the Faculty of Sciences in Lille, France. This was a blue-collar town, with numerous factories and distilleries. The Minister of Public Instruction of Lille encouraged the university faculty to conduct work and studies that would assist the industry of the surrounding countryside.

Pasteur took this advice to heart, taking his students on tours of the local factories and advising managers of his availability to help solve their problems. Thus, in 1856, M. Bigot, the father of one of his chemistry students, called upon Pasteur to help overcome problems in the manufacture of alcohol by fermentation of beetroot. Bigot's problem was that his fermentations, instead of producing alcohol, yielded lactic acid.

At that point in time, chemistry was just starting to take root as a true scientific discipline, wrenching itself from the work of the alchemist. The chemical processes involved in living animals were slowly being discovered, and the chemist, Lavoisier had showed, among other things, that sugar, the initial product of the fermentation process, could be broken down into alcohol, CO_2, and H_2O by placing a sugar solution on a heated plate of platinum. In addition, Woehler had amazed the scientific community by synthesizing urea, demonstrating for the first time that organic compounds, previously believed only to be synthesized by living animals, could be produced in a test tube. Pasteur's previous work on crystals also led to the routine discovery of the internal structure and analysis of complex organic compounds.

Given this environment in 1856, fermentation, which was used in the production of wine, beer, and vinegar, was thought to be a process involving the chemical breakdown of sugar into the desired molecules based upon the existence of unstablizing vibrations in the molecules. It was known at the time that yeast cells existed in the fermenting vats of wine, and had been recognized as live organisms, but they were believed to be a product of fermentation or catalytic agents that infuse the ingredients that allow fermentation to take place. Ridicule befell those few biologists who had concluded that yeast was the cause of, and not the result of, fermentation. Also at that time, the scientists of the community were not providing much assistance to the wine, beer, and vinegar producers, who were facing serious economic downturns directly related to the fermentation processes. Yields of alcohol fell off, wine grew sour or turned to vinegar, and vinegar, when desired, ended up as lactic acid instead. Most importantly, the quality and taste of beer was prone to change from vat to vat, making quality control impossible.

Into this world came Louis Pasteur, entering Mr. Bigot's factory with his microscope. Pasteur found that when alcohol was produced normally, the yeast cells were plump. However, when lactic acid would form instead of alcohol, rod-like microbes were mixed with the yeast cells. He also found that amyl alcohol and other complex organic compounds were formed during the fermentation process, which could not be explained by the simple catalytic breakdown of sugar shown by Lavoisier. Pasteur concluded that some added processes must be involved. Also, based on his earlier work on crystallography, he found that some of the compounds rotated light, and were, therefore, asymmetric. His early work had shown that only living cells produced asymmetrical compounds, and thus he extrapolated his findings to determine that living cells—yeast—were forming the alcohol from sugar, and that other microorganisms contaminated the fermentation, and turned the fermentation sour.

Over the next several years, Pasteur isolated and then identified specific microorganisms that led to both abnormal and normal fermentations in wine, beer, and vinegar production. He determined that if wine, beer, or milk were heated to moderately high temperatures for a short period of time and then cooled, living microorganisms could be killed, thereby sterilizing (later known as pasteurizing) the fermentation batches and preventing their degradation. Thus, if microbes and yeasts in pure cultures were added to sterile fermentation masses and air was prevented from entering the vats by sealing them, predictable fermentation would follow.

Pasteur's earlier work on crystallography, chemistry, and optics led him to formulate the theory that asymmetric molecules are the result of living forces, and his work developed the new science of stereochemistry. During his work in fermentation, he demonstrated that each type of fermentation is caused by the existence of a specific microorganism or ferment, which is a living organism that can be studied through cultivation in a sterile medium. This is the basis of microbiology today.

Following his work in fermentation, and his discovery that the living microorganisms could be controlled to prevent the spoilation of products, Pasteur went on to a successful career as a chemist, with several major discoveries to his name. For example, he debunked the theory of spontaneous generation, which held at that time that microbes could be generated spontaneously from spoiling matter. Through his work on fermentation, he proved that microorganisms found during fermentation and putrefaction came from the outside, such as from dust in the air, and destroyed every theory that supported the spontaneous generation argument. He also concluded that microscopic beings are generated from parents similar to themselves.

Pasteur went on to research and cure a devastating disease among silkworms that was destroying the French silk industry. He also discovered the germ theory of disease and the use of vaccines in humans to prevent those diseases. It was only through the teachings of Pasteur, Lister, and others that antiseptic medicine and surgery began saving many lives. Pasteur also made major advances in dealing with anthrax, rabies, and the use of vaccines in humans.

While experimenting with biochemical agents for use against an increasing rabies infection epidemic in France, Pasteur discovered that contagions were the cause of disease. He also identified different germs that were present in the human body during illness. With this information, he found the causes of several diseases, and also discovered how to protect uninfected people through the use of vaccines that he ultimately developed. Pasteur made successful vaccines for diphtheria, tetanus, anthrax, chicken cholera, silk worm disease, tuberculosis, and the plague. In 1858, he proved garlic could be used as an antibacterial agent, which he ultimately gave to people who were seriously ill or had developed plague. His work on sterilization in medical procedures was slow to be adopted by many hospitals, but during his lifetime he spent much of his time working in hospitals with doctors trying to find ways to sterilize the equipment and the rooms in which operations were performed.

In 1885, Pasteur was working on experiments with rabies vaccines involving dogs, but had not used the vaccine on humans because he was afraid of unanticipated results and his inability to isolate the substance causing rabies. However, as in the development of all significant scientific discoveries and inventions, fate played its hand. A 9-year old, Joseph Meister, appeared in Pasteur's laboratory on July 6, 1886 with his mother. The young boy had been bitten by a rabid dog, and he could hardly walk. Pasteur, up to that time, had successfully treated 40 dogs, but had never used his vaccine on a human. Pasteur then consulted with many of his physician colleagues, and with much hesitation and reluctance treated the youth with his vaccine. Joseph Meister recovered, and lived a long and healthy life. Following this, people bitten by rabid dogs in many countries, including Russia and the United States, came to Pasteur for treatment. Newspapers reported these treatments and cures with overwhelming interest, making Pasteur a legend. Funded by public and governmental funds, the Pasteur Institute was created in Paris, initially to treat victims of rabies. Eventually, other Pasteur Institutes were built, including three in the United States, to treat rabies and other diseases.

The treatment of rabies was the last major project of Louis Pasteur. At the age of 46, he suffered a serious stroke, and his general health began failing. After suffering additional strokes, he died in 1895.

The resources used in the preparation of this treatise indicate that Joseph Meister, the young nine-year-old who received the first treatment for rabies in 1886, worked in the Pasteur Institute in Paris as a gatekeeper. In 1940, 45 years after his treatment for rabies, he was ordered by the German occupiers of Paris to open Pasteur's crypt. Joseph Meister committed suicide rather than defile the final resting place of his legendary hero.

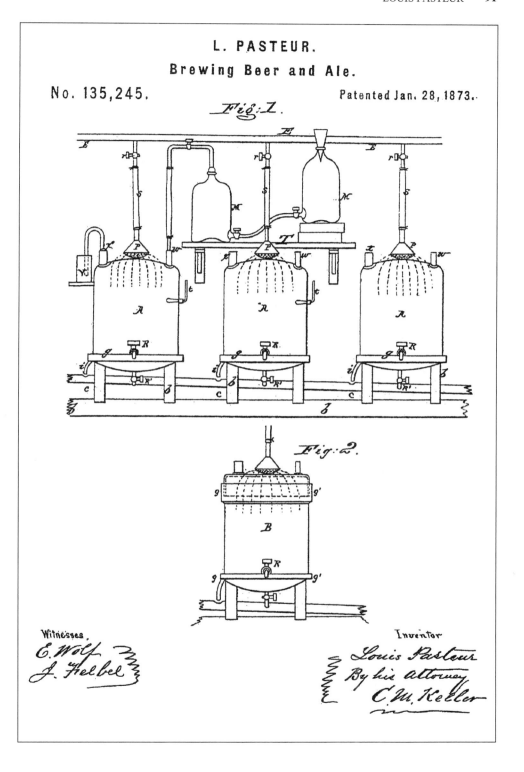

7 Requirement of Non-Obviousness for Patentability

7.1 DEVELOPMENT OF THE STANDARD OF NON-OBVIOUSNESS

The preceding chapter was, in part directed toward the requirement that an invention must be "novel" in order to be patentable. This represents a threshold hurdle to overcome, however, having established novelty alone does not automatically lead to the conclusion that your invention is patentable relative to the prior art. Thus, after it is established that the claimed invention differs structurally, or functionally, or both from the prior art, which means that the patent claim does not read literally on a single item of prior art, Section 103 of the Patent Statute (35 U.S.C.) requires that the claimed invention as a whole must also be *non-obvious* at the time the invention was made to a hypothetical "person having ordinary skill in the art to which the subject matter of the patented invention pertains." This condition deals with the level or degree of "invention" required to obtain a patent. Thus, the non-obviousness requirement comes into play only when the claimed invention is not identically disclosed or described in the prior art as set forth in Section 102 of the patent statute, which determines novelty. If the claimed invention is not novel, it is identically described in the prior art falling under one of the subsections of Section 102. If this occurs, no valid patent is possible, and the question of patentability is ended.

However, where the claimed invention is not identically described in any single piece of prior art, there is then the hurdle of non-obviousness that must be overcome to obtain a patent. The question becomes: does the invention for which you seek to obtain a patent represent sufficient innovation, or nonobviousness, over the prior art to support the grant of a patent.

7.2 HISTORICAL BACKGROUND

The first United States Patent Act in 1790 provided for the issuance of patents by the Secretaries of State, or the Department of War, or the Attorney General, or any two of them, who should deem the invention or discovery sufficiently useful or important. Three years later, the Patent Act of 1793 eliminated altogether the examination procedure in the grant of patents. However, the language regarding "useful" and "important" as to patents did reappear in the statute of 1836, which also reinstituted the patent examination process. This language was also included in all patent acts preceding the 1952 Patent Act, which is primarily the one in operation today, with periodic amendments.

In dealing with patents, the courts instituted certain criteria for innovation above and

Intellectual Property Law for Engineers and Scientists, by Howard B. Rockman
ISBN 0-471-44998-9 © 2004 The Institute of Electrical and Electronics Engineers

beyond the test of novelty. Thus case law began to develop around this test of "importance" for invention. However, the various cases decided by the courts set forth a great variety of definitions relating to the requirement for innovation, in addition to novelty, to support patentability. The question always has been, and still is, to determine whether a novel invention is a sufficient advance in the art that its disclosure to the public warrants granting the right to exclude others from use of the invention for a limited time period. This is the statement of the law as it exists today, and the answer to this question lies in the analysis of the technological advance of the particular invention.

The requirement that the subject matter of a patent grant be non-obvious was first embodied in statutory form in the 1952 Patent Act in Section 103, which states:

Conditions for Patentability: Non-Obvious Subject Matter

A patent may not be obtained though the invention is not identically disclosed or described as set forth in Section 102 of this title (novelty requirements), if the differences between the subject matter sought to be patented and the prior art are such that the subject matter as a whole would have been obvious at the time the invention was made to a person having ordinary skill in the art to which said subject matter pertains. The patentability shall not be negatived by the manner in which the invention was made. . . .

The legislative history of the 1952 Act, which incorporates Section 103, indicates that there was no provision in prior patent acts that corresponds to rejecting patents on the grounds of obviousness. However, the U.S. courts had been holding patents invalid on the grounds of lack of invention since at least as early as 1850. The statement about non-obviousness was purposely left broad in the statute, Congress hoping that the courts later would develop a more explicit statement of criteria that may be worked out to determine whether inventions are obvious or not in view of the prior art. Also, the legislative history indicates that the second sentence, relating to how the invention is made, states that patentability is not to be negated by the manner in which the invention is made. That is, it is immaterial whether or not the invention resulted from long toil and experimentation, or from a flash of genius. This specific provision overruled a series of prior Supreme Court and other court cases, which held that to meet the requirement of inventiveness, or nonobviousness, the invention had to be the result of a flash of genius, rather than something resulting from long efforts and constant empirical experimentation, as is the case with most modern innovation.

7.3   SUPREME COURT CASES PREDATING THE SECTION 103 NON-OBVIOUSNESS TEST

There were five Supreme Court decisions handed down between 1850 and 1950 that form the background to the introduction of the non-obviousness test for patentability into the United States patent system. My purpose is to give you a brief discussion of each of these cases, and advise you of the types of criteria that were used by the courts to determine whether or not your invention rises to the level of patentability, or is merely an obvious manifestation of the prior art. By understanding the thought process expounded by these Supreme Court justices, you should be in a good position to think about the non-obviousness of your invention.

7.3.1 *Hotchkiss v. Greenwood,* **Supreme Court, 1850**

In this case, the U.S. Patent Office had issued a patent on a mode of fastening a rod or shank to a knob, such as a doorknob. In this case, the knob was made of clay, however, the method of fastening the shank to the knob had been known and used by others in the prior art, and had been applied by others previously to the fastening of shanks to metallic knobs, but not to clay knobs. Apparently, clay knobs had been known and used before, and the shank and spindle by which the shank was attached to the knob were known before. However, this known means of attachment had never before been used to attach a shank to a knob made of potter's clay. It was shown that prior to this invention, metallic knobs had been attached to shanks by means of a cavity in the form of a dovetail and infusion of melted metal, which is the same mode claimed in the invention before the court considering the clay doorknob. It was decided by the Supreme Court that substituting a knob of clay was simply the substitution of one material for another.

The Supreme Court held in this case that the improvement, if any, consisted in the superiority of the material, clay versus metal, and this was not considered new over materials previously employed in making knobs. The difference between the patented invention and the prior art was merely formal, and destitute of ingenuity or invention. The Court also stated that the invention gave evidence of judgement and skill in the selection and adaptation of the materials used in the manufacture of the instrument for the purposes intended, but nothing more. In other words, the court felt that a skilled technician could merely substitute clay for metal knobs, and that would constitute the subject matter of the alleged invention. The court went on to say that "unless more ingenuity and skill in applying the old method of fastening the shank and the knob were required in the application of it to the clay or porcelain knob than were possessed by an ordinary mechanic acquainted with the business, there was an absence of that degree of skill and ingenuity which constitutes an essential element of every invention." In other words, the improvement here was the work of a skillful mechanic, not that of an inventor.

This was the first case the Supreme Court decided that added the requirement of "invention or non-obviousness" to the requirements for patentability. Remember that such non-obviousness requirement was not in the patent statute of 1836, under which this case of *Hotchkiss v. Greenwood* was decided.

7.3.2 *Atlantic Works v. Brady,* **Supreme Court, 1882**

The patent in question in this case involved a dredge boat construction, the invention consisting mainly of attaching a screw to the forward end of a propeller dredge boat, the boat being provided with tanks for settling the boat in the water. The dredge is operated by sinking the boat until the screw comes in contact with the mud and sand, which by the revolution of the screw, is thrown up and mingled and carried away with the current. The use of tanks for the purpose of keeping the vessel level while she settles was already old in the art, having been used in dry docks previously. It was also shown that the same tanks for leveling craft were used in many light-draft monitors during the "late war." I would like to quote directly from this case to show what the Supreme Court in 1882 felt was the difference between patentable invention and merely the exercise of technical skill:

> "The process of development in manufactures creates a constant demand for new appliances, which the skill of ordinary head-workmen and engineers is generally adequate to devise, and which, indeed, are the natural and proper outgrowth of such development. Each step forward

prepares the way for the next, and each is usually taken by spontaneous trials and attempts in a hundred places. To grant to a single party a monopoly of every slight advance made, except where the exercise of invention, somewhat above ordinary mechanical or engineering skill, is distinctly shown, is unjust in principal and injurious in its consequence."

The design of the patent laws is to reward those who make some substantial discovery or invention, which adds to our knowledge or makes a step in the useful arts. Such inventors are worthy of all favor. It was never the object of those laws (patent laws) to grant a monopoly for every trifling device, every shadow of a shade of an idea, which would naturally and spontaneously occur to any skilled mechanic or operator in the ordinary progress of manufactures. Such an indiscriminate creation of exclusive privileges tends rather to obstruct than to stimulate invention. It creates a class of speculative schemers who make it their business to watch the advancing wave of improvement, and gather its foam in the form of patented monopolies, which enable them to lay a heavy tax upon the industry of the country, without contributing anything to the real advancement of the arts."

As you can see, the Justices of the Supreme Court sometimes wax poetic when describing their ideas of what should be patentable and what should be not.

7.3.3 *Goodyear Rubber and Tire Company v. Ray-O-Vac Company,* Supreme Court, 1944

The patent in suit here was for a very narrow advance in a crowded art, and covered a leak-proof dry cell, where insulating material was placed around a conventional cylindrical zinc cup of a flashlight battery, and this was covered by an outside protective metal sheath which would enclose the insulated sidewalls of the zinc cup and tightly embrace both the upper and lower closures to prevent leakage of the electrolite and depolarizing mix constituting the internal portions of the battery.

The Supreme Court held that, viewed after the event with hindsight, the invention covered by this patent may seem simple. However, the court noted that during the prior period of 50 years in which flashlight batteries were used, no one devised a method of curing the defect of leakage. Once the method of the patent in suit was used, it became publicly and commercially successful. The court held that the fact of commercial success was entitled to weight in determining whether the improvement amounted to an "invention" and should in a close case tip the scales in favor of patentability. In this case, the leak proof battery patent was upheld.

7.3.4 *Cuno Engineering Corporation v. Automatic Devices Corporation,* Supreme Court, 1941

This case involved a patent on a cigarette lighter commonly found in automobiles. The prior art against which the obviousness of this cigarette lighter was tested were two patents, one covering a wireless or cordless cigarette lighter for a car, and another covering an electric lighter for cigars and cigarettes with a thermostatic control. The patent in question added to the so-called wireless or cordless lighter a thermostatic control responsive to the temperature of the heating coil, which automatically returned the plug to its off position after the heating coil had reached an appropriate maximum temperature. The plug was then manually removed from the dashboard of the car to light the smoking material. When replaced in the socket after use, the cigarette lighter was held in an open circuit position until next needed.

The court held that thermostatic controls of a heating unit operating to cut off an electric current energizing the unit when its temperature had reached its desired point were well known when the patentee made his invention. The court held that the advance of the inventor over the thermostatically controlled electric lighter was the use of the removable plug bearing the heating unit, which plug was shown in the other prior art patent to establish the automatic control circuit. The court said the question was whether it was invention (or non-obvious) to apply the automatic circuit of one patent to the removable heating unit in substitution for a circuit manually controlled as shown by another patent. The court in this case held that if an "improvement" is to obtain the privileged position of a patent, more ingenuity must be involved than the work of a mechanic skilled in the art. The court recognized that the principals set forth in the *Hotchkiss v. Greenwood* case applied to the adaptation or combination of old or well known devices for new uses. However, the court went on to say that: "the new device, however useful it may be, must reveal the flash of creative genius not merely the skill of the calling." In this case, the court went on to say that the patent in question did not reach this level of inventive genius. The so-called inventor merely incorporated the well known thermostat into the old wireless lighter to produce a more efficient, useful and convenient article. A new application of an old device may not be patented if the result claimed as new is the same in character as the original result. The use of a thermostat to break a circuit in a "wireless" cigar lighter is analogous to, or the same in character as, the use of such a device in electric heaters, toasters or irons, whatever may be the difference in detail of design. Ingenuity was required to effect the adaptation, but no more than that to be expected of a mechanic skilled in the art. Then, the Court went on to say, rather poetically: "Strict application of that test is necessary least in the constant demand for new appliances the heavy hand of tribute be laid on each slight technical logical advance in an art."

7.3.5 *The Great Atlantic and Pacific Tea Company v. Supermarket Equipment Corporation,* Supreme Court, 1950

The claims of the patent before the Supremes in this case asserted invention in a cashiers' counter, such as the check-out counter in a grocery store, equipped with a three-sided horizontally disposed U-shaped frame or rack, with no top or bottom. When pushed or pulled along the top of the check-out counter, the frame moved groceries deposited within it by a customer to the checking clerk, and left them there when pushed back to repeat the operation. I recall this device being used in grocery stores when I was young, and which have now been replaced by moving conveyor belts.

The Supreme Court noted that this device had been widely adopted and successfully used, but did it only bring old elements together? The court held that the mere aggregation of a number of old parts or elements which in the aggregation perform or produce no new or different function or operation than they performed individually before is not patentable invention. The court noted that there was no finding that the old elements which made up this device performed any additional or different function in the combination than they performed out of it. The court stated that the three-sided rack will draw or push goods put within it from one place to another—just what any such rack will do on any smooth surface—and the guide rails keep it from falling. The court held that a patent for a combination which only unites old elements with no new change in their respective functions, such as presented here, obviously withdrawals what technology is already known to others into the field of its monopoly and diminishes the resources available to skillful men. The court held that the patentee had added nothing to the total stock of knowledge, but had merely brought together segments of prior art in an attempt to claim them in congregation as a monopoly.

The Court continued by saying that the framers of the Constitution plainly did not want to grant exclusive rights freely. To justify a patent, the invention had to serve the ends of science—to push back the frontiers of chemistry, physics and the like; to make a distinctive contribution to scientific knowledge. The court went on to reaffirm the "inventive genius" test for patentability as set forth in the previously mentioned Cuno Engineering case. The Supreme Court in the present case stated: "the Constitution never sanctioned the patenting of gadgets. Patents serve a higher end—the advancement of science. An invention need not be as startling as an atomic bomb to be patentable. But it has to be of such quality and distinction that masters of the scientific field in which it falls will recognize it as an advance."

Thus, the Supreme Court in 1950 reinforced the "flash of genius test" as a test for patentability, thereby begging the question whether inventions which had taken a long time to develop would qualify as patentable inventions. Fortunately, this issue was directly taken up by the U.S. Congress, which in 1952 passed a new patent statute which specifically overruled the Cuno Engineering case "flash of genius" test, by stating that patentability of an invention will not be negatived by the manner in which the invention is made. Therefore, the "flash of genius" test is no longer applicable to determine patentability, and those inventions which resulted from dogged determination and perserverance over a period of time qualify as non-obvious and patentable, upon meeting the other criteria of patentability—falling into a category of patentable subject matter; utility for a stated purpose; and novelty over the prior art.

7.4   THE 1952 PATENT STATUTE AND THE CASE OF *GRAHAM V. JOHN DEERE COMPANY*

Previously I discussed the U.S. patent law of 1836, which was the basis for the existing modern patent law. In the 1836 law, the requirement of novelty was set forth in great detail, however there was no standard of non-obviousness written into the statute. The concept of an invention not only being novel, but also being non-obvious to one skilled in the art, was created over 150 years ago in the Supreme Court case of *Hotchkiss v. Greenwood*. This was the first case in which a court held that more than just novelty was required for patentability, even though the 1836 statute had specified nothing but novelty as a requirement for distinguishing over the prior art. Subsequent to the *Hotchkiss* case, thousands of cases were decided dealing with the subject of obviousness of inventions, without any apparent consistency or common thread through all these decisions. Thus, until only within the last 40 years or so, there was great confusion by the courts in applying the standard of what would be obvious to one skilled in the art differentiating an invention from the genre of the prior art.

In 1952, when the present patent statute was enacted, the drafters of the law included Section 103 which required that the invention be non-obvious, as well as novel and useful. However, the law did not state any single, generic, bold print rule as to how the law should be applied to enable an inventor or the courts to easily determine whether his/her invention was non-obvious compared to what had gone before.

The object of the non-obviousness clause of the patent statute was to indicate to the creative world that while everyone who does something different or new has created an "invention" unless the subject matter had been published or patented by someone else, a determination still had to be made whether the invention was non-obvious and therefore meritorious enough to support a patent grant. Even though you make an invention, because it is new to you, someone else unbeknownst to you may have come up with the same or a similar idea years before and obtained a patent on it or published it. These prior events may render your invention unpatentable, as not novel or non-obvious under the patent statute, however you have still created an "invention."

Thus, the drafters of the law in 1952 set forth no exact test to be used to determine obviousness, and indicated that the determination of what is obvious is still one of judgment to be determined case by case, invention by invention.

During my career in patent law, which began in 1959, most of the inventors and engineers that I have spoken to tend to tell me, at the onset, that the invention they have just developed would actually be obvious to anyone. Of course, with hindsight anything is obvious. Once the invention or the improvement has been shown, then everybody can say "Oh, I could have thought of that." However, that is not true. During your engineering and science careers, before you make a decision as to whether or not the project you are working on and the results of that project meet the standards of patentability, ask yourselves these five questions:

1. How long did a need exist for the improvement you came up with?
2. How many before you tried to find a way, but could not?
3. How long did the surrounding and analogous arts disclose the means or steps to do what you did?
4. How immediately was your invention recognized as an answer by those who use your new variant?
5. Has there been commercial success of your invention?

It wasn't until 1966, in a trilogy of cases, now referred to as the *Graham v. John Deere Company,* 383 U.S. 1 (1966) cases, that the Supreme Court set forth guidelines which now allow engineers, scientists and their attorneys to determine whether or not their invention will meet the requirement of non-obviousness necessary to secure a patent. The Supreme Court in the *Graham* case set the following test for determining obviousness:

1. Determine the scope and content of the prior art. This determination is made from an analysis of all prior art known by the inventor, and from additional prior art that may also be uncovered by a novelty search conducted prior to filing a patent application.
2. Next, determine the differences between the invention under consideration and the content of the prior art. Remember, if there are no differences, your invention is not novel and does not pass the first test for patentability, i.e., novelty.
3. Next, determine what is the level of ordinary skill in the art. Imagine a hypothetical person, skilled in the art, such as you are, and what that person would know and not know.
4. Keeping in mind the differences between the prior art and the invention you have just made, decide what modifications to the prior art would be necessary to make the prior art correspond to, or rise up to, your invention.

5. Determine whether the other prior art materials you are aware of, or even common knowledge that would be available to one skilled in the art, suggest the "necessary" modifications to the prior art you have determined from Step 4 above. If the answer to this question is yes, the invention is obvious and not patentable.

6. Keep in mind the so-called secondary considerations bearing on the question of non-obviousness:

    (a) What is the commercial success, if any, of the invention you are analyzing in comparison with the prior art. If your invention has achieved commercial success, it would therefore not have been obvious to modify the prior art to derive your invention.

    (b) Does the invention fill a long-felt, but as yet unresolved, need in the relevant industry?

    (c) The failure of others to solve the problem to which the invention is directed.

    (d) The invention provides a new or different function as well as an unexpected result.

    (e) A synergistic result is produced, wherein one plus one equals three.

    (f) The invention you have just derived directs one contrary to the teachings of the prior art.

In determining the test of obviousness, I refer to the term "prior art" or "references" that are used to make this comparison to your invention. This prior art is the same as defined under the statute providing for novelty as a requirement of patentability. If a patent publication or prior use or sale of a product does not fall within the definition of prior art under Section 102, it is not "prior art" that can be used in combination with other prior art to determine non-obviousness under Section 103.

In applying the test to determine non-obviousness, the relevant time period is the time when the invention was made. Therefore, when analyzing the prior art, be aware of the conception date of your invention, and compare that against the application filing dates of the reference patents. Remember that the date of your earliest conception of the invention, which was followed by diligent efforts to reduce the invention to practice, constitute your earliest invention date. If any publication or issued patent bears a date within a year of the time you expect to get a patent application on file, these materials may not constitute prior art. Rather than bore you with any more details, I would suggest that if this situation arises, the advice of a competent patent attorney would be very helpful in determining whether a patent or publication dated within the last year constitutes "prior art" or not. Also, when considering whether your invention can meet the standard of non-obviousness, please consider a few other points that may help you in making this decision:

1. Does the combination of the devices or processes shown in the prior art lead to a device or process which produces the same or a different result as your invention?

2. Does the device or process derived from combining the prior art function the same as your invention?

3. Is the combined device or process derived from the prior art as efficient as your invention?

4. Is the combined device or process derived from the prior art operative, that is will it work to produce the intended function and result of your invention?

5. Would the combined device or process from the prior art be more expensive to produce or operate compared to your invention?

All of these answers will help in making a determination whether or not the hurdle of non-obviousness has been overcome.

Here are a few additional factors taken from cases decided in the field of patent law regarding the question of non-obviousness over the past several years. For example, if the only difference between your invention and the prior art involves the selection or substitution of a known material due to its known suitability for its intended function or purpose, your invention may not be patentable. See, for example, the *Hotchkiss* Supreme Court case mentioned previously. Keep in mind, however, the common knowledge that a vast majority of all patentable inventions are combinations of known elements that are formed in a different and novel array to provide a new and unexpected result. Therefore, when determining whether the solution to the problem you have been working on is non-obvious over the "known elements," consider whether the result you have obtained is predictable or not from the known elements. As recently described to me by a sage colleague, the standard of meeting the requirement of non-obviousness is not "Eureka!" It is more along the lines of "that's cool."

If your invention involves the application of optimum ranges within ranges set forth in the prior art, or you merely provide mechanical or automatic means to replace a manual operation, without any further contribution to the art, you also may not be able to obtain a patent. Additionally, changes of size, degree, proportion and sequence of adding ingredients do not lend patentability, unless some new and unexpected result or function can be derived from such changes. For example, making a catalytic converter smaller to fit under smaller sized cars is not a patentable advance in the art, unless some new structure or function evolves from the change of size.

Similarly, a combination of elements set forth in your invention that produces an improved and unexpected result will lead to patentability, since the invention would be non-obvious. Also, if your invention omits one or more of the elements that are shown in the prior art devices, but your invention still retains the function of that or those elements in the resulting combination, you may have a patentable invention.

In summary, it is apparent from the above comments that determining whether your novel and useful invention would ultimately be declared to be non-obvious over the prior art, and therefore worthy of a patent, is one that is not easily arrived at. Therefore, one of the services that you should look for when engaging a patent attorney is that the patent attorney carefully look at all of the related prior art and make a determination whether your invention is both novel and unobvious. You should ensure that any report on patentability that your attorney submits to you does include an analysis of the question of non-obviousness as well as novelty. It would not be wise to spend the money to prepare a patent application where there is a high risk that the U.S. Patent & Trademark Office will reject the application on the grounds of obviousness. Do not try this at home, leave it to the professionals.

Having said all of the above regarding the test of non-obviousness, I feel it prudent to provide you with a certain factious example at this point to show how a determination of non-obviousness works through the thought processes. Assume that someone invents a general purpose, programmable, digital computer. And this computer is colored green. The inventor files a patent application claiming a green, digital computer. Assume also that the physical structure of the computer is old in the art, but never had one ever been colored green before, and there is not a single prior art reference or patent showing a green computer. Consider also that dozens of other colors and shades in the visible spectrum were used as colors for the same kind of computer.

The first question is whether the claimed green computer is novel over the prior art. This determination must be made first, because if there is no novelty, the question of unobviousness becomes moot. In this particular situation, the green computer is novel since it is not identically described in any single item of prior art. For purposes of our analysis, a green computer must be considered structurally different from a computer of any other color. Therefore, it is now appropriate to examine the "green" technology embodied in this computer to determine whether it is an unobvious advance over the prior art.

At first glance, you may determine that using the color green surely would be obvious compared to computers using all the other colors of the visible spectrum. However, further analysis may show that this answer is not correct. For example, given the same set of facts as above, assume that when the computer is green, the frequency band of the green color serves to absorb and concentrate ambient cosmic and ultra-violet rays that, in combination, change the static electrical charge in all of the components of the computer, including the conductive and semi-conductive elements in the computer. As a consequence, all the electrical and electronic operations are speeded up by a factor of 1.2, wherein the computer literally operates 1.2 times as fast and also is possibly 1.2 times more valuable than a computer that is not colored green. Given all of these new and unexpected results of using a green computer, the subject invention also passes the test of non-obviousness, since no one else ever used the color green to obtain these results in the computer.

The above example points out the fact that no structural or functional difference between your invention and the prior art may be ignored in determining the questions of novelty and unobviousness. The differences may be slim, however the subject matter as a whole may still be unobvious over the prior art to a person of ordinary skill in the relevant technology.

Alexander Graham Bell

TELEPHONE

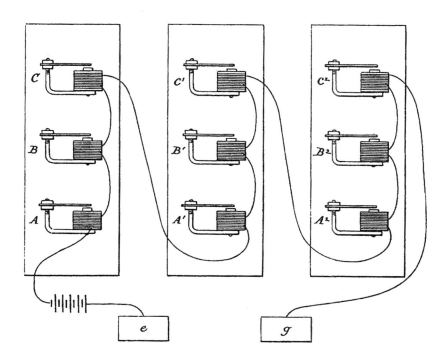

Alexander Graham Bell is credited with inventing the practical telephone, which can be defined as a device for transmitting human speech by electricity. The history of the development of the telephone shows that there were several others working on similar projects at the same time, such as Elisha Gray and Thomas Edison. For example, in the United Kingdom, some consider Gray as the telephone's inventor. As a result, the United States patent that was ultimately issued on Bell's telephone, and his ensuing telephone patents, were the subject of 600 patent infringement lawsuits, all won by Bell, and all upholding his patents.

Alexander Graham Bell was born in Edinburgh, Scotland on March 3, 1847. His father, Alexander Melville Bell, was a teacher who taught deaf and mute students how to speak. Bell's father also created a code of symbols, indicating positions of the lips, tongue, and throat in making sounds, helping the deaf learn to speak. This was known as "visible speech."

Alexander's mother, Eliza Bell, was practically totally deaf, and by pressing his lips against his mother's forehead, Bell discovered that he could make the bones in her head

Intellectual Property Law for Engineers and Scientists, by Howard B. Rockman
ISBN 0-471-44998-9 © 2004 The Institute of Electrical and Electronics Engineers

resonate to his voice. Bell was also a talented pianist who learned early on to define and discriminate pitch. He noticed that a chord struck on one piano would be echoed by a piano in another room, and that entire chords could be transmitted through the air, vibrating at the receiving end at the same pitch as transmitted. This observation eventually was involved in the development of the telephone.

After Bell's oldest and youngest brothers died of tuberculosis in Scotland, the family moved to Tutelo Heights, near Brantford, Ontario, Canada. Bell's father subsequently took a position in Boston, Massachusetts, teaching deaf children to speak, and his son began a successful teaching career in Boston. His students included George Sanders, the son of a successful leather merchant, and Mabel Hubbard, the daughter of a successful lawyer. Later in life, Mr. Hubbard and Mr. Sanders were to become Bell's chief financial backers, and Mabel Hubbard became his wife.

The early experiments of Bell that eventually led to the invention of the telephone did not even involve thinking about a telephone. Bell was trying to develop a multiple telegraph, one that could be used to convey several messages simultaneously, each at a different pitch. Telegraphy at that time involved transmission of an electrical current that was interrupted in a pattern known as the Morse Code. In the 1870s, Bell, Edison, and Elishia Gray were all seeking a telegraph device that could send upwards of four messages simultaneously. Bell's work on his multiple telegraph stemmed from Helmholtz's device, which used a single tuning fork that continually interrupted the circuit and a resonator that kept the other tuning forks in the system in constant vibration. The Helmholtz device was used to produce vowel sounds using electromechanical means, and Bell assumed that if the vowels could be transmitted over wires, so could other sounds, including the consonants and musical tones.

Bell found it difficult to determine how to make and break the current at the precise pitch required as the pitch was conveyed along a telegraph wire. While on vacation in 1874, he constructed an "ear phonoautograph" using a hay reed and the ear bones from a dead man mounted on a wooden frame. Sounds delivered to the ear bones caused the hay reed to trace the shape of the sound waves on a smoked glass. Using his previous knowledge of electricity, speaking machines, and pitch, Bell was inspired to conclude that the smoked glass could be rolled back and forth beneath the hay reed. This also led Bell to conclude that sound could be translated into visible waves, from which he theorized that vibrations of a reed could be transformed into an undulating electrical current and reproduced as sound. The undulating current concept was crucial to his later development of the telephone.

Bell initially conceived of a device made of a plurality of reeds extending over a magnet. As the reeds responded to one's voice, they would ultimately vibrate in the direction of and then away from the magnet, creating the undulating current. This "harp apparatus," as Bell himself called it, did not resemble the telephone that he ultimately developed.

In 1874, Bell sketched, but never built, his "harp apparatus" device, showing how undulating sound waves could be translated into electric currents of the same form. This sketched apparatus included two permanent horseshoe magnets with two steel reeds on each. Bell conceived that this would serve as a transceiver for two separate signals, the signals corresponding to each of the reeds. Bell used permanent magnets in his harp apparatus rather than the electromagnets he had previously used in his multiple telegraph experiments. He reasoned that if a magnet is moving away from a coil half of the time and moving toward the coil the other half of the time, the induced current should imitate the vibrating magnet, since the flux would be increasing half of the time when the magnet moves towards the coil, and decreasing the remaining half of the time when the magnet moves away from the coil. This periodic increasing and decreasing of the flux at discrete intervals would produce the same periodic induced current in the coil.

Bell postulated a device with a first steel reed having a specific harmonic mounted on a horseshoe-shaped permanent magnet, and a second reed having a different harmonic on the same magnet (a transceiver). He then thought of placing a third reed having the same harmonic of the first reed, and a fourth reed having the same harmonic as the second reed on a duplicate transceiver. When the first reed was vibrated, the third reed on the transceiver would also vibrate. Likewise, when the second reed was vibrated, the fourth reed on the transceiver also vibrated.

When the first reed vibrated toward the coil, the current became more positive or negative, depending upon which pole of the magnet the first reed was on and the winding pattern of the underlying coil. When the first reed vibrated away from the coil, an opposite current was induced. The signal was sent across as a sinusoidal wave, which was precisely the same wave form produced by the phonautograph on smoked glass.

This is what Bell referred to as his "undulating current," which became the primary feature of his first telephone patent, issued in 1876. This wave expressed in a graphical manner the vibratory movement of the air while the reeds were producing their musical tones, and the vibrations of the individual reeds attached to the permanent magnet resulted in a single undulating current waveform. Bell determined that if the waves from the two reeds could be combined to produce a more intricate wave, the proper combination of waves could be used to produce all sounds.

Bell used this mental model to develop the postulate that undulating waves traced into the smoked glass in his phonautograph could be transformed into undulating electric current, and then be reproduced as sound. This use of undulating current was different than the intermittent current used in telegraphy to produce dots and dashes. Bell also discovered that by combining undulating currents, the result would be a different sine curve produced for every combination of sounds, allowing discrimination among different messages. His future father-in-law, Gardiner Hubbard, who was his primary backer, urged Bell to direct his efforts towards the multiple telegraph, and forget trying to produce a "speaking" telegraph.

Bell's initial multiple transmitter and receiver (transceiver) made and broke contact with a dish of mercury that ultimately completed an interrupted circuit. At the receiving end, electromagnets attracted the tuning fork each time the circuit was completed, thus causing the fork to vibrate. Bell had thought through a complete system for his multiple telegraphy device, and had succeeded in patenting different parts of it by the spring of 1875. A key part of his thinking was that the multiple telegraphy system would transmit an undulatory current, as opposed to the intermittent or make-or-break current used in single-transmission telegraphy.

By June 2, 1875, Bell had constructed three multiple telegraph stations, each with three tuned relays. When Bell caused one of the reeds at the first station to vibrate, the corresponding reed at the second station also vibrated. His assistant, Mr. Watson, who was in another room with the third corresponding reed, advised Bell that the reed was stuck. To release the stuck reed, Watson vibrated it with his finger, and Bell noticed that the corresponding reed at Station II vibrated violently. Bell then placed his ear next to each of the other reeds at the second station in succession, and heard both the overtones and the pitch of the tuned reeds. He concluded from this incident that magneto-electric undulating currents generated by the vibration of an armature in front of an electromagnet could produce audible effects that could be utilized for multiple telegraphy and speech transmission. Later, Mr. Watson was to comment that the speaking telephone was born as a result of this experiment.

However, extensive work did remain before a workable electric telephone was developed. As a result of the stuck reed, Bell learned that a single reed, when dampened or stuck, could also induce a current that was capable of transmitting complex vibrations or sounds over a distance, and the multiple reeds of the harp structure were not necessary. Bell then asked Mr. Watson to construct a device in which a reed relay was attached to a membrane or diaphragm having a speaking cavity. As one spoke into the cavity, the membrane vibrated and these vibrations were translated into electric current by the dampened reed. The current thus generated was received by a similar device at the end of an electrical wire. The receiving device produced mumbling, rather than intelligible speech. However, Bell and Watson considered that they were heading in the right direction.

On January 20, 1876, Bell signed a patent application directed to his use of electrical undulations induced by the vibration of a body capable of inductive action to transmit sound. This was before speech had even been transmitted electrically. Bell's patent application was submitted to the United States Patent Office on February 14, 1876, four days after his 29th birthday, and merely a few hours before Elisha Gray submitted a caveat for a speaking telegraph. (A caveat was a document submitted by a potential inventor with the U.S. Patent Office, setting forth a broad outline of an invention they intended to make, but which was not complete. The use of caveats in the United States terminated circa 1909.)

When the Bell patent application was filed, he and Watson had still not developed a working device. On March 10, 1876, Bell removed the electromagnet from the device he and Watson had constructed that produced the mumbling transmission, and substituted a dish of water that was used as a spark arrester; i.e., the water acted as a resistance that prevented sparks in the telegraph relay. These liquid experiments led to the famous quote, "Watson, come here. I want you," which occurred on March 10, 1876. Thus, when Bell obtained his U.S. Patent No. 174,465 on March 7, 1876, it was three days before he finally achieved a working telephone.

Claim 5 of Bell's patent was rather broad, and reads as follows:

5. The method of, and apparatus for, transmitting vocal or other sounds telegraphically, as herein described, by causing electrical undulations, similar in form to the vibrations of the air accompanying the said vocal or other sound, substantially as set forth.

Subsequently, the basic Bell telephone patent was subject to 600 lawsuits of various kinds, mainly suits filed by Bell to prevent others from infringing on his patent.

The first lawsuit filed under the Bell patents was the so-called Dowd case, in which Western Union was the alleged primary infringing defendant. This lawsuit was filed on September 12, 1878 in the Circuit Court of the United States for the District of Massachusetts, and there is no published court decision because the case was settled after trial while the judge had the case under advisement. This first lawsuit turned out to be the heart of the ensuing litigation that took place over the next 20 years.

Bell had very little in the way of documents, correspondence, sketches, or drawings to help his memory regarding his work in developing the telephone. In his search for such documentation, Bell even asked his wife, Mabel, for the keys to a bureau were she kept his love letters written to her before they were married, in an attempt to find any statement that he might have made in those letters that would help fix the dates of his telephone experiments. Bell told Mabel that he did not have the remotest intention of publishing any of his love letters.

In the litigation against Western Union, Bell's attorney did not base his strategy on the concept of undulatory current as something that was new, but on the use of electricity in general for transmitting speech, as exemplified by the instruments described in the Bell patents. This strategy worked, because the Western Union lawyers had built their case around showing that undulatory currents were not new with Bell. Bell's case, however was predicated on the *application* of undulatory currents. This led to the Bell company winning control, with their patents, of the basic principle of telephony, not merely the particular devices used in telephony.

However, Bell still needed to present documentary evidence showing that he had worked on the telephone. During the spring and summer of 1879, Mabel Bell, his wife, and her cousin Mary Bletchford, went through all the old correspondence between Bell and his then fiancé, and also the notebooks that Bell was able to maintain. In the movie "The Story of Alexander Graham Bell" (1939), the Hollywood version of the story shows that the entire lawsuit depended upon one love letter submitted to the court by Mabel Bell. Thus, Hollywood used poetic license to turn a patent litigation matter into an interesting love story.

The lawsuit against Western Union was eventually settled before decision, when Western Union assigned its telephone patents to the Bell Company in exchange for Western Union being awarded 20% of rental receipts by Bell for the next 17 years. The Edison carbon transmitter patent, along with additional improvement patents, were obtained by the Bell Company as a result of the settlement, along with the network of agencies and customers of Western Union. Thus, after the settlement, the stock of American Bell Telephone Company nearly doubled in a few days.

The Bell Company's decision to settle the case was predicated not on the theory that there was any weakness in Bell's patents, but upon the fact that Western Union had brought other lawsuits against the Bell Company for infringement of the later improvement patents, such as the Edison transmitter. As in any litigation, the parties considered that victory by either side is not a certainty, but distraction and the expense of resources are certain. Therefore, Bell and his advisors felt that the settlement was the best business choice.

Two other Bell patent-related lawsuits are worthy of mention in this treatise. The first is the case of *American Bell Telephone Company v. Globe Telephone Company, Antonio Meucci, and others,* 31 Fed. 728 (SDNY, 1887). In this case, the defendants were attempting to invalidate broad Claim 5 of the basic telephone patent No. 174,465 obtained by Bell on March 7, 1876. The primary evidence offered in the defendant's attempt to invalidate the Bell patent was Meucci's allegation that he had developed a speaking telephone for domestic use as early as 1871, and since he was too poor to obtain a patent, his invention was made public by being published in *Eco D'Italia,* a local newspaper for Italian immigrants in New York in the latter half of the 19th century. Meucci had filed a caveat in the United States Patent Office on December 28, 1871 describing his device. The Globe Company, at the time of the suit, had never constructed any telephones, but was obtaining money from investors, after telling the investors that Globe had acquired patents that would be used to defeat the Bell patents, and that Globe's patents would protect the purchasers or licensees against the Bell Company patents. Investors were also told that the Meucci caveat would be used to defeat the Bell patents. The Globe Company realized that its own patents were worthless unless the Bell patent could be invalidated, and thus did not manufacture any telephones, so that the Bell Company could not accuse them of infringement. At the time of the trial, Mr. Meucci did not have any of his original devices to offer in evidence to show what it was he had developed, since his wife had sold them at a "garage sale" to raise money. The Meucci caveat was originally filed in 1871; it was renewed in December 1882, and again in December 1883. During that time, Mr. Meucci did not make any improvements on the device that was disclosed in his 1871 caveat.

Upon reviewing the evidence, the court in the Globe case held that the Meucci device resulted in nothing beyond conveying speech mechanically by means of a wire telephone. His caveat disclosed a metallic conductor as a sound conveying medium, and he merely supposed that by electrifying the apparatus or the operator, he could obtain a better result. He did not communicate his invention to anyone else who could appreciate it or assist him in perfecting and introducing his invention to the public, but between 1859 and 1871, he did file several patent applications for other inventions. Meucci was also in close association with one William E. Rider, who paid the expenses of his experiments. Therefore, the court in the *Bell v. Globe* case disregarded Mr. Meucci's claims of poverty. The relation with Rider continued until 1867, when Mr. Rider became convinced that Meucci's inventions were not sufficiently practical or profitable.

The court further held that the caveat of Meucci did not describe any elements of an electric speaking telephone, but that Meucci employed the then well-known physical conducting effect of metallic conductors to convey sound, and enhanced the results by electrically insulating both the conductor and the communicating parties. The caveat filed by Meucci consisted of isolating two persons by placing them upon glass insulators, and putting them in communication by means of a telegraph wire. He then amended this statement by stating that the person sending the message was insulated, with the person receiving the signal in free electrical communication with the ground. These conditions could also be reversed.

The court held that Meucci's device consisted of a mechanical telephone consisting of a mouthpiece and an earpiece connected by a wire, and that beyond this the invention of Meucci was only imagination. The patent attorney who prepared the caveat for Mr. Meucci told Meucci that his idea gave promises of usefulness, but would require many experiments to prove the reality of his concept. This case, as were all of the other cases in which the validity of the original Bell telephone patent was in dispute, was resolved by upholding the validity of the Bell patent.

Despite this court decision, over 100 years later, on June 11, 2002, the United States House of Representatives in Washington, D.C. passed a resolution honoring the achievements of Antonio Meucci. This resolution briefly sets forth the fact that Meucci developed his speaking device in 1871 so he could communicate with his ailing wife on a different floor of his house, that he published a description of his invention in New York's Italian language newspaper at the time, and that he was too poor to obtain patent protection or commercialization of his invention. The resolution also implies that Meucci submitted his earlier models to Western Union, who then lost them, but that before they were lost, Alexander Graham Bell conducted experiments in the same laboratory at Western Union where Meucci's earlier materials were stored. The resolution also refers to a lawsuit filed by the United States government on January 13, 1887 to annul the Bell patent on the grounds of fraud, which lawsuit is discussed a few paragraphs below. The resolution concludes that if Meucci had been able to pay the $10 fee to maintain his caveat after 1874, no patent on the telephone would have been issued to Alexander Graham Bell.

My continuing research into this resolution led me to the rebuttal comments of Edwin S. Grosvenor, published at `http://www.alecbell.org/meuccimemo.html`. In his memo, Mr. Grosvenor refers back to the case of *American Bell Telephone Company v.*

Globe and Meucci, and points to those facts in the court's decision that would completely repudiate the grounds set forth in the resolution of the U.S. House of Representatives of 2002. The Grosvenor article points out that the Meucci caveat disclosed a mouthpiece and an earpiece connected by a taut wire that transmitted vibrations of sounds mechanically (not electrically) over the wire. The Grosvenor article also states that Meucci had financial help and he was not destitute, and could have commercialized his invention had it been worth anything. Grosvenor thus concludes that the Meucci caveat, and indeed his "invention," does not describe or suggest any of the elements of electrical communication of voice, or the principle of undulating current that is set forth even in the broadest claim of the Bell patent.

Upon my review of the *American Bell Telephone Company v. Globe and Meucci* court decision of July 19, 1887, I conclude the comments of Mr. Grosvenor are more likely correct in comparison to the statements by the United States House of Representatives. I draw this conclusion knowing full well that Mr. Grosvenor is the great-grandson of Alexander Graham Bell.

Another incident that is of interest is the lawsuit filed by the United States government, referred to in the House of Representatives resolution discussed above, attempting to invalidate the Bell telephone patents on the grounds that they were obtained by fraud. One Dr. James Rogers of Tennessee conceived that a legal challenge to the Bell patents, having merit or not, would protect infringers for a period of time, even if the challenge were not legitimate. The purpose was to delay the American Bell Telephone Company from successfully suing infringers until the Bell patents expired. Rogers' son, an electrician, came up with a series of inventions, which apparently were primarily imagination. Casey Young, a former member of the U.S. Congress from Tennessee, and several associates incorporated the Pan-Electric Company, and 10% of the stock was given to Augustus H. Garland, a former governor of Arkansas, and at that time a Senator from Arkansas. Garland was also appointed as the attorney for Pan-Electric Company. Garland assured investors that the Rogers patents covered devices that did not infringe on the Bell patents, and thus was able to raise substantial investment capital for Pan-Electric.

In 1884, the Pan-Electric organizers convinced the United States House of Representatives to enact a bill granting authorization to the federal government to file lawsuits to invalidate patents under a listing of potential circumstances. The Senate failed to pass the act, but Grover Cleveland was elected President later that year, and he appointed none other than Augustus H. Garland, attorney for Pan-Electric, as United States Attorney General. The Pan-Electric principals asked Garland to file a lawsuit in the name of the United States seeking annulment of Bell's patents on the grounds that Bell had obtained his patents by fraud, and that Bell was not the first inventor of the telephone. Garland then left on a hunting trip in Arkansas, and the Solicitor General, one of the Attorney General's staff members, hastily granted the request while the Attorney General was away. The Secretary of the Interior upheld the decision to file the lawsuit, applying the reason that charges of fraud were being made against federal officials in the Patent Office, and the truth of these charges should be tested by the filing of a lawsuit at government expense against the American Bell Telephone Company.

The government lawsuit was filed in January 1887, and the initial government effort in the litigation to enjoin Bell from filing further lawsuits against infringers did not succeed. Previously, in 1885, the New York newspapers had exposed the intricate stock holdings of Pan-Electric by the United States Attorney General, members of Congress, and past and present members of the Federal Executive Branch. A congressional committee investigated the matter and concluded that Garland was not guilty of any misdeeds. Grover Cleveland retained Garland as Attorney General.

The government case lumbered through the litigation process, without ever reaching a result. The lawyer in charge of the government's case passed away in 1896, and the government let the case drop. During 1892, Bell spent a total of nine weeks, at intervals, testifying in the government lawsuit and providing a complete account of the development work that led to the invention of the telephone. In 1908, the American Bell Telephone Company printed the complete testimony of Alexander Graham Bell, both direct and cross-examination, in a 445 page document.

The government case at an interim point reached the United States Supreme Court on Bell's motion to dismiss the lawsuit. The government case against Bell was decided by the Supreme Court on November 12, 1888, which remanded the case to the lower court for further litigation. See *United States v. The American Bell Telephone Company,* 128 U.S. 315 (1888). The Court held that *if* Bell was aware when he filed his patent applications that the same subject matter had been previously discovered and put in operation by other persons, he was guilty of a fraud upon the public, and that the monopoly that the patents granted to him ought to be revoked and annulled. The Supreme Court held that the federal courts do have the power to grant such relief when it is proven that patents were obtained by fraud. The rationale of the Court's decision is that to obtain a patent, the inventor must know that he or she was the original inventor. However, the case never reached the point where the fraud allegations in the complaint were proven to be true or false.

The United States House of Representatives in its resolution of June 11, 2002 states merely that the government of the United States filed the lawsuit, and that the Supreme Court found the complaint viable and remanded the case for trial. The House of Representatives resolution, in my opinion, leaves out many of the salient details, and presents a disjointed and incorrect view of the invention of the telephone.

Bell subsequently worked on transmitting sounds on a beam of light, a precursor of today's fiber optic systems. He also did work on techniques for teaching speech to the deaf, and was instrumental in 1888 in founding the National Geographic Society. The entire story of Alexander Graham Bell, including his involvement in other inventions such as aircraft, would unduly lengthen this treatise. Therefore, the reader is directed to the resources listed in the Bibliography to gain a further understanding of the genius and works of Alexander Graham Bell.

Bell eventually obtained 18 patents in his own name, and 12 additional patents in which he was a joint inventor. Alexander Graham Bell died on August 2, 1922 near his home in Nova Scotia, Canada.

2 Sheets—Sheet 1.

A. G. BELL.
TELEGRAPHY.

o. 174,465.   Patented March 7, 1876.

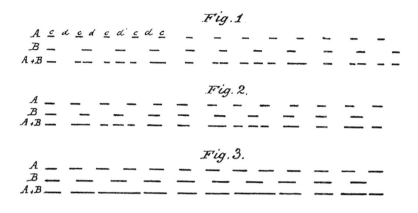

Fig.1

Fig.2

Fig.3

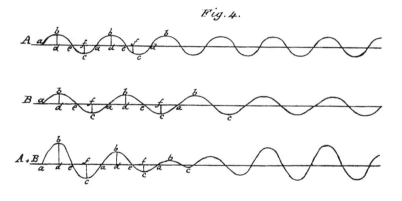

Fig.4

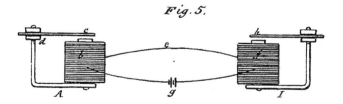

Fig.5

Witnesses   Inventor:

Ewell Hoick,   A. Graham Bell

H. J. Hutchinson   by attys Pollock & Baily

8 The Patenting Process

8.1 WHO MAY OBTAIN A PATENT

8.1.1 Inventorship and Ownership

United States patents are granted only to the first and original inventor or joint inventors, or anyone asserting rights obtained from the inventor, such as an employer to whom the inventor(s) are obligated to assign their inventions. It must be understood that one who merely recognizes the commercial merits of an existing product or idea, or who discovers technology in an ancient document or in a foreign country may not properly receive a patent. The invention must have been invented by the person or persons applying for the patent. In the United States, a corporation or business entity cannot pursue patent protection on a development independently of the inventor. However, the common practice in the United States is for employed inventors to assign patent rights to their employers, usually as a condition of employment. The patent assignment document is usually signed on the first day of employment along with tax documents and confidentiality agreements.

An invention can be made by one, two or any number of persons. Thus, many patent applications frequently name joint inventors. However the following must be kept in mind amongst the joint inventors. Unless there is an agreement or an obligation to assign the patent to one or a few of the inventors, or to a certain third party, such as the employer, each inventor will end up with the right to exploit the invention, with no duty to account to the other inventor or inventors for his/her actions, or his/her royalties. This would be true regardless of the percentage of the patent any one joint inventor owns. Also, none of the joint inventors has the right to exclude any of the other joint inventors from practicing the invention, nor to prevent any joint inventor from granting licenses to others under the patent rights.

Normally, the question of ownership of an invention, and of the patent rights covering that invention, are handled in a corporate or large entity environment by obligating all of the inventors to give all of the rights in the patents to the employer by way of assignment from the individual inventors as a condition of employment. Thus, if several inventors combine to produce an invention on their own, outside of a corporate structure for example, it is extremely important that the rights, obligations and limitations of the joint inventors vis-à-vis the invention be defined in a written agreement before the patent application is even filed or ultimately issues to prevent problems in the future. In such cases, the number of inventors may form a separate new entity, such as their own corporation or partnership, to which the patent rights are assigned. Then, it becomes the duty of the management of the new corporation or partnership to decide the direction of and limitations on exploitation of the invention, and the distribution of the rewards from that exploitation.

Intellectual Property Law for Engineers and Scientists, by Howard B. Rockman
ISBN 0-471-44998-9 © 2004 The Institute of Electrical and Electronics Engineers

It is not uncommon for several inventors, working independently of each other, to develop an invention at the same time, and for each to file for patent protection covering their invention. This is sometimes true, for example, in the pharmaceutical field, where several different companies are seeking a cure or treatment for a certain disease, and have all started with the same known "prior art" treatments. Each of these inventors or groups of inventors may arrive at the same end point independently. In this situation, who gets the patent? Answer: The U.S. Patent and Trademark Office has established a procedure to resolve this issue, which procedure is denoted as an "interference" proceeding. I myself have been through several interference proceedings during my career, and the word "complex" only begins to define these particular proceedings.

In an interference proceeding, the question of who is the first true and original inventor is determined through presentation of facts to a Board within the U.S. Patent and Trademark Office. Only the true and original inventor, or group of inventors, may obtain the patent. The inventor who first filed the patent application is not necessarily the one who obtains the patent. Under interference proceedings, the first applicant for the invention has a distinct advantage in the contest, because of the rules governing the contest. However, rights may be lost to a contending inventor who was not the first to file, but who has valuable records proving that the second to file a patent application is actually the earlier inventor, and his/her inventorship was followed by diligent acts and efforts to reduce the invention to practice following its conception.

As indicated above, the determination of the inventor in an interference proceeding involves resolution of complex factual and legal issues. This treatise is not long enough to cover the entire interference proceeding. However, it is important to stress at this juncture that witnessed and well kept records covering your conception and development of an invention are important, as is diligent activity toward reduction to practice and an early filing date for the patent application. I recall defending a doctor in a patent litigation, where he had developed his own invention, which invention was also accused of infringing someone elses patent. My doctor-inventor client first conceived of his idea on a paper cocktail napkin while in a restaurant. When I met my client for the first time, I noticed that the cocktail napkin with the penciled inscriptions relating to his invention was framed behind glass on the wall of his office. This is not unusual, since acts of conception for inventions are usually proven by yellowed or stained lab notebook pages, paper cocktail napkins, or other scraps of paper showing sketches of the early conception of the invention.

For those of you who are classic movie buffs as well as have some interest in intellectual property matters, I recommend renting the movie (if available) produced in 1939 entitled "The Story of Alexander Graham Bell," starring Don Ameche and telling the story of Bell's life and invention of the telephone. In the final moments of the film, a contest has developed to determine who first invented the telephone, Alexander Graham Bell or another team of engineers, and thus who was entitled to the patent on the telephone. In true Hollywood fashion, the earliest conception of the telephone, by this telling, appeared on the back of a love letter Alexander Graham Bell had written to his fiance, played by Loretta Young, before they were married. Other than that document, Bell was unable to produce a single piece of paper showing his conception of the telephone invention. In acceptable gentlemanly fashion, Alexander Graham Bell refused to have this intimate note produced in evidence and made public. However, his then wife and former fiance, grabbed the note from his hand in the courtroom, ran up to the Judge and handed it to the Judge to offer the letter in evidence. As a result, the Bell Telephone Companies flourished.

The recommendation to keep careful records of the conception and development of your invention cannot be overstated. These records, where possible, should also be signed by a witness so that the authenticity of the records can be proven when necessary. Also, it is important to file a patent application at the earliest practical time, preferably before any public description or commercial development or public use of the invention occurs, so that all foreign patent rights are also maintained without question.

8.1.2   True Inventors Must Be Named

In the United States, patent applications must be originally filed in the names of the inventor, or inventors if there is more than one. The patent application, upon filing, can be immediately assigned to the company for whom the inventors work and have a previous assignment agreement. Also, the inventors may have decided prior to filing the application that they desire to assign the patent rights either among each other or to other people or companies.

This U.S. practice differs from the law or procedure in most other developed countries, where corporations themselves for whom the inventors work can file a patent application in the name of the company. However, it is important that in the United States, only inventors can initially be named as applicants for the patent. An assignment document may be filed along with the initial patent application, or later, in which the inventors assign their rights over to their employers or others.

Regardless of any assignment, it is imperative in the United States that the actual, true inventors be named as the inventors in a patent application. The patent laws do not allow those to be named as inventors who did not contribute to the conception or reduction to practice of the invention. In several instances I have noted during my practice, politics within a business environment may result in inventors being named who have nothing to do with the actual conception or reduction to practice of the invention. This should be avoided at all costs. After the patent issues, and the owner attempts to enforce the patent against an infringer, the acts of invention by the named inventors will be part of the discovery and trial testimony in the case. If it is ultimately determined that individuals who are named are not the true inventors, the patent's validity and/or enforceability could be seriously jeopardized. Therefore, when working with a patent attorney, the inventors must ensure that all of the proper inventors are named, and also be sure that those who are not inventors do not appear on the application as inventors.

To determine the identity of actual inventors on a project that involves several people, I have applied a simple mental test, which you may also use. The addition of technically known features to a development project usually does not qualify as contributing to the "invention." Thus, one who can take a sketch appearing on a piece of paper and create a workable and valuable product, composition of matter, or other item from the sketch is normally not named as an inventor. By contrast, an inventor is one who starts with a blank piece of paper and places the sketch on the sheet which the technician eventually works from. Therefore, in determining who the inventors are to be named in a patent application, it is important to determine who started with the blank sheet of paper, and who acted only in a purely technical capacity and carried out the invention that was actually conceived and reduced to practice by others. Management should understand that there is no room for politics in the naming of inventors in patent applications.

8.2   PROPER DOCUMENTATION OF THE INVENTION

8.2.1   Conception

The act of conception relates to the first concept, idea or informal description of a working example of the invention made by the inventor or inventors. Usually, the first conception of an invention takes place either on a computer screen, on small scraps of paper where the idea was initially set down, or possibly on other media of recording the inventive idea, such as a dictating machine.

It is important to note or make a record of the earliest date of conception of your invention because conception followed by diligence in reducing the invention to practice, in a working model or a complete illustration of a working model, determines the date of invention that that inventor can rely upon in the event of conflicting inventorship allegations such as give rise to an interference. As stated above, my experience has shown that the initial act of conception can be proven by presenting evidence of comments made to others in the project control group which they recall, sketches on restaurant or tavern napkins, or stained lab notebook papers or prints. I also suggest that a paper file be maintained of computer-generated prints of your conception efforts. It is important to note that information regarding an inventor's claim of the first invention date is not submitted to the U.S. Patent and Trademark Office with the patent application, unless an interference proceeding is declared between two inventors, and it becomes a matter of evidentiary proof to establish the earliest date of invention. When a patent application is ultimately filed covering your invention, the patent examiner knows only the date the application was filed, and therefore draws the assumption that the filing date is your invention date, although it is understood that it takes time to prepare a patent application and that your actual invention date is prior to the filing date. When the patent examiner applies a reference (prior art) patent against your invention during the examination process, and that patent issued less than one year from your patent application filing date, that patent is not technically "prior art" since it was not publicly known more than a year before your invention. However, the filing date of the reference patent may be prior to the filing date of your patent application, and therefore the patent examiner draws the assumption that the inventor of the subject matter of the prior art reference invented his or her invention before your invention date, since your invention date before the patent examiner is, at this point, your application filing date. It is possible to eliminate such a reference patent as "prior art" if you can prove that your invention date was prior to the filing date of that particular reference patent. Thus, even though a prior issued patent may show similarities with your invention, you may be able to prove that you actually conceived of your invention prior to the filing date of the reference patent. This would eliminate that reference as being applicable to your invention, and ultimately you may obtain your patent. This is only one of the reasons why it is important to maintain records showing conception of your invention, even though such records may never be furnished to the U.S. Patent and Trademark Office.

One comment made above is worthy of repetition. Most inventors today work by themselves, in offices, cells or cubicles, when developing an invention. It is important, however, that early work on an invention be somehow witnessed by others and documented, so that at a later time, a second party or document can corroborate your first date of invention. Working alone on your idea without disclosing the same to other people within your working group and having them witness and sign off on your invention is a bad practice. Certain corporations with which I have been involved require their inventors to keep notes in lab or log books, and to have each page of the lab or log book witnessed by another person in the group at the end of each day.

The reason for this exercise is that whenever an inventor is required to testify in court or any other judicial proceeding that he or she was the first inventor of a certain invention, the inventor's testimony must be corroborated by other documentation or testimony of live witnesses that the inventor actually did conceive the invention when they said they did. It is obvious that anyone can sit on a witness stand and testify that they had invented a certain device or process before someone else, but unless they have independent proof of such conception, their evidence will not be accepted by the court. Therefore, keep in mind as you develop inventions throughout your careers, that each step you take may ultimately have to be corroborated by some other person or some documentation to prove the veracity of your statements regarding conception.

8.2.2   Reduction to Practice

The act of conception followed diligently by steps leading to a reduction to practice of the invention are the two components which equal the act of invention. Remember however, that the reduction to practice need not culminate in a working embodiment or model of the invention. Illustrations, drawings, and sketches of a workable concept also constitute a reduction to practice if they adequately describe the invention to one of ordinary skill in the related art. Thus, you need not have a working model to file a patent application. When your patent application illustrates in drawings how your invention works, and includes a complete written description of the invention, in most instances, the filing of the patent application itself constitutes a constructive reduction to practice of your invention. Thus, even though you do not have a working model of your invention, drawings and/or sketches that are sufficient to show how your invention will work or constructed are sufficient to start the patenting process on its way.

The reduction to practice, however, must be of the complete invention that you ultimately are going to be claiming as the invention to be covered by your patent. The subject matter of claiming your invention is covered in detail in Chapter 11. Thus, it is important to conclude from the facts surrounding your conception, diligent efforts, and reduction to practice that the invention will work for its intended purposes, and will work the way you will ultimately describe the invention in your patent application.

Ultimately, using drawings showing the structure and function of your invention, and a corresponding written description of the structure and operation of your invention, a patent application will be prepared and filed with the U.S. Patent & Trademark Office. Therefore, it is important that prior to meeting with a patent attorney or agent, that you have a complete invention to submit for patenting, which includes the complete reduction to practice of the invention, either on paper or on a computer screen, or which can be understood with the help of a working model. Again, it is not necessary to have a working model of the invention before you proceed to discuss the patenting process with the patent professional. The importance of filing a patent application as early as possible has been stressed in previous comments; it is not necessary or even recommended to wait until you have a working model of your invention before beginning the patenting process.

An "actual reduction to practice" consists of the production and operation of a working model of your invention. A "constructive reduction to practice," which is more common, consists of an expression of the invention in a written or electronic medium, such that one skilled in the art could read that expression of your invention and understand the structure and operation of the invention. Again, the constructive reduction to practice must be a description of a complete and operable invention.

8.2.3   Witnesses

In most patent litigation, if not all, the validity of the patent asserted against the infringer is challenged by the accused infringer. If the patent is invalid, there can be no infringement. In order to overcome the challenge to the validity of the patent, it is important that the inventor establish the acts of conception and reduction to practice which support the patentability of the invention. At this point, documents such as I mentioned in the movie about Alexander Graham Bell, as well as cocktail napkins and lab notebook pages with sketches on them, become evidence submitted at the trial. These documentary pieces of paper and scraps of other materials are usually challenged by the defense lawyer as lacking authenticity. By having your relevant documents signed, dated and witnessed by other parties, these other parties can then testify at trial that they saw and signed those documents, thus proving their authenticity. Also, if you tell somebody within your project control group about your invention, they can testify that they discussed the invention with you at that time. However, it is important to remember that the invention should not be discussed with anybody working outside of the project control group involved in the development and/or production of the invention. Public disclosure of the invention during its development stage and reduction to practice stage should be avoided, or else valuable patent and trade secret rights can be lost.

8.3   THE INVENTION DISCLOSURE AND INVENTION DISCLOSURE MEETING

8.3.1   Preparation of a Complete Description of the Invention, How the Invention Operates, and What Advantageous Results Are Obtained by the Invention

The patent application ultimately prepared covering the invention must contain sketches or illustrations showing the important elements of the invention, where the invention comprises an article of manufacture, machinery, an electronic circuit, electrical circuit or the like. The application should also include a complete description of the structure of the invention followed by a description of one cycle of operation of the described structure. The description of the structure and operation of your invention are keyed to the drawings through the use of reference numerals and lead lines identifying parts in the drawing that are described in the patent specification, somewhat similar to technical drawings. Therefore, it is important that the inventor or inventors prepare an adequate disclosure of the invention, with sketches and a description of the structure and of operation, prior to meeting with the patent professional at an invention disclosure meeting. It is no secret that patent agents and lawyers charge for their time, and an inventor can save substantial time, and thus money, by shortening the time the patent lawyer has to spend preparing the patent application. Therefore, by preparing detailed sketches and descriptions of the invention for presentation to the patent professional, hundreds and possibly thousands of dollars can be saved in the cost of obtaining and prosecuting the patent application. There are additional materials and information that the inventor or inventors should bring to the invention disclosure meeting with the patent professional, which will be covered in more detail as this chapter proceeds.

The disclosure of the invention must be of the best mode of practicing the invention known to the inventor at the time of the invention disclosure meeting. Since there is a time lag between the first meeting with the patent attorney and the actual completion of the patent application, if the invention has been improved during that time period, the later developments must be described to the patent attorney so that the latest, best mode of the invention can be included in the patent application upon filing. Also, if the inventor or inventors have developed alternative embodiments of the invention during this time period, these should be described so the patent attorney can determine which of the alternative embodiments should also be described in the patent application. Each and every remote possible embodiment does not need to be described, but the presentation of alternative embodiments helps the lawyer draft the description and claims in the patent application to provide broad enough protection to cover any manifestation of the invention that a potential infringer could develop.

Your initial invention disclosure must be clear, although it is not necessary that it be typewritten. Also, a good disclosure is not necessarily long, if the important features of the invention and their operation and advantages are adequately disclosed. When submitting your disclosure, always give the benefit of the doubt to including more in your disclosure rather than omitting information. The patent attorney can help decide what information you provide which should be made part of the patent application, and which should not. Any drawings or sketches you prepare to submit to the patent attorney should be clear and sufficiently detailed, and coordinated with your written description. This is accomplished by numbering the various parts of the invention on the drawing and keying the numbers with the written disclosure. If you submit alternative embodiments, also submit the drawings or illustrations directed to those alternatives. If a model of the invention has been prepared, submit the model to the patent attorney with the other descriptive materials. Photographs of your model can be used as the basis for the drawings initially filed with the patent application.

The key factor in preparing the initial disclosure of the invention and its different embodiments is to remember to present all information you know about your invention, and the environment in which it functions, to the patent attorney, leaving nothing out. The more information about your invention in the patent application, the more difficult it is for a potential infringer to design around your patent coverage. As will be explained in Chapter 11, the claims in your patent application will be drawn to cover all embodiments of your invention, and hopefully these claims will later be interpreted to cover those competing devices that are marketed in the future that are directed toward solving the same problems that your invention is directed toward solving.

8.3.2 Dates of First Public Disclosure, If Any, and What Was Disclosed

As we have already discussed, if your invention was in public use or on sale, or offered for sale in the United States more than a year before the date that the invention is initially disclosed to the patent attorney, patent protection cannot be obtained for that particular invention. In those cases, I have usually advised inventors to develop an improvement to their invention, and then a patent application can be filed covering the improvement. However, the prior activities of the inventor more than a year before the filing of the patent application may have destroyed any patent rights the inventor may obtain in the original invention.

Also, determine whether or not there has been a public disclosure or public knowledge of the invention less than a year before the date of the invention disclosure meeting, since it is important to know whether foreign patent rights have been affected by such disclosure. It is also important to know when the one-year U.S. "statutory bar" will be effective due to a public disclosure of the invention, to enable a patent application to be filed before the bar date.

In making your disclosure to the patent attorney, it is important to indicate what acts took place and what facts surround the circumstances relating to any prior disclosure of your invention that was made to others, either prior to a year or within a year of the invention disclosure meeting. It is possible that the public disclosures you made were only of the experimental version of your invention, and therefore did not comprise disclosure of a complete invention such as will destroy patent rights. If there has been no prior public disclosure of the invention, the patent attorney will most assuredly advise you to refrain from disclosing, publicly using, selling or offering to sell the invention prior to the date the patent application is actually lodged with the United States Patent & Trademark Office. The potential adverse affect of such public disclosures on patent rights need not be repeated.

You must also disclose to the patent attorney how you derived the concept of your invention. Obviously, if you derive the invention from a showing of the same invention from another source, you are not the first inventor and cannot obtain the patent. It is important to recall that those statements in the patent statutes, particularly 35 U.S.C. Section 102(b), that define who may obtain a patent and who may not, apply differently to events and publications inside and outside of the United States. Patents, publications, and other written public disclosures act as bars to patentability when they occur or exist anywhere, either inside or outside the United States. Public sale and use of an invention in foreign jurisdictions does not affect the applicant's ability to obtain a patent covering that invention in the United States. However, an applicant cannot discover the invention in another country and apply for a patent in the United States, since the applicant could not comply with that portion of the statute requiring that the inventor certify that he or she is the original and first inventor.

Since "experimental use" is not a public use of a complete invention and therefore is not a bar to obtaining a U.S. patent, when meeting with the patent attorney for the first time the inventor should, in describing all outside uses and showings of the invention to others, present sufficient facts to enable the patent attorney to determine whether or not such use could be classified as "experimental" or not. Thus, even though you may have previously exposed a portion of the subject of the invention to third parties, the attorney may advise you that this is not necessarily a bar to patentability. Also, it is important to advise the attorney of any prior publication(s) by the inventor or inventors to determine when and which features of the invention were disclosed, and which were not disclosed in such prior publications. Non-disclosed features can still form the subject matter of a patent application.

8.3.3   Advantages of the Invention Over Known Devices/Processes

After disclosing to the patent professional your information about the structure, operation/function and results achieved by your invention, it is important to disclose to the patent professional the advantages of your invention, and how those advantages are realized from the structure of the invention, the operation or function of that structure, and the results achieved by the operation and/or function of that structure. In other words, what structure and/or function of the invention produces the advantages over the prior art. The advantages should be expressed both in broad terms and in more limited terms. These advantages provide the "selling points" for persuading the patent examiner that the invention is indeed a step forward in the useful arts. Such advantages also may assist in defining the "contribution" to the advance in the art that this particular invention offers to the public. More importantly, I have personally noticed that the courts tend to rely upon the advantages of the invention and the contribution of the inventor to the advance in art to base their decisions upholding patentability. If the patent attorney at the initial meeting does not ask you what advantages are provided by the invention, tell him anyway. In my view, it is most important.

8.3.4 What Prior Art Is The Inventor Aware of for Disclosure to the Patent Examiner

An important inquiry during your initial invention disclosure meeting with the patent attorney is to determine what knowledge you, the inventor, has of "prior art" relating to the subject matter of the invention. This involves the inventor's knowledge of printed publications, devices already existing in the market, issued patents and any other prior acts or materials, electronic or published in print, of the inventor or others, that may relate to the invention. The Patent and Trademark Office has enacted Rule 56 (37 C.F.R. §1.56) *requiring* an inventor, and his or her attorney or agent, to disclose "information they are aware of which is material to the examination of the application" to the patent examiner during the examination process. "Material" prior art is that which the examiner would consider material to patentability in deciding whether or not to issue the patent from the application. Thus, most patent attorneys prepare an Information Disclosure Statement to be submitted with the application, setting forth all prior art that the inventor and the attorney together are aware of that relates to the examination of the application. This would include all prior art uncovered by a novelty search conducted prior to filing the patent application, as well as any additional relevant prior art information known to the inventor and the patent attorney.

There is a twofold purpose to Rule 56. First, you are required to advise the patent examiner of prior art of which you are aware. The applicant and the attorney are held to a strict duty of candor in making a showing before the U.S. Patent and Trademark Office of the reasons they believe the inventor to be the first inventor, and that the inventor is actually the first inventor. It is not an option to attempt to hide prior art from the patent examiner to obtain issuance of a patent. The disclosure of the known prior art to the examiner, beside including all patents and publications that the inventor and the attorney are aware of that are material to examination, also includes any activities of the inventor which are material to consideration of possible statutory bars of the patent under 35 U.S.C. §102(b). For example, this would include the inventor's related activities more than one year prior to the expected filing date, along with a showing why such activities are only experimental or technical testing activities, and do not give rise to public use, offer-for-sale or on-sale bars to patentability. The patent examiner must be given the opportunity to consider these activities as "prior art," and the applicant during the course of prosecution of the patent application will have the opportunity to explain away such activities as "experimental use."

Second, the patent attorney prepares a patent application with a view towards ultimately standing before a Federal Court, with the inventor beside him or her, and explaining to the court every step taken in developing the invention and during patent prosecution. Opposing counsel will introduce into evidence all prior art which is believed relevant in an effort to invalidate the patent. Case law governing patent litigation generally holds that the court can give short shrift or ignore all prior art offered by an accused infringer, if that prior art was previously considered by the patent examiner during examination. Thus, defense counsel is in the position of presenting only prior art that was not previously considered by the patent examiner. It follows that the more prior art presented and considered by the patent examiner and introduced into the prosecution history of the patent application, the shorter the playing field for defense counsel when it becomes imperative to introduce additional prior art in an attempt to invalidate the patent. Thus, it is definitely to the inventor's advantage to have as much prior art as possible introduced into the record of the patent prosecution, as a means of strengthening the patent.

8.3.5   Additional Matters Discussed During the Invention Disclosure Meeting Between the Inventor and the Patent Attorney

Confidentiality of the Meeting   The meeting at which the inventor discloses the invention to the patent attorney is held in strict confidence, and the confidentiality of the invention is protected by the attorney/client privilege. This ensures that the client need not fear that the attorney will "steal" the invention. If the inventor is not satisfied with this explanation, the attorney can sign a non-disclosure agreement binding the attorney to secrecy regarding the invention. However, the cannons of ethics which bind an attorney to confidentiality regarding information passing between the client and the attorney are sufficient to re-assure the inventor of the confidentiality of his/her invention. In view of the fact that an attorney may lose his or her license to practice law, and therefore their ability to earn a living, upon violating the cannons of ethics of the profession, it is extremely rare, and I have never known it to happen, that an attorney would attempt to misappropriate the invention of one of his/her clients.

Does the Invention Qualify for Patent Protection   Once the disclosure of the invention has been provided to the patent attorney, the attorney must decide and discuss with the inventor whether the subject matter is sufficiently concrete, and not merely conceptual, to qualify for patent protection. Next, it must be determined whether the invention falls within one of the statutory classes covered under the patent laws. In other words, is the invention a process, machine, manufacture or a composition of matter, and/or any new and useful improvement thereof. The patent attorney must also determine whether an article patent, method patent, design patent or a combination of several of these would best serve your purposes. Also, the possibility of using trade secret, trademark and copyright protection must also be discussed, depending upon the nature of the invention.

Preliminary Novelty Inquiry   The inventor must disclose to the attorney at the patent disclosure meeting all material information known to the inventor which is relevant to related prior technology, either of the inventor or of others. For example, any information or activities the inventor has knowledge of regarding use or disclosure of a similar device or process, or whether there are any third party publications, articles or prior patents which disclose the invention of which the inventor is aware, should be discussed. These articles, patents and other materials should also be produced to the patent attorney. All of such printed information in books, articles, brochures and patent publications, as well as general knowledge and items that are available to the public are all included within the definition of "prior art" against which the novelty of the invention is measured.

Chapter 9 discusses the pre-examination novelty search that is normally conducted to discover prior art that may bear on the patentability of your invention. This search will ultimately disclose whether or not there is a single prior art publication or event that would destroy novelty under 35 U.S.C. §102(a) or (b), or whether the invention is rendered obvious through a combination of prior art materials under 35 U.S.C. §103.

Determining the Date of Invention   The inventor should also disclose to the patent attorney the events and the dates of those events relating to the conception, diligence, and reduction to practice of the invention. This includes the initial activities of the inventor in conceiving the invention, and the sketches and rough drawings, usually on scrap paper, cocktail napkins or lab notebooks discussed previously. The date of invention is not disclosed to the patent examiner, however this information is important if an interference is later declared, or if a prior art patent that issued less than a year from the filing date of your patent application is applied by the patent examiner during prosecution of your patent application. In the latter case, knowledge of the invention date will assist the patent attorney in overcoming and eliminating that piece of prior art.

Will the Invention Work as Claimed   Sufficient information must be given to the patent attorney by the inventor to ensure that the invention will work for its intended purposes. The Constitutional mandate states that patents can only be granted for advances in the "useful" arts. A patent cannot be granted for an inoperative device or method, such as a perpetual motion machine, and is subject to post grant cancellation if the device is proven to be inoperative. Thus the inventor should be prepared at the initial invention disclosure meeting to provide sufficient information establishing the workability of the invention. A model need not be presented to the patent attorney since the patent attorney has a technical background.

A Brief Comment Regarding Foreign Patent Rights   The inventor should ask the patent attorney to explain the ability to obtain foreign patent rights covering the invention, considering the possibility of any prior disclosure by the inventor that may have adversely affected such foreign patent rights. The attorney should explain to the inventor whether or not there has been any affect on foreign patent rights due to the prior activities of the inventor before the initial invention disclosure meeting. The subject of foreign patent rights is covered in more detail in Chapter 17.

What the Prior Art Lacks   The inventor should disclose to the patent attorney those problems which exist in the art, and which the proposed invention is designed to solve. Also, the inventor should describe what prior art devices or process he or she is aware of that have attempted to solve the same problems, and how the prior art devices have failed to solve such problems. The inventor should then proceed to explain how his/her invention which is being considered for patentability particularly solves those problems in the prior art that no one else has been able to solve. This information is important for the preparation of a persuasive patent application.

Inventor's Concept of Novel Features   The inventor next describes his or her understanding of what is believed to be novel about the invention for which a patent is being sought. There may be one or more points of novelty. Remember, no novelty search has yet been conducted to determine what actually may be novel about the invention, so the only reference point at this meeting is that of the inventor's knowledge.

Although the inventor will explain what he/she believes the novelty to be, it is always prudent to conduct a novelty search of prior art patents in the public search facilities of the U.S. Patent and Trademark Office to determine more precisely what the point of novelty is, and upon what features of the invention it can be expected that valid patent claims can be obtained. This patent novelty search, and indeed the examination process itself, may indicate to the inventor that the initial thoughts regarding novelty were not exactly correct, but that other novel features do reside in the invention for which patentability can be claimed. This process is known as "shifting the point of novelty" and is quite common in the prosecution and development of patents.

To prepare a patent application that will support all points of novelty, all of the structure, operation and advantages of the invention, as well as the results of the invention, should be clearly disclosed to the attorney by the inventor. Thus, the patent application will be drafted with all elements discussed, so that if the point of novelty shifts, the new novel elements relied upon will be discussed in the application. Thus, it is important to present a full disclosure of the invention to the patent attorney.

Obviousness   As mentioned previously, the inventor cannot obtain a patent if the differences between the subject matter sought to be patented and the prior art are such that the subject matter as a whole would have been obvious at the time of the invention to a person having ordinary skill in the art to which the subject matter pertains. Thus, you must furnish sufficient information to the patent attorney as to the relevant prior art and prior activities that you are aware of to allow the patent attorney to determine whether or not any differences between your invention and the prior art could be considered obvious. This is a cost benefit consideration, since it is folly to file a patent application where you are advised that a patent may never be obtained because the differences between the invention and the prior art would be obvious to one skilled in the art.

Enablement   A patent application must be drafted so that one skilled in the art can read the issuing patent 20 years from its date of filing and reconstruct the invention, without undue experimentation, from the information contained in the patent. If such complete information is not presented, the patent itself may be declared invalid by a court of law when attempted to be enforced against an infringer, on the basis that the patent itself eliminates certain essential material that is necessary to enable one to practice the invention. Therefore, it is not wise to hold back secret information from the patent attorney which would be required to furnish a complete operating working paper on how to reconstruct and operate the invention in the patent application. The enablement requirement has been very strictly construed by the courts in recent decisions, and a lack of an enabling disclosure has been the basis for invalidating several patents. Therefore, it is important to remember the enablement requirement when providing descriptive information that goes into the patent application. Keep in mind also that technical details such as dimensions, materials and the like need not be set forth in the patent application, unless these details are relevant to the operation, novelty, or non-obviousness of the invention.

The Best Mode Requirement   Since the patent statutes require that the "best mode" of the invention contemplated by the inventor at the time of filing the patent application be described in the application as filed, you, as the inventor, must describe to the patent attorney the best mode of carrying out the invention as of the date of your invention disclosure meeting. You must also keep your patent attorney advised of further significant developments in the progress of the invention while the patent application is being prepared, so that on the filing date, the application will contain the best mode of the invention. This may require that you, the inventor, take a day off of work to allow the patent professional to complete and file the application before you make any further improvements.

8.3.6   Invention Disclosure Form

At the end of this chapter is a sample invention disclosure form (Fig. 8-1) which I use quite often in my practice, which should be completed by the inventor prior to the first invention disclosure meeting, and then brought to the meeting for discussion. Better yet, the disclosure form and materials should be forwarded to the patent attorney prior to the meeting. This will shorten the meeting, and provide the patent attorney with most of the information for review prior to the meeting. Also, the inventor should come to this meeting with all prints, drawings, sketches, photos and written material that describe the structure, operation and advantages of the invention.

BARNES & THORNBURG

Suite 4400
One North Wacker Drive
Chicago, Illinois 60606-2809 U.S.A.

Howard B. Rockman
(312) 214-4812
Email: brockman@btlaw.com

INVENTION DISCLOSURE FORM
(CONFIDENTIAL)

This form is used to identify and screen inventions submitted by clients for patentability evaluations, the preparation of an application for patent, and for considering other appropriate types of proprietary protection. For purposes of completing this form, an "invention" may be just about anything. The typical subjects regarded as an invention include a useful idea, concept, method, process, machine, algorithm, device, article of manufacture, composition of matter, apparatus, improvement, or development.

This form is 4 pages long. Your signature and the date should be on the last page.

Answer all questions. Attach additional pages, copies of your notes, sketches, blueprints, computer-generated drawings, or other materials to explain your responses and provide full details of your disclosure.

*   *   *   *   *   *   *   *   *   *   *   *   *

1.   Client Name:_____ Client Matter:_____

2.   Date of Submission of this Disclosure:_____

3.   (a) This submission is by: (Person's) Name:_____

     (b) Address:_____

4.   Title of Invention:_____

5.   Using text, and drawings if appropriate, answer the following questions, separately and specifically, as each relates to the invention. Additional pages may be necessary for the completion of this section.

     (a)   What is the purpose of the invention? _____

     _____

     _____

     (b)   How is the invention made and/or assembled? _____

     _____

     _____

Chicago   Elkhart   Fort Wayne   Grand Rapids   Indianapolis   South Bend   Washington, D.C.

Figure 8.1. Sample invention disclosure form.

(c)   How does the invention work? _____

_____

_____

(d)   What were the prior methods, techniques or devices used to accomplish the purpose or comparable aim of the invention? _____

_____

_____

(e)   What were the disadvantages of these methods, techniques or devices? _____

_____

_____

(f)   What are the advantages of the invention over the prior methods, techniques or devices? _____

_____

_____

(g)   Practically, where will the invention be useful and to what extent will it be used?

_____

_____

6.   State the earliest date and place the invention was conceived and include a brief description of circumstances:

Date: _____   Place: _____

Circumstances: _____

_____

7.   State the date and present location of:

	Date	Present Location
(a) first sketch or drawing of invention:	_____	_____
(b) first written description:	_____	_____

Figure 8.1. *continued.*

8.   If a test has been made or an operating mode, breadboard, or prototype constructed:

   (a)   For any test, state the date and place; describe any general results; and identify witnesses to the tests.

   Date: _____   Place: _____

   Results: _____

   Witnesses: _____

   (b)   For any model, breadboard or prototype state the date of completion; fabricator of the model or prototype; and present location of the model or prototype:

   Date: _____   Fabricator: _____

   Present location: _____

9.   State the names and dates of any disclosure of the invention to other persons:

   (a)   To employees of the client:

   Names: _____

   Date: _____

   (b)   Other persons and dates of disclosure:

   Names: _____

   Company: _____   Date: _____

10.   Has any publication, submission for publication or written report of the invention been made?

   _____ Yes   _____ No

   If "Yes," provide details: _____

   _____

11.   Was the invention made in performance of work for a customer?

   _____ Yes   _____ No

   If "Yes," provide contract or job: _____

Figure 8.1.   *continued.*

12.   If an embodiment of the invention has left your possession, custody, or control or that of your employer or has otherwise been shipped from you or your employer's premises, state the date and circumstances of shipment:

Date: _____   Circumstances: _____

_____

_____

13.   If the invention was made for internal use (rather than for use by third party customers) state the first date on which use of the invention was made in commercial production. Identify whether such use was a test. Briefly describe circumstances and results:

Date: _____   Test? _____ Yes _____ No

Circumstances and results: _____

_____

_____

14.   List commercial products, publications or patents related to the invention, or prior art related to the invention, if you know of any:

_____

_____

_____

15.   Attach all drawings, sketches, photos, computer-generated drawings or text material, and/or notebook entries made in the course of development of the invention which show or describe the invention.

16.   Who do you consider to be the inventor(s)? More than one person may be named.

Name: _____   Address: _____

_____

_____

Name: _____   Address: _____

_____

_____

17.   Your Signature: _____   Date: _____

Figure 8.1. *continued.*

Thomas Edison

THE LIGHT BULB

The icon of an American inventor is probably Thomas Alva Edison, who invented the phonograph, the first practical electric light bulb, an automatic timer for a telegraph, an electric voting machine, improvements in the telegraph and telephone, and electrical systems to power his light bulb. Besides being an inventor, Edison was also a shrewd businessman, and the methods he used to carry his inventions to the public, to his profit, involved many activities that might be deemed questionable given today's business ethics. This essay is limited to Edison's life and his invention of the light bulb. The battle between DC and AC current involving Edison, Telsa, and Westinghouse will be discussed in the essay "Current Events" following Chapter 27.

Thomas A. Edison was born on February 11, 1847 in Milan, Ohio, the youngest child of Samuel and Nancy Edison. At the age of sevem, Edison and his family moved to Port Huron, Michigan. Edison reportedly had hearing problems as a child, and although he had difficulty with his lessons in school, he became an avid reader, and by the age of 10 had established a laboratory in the basement of his house. Edison learned reading, writing, and arithmetic from his mother, who had taken him out of school because of his hearing problem. He spent most of his free time reading technical and scientific journals. When his mother got tired of the odors coming from the basement, Edison obtained a job as a train boy on the Grand Trunk Railway, and built a new laboratory in an empty freight car at the age of 12. Edison's laboratory in the box car was shut down when it caused a fire on the train. While working for the railroad, he saved the life of a child of one of the station officials who had fallen on the tracks in front of an oncoming train. To reward Edison for saving his son, the father began teaching Edison how to use the train system's telegraph.

From 1862 to 1868, Edison was employed as a telegrapher throughout the Midwest, New England, the South, and Canada. During this time, he invented a repeating telegraph, allowing automatic transmission of telegraphic messages. In 1869, his inventions, including the duplex telegraph, message printer, and an improved stock ticker, were doing so well that he began a career of full-time inventing and business development. He became a highly visible inventor as a result of his inventions in telegraphy, which was the primary system used by business and finance concerns in those days to obtain information necessary to control their businesses.

Edison moved to New York City in 1869. He sold his inventions for $40,000, allowing him to establish his first laboratory and manufacturing facility in Newark, New Jersey in 1871. He also married Mary Stilwell and began his family. In 1876, Edison sold his Newark, New Jersey facility and moved to Menlo Park, New Jersey, 25 miles away from New York City. Edison, along with two assistants, Charles Batchelor and John Kruesi, moved into the Menlo Park facility in March 1876. This laboratory employed many highly skilled technicians, and became the prototype for later modern facilities devoted to only research and development, such as Bell Laboratories.

In 1877, urged by Western Union, Edison created a carbon-button transmitter for use in telephone speakers and microphones that is still in use today. While experimenting with devices for recording telegraph signals, Edison developed the phonograph, which moved him to the top of the charts as an inventor in the late 19th century. However, it took 10 years for the phonograph to be available as a commercial product. Edison also invented the first talking moving pictures in 1913. He held 1,093 patents, leading all other American inventors in that category.

Edison was not the first to develop an electric light bulb. In the latter half of the 19th century, gas lights, oil lamps, and candles were used to light homes and offices. Electric arc lights, which used high-voltage electricity to create a spark between two pieces of carbon, could only be used outdoors, such as in street lamps, lighthouses, and other public areas. The carbon arc created a blindingly bright light, which could not be "subdivided" to make small electric lights, which were unknown at the time. An arc light produced a light of approximately 4,000 candle power, compared to the 10 or 20 candle power light produced by gas in the home. Arc lights were also operated by inefficient generators. When Edison began his experiments with light, it was known that an incandescent light could be made moderate enough for indoor use if the device could be constructed so that it would not extinguish itself rapidly. Prior to Edison's work, all of the filament elements used in incandescent light experiments either burned up in the heat or melted. These experiments had preceded Edison by approximately 20 years, without any meaningful advance.

An English inventor, Sir Joseph Wilson Swan, is credited with inventing the first electric light bulb which he demonstrated in 1878. However, the filament had a short life and the bulb was not practical. The Swan invention, which used high current and low voltage is still used in flashlights and in automobiles. One of the approaches used prior to Edison to obtain a practical electric light was to use filament materials composed of platinum that had a relatively high melting point and did not oxidize. The platinum material always reached its melting point despite efforts to prevent this from happening. A second pre-Edison approach was to use a filament material such as carbon, whose melting point was so high that melting would not be a problem. However, the use of carbon in the lamp usually resulted in combustion of the carbon, despite the use of vacuum pumps to evacuate air from the bulb.

In mid-1878, Edison was described as ill and very tired from the burdens of maintaining his position as the premier inventor in the United States. In the summer of 1878, he took a vacation to Wyoming with other scientists to view a solar eclipse. The other scientists on the trip discussed the fact that their compatriots were not able to come up with an electric light to replace the gas, oil, and carbon lights presently in use. Upon his return from vacation, Edison visited the workshop of William Wallace in Connecticut, where Mr. Wallace had on display an electric arc lighting system comprised of eight electric lights that were all lit at the same time by an electric generator, each arc light being equal to 4,000 candles. Again, the subdivision of this light into smaller light units was then unknown. Edison realized that he had a window of opportunity to develop a subdivided electric light, since the demonstration by Mr. Wallace showed him that science had not yet reached the point of making a practical, subdivided electric light suitable for home use.

When he returned to Menlo Park, Edison, with the help of Charles Batchelor, started experimenting to produce a practical subdivided electric light. They began by constructing lamps using spirals of platinum wire as the filaments or "burners." They controlled these lamps with regulating devices designed to halt the current to the bulb if the platinum reached its melting point. Edison was so confident that he had solved the problem that he publicly announced that in "a few weeks" he would have a practical light bulb available. As a result of his announcement in 1878 that he was nearing completion of a practical light bulb, the stock exchanges witnessed a vast drop in gas company stocks, while others sought to invest in the new technology. Thus, Edison started the Edison Electric Light Company, whose backers were J. P. Morgan and the Vanderbilt family. Following his announcement, Edison and his workers continued their experiments, including testing generators to power the system and to prepare patent applications. Beside working on the light bulb, Edison felt it was important to construct and market an electric generating system that could be used to power the light bulbs he would sell to the public.

After the "few weeks" went by, his light bulb still did not work. The lamps using the platinum filaments flickered out of control, the filaments either broke or melted, and any light that was produced was too low. Edison, up to this time, was working on his own mental juices, and had not investigated prior work on incandescent lights to see what had been done by others, nor did he derive the details of the distribution and generation systems necessary to provide electricity to light his bulbs.

In November, 1878, Edison did two things. First, he hired a young physist, Francis Upton, which impressed his investors with the fact that he was ready to use the latest in modern science to assist in developing his inventions. Second, he began reviewing the state-of-the-art as to every lighting system extant at that time. He reviewed the work of his competitors, studied prior patents, and, in effect, began all over again, looking for the proper filament for his light bulb.

Edison's team saw that the amount of electrical current required to operate previously devised electric lighting systems was large. Edison was attempting to develop a light bulb that would provide the same convenience of gas light, and make it possible to turn one light on or off without affecting other lights. This led him to conclude that the lights would have to be in a parallel circuit, not a series circuit, since electric current would have to be delivered independently to each lamp. Although generally known, Edison's team also noted that a system required to light a plurality of lamps would require either a high voltage or large current. Large currents required thicker conducting wires, and copper was an expensive commodity in the late 19th century. If a system were developed using small currents and large voltages, each lamp would require a high resistance, which is the solution that Edison settled upon.

At that time, Edison was using platinum as the filament in his light bulb experiments. However, small lengths of platinum provided a low resistance, so Edison began using long spirals of thin platinum wire as filaments. These broke easily upon being heated to an incandescent temperature. For an extended period of time in 1879, Edison's team failed in their attempts to create spiral filaments sufficient for a long-lasting light bulb. What he did discover was that when efficient vacuum pumps were used to evacuate the air in the light bulb, the life of the platinum burner was extended, though not long enough for practicality.

During the early part of 1879, Edison and his team continued their light bulb experiments, and they also devoted a portion of their efforts to creating a generator that would create a high-voltage system to light their bulbs. By the middle of 1879, Edison and his team still could not make the platinum filament lamp operate properly. In approximately October, 1879, Edison and his team gave up on platinum and looked for other materials from which their filaments could be made. As a result of their intensive research efforts, the fact that carbon would provide the desired results was determined in a matter of a few weeks. Carbon had been used previously in the electric lamps of other inventors, but in those experiments the carbon either disintegrated or burned up. However, carbon appeared to be workable in the high vacuum created in Edison's bulbs. Edison had been familiar with carbon, which he had used in his telephone receiver invention.

The records of Edison's laboratory indicate that in the middle of October, 1879, Batchelor and Upton were making notes of their measurements of carbon's resistance and how to shape the carbon strands into spiral configurations. However, the carbon spirals always seemed to break. Batchelor's notes indicate that by October 22, the team had performed experiments using several inches of carbonized cotton thread, which had a resistance of 100 ohms, significantly larger than the resistance of platinum. This lamp appeared to be as bright as a gas lamp, and did not flicker out. In the end, and after all the time, money, and experimentation, the result, using hindsight, was simply a glass globe with the air evacuated, in which a short strand of carbonized thread was mounted between two electrodes.

On New Years Eve of 1879, a public demonstration of the light bulb was made in Edison's Menlo Park laboratory. The event was heavily attended by the press, shooting Edison's popularity way up in the ratings. Edison filed for a patent on his invention on November 4, 1879, and the patent on the first practical light bulb was issued on January 27, 1880. Also, by the first demonstration, Edison's workers had discovered that Bristol board made more reliable filaments than cotton thread.

Edison and his team not only invented the practical electric bulb, but an entire electric lighting system with all of the equipment required to make the incandescent light economical, operable, safe, and practical. For example, to make his system work, Edison also had to develop, create, and invent light sockets with on/off switches, safety fuses and insulating materials, constant-voltage delivery systems, an underground conductor network, improved electrical generating dynamos, a durable long-lasting light bulb, and parallel electric circuits. The Edison Electric Company established its first commercial central power station on Pearl Street in lower Manhattan in New York City in 1882, furnishing electric power to a small area of the city. Other buildings set up dynamos in the basement to provide electricity for the building.

By the end of the 1880s, central electric power producing stations were established in many U.S. cities, each being limited to a few blocks in area due to the ineffective transmission of direct current (DC) electricity, to which Edison was wedded until his fight with the creators of alternating current, circuits, and systems was over many years later. Edison created many electric companies, and on April 24, 1889 they were all brought together to form the Edison General Electric Company. In 1892, Edison General Electric merged with Thompson-Hudson, it's leading competitor, the name Edison was dropped from the company name, and the company became General Electric Company. After the turn of the century, and facing financial difficulty, Edison sold his stock in the General Electric Company. To this day, the General Electric Company is a leading producer of electrical and electronic systems and equipment, including light bulbs. Edison never controlled the Edison General Electric Company, since the amount of capital required to develop the electrical and lighting industry necessitated the involvement of investment bankers, such as J. P. Morgan, and financers such as Vanderbilt.

In November, 1887, Edison moved his research and development team to a new facility in West Orange, New Jersey. He then began working on the phonograph, which project he had set aside when developing the electric light bulb in the late 1870s. By 1890, Edison was manufacturing phonographs for both home and business. He also developed the entire system to make the phonograph work, including the records, equipment to record sound on the records, and equipment to manufacture both the records and the phonographs. Edison used cylindrical paraffin records to produce sound, but in later years the circular recording disk was developed, putting Edison out of the record business. Regarding movies, Edison also developed the complete system needed to both make movies and to show motion pictures, and in 1913 introduced the first talking movies. By 1918, the motion picture industry, which he was instrumental in creating, became so competitive that Edison got out of this business altogether.

On June 8, 1903, Thomas Alva Edison signed an agreement with his son, Thomas A. Edison, Jr., whereby Edison's son agreed not to use his own name in a business enterprise in exchange for a weekly allowance of $35.

One of the commentators relied upon during my research noted that the public, in the latter part of the 19th century, looked upon the developments of scientific technology as a source of hope, not with distrust. This commentator felt that the positive public attitude garnered toward the power of science and technology as a result of Edison's work, among others, is one of the most important legacies to emanate from the technological developments of that era.

In 1884, Edison's first wife Mary passed away, leaving him with three small children. He married Mina Miller in 1886. Thomas Alva Edison died in West Orange, New Jersey on October 18, 1931. Today, he has truly attained folk hero status based upon his inventions.

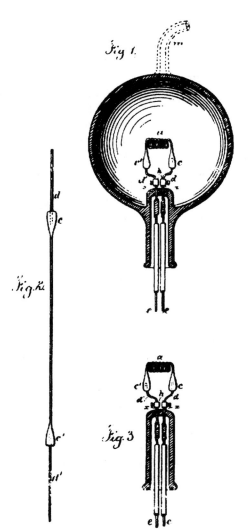

T. A. EDISON.
Electric-Lamp.

No. 223,898. Patented Jan. 27, 1880.

9 Novelty, Infringement, and Other Searches

9.1 THE NOVELTY SEARCH

Since one of the most important aspects of obtaining a patent on your invention is to compare your invention to the state of the prior art, the best way to gain an understanding of the content of the prior art is to conduct a novelty, or patentability search. The search occurs after the patent attorney gains a full understanding of your invention from the disclosure meeting, and after you have described to the patent attorney all of the prior art materials with which you are familiar. Since the novelty search expands the scope of knowledge available to the inventor regarding technology related to the invention, the novelty search provides the first real chance to explore the prior art surrounding your invention in significant detail.

The most complete and accessible library of prior art is housed in the public search room of the U.S. Patent and Trademark Office, where the public is admitted. However, patent lawyers and other patent professionals outside of the Washington, D.C. area usually employ the services of Washington, D.C. or Arlington, Virginia associates who can conduct patent searches using the public search facilities of the U.S. Patent and Trademark Office. These searchers can also obtain additional information housed in the U.S. Patent & Trademark Office scientific library, such as technical journals and foreign patents lodged there. Additionally, U.S. patents issuing since the year 1790 can be searched on the U.S. Patent & Trademark Office website (www.uspto.gov), and further prior art can be accessed on other available websites. It is barely possible for an inventor to make his/her own preliminary novelty search, therefore it is usually wise, and cost beneficial to have an experienced professional conduct the search.

The patent searcher will normally provide the patent attorney with copies of relevant patents and other materials uncovered during the search, but the searcher normally does not provide his or her review or evaluation of the patents, nor does the searcher usually provide a legal patentability opinion. The results of the search are commonly forwarded to your patent attorney, who conducts an evaluation of the content of the prior art, and provides you with a legal opinion as to whether or not your invention is sufficiently novel and nonobvious over the prior art to support the granting of a patent. The report you receive from your patent attorney should a) set forth an evaluation of each relevant reference uncovered by the search, commenting on what each reference does and does not show relevant to your invention, and b) comment on whether any combination of the uncovered references might be used by a patent examiner to support an argument that your invention is obvious in view of the teachings of these references.

Searching may also be conducted at the Patent Depository Libraries consisting of patent copies on microfilm located in several public libraries across the country. For example, the Chicago Public Library in downtown Chicago is such a Patent Depository Library. If you desire to conduct a novelty search at one of these libraries, you will find the reference librarians extremely helpful. However, experience shows that inventors trying to conduct a patent search through these Patent Depository Libraries should plan to spend a considerable amount of time to obtain information as to the class and subclass relating to their invention, and then to locate the patents they deem pertinent. My experience has shown that it is extremely time and cost beneficial to have a professional conduct a patent search for you, rather than to try and conduct a meaningful search yourself at these libraries.

It is important to keep in mind that in certain circumstances, it may be practical to forego a search before filing a patent application. Thus, if the subject matter is too difficult to search, or the product has been scheduled for production before a search can be conducted, or where the inventor has a keen knowledge of the prior art, you may decide that it is not cost beneficial to conduct a search, and to file the patent application as soon as possible.

If the search reveals that the invention is not patentable, this will save the inventor the cost of filing the patent application. On the other hand, if the search reveals that the invention is novel, the search provides an additional valuable function in furnishing useful background information and advice to the patent attorney as to the scope of the prior art, enabling the patent attorney to draft more effective patent claims covering your invention over the prior art. Further, as stated previously, the patent search develops a library of technical information the inventor can use in further development of the invention to which the search was directed, or improvements to his or her invention. This of course must be done without infringing any of the unexpired patents uncovered by the search. The subject of patent infringement will be covered in Chapter 18.

9.2 SEARCH PARAMETERS

The patent attorney you have contacted normally will not perform the search him or herself, and solicits the services of an experienced patent searcher. Therefore, the patent attorney must be able to furnish the searcher sufficiently accurate information regarding the description of the invention, its function, its advantages, objectives and purpose, so that the searcher's direction will be focused on the important features of the invention that the inventor has determined provide novelty and non-obviousness. Note also that the information about your invention furnished to the search associate by your patent attorney constitutes a confidential disclosure, and the confidentiality of that disclosure is protected by the searcher as the search is conducted. Thus, the disclosure of the invention to the search associate does not jeopardize any U.S. or foreign patent rights.

Since the subject matter located in the public search facilities of the U.S. Patent and Trademark Office, and in the Patent Depository Libraries located throughout the country is finite in quantity, no search of these libraries can, by definition, constitute a complete novelty and non-obviousness search in view of all publicly available or generally known information relating to your invention which bears upon the questions of novelty and non-obviousness. To conduct a search of all publicly known prior art world-wide would be cost prohibitive, if possible at all. Thus, do not be surprised if the patent examiner, or an accused infringer, uncovers prior art not uncovered by your search. Any later-appearing relevant prior art materials you become aware of during the prosecution of your patent application before the U.S. Patent & Trademark Office must be submitted to the patent examiner for consideration. Any relevant prior art you became aware of after your patent issues may be submitted to the patent examiner for consideration in a reexamination proceeding. The advantage of the reexamination proceeding is to have the patent examiner consider the later-found prior art, and to decide that the claims of your patent define novelty over the later found prior art. Note that reexamination proceedings will be covered later in Chapter 12, Section 12.11.

Besides the material lodged in the United States Patent and Trademark Office public search facilities and the Patent Depository Libraries, other sources of information that constitute the prior art are foreign patents and published U.S. and foreign patent applications, information in scientific journals, technical bulletins, product literature and brochures, safety data sheets, trade publications, press releases, product or service catalogs, and the myriad of information posted on the internet. In the best of all possible worlds, it would be desirable to be able to evaluate patentability with reference to all existing relevant prior art, however to amass this amount of information is a practical impossibility. Thus, the patent searcher usually looks only to United States patents, relative scientific or technical literature that is available, such as on the internet, and foreign patents and published patent applications where available.

Where the invention is of significant importance to the inventor or the inventor's employer, a search of foreign patents can be obtained by the Patent Depository of the European Patent Office in the Hague, the Netherlands. Also if necessary, you could write to search associates in Japan, Taiwan, Hong Kong, and other areas of technical innovation throughout the world to conduct searches at their national Patent Offices. However, the extent of the search, as anything else, must be weighed against its cost and expected benefit. It is normally concluded that the patent search conducted in the public search facilities of the United States Patent & Trademark Office provides prior art material that reliably may be extrapolated to the full content of the prior art, at a reasonable cost.

9.3   DIFFERENT TYPES OF SEARCHES

In addition to the novelty and non-obviousness search, there are other searches that can be conducted. Keep in mind that the novelty/non-obviousness search discussed above asks the question "Is the invention sufficiently novel and non-obvious to be patentable?" Or to put it in a more practical way, "Should the inventor proceed to spend his or her resources to obtain a patent?".

9.3.1   Infringement Search

Since others normally have obtained patents in the related field to which your invention pertains, an infringement search should also be conducted upon completion of the development of the product or process embodying your invention, which search asks the question "Will my new invention, as embodied in a marketable product or process, infringe another unexpired patent of which we are currently unaware?" By way of example, suppose your new invention relates to a pencil having an eraser on one end. It would be important to find out whether anyone holds a patent on a pencil alone, because the manufacture and sale of your pencil plus eraser will infringe the earlier patent owner's right to exclusively make, use or sell pencils. Thus, the purpose of an infringement search is to uncover prior active patents to determine whether your invention, or any subset of your invention, would be covered by claims of another unexpired patent.

In conducting an infringement search, each claim of the patents uncovered by your search that are not expired must be examined to determine whether your invention may be covered by any of these claims. If only a single claim in a patent reads on your product or process, that patent is infringed. If it is found that there is a possibility of an infringement issue arising upon the marketing of your new product or process, a right-to-use search may be appropriate (see Section 9.3.3). Alternatively, it may be possible to create a modification of your invention or device which designs around the patent claims that potentially cause infringement problems. In so doing, you are attempting to avoid infringement.

9.3.2   State-of-the-Art Search

Another type of search that can be conducted is the state-of-the-art search, which asks the question "What is the general state of the art or technology concerning the area of my invention?" The results of this search are broader in scope than a novelty and non-obviousness search, but the search is still limited to the technology related to your invention. This type of search normally results in a collection of patents which yield valuable technical data and knowledge concerning the area of related technology, and may be useful to the inventor in further development of the invention, so long as potential infringement problems are avoided.

9.3.3   Right-to-Use Search

A further type of search, alluded to above, is the right-to-use search. This is also commonly called a validity search. This search attempts to answer the question "Even if it appears that the invention or device under analysis infringes another unexpired issued patent, is there a basis for determining that the potentially infringed patent cannot or should not be enforced with respect to my invention?" In this type of search, the patent attorney normally analyzes how the potentially infringed issued patent was obtained by reviewing the prosecution history or "file wrapper" of the subject patent before the U.S. Patent & Trademark Office. This analysis includes an evaluation of the prior art applied by the patent examiner against the claims of the potentially infringed patent. Very often in obtaining a patent and avoiding the prior art, the patent attorney, during prosecution of that patent and amending the claims, will represent to the patent examiner that the language and scope of the patent claims are somehow limited to specific structure or process steps not shown in the applied art. Such admissions by the patentee's attorney in the prosecution history can be used to show that an accused device falls outside a particular claim limitation. The prosecution history analysis attempts to find these limitations, or loopholes, in the scope of protection of the potentially infringed patent. From the relevant communications and changes to the claims made by the attorney to the Patent Examiner in the prosecution of the potentially infringed patent, your attorney can determine whether or not your invention falls inside or outside the issued patent's scope of protection.

Following such an analysis, if it is determined that your invention may still potentially infringe one or more claims of the issued patent in question, a right-to-use search is requested from a searcher in an effort to obtain prior art not considered previously by the patent examiner which would render the claims in question anticipated or obvious, and therefore invalid.

9.4   DATABASE SEARCHES

The searches conducted up to a few years ago were conducted by the searcher manually leafing through the collections of paper patents in the public search facilities of the U.S. Patent & Trademark Office. However, most search associates today use a computer database in conducting their searches.

The website of the U.S. Patent & Trademark Office (www.uspto.gov) provides one with the ability to search all patents issued in the United States since the year 1976 using key-word search techniques. Patents issuing between 1790 and 1975 are available in image format only if you know the patent number. Thus, today both manual and computer database searching are combined to conduct a complete search. Assuming that the inventor and patent attorney have provided the searcher with the identity of the inventor's largest competitors in the area of technology covered by the search, the searcher can then use the U.S. Patent & Trademark Office's database to obtain a list of all patents and the titles of these patents owned by each competitor subsequent to 1976. This will enable the searcher to pinpoint particular patents, and furnish the patent attorney and the inventor with a precise list of relevant patents owned by such competitors.

The U.S. Patent & Trademark Office database also allows searching by subject matter back to 1976, through the incorporation of key words into the search. Thus, if you are looking at a combination of electrical heating elements particularly useful for heating engine blocks, by typing the key words "heater" and "engine block" into the computer search engine, you will obtain the numbers of referenced patents issuing since 1976 that correspond to that key word search. Thus, it is important to provide your patent attorney with as much information as possible regarding the terms used in defining the technology to be searched so that these terms may be keyed into the database search.

9.4.1   U.S. Patent and Trademark Office Patent Classification System

Because of the vast number of patents that are filed and cross-referenced, the U.S. Patent & Trademark Office employs a numerical classification system to identify the many areas of technology. Class and subclass numerical designators pinpoint the specific technology and art to be searched. By examining the first page of a patent, the numbers of the classification system appear as "Field of Search." All of these classifications are listed in a rather thick classification manual. The entire manual is posted on the U.S. Patent & Trademark Office website (www.uspto.gov).

The manual classifies all patents according to subject matter by classes and subclasses. There are well over 400 classes and 20,000 subclasses which cover practically every category of technology and type of invention known. The patent classification manual is basically a table of contents to issued patents, and the searcher uses the manual to determine which classes and subclasses relate to your technology.

The patent classification system does more than divide patents into manageable related groups. The system divides the patent examiners into their own art groups, or areas of expertise. Thus, when directing a search, the attorney can particularly relate the scope of that search to the potential patent examiner's specific area of knowledge. For example, when I was a member of the United States Patent Office examining corps in the early days of my career, I examined patent applications directed to automatic transmissions, automatic transmission fluid control systems, differential drive mechanisms for vehicles, and locking devices to override the differential action upon slippage of one of the wheels. By examining patent applications in these areas of technology on a daily basis, I gained a degree of expertise in these particular technology areas. Thus, as new patent applications were filed that related to my area of technological expertise, it was easy for me to understand the technology, and the alleged advance in the technology. The work of the patent examiner will be covered in Chapter 12.

George Eastman

PRACTICAL PHOTOGRAPHY

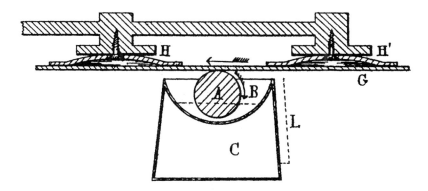

George Eastman is responsible for making photography practical, widely available, and more convenient, since his invention made it possible to take a camera anywhere. He was born on July 12, 1854 in the same house in which his father was born in the village of Waterville, New York. When George was five, his family moved to Rochester, NY, where his oldest sibling established the Eastman Commercial College. When the college failed and George's father died, the family became financially unstable.

George quit school at the age of fourteen to start working to support the family. He had several jobs working at insurance firms and the Rochester Savings Bank, and his pay ranged from three to fifteen dollars per week. When Eastman was twenty-four, he made plans to take a trip to Santo Domingo. Following a suggestion from a coworker at the bank, Eastman bought a photographic outfit equipped with all the supplies needed for wet-plate photography. His camera was as big as a sewing machine and required a heavy tripod as a support. He also purchased plate holders, chemicals, tanks, and a tent, all of which were necessary to be able to apply photosensitive emulsion on glass plates, expose the emulsion, and then develop the images before the emulsion dried. This amounted to approximately 50 pounds of equipment. Eastman said that the equipment "was a pack-horse load."

After all this, Eastman did not make the trip, but he was enticed to find an easier way to take pictures. In 1877, after reading in British journals about photographers creating their own dry gelatin emulsions, which meant that even after the plates became dry they were still sensitive to light, Eastman decided he would do the same. Beginning with a formula he obtained from one of the British journals, he worked on creating his own gelatin emulsions almost nonstop. After three years of working in the bank during the day, and experimenting in his mother's kitchen at night, he came up with a formula for dry plates that worked, and by 1880 he had obtained patents covering both his formula and a machine that prepared large numbers of plates.

Eastman leased a floor of a building in Rochester in April 1880 to begin manufacturing his dry plates for sale. His company prospered and grew, but faced a downturn at least once when plates went bad in the hands of dealers and Eastman recalled them and replaced the faulty plates with good ones. This recall was costly, but it greatly enhanced Eastman's reputation.

In 1884, Eastman started working on ways to make a photographic film lighter than the dry plates that were backed by glass. His first attempt was to put the photographic emulsion on a flexible backing such as paper, and then load it into a roll holder. Despite some flaws, this development was a huge success, and Eastman patented a paper-backed film in 1884. Eastman found that imperfections on or in the texture of the paper were transferred to the developed image. He then decided to eliminate this problem by applying a soluble layer of gelatin over the insoluble light-sensitive gelatin layer. After development, the soluble gelatin layer bearing the image was lifted off, and the insoluble layer was transferred to a sheet of clear gelatin and varnished with collodion, a cellulose mixture that hardened into a rigid, transparent film. His development of transparent roll film and a roll holder resulted in the introduction of the Kodak® Camera in 1888, the first camera built to hold roll film. Film rolls capable of holding 100 pictures were loaded in the camera. After exposure, the entire camera and film were sent back to Eastman's company, where the film was developed, the camera was reloaded and returned to the customer, all for $25.00.

A year later, Eastman created flexible transparent film, which proved vital to the development of the motion picture industry. In 1892, he established the Eastman Kodak Company at Rochester, New York. In 1900, the Kodak Brownie became the first roll-film, hand-held camera.

George Eastman was also very generous with the fortune he earned, donating in excess of $75 million to a multitude of projects. He endowed the Eastman School of Music in 1918 and the University of Rochester School of Medicine and Dentistry in 1921. He also gave $20 million to the Massachusetts Institute of Technology.

On one day in 1924, George Eastman donated $30 million to the University of Rochester, M.I.T., Hampton Institute, and Tuskegee Institute. The latter two were schools for African-American students, whose education was a particular concern of George Eastman.

Near the end of his life, Eastman became quite ill and became progressively disabled as a result of hardening of the cells in his lower spinal cord. He died at age 77 of his own hand on March 14, 1932.

G. EASTMAN.
Method and Apparatus for Coating Plates for use in
Photography.

No. 226,503.   Patented April 13, 1880.

Fig. 1.

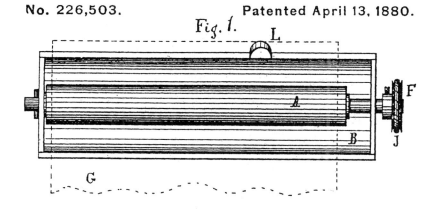

Fig. 2.

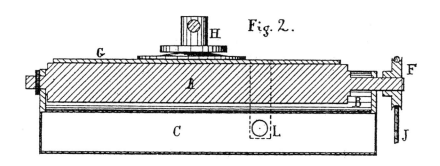

Fig. 3.

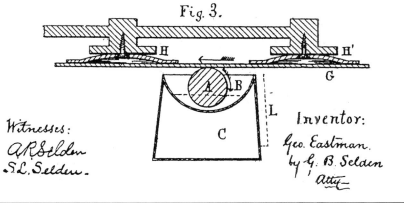

Witnesses:
A.R.Selden
S.L.Selden.

Inventor:
Geo. Eastman.
by G. B. Selden
atty.

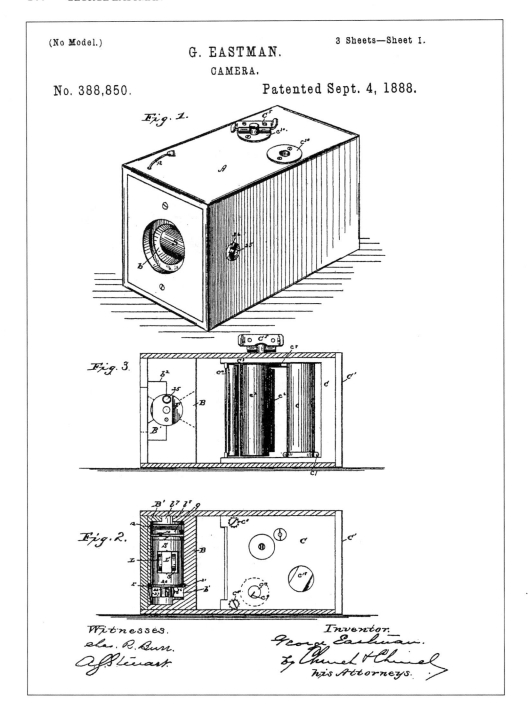

(No Model.)

3 Sheets—Sheet 1.

G. EASTMAN.

CAMERA.

No. 388,850.

Patented Sept. 4, 1888.

Fig. 1.

Fig. 3.

Fig. 2.

Witnesses.
ela. R. Burr.
A. J. Stewart.

Inventor.
George Eastman.
By Church & Church
his Attorneys.

10 Patent Application

10.1 INTRODUCTION

This chapter discusses what information goes into a properly prepared patent application, so you will be able to adequately review an application when presented for your review and comments prior to filing the application. One of the important requirements of the Patent Law is that an inventor must review his/her patent application for correctness before it is filed with the U.S. Patent and Trademark Office. This chapter also briefly summarizes the history of patent application content, leading up to the present system and its requirements for a properly filed application. Also discussed are the goals intended to be met in the preparation of a properly prepared application, the use of provisional patent applications, and how to conduct a rigid review of a patent application covering your invention.

10.2 REGISTRATION SYSTEM EVOLVING INTO AN EXAMINATION SYSTEM

You will recall from earlier chapters that from the year 1793 until 1836, there was no patent examination system in the United States, and inventors were merely required to furnish the government with a description of their invention, and the government would then register that explanation. This procedure caused immense difficulty when infringers were brought to court, and the court had the burden of determining just what the inventor was claiming as his or her invention, without any direct statement in the registration certificate that defined the novel point or points of the invention. Thus, the courts had no knowledge of the prior art against which the novelty of the "invention" could be measured.

This system changed in 1836, owing to the efforts primarily of Senator John Ruggles. Congress created a Patent Office, an examination system was created, and inventors were required not only to describe their invention in their applications for a patent, they had to specifically set forth what it was they were urging as novel over the prior art. The requirements of the system today are basically the same as established in 1836, even as the level of technology has increased approximately one hundred fold. One of my favorite tests to measure advances in technology between 1836 and the present is to determine how fast a human being could possibly travel in 1836 using any means possible, for example, a horse, and how fast a human being can travel today using any means possible, for example, a space shuttle. The answer may stagger your imagination.

Intellectual Property Law for Engineers and Scientists, by Howard B. Rockman
ISBN 0-471-44998-9 © 2004 The Institute of Electrical and Electronics Engineers

10.3   GOAL OF A PROPERLY PREPARED PATENT APPLICATION

Based upon historical development, the patent application today provides the foundation to define the proper description and scope of patent protection sought by an inventor. The patent application also must result in an issued patent that will advise the public of the strict definitions of the metes and bounds of the technology protection you have obtained from the government. Competitors must be able to easily ascertain what they can produce and what they can't produce in view of the patent fence that you have erected through your patent. The patent application must also describe each important detail of the structure and operation of your invention, as well as include claims specifically defining the limits of your protection. The claims must also define your invention beyond the state of the prior art. And again, your patent is ultimately a technical paper advising posterity of the advance in technology embodied in your invention. Remember, that the history of the patent laws stresses that the 20-year exclusive position in your invention is granted as consideration for the full and complete disclosure of your invention to the public.

In my law school course, where I teach students desiring to become patent attorneys, I begin my lecture on patent application preparation by indicating that the application is basically a sales document, where you are selling the concept to the patent examiner that the application defines an invention, without question, and that the only issue for examination is to ensure that the invention has been adequately defined over the prior art.

The patent application itself, in broad terms, consists initially of a statement of the field or art to which the invention pertains. This is followed by setting forth the problem which the invention is directed toward resolving, and a statement of how others have attempted to solve the same problem and failed. This is followed by stating that your invention will achieve certain advantages, results, and/or objectives that are not achieved by the technology shown in the prior art, and this is followed by a statement, in summary form, of the specific structure, elements and/or function of your invention which provide these advantages, objectives and results.

Following the above in a patent application is a brief description of the various drawing views, followed by a complete description of the invention which sets forth in concise detail a description of the complete structure of the invention, referring only to important elements of the invention, followed by a description of at least one cycle of operation. This is followed by the all important claims which will be discussed in the next chapter.

The above general "outline" for a patent application usually varies among some patent attorneys. For example, some patent applications are drafted without reference to advantages, results or objectives. Whatever preparation technique was used to prepare your application, ensure yourself that all aspects of your invention are clearly covered in the patent application.

10.4   PROVISIONAL PATENT APPLICATIONS

The U.S. Patent Laws were amended several years ago to allow the filing of provisional, or incomplete, patent applications in order to secure to the inventor a filing date prior to the time a complete patent application could be prepared, and requiring that the complete application be filed within one year from filing the provisional patent application. The purpose of the change in the law was to allow an inventor to establish a priority date as to his or her invention, without depending upon the workload, or the speed of preparation, of a patent attorney.

A provisional patent application (to the extent it is an "application" since no patent can ever issue from a provisional patent application) can be filed without any claims, without any declaration of inventorship by the inventor or inventors, and without a disclosure of prior art know by the inventor. The provisional application is basically a "shorthand" way of filing your novel technical information with the U.S. Patent & Trademark Office, indicating that within one year you expect to file a regular, non-provisional patent application covering the same technology. The purpose of the provisional application is to "save the date."

To place a provisional patent application on file, the inventor and/or his or her attorney file, among other things, a cover sheet that identifies the application as a provisional application, the identity of all the inventors usually in the form of an unsigned declaration setting forth the names and addresses of the inventors, and materials usually furnished by the inventor constituting a description and drawings of the invention, which need not necessarily be in the form of a normal patent application. The description and the drawings must be sufficient to allow the patent examiner and anyone else to understand the invention, since within a year a regular patent application will be filed, and the provisional application will become part of the prosecution history available to the public upon issuance of the patent from the regular patent application. The provisional application material must include all of the technology you include in the claims of your regular, non-provisional patent application when the latter is filed.

The reason I challenge the definition of a provisional patent application as being an "application" is that the rules clearly state that no provisional application will be examined for patentability, nor will it ever issue as a U.S. patent. The provisional patent application provides an early priority date if a regular, non-provisional patent application, or a foreign patent application, is subsequently filed within one year. Also, the priority period provided by the provisional application is not included in the 20 year term of the patent counting from the date of filing the regular application. Note further that provisional patent applications cannot be filed for design inventions.

The term "Patent Pending" may be used in connection with inventions that are the subject of provisional patent applications. Since 12 months after the filing of the provisional application, the application becomes automatically abandoned, it is important to file the regular patent application within that 12-month period or you will lose your priority filing date. It is possible to file a second provisional patent application based on the first one, but the second provisional application cannot claim the priority date of the first provisional patent application. The provisional patent application process was recently initiated, and the law governing this procedure is still developing.

10.5 REGULAR, NON-PROVISIONAL PATENT APPLICATION

As you probably have discerned by now, a patent application is the series of documents filed with the U.S. Patent & Trademark Office with the objective of the application proceeding through an examination process and ultimately issuing as a patent. The most important thing to keep in mind when reviewing your application, and in furnishing your patent attorney with information about your invention, is that once the application is filed with the U.S. Patent & Trademark Office, amendments can be made to the application during prosecution only within the framework of the material in the application as originally filed. There is a very strict rule that prohibits the introduction of "new matter" into any pending patent application. New matter is defined as any subject matter that is not described, shown or suggested in the four corners of the patent application as first filed. Thus, by way of example, if the inventor develops a new embodiment or an additional improvement to the invention covered by the filed patent application, that new material covering the new embodiment or additional improvement cannot be placed in the pending patent application. A new patent application, designated a "continuation-in-part- application," which will be described in Chapter 12, Section 12.10.2, can be filed to cover the new material related to the invention. As such, the inventor will ultimately end up with two or more patents. Therefore, it is important when assisting the patent attorney preparing your patent application, that all of the subject matter relating to your invention, including all new material, improvements and new advantages, be disclosed to the patent attorney for inclusion in the originally filed application.

It is also important that you provide the patent attorney with full knowledge of a completely conceived invention, the best mode contemplated for practicing the invention, and sufficient information to enable one skilled in the art to practice the invention without undue experimentation upon expiration of the patent. As stated previously, it is also important to provide your patent attorney with all prior art of which you are aware. The attorney may introduce some of the prior art in the body of the patent application itself in describing prior attempts at solutions to the same problem to which your invention is directed.

10.6   CONTENT OF A REGULAR PATENT APPLICATION

When working with your patent attorney, you will be asked to assist in the preparation of the application by initially furnishing all information relating to the structure and operation of your invention. There are many ways of describing an invention, however over the years and aided by court decisions as to what the content of a patent application should be, and having the U.S. Patent & Trademark Office codify rules as to what they expect in a patent application, a somewhat definitive content of a patent application has developed. As a result, most patent attorneys today use a similar "format" in preparing their patent applications. While this format may vary, the following sets forth the most acceptable way of presenting your material to the patent examiner in the judgement of the author.

10.6.1   Title of the Invention

The title of the invention should broadly describe the purpose of the invention, or the structure of the invention. Thus, the title could be "Apparatus for Preheating Engine Blocks" or "Process for Detasseling Corn," or something similar. Note that the U.S. Patent & Trademark Office website lists patents owned by inventors, corporations and other entities by their title and patent number, which enables easier searching for relevant patents if the title is descriptive of the disclosed invention to a certain degree.

10.6.2   Cross-Reference to Other Applications

In many instances, your patent application will be a continuation, continuation-in- part or division of a previously filed related patent application, or dependent upon a previously filed provisionally filed patent application. In order to properly establish the chain of the parent patent application(s) in your present application, it is necessary to place a statement in your current patent application referring to these earlier applications. This sets forth the continuity of these patent applications, and allows later filed patent applications to rely upon the earlier filing date of the parent application for commonly disclosed subject matter.

It is important to note that patent applications that have not issued are maintained in secrecy during the term of their prosecution, except for the publication of certain applications (filed after November 29, 2000) eighteen months after their filing date, which applications ultimately are to be filed overseas. However, when a patent does issue, any abandoned or previously identified patent application mentioned in the specification of that issued patent becomes available for public scrutiny.

10.6.3 Background of the Invention

Definition of the Field of the Invention   This portion of the specification comprises a very brief statement of the invention in general terms, which identifies the art or technology to which the subject matter of the invention pertains. Usually, a broad statement of the related art, followed by a specific statement identifying a particular branch or subdivision of the art to which the invention relates is set forth. A statement as to the utility of the invention is usually also included.

Brief Description of the Problems That Exist in the Prior Art Which Your Invention is Directed Toward Solving   This portion of the patent application describes the problems which your invention is directed toward solving, followed by statements describing the content of known prior art which represent attempts to solve the same or similar problems in the past. The prior art is described, in brief terms, as what is disclosed in the reference patents or articles, followed by brief statements as to specific limitations or disadvantages of the prior art in terms of your invention, that is, what the prior art does not disclose. This indicates to the reader of the patent the problems in the prior art that are not solved, and which your invention is directed towards solving.

The discussion of prior art in this portion of the application is in addition to any prior art statement (Information Disclosure Statement or IDS) which is submitted to the United States Patent and Trademark Office pursuant to Rule 56 (37 C.F.R. 1.56). The IDS merely lists prior art that the patent examiner should consider during examination, and should not be substituted for the portion of the patent application specification setting forth the content and shortcomings of the prior art. The language chosen in this portion of the patent application should emphasize the advantages of your invention over the prior art, and set forth the problems that remain unsolved by the prior art, which problems your invention solves.

The Results, Objectives and Advantages of Your Invention, Not Achieved by the Prior Art   The next portion of the patent specification sets forth the results, advantages and objectives sought to be obtained by your invention. At this stage of the application, these objectives, advantages and results are stated without describing the structure or elements by which these results are obtained, or the function of the invention. As discussed in Chapter 11, the claims of the patent application are directed to defining the structure, steps or elements of your invention, and the function of these elements; while the portion of the specification referred to now sets forth the objectives, advantages and results of using the elements, steps and functions set forth in the claims. Conversely, the claims do not recite results. While the claims are intended to describe what the invention is, your statement of objects, advantages and results are intended to describe what the invention accomplishes. These are statements of the broad aims to be achieved by the invention which are not achieved by the prior art.

The entire background portion of the specification is what I refer to as "the sales pitch" of the patent application. This is where you explain the differences between your invention's objectives and the prior art, set forth the advantages of your invention over the prior art, and the problems your invention solves. This is the portion of the patent specification that will be referred to during the prosecution stage to convince the patent examiner that the only issue is the scope of the claims, not whether or not the application sets forth inventive subject matter. Well thought out statements of objectives and results help the examiner reach this intended result.

10.6.4   Brief Summary of the Important Elements of the Invention

This section of the patent application specification includes a brief summary of the invention, setting forth its substance and function, and immediately precedes the description of the drawings and the illustrated embodiments of the invention. The summary should set out the exact nature, operation and purpose of the invention, and usually paraphrases the subject matter of the broadest claim. The summary of the invention is normally concise and reasonably general, and usually contains references to structure to enable the reader to understand the nature of the invention from the summary.

10.6.5   Brief Description of the Drawings Which Illustrate the Invention

When drawings are submitted with the patent application, this portion of the specification sets forth a brief series of indented subparagraphs comprising descriptions for each figure shown. These subparagraphs are extremely brief, and specify information allowing the reader to determine what view of the invention they are looking at. The drawings are usually described in terms of perspective, plan, elevation, section, fragmentary, schematic, or exploded views. As stated before, in most chemical cases, there are no drawings submitted with the application.

10.6.6   Detailed Description of the Illustrated Embodiment of the Invention

This is the longest section of the patent application, and contains the detailed description of the invention's structure, followed normally by a description of one cycle of operation of the structure, where there is a cycle of operation. For example, compositions of matter do not have an operation to describe, except probably the method of making the composition. The description of the invention in this portion of the specification also describes the interrelationship between the elements of the invention, and their cooperation with each other. The description of the invention must be set forth with such particularity to enable any person skilled in the art to make and use the claimed invention without undue experimentation once the patent expires. Since the extent of the knowledge of those skilled in the art varies from art to art, the level of detail varies from patent application to patent application. However, any doubt as to the amount of detail which should be included in the description of the invention should be resolved by adding detail. Remember that once the patent application is filed, no new matter can be added to the specification. Therefore, it is important to include all material elements and functions in the patent specification as initially written.

Normally, in describing a mechanical or electrical invention, the structure is defined in a logical way usually from an input to an output, or from a base upward in constructing the invention. In the chemical field, detailed descriptions include a wide range of specific examples or embodiments of the invention, as well as all known equivalents of the specific elements of the invention. In non-chemical cases, the detailed description need only cover one specific embodiment of the invention, however, it is preferable that alternate embodiments of the invention be set forth in the specification to advise the reader of the issued patent that several embodiments of the invention are covered by the issued patent's claims.

Since there is a requirement that the detailed description of the patent application set forth the "best mode" of the invention contemplated by the inventor at the time the application is filed, you must ensure yourself that the best mode is set forth in the application. This requires that if you have performed additional work on the invention while the patent attorney was preparing the patent specification, you must add the additional material to the application after the application has been drafted and furnished to you for review and comment. Failure to do so may result in the invalidity of any issued patent. Keep in mind that a "best mode" of the invention discovered one day after or subsequent to the filing of the application is of no consequence. That "mode" can be covered in a subsequently filed patent application.

The patent specification also points out features of the subject invention which produce the previously described advantages, and comprise improvements over the prior art. This again is part of the "sales" presentation advising the patent examiner how the invention differs from past technology. The specification can also point out how your invention solves a long standing problem or need in the prior art. This will reinforce the argument that the invention was not obvious to one skilled in the art.

Upon reviewing the patent application once it is completed by the patent attorney, ensure yourself that the description of your invention is correct, complete, and is set forth in a logical, flowing manner. The description of the structure should be in an easy to understand format, and the statement of operation or function should also be logical, starting from an input and working through to the output, or from the beginning of the operation to the end.

Also, when reviewing the patent application submitted by the patent attorney, determine whether you believe that the patent examiner, when he or she reads the application, will determine instantaneously that there is an invention described in the patent application. Also, ensure that the patent attorney has adequately defined all of the novel features of your invention.

To obtain a filing date for the patent application, it must be filed with the U.S. Patent & Trademark Office with at least one claim, all the pages of the specification, and all the drawings. If any one of these elements is omitted, no filing date will be assigned to the application.

If you determine from reading the prior art that was obtained through a pre-filing novelty search, that the patent examiner may make an argument of lack of novelty based on the prior art, the patent application specification should anticipate these arguments and furnish rebuttal information in the specification itself. Therefore, when reviewing the patent application, be sure that you understand the differences between your invention and the disclosures of the prior art of which you are aware.

In the patent specification, technical details such as dimensions, materials of construction, circuit components, values and the like may be omitted, unless they are critical to the novelty or understanding of the invention. However, all details critical to the practice of the invention must be set forth. Again, my recommendation is to err on the side of inclusion if you cannot determine the essentiality of all details. Also, remember that if your issued patent is ultimately subjected to enforcement in a court of law, the ultimate reader of the patent may be a federal judge and/or jury who have no technical knowledge whatsoever. Therefore, when reviewing the patent application, review it from the standpoint that some day a non-technical person may have to determine the scope and content of the issued patent.

The specification must also include sufficient information to enable a person skilled in the art to make and use the invention. If it is found that the specification is not complete, or describes an inoperable invention, the issued patent ultimately could be held to be unenforceable. It has been my experience that a properly prepared patent application is a finite merger of proper technical disclosure and description, and excellent use of the English language, all applied to technology.

The description portion of the patent specification concludes with a general statement of intent not to restrict the invention to the precise embodiments described, but to have the patent cover any device or process which falls within the scope of the claims that are ultimately allowed by the patent examiner.

10.6.7   Claims Distinctly and Precisely Pointing Out the Definition of the Invention

As a preface to Chapter 11, which discusses patent claims in detail, it suffices to say that the claims of a patent application should be written broad enough to cover any competing device or process that may be marketed in the future, and at the same time the claims are written limited enough so they do not cover, or "read on," the prior art. The construction of the claims usually turns on the combined efforts of the inventor and the patent attorney, working in conjunction to ensure that the fine line of invention over the prior art is adequately defined.

10.6.8   The Abstract

The U.S. Patent & Trademark Office rules require that the patent application include an "Abstract of the Invention" of not more than 250 words, briefly describing the novel features of the invention. The Abstract is reprinted on the first page of the issued patent, which is normally called the information page. The purpose of the Abstract is to provide a reader with the "heart" of your invention in a few concise sentences. Usually, the patent attorney will divide the broadest claim of the patent application into a series of short sentences which eliminate the legalese of the broad claim. By reading the Abstract, one reviewing the issued patent should be able to decide if they desire to read further.

It is important that the Abstract be worded with the same degree of care as the rest of the patent application. In at least one reported decision, the Court of Appeals of the Federal Circuit (CAFC) has referred to the Abstract in deciding to limit the scope of claim coverage of a patent.

10.7   YOUR REVIEW OF YOUR PATENT APPLICATION

Once the patent application is prepared by the patent attorney, the application must be forwarded to the inventor for the inventor's review and comment. It is a requirement of the patent laws that the inventor must review the patent application prior to signing the formal papers, known as the Declaration or Oath, wherein the inventor declares that he/she believes himself or herself to be the first original and sole or joint inventors of the subject matter of the application.

Upon reviewing your completed patent application, you must ensure that the invention has been adequately described, and that the claims adequately cover the invention. If, upon your review, you determine that a competitor can "design around" your broad claims, advise your patent attorney, who will suggest adding even broader claims to the application to cover your "design around" embodiment. I refer to this analysis as having the inventor assume the role of "devil's advocate" vis-à-vis the claims of the patent application.

I advise my clients that we, as patent attorneys, have no pride of authorship, and therefore the inventor can make any and all additions, changes or comments they deem necessary. If the patent attorney concludes that certain of these recommended changes by the inventor may add limitations to the patent application rather than broadening the scope, the patent attorney will then discuss these proposed changes with the inventor. Ultimately, once the patent application is approved by both the inventor and the patent attorney, the formal documents supporting the application are signed, and the application is filed with the U.S. Patent & Trademark Office to await examination.

10.8   EXECUTION OF DECLARATION, POWER OF ATTORNEY, AND ASSIGNMENT WHEN APPLICATION COMPLETED

Upon completion of the review of your patent application, including the claims which are covered in detail in Chapter 11, documents commonly known as the "formal papers" are completed and furnished to the U.S. Patent & Trademark Office along with the application. These papers constitute a Declaration (or Oath) that the inventor or inventor(s) are the sole or joint inventors of the subject matter described in the claims of the patent application, and that they believe themselves to be the first and original inventor(s) of the claimed invention.

Where the patent application has been prepared by a patent attorney who will be responsible for the continued prosecution of the application through the U.S. Patent & Trademark Office, a Power of Attorney form is executed by the inventor(s), providing the attorney with the power to prosecute the application further on behalf of the inventor(s).

If the invention is to be owned by a corporation or other entity or group of entities other than the inventor or inventors, an Assignment document signed by the inventors, granting all rights, title and interest, or portions thereof, of the invention to the assignee is also prepared for official recording. The assignment document, the formal papers, and the patent application are then submitted to the U.S. Patent & Trademark Office with the appropriate government filing fee. The Assignment document is recorded, and returned to your attorney. The patent application, with the formal papers, awaits examination.

In addition, to comply with the provision of the U.S. Patent & Trademark Office rules that the inventor and the inventor's attorney must submit all prior art that they are aware of to the patent examiner, it is normal practice for the patent attorney to prepare and file with the patent application, or shortly thereafter, an Information Disclosure Statement (IDS), which lists prior art known by the applicant and the attorney, for consideration by the patent examiner. The IDS consists of:

1. A list of all patents, publications or other information submitted by the applicant for consideration by the patent examiner;
2. A legible copy of each U.S. patent, foreign patent publication or portions thereof and other information identified in the IDS except that no copy of a pending U.S. patent application need be included;
3. An explanation of the relevance of any patent publication or information not in the English language.

The IDS is normally submitted to the United States Patent & Trademark Office along with the completed patent application to initiate the examination process. The IDS can also be submitted to the patent examiner at any time prior to the initial examination, without monetary penalty. Also, the inventor and the inventor's attorney have a continuing obligation to submit material prior art they become aware of to the patent examiner up to the date the patent issues. This is an important point to remember, and cannot be stressed enough.

Ottmar Mergenthaler

THE LINOTYPE™ HOT-TYPE COMPOSING MACHINE

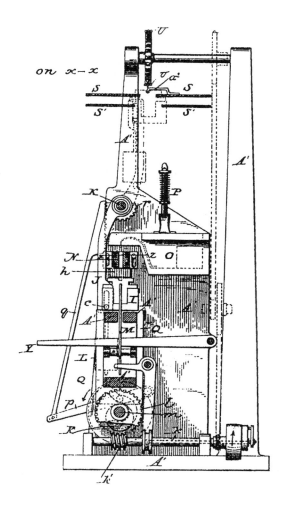

Ottmar Mergenthaler's contribution to the state of the printing art in 1886 is today considered by many as the most important advance in printing since Guttenburg's invention of movable type approximately 400 years previously.

Ottmar Mergenthaler was born on May 11, 1854 in Hachtel, Baden Wuerttemberg, in what is now Germany. His mechanical ability surfaced early. The clock in the Lutheran church bell tower in his family's home town had stood still for many years. No one had been able to repair it, not even skilled clock repairers. One evening, the bell suddenly rang because fourteen-year-old Ottmar Mergenthaler had fixed the clock. As a matter of fact, his ambition at that time was to become a watch maker, and he spent four years as an apprentice to a relative of his family learning the watch- and clock-making trade.

In 1872, Mergenthaler noticed that soldiers were returning from the Franco-Prussian Wars, and he thought that his opportunities for advancement would be better in the United States. On October 26, 1872, a ship carrying the 18 year old Mergenthaler in steerage with only a wooden suitcase docked in Baltimore, Maryland. He immediately went to Washington to work in a knife and tool shop operated by the son of the relative to whom Mergenthaler was previously apprenticed in Germany. However, business was rather poor in Washington at the time, and in 1874 Mergenthaler moved to Baltimore along with the rest of the knife and tool shop in which he was working.

The shop that Mergenthaler was working in designed and constructed clocks, bells, weather devices, and patent models for inventors who were seeking to patent their inventions. One day in 1876, an inventor named Charles Moore came into the shop looking to have a patent model made for a typing machine he had designed that printed characters in lithographic ink on paper strips. The impressions of the characters were mounted on a backing sheet, and the words were transferred to a lithographic stone ultimately for printing. Moore stated that he held a patent on a transfer typewriter used for making newspapers by eliminating type-setting by hand. However, his prior invention did not work and he asked Mergenthaler whether a better model could be constructed. Mergenthaler noted that Moore's design was problematic, and Mergenthaler started working on improvements. Two years later, in 1878, Mergenthaler had constructed a machine that stamped letters and words on cardboard; however, this was not what Mergenthaler ultimately wanted to develop.

Mergenthaler continued working and eventually improved the reliability of Moore's typing machine. However, insurmountable problems in transferring the lithographic images resulted in this process being abandoned. In 1878, one of Moore's backers proposed the development of a stereotypic process in which the typing machine would impress characters into papier-maché strips. Mergenthaler devised a rotary impression machine, and obtained his first patent on this machine, but, eventually, this process was not satisfactory, and was abandoned.

In 1883, this backer, one James O. Clephane, financed Mergenthaler's attempts to develop a new machine that Mergenthaler had first conceived in 1879. Mergenthaler developed a band machine using long tapered metal bands with raised characters that created impressions of type characters in lines on papier-maché strips. Difficulties arose using this machine and in making satisfactory castings. In 1884, Mergenthaler developed a second machine using bands of indented characters that were located in the machine in such a way that lines of type could be cast from molten lead. This became Mergenthaler's initial Linotype machine. Mergenthaler's backers then formed the National Typographic Company, and named Mergenthaler as manager of its Baltimore factory. The name of the company was changed to Mergenthaler Printing Company in 1885.

However, Mergenthaler realized that the second band machine that he had developed would still not produce type of the quality of hand-set type. He then proposed a third machine, using matrices, or molds, of single characters that would immediately cast the characters in molten metal in the same machine. This principle of circulating single matrices became the foundation of all subsequent Linotype machines. When a Linotype operator pressed a key, that stroke identified which letter molds were to be retrieved from the magazines in the machine. The machine then assembled a row of metal molds of characters, called matrices. Molten lead was then poured into the matrices, producing a line of type, but in reverse. Thus, the type would read properly when ink was applied to it and the image was transferred to the printed page. The matrices were automatically restored by the machine to the magazines after the lead was poured. It has been reported that Mergenthaler got the idea for his brass matrices from the wooden molds used to make Christmas cookies in Germany.

The first commercial machine using this structure was completed in 1886 and installed at the plant of the *New York Tribune* to set both newspaper type and a 500 page book. Whitelaw Reid, the publisher of the Tribune, saw the potential of this machine and provided additional money to the Mergenthaler Printing Company.

By 1888, the usefulness and reliability of the Mergenthaler Linotype machine was noticed by Mr. Reid, and he wanted machines produced quickly for sale, but Mergenthaler still wanted a perfect machine. At that time, unable to resolve his differences with the company, Mergenthaler resigned as factory manager. Reid ultimately moved the factory to Brooklyn, New York. Mergenthaler responded by opening his own shop in Baltimore, where he developed improved Linotype machines that were built in both the Brooklyn and Baltimore shops.

In 1891, Mergenthaler perfected his newer Model I Linotype machine, overcoming the difficulties faced by newspaper publishers with the earlier machine. In 1895, 2,608 Model I machines were installed at 385 locations in the United States. It was in this year that the Linotype machine was recognized by the printing industry as the first revolutionary advance over the hand typesetting procedures invented by Johann Guttenberg circa 1450.

Prior to Mergenthaler's death in 1899, the Mergenthaler Company was compelled to defend its patent rights in patent interference proceedings, and sued infringers who were manufacturing competing machines. In 1895, the Mergenthaler Company also acquired a competitor, and along with it the patent rights for the double-wedge spaceband, which justified the lines of type. In 1913, Mergenthaler's principal patents expired and competing hot-metal typesetting machines immediately entered the market.

It was not until after World War II that the use of Mergenthaler's hot-type systems began declining in use. The development of offset printing, cold-type and photocomposition, and, ultimately, computers compelled the Mergenthaler Company to stop production of Linotype machines in 1971, but by that time the company had built approximately 90,000 Linotype machines. Several thousands of these machines are probably still in use in the United States and elsewhere.

Mergenthaler's contribution to the printing industry cannot be overlooked. The use of the Linotype machines geometrically increased the dissemination of ideas, concepts, and information throughout the literate world. The Guttenberg system allowed printers to set type by hand one letter at a time. The Linotype machine could set a complete line of type using a 90-character keyboard. Mergenthaler's machine allowed newspapers to compose pages five times faster than using hand-set type, and one Linotype operator could perform the work of six hand-setting typographers.

Mergenthaler died on October 28, 1899 in his home in Baltimore, Maryland. The church in which his funeral services were held, the Old Zion Lutheran Church, to this day has a stained glass window featuring Mergenthaler's first Linotype machine.

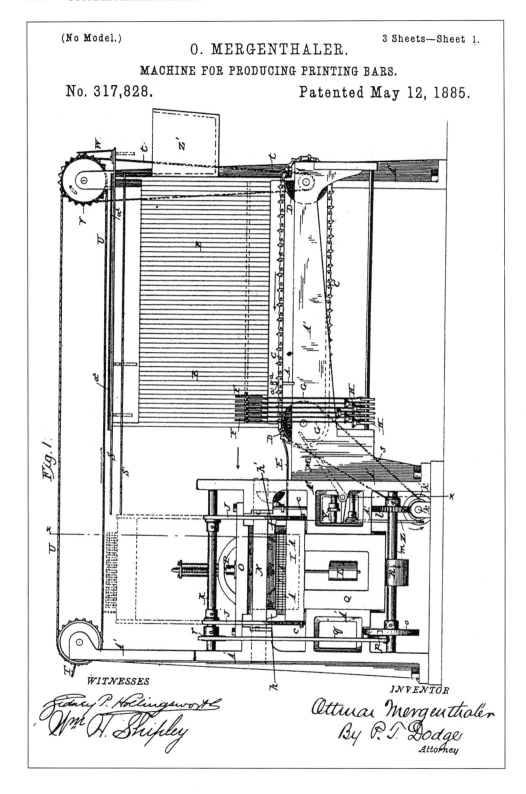

(No Model.)   3 Sheets—Sheet 1.

O. MERGENTHALER.
MACHINE FOR PRODUCING PRINTING BARS.

No. 317,828.   Patented May 12, 1885.

Fig. 1.

WITNESSES   INVENTOR

Sidney P. Hollingsworth   Ottmar Mergenthaler
Wm H. Shipley   By P. T. Dodge
                                                Attorney

11 Claims of a Patent Application

11.1 INTRODUCTION TO PATENT CLAIMS

Upon completion of the draft of your patent application and prior to its filing with the U.S. Patent & Trademark Office, your patent attorney will furnish you with a copy of the draft application for your review, comments, additions and corrections. As you read the application, all goes well until you reach a series of numbered "paragraphs" at the end of the application. All of a sudden you are reading English language statements that appear to be written by a patent attorney from a different planet. These numbered "paragraphs" are the claims of your patent which serve many purposes, the two primary among them being to define the limits where your invention transcends the prior art, and to provide notice to competitors and potential infringers of the exclusive territory you have fenced in by your patent grant. In this chapter, we shall discuss the historical origin of these somewhat arcane claims, an explanation of what patent claims are, different types of claims, and most importantly, a short guide on how to read and understand the claims your patent attorney has drafted to cover your invention.

11.2 HISTORICAL DEVELOPMENT OF PATENT CLAIMS

The requirement of claims in a patent evolved from problems courts were having understanding the novel features of a patent "registration certificate" that deserved exclusivity. Congress ultimately recognized the existence of this problem, and took steps to remedy the situation.

11.2.1 Court Decisions

As mentioned in Chapter 4, in 1790 the United States enacted its first patent law, which called for an examination procedure by two out of three high government officials. Well, apparently they got tired of this practice in a hurry, because three years later the second Patent Act of 1793 was enacted which did away with the examination procedure altogether. From 1793 to 1836, all an inventor was required to do was submit a statement of his/her invention to the government, and the government would register that statement as a patent without any examination.

Once an inventor obtained a registration certificate, and an infringer appeared on the horizon, the inventor filed a lawsuit in the federal courts accusing the interloper with patent infringement. It was then up to the courts to determine whether or not the infringer had actually adopted the patented invention in the alleged infringing device or method. However, in the majority of those cases where there was not an exact duplication of the protected invention, as is the case in most infringement controversies even to the present time, it was each court's burden to define what the invention was from reading the inven-

Intellectual Property Law for Engineers and Scientists, by Howard B. Rockman
ISBN 0-471-44998-9 © 2004 The Institute of Electrical and Electronics Engineers

tor's description, to determine what was novel about the invention covered by the certificate, and then to determine whether or not the infringer had embodied the novelty of the invention in the alleged infringing device. The court's analysis was complicated by the fact that there was nothing in the patent registration certificate that indicated what the inventor claimed was novel, and conversely, what was common throughout the prior art. This caused frustration amongst the courts, and difficulty in determining acts of infringement.

Consider the time also. This was a period when the United States was largely agrarian, but was also moving into the industrial age. Industry and even farming depended to a large degree on mechanical devices that would increase the power and leverage that could be applied to an object beyond that of human strength. The steam engine was still in the distant future, electricity had still to be evolved as a medium for controlling mechanical movements, and the term "physics" had not even entered common parlance. However, by 1836, at least one U.S. senator, Senator John Ruggles, saw a need to assist the courts by recommending the enactment of an examination system, the establishment of a Patent Office that would examine patent applications for novelty of submitted inventions, and take the burden of determining what is novel in an invention from the courts. The proposed new system provided a government determination whereby patents would not be issued until the inventor was able to prove to a Patent Office examiner that the invention did incorporate novel features.

11.2.2   1836 Patent Law

The U.S. Patent Law of 1836 was enacted in response to continuing public and judicial outcries with regard to the state of the patent law, which still substantially relied upon the Patent Act of 1793. Senator Ruggles, newly appointed from Maine in 1835, had long practiced law in his state, was a justice of the state's Supreme Court before being appointed to the Senate, had a strong interest in mechanics and engineering and had a desire to become a patentee in his own right. Senator Ruggles set out to determine what was causing the inadequacies in the operation of the patent law, and in 1835 expressed to the Senate the complaints he had heard from the Patent Office and the courts. He asked the Senate to appoint a committee to consider the Patent Office situation and, as is common in all political and societal situations, he himself was appointed chairman of the committee to conduct the investigation. He discovered that the heart of the matter was that the Patent Office was obligated to issue a patent if technical and filing requirements were satisfied, regardless of novelty. After the patent issued, it was up to the courts to decide what exclusive rights, if any, existed with respect to the issued patent, and whether the patent was infringed.

The head of the Patent Office at that time also urged upon Senator Ruggles that the Patent Office should be able to prevent the issuance of a patent for an invention which was not novel, or which claimed invention in technology disclosed in an earlier patent. This could be performed by an examination system for novelty. Although England at that time had a system that allowed patents for imported inventions, it was felt that the United States system should be confined to patents relating only to new inventions. It became clear to Senator Ruggles that patents should be allowed only for such inventions as are in fact new, and entitled by the merit of originality and utility to be protected by law. Note that the question of non-obviousness of an invention was not a factor in 1836. As stated previously, the concept of non-obviousness did not arise in the United States until 1850 in the courts, and in 1952 in the legislature.

The law of 1836 required that each patent contain a specification comprising a description of the invention in full, clear and exact terms, and that the specification "particularly specify and point out the part, improvement, or combination claimed to be the invention." The exact language of the Patent Act of 1836 defining the specification and claims is as follows:

> "But before any inventor shall receive a patent for any such new invention or discovery, he shall deliver a written description of his invention or discovery, and the manner and process of making, constructing, using, and compounding the same, in such full, clear and exact terms, avoiding unnecessary prolixity, as to enable any person skilled in the art or science to which it appertains, or with which it is most nearly connected, to make, construct, compound, and use the same; and in case of any machine he shall fully explain the principle, and the several modes in which he has contemplated the application of that principle, whereby which it may be distinguished from other inventions; and shall particularly specify and point out the part, improvement or combination which he claims as his own invention or discovery."

Thus, for the first time in the United States, an inventor was obligated to set forth a written statement in the patent application defining what was novel in his or her invention, as compared to the prior art. Since the inventor was therefore "claiming" that portion of his or her invention that was novel, these statements in the patents became known as claims, and in a later Patent Statute, the claims were required to be separate "paragraphs" at the end of the specification, as they are in any modern patent document. At present, over 165 years later, the requirements of a patent application are the same.

11.3   WHAT CLAIMS ARE

The present U.S. patent law defines the claims of a patent application in quite the same manner as described in the Patent Law of 1836, set forth above. The patent application claims set forth in words the content and scope of the property rights the inventor is attempting to secure through the patent grant. Each claim defines a separate and distinct property right. Thus, the claims of a patent define the subject matter of the invention and serve as the metes and bounds of the legal rights conferred by the patent. The claims also serve to provide notice to the public of the precise area of technology that is "fenced in" by the exclusive rights of your patent grant, so that competitors and would-be infringers know where not to tread.

A patent claim recites the structural and/or functional elements of the invention, or the method steps of a process, or the constituent parts of a composition of matter. Language concerning the structural and/or functional relationships between elements or method steps is usually included in patent claims to clarify how the article or the method operates, and how the combination of elements "fit together" to place your invention in its proper environment. As is true with any definition, the language in a patent claim can be broad or can be specific. Most patents contain several claims written in broad, intermediate and specific terms to define the invention. The broader the language allowed in a patent claim, the broader the scope of protection of the patent grant. The breath of a patent claim, however, is limited in that the claim cannot read on the prior art. Stated another way, each patent claim must define over the prior art.

Thus, your patent attorney's objective in drafting patent claims is to initially submit to the patent examiner the broadest claims that you deem possible, to cover your invention in the broadest possible scope. The examiner will then apply prior art to the claims, and if necessary, will require that the claims be limited to the novelty of the invention in more specific terms such that the claims do not also encompass what is previously in the prior art, or in the public domain. This balancing of the description of the invention is the primary art of the patent attorney. In my humble estimation, without proper training and experience, it would be practically impossible for one to draft a valuable patent claim that is sufficiently broad to cover the invention, and yet not read on the prior art.

A patent application normally contains more than one claim, varying in degree of breadth. Thus, if one or more claims of the patent are held invalid as reading on prior art not applied by the patent examiner, as may result in a reexamination proceeding, or in court during an infringement case in an effort by an accused infringer to invalidate the patent, certain other claims of the patent of less breadth are still held valid and possibly infringed. Note that while a tract of land can only be described by one definition, inventions can be described by many claims, varying in scope and breadth from broad to narrow. Prudence dictates including several claims of varying scope in your patent application so that the patent survives if one or more claims are ultimately held invalid.

One of the key concepts in drafting patent claims is to draft claims which do not read on the prior art, and yet define your invention in such terms that any competitor in the future who tries to compete with you cannot produce a duplicate or near-duplicate of your invention without falling within the scope of your patent's claims. A great deal of foresight is required to prepare patent claims that will encompass any future competing device or process within the claim language. This requires looking beyond the precise physical structure embodied in the invention, and visualizing how the same results, objectives and/or advantages of the invention may be obtained by more or less obvious modifications or substitutions of elements or steps. Thus, the patent attorney, while drafting the claim, at the same time considers how to avoid or "design around" the claim he or she is drafting, as if they were a competitor. The patent attorney, with input from the inventor, then adjusts the claim language to close the loophole that has just been created in his or her own mind. Since most patent attorneys and inventors do not have access to working crystal balls, the requirement of drafting valuable patent claims calls into play a significant amount of imagination applied to the technology field related to the invention. This, in my opinion, is one of those great junction points between science and art, bonded together by the adhesive of imagination.

When one first reads a patent claim, and indeed the same has been true for my students at the law school where I teach patent claim drafting, the claims appear awkward and difficult to read. However, properly drafted patent claims do make sense, and further in this chapter at Section 11.10, I will provide you with information on how to read and understand patent claims. When drafting a patent application, including the claims, the patent attorney realizes that the audience for the patent application, and the patent issuing therefrom, is first the inventor, second the patent examiner, third the competitor's of the inventor, and fourth, if infringement ensues, a judge and jury. Thus, the claims ultimately have to be explained to, understood and interpreted by those with little or no technical knowledge, for example, the judge and jury.

Existing patent law (35 U.S.C. Section 112) requires that the patent application comprise claims that particularly point out and distinctly claim the subject matter that the applicant regards as his or her invention. This brief statement encompasses all of the above comments regarding the subject of patent claim scope and content. No other guidelines are set forth in the patent law regarding the procedure for properly drafting a patent claim.

In determining whether or not a patent is infringed, it is the patent claims that are measured against the alleged infringing device, not the detailed description of the invention in the specification of the patent. If the alleged infringing device falls within the scope of only one of the claims of your patent, infringement is made out. In addition, multiple claims in a patent may legally form the basis for parceling out several different licenses for different embodiments of the invention, each claim supporting a separate license. Since the claims are always preceded by the patent specification, the claims use language which is supported by the language and description of the invention in the specification. The patent claims are also supported by the drawings which appear with the patent application, when necessary. Thus, the patent document itself is taken as a whole to determine the scope and content of the invention set forth in the claims.

Another major function of patent claims is that they ultimately advise a potential infringer of the metes and bounds of the invention that falls within the scope of the issued patent's protection. Therefore, the potential infringer is duly advised to work around the patent claims in attempting to develop a competing device. This type of "hopscotching" around patent claims has led to the advancement of the arts to which the patent laws are directed. Believe it or not, in my experience, this process works to constantly move technology forward.

11.4 YOUR REVIEW OF THE CLAIMS OF YOUR PATENT APPLICATION

As potential inventors, each of you should remember that once a patent application directed to your invention is initially drafted, it is next submitted to you for review. When conducting your review, pay careful attention to the claims to ensure yourself that the claims 1) adequately describe your invention and 2) are broad enough to prevent a competing device from being made with minor alterations, and therefore get around your patent claims while accomplishing the same purposes, advantages and results as your invention. Therefore, when reviewing patent applications over your career, review the claims carefully to ensure that your invention is being adequately protected.

I also recommend that you discuss the scope of the claims at each stage of the patent application preparation and prosecution with your patent attorney to ensure that you have achieved the broadest possible protection. While claims are placed last in the patent application, their importance is decidedly first, since the claims must properly cover the invention, or the rights covered by the patent grant issuing from your patent application diminish in value. Indeed, the prosecution of a patent application largely involves comments back and forth between the inventor, the patent attorney and the patent examiner, ensuring that the claims are written in acceptable form, and clearly define the invention over the prior art.

The most effective patent application is the result of a joint effort between the inventor and the patent attorney. Thus, there should always be total communication between the two, and the lawyer should always be given all the relevant information for his job relating to preparing the patent application. Nothing should be held back by the inventor. Basically, a patent application, including the claims, is a complex document, and the inventor usually provides the information, with the patent attorney drafting the application. The review of the application, however, is a joint effort between the inventor and the patent attorney. I always advise my clients that I have no pride of authorship, and that each inventor is to review the entire application carefully to determine if there are any corrections or additions to be made to place the application in final form. If you as the inventor suggest adding certain elements to the claims, be prepared to have the patent attorney advise you that adding elements to patent application claims may unnecessarily limit the scope of the claims, and therefore the language initially prepared and inserted by the patent attorney may be the broadest way to go.

11.5 DISTINGUISHING DIFFERENT TYPES OF CLAIMS

Upon reviewing your patent application, you may encounter different types of claims, including those known as apparatus claims, means-plus-function claims, and method or process claims. The first two are used to define machines and articles of manufacture, while method claims define a series of novel and non-obvious steps of a process of doing something, such as transforming a piece of matter from one state to another, or the operation of a piece of machinery, or a computer program. Apparatus claims set forth the elements of the covered machine, or article of manufacture, the physical relationship between the elements comprising the invention, and the functional relationship between those elements. These features of apparatus claims are set forth in more detail in Section 11.10.3 of this chapter. Means-plus-function claims also cover machines and articles of manufacture, but in a format that describes each, or some, of the claimed elements in terms of the function they perform, rather than their physical structure. For example, you are now reading a "book." In means-plus-function terminology, this "book" would be defined as a "means for conveying information." This type of terminology is used to provide a broad scope of claim coverage to your patent. Consider, for example, that the term "book" narrowly defines a physical structure with information set forth on pages. On the other hand, a "means for conveying information" has a broader scope, encompassing a computer, an audio book system, a billboard, or any other information conveying medium. However, there is a limit. Means-plus-function claims are limited to covering only the corresponding structure described in your patent specification, or equivalent structure (the latter being determined on a case by case basis). Therefore, whenever you see an element of your invention described in your patent application claims in terms of "means-plus-function," be sure that all known substitutions and equivalents for that structure are also defined in the specification of your patent application. A sample of an apparatus, means-plus-function and method claim is set forth below, describing a simple electrically driven clock.

- Apparatus Claim:
  An electrically operated timepiece, comprising:
  —a cylindrical housing;
  —an electric motor mounted in the housing;
  —a clock face mounted on the cylindrical housing, the clock face having a centrally disposed aperture;
  —a pair of rotatable shafts driven by the electric motor, the shafts extending through the aperture and one shaft coaxially disposed around the other shaft;
  —a first minute hand attached to and rotated by the one shaft at a rotational speed of one rotation per hour; and
  —a second hour hand attached to and rotated by the other shaft at a rotational speed of one rotation every twelve hours.

- Means Plus Function Claim:

  An electrically operated timepiece, comprising:

  —a cylindrical housing;

  —means indicating hours and minutes mounted on an opening of the housing;

  —means mounted in the housing for providing rotational movement to a pair of shafts, one shaft coaxially mounted around the other shaft;

  —means mounted to each of said shafts to designate hours and minutes on the hour and minute indicating means;

  —the means for providing rotational movement to the shafts driving one shaft at a rotational speed of one rotation per hour and driving the other shaft at a rotational speed of one rotation every twelve hours.

- Method Claim:

  A method of indicating time on a clockface using a pair of rotating hands comprising the steps of:

  —placing both of said hands adjacent the clockface;

  —rotating one of the hands at a first rotational speed of one rotation every hour; and

  —rotating the other hand at a rotational speed of one rotation every twelve hours.

11.6   MORE ON METHOD OR PROCESS CLAIMS

If the invention is a new method, or a new use for an old product which is expressed as a method (see below), the patent claims recite the steps of the method or process of doing something which is considered novel. These claims normally do not require reciting the mechanical relationship between parts, but merely require the recitation of the steps of the novel and non-obvious process, something like writing a recipe in a cookbook. The ideal method patent claim recites as little structure as possible in carrying out the method. For example, if the process uses a heating or cooling step, you do not recite the heater or the cooling compressor. You merely recite the step of heating or cooling. However, where structure is necessary for an understanding of the process, the method claim will include such structure.

In mechanical or electrical inventions, the operation of the patented structure may also involve a novel method or process. If you determine that this is so, advise the patent attorney that novelty not only resides in the structure and function of the device itself, but also in the method used by the device. Thus, the patent attorney should include method claims drawn to the novel process used by the machinery or electrical or electronic circuit, in addition to claims directed to the apparatus.

In patent law, the terms "process" and "method" are used interchangeably. The term process also includes "a new use of a known process, machine, manufacture, composition of matter, or material." Thus, if you have a new way of using a device or apparatus that has been on the market for years, or even centuries, you may obtain a patent on the method of using that old device to accomplish the new process. Consider, for example, drafting a claim for a method of using beer to prevent baldness. No, I haven't figured that one out yet; I just pose it as a hypothetical.

As in apparatus claims, method claims may be broad, intermediate or narrow. The steps in a method claim must be recited in a logical order, however, a process can infringe a method claim even though the accused process does not accomplish the steps in the same order as recited in the claims. Also, if the claims of the method patent recite that the steps must be performed in a specific order, then there is no infringement unless the steps are carried out by the accused infringing process in the same order set forth in the claims. Thus, if sequence numbers or letters, or any indication of sequence or order are set forth in a method claim, more than likely that claim will be limited to cover only the sequence of steps in the order recited in the claim. The rule is, therefore, that the novel steps of the method claim may be recited in any order, unless a particular order is crucial for the operation of the method, or for the novelty or non-obviousness of the method.

Among the elements of method claims are acts, manipulative steps, or even thought processes which are in some cases performed upon an article. The essence of a method claim and the key to patentability in these situations involves the change of the item being worked upon to an altered condition by the new method. Steps such as "determining," "establishing," etc., are used as steps in method claims. Method claims are also required to particularly point out and distinctly claim the steps of the method the inventor considers as novel to support patentability.

When submitting your invention disclosures to a patent attorney in the future, if at all possible recommend that method claims be included where practicable, even with regard to mechanical and electrical inventions. The reason lies in a piece of legislation called the U.S. Process Patent Act of 1988. This law was created to allow U.S. courts to enforce method claims in U.S. patents against articles imported into the United States, where the articles were manufactured overseas using the method or methods encompassed by a United States patent. Prior to 1988, any article imported into the United States which did not infringe a U.S. apparatus patent did not constitute infringement of a method patent where the patented method was not performed in the United States. This 1988 legislation changed the law, and it is important to note that method claims now have a broader applicability to stop the importation of goods where an infringing process has been utilized overseas.

11.7   COMPOSITION OF MATTER CLAIMS

Very briefly, inventions and patents can be directed to new compositions of matter which are novel combinations of chemical substances. These patent claims usually are drafted in single lines setting forth the new chemical composition. Thus, these types of patents do not describe moving parts, electrical circuits, or processes of performing an act on another article. They are patents and claims directed to new compounds, using a new combination of chemical substances.

11.8   DESIGN PATENT CLAIM

A design patent includes drawings of a novel design of the non-functional features of an article of manufacture, and has a single claim which merely recites:

"The ornamental design for a (product) substantially as shown."

A design patent, as discussed in detail in Chapter 13, consists of a series of illustrations which show all the views of the particular item for which design protection is sought. The claim of the design patent will cover only the nonfunctional esthetic features of the product disclosed. Any functional features, of course, have to be covered by article patents to obtain protection.

11.9   DEPENDENT CLAIMS

In looking at a patent, you will sometimes note that certain claims depend from other claims previously recited in the patent. Any claim which depends from a previous claim is known as a "dependent claim," and is merely a shorthand way of incorporating by reference every element of the previous or base claim or claims into the new claim. Thus, if claim 2 depends upon claim 1 in a patent, claim 2 incorporates by reference all of the elements of claim 1, and adds the elements recited in claim 2. You will find, for example, that a dependent claim repeats the major elements of the preamble of the base claim, followed by words such as "as recited in claim 1."

Dependent claims are used to modify the parent claim by:

1. Adding an element not included in the parent claim; and/or
2. Qualifying an existing element of the parent claim; and/or
3. Qualifying a relationship between previously recited elements in the parent claim.

A dependent claim can also depend from a prior dependent claim. Such claim will incorporate by reference the elements of both the base claim and the intermediate claim or claims. Thus, to infringe such claim, the infringing device must incorporate all of the subject matter from the first claim and each intervening dependant claim. Care must be taken in drafting dependent claims so that the latter claims are not excessively limited by having too many elements incorporated by reference. The more elements set forth in the claim, the easier it is for a competitor to avoid infringement by eliminating or modifying one of the claimed elements.

11.10   HOW TO READ AND UNDERSTAND PATENT CLAIMS DRAFTED BY YOUR PATENT ATTORNEY

To comprehend how to read and understand patent claims, in my judgment furnishing you with a brief summary of how claims are drafted by a patent attorney is the best way to demonstrate how these arcane forms of the English language are derived. Consider for example a computer. Patent claims directed to the computer may read as follows:

1. An apparatus for storing, manipulating and displaying data upon the command of an operator, comprising:
   (a) a central processing unit including data storage disks and access elements that provide selective access to and manipulation of data stored on the disks;
   (b) a keyboard electronically connected to the access elements in the central processing unit, the keyboard having a plurality of keys which, when actuated, access and manipulate selected data stored on the disks; and

(c) a display device electronically connected to the central processing unit displaying selectively accessed data upon actuation of the keys of the keyboard.

2. The apparatus for storing, manipulating and displaying data of claim 1 wherein the display device is a plasma display screen.

3. The apparatus for storing, manipulating and displaying data of claim 1 wherein the display device is a cathode-ray tube.

I will now describe how these claims are structured, as a patent attorney would draft and view the claims.

11.10.1 Preamble

The initial portion of this claim, which reads "An apparatus for storing, manipulating and displaying data upon the command of an operator," is referred to as the "preamble" of the claim.

The preamble sets forth the category of the patentable invention that is ultimately being claimed, and includes a recitation of the purpose or object of the device in terms of results. Thus, the preamble sets forth information about the environment in which invention operates.

The preamble of my example indicates that the invention lies in an apparatus for storing, manipulating and displaying data upon the command of an operator. This lets you know, for example, that the invention is not directed to an agricultural combine, or to a chemical process. The environment of the invention is clearly set forth in the preamble.

By way of another example, where the invention sets forth a machine to perform work upon an object or a work piece, and the invention is in the combination of machine elements, the specific operation to be performed upon the work piece by the machine is clearly set out in the preamble. For example, "A machine for making paper" would be a proper preamble for a claim directed to a paper making machine. Likewise, a sample claim preamble would be: "A connector for the transmission of high voltage electricity," or "A composition for fertilizing the soil." Thus, the preamble may also set forth the intended purpose for the inventive structure.

An example of a method claim preamble would be "A method of treating a liquid mixture containing partial oxidation products of different molecular weights in the range of aldehyde fatty acids." Yet another example is "An improvement in methods for manufacturing rubber tires from molten rubber, in which the molten rubber is formed at high temperatures and subject to the application of high pressure."

11.10.2 Transition Phrase

The transition phrase of a patent claim leads from the preamble to the recitation of the specifically related elements of the claim, and uses the participle form of a verb: "comprising," "consisting of," "including," or "consisting essentially of." In the above example, in Claim 1, the transition phrase is "comprising:" in line 2. With reference to the ultimate of details, the transition phrase is separated from the preamble by a comma, and followed by a colon in accepted patent parlance. And believe it or not, the transition phrase, even though one word, substantially affects the scope of coverage of the claim.

The term "comprising" used as a transition phrase in a patent claim means the same as "including." When the transition phrase "comprising" is used, the scope of the invention set forth in the claim is "open ended" and may contain other elements besides the enumerated elements. In other words, when the word "comprised" is used as the transition phrase, it literally means "including the following elements, but not excluding other elements." Therefore, prior art having your recited elements, plus others, still invalidates your claim. Likewise, an infringing device having each of the recited elements, plus others, still infringes your claim.

To the contrary, the terms "consisting of," or "consisting essentially of" are restrictive or "closed end" transition forms, and define an embodiment of the claimed invention that is made up only of the recited elements. The sole exception is that if trace amounts or impurities of non-recited ingredients are found in a composition of matter alleged to infringe a patent claim, the trace amounts are not taken into account for the infringement analysis. These restrictive transition word forms are normally found in chemical patent claims to cover a product which can be constructed by eliminating certain previously used components, or eliminating certain steps shown in the prior art.

Therefore, it is important to ensure that your patent attorney has properly used the words "comprising" or "consisting of" in patent claims to make sure that the patent claims are not unduly restrictive.

11.10.3 The Body of the Claim

Elements   The body of the claim, which constitutes sub-paragraphs (a), (b) and (c) in the example claim above, recites the main and necessary elements of the invention, while setting forth only those minimum number of elements required to define the operable inventive combination in its workable environment. The elements are the structural parts of a machine or article, the steps of a process, or the ingredients of a composition of matter. The definition of the elements in a claim also includes a description of the structural relationship between the elements, that is, how the elements are combined, connected, operatively connected or otherwise physically associated with each other.

Functional Relationship of the Elements   The body of a patent claim also sets forth a statement of the functional relationship between each of the elements recited, describing how the elements function and cooperate in their structural relationship to form the inventive combination and to accomplish the result set forth in the preamble. Each claim should also recite a statement of those elements and features, and/or characteristics of those elements or features, which produce the beneficial results and define the novelty of the inventive combination.

Results Should Not Be in the Claim   As stated above, the elements and functional relationship of the elements are recited in the body portion of the claim to define the novel features of the invention which accomplish the beneficial results set forth in the preamble. However, results and objectives of the subject invention are not recited in the body portion of the claims. Only structure, structural relationships, and functional relationships of the elements are recited in the body of the claims. Results should be omitted, and left to the claim's preamble and to the specification portion of the patent application that appears before the claims.

Two Dependent Claims   Claims 2 and 3 of the above example are each dependent claims, which qualify an existing element of the parent claim, that is, the display device, or screen as it is commonly known. Claim 2 specifies that the display device of Claim 1 is a plasma display screen, while Claim 3 recites that the display device of claim 1 is a cathode-ray tube. Note that Claims 2 and 3 are each more limited in scope than Claim 1.

Nicolaus Otto

THE INTERNAL COMBUSTION ENGINE

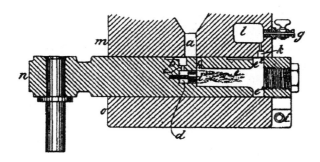

The most universal method of producing power today in both moving vehicles and in stationary factories and other facilities is the internal combustion engine. Today's internal combustion engines operate in practically the same way as the ones that were developed during the latter part of the 19th century.

The first self-propelled, over-the-road vehicles were powered by steam engines. The earliest of such vehicles was built by Nicolas J. Cugnot of France in 1769. However, steam-propelled vehicles were fueled by coal and were inefficient, and those with an interest in mechanics in the 19th century endeavored to provide more efficient power for both moving vehicles and stationary power sources. It was the invention of the four-stroke internal combustion engine, operating on liquid fuel, that provided the means for developing and producing the millions of motor vehicles in operation today.

The development of the internal combustion engine dates back, believe it or not, to the year 1680 when a Dutch physicist, Christian Huygens, designed an internal combustion engine fueled with gun powder. However, Huygens never built his engine. More than a century later, in 1807, Francois Isaac de Rivas, of Switzerland, designed an unsuccessful vehicle using an internal combustion engine powered by a blend of oxygen and hydrogen as fuel.

In 1858, a Belgian engineer, Jean Joseph Étienne Lenoir, developed and in 1860 obtained a patent on a two-stroke, coal-gas-fueled internal combustion engine using electric spark ignition. In 1863, Lenoir improved his engine, using petroleum and a carburetor, which he attached to a wagon that completed a fifty mile overland tour. This was the first workable internal combustion engine.

In 1862, Alphonse Beau de Rochas of France obtained French patent number 52,593 for a four-stroke engine. However, de Rochas never constructed this engine. In 1864, an Austrian, Siegfried Marcus, constructed a single-cylinder internal combustion engine, which he attached to a cart that completed a fifty foot tour. The modern four-cycle gaso-

Intellectual Property Law for Engineers and Scientists, by Howard B. Rockman
ISBN 0-471-44998-9 © 2004 The Institute of Electrical and Electronics Engineers

line powered internal combustion engine that is used practically universally today is primarily the creation of Nicolaus Otto. His Otto cycle engine, which was named after him, was conceived in 1861, and later constructed, successfully tested, and used in 1876.

Nicolaus August Otto was born on June 14, 1832 in Holzhausen, Germany. At the age of 16, Otto dropped out of high school and worked successfully as a clerk in a grocery store and as a traveling salesman, marketing sugar, kitchenware, and tea to grocery stores. According to his biographers, Otto took these positions to make enough money to marry the love of his life, Ann, who he met at a carnival in Cologne in 1858 when he was 26.

Throughout his selling career, Otto maintained a keen interest in mechanical devices, particularly the technology of engines related to horse drawn carriages and small factories. Kurt Rathke, in his biography of Otto, indicates that Otto was inspired in his technology dreams by watching smoke rise from a chimney while sitting on a park bench. Like all inventors and discoverers, Otto was effectively drawn into his development work by his intense characteristics of curiosity, fascination, and wonder. According to Rathke, Otto made the decision that the explosion in a gas engine, which he compared to the chimney, should receive a rich fuel mixture. Otto's idea was to allow fresh air to enter the engine first and mix with unburned gases from the previous working stroke. After that, the fuel mixture be would be inducted.

In approximately 1860, Otto learned about Lenoir's successful experiments with two-stroke internal combustion engines. However, the Lenoir engine did not achieve popular success. Not only did the engine have a less than reliable electrical ignition system, but it consumed expensive gas, almost 100 cubic feet of gas per horsepower per hour. In addition, the Lenoir engine required massive amounts of cooling water, and the heat generated usually ruined the bearings unless they were inordinately oiled; when not oiled, the engine seized. Otto concluded that the Lenoir engine would be improved if operated with a liquid, rather than gas, fuel.

While employed as a salesman in 1861, Otto had been sharing his ideas on internal combustion technology with Ugen Langen, the proprietor of a sugar factory, who was also a technician. Otto confided his ideas to Langen during his trips to Langen's shop to buy and sell sugar. In 1864–1865, Langen and Otto established N.A. Otto & Cie., the first company in the world to manufacture engines. Gottlieb Daimlar and Wilhelm Maybach later joined N.A. Otto & Cie. The company still exists today under the name Deutz AG, Köln, which remains one of the largest engine producing companies in the world. In 1867, two years after the company was formed, Langen and Otto were awarded a gold medal at the Paris World Exhibition for their development and construction of a two-stroke atmospheric gas engine. The award was given for the development of the most economical power for small businesses.

Otto, however, continued in his attempts to develop and perfect his idea of a four-stroke internal combustion, high-compression engine that would use all types of fuels and be suitable for all types of applications. In May 1876, Otto realized his ambition when he built the first practical high-compression, four-stroke liquid-fuel-powered engine with an ignition device. The engine's first stroke drew in a combustible mixture of air and fuel. The second stroke of the piston compressed the mixture, and the compressed air–fuel mixture was exploded by the ignition system. The expansion of the exploded air–fuel mixture drove the piston downward for its third stroke. The fourth stroke of the piston, moving upward, exhausted the burnt fuel, and evacuated the cylinder to begin the cycle again. Otto patented his four-cycle internal combustion engine in 1877. Due to its relative quietness, efficiency, and reliability, more than thirty thousand of Otto's engines were sold during the 10 years following its development in 1876. Gottlieb Daimlar attached Otto's engine to a bicycle to make what is considered to be the first motorcycle. Karl Benz built his first three-wheeled automobile incorporating an Otto engine. Otto never became involved directly in automobile production, but it is unquestioned that his four-stroke engine, which was the first practical alternative to the steam engine, began the era of modern automobile and heavy vehicle production.

After developing his four-stroke engine in 1876, Otto developed the first magneto engine ignition system using low voltage in 1884. In 1882, Otto, along with Alexander Graham Bell, was awarded an honorary Doctorate degree by the University of Wurzburg. Ultimately, Otto's Patent No. 365,701 on his original liquid fuel engine of 1877 was invalidated based upon the previous de Rochas patent for the four-stroke engine that Rochas never built. Thus, although Rochas put his ideas on paper, Otto was the first to build a working engine based upon the four-cycle combustion process principle. Further, on October 23, 1877, an additional patent for a liquid-fuel engine was issued to Otto and to Francis and William Crossley.

Nicolaus Otto died at age 59 on January 26, 1891 in Cologne. His engine was the prototype of internal combustion engines built from 1876 to today.

Oh, and by the way, he ultimately did make enough money to marry his sweetheart, Ann.

(No Model.)

N. A. OTTO.
GAS MOTOR ENGINE.

No. 365,701.

Patented June 28, 1887.

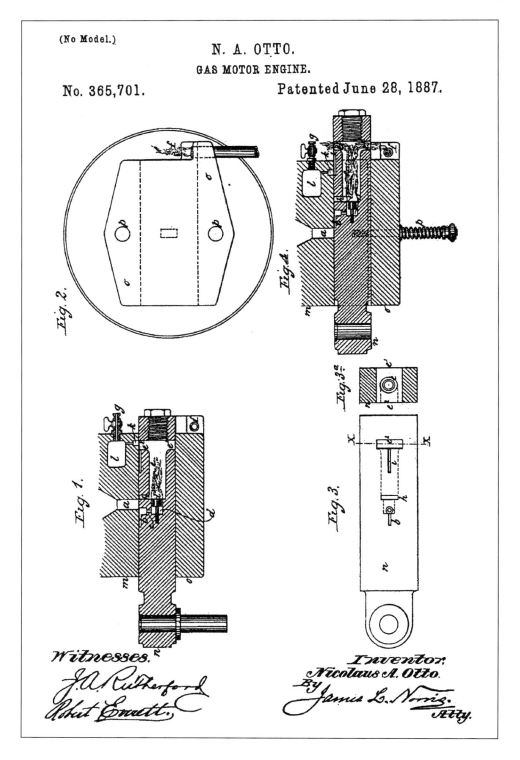

Fig. 2.

Fig. 4.

Fig. 3ª

Fig. 1.

Fig. 3.

Witnesses.
J. A. Rutherford
Robut Emett.

Inventor.
Nicolaus A. Otto.
By James L. Norris.
Atty.

Rudolf Diesel

THE INTERNAL COMBUSTION ENGINE

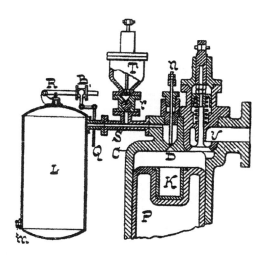

The second major inventor in the field of internal combustion engines is definitely Rudolf Diesel, who was born in Paris in 1858, the son of Bavarian immigrants. He was educated at the Munich Polytechnic School, and was employed as a refrigerator engineer after graduation. His interests, however centered upon engine design, and in 1893 he authored a treatise describing an internal combustion engine. In 1894, he filed for a patent in Germany for his new invention, named the Diesel engine. His engine exploded and nearly killed him. However, this engine was the first to prove that fuel could be ignited without an ignition spark. His first successful engine was operated in 1897. In 1898, he obtained U.S. Patent No. 608,845 for his Diesel internal combustion engine.

During his studies at the Munich Polytechnic, Diesel was inspired by a thermodynamics lecture in 1878 by Carl Linde, in which Linde espoused on the relatively poor efficiency of steam engines, and made comparisons to the theory by the French physicist Sadi Carnot, whose cyclic pressure and volume process foresaw higher energy efficiencies in power production. It is reported that Diesel made a lecture note to study whether it was possible to fully realize the Carnot cycle. The result of his lifetime of studies was to be the Diesel engine, which even today is the internal combustion engine having the highest degree of efficiency.

After completing his studies, Diesel returned to Paris where for about 10 years he was the manager of the French branch of the German Linde Ice Machine Company. In 1890, he returned to Berlin where he took over management of Linde's technical office. One day, Diesel noticed a pneumatic cigarette lighter in which small pieces of tinder were held in a small glass tube. A piston was used to compress the air in the tube, and the tinder glowed. This vision started him on the path to developing the Diesel engine.

During this time, Diesel's obsession with creating an efficient internal combustion engine led him to file a patent application, which issued on February 23, 1983—German Patent No. 67207, entitled "Working Method and Design for Combustion Engines." This patent application was based upon Diesel's theoretical ideas, and he realized that to reduce these theories to practical use required substantial resources. He sought support from several companies, one of them being Machinenfabrik Augsburg-Nurenberg (MAN), of Germany. With funding from MAN and others, Diesel began his own business and used the MAN facilities to develop his engine. As early as July 1893, he completed a test engine in Augsburg, which could not run on its own. He then built a second prototype in the summer of 1894 which did function and was 16.6% efficient, but was not suitable for Diesel's intended uses. On New Years Eve of 1896, the third Augsburg prototype of his engine was demonstrated, with a theoretical mechanical efficiency of over 75%.

Diesel's work leading up to the development of these engines began with the second law of thermodynamics and the maximum efficiency espoused for the Carnot cycle. Thus, Diesel began his work to enhance existing internal combustion engines of the day based upon purely theoretical considerations, using natural physical processes to provide the necessary heat transfer. In 1893, he wrote a famous thesis entitled "Theory for the Construction of a Rational Thermal Engine to Replace the Steam Engine and Other Internal Combustion Engines Currently in Use." Diesel's hypothesis embodied raising the temperature of pure air to an extremely high degree through aggressive adiabatic compression in a piston/cylinder engine. As the pistons started to descend, fuel would enter the cylinder in exact quantities at the proper time and self-ignite. The heat of combustion at any time would replace the heat lost through expansion. Thus, the total energy in the fuel during the expansion phase would be converted to mechanical energy, and no heat would be wasted. This theory was based on the closed Carnot cycle implementation, including the compression phase, to determine the efficiency of the engine.

Diesel's self-ignition principle was considered to be embedded in thermodynamic considerations. Self-ignition occurred during the compression phase when maximum pressure was realized at the beginning of isothermal expansion, leading to higher temperatures in the cylinder. Thus, the injected fuel spontaneously ignited at these high temperatures. Diesel considered using pulverized coal as fuel, in addition to other elements such as gas, petroleum, peanut oil, and even hemp.

Over his years of development, Diesel ran into many problems with his engine, one of which was fuel injection. For example, the air compression and injection system in the Diesel engine meant the injection of heavy and space-consuming aggregate.

In 1893, the Diesel engine was not considered suitable as a motor vehicle propulsion system. The Otto internal combustion engine, which required a spark to ignite the air–fuel mixture, used an externally supplied ignition system. Meanwhile, the Diesel engine ignited on its own when the air in the cylinder was compressed and heated, so that the fuel introduced just before the compression stroke ignited in the hot air. This fundamental difference between the Otto engine and the Diesel engine resulted in greater weight and dimension requirements for the Diesel engine. Thus, the initial Diesel engines were only suitable for static power sources when they were first successfully developed. The main reason for the size and weight differential was that the introduction of the fuel into the cylinder in a Diesel engine under high pressure required that the fuel be induced using pressurized air, which was possible only with pumps or pressure inducers that were not only heavy, but also part of the engine.

Diesel originally thought that the efficient small engine that he would develop would enable independent artisans and craftsmen to compete effectively against competition from large industries that monopolized the power source industry, which at that time was powered by the oversized and expensive fuel-wasting steam engine. Diesel never realized his goal of using his engine to assist small businessmen. Instead, large industries quickly adopted his engine, and Diesel became wealthy from his royalties.

Diesel's work in developing his engine was not without controversy. He had persuaded professors at a number of universities that his ideas, although theoretical, were valid. However, many of these professors were more practice-oriented than their counterparts at the newer, theoretically oriented technical universities. A chasm erupted between those who favored fundamental theory and those who favored technical applications.

Diesel worked from 1893 to 1897 developing his engine at MAN. After 1897, Diesel figured that he had completed his engine, and turned to marketing it. However, it was not ready for the market and needed eleven more years of improvement through the help of additional engineers. During this process, he apparently was not very hospitable to other engine designers, and derided their work.

Diesel ran into problems not only in the interface between thermodynamics and mechanical engineering but because, in the late 19th century, practical material applications lacked a sound material science basis. The Diesel engine required materials that could withstand heavy stresses caused by high pressures attained during the combustion stages. Thus, one of Diesel's research projects led him to read an entire book on the material science of machine elements by Carl Bach. This analysis took almost a year, and delayed his development of the Diesel engine by an equal amount of time. Diesel did use the information from the Bach text to achieve the calculations and dimensioning of the different components of his engine.

Even now, due to the weight and noise of Diesel engines, their use is primarily limited to stationary power-developing machines and in ships, trucks, submarines, and larger utility vehicles. It was not until 1920 that the Diesel engine, with an injection pump delivering a metered amount of fuel into the combustion chambers, gained acceptance in vehicle manufacture, and it was not until 1936 that Daimler-Benz unveiled the first real Diesel passenger car. Because of its low fuel consumption and sturdiness, the Diesel engine made an ideal taxicab engine. Long after the Second World War, the heaviness, low performance, and low driving comfort of Diesel-equipped automobiles made them second choice for consumers compared to the engine that Otto developed. During the first oil crisis of 1973–1974, the Diesel engine gained a greater share of the automobile market. However, as long as relatively low gasoline prices prevail, it appears that the Otto cycle engine will outsell the Diesel cycle engine in the passenger automotive field.

The criticisms that were aimed at Diesel seemed to have had an effect on him. Many felt that it was the development work following his early theoretical efforts that actually achieved the successful working of a Diesel engine. Diesel himself felt that the Diesel engine was his idea and that he was the one who gave it its start. Apparently, Diesel failed to see that his engine was made viable by the addition of inventive thinking by many additional bright engineers. In September, 1913, Rudolf Diesel boarded the mail ship Dresden sailing from Antwerp to Harwich, England across the English Channel. He was not seen departing from the boat when it landed and he was never seen again after that. His disappearance is one of the great mysteries of the modern era. There have been many stories told about plots against Diesel; however, the majority opinion of those who have investigated the subject matter concludes that he committed suicide.

During my research, I came across what I consider to be an interesting footnote. Diesel expected that his engine would be powered by vegetable oils, including hemp, as well as seed oils. It appears that at the 1900 World Fair, Diesel ran his engines on peanut oil and that Henry Ford, at one time, demonstrated that automobiles equipped with Diesel engines could run on hemp. Pollution abatement was important to Diesel and he saw his engine as reducing the pollution formed by the petroleum engines of his time. The report that I read indicated that heavy moneyed interests who were invested in timber and petroleum resources saw hemp-operated engines as a threat to their investments.

As most of you know, hemp, or *Cannabis sativa,* is the same plant that produces the controlled substance, psychoactive marijuana. Hemp has been used from the dawn of history for food, clothing, building materials, medicine, and, of importance to this discussion, fuel. In the 1920s and 1930s in the United States, reformers heated up the movement to ban the possession and use of marijuana, and the hemp plant from which it originated. Also, the petrochemical and pulp–paper industries of that time would have faced stiff competition if hemp's commercial potential were fully developed. For example, major chemical companies had developed and patented fuel additives such as tetraethyl lead and the sulfite and sulfate methods for producing pulp paper and many synthetic products.

Meanwhile, potential competitors were developing synthetic products from renewable biomass origins, including hemp. The hemp decorticator patented by George W. Schlichten in 1919, U.S. Patent No. 1,308,376, potentially could eliminate a large portion of the need for wood pulp paper. Consider that drafts of the United States Declaration of Independence and Constitution were written on hemp paper. At least one car manufacturer announced its aim to replace products made from petroleum hydrocarbons with products produced from cannabis carbohydrates. To counter this prospective competition, those who had a vested interest in the petrochemical and pulp paper processing industries lobbied the United States Treasury Department for the prohibition of cannabis, or hemp.

Since hemp was a local crop, the United States Congress could control only interstate or international shipments of hemp. Efforts to have each state pass a uniform law banning the production of hemp failed in all but 10 states by 1935. However, with continued pressure by "reformers" and certain moneyed interests, with less than three month's deliberation, the United States Congress ultimately passed the Marijuana Tax Act, which imposed a prohibitive transfer tax and an excise tax upon certain dealings in marijuana, including hemp seed and hemp oil. The legislation was signed by President Roosevelt on August 2, 1937.

For more excellently enumerated details on why there is no present movement to adopt hemp oil as a fuel for diesel engines, I refer you to "The Great Book of Hemp," by Rowan Robinson (Park Street Press, Rochester, VT, 1996).

Diesel was looking for an engine to approach the thermodynamic limit established by Carnot in 1824. His object was to expand the fuel in the cylinder at constant pressure. He patented this concept in 1892, while working for Linde in Berlin. This meant that his engines had to run at low speeds, with limited power. Diesel insisted that they be run this way, which delayed their successful development. Although Rudolf Diesel was not able to realize the theoretical Carnot cycle in his engine, which was his idea from the very beginning, he did create the most efficient internal combustion machine that, to date, remains the internal combustion engine that operates most economically compared to all others.

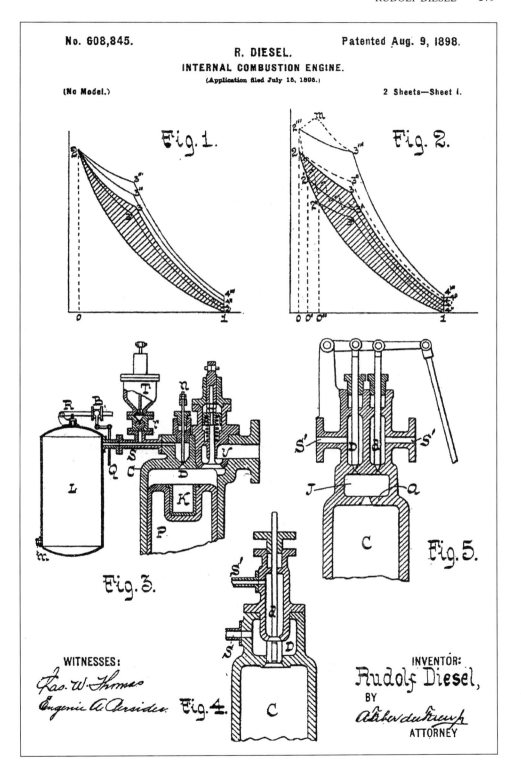

No. 608,845.

R. DIESEL.

Patented Aug. 9, 1898.

INTERNAL COMBUSTION ENGINE.

(Application filed July 15, 1895.)

(No Model.)

2 Sheets—Sheet 1.

Fig. 1.   Fig. 2.

Fig. 3.   Fig. 5.

Fig. 4.

WITNESSES:

Jas. W. Thomas

Eugenie A. Arsides

INVENTOR:

Rudolf Diesel,

BY

Arthur du Frarp

ATTORNEY

12 Prosecution of a Patent Application

12.1 U.S. PATENT EXAMINATION PROCESS

Once your patent application is filed with the U.S. Patent & Trademark Office, it is examined for compliance with technical filing requirements, novelty and non-obviousness. An examiner will report the results of the examination to your patent attorney, or directly to you if you have filed your application on your own. In most cases, the application will not be allowed after this first report, and you and your attorney will be required to confer to review the patent examiner's action, and to file a response that overcomes the examiner's objections and/ or rejections. This back and forth process may continue over several exchanges between your attorney and the examiner. The purpose of this chapter is to provide you with information regarding the patent examination process, which in turn will enable you to understand the content of the report from the examiner, and how to assist your attorney in preparing a persuasive response, and obtain issuance of your patent.

12.2 THE PATENT EXAMINATION SYSTEM—A LITTLE MORE HISTORY

This chapter starts after your patent application has been completed and reviewed, you signed the formal papers, and the application was forwarded for examination by a patent examiner, who is an employee of the U.S. Patent & Trademark Office, a federal agency. The patent examination process that takes place today is, in substance, the same as the procedure established by Senator Ruggles' Patent Act of 1836—except for the short time in the late 1800s that the Commissioner of Patents closed the Patent Office, since he believed that nothing further of any use could be invented. Also recall that prior to 1952, the patent examiners only examined a claimed invention for novelty. It wasn't until the 1952 Patent Act that non-obviousness was made a statutory requirement for the issuance of a patent by the U.S. Patent Office, as it was called then.

12.3 FILING THE PATENT APPLICATION WITH THE U.S. PATENT AND TRADEMARK OFFICE

Upon arriving at the U.S. Patent & Trademark Office, your patent application receives a filing date and is assigned an application serial number. When the application issues as a patent it receives a patent number, which is different than, and unrelated to, the application serial number. The filing date is the date your application was remitted by express

Intellectual Property Law for Engineers and Scientists, by Howard B. Rockman
ISBN 0-471-44998-9 © 2004 The Institute of Electrical and Electronics Engineers

courier, such as the Express Mail service of the U.S. Postal Service, to the United States Patent & Trademark Office, not the date the application was actually received. Thus, using an express courier service to file your application allows you to obtain an earlier filing date than if other means of transmittal are used.

The assigned filing date establishes the effective filing date of the application, which also establishes an invention priority date, which is important in defining prior art, in perfecting foreign patent rights, and in establishing certain priority rights if another application claiming somewhat the same invention as yours, is filed close in time to your application. Also, once the application receives a filing date, the running of any statutory bar period stops, and commercialization and public disclosure of the invention can begin without fear of losing U.S. or foreign patent rights as a result of the statutory bar or public disclosure restraints discussed previously. The serial number and filing date also serve to identify and provide access to the patent application by the patent examiner and by your patent attorney during the examination and prosecution of the application. Note also that sole inventors, small groups of inventors, and those inventors not under any obligation to assign their invention and patents to a company or entity having more than 500 employees are entitled to reduced government filing, issue and other fees charged by the United States Patent & Trademark Office for examining and issuing patents.

After your patent application is granted a serial number and filing date, the application is assigned to an Art Unit of the Patent & Trademark Office, which comprises a group of patent examiners who handle patent applications in the technology area to which your application is directed. Once in the appropriate Art Unit, the application is placed on the docket of (assigned to) an individual patent examiner who has a technical degree and expertise in the technology of your invention, and who has examined many other patent applications in the same genre of technology. Due to the backlog of patent applications awaiting examination by the corps of patent examiners, it may take from 8 months to 2 years for your application to reach its initial examination. After examining your application, the patent examiner prepares a written report of the examination results, and forwards the report to your attorney. Your attorney will notify you of the content of the report, and you and your attorney will discuss an appropriate response to the examination report. Both the examination process and the response process are discussed later in this chapter at Sections 12.4 to 12.6.

Patent applications filed prior to November 29, 2000 remain in secrecy until they issue as a patent. Those patent applications filed after November 29, 2000 are published prior to issuance eighteen (18) months after their filing date, unless the applicant or his/her attorney states in writing upon filing the application that there is no present intention of filing foreign counterpart patent applications. If the applicant later changes his/her mind, the U.S. Patent & Trademark Office is so notified, and the U.S. patent application is published at the eighteenth month date, or thereafter if that point in time has passed. Currently, the U.S. Patent & Trademark Office is electronically publishing patent applications eighteen months after filing, and not on paper. That procedure may or may not change in the future.

Keep in mind, therefore, that the novelty search conducted prior to filing your patent application will not uncover pending patent applications that are maintained in secrecy by the U.S. Patent & Trademark Office until they issue. By logging on to the U.S. Patent & Trademark Office website (www.uspto.gov), you and/or your patent attorney or searcher can access those patent applications published upon reaching eighteen months of pendency, where no intent to forego foreign patent application filings has been noted in the record of the patent application.

12.4 EXAMINATION OF THE PATENT APPLICATION

Upon reaching a new (not previously examined) patent application, the patent examiner reviews the application to ensure that three primary criteria are met. First the patent examiner verifies that all technical filing requirements have been met. For example, is there a complete specification with at least one claim? Are drawings present, if drawings are described in the specification? Is a signed Declaration or Oath in the file? Has the fee been paid? Has the patent application been assigned to the proper Art Unit? Is one invention or more than one distinct invention claimed in the application? Is the specification in understandable English, and are the claims clearly worded and in proper form, for example, proper multiple dependency? Discrepancies sometimes occur in patent applications initially drafted abroad to be filed first in a foreign country, which applications are then translated and filed in the U.S. Patent & Trademark Office in the format of the first filed country. These discrepancies are normally corrected in the response of your patent attorney to the first communication from the patent examiner, as will be explained further in Section 12.6.

Second, the patent examiner ensures that the claimed invention falls into one of the categories of patentable subject matter set forth in 35 U.S.C. 101. For example, if the invention is set forth in the claims in purely conceptual terms, with no structure or function to embody or define the invention, the application will be rejected. An example would be a claim which reads: "A fibrous cloth having a tendency to wear rough rather than smooth." In addition, if the patent examiner, based upon his/her expertise in the related technical field, deems that the claimed or described invention will not work for its intended use, or if the invention has no use at all, the application will be rejected. Additional non-statutory, and thus non-patentable subject matter includes:

1. Printed matter;
2. Naturally occurring articles, such as a shrimp with the head and digestive tract removed;
3. Scientific principles; and
4. Inventions concerned with atomic energy, which are dealt with in the U.S. Atomic Energy Act.

Several years ago, methods of doing business and software algorithms were on the above list. However, these two categories are now defined as patentable subject matter. The same is true for genetically modified living creatures.

Third, the patent examiner determines whether the claims of the application define an invention which is novel and non-obvious compared to the prior art. Recall that filed with your patent application is the Information Disclosure Statement, and copies of all prior art you and your attorney are aware of that could be material at this stage of examination of your claimed invention. After reading your specification and claims to the point of understanding what the claims define as novel about your invention, the patent examiner determines the appropriate class and subclass of the prior art which should be searched to uncover issued patents and published articles related to your claimed invention. The relevant prior art is stored and classified in a search area within the confines of the patent examiner's Art Unit and on computer data bases. The examiner next searches the relevant classes and subclasses to determine the closest related prior art, using state-of-the-art electronic search databases to assist in conducting the search. If deemed necessary, the patent examiner also searches analogous prior art classes and subclasses to possibly find references relating to portions or details of your claimed invention to be combined with references found in the initial search. For example, during my term as a patent examiner, the automatic vehicle transmissions in my area of technology responsibility incorporated parallel systems of planetary gear sets, with brakes and clutches controlling the braking or movement of single or multiple elements of the gear sets. On numerous occasions, I consulted with examiners in the brake art and in the clutch art to determine the novelty, or lack thereof, of brake and clutch elements embodied in the transmission claimed in a patent application I was examining. When deemed necessary, I extended my search to the analogous brake and/or clutch classes and subclasses.

The search by the patent examiner is conducted to determine whether the submitted claims in your application define an invention which is totally shown or taught in a single prior art reference under 35 U.S.C. §102, or whether your claimed invention would be obvious to one of ordinary skill in the related art, as concluded from the content of a combination of two or more prior art references under 35 U.S.C. §103.

12.5 RESULTS OF THE EXAMINATION ARE REPORTED IN AN "OFFICE ACTION"

Upon completing the examination of your patent application, the patent examiner is required by the Patent Statute to prepare a written report of the results of the examination, including furnishing copies of all prior art references cited in the examination report with the exception of those prior art references furnished to the examiner with your Information Disclosure Statement. This examination report is commonly known as an "Office Action," and is forwarded to your patent attorney, or to the applicant in the rare case where the inventor is not represented by an attorney. Where your patent application has been prepared and filed by your patent attorney, and you have executed a Power of Attorney, the patent examiner will communicate only with your attorney, who reviews the Office Action upon receiving same.

The Office Action must set forth in detail the patent examiner's position on all of the claims in your application regarding novelty and/or obviousness issues, and present comments on other technical matters that must be corrected to place the patent application in proper form. The U.S. Patent & Trademark Office rules require that the Office Action be complete, and that it clearly set forth all reasons supporting the examiner's decisions. The purpose of this clarity requirement is that upon receipt of the Office Action, the applicant and his/her attorney must decide, based upon the examiner's comments, whether it is worthwhile to continue with the expenditure of resources to further the prosecution of the patent application. In many instances, the examiner will suggest language changes in the claims that in the examiner's opinion may assist in defining your invention over the prior art, or which may overcome some technical objection to a portion of the application.

Since a patent application is normally written with claims that attempt to define the invention in the broadest possible terms to elicit citation by the patent examiner of the most relevant prior art, most patent applications do not result in allowance of the claims or issued patents upon the first examination. Therefore, expect the first Office Action to normally be a "rejection." Actually, in the vast majority of patent applications, the examiners reject all, or some, of the claims in the first Office Action. Not to worry, however. Read on to find out how such rejections are responded to and overcome!

12.6   YOUR AND YOUR ATTORNEY'S RESPONSE TO THE OFFICE ACTION

Upon your attorney's receipt of the Office Action from the patent examiner, he can be expected to quickly review the claims, the Office Action, and the prior art cited and applied by the patent examiner. The purpose is to determine whether or not the cited prior art can be overcome by proper amendment and/or argument back to the patent examiner, or whether the prior art so closely resembles the claimed invention that in the patent attorney's opinion, patent protection may not obtainable.

A copy of the Office Action and all cited and applied prior art, as well as the attorney's comments are then forwarded to the inventor for review, and to determine if the inventor still is interested in protecting the invention. The first inquiry is whether the client desires to pursue the patenting process, since it is quite possible that in the 8 to 12 months it took the U.S. Patent & Trademark Office to act upon the patent application, the invention may no longer be of importance to the applicant, and thus the expenditure of further resources on patent prosecution should be ended. Note also that since the term of a patent dates from its filing date, and not its issue date, and enforcement of the patent cannot begin until the issue date, it is important that you receive from your patent attorney the Office Action and any relevant comments at the earliest possible time so that no delay is encountered in ultimate issuance of the patent.

The letter to you accompanying the Office Action and prior art furnished by your attorney should also request your input as to whether or not the prior art can be overcome based upon your review. You will be requested to examine the prior art in detail, and to furnish the patent attorney with all differences between the prior art and your invention in structure, function, and/or results obtained. In most instances, you as the inventor can observe several specific differences between your invention and the prior art that escaped the eyes of the patent attorney. If necessary, you can confer with the patent attorney directly to obtain a further understanding of the content of the prior art cited and applied by the patent examiner in examining the claims of your patent application.

If you and your employer have decided that it is advantageous to continue with the prosecution of the application, a response must be furnished to the patent examiner within three months. An additional three months can be "purchased" from the Patent & Trademark Office in one month increments, however it is the normal practice of the patent attorney to respond to the patent examiner within the initial three months to avoid unnecessary costs. Delaying beyond the three month period only increases the expense of prosecution. Note also that an extension of time up to six months is the maximum response time allowed. If the patent examiner has not received a response within that six month period, the patent application goes abandoned, and further difficulty and expense may be incurred in trying to resurrect the abandoned application.

Recall that in the Office Action, the patent examiner may have determined that the invention itself, compared to the prior art, is just not patentable. Or, the examiner may have recognized that the patent specification does describe a patentable invention, and the only argument is over the form and scope of the claims, which the examiner may determine read on the prior art based upon the examiner's interpretation of that prior art. Ultimately, it is the purpose of your response to have the patent examiner recognize both the existence of a patentable invention, and confirm that the form and scope of the claims adequately define that patentable invention over the content of the prior art. Keep in mind also that if the patent examiner is not ultimately satisfied about the patentability of your claimed invention, an appeal process is also available.

Upon your receipt of the Office Action and prior art from your patent attorney, you should immediately review these materials to determine what type of response will be necessary to overcome the examiner's position. For example, you may have personal knowledge of one of the devices disclosed in the prior art, and also have personal knowledge that the disclosed device is inoperative, or functions poorly. To submit that information to the patent examiner, a Declaration or Affidavit from you may be necessary. Since it will take time to prepare such Declaration or Affidavit, the patent attorney should be notified shortly after your review of the prior art that you have noticed this discrepancy in the prior art, and that a Declaration or Affidavit should be prepared. Also, if there are any other comments that you desire to place in the record of the patent application in support of patentability, a Declaration or Affidavit setting forth your comments should also be prepared.

After reviewing the Office Action, discuss with your patent attorney the possible benefits of interviewing the examiner, in person or by phone, to limit or clarify the rejections and/or objections lodged against your application. This may lead to a clearer understanding of how the examiner reads the prior art, and may avoid the necessity of making unnecessary limiting amendments to your claims, or making written comments in response to the Office Action that later may limit the scope of your claim language.

In responding to the patent examiner's position, it may be advisable to amend the claims to limit their scope to overcome the prior art. This can be accomplished so long as the amendments do not introduce any new matter or new material into the patent application. Conversely, it may be the position of you and your attorney that the patent examiner has completely misinterpreted the prior art, and that the prior art references cited by the examiner do not in any way anticipate or render obvious your claimed invention. In such case, the response to the patent examiner may not be an amendment to the claims, but may instead proffer strenuous arguments showing the technical reasoning why the patent examiner's interpretation of the prior art is incorrect. In a section headed REMARKS in the response to the Office Action, comments and arguments are made in support of your position of allowability of the claims in the application, whether they have been amended or whether they remain the same. In addition, amendments may be made to the claims to eliminate any discerned ambiguity or indefiniteness noticed by the patent examiner.

It is important to use the minimum number of arguments in supporting amendments to your claims, since the old expression that anything you say may be held against you is particularly true in patent prosecution. For example, if you strenuously argue that your patent claims a coil spring as a resilient element to avoid a showing in a prior art reference, and a potential infringer later uses a spongy material as a resilient element, your patent may be limited to the coil spring and not be construed to encompass the spongy material. Therefore, the patent attorney and the inventor should be careful in the language they choose in responding to the patent examiner so as not to add limitations to the scope of the claims that are unintentional.

It is also important to ensure that the arguments made in your response to the patent examiner relate to subject matter that is recited in the claims of your patent. It is the claims that define the invention, not the patent specification, and the differences between the prior art and your invention must be recited in those claims, and those differences should be pointed out to the examiner in your response to the Office Action.

You as the inventor should assure yourself that when the claims of your patent application are amended, the patent attorney has not unduly limited the scope of your invention. Therefore, I recommend that you instruct your patent attorney to furnish you with a copy of the amendments to the claims that he or she suggests sending back to the patent examiner in response to the Office Action, so that you may determine whether you can "design around" the claims as amended. If you can easily get around these claims, then changes will have to be made again so that your invention is not unduly limited by the amended claims.

The response to the Office Action also corrects any technical errors in the filing requirements that the examiner notes, as well as any typographical errors or other errors that are encompassed within the four corners of the patent application.

Keep in mind that the patent examination process should not be deemed an adversarial process. The examiners adhere to the policy of wanting to issue claims. You and your patent attorney or agent just have to convince the examiner that you are not asking for more claim coverage than you deserve in view of the point art.

12.7   FURTHER PATENT PROSECUTION

Following you and your attorney's response to the initial Office Action of the patent examiner, the examiner may issue a second Office Action rejecting the same claims, or finding that some previously rejected claims still fail to define novelty or non-obviousness over the prior art, while other claims have been found allowable. Or, the examiner may issue a Notice of Allowance indicating that the examiner has found that all claims in the application, including those that have been amended, define a patentable invention over the prior art. In this latter case, the application will subsequently issue as a patent after the "Issue Fee" has been submitted to the U.S. Patent & Trademark Office.

In those cases where the second Office Action reports that certain of the claims still fail to define your invention over the prior art, this Office Action may be designated a "final" rejection, which isn't really final. You and your attorney have one more chance to respond to the final rejection, either amending the claims or furnishing arguments in response to the comments of the patent examiner in the Final Office Action, or both. If you and your attorney are persuasive in this "Amendment After Final," the application will be allowed by the examiner by withdrawing his/her objection and rejection of the claims, and ultimately your patent will issue.

If you and your attorney's response to the Final Office Action is not persuasive you may 1) pay an additional filing fee and continue the prosecution of the patent application by submitting further arguments and amendments in an attempt to change the examiner's position, or 2) let the application become abandoned. Or a third option, where you conclude that the patent examiner is in error, such as in his or her interpretation of the content of one or more of the prior art references, is to file an appeal before the U.S. Patent & Trademark Office Board of Appeals and Interferences. This board has the authority to overturn the patent examiner based upon the persuasive arguments of your patent attorney, which you play a major role in preparing. If the patent examiner is overturned by the Board of Appeals and Interferences in his or her rejection or objection to the claims, ultimately your patent will issue.

12.8   ISSUANCE OF THE PATENT

After all of the claims remaining in the patent application have been allowed by the patent examiner, and all technical matters in the application have been taken care of, such as the correction of typographical errors, for example, a Notice of Allowance is transmitted by the patent examiner to your attorney, along with a notification that the Issue Fee must be paid within a certain time period. Also, the Notice of Allowance may require that formal drawings of your invention be submitted, if the application was originally filed with informal drawings which did not comply with the U.S. Patent & Trademark Office requirements for illustrating the invention.

Upon compliance with the requirements noted in the Notice of Allowance, the patent application is advanced to be printed, sealed and issued as a U.S. Patent. At this point, your patent application stands in line behind other previously issued patents also waiting to be printed. Your application waits in this line for approximately 8–12 weeks before issuing as a patent, reminiscent of the line at Space Mountain at Disney World.

The Patent Statute, at 35 U.S.C. §282, decrees that once a U.S. Patent issues following the examination procedure, the issued patent is presumed by law to be a valid patent. Further, the law states that each claim of the issued patent shall be presumed valid independently of the validity of the other claims, whether they are dependent claims or not. Also, a dependent claim shall be presumed valid even though it may depend upon an invalid claim. The law is strict that the burden of establishing invalidity of a patent or any claim of a patent shall rest on the party asserting such invalidity.

The presumption of validity of a patent means that an accused infringer has the burden of establishing by "competent evidence" that the patent is not valid, usually as a defense to a charge of infringement in a lawsuit. As mentioned previously, this "competent evidence" presented by the alleged infringer must be prior art material that has not previously been seen by the patent examiner during the prosecution of the asserted patent. Again, this highlights the importance of having the patent examiner review all of the prior art that you can present to the examiner, so that the presumption of validity of the patent is ultimately strengthened.

Note also that, under the law, a presumption is a fact that stands only until it is successfully rebutted. Therefore, even though the issued patent is presumed valid, an alleged infringer in a lawsuit is permitted to present evidence of prior art not previously seen by the patent examiner in an attempt to overcome the presumption of validity. If the alleged infringer is successful, the patent will ultimately be held invalid, and the infringer will not be held liable for any acts of infringement of the invalid patent.

12.9 INFRINGEMENT DURING DEPENDENCY OF THE PATENT

A patent cannot be enforced against an alleged infringer until the patent has issued from the U.S. Patent & Trademark Office. However, a procedure has been established within the Patent & Trademark Office to advance examination of your patent application where an alleged infringement has been noticed on the horizon. Therefore, where you and/or your company discover that someone is producing and marketing a product which is potentially infringing the claims of your pending patent application, it is important for you to advise your patent attorney immediately. At that point, your attorney will examine the potentially infringing product, determine whether the claims of your pending application cover that particular product, and if the answer is yes, a "Petition to Make Special" will be prepared and filed with the U.S. Patent & Trademark Office requesting the authorities at the Patent & Trademark Office to instruct the examiner to expedite examination and issuance of your patent application.

Note also that your patent application may not contain claims that read on the potentially infringing device, but the specification of your application may be written so that claims can be amended or added that would cover the infringing device, without adding "new matter" to your patent application. Your attorney then will prepare new or amended claims to cover the infringing device, assuming such new claims (1) will not read on the prior art, and (2) are supported by the disclosure of the originally filed patent application.

If the U.S. Patent & Trademark Office first determines that the evidence submitted in your Petition to Make Special warrants expedited examination of the application, the Examiner will be so advised. The Examiner will then act on your case out of order, and provide you with an immediate examination and Office Action. This examination may result in a further rejection of your claims, and it will then be incumbent upon you and your attorney to respond to the patent examiner as quickly as possible to maintain the expedited examination process.

Although you have created an expedited examination process, it will take some time to issue the patent, since the patent examination process cannot be completed immediately. For example, one of my clients had a patent application pending three years ago, and noticed an infringement, as a matter of fact several infringements, in the market. We filed our Petition to Make Special, and it still took three years of arguing with the patent examiner and ultimately having the examiner overturned by the Board of Appeals and Interferences before the patent issued. When the patent issued, the infringers agreed to stop manufacturing the product covered by the patent, after a free ride on my client's technology for three years.

Note also that once the issue fee is paid and the patent application is set in line to be printed as a patent, that printing process takes eight to twelve weeks, and nothing on this earth can change that. Ultimately, however, your patent will issue and all alleged infringements that can be proven will have to stop.

12.10   ADDITIONAL PROBABLE PATENT PROSECUTION EVENTS

12.10.1   Continuation Patent Applications

As stated previously, you and your attorney may not obtain allowance of all the claims following the second action upon your application by the patent examiner. A continuation application is a procedural vehicle which is used to continue the prosecution of the patent application after the final rejection, and the refusal of the examiner to allow the application after the response to the final rejection. Also, a continuation application can be filed at any other time during prosecution of your application, however, this is normally unnecessary until after a final rejection. The rationale behind filing a continuation application is, in my opinion, that for the fee you pay initially, you are entitled to two Office Actions and consideration of one amendment after the Final Office Action. At this point, if the examiner decides that the application is not yet in condition for allowance, you must file a continuation application and pay a new filing fee to be entitled to further prosecution. In other words, for your initial filing fee, you get two bites at the apple. For an additional fee, you obtain more bites.

Technically, a continuation application, or a request for continuing prosecution, is defined as the second patent application for the same invention claimed and disclosed in the first or parent application, where the continuation application is placed on file before the first, or parent, patent application becomes abandoned, has issued as a patent, or has otherwise had proceedings terminated. The continuation application is afforded the benefit of the earlier filing date, or priority date, of the parent application. This is important, since by the time a continuation application has been filed, the invention may have been placed in public use by the inventor. Therefore, if the continuation application were not granted the benefit of the earlier filing date, the continuation application may not meet the requirement that the application be filed within one year of public use or sale of the disclosed invention. Note also that no new matter may be inserted into the continuation application that is not included in the original application.

One other point bears mentioning. As a result of the examination process of your patent application, certain broad claims may still be facing rejection, while more limited claims may have been allowed. If you have a reasonable basis for concluding that your broad claims do define patentable subject matter over the prior art, and that these claims do define important technology, it may be advisable to file a continuation patent application containing only those yet non-allowed claims, and to have the first, or parent application issue with the more limited claims. You can then continue to persuade the examiner that the non-allowed claims in your continuation application are allowable over the prior art applied by the examiner, and that your second application with the broader claims should also issue as a patent. In this case, it is permissible to have two patents covering the same invention, one with broad claims, and one with narrower claims. Both of these patents will expire on the same day, for example, 20 years from the filing date of the original, or parent, patent application.

12.10.2 Continuation-in-Part Patent Applications

A continuation-in-part patent application is one filed during the pendency of any earlier filed patent application, and which includes new subject matter which is not disclosed in the earlier application, and which would constitute new matter if attempted to be added to the earlier or parent application. The continuation-in-part application repeats substantially most of the parent application, and adds drawings, descriptive material and claims regarding the new subject matter in the application. A continuation-in-part application effectively ends up with two application filing dates: one for the originally disclosed subject matter which dates back to the original parent application, and a new filing date pertaining to the added material.

12.10.3 Divisional Patent Applications

The Patent Statutes and U.S. Patent & Trademark Office policy require that one patent is issued for every one invention. If more than one invention is disclosed in a patent application upon filing, the examiner uses a form of objection designated a Restriction Requirement to compel the inventor and the attorney to comply with this policy. Thus, if two or more independent and distinct inventions are claimed in one patent application, the Commissioner of Patents may require the application to be restricted to one of the inventions for examination. You will receive this action from the patent examiner when there is no disclosed relationship between two or more claimed inventions in an application, or when the inventions are related but are capable of separate use and are patentably distinguishable.

Although one invention may be claimed in a single patent application, a reasonable number of species or varying embodiments of the single invention may be described and claimed in the application if there is an allowable generic claim covering all of the species or embodiments.

In response to a restriction requirement by the examiner, the inventor's attorney elects one of the inventions for continued prosecution in the parent application. The claims to non-elected inventions are withdrawn from further consideration. Ultimately, before the originally filed application issues as a patent on the elected invention, a second or divisional patent application is filed including the non-elected claims to the separate and distinctive invention or inventions. That application then proceeds ultimately towards issue or abandonment. If that application issues, the inventor then has two patents covering each of the inventions. In certain instances, more than two inventions can be filed in an initial application, and several restriction requirements are requested by the examiner. In that case, it is possible that a multitude of patents may issue from the single originally filed patent application.

It is a common practice amongst the patent profession to file a patent application knowing ahead of time that there may be several inventions set forth and claimed in the application, and that ultimately divisional patent applications will be required. It is more expeditious and usually less expensive to group the inventions in a single application initially, obtain an early filing date, and deal with the separate invention issue and divisional applications as prosecution of the applications proceeds.

12.11 RE-EXAMINATION BY THE APPLICANT, THE INFRINGER, OR THE COMMISSIONER OF PATENTS

Any person, either the applicant or anyone else, at any time during the period of enforceability of an issued patent, may file a request with the U.S. Patent & Trademark Office for re-examination of any or all of the claims of the issued patent. Such request must be based upon pertinent and applicable prior art patents or other printed publications that were not previously reviewed by the patent examiner during the prosecution of the patent in question. The U.S. Patent & Trademark Office will initially determine whether or not the newly submitted prior art raises new questions of materiality and patentability, and then decide whether or not a re-examination should be conducted. If it is determined that no re-examination is to be conducted, the U.S. Patent & Trademark Office will then so notify the person seeking the re-examination. If the Patent & Trademark Office decides that the new prior art submitted is material to certain or all of the claims of the issued patent, a re-examination procedure will be established, and the request will be sent to the original patent examiner for handling.

Re-examination proceedings can arise in several different ways. First, if a lawsuit is filed against an alleged infringer, and the alleged infringer introduces prior art during the lawsuit that was not considered by the examiner during prosecution of the patent, the patent owner during the pendency of the lawsuit has the right to go back to the Patent & Trademark Office, submit this new prior art to the patent examiner for re-examination, and hopefully obtain a decision that the new prior art is no more pertinent to the issued patent than the prior art previously applied by the examiner during prosecution of the patent. In that case, the owner of the patent in the litigation has thus eliminated that patent as prior art for consideration by the judge or jury.

Also, the defendant or potential infringer in litigation, may submit prior art to the Patent & Trademark Office in an attempt to have the examiner determine that the patent is invalid, rather than to cast the lot of invalidity before a judge or jury. Further, the Commissioner of Patents, on his or her own volition, may seek re-examination of a patent on a myriad of grounds.

Note that during a re-examination proceeding, the patent owner can amend the claims to possibly avoid the new prior art, and then emerge with a reexamined patent that may be stronger and may still cover a potentially infringing device. This amendment process during a re-examination allows the claims to be narrowed in coverage, but not to be broadened.

12.12   RE-ISSUE PATENTS

A re-issue patent application is filed, when necessary, after a patent has issued and review of the issued patent indicates that an "error" has occurred. One such "error" can be that the scope of claim coverage if the patent is too limited, without any deceptive intent. Therefore, it is possible to file for re-issuance of a patent within the first two years of its enforceable life to obtain broader claim coverage. After two years from the date of issue of the patent, a broadening re-issue is not allowed. Note that the re-issue patent has the same life as the patent from which it has been re-issued, that is, 20 years from the date of filing of the original patent application.

Narrowing re-issue patent applications may be filed at any time during the life of the issued parent patent. Several reasons to consider when thinking of filing a re-issue patent application are: 1) to present claims of modified scope for evaluation over additional prior art, 2) to correct a misjoinder of inventors, 3) to claim the benefit of an earlier filing date, 4) to obtain broader claim coverage within the first two years, and 5) to obtain enhanced validity of the patent. The problem with re-issues is that once a request to re-issue a patent has been filed, the patent undergoes a new examination process, and the possibility exists that the examiner may uncover additional prior art that was overlooked before and reject the claims. This is a risk that has to be evaluated before submitting a patent for re-issue, and the risk can be minimized by conducting a search of the prior art prior to submitting the patent for re-issue.

◆ INVENTORS AND INVENTIONS ◆

Nikola Tesla

AC INDUCTION MOTOR AND RADIO

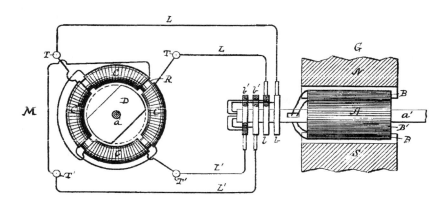

Some consider Nikola Tesla to embody the essence of genius, and to be one of the world's greatest inventors. His name is connected with innovations such as the Tesla coil transformer, the induction motor, the rotating magnetic field principle, polyphase alternating current systems, radio and wireless communication, fluorescent lights, and other technologies. He is named as an inventor in over 700 patents.

Nikola Tesla, who was to become the master of alternating current electricity at the turn of the 19th century, was born at the stroke of midnight between July 9th and 10th, 1856, in Smiljan, Croatia, a province of Lika, which was then part of the Austro-Hungarian Empire. Though born in Croatia, he was the son of a Serbian Orthodox priest and a Serbian mother, from whom he inherited a photographic memory. Just as Mozart could visualize completely scored and orchestrated music in his head, Nikola Tesla had the ability to visualize completely structured and operating technology and inventions in his mind, without resorting to experiments, drawings, or prototype models. In his high school math classes, he would shout out answers to complicated problems without the use of pencil or paper. Alas, he therefore needed no sketches, models or experiments to "complete" his inventions, and, as a result, he left little in the way of records or evidence of many of his innovative uses of electricity. His practice was to make a working model of his inventions after he worked out all of the details and made necessary modifications in his imagination.

Tesla began his electrical engineering education in 1875 at the Polytechnic College of Graz, Austria. In 1881, he took a position in the Central Telegraph Office of the Hungarian government in Budapest, which was also associated with Thomas Edison's telegraph subsidiary. While an undergraduate student, Tesla first noticed the problems with the induction motors of that time. He noticed that a direct-current Gramme dynamo being oper-

Intellectual Property Law for Engineers and Scientists, by Howard B. Rockman **193**
ISBN 0-471-44998-9 © 2004 The Institute of Electrical and Electronics Engineers

ated in a classroom demonstration as a motor was creating sparks between the brushes and the commutator. His professor did not think much of Tesla's suggestion that motors without commutators could be developed by switching to alternating current. At that time, Tesla had no idea how to accomplish his idea, but he was intrigued. He came to the United States in 1884 to work with Thomas Edison. Later, he was to form his own company, and he continued to experiment and invent for the rest of his life. He died on January 7, 1943 of heart failure at the age of 86.

I have purposely skipped over many important facets of the life of Nikola Tesla, as I am compelled to do for the sake of brevity. For those of you who desire to learn more about one of the most amazing technical intellects of his, or any, time, I recommend reading *Tesla, Man Out of Time* by Margaret Cheney (Dorset Press, New York, 1989), as well as other works referenced in Ms. Cheney's book. However, there are two facets of the life and work of Tesla that are worthy of remark in this treatise.

First, after leaving the Polytechnic at Graz, Tesla kept the image of the sparking dynamo in the midregions of his mind. In about 1881–1882, while he was in Budapest, after recovering from what doctors had diagnosed as a "nervous breakdown," Tesla was walking with a friend, Anital Szigety, in the city park, and was reciting poetry—Goethe's *Faust* as the story is told. Then, as the seed of an idea came to him, he took a stick and drew a sketch in the dust on the ground of the park. He sketched a motor in the dirt, and said to his friend, "Watch me reverse it." That same diagram was displayed 6 years later at an appearance Tesla made before the American Institute of Electrical Engineers. His demonstration was considered to be a new scientific principle, and it later transformed the world of power system technology.

Tesla had conceived, in the dust, not only a new motor, but the principle of the rotating magnetic field created by two or more alternating currents that were out of phase with each other. He had eliminated the requirement for a commutator (which reverses the direction of direct electric current), and the brushes necessary for providing a path for the current used in prior DC motors.

Alternating current had been employed prior to Tesla by Elihu Thomson to power arc lights, and in transformers for modifying power transmission voltages. The first AC transformer was developed and patented by Europeans Gaulard and Gibbs, and the U.S. rights to their invention were bought by George Westinghouse, an early advocate of AC electrification. However, there was no successful, practical AC motor until later when Tesla invented his induction motor.

In 1882, Tesla took a position with the Edison telephone subsidiary in Paris, where he learned of Edison's revulsion at the mere mention of alternating current. Tesla's responsibilities included investigating and curing the shortcomings of Edison power facilities in Germany and France. While in Strasbourg, Alsace on company business, he built his first AC induction motor, which used a rotating magnetic field and an armature that rotated without commutation. By the end of the summer of 1883, Tesla had twice repeated his experiments, and became convinced that AC was the power of the future.

Tesla was next asked to repair a railroad station lighting facility that lost a wall portion caused as a result of a DC short circuit during the grand opening of the station. Tesla was promised a bonus if he could solve the problem, but after successfully getting the system operational, he was denied his bonus and he resigned. However, Charles Batchelor, the manager of the Paris plant and a close assistant to Edison over the years, saw Tesla's talents, and recommended Tesla for a position at Edison's Menlo Park research center in the United States. Batchelor wrote a glowing letter of recommendation to Edison, that in the words of Margaret Cheney (ibid.,. p. 26) involved "introducing the one egocentric genius to the other." Everyone agreed, and at age 28, Nikola Tesla landed in the United States in 1884. Edison was then 32 years of age.

While working for Edison, Tesla at the beginning impressed Edison with his skills, and was awarded broad freedom in tackling the operation and design problems of Edison's electric power systems. Tesla devised a way in which the outdated Edison dynamos could become more efficient, and was promised (again) a $50,000 bonus if he could succeed. Tesla then redesigned and improved over twenty dynamos, and installed automatic controls.

Edison's sometimes faulty dynamos powered all of the new-fangled electrical devices in New York City. The electrically operated trolley cars frightened nearby pedestrians as well as the riders. The citizens of Brooklyn, who felt particularly victimized by malicious electric trolleys, became known as "Trolley Dodgers." When the borough of Brooklyn was endowed with a baseball franchise, the team was naturally anointed the Brooklyn Dodgers.

Edison's and Tesla's different approaches to problem solving soon drove a wedge between the two geniuses. Edison used the empirical approach, trying out solutions and employing a process of elimination until one worked. Tesla, meanwhile, was analytical, using theory and calculation to solve difficult situations. On top of this, Edison saw Tesla's interest in AC as a threat to his myopic and total devotion to DC, partly because Edison thought (incorrectly) that only DC could light his incandescent bulbs.

After Tesla's redesign of the Edison dynamos was complete, he asked for his $50,000 bonus. Tesla's supporters report that Edison merely replied that Tesla simply misunderstood America's (and Edison's) sense of humor. Tesla, feeling cheated by another Edison Company, resigned. He was then approached by investors, who helped him create the Tesla Electric Light Company, with the aim of producing better electric arc lights for street and factory lighting. Tesla developed an arc lamp that was simple, safe, and cost less than available gas lights. However, even though successful, Tesla was forced out of his own company with little compensation. The years 1886–1887 saw slow economic times, and Tesla barely survived, working as a street laborer. Meanwhile, his arc-lighting inventions resulted in the award of seven patents, plus other patents related to light.

Lady Luck came to Tesla's rescue. The foreman of Tesla's street labor crew knew of his induction motor, and introduced Tesla to A. K. Brown, the manager of Western Union, who happened to have an interest in alternating current. Brown assisted Tesla in forming the Tesla Electric Company, with the goal of developing and building the AC induction motor and system that Tesla sketched in the Budapest dust in 1882, and had successfully built in Alsace in 1883.

In 1888, Tesla was awarded U.S. Patent No. 381,968, titled "Electric Magnetic Motor." He also obtained U.S. Patents Nos. 381,969, 381,970, 382,279, 382,280, 382,281, and 382,282 for a complete AC system, including his single and polyphase motors, split-phase induction motors, a distributor system, and polyphase transformers for producing, transmitting, and using electricity. Only his first induction motor patent is reprinted here; the remaining patents can be found at the U.S. Patent & Trademark Office website, www.uspto.gov.

At the Chicago Columbian Exposition of 1893, Westinghouse, using Tesla's AC power system, lit up the entire City of Tomorrow, started fountains and machinery, and raised banners and flags. AC was a hit and was here to stay. The Tesla polyphase system is used today practically everywhere. Compared to DC, higher voltages could be generated through Tesla's AC systems, and the transmission of electricity became possible over hundreds of miles and more, compared to DC requiring electrical substations every few miles. Edison's light bulb could be switched on using either AC or DC. For more on this aspect of Tesla's life, see the essay "Current Events," following Chapter 27.

The second Tesla saga involves the radio, whose invention is popularly credited to Guglielmo Marconi. However, the Teslaites dispute this conclusion. They argue that as a child, Tesla had a fascination with rain and lightning, observing that "the electrical energy enclosed in the precipitation of the water was inconsiderable, the function of the lightning being much like that of a sensitive trigger." Tesla's vision was to control lightning, and with it enhance the world's water supply. He considered the technology needed to develop electric forces of the magnitude of those found in nature similar to that required to successfully transmit energy without wires. (see N. Tesla, "Inventions," p. 62.)

In February 1892, Sir William Crookes published an article suggesting the use of Hertzian waves for wireless telegraphy by the then-known means of generating electromagnetic waves of any desired wave length, and transmitting the waves through the air to a receiver. The sending and receiving devices would be attuned to a definite wavelength. Crooke's hypothesis confirmed Tesla's thoughts on using the air to transmit electrical signals and energy.

One year later, in speeches in 1893 before the Franklin Institute in Philadelphia and the National Electric Light Association in St. Louis, Tesla presented, in detail, the principles of the transmission of electrical signals through the air. His supporters point to the fact that during the St. Louis speech in 1893, Tesla presented the first public demonstration of adjustable high-frequency oscillations for transmission of wireless messages. Marconi made his "first" radio transmission in 1895.

Figures 1 and 2 from Tesla's speeches delivered in Philadelphia and St. Louis in February and March, 1893 are shown below. Figure 1 diagrams the laboratory setup Tesla used to produce high-frequency currents from either continuous or low-frequency alternating currents utilizing then-known dynamos. In conjunction with the portion of his presentation relating to Figure 2, Tesla proposed that the high-frequency currents could be used to

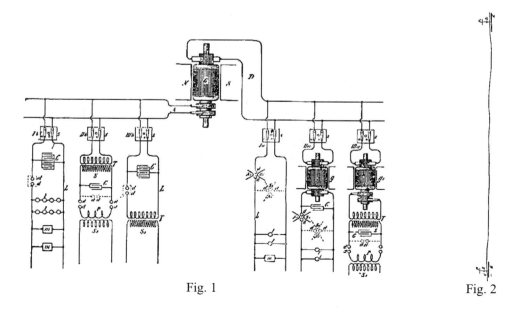

Fig. 1   Fig. 2

produce electric waves for the transmission of wireless telegraph messages. Tesla, referring to Figure 2, described in his speeches a system of creating electromagnetic waves from a source of high-frequency currents, with an elevated conducting surface connected to a terminal of the source, and the other source terminal connected to underground pipes, or to earth. These figures have been relied upon by Tesla supporters and the Supreme Court to support the conclusion that Tesla was the first to demonstrate the transmission of wireless signals.

Tesla's St. Louis transmitter circuit assembly consisted of a high-voltage (5 kilovolts) pole-type, oil-filled transformer connected to a condenser consisting of a bank of Leyden jars, a coil, a spark gap, and a wire extending to the top of the room. His receiver circuit assembly, 30 feet away, included a similar wire suspended from the ceiling and an identical coil and bank of condenser Leyden jars. However, instead of the spark gap used in the transmitter, the receiver included a Geissler tube that would glow upon the application of voltage. No wires connected the receiver and transmitter.

When Tesla powered up the transmitter circuit assembly, corona appeared at the foil edges of the Leyden jars. The spark gap made a noisy discharge, and electromagnetic waves radiated from the transmitter antenna (although these waves were invisible). At the receiver assembly, the Geissler tube became excited by the electromagnetic waves, and lit up.

This demonstration by Tesla, his supporters argue, displayed all of the fundamental principles of radio:

1. An arrangement of four circuits
2. An open antenna circuit coupled through a transformer to a closed charging circuit
3. An open antenna circuit at the receiver similarly coupled to a closed detector circuit
4. The open and closed circuits in the transmitting and receiving circuits in electrical synchronized resonance with each other
5. Achieving synchronized resonance by adjusting the length of wire in the secondary winding of the oscillation transformer in the transmitter, and similarly in the receiver, such that the antenna circuit is resonant with the frequency developed in the charging circuit of the transmitter
6. The primary coil and the secondary coil of the receiver are preferably carefully adjusted to vibrate synchronously with the transmitting coil.

As a prologue to the subsequent patent battles between Tesla and Marconi, it must be mentioned that Sir Oliver Lodge, in 1894, built a system that transmitted wireless telegraph signals using Hertzian waves over a 150 yard distance. Lodge adjusted the tuning of his device by varying the self-inductance of the antenna circuits. Lodge demonstrated that the adjustment of wavelengths and, thus, frequency in the circuits, was accomplished by varying either or both the inductance and capacity, which are the factors controlling wavelength, and hence frequency, in the antenna circuits. Tuning the radio circuit by varying inductance was not demonstrated by Tesla in 1893.

In 1896, Marconi demonstrated in London a wireless radio transmitter and receiver. Margaret Cheney, in her book "Tesla, Man Out of Time," on page 69, reports that the Marconi wireless device was identical to Lodge's, and exactly what Tesla had discussed in his widely published and circulated 1893 lectures, which had been translated into several languages.

Tesla's first U.S. radio patent application for a remote controlled device was filed on July 1, 1898, and granted on November 8, 1898 as No. 613,809. Tesla's second radio patent application (for wireless signal and power transmission) was filed on September 2, 1897, and was granted on March 20, 1900 as No. 645,576. Marconi's first U.S. patent application was granted on July 13, 1897 as U.S. Patent No. 586,193, and reissued on June 4, 1901 as Re. No. 11,913.

Marconi's second patent was filed on November 10, 1900, and was initially rejected as lacking novelty over the Lodge prior art. Marconi's attorneys then submitted a new specification and claims, canceling the initially filed material. The patent examiner consistently rejected Marconi's second set of claims in view of the Tesla, Lodge, and Braun prior art, and refused to believe Marconi's assertion that he had no knowledge of the "Tesla Oscillator," which had been widely described in the technical press. After the application was abandoned, and after a first refusal by the Commissioner of Patents to revive the Marconi application, Marconi's attorneys requested reconsideration of the Commissioner's decision. Reconsideration was granted, and the Marconi application was given to a different patent examiner who allowed the application. Marconi's U.S. Patent No. 763,772 was granted on June 28, 1904.

The second patent examiner decided that Marconi's claims directed to the use of variable inductance to tune the antenna circuits were distinguishable from prior art of Stone that showed adjusting the length of the antenna conductor to tune the antenna circuits. However, this conclusion overlooked Lodge's prior U.S. Patent No. 609,154, which disclosed a variable inductance in the aerial circuit.

Marconi, however, was an excellent marketer, and his Marconi Worldwide Wireless Company gained the lead in developing and commercializing radio. Eventually, on August 4, 1915, Tesla sued Marconi for infringing Tesla's wireless patent. However, Tesla lacked the financial resources to pursue his case.

Then, on July 29, 1916, the Marconi Wireless Telegraph Company of America filed a lawsuit against the United States government charging infringement during the First World War of Marconi's U.S. Patent No. 763,772 and three other patents. The lower court held claim 16 of the Marconi patent valid and infringed, and awarded Marconi's company $42,894.93 in damages. The lower court had also held that Marconi's reissue patent, No. 11,913, was not infringed, and Marconi did not appeal this ruling. On November 20, 1919, all of the assets, including the patents, of Marconi's company were assigned to the Radio Corporation of America, but the Marconi Company retained the right to prosecute the lawsuit against the U.S. government. Marconi's case lumbered through the federal court system for the next 27 years, culminating in a decision by the United States Supreme Court on June 21, 1943, holding claim 16 of Marconi's Patent No. 763,772 invalid in view of the prior public disclosures and patents of Nikola Tesla, Lodge, and others, thus awarding priority of invention of the radio to Tesla and his 1893 presentation in St. Louis. See *Marconi Wireless Telegraph Co. of America v. United States,* 320 U.S.1 (1943).

The Supreme Court defined the "invention" in the Marconi Patent No. 763,772 as:

> . . . [T]he use of two high frequency circuits in the transmitter and two in the receiver, all four so adjusted as to be resonant to the same frequency or multiples of it. The circuits are so constructed that the electrical impulses in the antenna circuit of the transmitter vibrate longer with the application to the transmitter of a given amount of electrical energy than has been the case in the previous structures known to the art, and the selectivity and sensitivity of the receiver is likewise enhanced. Thus increased efficiency in the transmission and reception of signals is obtained.

This definition is not specifically directed to the transmission of voice and music, which was made possible subsequently by de Forest, whose Audion provided variable frequency modulation.

In its 80 page opinion, The Supreme Court found that the Tesla '576 patent, which was issued before Marconi's '772 patent was even applied for, disclosed a four-circuit system, two each at the receiver and transmitter, and suggested that all four circuits be tuned to the same frequency. Although Tesla's device was designed primarily for the transmission of energy to any form of energy-consuming device, Tesla also recognized that his system could be used, without change, for wireless communication of intelligible messages. Tesla's '576 patent disclosed the following features of the Marconi '772 patent:

> A charging circuit in the transmitter for causing oscillations of the desired frequency, coupled, through a transformer, with the open antenna circuit, and the synchronization of the two circuits by the proper disposition of the inductance in either the closed or the antenna circuit or both. By this and the added disclosure of the two-circuit arrangement in the receiver with similar adjustment, he [Tesla] anticipated the four circuit tuned combination of Marconi. (80 U.S. at pp. 15, 16).

The Court also held that a feature of Marconi's patented device not shown by Tesla's patent for the use of a variable inductance to adjust the tuning of the antenna circuit of both transmitter and receiver was developed by Lodge (U.S. Patent No. 609,154) after Tesla's patent but before Marconi's patent.

Thus, among his other acts of inventive genius, the Tesla supporters point to this 1943 U.S. Supreme Court decision, and the facts referred to by the Court, as defining Nikola Tesla as the true inventor of radio.

(No Model.)   4 Sheets—Sheet 1.

N. TESLA.
ELECTRO MAGNETIC MOTOR.

No. 381,968.   Patented May 1, 1888.

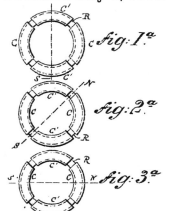

Fig:1   Fig:1ª

Fig:2   Fig:2ª

Fig:3   Fig:3ª

Fig:4   Fig:4ª

Fig:5   Fig:5ª

Fig:6   Fig:6ª

Fig:7   Fig:7ª

Fig:8   Fig:8ª

WITNESSES: INVENTOR.

Frank E. Hartley   Nikola Tesla,
Frank B. Murphy   BY
                                             Duncan, Curtis & Page
                                                  ATTORNEYS.

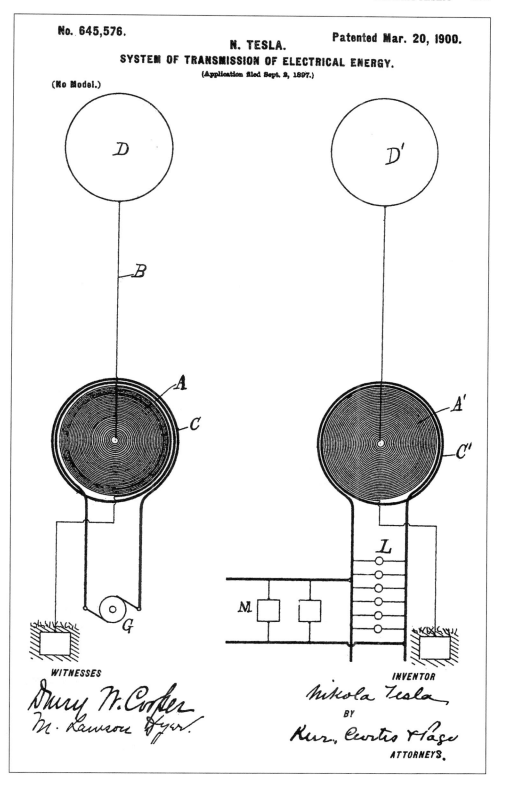

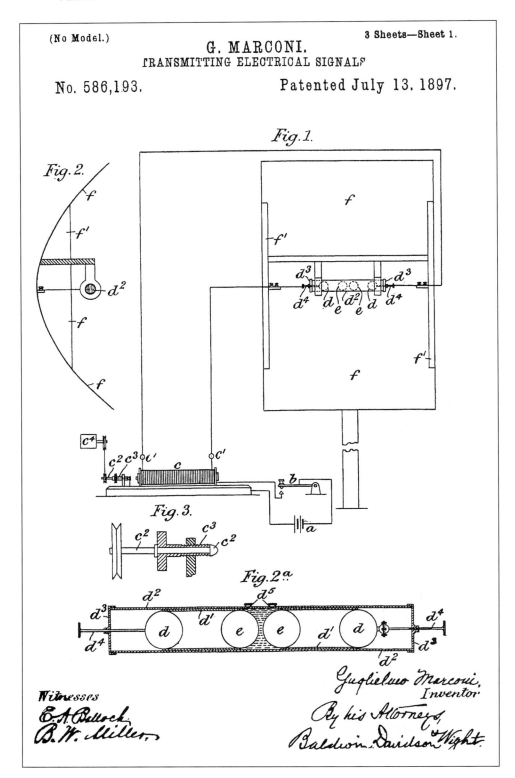

(No Model.)   3 Sheets—Sheet 1.

G. MARCONI.
TRANSMITTING ELECTRICAL SIGNALS

No. 586,193.   Patented July 13, 1897.

Fig.1.

Fig.2.

Fig.3.

Fig.2ª.

Guglielmo Marconi,
Inventor

By his Attorneys,
Baldwin Davidson & Wight.

Witnesses
E. A. Bullock.
B. W. Miller.

13 Design Patents

13.1 COVERAGE OF DESIGN PATENTS

In recent years, the coverage afforded by design patents has increased in importance in protecting product designs from slavish copying. Design patents covering new, original, ornamental and non-functional aesthetic designs of an "article of manufacture" are authorized by 35 U.S.C. §171-173. "Ornamentability" of the article of manufacture is a requirement for design patents, as distinguished from the requirement for "utility" in article patents. To establish patentability of a design, the novel features of the design must not be found in the prior art, and the design features must be non-obvious over the prior art in the view of a designer with ordinary skill in the art. The spirit of the design patent statute is to encourage development of the decorative arts.

Design patents are enforceable for a period of fourteen years from date of issue, and they are not renewable. Importantly, functional features of the article of manufacture covered by a design patent are excluded from protection by the design patent. Such functional features should properly be protected by an article patent. Design patent protection covers the design features of the article shown in the patent illustrations. However, all illustrated features which are dictated solely by function cannot be protected by the design patent.

A new and non-obvious design which incorporates a mixture of design and function is protectable by a design patent, which will be interpreted as protecting only the design features. However, if the shape of every part of the article is dictated by the utility to be performed by the article, design patent protection is not warranted. Thus, even though an article illustrated in a design patent may embody a mechanical function, the design patent is acceptable and valid provided that the design is also pleasing, attractive, novel, useful, and the result of invention. *R.E. Dietz Co. v. Burr and Starkweather Co.,* 243 Fed. 592, 594 (2 Cir. 1917).

It is interesting to note that the first U.S. design patent statute enacted in 1842 originally referred to protection of "useful" designs. This was changed in the 1902 statute to "ornamental" designs.

The "claim" of a design patent covers only the design illustrated in the patent document, and the patent document includes no written text description of what the patent covers. Normally, all six views (front, back, two sides, top and bottom) of the article covered by the design patent are illustrated. Occasionally, it is helpful to include perspective drawings of the design in the patent.

A properly drawn design patent should illustrate only the design features of the article it covers in solid lines, and functional and non-aesthetic features should be illustrated by the use of phantom or dotted lines. This illustrating technique will define only the ornamental features of the article as being covered by the patent. Thus, if an infringer copies the protected ornamental elements of your product, but alters the design of the functional features of its competing product, your design patent can be used to prevent adoption of

Intellectual Property Law for Engineers and Scientists, by Howard B. Rockman
ISBN 0-471-44998-9 © 2004 The Institute of Electrical and Electronics Engineers

the ornamental design by the infringer, regardless of the shape of the remainder of the infringing device.

Both utility and design patents can cover the same product or article of manufacture. The utility patent covers the structure and function of a useful invention; the design patent protects only the novel, non-functional ornamental features of the design of the product.

A design is a unitary thing and all of its portions are material in that they contribute to the appearance which constitutes the design. *Ex. parte Daniels,* 40 U.S.P.Q. 2nd 1394 (Bd. of Pat. App. & Int'f. 1996). However, a design patent may be utilized to cover a design embodied in only a portion or part of an entire article of manufacture. Also, design protection can be directed to the article's configuration itself, or cover surface ornamentation of the article.

A United States design patent corresponds in effect and coverage to a design model registration or an industrial design obtained under the laws of various foreign countries. Therefore, the design model registration systems or industrial design systems of other countries can be used to cover your new design in those foreign countries that do not have design patent protection per se.

13.2   INFRINGEMENT OF A DESIGN PATENT

To determine whether a design of an article of manufacture falls within the scope of coverage of an existing design patent, the Supreme Court established a test in the 1872 case of *Gorham Manufacturing Company v. White,* 81 U.S. 511 (U.S. Supreme Court 1872). Over 125 years later, the Gorham test is still the standard for design patent infringement in the United States. The Gorham test, which is also commonly known as the "Ordinary Observer" test states that:

> "If in the eye of an ordinary observer, giving such attention as a purchaser usually gives, two designs are substantially the same, if the resemblance is such as to deceive such an observer, inducing him to purchase one supposing it to be the other, the first one patented is infringed by the other."

Thus, a second design does not have to be identical to the illustration in a design patent to constitute infringement of that patent. All that needs to be proven is that an ordinary purchaser would be deceived by the second design into thinking it was the first design.

13.3   IMPORTANCE OF DESIGN PATENTS

Where a new product being introduced to the market comprises novel ornamentation, either in its product configuration or in its surface design, a design patent should be obtained to protect the marketing, advertising and promotional value of that design. There have been many instances where copiers will substitute the inner workings of a product with sub-par components to make the product inferior and less costly to produce, but still copy the complete outside design or ornamentation of the product. The next thing that happens is the copied product is offered to your customers at a price you can't afford to match. Those of you who have purchased "fine" watches at ridiculously low prices from street vendors may have an idea of what I mean. Design patent protection affords the producer of the "original" to prevent such copies from reaching the marketplace.

More importantly, many products today comprising articles of manufacture are copied in their totality, both mechanically and/or electronically, in overall product design, packaging, and even accompanying literature such as instruction booklets. If a "knock-off" product looks like a widely sold and advertised product, the copy of the product could be marketed at a significantly lower price, since the copier has no research and development costs, design development costs, or advertising costs. In my experience, this type of product design knock-off copying is quite prevalent, and obtaining design patent protection covering your product's appearance which is viewable by the consumer has taken on new importance with the advent of increased globalization of marketing and sales. Thus, it is the author's recommendation that when you consider obtaining article patent coverage for your invention, you also consider whether the design of your product is novel enough and unobvious enough to support a design patent. Design patents are normally considerably less expensive to obtain than article patents, and in the judgement of this warrior, are well worth the minimal expense. Therefore, do not overlook the possibility of obtaining design patent protection when you discuss intellectual property protection for your new product configuration or ornamentation.

13.4 EXAMPLES OF DESIGN PATENTS

Appended at the end of this chapter is a design patent No. D291,645 to Bruno covering an oiling can design. This is an example of a design patent covering a product configuration.

Interestingly, in 1967, the U.S. Court of Customs and Patent Appeals (the predecessor to today's Court of Appeals of the Federal Circuit) decided that the continuous flow or spray of water in motion in a particular pattern produced by a water fountain constituted patentable design subject matter, as an article of manufacture defined by the patent statute. The case is *In re Hruby,* 153 U.S.P.Q. 61 (CCPA 1967). An illustration of the design submitted for protection and covered by that design patent is shown in Figure 13.1.

The court held that even though the water sprays cannot exist by themselves, and are dependent on the existence of the nozzles and water under pressure, the spray itself is a three-dimensional design. The existence of the design was seen by the court as dependent on something outside of itself, such as the nozzles and water pressure, similar to the design of hosiery not being apparent until placed on one's leg. Thus, the water spray design was held to be an "article of manufacture."

13.5 DESIGN PATENTS ON COMPUTER SCREEN ICONS

Both the United States Patent and Trademark Office and the courts have traditionally held that a picture, such as a photograph, standing alone is not proper subject matter for a design patent. The design must be part of an "article of manufacture." See *In Re Schnell,* 46 Fed. 2nd 203 (CCPA 1931). However, the U.S. Patent and Trademark Office has, in the last few years, instructed its design patent examiners to accept design patent applications directed to novel and non-obvious computer displayed icons. In the application, the patent applicant must claim, and illustrate, the icon in association with a computer screen, monitor or other visual display device. See Manual of Patent

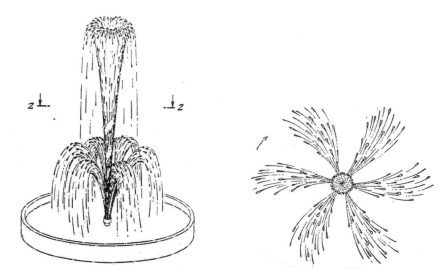

Figure 13.1. Illustration of patent of the case *In re Hruby.*

Examining Procedure, Section 1504.01 (8th Edition, August 2001, U.S. Patent & Trademark Office, pp. 1500-12 to 14).

13.6 DESIGN PATENTS CONTRASTED WITH COPYRIGHTS

The Design Patent Law and the Copyright Law are closely related, yet there are material differences between them. A design patent, according to 35 U.S.C. §171, may be obtained on any new, original and ornamental design for an article of manufacture. The article must provide an aesthetically pleasing appearance to the eye of the beholder, and the design must be primarily ornamental and not solely dictated by function or the performance of the article. To obtain design patent protection, the remaining provisions of the patent law must also be complied with. Therefore the design must be novel and non-obvious.

In contrast, the copyright law covers original works of authorship, such as a work of art, or a label used for an article of merchandise, or technical drawings. However, there is a certain degree of overlap. Consider, for example, a decorative column used as a support for a balcony. Copyright protection would be available for the original artistic features of the column. In addition, design patent protection would be obtainable if the decorative column design was new and non-obvious.

Copyrightable works are endowed with exclusive rights as soon as the works are in a sufficiently stable form, such as fixed in any tangible medium of expression as set forth in 17 U.S.C. §102(a) of the U.S. Copyright Law. However, to obtain design patent protection, an application must be filed with the U.S. Patent and Trademark Office, and the application must survive an examination process.

The examination process for a U.S. copyright application is much less stringent than examination of a design patent application. The requirement of originality for copyright protection is a relatively lenient standard, requiring only that the named author actually created, for example, originated, the work, and the work was not copied from another source. In addition, only a minimal amount of creative authorship is required for a work to fall under one of the categories of copyrightable subject matter. Copyrightable subject matter need not be strikingly unique or novel. In other words, the originality required to support a copyright is independent creation, and not novelty. As a result, the search for prior art that is normally conducted by an infringer to challenge the validity of a patent has no bearing in copyright cases.

Regarding infringement criteria, any product which is "substantially similar" to a patented design infringes the design patent, whether the infringer copied or even knew about the design patent or the product covered by the design patent. In contrast, one is liable for copyright infringement only if they are proven to have "copied" the work protected by copyright. Also, unlike design patent infringement, copyright infringement could possibly lead to criminal liability.

United States Patent [19]

Bruno

[11] **Patent Number:**   **Des. 291,645**

[45]   **Date of Patent:**   ∗∗ **Sep. 1, 1987**

[54] **COOKING OIL CAN**

[75] Inventor: **Pasquale Bruno,** Chicago, Ill.

[73] Assignee: **Amco Corporation,** Chicago, Ill.

[∗∗] Term: **14 Years**

[21] Appl. No.: **882,693**

[22] Filed: **Jul. 7, 1986**

[52] U.S. Cl. D7/321; D7/58;
D9/374; D9/376; D23/11

[58] **Field of Search** D7/300, 312, 321, 322,
D7/58; D9/376, 374, 373, 375; D23/5, 11

[56] **References Cited**

U.S. PATENT DOCUMENTS

D. 2,504	11/1866	Hauck	D9/374
D. 2,681	6/1867	Jones	D7/321
D. 2,862	1/1868	Hauck	D9/374
3,031	4/1843	Cornelius .	
D. 85,355	10/1931	Voisine .	
95,948	10/1869	Staples .	
D. 170,639	10/1953	Hoffman, Jr.	D9/375
D. 193,120	6/1962	Gerber .	
D. 196,146	8/1963	Lello .	
D. 241,248	8/1976	Burke et al.	D23/11
D. 251,129	2/1979	Behling	D23/11
D. 259,767	7/1981	MacFarlane	D9/374
D. 267,473	1/1983	Telzrow	D9/374
D. 267,630	1/1983	MacFarlane	D9/374
D. 278,799	5/1985	Maynard	D9/376
1,641,051	8/1927	Rheney .	
1,849,950	3/1932	Murdock .	
4,030,664	6/1977	Tisbo et al.	D23/11 X

OTHER PUBLICATIONS

HFD–*Retailing Home Furnishings,* Jul. 13, 1981, Sec. D, p. 8, bottom r. panel "Cooking With Oil" Stainless Steel Oil Can, Mark Louis Co.

Primary Examiner—Winifred E. Herrmann
Attorney, Agent, or Firm—Laff, Whitesel, Conte & Saret

[57]   **CLAIM**

The ornamental design for a cooking oil can, substantially as shown.

DESCRIPTION

FIG. 1 is a left side elevational view of a cooking oil can showing my new design;
FIG. 2 is a front elevational view thereof;
FIG. 3 is a top plan view thereof;
FIG. 4 is a right side elevational view thereof;
FIG. 5 is a rear elevational view thereof; and
FIG. 6 is a bottom plan view thereof.

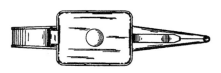

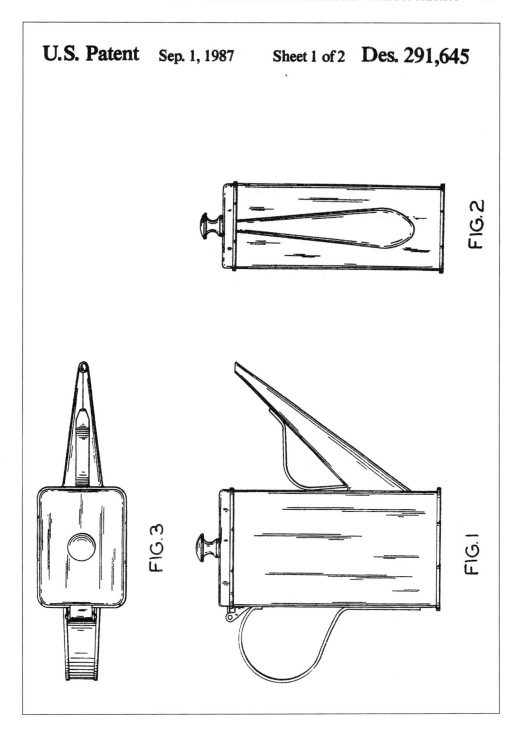

FIG.2

FIG.3

FIG.1

U.S. Patent Sep. 1, 1987 Sheet 2 of 2 **Des. 291,645**

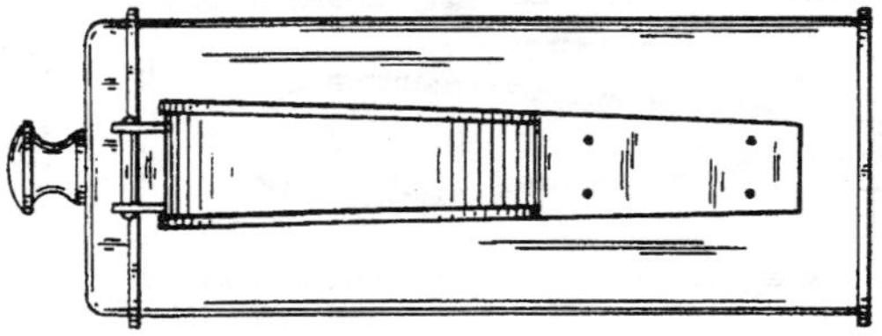

FIG.5

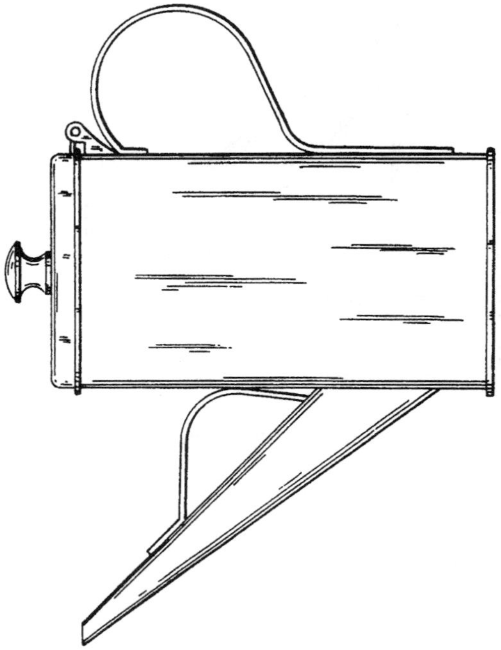

FIG.4

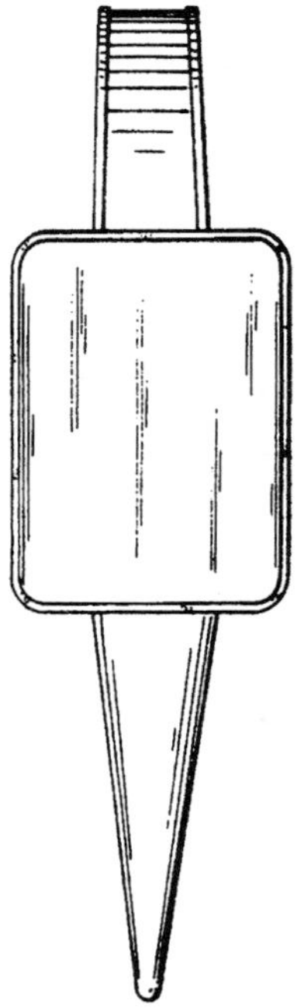

FIG.6

Herman Hollerith

TABULATING MACHINE

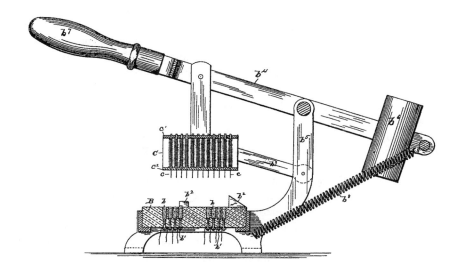

Herman Hollerith was the man who initially made it easy for the government to determine how many people live in the United States. Beginning in 1890, the U.S. Census was tabulated with the help of Hollerith's statistics tabulating machine.

Hollerith was the son of German immigrants who came to the United States in 1848. Although never particularly good in public school because of spelling problems, with the help of the family's Lutheran minister as a tutor he was able to enroll in the City College of New York and also receive an engineering degree with distinction from the Columbia School of Mines (now part of Columbia University) in 1879. One of Hollerith's teachers, W. P. Trowbridge, was very impressed with him and made him his assistant. Hollerith accepted and started working at Columbia University and later the Census Bureau when Professor Trowbridge was appointed as Chief Special Agent to the Census Bureau. While working for the Census Bureau, Hollerith appreciated that there was a need to find a better, faster way to mechanically manipulate large amounts of statistical and other data. During his time at the Census Bureau, Hollerith met Dr. John Shaw Billings, from whom the idea for a tabulating machine first came. Dr. Billings suggested "something on the principal of the Jacquard loom, whereby holes in a card regulate the pattern to be woven."

In 1882, Hollerith began teaching mechanical engineering at the Massachusetts Institute of Technology. During this time, he began working with Dr. Billings' idea, examining how the Jacquard loom worked, and if its principles could be used for his intended tabulating purposes. Although the loom idea would not work for the census, the idea of punch cards seemed to provide a very efficient way to store information. Another idea came to Hollerith on a train ride as he watched the conductor punch tickets, which led to an easier way to punch information on cardboard cards.

Hollerith then began working on a tabulating system, first using a perforated paper tape, and later cards, and he filed for his first of thirty plus patents in 1884. He developed a hand-fed "press" that sensed the holes in punched cards. A wire would pass through the holes into a cup of mercury beneath the card, closing an electrical circuit and creating an electrical impulse. This process triggered mechanical counters and sorter bins and tabulated the appropriate data. His system, including keyboard punch tabulator and sorter elements, allowed the official 1890 population count to be tallied between September 1890 and December 12, 1890, instead of the budgeted two years if tabulating were done manually. The total cost was five million dollars below forecast. His later machines mechanized the card feeding process, added numbers, and sorted cards, in addition to merely counting data. In 1896, Hollerith founded the Tabulating Machine Company.

The U.S. Census Bureau again used Hollerith's system for the 1900 census, but because Hollerith had a monopoly on tabulating machines, he set the price at a rather steep level. To counter this, for the 1910 census, the Census Bureau developed its own, more advanced tabulating machines, although it was hard to get around Hollerith's patents. But James Powers, the engineer who developed the new machine, was allowed to obtain patent rights in his own name.

Powers then left the Census Bureau to start his own company, the Powers Tabulating Machine Company, that rivaled Hollerith's Tabulating Machine Company. After a merger in 1911 with another company, Hollerith's company became the Computer Tabulating Recording Company, for which Hollerith acted as a consultant until he retired in 1921. In 1924, Arthur Watson, president of Computer Tabulating Recording Company changed the company's name to International Business Machines Corporation (IBM). Herman Hollerith died in 1929.

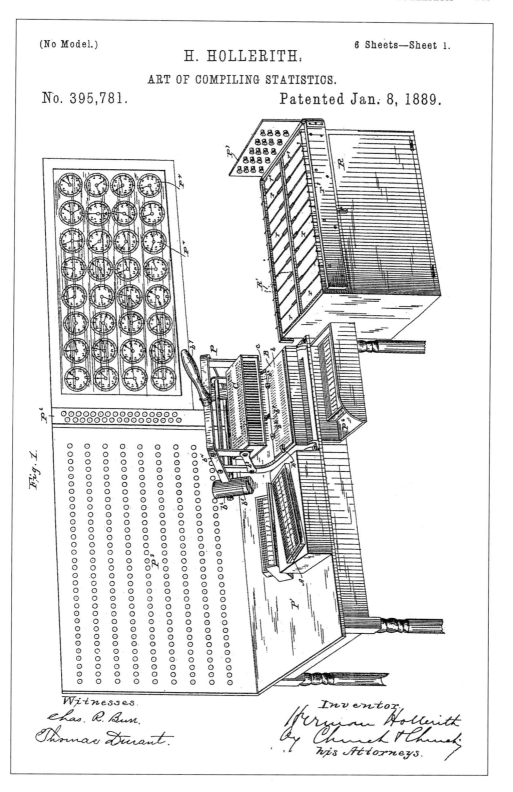

6 Sheets—Sheet 1.

H. HOLLERITH.
ART OF COMPILING STATISTICS.

No. 395,781.   Patented Jan. 8, 1889.

Fig. I.

Witnesses.
Chas. R. Burr.
Thomas Durant.

Inventor,
Herman Hollerith
By Church & Church,
his Attorneys.

(No Model.)   3 Sheets—Sheet 1.

H. HOLLERITH.
ART OF COMPILING STATISTICS.

No. 395,782.   Patented Jan. 8, 1889.

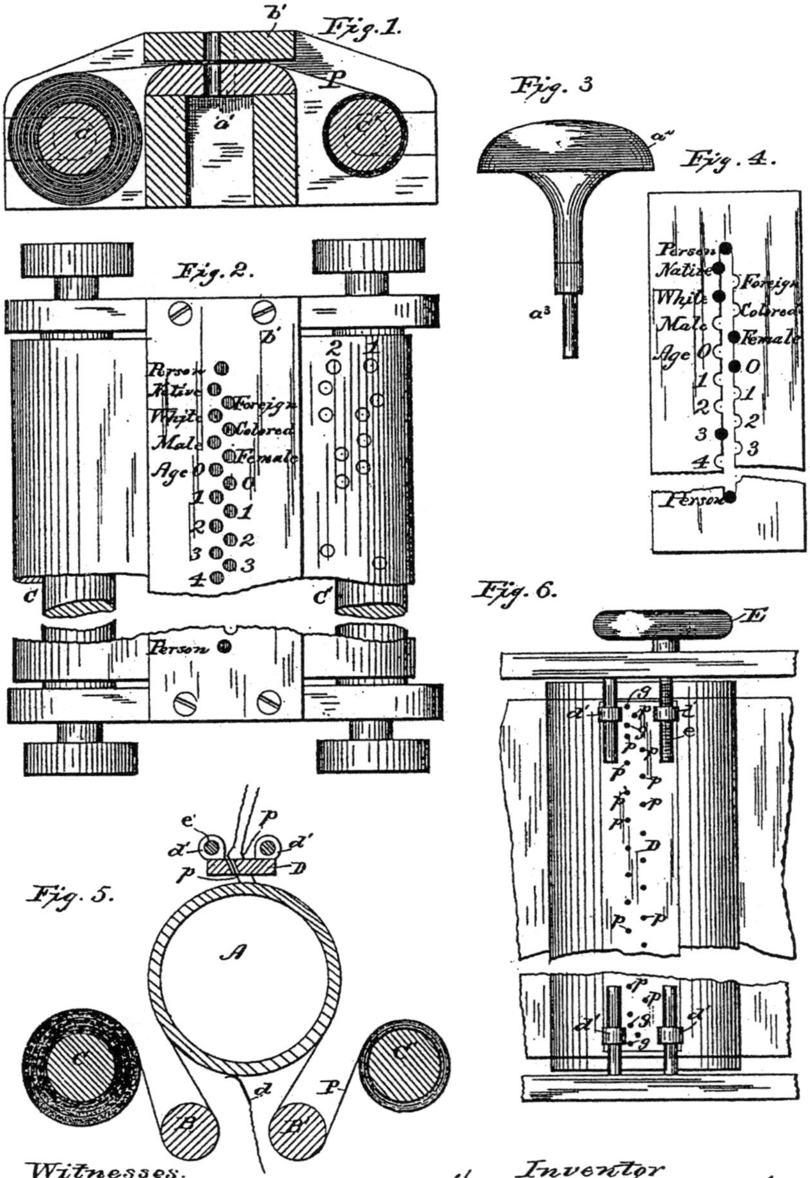

Fig. 1.
Fig. 2.
Fig. 3.
Fig. 4.
Fig. 5.
Fig. 6.

Witnesses.
Chas. R. Bull.
A. L. Stewart.

Inventor
Herman Hollerith
by Church & Church
his Attorneys.

14 Protection of Computer-Related Inventions

14.1 INTRODUCTION

One of the most frequently asked questions of patent attorneys during the past twenty five years has been: "Is computer software patentable?" The answer has progressed over time from a flat "no," through the stage of a "definite maybe," to the current "yes, if specific criteria are met." The purpose of this chapter is to provide you, the computer-related and software developing engineer or scientist, with sufficient information to (1) determine whether the computer-related technology you develop constitutes patentable subject matter, and (2) if it does, how to ensure that the patent application prepared to cover your invention is sufficiently crafted to obtain ultimate issuance of a patent. The pertinent rules established by the courts and the U.S. Patent and Trademark Office are not for the faint hearted, and the devil is in the details. The following sections include several examples in an attempt to clarify the concepts.

14.2 TORTUROUS PATH THROUGH THE COURTS

The discipline of computer science began when general-purpose computers reached the capacity to run a large variety of programs. At this point, designers of programs (software) began to distinguish themselves from the designers of the machines on which the software ran (hardware). Other than the programmers themselves, and the hardware engineers, not many people understood the nature of software at this time. In the 1950s and early 1960s, patent applications were filed covering software inventions, and the U.S. Patent and Trademark Office rejected them all, stating that software was definitely not patentable subject matter. Those programmers who were able to obtain patents did not obtain the patent on the software itself, but on combinations of hardware and software since the hardware was a "machine." Through a long and torturous path, the Supreme Court and the Court of Appeals for the Federal Circuit (the "CAFC") began to understand computer programming, and its value to business and society in general. The pendulum swung, and rules and guidelines now exist to enable patent protection for computer-related inventions, even those embedded in software, if the program meets certain criteria.

14.2.1 *Gottschalk v. Benson,* 1972

The first relevant Supreme Court case regarding computer-related inventions is *Gottschalk v. Benson,* 409 U.S. 63 (1972). The patent application in the Benson case was directed "to the processing of data by program, and more particularly to the programmed conversion of numerical information" in a general-purpose digital computer. The claimed

Intellectual Property Law for Engineers and Scientists, by Howard B. Rockman
ISBN 0-471-44998-9 © 2004 The Institute of Electrical and Electronics Engineers

invention was a method for converting binary-coded decimal (BCD) numerals into pure binary numerals. The claims in the patent application were not limited to any particular art or technology, to any particular apparatus or machinery, or to any particular end use. The U.S. Patent and Trademark Office rejected the application as not defining statutory patentable subject matter. However, the claims were held to constitute patentable subject matter on appeal to the Court of Customs and Patent Appeals (the predecessor of the CAFC). The Supreme Court agreed to hear the case, which was appealed by the Patent Office.

The question before the Supreme Court was whether the method described and claimed in the Benson patent application was a "process" within the meaning of patentable subject matter under patent statutes. The Supreme Court determined that the conversion of BCD numerals into pure binary numerals can be performed mentally through use of a table showing how decimal numbers are expressed as binary symbols using only a zero and a one. The method sought to be patented varies the ordinary arithmetic steps a human would use by changing the order of the steps, changing the symbolism for writing the multiplier used in some steps, and by taking subtotals after each successive operation. The mathematical procedures claimed in the patent application could be carried out in existing computers long in use, with no new machinery being necessary, and the procedures could also be performed without a computer.

The Court held that one may not patent an idea, and in practical effect that would be the result if the formula in this case for converting BCD numerals to binary numerals were patented. The Benson mathematical formula, the Court said, has no substantial practical application except in connection with a digital computer, which means if the appellate court judgment allowing the patent to issue were confirmed, the patent would wholly preempt others from using the mathematical formula, and in practical effect would be a patent on the algorithm itself. The Court went on to say that it may be that the patent law should be extended to cover these programs, however the President's Commission on the Patent System rejected the proposal that these programs constitute patentable subject matter.

The decision of the Supreme Court in the Benson case appears to be founded on the principal that a patent should not be allowed for inventions that are basic and fundamental to future advances in technology, since these patents would unduly burden future inventors by patenting fundamental tools of science and decreasing the incentives for improvements. One possible rational for deciding that algorithms are not patentable subject matter, as the Court did in the Benson case, is that "the underlying notion is that a scientific principal, such as that expressed in the patent applicant's algorithm, reveals a relationship that has always existed."

14.2.2 *Diamond v. Diehr*, 1981

The next case on computer-related inventions decided by the Supreme Court is *Diamond v. Diehr,* 450 U.S. 175 (1981). The patent before the Court this time claimed a process for curing synthetic rubber, including several steps utilizing a mathematical formula and a programmed digital computer. The Court held that the claimed physical and chemical process for molding precision synthetic rubber products was patentable subject matter, since the patent application claims covered the step-by-step transformation of an article, in this case raw, uncured, synthetic rubber, into a different state or thing. The claims described a method, beginning with the loading of a mold with raw, uncured rubber and ending with the eventual opening of the press at the conclusion of the cure. The Court's conclusion was not altered by the fact that several steps of the process involved a mathematical equation and a programmed digital computer.

The Court, in the Diehr case, differentiated its decision from the *Benson* case, the latter involving an algorithm used to convert binary code decimal numbers to equivalent pure binary numbers, which was held to constitute unpatentable subject matter. The sole practical application of the Benson algorithm was in connection with the programming of a general purpose digital computer. In the *Benson* case, the Court defined an "algorithm" as "a procedure for solving a given type of mathematical problem," and concluded that such an algorithm, or mathematical formula, is comparable to a law of nature which cannot be the subject of a patent grant.

In the Diehr case, however, the patent claims were not directed to a mathematical formula. Instead, they were directed to a process of curing synthetic rubber. The Diehr process admittedly employed a mathematical equation, but the patent applicants did not seek to preempt the use of that equation. They only sought to foreclose others from using that equation in conjunction with all of the other steps in their claimed process, including steps of processing the rubber. The Court held that one does not need a computer to cure natural or synthetic rubber, but if the use of the computer incorporated in the claimed process lessens the possibility of over-curing or under-curing, the process as a whole does not become unpatentable subject matter.

The Court in the *Diehr* case concluded that a patent claim drawn to subject matter otherwise protectable by a patent, does not become unpatentable simply because it uses a mathematical formula, computer program or a digital computer. The court also held that an application of a law of nature or mathematical formula to a known structure or process may well be deserving of patent protection. Thus, while a scientific truth, or the mathematical expression of that truth, is not patentable, a novel and useful structure or process created with the aid of that knowledge and scientific truth is patentable subject matter, once the criteria of novelty and unobviousness are also satisfied.

14.2.3 *Arrhythmia v. Corazonix,* 1992

In the 1992 CAFC case of *Arrhythmia Research Technology, Inc. v. Corazonix Corp.* 958 Fed. 2d 1053 (Fed. Cir. 1992), the patent claims in question related to a method of detecting those heart attack victims who were more at risk for suffering later complications. The claimed technique involved measuring and then processing electrocardiograph signals. In sustaining the claims as being directed to patentable subject matter, the CAFC reasoned that although the claims recited a mathematical algorithm, the number obtained from the algorithm is not just an abstraction, it is a measure in microvolts of a specified heart activity. In this case, the apparatus claims of the patent application called for a "means" for converting electrocardiograph signals from analog form to digital form. The patent application specification described this "means" as a conventional analog-to-digital converter. Calculations performed on a microcomputer were stored in the form of electrical signals. The computer-performed operations transformed a particular input signal to a different output signal. The Court reasoned that "The claimed invention . . . converts one physical thing into another physical thing just as any other electrical circuitry would do," relying on a prior 1980 decision finding that patent claims directed to an apparatus for analyzing seismic signals, including mathematically described means for "sonogramming," "dividing," and "plotting" described patentable subject matter.

Therefore, the court determined that data or signals are not abstractions; they are related to the patient's heart functions. It is clear from this decision that an electronic apparatus or device for transforming electrical signals constitutes patentable subject matter.

14.2.4 *In re: Alappat,* 1994

In the 1994 CAFC case of *In re Alappat,* 33 Fed. 3d 1526 (Fed. Cir. 1994), the invention under consideration was an improved technique for reducing apparent discontinuities or jaggedness in the display of wave forms on an osciloscope. Specific mathematical formulae were used to interpolate between data points to display a continuous line on the osciloscope rather than discrete points. The patent application claims recited features representing circuitry elements that performed mathematical calculations. The CAFC held that the claimed invention, as a whole, constituted patentable subject matter directed to a combination of interrelated elements which combine to form a machine for converting discrete wave form data samples into anti-aliased pixel illumination intensity data to be displayed on a display device. This is not a disembodied mathematical concept which may be characterized as an abstract idea, but rather a specific machine to produce a "useful, concrete and tangible result."

Although the Alappat invention was only directed to a new process that could be implemented on existing hardware, the majority of the court felt that the patentable invention was still in a "new machine." The court said that "such programming creates a new machine, because the general-purpose computer in effect becomes a special purpose computer once it is programmed to perform particular functions pursuant to instructions from program software." Thus, the court appears to be holding that a standard computer, when programmed to do a certain function, becomes a "new machine," and new machines constitute patentable subject matter. Under this analysis, the court looked at the software and hardware that it operates as a single unit, and each time a new piece of software is added to the hardware, a new machine totality is created.

14.2.5 The Guidelines

In the 1995 CAFC case of *In re Beauregard,* 53 Fed. 3d 1583 (Fed. Cir. 1995), IBM appealed the U.S. Patent and Trademark Office's rejection of a patent application directed to "software contained on a floppy disk." During the pendency of this appeal, the Patent and Trademark Office made a decision that it would not oppose this particular type of patent claim, and stated to the CAFC that it would soon issue guidelines for the examination of software patents. In early 1996, the U.S. Patent and Trademark Office issued new examining procedures for software patent applications, titled "Examination Guidelines for Computer-Related Inventions," which can be found at 61 Fed. Reg. 7478 (1996) ("the guidelines").

The guidelines recognize that abstract ideas, natural phenomenon and laws of nature are non-statutory and non-patentable subject matter under the patent laws. These three important exclusions recognize that subject matter that is not a practical application or use of an idea, a law of nature or a natural phenomenon is not patentable. Thus, the guidelines base the patentability of software upon its utility, and place reliance upon the patent applicant's total invention disclosure in the patent application to establish that the patent application is directed to patentable subject matter.

Where a use or uses for specific hardware or specific software are adequately described in the patent application specification to support a claim, the claim will probably be found to define patentable subject matter. However, patent application disclosures set forth in generalities without establishing a concrete use for the invention will probably not lead to the grant of a patent. While the guidelines do not have the force of law, many courts have relied upon these guidelines in reaching their decisions on the patentability of software-related inventions, and to date no court has seen fit to overturn the effect of the guidelines. The guidelines reflect the position of the government agency charged with the responsibility of issuing patents, and courts have on more than one occasion given weight to views of the experts of the U.S. Patent and Trademark Office.

14.2.6   The *State Street* "Finale"

Of major importance is the CAFC case of *State Street Bank and Trust Company v. Signature Financial Group, Inc.,* 149 Fed. 3d 1368 (Fed. Cir. 1998). Signature owned a patent entitled "Data Processing System for Hub and Spoke Financial Services Configuration," which patent was generally directed to a data processing system for implementing an investment structure developed for use in Signature's business as an administrator and accounting agent for mutual funds. The program facilitates a structure whereby mutual funds (spokes) pool their assets in an investment portfolio (hub) organized as a partnership. This investment configuration provides an administrator of the mutual fund with the advantageous combination of economies of scale in administrating investments, coupled with the tax advantages of a partnership. State Street, after unsuccessfully trying to negotiate a license under the Signature patent, brought a court action, alleging amongst other things that the Signature patent did not claim statutory subject matter under the patent laws.

The patented system provides a way for daily allocation of assets for two or more spokes that are invested in the same hub, and determines the percentage share that each spoke maintains in the hub while taking into consideration daily changes both in the value of the hub's investment securities and in the concomitant amount of each spoke's asset. The system ultimately enables the determination of the true asset value of each spoke and an accurate calculation of allocation ratios between or among spokes.

A mutual fund administrator is required to calculate the value of the shares in the fund to the nearest penny within as little as an hour and a half after the stock market closes each day. Given the complexity of these calculations, a computer or equivalent device is a virtual necessity. The patent claims in question were in "means plus function" format. The CAFC held that the patent claims were properly construed as being directed toward a machine which included "means" as the structural elements.

The decision of the CAFC in the *State Street* case is reprinted in pertinent part at the end of this chapter. In that decision, note that the court paraphrases the seven elements of the patent claim, and shows how the term "means" defines a particular physical structure, such as a personal computer, a data disk, etc. Claim 1 of the subject patent was construed as being directed to a machine, namely, a data processing system for managing a financial services configuration. The machine is made up, at the very least, of the specific structures disclosed in the written description in the patent, and those structures correspond to the "means plus function" elements recited in the claim. The court went on to state that a machine is proper patentable subject matter.

The *State Street* decision includes a very important analysis indicating that the lower court erred in concluding that the subject matter fell into two exceptions to the patentable subject matter classification, that being mathematical algorithms and business methods. Prior to the *State Street* case, mathematical algorithms and business methods were not considered patentable subject matter. However, *State Street* substantially changed all that. The court repeated a previous comment by the Supreme Court that Congress intended Section 101 of the Patent Statute, which defines patentable subject matter, to extend to "anything under the sun that is made by man." An analysis of the "Mathematical Algorithm" portion of the *State Street* decision follows. The "Business Method" portion of *State Street* is discussed at Chapter 16, Section 16.1.

14.2.7   The "Mathematical Algorithm" Exception Analysis of *State Street*

Prior to the *State Street* decision, the Supreme Court in the *Diehr* case had identified three categories of subject matter that are unpatentable, namely laws of nature, natural phenomenon, and abstract ideas. This is the law today. In the *Diehr* case, the Court also held that mathematical algorithms are not patentable subject matter to the extent that, standing alone, they are merely abstract ideas, and did not reach the level of patentability until reduced to some type of practical application resulting in a "useful, concrete and tangible result."

Unpatentable mathematical algorithms are identifiable by showing that they are merely abstract ideas constituting disembodied concepts or truths that are not "useful." Thus, to be patentable, a mathematical algorithm must be applied in a "useful" way. For example, in the *Alappat* case, it was held that data transformed by a machine through a series of mathematical calculations to produce a smooth wave form display on a rasterizer monitor constituted a practical application of an abstract idea, because it produced a useful, concrete and tangible result, i.e.: a smooth wave form.

In the *State Street* case, the court held that the transformation of data, representing discrete dollar amounts, by a machine through a series of mathematical calculations into a final share price, constitutes a patentable practical allocation of a mathematical algorithm, formula, or calculation because it produces a useful, concrete and tangible result. That result is a final share price momentarily fixed for recording and reporting purposes, and even accepted and relied upon by regulatory authorities and in subsequent trades.

The question of whether a computer-related invention encompasses patentable subject matter should focus on the central characteristics of the subject matter, and in particular its practical utility. In *State Street,* the machine programmed with the hub and spoke software produced a useful, concrete and tangible result, defining statutory and patentable subject matter. This is true even though the useful result is expressed in numbers, such as price, profit, percentage, cost or loss.

Based upon the *State Street* case, inventors applying for patents covering software inventions can now, and should, describe and claim their inventions in terms of a process having a stated utility. These applicants do not have to rely solely on claiming the software in association with a machine, such as a computer system or CPU.

14.2.8   *AT&T v. Excel Communications*

The 1999 CAFC case of *AT&T v. Excel Communications,* 172 Fed. 3d 1352 (Fed. Cir. 1999) confirmed the *State Street* holding by stating: "The mere fact that a claimed invention involves inputting numbers, calculating numbers, outputting numbers, and storing numbers, in and of itself, would not render it nonstatutory subject matter, unless, of course, its operation does not produce a useful, concrete and tangible result." In the *AT&T* case, the court found a tangible and useful result was produced, because the claimed process facilitated differential billing of long-distance phone calls.

A more fundamental question now appears on the horizon for consideration. That is whether even pure mathematics can now be patented. See, for example, U.S. Patent No. 4,744,028, reprinted as Fig. 14.1 on the following pages, covering a new linear algebra technique for allocating scarce resources in a large system such as a telephone network.

14.3   PROPER PROTECTION OF COMPUTER-RELATED SOFTWARE

After the CAFC decided that computer related inventions, including software and hardware, constituted patentable subject matter, the U.S. Patent and Trademark Office guidelines were issued to assist the patent examiners in the examination of patent applications directed to such inventions. As of the writing of this text, these guidelines do not have the force of law, however courts and the U.S. Patent and Trademark Office have been relying upon these guidelines in the examination, allowance and interpretation of computer related patents. In addition to these guidelines, the "Manual of Patent Examining Procedure" (MPEP) published by the U.S. Patent and Trademark Office incorporates significant useful information to not only assist the examiner, but to guide an inventor of a computer-related invention in ensuring that his/her patent application properly defines patentable subject matter.

"Computer-related inventions," according to the MPEP, includes inventions implemented in a computer, and inventions employing computer-readable media. The following discussion is equally applicable to claimed inventions implemented in either hardware or software.

14.3.1   How to Prepare a Proper Patent Application Covering Computer-Related Inventions

Specification   Your patent application covering a computer-related invention should set forth precisely what you, the inventor, have invented and are seeking to patent. The specification of the application should pointedly state how the claims relate to and define the specific point of novelty of your invention.

Before the recent changes in the patent law of computer-related inventions, discussed previously, the patent examiners rejected applications that merely recited a "mathematical algorithm." Today, however, the examiners are advised to review the complete specification, including the detailed description of the invention, any embodiments that are described, the claims and most importantly, specific, substantial and credible utility or usefulness asserted for the invention.

After the *State Street* case, the U.S. Patent and Trademark Office follows the rule that the invention as claimed, as a whole, must accomplish a practical application; that is it must produce a useful, concrete and tangible result. Thus, your patent application should set forth a "real world" value, as opposed to subject matter that represents nothing more than an idea or concept, or is simply a starting point for future investigation or research. Thus, it is important that the complete disclosure in your patent application contain an indication of all practical applications for the claimed invention, along with a description of

United States Patent [19]

Karmarkar

[11]   **Patent Number: 4,744,028**

[45]   **Date of Patent: May 10, 1988**

[54]   **METHODS AND APPARATUS FOR EFFICIENT RESOURCE ALLOCATION**

[75]   Inventor: **Narendra K. Karmarkar,** Somerset, N.J.

[73]   Assignee: **American Telephone and Telegraph Company, AT&T Bell Laboratories,** Murray Hill, N.J.

[21]   Appl. No.:   **725,342**

[22]   Filed: **Apr. 19, 1985**

[51]   Int. Cl.⁴ G06F 15/20; H04Q 3/66; H04M 7/00

[52]   **U.S. Cl.** **364/402**

[58]   **Field of Search** 364/402; 379/113, 221; 340/524

[56]   **References Cited**

U.S. PATENT DOCUMENTS

4,364,115	12/1982	Asai	364/765
4,479,176	10/1984	Grimshaw	369/168
4,481,600	11/1984	Asai	364/765

OTHER PUBLICATIONS

Linear Programming and Extensions, G. B. Dantzig, 1963.
Hacijan, L. G., A Polynomiar Algorithm in Linear Programming, Soviet Math. Dokl, vol. 20, #1, 1979.
Bland, R. G. et al., The Elipsoid Method: A Survey, vol. 29, No. 6, Operations Research 1981.
A New Polynomial-Time Algorithm Ser Linear Programming, N. Karmarkar, ACM 1984.
Design and Optimization of Networks with Dynamic Routing, G. R. Ash et al., The Bell System Tech. Journal, vol. 60, No. 8, 10/1981, p. 1787.
G. R. Ash et al., Servicing and Real-Time Control of Networks with Dynamic Routing, The Bell System Tech. Journal, vol. 60, No. 8, 10/1981, p. 1821.
"The Ellipsoid Method and its Consequences in Combinatorial Optimization," Combinatorica 1(2), Grotschel et al., 1981, pp. 169-197.

Primary Examiner—Joseph Ruggiero
Assistant Examiner—Charles B. Meyer
Attorney, Agent, or Firm—Robert O. Nimtz; Henry T. Brendzel

[57]   **ABSTRACT**

A method and apparatus for optimizing resource allocations is disclosed which proceeds in the interior of the solution space polytope instead of on the surface (as does the simplex method), and instead of exterior to the polytope (as does the ellipsoid method). Each successive approximation of the solution point, and the polytope, are normalized such that the solution point is at the center of the normalized polytope. The objective function is then projected into the normalized space and the next step is taken in the interior of the polytope, in the direction of steepest-descent of the objective function gradient and of such a magnitude as to remain within the interior of the polytope. The process is repeated until the optimum solution is closely approximated. The optimization method is sufficiently fast to be useful in real time control systems requiring more or less continual allocation optimization in a changing environment, and in allocation systems heretofore too large for practical implementation by linear programming methods.

36 Claims, 5 Drawing Sheets

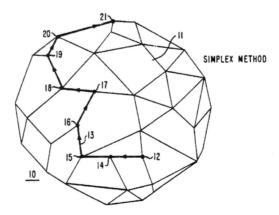

SIMPLEX METHOD

Figure 14.1. U.S. Patent Number 4,744,028.

13

4,744,028

14

links, i.e., c is the cost coefficient and x is the link load. The constraint coefficients (a_{ij}) represent the capacity of the transmission lines (which cannot be exceeded) and the traffic loads (which must be served). As in the general system of FIG. 6, only positive values of link loads are permissible ($x_i \geq 0$).

More specifically, a telephone routing system can be represented as a linear program model as shown in the Ash reference:

$$\text{Minimize:} \quad \sum_{i=1}^{L} M_i a_i \tag{15}$$

$$\text{Subject To:} \quad \sum_{k=1}^{K} \sum_{j=1}^{J_k^h} P_{jk}^{ih} \, r_{jk}^h \leq a_i,$$

$$i = 1, 2, \ldots, L; \, h = 1, 2, \ldots, H$$

$$\sum_{j=1}^{J_k^h} \frac{r_{jk}^h}{1 - g_{jk}^h} = R_k^h,$$

$$h = 1, 2, \ldots, H; \, k = 1, 2, \ldots, K$$

$$r_{jk}^h \geq 0, \; a_i \geq 0$$

where

L = the total number of links in the network,
K = the number of demand pairs (offered load),
H = the number of design hours,
J_k^h = the number of routes for demand pair k in hour h,
P_{jk}^{ih} = the proportion of carried load on route j for point-to-point demand pair k on link i in hour h,
M_i = the incremental link cost metric in terms of dollar cost per erland of carried traffic for link i,
R_k^h = the offered load to demand pair k in hour h,
r_{jk}^h = the carried load on route j of demand pair k in hour h,
A_i^h = the offered load to link i in hour h,
a_i = the maximum carried load on link i over all hours,
g_{jk}^h = the route blocking on route j of demand pair k in hour h, and
b_i^h = the blocking on link i in hour h.

A system for solving this type of LP model is shown in FIG. 8.

FIG. 8 shows an iterative loop for route formulation for telephone network 100. The apparatus of FIG. 7 finds the shortest (most economical) paths, e.g., 101, 102, 103, between points, e.g., 104, 105, in the network 100. Acceptable blocking levels are assumed (or actual blocking is measured in box 106) and router 107 forms paths 101, 102, 103 into candidate routes (sequences of paths). Router 107 also determines the proportion of traffic flow offered to each path in the route for each unit of offered load, where this traffic load is continually provided by box 109. The linear program controler 108 then assigns traffic flows to the candidate routes to minimize overall network routing costs. The output from linear programming controller 108 is the optimum routing plan which can then be used by routing tables 110 to control the flow of traffic on each link.

The telephone routing apparatus of FIG. 8 can be used to control the telephone network continually or at regular intervals. Thus, with the much faster procedures of FIGS. 4 and 5, it is possible to use the apparatus of FIG. 8 to dynamically control the telephone network in the presence of changing demand and changing link availability.

It can be seen that the solution to the telephone routine problem provides the optimal traffic load to be placed on each transmission link, and hence the optimum routing for all telephone calls. Moreover, since the national telephone network includes a large number of such links, the time required to solve the problem is of considerable importance to the actual usefulness of the solution. Traffic loading changes, linkage outages and link cost variations all affect the optimal allocation. Routing control must therefore be provided before the problem itself changes significantly. While heuristic methods are of assistance in this regard, a much faster linear programming method is also of extreme usefulness, particularly in handling unexpected (unpredictable) loads.

Other problems which would benefit from the new procedures herein described include industrial process control, deployment of personnel to provide customer services, blending of ingredients to form commercial products, oil refinery product mix, assignments of computer resources to a plurality of users, and many others. In each case, the cost (or benefit) coefficients must be measured or otherwise determined, the constraint limits must be established and the contributions of all of the decision variables to these constraints also measured or determined. The result of executing the procedures is, in each case, the specification of a set of control parameters which, when applied to the real world situation, will produce an optimum process or apparatus.

It should be noted that the matrices involved in most practical linear programming problems are sparse matrices and that sparse matrix techniques can also be used in evaluating the search direction p in FIGS. 4 and 5.

While the present inventor has constructed a new method for solving linear programming problems, it is to be understood that the claims of this invention relate only to the application of this novel method to arrangements that determine the optimum allocation of resources in real world technological and industrial systems that lend themselves to a linear representation of the variables and constraints characterizing the system, i.e., physical arrangements that determine how resources are actually applied to optimize the performance of processes, machines, manufactures or compositions of matter. All other uses of the new method, such as computation research, algorithm research, or linear algebra research activities, form no part of the present invention. Similarly, use of the new method in non-technological or non-industrial systems likewise form no part of the present invention.

What is claimed is:

1. A method for allocating the available telecommunication transmission facilities among the subscribers demanding service at a particular time so as to reduce the total cost of operating said transmission facilities, where the available transmission facilities, the subscribers, and the total cost are related in a linear manner, said method comprising the steps of:

tentatively and iteratively reassigning said available telecommunications transmission facilities to said subscribers so as to reduce said total costs at each said reassignment,

each said reassignment being determined by normalizing the previous assignment with respect to constraints on said allocations,

terminating said iterative reassigning steps when said costs are below a preselected threshold, and

allocating said transmission facilities in accordance with the reduced cost assignment.

Figure 14.1. *continued.*

4,744,028

15

2. A telecommunications transmission system comprising:

a plurality of links interconnecting a plurality of telecommunication switching nodes, and

means for assigning traffic arising at each of said nodes to said links so as to reduce the cost of carrying said traffic, said assigning means including

means for iteratively selecting estimates of said reduced cost assignments such that each said iterative selection represents assignment values entirely in the interior of the multidimensional convex solution space representing the physical constrains on said assignments.

3. A method of allocating available user facilities among a plurality of users so as to reduce the cost of providing said facilities, said method comprising the steps of

tentatively and iteratively reassigning said facilities among said users so as to reduce said costs at each said reassignment,

each said iterative reassignment being determined by centralizing the previous assignment with respect to constraints on said allocations,

terminating said iterative reassignment step when said costs are at a below a preselected limit, and

allocating said available user facilities among said users in accordance with the final iterative reassignment.

4. The method according to claim 3 wherein said facilities comprise telecommunication transmission facilities and said users comprise telephone subscribers.

5. The method according to claim 3 wherein said facilities comprise information handling facilities.

6. The method according to claim 3 wherein said facilities comprise data processing facilities.

7. The method according to claim 3 wherein said facilities comprise manufacturing facilities.

8. An optimized resource allocation system comprising:

a first plurality of physical resources available for use,

a second plurality of resource users using said physical resources, and

means for assigning said resource users to said physical resources so as to reduce the cost of providing said resources, said assigning means including

means for iteratively and tentatively selecting feasible ones of said assignments such that, at each iteration, each of said feasible assignments is centered within the interior of a normalized multidimensional convex feasible solution space, and

means for allocating said physical resources in accordance with the final one of said tentative assignments.

9. The allocation system according to claim 8 wherein said physical resources comprise telecommunications facilities and said users comprise telephone subscribers.

10. The allocation system according to claim 8 wherein said physical resources comprise information handling facilities.

11. The allocation system according to claim 8 wherein said physical resources comprise data processing facilities.

12. The allocation system according to claim 8 wherein said physical facilities comprise manufacturing facilities.

16

13. A system for optimizing the performance of a controlled process in accordance with an optimizing criterion, said system comprising:

process control devices for controlling said process in response to control signal sets,

a plurality of sensors for sensing variable conditions affecting the operation of said process,

a plurality of data input devices for prescribing conditions affecting the operation of said process, and

a linear programming controller responsive to said sensors and said input devices for providing optimum control signal sets to said process control devices,

said controller including means for iteratively identifying successive tentative strictly feasible control signal sets and selecting each next tentative control signal set in the direction of the steepest gradient of a normalized version of said optimizing criteria.

14. A controller for optimizing the operation of a controlled system comprising:

means for determining the physical constraints and constraint limits on the operation of said system,

means for prescribing performance measurement criteria for the operation of said system,

means for successively identifying tentative sets of operational control values strictly satisfying said constraints and said constraint limits,

means for normalizing said tentative sets of control values so as to equidistance said control values from said constraint limits, and

means for selecting each next successive set of normalized control values in accordance with said prescribed performance measurement criteria.

15. A method for allocating physical resources using a linear programming model including the steps of:

prescribing a linear programming model with an objective function and a plurality of constraints which adequately describes feasible allocations of said physical resources,

identifying a tentative physical resource allocation which is strictly feasible,

iteratively improving said tentative resource allocation by normalizing said tentative resource allocation with respect to said constraints and altering said tentative resource allocations in the direction specified by said objective function, and

allocating said resources in accordance with the most improved tentative resource allocation.

16. The improvement in linear programming methods for optimally allocating physical resources among a plurality of users which includes the steps of:

iterating on only strictly feasible allocations, and

normalizing each strictly feasible allocation with respect to the constraints on said allocations.

17. A system for allocating technological resources among a plurality of user entities, each said allocation having constraints imposed thereon and quantifiable costs or quantifiable benefits associated therewith, said system including resource allocation elements disposed by a resource allocating mechanism including:

means for representing said constraints as a multidimensional convex polytope having facets representing said constraints and having a surface representing preferred resource allocations,

means for tentatively selecting an allocation of said resources corresponding to a point in the interior of said polytope as a beginning point,

Figure 14.1. *continued.*

4,744,028

17

means for stepping from said beginning point to a succession of points in the interior of said polytope, each succeeding point representing a more optimal allocation than the preceding point, and

means for deploying the elements of said system to accommodate the preferred resource allocation specified by a point on said surface.

18. A technological resource allocation system for allocating technological resources among a plurality of resource users subject to constraints on said allocations and in such a manner as to reduce the total cost of said allocations, the allocations made in said system being determined in accordance with a method comprising the following steps:

(1) receiving information concerning availability of said technological resources, said users, said constraints, and said costs,

(2) representing said constraints as a polytope in multidimensional space,

(3) representing said allocation costs as a vector in said multidimensional space,

(4) selecting an initial allocation point located in the interior of said polytope,

(5) normalizing said polytope such that said initial allocation point is substantially at its center,

(6) determining the direction of said cost vector projected into the null space of said constraints within said normalized polytope,

(7) selecting a new allocation point in said normalized polytope in a direction opposite to the direction of said projected cost vector, and

(8) repeating steps (4) through (7) for said new allocation point,

(9) allocating said technological resources to said users in accordance with the latest one of said new allocation point.

19. A system comprising a plurality of resources achieving a plurality of end results and employing a recursive method for allocating said resources to achieve said end results, wherein a present resource allocation arrangement x^i is replaced by an improved resource allocation arrangement x^{i+1} which is derived from x^i by the equation $x^{i+1} = \Phi\{X^i\}$ and which becomes the present resource allocation arrangement of the next iteration, the function Φ comprising:

(1) arranging the components of said present resource allocation arrangement along the diagonal of an otherwise empty matrix D;

(2) forming a matrix B by developing the matrix product AD and augmenting the developed product with a last row of n 1's;

(3) developing a vector c_p by obtaining the value of $[I - B^T(BB^T)B]^{-1}Dc$ where I is the identity matrix;

(4) dividing c_p by its magnitude to develop a normalized pointer $\hat{c}_p$;

(5) creating a transformed new estimate x^{i+1} of x by subtracting $\alpha\hat{c}_p$ from said current transformed estimate x^i of x, where α is less than unity;

(6) creating an untransformed new estimate of x by evaluating Dx^{i+1}/e^TDx^{i+1} where $e = \{1, 1, \ldots, 1\}$; and

(7) applying said new estimate x^{i+1} of x to said system.

20. The method of allocating industrial resources among a plurality of resource users, each said allocation having physical constraints on resource use and quantifiable costs or benefits associated with each said allocation, said method comprising the steps of

18

(1) receiving information concerning availability of said industrial resources, said users, said constraints, and said costs,

(2) representing said physical constraints with a system of linear relationships together defining a multidimensional polytope having a facet representing each of said physical constraints,

(3) selecting a tentative set of allocations of said resources represented by an interior point within said polytope as a beginning allocation point,

(4) transforming said polytope to place said beginning allocation point substantially at the geometrical center of said transformed polytope and all said facets at substantially equal distances from said center,

(5) moving from said beginning allocation point to another allocation point interior to said rescaled polytope but closer to the surface of said rescaled polytope,

(6) transforming said another allocation point back to the original scale of said polytope,

(7) repeating steps (4) through (6) until a point interior to said polytope is selected which is substantially coincident with said surface,

(8) identifying the allocation values associated with said point substantially coincident with said surface, and

(9) allocating said resources in accordance with the resource allocation values so identified.

21. A system for allocating industrial resources among a plurality of resource consumers, each resource allocation being physically constrained and having quantifiable costs associated with said allocation, said system providing allocations of said resources determined in accordance with a method comprising the steps of:

(1) representing said physical constraints as a system of linear relationships defining a closed convex multidimensional solid,

(2) selecting a resource allocation corresponding to a point interior to said multidimensional solid as a beginning point,

(3) transforming said closed solid so as to place said selected beginning point substantially at the geometric center of said transformed solid and the surfaces of said solid substantially equidistant from said center,

(4) selecting another allocation of said resources corresponding to another point interior to said rescaled closed solid but closer to said surface than said beginning point,

(5) repeating steps (3) and (4) with the new allocations until a selected allocation substantially corresponds to a point on the surface of said solid, and arranging said system to allocate said resources in accordance with the final industrial resource allocation associated with said point on the surface of said solid.

22. A linear programming controller for use with a general purpose digital computer, said controller comprising:

a computer program storage medium having a computer program stored thereon for execution by said digital computer, said program comprising

means for processing a plurality of linear relationships defining a multidimensional convex polytope representing the set of feasible solutions to said plurality of linear relationships, and

Figure 14.1. *continued.*

4,744,028

19

means, including a function to be optimized, for identifying that point on the boundary of said polytope representing the optimum solution to said plurality of linear relationships by proceeding in successive steps along a strictly feasible solution path entirely contained within the interior of said polytope.

23. A method for allocating physical resources among a plurality of resource users subject to constraints on said allocations and in such a manner as to reduce related allocation costs, said method comprising the steps of:

(1) representing said constraints as a polytope in multidimensional space,

(2) representing said allocation costs as a vector in said multidimensional space,

(3) selecting an initial allocation point located in the interior of said polytope,

(4) transforming said polytope into an equivalent space with said initial allocation point substantially at its center,

(5) determining the direction of said cost vector in said equivalent space,

(6) selecting a new allocation point in said equivalent space in a direction opposite to the direction of said cost vector,

(7) transforming said new allocation point back to the original space of said polytope,

(8) repeating steps (4) through (7) for said new allocation point,

(9) terminating the iterative process defined in steps (4) through (8) when evaluated allocation costs fall below a preselected threshold, and

(10) allocating said physical resources among said plurality of resource users in accordance with the latest one of said new allocation point.

24. A method for allocating industrial or technological resources x_i ($i=1$, n) among a plurality of resource users subject to constraints $A_{ij}x_i \leqq b_j$ and $x_i \geqq 0$ ($i=1$, n; $j=1$, m) in such a manner as to optimize a cost function $c_i^T \cdot x_i$, said method comprising the steps of:

(1) selecting an initial allocation $x^{start}=(x_1^{start}, x_2^{start}, \ldots, x_n^{start})$ meeting said constraints,

(2) using the projective transformation

$$x_i' = \frac{D^{-1}x}{e^T D^{-1}x}$$

where

$$D = \mathrm{diag}.\{x_1^{start}, x_2^{start}, \ldots, x_n^{start}\},$$

and

$$e = (1, 1, 1, \ldots, 1),$$

to transform said constraints into an affine space with x^{start} substantially at its center,

(3) determining the cost function vector c_p in said affine space by the relationship

$$c_p = \{I - B^T(BB^T)^{-1}B\}Dc$$

where

I is the identity matrix,
c is the cost vector,
D is defined above, and

$$B = (AD/e^T),$$

20

(4) normalizing said cost function vector c_p by the relationship

$$\hat{c}_p = \frac{c_p}{|c_p|},$$

(5) selecting a new initial allocation b′ in said affine space given by

$$b' = x'^{start} - \alpha r \hat{c}_p,$$

where

r is the radius of the largest inscribed sphere in said affine space and is given by

$$r = \frac{1}{n(n-1)},$$

and
α is less than unity,

(6) transforming said new new initial allocation point back to the original space with the transformation

$$b = \frac{Db'}{e^T Db'},$$

and

(7) repeating steps (2) through (6) using b instead of a_o as the new initial allocation

(8) allocating said industrial or technological resources in accordance with said new allocation b′.

25. A method for improving overall cost in a system having a plurality n of industrial resources operating in concert to achieve a plurality of technological end results b_j, each of said resources providing a contribution to each of said end results with an attendant cost coefficient and subject to constraints characterizing said system, where vector b represents said plurality of end results, vector x represents the set of said contributions required of said plurality of resources, vector c represents the set of said cost coefficients, and matrix A represents said system constraints,

CHARACTERIZED BY:

selecting a set of contributions x^{curr} satisfying said system constraints as a current estimate of x;

arranging said current estimate x^{curr} along the diagonal of an otherwise empty matrix D;

forming a matrix B by developing the matrix product AD and augmenting the developed product with a last row of n 1's;

developing a pointer vector c_p by evaluating $[I - B^T(BB^T)^{-1}B]Dc$ where I is the identity matrix;

dividing c_p by its magnitude to develop a normalized pointer $\hat{c}_p$;

creating a transformed new estimate x^1 of x by subtracting αc_p from e/n, where α is less than unity,

creating an untransformed new estimate x^{next} of x by evaluating Dx′/e Dx′ where $e = \{1,1, \ldots 1\}$; and applying said new estimate x^{next} of x to said system.

26. Method for allocating industrial or technological resources, said method comprising:

the determination of values for controllable physical variables associated with said resources,

Figure 14.1. *continued.*

4,744,028

21

the set of feasible combinations of said physical variables being a convex set and said determination to be effected so as to enhance the value of an objective function of said physical variables,

said determination comprising a sequence of steps such that at each step tentative values for said physical variables are replaced

said replacing based on choosing a direction in a set which is obtained by centralizing said convex set; and

allocating said resources in accordance with the last step in said sequence of steps of replacing tentative values of said physical resources.

27. A method of optimizing the allocation of resources in a system characterized by a linear objective function, each element of which represents a specific resource allocation attributable to an individual entity of the system, and comprises a variable and a known variable coefficient, and by one or more constraint linear forms expressed in terms of one or more of the variables of the objective function, said method comprising the steps of

(1) determining an initial value for each of the variables of the objective function such that a vector in n-dimensional space defined by the initial values resides inside a polytope defined by the constraint linear forms,

(2) transforming the polytope including the initial vector and the constraint linear forms into a simplex $S\{x|x>=0, \Sigma x_i=1\}$ having the origin of the initial vector located substantially at its center,

(3) projecting the transformed initial vector orthogonally onto the simplex,

(4) determining the direction of the projection of the transformed initial vector in said simplex,

(5) determining a new starting point for a new initial vector by moving from the center e/n of the simplex S in a direction opposite to said determined direction by a distance in said simplex equal to a multiple of the radius of the largest sphere inscribed in said simplex and centered at the origin of the transformed initial vector,

(6) transforming said new starting point back into the polytope space,

(7) repeating steps (2) through (6), substituting, for the initial values of the objective function variables, values defined by said transformed new starting point, until a satisfactory minimization of the objective function is obtained, and

allocating system resources to the individual system entities according to the final values of the elements of the objective function.

28. The method of claim 27 wherein step (2) further comprises the step of:

generating a matrix B by multiplying a diagonal matrix of the initial values of the variables of the objective function by a matrix of the coefficients of the constraint linear forms, and adding an additional lower-most row to matrix B containing a value of unity in each matrix position of the row.

29. The method of claim 27 wherein step (3) further comprises the step of

computing the orthogonal projection of the transformed initial vector from the matrix equation $[I-B^T(BB^T)^{-1}B]$ times the diagonal matrix of the initial variable values times the initial vector, where I is the identity matrix and B^T is the transpose of the B matrix, and

22

normalizing said orthogonal projection.

30. The method of claim 27 wherein step (5) further comprises the step of:

calculating a new transformed initial vector from the value of $(x^{start}-\alpha r)$ times said transformed cost vector, where $x^{start}=e/n$, r is the radius of said inscribed sphere and α is a preselected constant.

31. The invention of claim 30 further comprising the step of:

computing said radius from the formula $1/\sqrt{n(n-1)}$.

32. A method of optimizing an allocation of resources in a system characterized by an n-dimensional objective function, each element of which represents a specific resource allocation attributable to an individual entity of the system and comprises a variable and a known variable coefficient, and by one or more constraint relationships expressed in terms of one or more of the variables of the objective function, said method comprising the steps of:

(1) determining an initial value for each of the variables of the objective function such that an initial vector defined by the initial values resides inside a polytope defined by the constraint relationships,

(2) transforming the polytope, including the initial vector and the constraint relationships, into a simplex $S=\{x|x_1\geqq 0, \geqq x_i=1\}$ in which the transformed initial vector is located substantially at the center of the simplex,

(3) projecting the transformed vector of said objective function orthogonally onto the null space of the transformed constraint relationships,

(4) determining the direction of the projection of the transformed objective function,

(5) determining a new value for each of the variables of the objective function by moving from the center e/n of said simplex, a distance equal to a predefined multiple of the radius of the largest sphere contained within the simplex and centered at the origin of the transformed initial vector,

(6) transforming said new values back into the original variables,

(7) repeating steps (2) through (6), substituting said new values for the initial values of the objective function variables, until a satisfactory minimization of the objective function is obtained, and

(8) allocating system resources to the individual system entities according to the final values of the elements of the objective function.

33. The method of claim 32 wherein step (2) further comprises the step of:

generating a matrix B by multiplying a diagonal matrix of the initial values of the variables of the objective function by a matrix of the coefficients of the constraint relationships, and

adding an additional lowermost row to matrix B containing a value of unity in each matrix position of the row.

34. The method of claim 33 wherein step (3) further comprises the step of:

computing the orthogonal projection of the transformed initial vector from the matrix equation $[I-B^T(BB^T)^{-1}B]$ times the initial vector, where I is the identity matrix, and B^T is the transpose of the B matrix, and

normalizing said orthogonal projection in a predefined manner.

35. A linear programming system for optimally allocating physical resources in which feasible allocations

Figure 14.1. *continued.*

4,744,028

23

are bounded by a closed, multidimensional, feasible allocation space, and in which optimum allocation involves at least one step from a less optimum allocation to a more optimum allocation, said system including first means responsive to said physical resources and to said allocation, second means for developing a resource allocation directive based on said first means, and third means for allocating said physical resources,

characterized in that:

said allocation space is rescaled so as to initiate said step substantially at the center of the rescaled feasible allocation space.

24

36. A linear programming method for optimally allocating physical resources where feasible physical resource allocations are bounded by a closed, multidimensional, feasible physical resource allocation space, and where optimum allocation involves at least one step from a less optimum allocation to a more optimum allocation,

characterized by the step of:

rescaling said physical resource allocation space so as to initiate said step substantially at the center of the rescaled space.

*   *   *   *   *

15

20

25

30

35

40

45

50

55

60

65

Figure 14.1. *continued.*

the significant functionality of your computer-related invention for which a patent is sought.

The U.S. Patent and Trademark Office takes the position that merely claiming non-functional descriptive materials stored in a computer-readable medium does not make the invention eligible for a patent. For example, a patent application claim directed to a word processing file stored on a disk may satisfy the utility requirement, since it has real world value. However, the mere fact that the claim may satisfy the "utility" requirement, does not mean that a useful result is achieved under the "practical application" requirement. The claimed invention, as a whole, must produce a useful, concrete and tangible result to have practical application.

In its guidelines, the U.S. Patent and Trademark Office has set forth certain examples of computer-related inventions that have been determined to have a practical application, and as producing a useful, concrete and tangible result:

a. A long-distance telephone billing process containing mathematical algorithms, since the claimed process applies the Boolean principal to produce a useful, concrete, and tangible result without pre-empting other uses of the mathematical principal.

b. The transformation of data, representing discrete dollar amounts, by a machine through a series of mathematical calculations into a final share price. This constitutes a practical application of a mathematical algorithm, formula or calculation, since it produces a useful, concrete and tangible result, that is a final share price momentarily fixed for recording and reporting purposes.

c. Patent claims drawn to a rasterizer for converting discrete wave form data samples into an anti-aliased pixel illumination intensity data to be displayed on the display means (monitor), since these claims define a specific machine to produce a useful, concrete and tangible result.

The important thing to remember is that the inventor and the patent application provide suffcient information to set forth concrete evidence why the invention is believed to be useful. The patent examiners will focus their efforts on statements made in the patent specification that identify all practical applications for the invention. The patent applicant may assert more than one practical application, however only one such practical application asserted in the application is necessary to satisfy the utility requirement. The examiners will also review the application specification to ensure the presence of a description of that structure and/or those functional elements that are necessary to accomplish at least one asserted practical application of the invention. Therefore, a word to the wise. Be sure when reviewing your patent application directed to a computer-related invention that utility is clearly set forth in the specification.

It is also important that the patent application explicitly explain the relative significance of the various features of the invention. The application should include the following detailed information:

a. What the programmed computer does when it performs the processes dictated by the software, that is, the functionality of the programmed computer. For example, it is true that a modern digital computer manipulates data, usually in binary form, by performing mathematical operations, such as addition, subtraction, multiplication, division or bit shifting. But this is only how the computer does what it does. Of importance is the significance of the data and their manipulation in the real world, that is, what the computer is doing.

b. How the computer is to be configured to provide the functionality set forth in the patent application specification. For example, describe those elements which constitute the programmed computer, and how those elements are configured and interrelated to provide the specified functionality.

c. Where applicable, the specification should set forth the relationship of the programmed computer to other subject matter outside the computer that constitutes the invention. This would include machines, devices, materials or process steps other than those that are part of or performed by the programmed computer. The specification should also adequately explain the role of the programmed computer in the overall process performed by the machine, and how the programmed computer is to be integrated with the other elements of the apparatus used in the process.

d. Where software constitutes a part of the best mode of carrying out the invention, include a description of such best mode including a disclosure of the functions of the software. However, charts or source code listings are not a requirement for adequately disclosing the functions of the software.

The disclosure of a software program per se is not necessary to satisfy the "best mode" requirement where the functions of the software program are readily apparent from the patent application specification, and one skilled in the art could generate the necessary software program to implement the disclosed functions.

14.3.2 Claims

The claims identify the boundaries of the protection sought by a patent applicant and the claims are looked at to understand and define what the inventor has indicated is the invention to be patented. In computer-related patent applications, the physical structure or material in a patent claim may consist of hardware or a combination of hardware and software. The elements in a patent claim must relate to those same elements that describe the particular limitation in the specification. When a patent examiner reviews the application, this relationship of claim elements to the description in the specification ensures that the patent examiner correctly interprets each claim limitation.

Language in patent claims that merely suggests or makes optional, but does not require steps to be performed, or does not limit a patent claim to a particular structure, does not adequately limit the scope of the claim to a particular structure, and does not adequately limit the scope of the claim. Examples of language in a patent claim for a computer-related invention that may cause problems are:

a. Statements of intended use or field of use,

b. "Adapted to" or "adapted for" statements,

c. "Wherein" or "whereby" clauses.

If the patent claims define a means or a step, followed by a functional limitation, the specification must include the corresponding structure, material or acts for performing the stated function. If the patent application specification defines what is meant by the claim language, the claim limitation will be interpreted as having that meaning and its equivalent. This will avoid any problems in determining the scope of the claimed limitation. With computer-related inventions, conventional programming need not be supplied in the application. The recommended procedure is to use flow diagrams to illustrate and describe the process.

In reviewing the claims of your computer-related patent application, ensure that each claim includes all of the elements which you consider essential and critical to the structure and functioning of the invention. If the desired patentability is based on specific ranges, the specification must show that these ranges are critical.

14.3.3 Determination of Whether a Computer-Related Invention Defines Patentable Subject Matter Under the Patent Laws

A patent application directed to a computer-related invention that is found to be directed to non-patentable subject matter falls into the same general category as non-statutory subject matter in other arts, namely, natural phenomena such as magnetism, and abstract ideas or laws of nature which constitute "descriptive material."

"Descriptive material" that falls outside the realm of patentability can be characterized as either "functional descriptive material" or "non-functional descriptive material." In this context, "functional descriptive material" consists of data structures and computer programs which impart functionality when employed as a computer component. "Data structure" is defined as the physical or logical relationship among data elements, designed to support specific data manipulation functions. This definition is derived from the *IEEE Standard Dictionary of Electrical and Electronics Terms,* at page 308 (Fifth Edition 1993). "Non-functional descriptive material" includes, but is not limited to music, literary works, and a compilation or mere arrangement of data.

Both functional and non-functional descriptive material are not patentable subject matter when claimed in a patent application as descriptive material by themselves. When functional descriptive materials are recorded on a computer-readable medium, the descriptive material becomes structurally and functionally interrelated to the medium, and will be considered as patentable subject matter in most cases, since use of technology permits the function of the descriptive material to be realized. For example, a patent directed to data structure stored on a computer-readable medium that increases computer efficiency was held to constitute patentable subject matter. Also, a patent claim to a computer having a specific data structure stored in memory was held to be patentable product-by-process subject matter. Similarly, a patent claim directed to a data structure standing alone was held to be non-patentable subject matter.

Where non-functional descriptive material is recorded on a computer-readable medium, it does not define patentable subject matter since no requisite functionality is present to satisfy the practical application requirement of the patent statutes. Thus, music per se is not a computer component, and does not become patentable by merely placing it on a compact disk. Protection for this type of work is provided under the Copyright Law, which is discussed in Chapter 22, Section 22.10 of this text.

Certain patent applications have been filed claiming an invention in processes that do nothing more than solve mathematical problems or manipulate abstract ideas or concepts. Such patent applications are more complex in determining whether the subject matter can be patented. If the "acts" of a process manipulate only numbers, abstract concepts or ideas, or signals representing any of the foregoing, the acts are not being applied to appropriate patentable subject matter. Thus, a process consisting solely of mathematical operations, such as converting one set of numbers into another set of numbers, does not manipulate appropriate subject matter and thus cannot constitute a patentable process.

Nonpatentable processes can be defined as:

a. Claimed subject matter that consists solely of mathematical operations without some claimed practical application, such as executing a mathematical algorithm, or

b. Claims which define subject matter that simply manipulates abstract ideas, such as a bid or a bubble hierarchy, without some claimed practical application.

To complicate matters, the Supreme Court in its decisions regarding computer-related inventions has not been clear to state exactly what kind of mathematical subject matter may or may not be patented. The Supreme Court has used terms such as "mathematical algorithm," "mathematical formula," and "mathematical equation" in describing types of mathematical subject matter that are not entitled to patent protection, standing alone.

Certain mathematical algorithms are not patentable subject matter because they represent a mathematical definition of a law of nature or a natural phenomenon. By way of example, an algorithm representing the formula $E = mc^2$ is a "law of nature"—it defines a "fundamental scientific truth," that being the relationship between energy and mass. Someone claiming an invention in a process which consists solely of the steps that one must follow to solve the mathematical representation of $E = mc^2$ would find his or her application rejected as being indistinguishable from the law of nature. Thus, if a patent application such as this were granted, the patent would not allow others to solve the mathematical representation of $E = mc^2$. A patent cannot be granted on such a process. However, although $E = mc^2$ is not patentable, that does not preclude the equation from being included in a patent claim.

14.3.4 Functional Descriptive Material: "Data Structures" Representing Descriptive Material *per se* or Computer Programs Representing Computer Listings *per se*

Data structures not claimed as embodied in a computer-readable medium constitute descriptive material *per se*, and are not patentable because they are not capable of causing functional change in the computer. Such data structures do not define any structural and functional interrelationships between the data structure and other claimed aspects of the invention which permit the functionality of the data structure to be realized. Such claimed structures are distinguishable from a computer-readable medium encoded with a data structure defining structural and functional interrelationships between the data structure and the computer software and hardware components which permit the data structure's functionality to be realized.

Similarly, computer programs set forth as computer listings *per se,* that is, the descriptions or expressions of the programs, are not physical "things." They are neither computer components nor processes, as they are not "acts" being performed. Such computer programs also do not define any structural or functional interrelationships between the computer program and other claimed elements of the computer which permit the computer program's functionality to be obtained. Again, such computer listings *per se* must be distinguished from a claimed computer readable medium encoded with a computer program, which is a computer element which defines structural and functional interrelationships between the computer program and the rest of the computer. This latter computer-readable medium is patentable. Thus, it is important to ensure that your patent application clearly distinguishes between descriptive material *per se,* and language that defines structural and functional interrelationships between the elements of the computer program and/or the computer.

Where the computer program is set forth in a patent claim as part of an otherwise patentable article of manufacture or machine, the patent claim remains patentable irrespective of the fact that the computer program is included in the claim. The same result occurs when a computer program is used in a computerized process where the computer executes the instructions set forth in the computer program. However, where the claimed invention, taken as a whole, is directed to a mere program listing, that is, to only its description or expression, such claim constitutes descriptive material *per se* and hence is not patentable.

It must be remembered that a computer program is merely a set of instructions capable of being executed by a computer, and the computer program itself is not a process. Thus, a patent claim on a computer program without the computer-readable medium needed to realize the computer program's functionality, is not patentable since it constitutes functional descriptive material. When a computer program is claimed as an invention in a process where the computer is executing the computer program's instructions, that claim will be treated as a process claim. When a computer program is recited in conjunction with a physical structure such as a computer memory, the patent examiners will treat that claim as a product claim.

14.3.5 Non-Functional Descriptive Material

Descriptive material that cannot exhibit any functional interrelationship with the way in which computing processes are performed does not constitute patentable subject matter. Where certain types of descriptive material, such as music, literature, art, photographs and minor arrangements and compilations of facts or data, are merely stored so as to be read or outputted by a computer without creating any functional interrelationship, either as part of the stored data or as part of the computing process performed by the computer, such descriptive material alone does not impart functionality either to the data so structured or to the computer. Such descriptive material does not fall within the category of patentable subject matter. Data consists of facts, which become information when the data is seen in context and conveys meaning to people. Computers process data without any understanding of what that data represents.

Music is commonly sold to consumers in a format of a compact disc, and the known compact disc acts as nothing more than a carrier for non-functional descriptive material. This purely non-functional descriptive material cannot alone provide the practical application, which constitutes the physical disc.

Non-functional descriptive material may be claimed as inventive in combination with other functional descriptive multi-medium material on a computer-readable medium to provide the necessary functional and structural interrelationship to satisfy the requirements for patentability. By way of example, a computer that recognizes a particular grouping of musical notes read from memory, and upon recognizing that particular sequence, causes another defined series of notes to be played, defines a functional interrelationship among that data and the computing process performed when utilizing that data.

Thus, this latter example provides patentable subject matter because it implements a process as defined under the patent law.

14.3.6 Natural Phenomena Such as Electricity and Magnetism

Patent claims directed to nothing but the physical characteristics of a form of energy, such as a frequency, voltage, or the strength of a magnetic field, or a defined energy or magnetism per se, do not qualify as being directed toward patentable subject matter. However, a single claim directed to a practical application of electromagnetic energy is defined as covering patentable subject matter, regardless of its transitory nature.

14.4 STATUTORY SUBJECT MATTER

14.4.1 Types of Claimed Subject Matter

The legal principals are the same in defining whether a patent application is directed to a machine or a process when determining whether patentable subject matter is presented.

a. Statutory Product Claims. "Products" in the patent law are defined as either machines, manufactures or compositions of matter.

—A "machine" is defined as "a concrete thing, consisting of parts or of certain devices and combinations of devices."

—A "manufacture" is defined as "the production of articles for use from raw or prepared materials by giving to these materials new forms, qualities, properties or combinations, whether by hand labor or by machinery."

—A composition of matter is "a composition of two or more substances or a composite article, whether it be the result of chemical union, or of mechanical mixture or whether it be a gas, fluid, powder or solid."

If a patent application is directed to a machine or manufacture, and identifies the physical structure of the machine, or manufacture, in terms of its hardware or its hardware and software combination, the application is directed to patentable subject matter. A claim submitted in a patent application limited to a machine or manufacture which has a practical application in the technological arts also defines patentable subject matter. In the *Alappat* case, 33 Fed.3rd at 1544, the CAFC stated "the claimed invention as a whole is directed to a combination of interrelated elements which combine to form a machine for converting discrete waveform data samples into anti-aliased pixel illumination intensity data to be displayed on a display means (such as a computer screen). This is not a disembodied mathematical concept which may be characterized as an 'abstract idea' but rather a specific machine to produce a useful, concrete and tangible result."

b. Statutory Process Claims. If your patentable invention is one that requires one or more acts or steps to be performed, your invention is defined as a process. To constitute patentable statutory subject matter, a claimed computer-related process must either:

1. Result in a physical transformation outside the computer for which a practical

application in the technical arts is either disclosed in the patent application specification, or would have been known to a person skilled in the art, or

2. Be limited to a practical application within the technological arts. For example, in the case of *Diamond v. Diehr,* 450 US at 183-184, the CAFC stated:

   "a [patentable] process is a mode of treatment of certain materials to produce a given result. It is an act, or a series of acts, performed upon the subject matter to be transformed and reduced to a different state or thing. . . . The process requires that certain things should be done with certain substances and in a certain order; but the tools to be used in doing this may be of secondary sequence."

Even though a scientific principle *per se* may be unpatentable, the practical application of that principle may be patentable. If a physical transformation occurs outside of the computer, the patent application disclosing that invention must permit a skilled artisan to practice the claimed invention, that is, to put it to a practical use. It is necessary for the claimed invention to be read as a whole to produce a practical result if there is only a transformation of signals or data inside a computer, or if a claimed process merely manipulates concepts or converts one set of numbers into another.

14.4.2 Safe Harbors

An inventive process clearly falls within the category of patentable subject matter if it results in a physical transformation outside the computer. These types of patentable subject matter are characterized as "safe harbors."

Independent Physical Acts, or Post-Computer Process Activity   A process defines patentable subject matter if it requires physical acts to be performed outside the computer independent of and following the steps to be performed by a programmed computer, where those acts involve the manipulation of tangible physical objects that result in the object having a different physical attribute or structure. Thus, a process claim is patentable if it includes one or more post-computer process steps that result in a physical transformation outside the computer, beyond merely conveying the direct result of the computer operation.

Examples of this type of process which constitute patentable subject matter include the following:

1. A method of curing rubber in a mold which relies upon updating process parameters, using a computer processor to determine a time period for curing rubber, using the computer processor to determine when the time period has been reached in the curing process, and then opening the mold at that stage.

2. A method of controlling a mechanical robot which relies upon storing data in a computer that represents various types of mechanical movements of the robot, using a computer processor to calculate positioning of the robot in relation to given tasks to be performed by the robot, and controlling the robot's movement and position based on the calculated position.

In contrast, the following are examples of computer related processes that do not achieve a practical application and are not patentable:

1. The step of "updating alarm limits" that constitutes merely changing the number value of a variable to represent the result of the calculation.

2. A final step of "equating" the process outputs to the values of the last set of process inputs, since the process merely stores the result of calculations.

3. A step of "transmitting electrical signals representing" the result of calculations. The computer was instructed to transmit electrical signals representing the results of its calculations, and did not constitute the type of "post solution activity" found patentable in previous cases. The final transmitting step was held to constitute nothing more than reading out the result of the calculations.

4. A step of displaying a calculation as a gray code scale.

Manipulation of Data Representing Physical Objects or Activities; Pre-Computer Process Activity   Another process incorporating patentable subject matter is one that requires the measurements of physical objects or activities to be transformed outside of the computer into computer data, where the data comprises signals corresponding to physical objects or activities external to the computer system, and where the process causes a physical transformation of the signals which are intangible representations of the physical objects or activities.

Examples of this type of patentable process include:

1. A method of using a computer processor to analyze electrical signals and data representative of human cardiac activity by converting the signals to time segments, applying the time segments in reverse order to a high pass filter means, using the computer processor to determine the amplitude of the high pass filter's output, and using the computer processor to compare the value to a predetermined value. In this example, the data is an intangible representation of physical activity, that being human cardiac activity. The transformation occurs when heart activity is measured and an electrical signal is produced. This process has "real world value" in predicting vulnerability to ventricular tachycardia immediately after a heart attack.

2. A method of using a computer processor to receive data representing Computerized Axial Tomography (CAT) scan images of a patient, performing a calculation to determine the difference between a local value at a data point and an average value of the data in a region surrounding the point, displaying the difference as a gray scale for each point in the image, and displaying the resultant image. In this example, the data is an intangible representation of a physical object, that being the portions of the anatomy of the patient. The transformation occurs when the condition of the human body is measured with x-rays and the x-rays are converted into electrical digital signals that represent the condition of the human body. The real-world value of the invention lies in creating a new CAT scan image of body tissue without the presence of bones.

3. A method of using a computer processor to conduct seismic exploration, by imparting spherical seismic energy waves into the earth from a seismic source, generating a plurality of reflected signals in response to the seismic energy waves at a set of receiver positions in an array, and sending the reflection signals to produce a signal simulating the reflection response of the earth to the seismic energy. In this example, the electrical signals processed by the computer represent reflected seismic energy. The transformation occurs by converting the spherical seismic energy waves

into electrical signals which provide a geophysical representation of formations below the earth's surface. Geophysical exploration of formations below the surface of the earth has real world value.

Following are additional examples of processes that limit the claimed invention to the safe harbor definition of patentable subject matter:

1. A method of conducting seismic exploration which requires generating and manipulating signals from seismic energy waves before "summing" the values represented by the signals.
2. A method of displaying x-ray attenuation data as a signed gray scale signal in a "field" using a particular algorithm, where the antecedent steps require generating the data using a particular machine, such as a computer tomography scanner.

The following are examples of processes relating to precomputing that do not meet the "safe harbor" requirements for patentable subject matter:

- Perturbing" the values of a set of processed inputs, where the subject matter "perturbed" was a number and the act of "perturbing" consists of substituting the numerical values of variables. The step of perturbing the values of a set of process inputs, in addition to being a mathematical operation, appears to be a data-gathering step of the type that is insufficient to change a non-patentable method of calculation into a patentable process. In this instance, the "perturbed" process inputs were not even measured values of physical phenomena, but were instead derived by numerically changing the values in the previous set of processed inputs.
- Selecting a set of arbitrary measurement point values.

14.4.3 Computer-Related Processes Limited to a Practical Application in the Technological Arts

If a claim in a patent application does not clearly fall into one or both of the "safe harbors" mentioned above, the patent claim and invention may still constitute patentable subject matter if the claimed subject matter is limited to a practical application in the technological arts.

There is always some form of physical transformation within a computer because a computer acts on signals and transforms them during its operation, and changes the state of its components during the execution of the process. Even though this physical transformation occurs within a computer, such activity is not determinative of whether the process qualifies as statutory subject matter under the patent laws. What is determinative of patentable subject matter is not how the computer performs a process, but what the computer does to achieve a practical application.

A process that merely manipulates an abstract idea or performs a purely mathematical algorithm constitutes non-patentable subject matter despite the fact that it might inherently have some usefulness. To qualify such subject matter as patentable, the process must be described as having a practical application of the abstract idea or mathematical algorithm in the technological arts. An inventive process is limited to a practical application when the process, as claimed in the patent application, produces a concrete, tangible and useful result. Likewise, an invention to a machine constitutes patentable subject matter when the machine, as claimed in the patent application, produces a concrete, tangible and useful result. For example, a computer process that simply calculates a mathematical algorithm that models noise does not constitute patentable subject matter. However, a claimed process for digitally filtering noise employing the mathematical algorithm is patentable.

Examples of claimed processes that have been found to constitute useful patentable subject matter are as follows:

1. A computerized method of optimally controlling transfer, storage, or general retrieval of data between cache and hard disk storage devices, such that the most frequently used data is readily available.

2. A method of controlling parallel processors to accomplish multi-tasking of several computing tasks to maximize computing efficiency.

3. A method of making a word processor by storing an executable word processing application program in a general purpose digital computer's memory, and executing the stored program to impart word processing functionality to the general purpose digital computer by changing the state of the computer's arithmetic logic unit when program instructions of the word processing program are executed.

4. A digital filtering process for removing noise from a digital signal comprising the steps of calculating a mathematical algorithm to produce a correction signal and subtracting the correction signal from the digital signal to remove the noise.

14.5 PREPARING A PATENT APPLICATION FOR THE COMPUTER-RELATED INVENTION

As stated previously, all patent applications must contain an adequate written description of the invention that enables someone skilled in the art to which the invention pertains to duplicate the invention without undue experimentation upon expiration of the patent. The application must also clearly set forth the subject matter that the applicant regards as the invention, and the claims must distinctly point out and distinctly claim the invention. Without such clarity and precision, the patent application, particularly those pertaining to computer-related inventions, will be rejected by the patent examiners.

14.5.1 Claims of the Patent Application of a Computer-Related Invention Must Set Forth the Subject Matter the Inventor Considers as the Invention

The claims of the computer-related patent application need not explicitly recite every feature of the invention. For example, if the invention is a particular computer, the claims of the application do not have to recite every element or feature of the computer. The claims should be prepared in a form that emphasizes what the inventor has invented, that is, what is new in the combination rather than old.

Computer-related patent claims may often be drafted in terms of a "means" to perform a particular "function," or the "means plus function" format as it is known among the patent professionals. Means plus function language in a patent claim must be preceded by the description of the invention in the specification which makes it clear that the "means" corresponds to a well-defined structure of a computer or computer component implemented in either hardware, or software, and its associated hardware platform. Examples of defining such elements in claims are as follows:

1. A programmed computer with a particular functionality implemented in hardware or hardware and software.
2. A logic circuit or other component of a programmed computer that performs a series of specifically identified operations dictated by a computer program.
3. A computer memory encoded with executable instructions representing a computer program that can cause a computer to function in a particular manner.

The scope of a "means" limitation in a patent claim is defined as the corresponding structure or material, for example, a specific logic circuit, as set forth in the written specification that precedes and supports the claim, and equivalents of that corresponding structure. For example, if the patent application discloses only functions to be performed and provides no express, implied or inherent disclosure of hardware or a combination of hardware and software that performs the functions, the patent application will be faulted as having not disclosed any "structure" which corresponds to the "means" in the claims.

Therefore, it is important that the computer-related invention covered in your patent application be described as including at least one specific structure or material that corresponds to the "means" used in the claim. If the corresponding structure is disclosed as a memory or logic circuit that has been configured in some manner to perform the particular claimed function, for example using a defined computer program, the application has then disclosed "structure" properly which corresponds to the claimed "means".

When a claim or part of a claim in a patent application is defined in computer program code, whether in source or object code format, a person skilled in the art must be able to ascertain the metes and bounds of the invention from the language in the claim. In certain circumstances, as where self-documenting program code is employed, use of programming language in a patent application claim would be permissible because such program source code presents a suffciently high level language and descriptive identifiers to make it universally understood to others in the programming art without the programmer having to insert any comments. The MPEP recommends that patent applicants in their application should be encouraged to functionally define the steps the computer would perform, rather than simply reciting source or object code instructions. This is a matter you should surely bring to the attention of the patent professional preparing your computer-related patent application, where applicable.

14.5.2 Computer-Related Patent Application Must Contain an Adequate Written Description and an Enabling Disclosure

Adequate Written Description   All patent applications must contain an adequate written description of the invention that is intended to be covered by the patent issuing from the application. For the written description requirement to be satisfied, a patent applicant's specification must reasonably convey to those skilled in the art that the inventor was in possession of the claimed invention as of the date of the invention. The claimed invention subject matter need not be described literally, that is, using the same terms, in order for the disclosure to satisfy the description requirements. Software aspects of inventions may be described functionally.

Enabling Disclosure   A computer or software inventor's patent application must contain a specification that will enable a person skilled in the art to make and use the claimed invention without undue experimentation. Obviously, in computer-related inventions, the type of experimentation necessary may be rather complex. However, the fact that experimentation is complex will not make it "undue" if a person skilled in the art typically engages in such complex experimentation.

The disclosure in a patent application for a computer-related invention must enable a skilled artisan to configure the computer to possess the requisite functionality, and where applicable, interrelate the computer with other elements to yield the claimed invention, without undue experimentation. It is important that the patent specification for a computer related invention disclose how to configure a computer to possess the requisite functionality, or how to integrate the program's computer with other elements of the invention, unless a skilled artisan would know how to do so without such disclosure. A proper disclosure of computer-related inventions has been found in the following situations:

1. Where a programmer of reasonable skill could write a satisfactory program with ordinary effort based on the disclosure in the patent application.

2. The invention was adequately disclosed for purposes of enablement even though all of the circuitry of a word processor was not disclosed, since the undisclosed circuitry was deemed inconsequential because it did not pertain to the claimed circuit in the patent application.

3. A computerized method of generating printed architectural specifications dependent on the use of a glossary of predefined standard phases and an error checking feature was enabled by an over-all disclosure generally defining errors.

4. The enablement requirement was satisfied by the employment of block diagrams and descriptions of their functions, since the represented structure was conventional and could be determined without undue experimentation.

5. A software invention did not require a detailed description of all the circuitry in the complete hardware system.

Many computer related patent applications describe inventions that involve more than one field of technology. For such applications, the disclosure set forth in the patent application specification must satisfy the enablement standard for each aspect of the invention. Thus, when an invention, in its different aspects, involves separate and distinct arts, that specification is adequate which enables those skilled in each art, since they have the best chance of being enabled from the invention disclosure and to carry out the aspect proper to their specialty. For example, if the invention in question relates to a computer controlled fuel injection system, the patent application must enable a person skilled in the electronic computer art, in cooperation with a person skilled in the fuel injection art, to make and use the disclosed invention. Likewise, for example, a proper specification to an invention for a programmed computer that determines and displays three dimensional structure of a chemical compound must:

1. Enable the invention to a person skilled in the art of molecular modelling to understand and practice the underlying molecular modelling processes, and

2. Enable a person skilled in the art of computer programming to create a program that directs a computer to create and display an image representing the three dimension-

al structure of the compound.

Many patent applications directed to computer-related inventions comprise a disclosure that describes a programmed computer by outlining the significant elements of the programmed computer using a functional block diagram. To avoid an adverse examination position on the application, the application specification should include, along with the functional block diagram, a disclosure that provides information that adequately describes each "element" in hardware, or hardware and its associated software, and how such elements are interrelated. In other words, the patent specification must itself inform those skilled in the art about the invention, and not merely direct those skilled in the art to find out information for themselves. Thus, the disclosure must constitute more than a sketchy explanation of flow diagrams or a bare group of program listings together with a reference to a proprietary computer on which they must be run, to satisfy the requirement that the patent specification enable one skilled in the art to perform the invention without undue experimentation.

14.6   THE COMPUTER-RELATED INVENTION MUST STILL BE NOVEL AND NON-OBVIOUS

Once your patent specification establishes that the computer-related invention covered in your application constitutes "patentable subject matter," as discussed in the previous sections of this chapter, the claimed invention must still meet the requirements of novelty and non-obviousness. All of the factors considered previously to establish novelty and non-obviousness apply without any modification to computer-related inventions. Moreover, merely using a computer to automate a known process does not by itself impart novelty or non-obviousness to the process.

If the difference between the relevant prior art and the invention you are claiming to be patentable in your patent application is limited to descriptive materials stored on or employed by a computer, it must be determined whether the descriptive material is functional descriptive material or non-functional descriptive material, as described previously at Sections 14.3.3 to 14.3.5 of this chapter. If the functional descriptive material stored on or employed by the computer would not have been suggested by the prior art, then your invention is patentable over the prior art. However, non-functional descriptive material cannot render non-obvious an invention that would have otherwise been obvious. Situations involving non-novel and obvious non-functional descriptive material are set forth in the following example:

1. A computer-readable storage medium that differs from the prior art solely with respect to non-functional descriptive material, such as music or a literary work, encoded on the medium;

2. A computer that differs from the prior art solely with respect to nonfunctional descriptive material that cannot alter how the machine functions, that is, the descriptive material does not reconfigure the computer; or

3. A process that differs from the prior art only with respect to nonfunctional descriptive material that cannot alter how the process steps are to be performed to achieve the utility of the invention.

Thus, if the prior art suggests storing a song on a disk, merely choosing a particular song to store on the disk would be presumed to be well within the level of ordinary skill in the art. In this case, the difference between the prior art and the claimed invention would only be a non-patentable rearrangement of non-functional descriptive material on the known disk.

14.7 COMPUTER PROGRAMMING AND A SUFFICIENT DISCLOSURE

In patent applications directed to all inventions that are sought to be patented, the requirements for sufficient disclosure of the invention is the same, and thus incorporates those patent applications involving computer programming. As stated previously, the application specification must sufficiently enable someone to make and use the invention set forth in the claims of the patent application.

In applications involving computer programs, software, firmware, or block diagram illustrations where in one or more of the block diagram, elements are at least partially comprised of a computer software component, the U.S. Patent and Trademark Office guidelines state certain requirements to ensure that the disclosure sufficiently describes the invention. The sufficiency of disclosure in computer-related patent applications necessarily requires an inquiry into both the sufficiency of the disclosed hardware as well as the disclosed software, due to the interrelationship and interdependence of computer hardware and software.

To satisfy the "written description" requirement, the description in the patent application must ensure that the inventor had possession of the specific subject matter claimed to be novel and non-obvious as of the filing date of the application. Thus, this writer suggests that the patent specification, when filed, contain a complete disclosure of the invention recited in the claims, and that the inventor review the patent application carefully before filing to ensure that this is the case.

As discussed previously at Chapter 8, Section 8.3.5, the inventor is required to submit to the U.S. Patent and Trademark Office the best mode of carrying out and practicing the invention known to the inventor upon the date of filing the application. As a general rule, where software constitutes part of a best mode of carrying out an invention, a description of such best mode is satisfied by disclosure of the functions of the software. Normally, writing code for such software is within the skill of the art, and does not require undue experimentation once its functions have been disclosed. Neither a flow chart nor a source code listing is a requirement for adequately disclosing the functions of software. This is a very important point, and avoids the necessity of having to divulge source codes to support a patent application. Customarily, flow charts are used to convey the proper functionality.

14.7.1 What Constitutes an Adequate Disclosure in Computer Programming Patent Applications

In most computer-related patent applications, it is not unusual for the claimed invention to involve two areas of prior art, or more than one technology. For example, an appropriately programmed computer and an area of application of the computer. Regarding the "skilled in the art" standard in such patent applications, the knowledge of persons skilled in both technologies must be considered in preparing a patent application specification that will meet the requirement of sufficiency of disclosure.

In a typical computer-related patent application, system components are often represented by a "block diagram" representing the elements of the system, functionally labeled and interconnected by straight lines. The U.S. Patent and Trademark Office, during the examination procedure, categorizes such block diagram disclosures into (a) systems which include, but are more comprehensive then a computer, and (b) systems wherein the block elements are totally within the confines of the computer.

Block Elements More Comprehensive Than a Computer   In this first category, your block diagram includes a representation of a computer as well as other system hardware and/or software components. The diverse functions attributed to each block element should be particularly set forth in the specification, including how such a component could be implemented. If more than routine experimentation would be required by one of ordinary skill in the art to implement such a component or components, the specification will most likely be challenged by the examiner as inadequate. Additionally, the specification should set forth whether certain of the hardware or software components depicted as block diagrams are themselves complex assemblies which have widely different characteristics and which must be precisely explained as to their coordination with other complex assemblies.

It is proper in a patent application to refer to prior art patents or publications to demonstrate that particular block diagram hardware or software components are old in the art. Although, it may not always be self-evident to the patent examiner how such components are to be interconnected to function in the disclosed complex manner. The higher the complexity of the invention described and claimed in your computer-related patent application, the more explanation is necessary to avoid an adverse comment by the examiner that the invention is not adequately described.

In addition, in complex systems including a digital computer, a microprocessor, and/or a complex control system as one of many block diagram elements, the timing between various system elements may be of extreme importance. In such cases, I recommend that a timing chart relating the timed sequences for each element be included. If this is omitted, an unreasonable amount of work, time and effort may be required to decipher the detailed relationships that the inventor in the application states that he or she has solved.

Consider, for example, a block diagram disclosure in a patent application of a complex system which includes a microprocessor and other system components controlled by the microprocessor. A mere reference to prior art that is commercially available covering the microprocessor, without any description of the precise operations to be performed by the microprocessor, will most likely be determined as failing to disclose how such microprocessor could be properly programmed to either perform any required calculation or to coordinate the other system components in the proper timed sequence to perform the functions disclosed. If, in such a system, a particular program is disclosed, you should ensure that the patent specification teaches that the scope of the disclosure is commensurate with the scope of the functions contributed to the program in the claims of the patent application. If the disclosure fails to disclose any program, and if more than routine experimentation would be required by one skilled in the art to generate such a program, the patent application will be challenged by the examiner.

The amount of experimentation that is considered "routine" by one skilled in the art will vary depending on the facts and circumstances of individual inventions. The amount of required experimentation must, however, be reasonable. For example, one court found that the amount of experimentation involved by one skilled in the art was reasonable where a skilled programmer could write a general computer program directed to one of the embodiments of the invention shown in the patent application within four hours. In another case, where the opposite result was reached, it was shown that those skilled in the art would take one to two man-years to develop a particular program from the disclosure in the patent application. This latter situation would be clearly unreasonable.

Block Elements Within a Computer   The second category of block diagram patent application cases occurs most frequently with regard to pure data processing inventions, where the combination of block elements is totally within the confines of a computer, there being no interface with external apparatus other than normal input/output devices. To provide an enabling disclosure for such inventions, it is recommended that the disclosure contain (1) a reference to and a teaching of reliance upon an identified prior art computer system, and (2) an operative computer program for the referenced prior art computer system. The specification should show that the individual program's steps are specifically interrelated with the operative structure of elements in the referenced prior art computer system. The application should not merely set forth a sketchy explanation of flow diagrams or a bare bones group of program listings together with reference to a proprietary computer in which they might be run. The disclosure should provide considerable detail in explaining the interrelationships between the disclosed hardware and software elements. Because of the significance of the program listing and the reference to and reliance on an identified prior art computer system, absent either of the items, a block element disclosure within the confines of a computer must present ample disclosure in the same manner as the first category of block diagram cases discussed in the immediately proceeding section.

Regardless of whether a patent specification discloses block elements more comprehensive than a computer, or block elements totally within the confines of a computer, the specification must be adequate to teach how to practice the claimed invention. If such practice of the invention requires a particular apparatus, the application must therefore provide a sufficient disclosure of that apparatus.

There is no universally applicable rule that exists for determining whether a patent application specification involving computer programs is sufficiently or insufficiently disclosed. However, disclosures which fail to include either the computer program itself, or a reasonably detailed flow chart which delineates the sequence of operations the program must perform, will most likely be rejected by the patent examiner in the first instance. In programming patent applications, software disclosure only includes a flow chart. As the complexity of functions and the generality of the individual components of the flow chart increase, the chance of the application being held to constitute an insufficient disclosure based on such a flow chart increases, since the likelihood increases of more than routine experimentation being required to generate a working program from the flow chart.

It is imperative that the inventor in a computer program patent application show that his or her specification would enable one of ordinary skill in the art to make and use the claimed invention without resorting to undue experimentation. In certain instances, efforts to meet this burden involve submitting affidavits or declarations from the inventor, or others on the inventor's development team, referencing prior art patents or technical publications, arguments of the patent professional or attorney prosecuting the application, or combinations of these approaches, to establish that one of ordinary skill in the computer arts could practice the invention.

14.7.2 Affidavit or Declaration Practice

When submitting evidence to support the degree of skill necessary to practice the invention from the disclosure in a patent application, affidavits or declarations from inventors or others may be submitted to the patent examiner setting forth facts necessary to establish what the level of ordinary skill is in the art. One must be careful when submitting such information that the person making the declaration or affidavit is not established as having a level of skill higher than that required by a "routineer," or one of ordinary skill in the related art.

Such affidavits and declarations should not merely set forth conclusions or opinions, without facts to support or bolster these conclusions. For example, in one case the patent application included broadly worded block diagrams of the inventive structure, but no flow charts or program listings of the programs of the controller to control a message switching system. No evidence was submitted in the affidavits as to the number of programmers, the number of hours required to develop the program, and the level of skill of programmers needed to produce the program required to practice the invention, starting with the patent application disclosure. Thus, affidavits and declarations submitted to establish the skill of one of ordinary skill in the art should present factual evidence directed to the amount of time, effort and level of knowledge required for the practice of the invention from the disclosure alone.

14.7.3 Referencing Prior Art Documents

In computer programming patent applications, it is necessary to identify a prior art computer system for purposes of enabling the computer program in question. However, merely citing extracts from technical publications in an affidavit or declaration is not sufficient, if it is not made clear that a person skilled in the art would know which, or what parts, of the cited circuits in the prior art could be used to construct the invention described in the patent specification, or how they could be interconnected to act in combination to produce the required results. Such a submittal is less critical where the circuits comprising the inventive system are essentially standard components comprising an identified prior art computer system and a standard device attached to the system.

Also, it is important that such prior art patents used as a basis for enablement must have an issue date earlier than the effective filing date of your patent application. Also, do not rely only on arguments of your patent attorney or agent in the prosecution of the patent application to support the adequacy of the disclosure. Factual affidavits or declarations should be supplied to support the enablement requirement.

STATE STREET BANK & TRUST CO., Plaintiff-Appellee, v. SIGNATURE
FINANCIAL GROUP, INC., Defendant-Appellant.

96-1327

UNITED STATES COURT OF APPEALS FOR THE FEDERAL CIRCUIT

149 F.3d 1368; 1998 U.S. App. LEXIS 16869; 47 U.S.P.Q.2D (BNA) 1596

July 23, 1998, Decided

SUBSEQUENT HISTORY:
[**1] Certiorari Denied January 11, 1999

PRIOR HISTORY:
Appealed from: U.S. District Court for the District of
Massachusetts. Judge Patti B. Saris.

DISPOSITION:
REVERSED and REMANDED.

CASE SUMMARY

PROCEDURAL POSTURE: Defendant appealed a
decision from the United States District Court for the
District of Massachusetts, which granted plaintiff's
motion for summary judgment and found defendant's
patent invalid on the ground that the claimed subject
matter was not encompassed by *35 U.S.C.S. § 101*.

OVERVIEW: The patent was directed to a data
processing system for implementing an investment
structure for the administration and accounting of mutual
funds. In reversing the decision the court held that
plaintiff was not entitled to the grant of summary
judgment of invalidity of the patent under § 101 as a
matter of law, because the patent claims were directed to
statutory subject matter. Section 101 defined patentable
subject matter to include any new and useful process,
machine, manufacture, or composition of matter. Three
categories of subject matter that were not patentable
were laws of nature, natural phenomena, and abstract
ideas. Although an invention which consisted solely of a
mathematical algorithm which represented nothing more
than an abstract idea was not patentable, mathematical

algorithms which were reduced to some type of practical
application with a useful concrete result were. The court
found that the patent in question fell within this category,
which rendered it statutory subject matter, even though
the useful result was expressed in numbers, such as price,
profit, percentage, cost, or loss.

OUTCOME: The court reversed the decision and
remanded the case for further proceedings because the
claimed process was patentable subject matter under the
statute.

LexisNexis(TM) HEADNOTES - Core Concepts

*Civil Procedure > Summary Judgment > Summary
Judgment Standard*
*Civil Procedure > Appeals > Standards of Review > De
Novo Review*
[HN1] On appeal, the court is not bound to give
deference to the district court's grant of summary
judgment, but must make an independent determination
that the standards for summary judgment have been met.
Summary judgment is properly granted where there are
no genuine issues of material fact and the moving party
is entitled to judgment as a matter of law. Fed. R. Civ. P.
56(c).

*Patent Law > Jurisdiction & Review > Standards of
Review*
[HN2] The substantive issue of whether a patent is
invalid for failure to claim statutory subject matter under
35 U.S.C.S. § 101, is a matter of both claim construction
and statutory construction. The court reviews claim
construction de novo including any allegedly fact-based
questions relating to claim construction. The court also
reviews statutory construction de novo.

Page 2

149 F.3d 1368, *; 1998 U.S. App. LEXIS 16869, **;
47 U.S.P.Q.2D (BNA) 1596

Patent Law > Patentable Subject Matter > Products
[HN3] A "machine" is proper statutory subject matter under *35 U.S.C.S. § 101.*

Patent Law > Patentable Subject Matter > Products
Patent Law > Patentable Subject Matter > Processes
[HN4] For the purposes of a *35 U.S.C.S. § 101* analysis, it is of little relevance whether a claim is directed to a "machine" or a "process," as long as it falls within at least one of the four enumerated categories of patentable subject matter, "machine" and "process" being such categories.

Patent Law > Patentable Subject Matter
[HN5] See *35 U.S.C.S. § 101.*

Patent Law > Patentable Subject Matter
[HN6] The plain and unambiguous meaning of *35 U.S.C.S. § 101* is that any invention falling within one of the four stated categories of statutory subject matter may be patented, provided it meets the other requirements for patentability set forth in *35 U.S.C.S. § § 102,* 103, and 112, P2.

Patent Law > Patentable Subject Matter
[HN7] Congress intends *35 U.S.C.S. § 101* to extend to anything under the sun that is made by man. Thus, it is improper to read limitations into § 101 on the subject matter that may be patented where the legislative history indicates that Congress clearly did not intend such limitations.

Patent Law > Patentable Subject Matter > Computer Software & Mental Steps
[HN8] The court has identified three categories of subject matter that are unpatentable, namely laws of nature, natural phenomena, and abstract ideas. Mathematical algorithms are not patentable subject matter to the extent that they are merely abstract ideas. Certain types of mathematical subject matter, standing alone, represent nothing more than abstract ideas until reduced to some type of practical application, i.e., a useful, concrete and tangible result.

Patent Law > Patentable Subject Matter > Computer Software & Mental Steps
[HN9] Unpatentable mathematical algorithms are identifiable by showing they are merely abstract ideas constituting disembodied concepts or truths that are not "useful." From a practical standpoint, this means that to be patentable an algorithm must be applied in a "useful" way.

Patent Law > Patentable Subject Matter > Computer Software & Mental Steps

[HN10] The transformation of data, representing discrete dollar amounts, by a machine through a series of mathematical calculations into a final share price, constitutes a practical application of a mathematical algorithm, formula, or calculation, because it produces a useful, concrete and tangible result--a final share price momentarily fixed for recording and reporting purposes and even accepted and relied upon by regulatory authorities and in subsequent trades.

Patent Law > Patentable Subject Matter > Computer Software & Mental Steps
[HN11] The mere fact that a claimed invention involves inputting numbers, calculating numbers, outputting numbers, and storing numbers, in and of itself, would not render it nonstatutory subject matter, unless, of course, its operation does not produce a "useful, concrete and tangible result."

Patent Law > Patentable Subject Matter > Computer Software & Mental Steps
[HN12] A process is not unpatentable simply because it contains a law of nature or a mathematical algorithm.

Patent Law > Patentable Subject Matter
[HN13] The question of whether a claim encompasses statutory subject matter should not focus on which of the four categories of subject matter a claim is directed to -- process, machine, manufacture, or composition of matter--but rather on the essential characteristics of the subject matter, in particular, its practical utility.

Patent Law > Patentable Subject Matter > Processes
[HN14] Business methods are subject to the same legal requirements for patentability as applied to any other process or method.

Patent Law > Patentable Subject Matter > Processes
[HN15] Claims should not be categorized as methods of doing business. Instead such claims should be treated like any other process claims.

COUNSEL:
William L. Patton, Ropes & Gray, of Boston, Massachusetts, argued for plaintiff-appellee. With him on the brief were James L. Sigel and James S. DeGraw. Also on the brief was Maurice E. Gauthier, Samuels, Gauthier, Stevens & Reppert.

Steven L. Friedman, Dilworth, Paxson, Kalish & Kauffman LLP, of Philadelphia, Pennsylvania, argued for defendant-appellant. With him on the brief were Steven J. Henry, Wolf, Greenfield & Sacks, P.C., of Boston, Massachusetts; and Philip G. Koenig, Pittas Koenig, of Winchester, Massachusetts.

149 F.3d 1368, *; 1998 U.S. App. LEXIS 16869, **;
47 U.S.P.Q.2D (BNA) 1596

William T. Ellis, Foley & Lardner, of Washington, D.C., for amicus curiae Information Technology Industry Council. With him on the brief were Harold C. Wegner, Richard L. Schwaab, and Mary Michelle Kile. Of counsel was John F. Cooney, Venable, Baetjer, Howard & Civiletti, LLP.

Robert C. Scheinfeld, Baker & Botts, L.L.P., of New York, New York, for amicus curiae Mastercard International Service. With him on the brief was Lawrence T. Kass. Of counsel on the brief for amicus curiae VISA International Service Association were Laurie [**2] S. Hane, Donald S. Chisum, and Alan L. Durham, Morrison & Foerster LLP, of Palo Alto, California.

JUDGES:
Before RICH, PLAGER, and BRYSON, Circuit Judges.

OPINIONBY:
RICH

[*1107] *1370 RICH, Circuit Judge.

Signature Financial Group, Inc. (Signature) appeals from the decision of the United States District Court for the District of Massachusetts granting a motion for summary judgment in favor of State Street Bank & Trust Co. (State Street), finding U.S. Patent No. *5,193,056* (the *'056* patent) invalid on the ground that the claimed subject matter is not encompassed by *35 U.S.C. § 101* (1994). See *State Street Bank & Trust Co. v. Signature Financial Group, Inc., 927 F. Supp. 502, 38 U.S.P.Q.2D (BNA) 1530 (D. Mass. 1996)*. We reverse and remand because we conclude that the patent claims are directed to statutory subject matter.

OPINION:

BACKGROUND

Signature is the assignee of the *'056* patent which is entitled "Data Processing System for Hub and Spoke Financial Services Configuration." The *'056* patent issued to Signature on 9 March 1993, naming R. Todd Boes as the inventor. The *'056* patent is generally directed to a data processing system (the system) for implementing an investment structure which was developed [**3] for use in Signature's business as an administrator and accounting agent for mutual funds. In essence, the system, identified by the proprietary name Hub and Spoke (R), facilitates a structure whereby mutual funds (Spokes) pool their assets in an investment portfolio (Hub) organized as a partnership. This investment configuration provides the administrator of a mutual fund with the advantageous combination of economies of scale in administering investments coupled with the tax advantages of a partnership.

State Street and Signature are both in the business of acting as custodians and accounting agents for multi-tiered partnership fund financial services. State Street negotiated with Signature for a license to use its patented data processing system described and claimed in the *'056* patent. When negotiations broke down, State Street brought a declaratory judgment action asserting invalidity, unenforceability, and noninfringement in Massachusetts district court, and then filed a motion for partial summary judgment of patent invalidity for failure to claim statutory subject matter under § 101. The motion was granted and this appeal followed.

DISCUSSION

[HN1] On appeal, we are not bound [**4] to give deference to the district court's grant of summary judgment, but must make an independent determination that the standards for summary judgment have been met. *Vas-Cath, Inc. v. Mahurkar, 935 F.2d 1555, 1560, 19 U.S.P.Q.2D (BNA) 1111, 1114 (Fed. Cir. 1991)*. Summary judgment is properly granted where there are no genuine issues of material fact and the moving party is entitled to judgment as a matter of law. Fed. R. Civ. P. 56(c). [HN2] The substantive issue at hand, whether the *'056* patent is invalid for failure to claim statutory subject matter under § 101, is a matter of both claim construction and statutory construction. "We review claim construction de novo including any allegedly fact-based questions relating to claim construction." *Cybor Corp. v. FAS Techs., 138 F.3d 1448, 1451, 46 U.S.P.Q.2D (BNA) 1169, 1174 (Fed. Cir. 1998)* (in banc). We also review statutory construction de novo. See *Romero v. United States, 38 F.3d 1204, 1207 (Fed. Cir. 1994)*. We hold that declaratory judgment plaintiff State Street was not entitled to the grant of summary judgment of invalidity of the *'056* patent under § 101 as a matter of law, because the patent claims are directed to statutory [**5] subject matter.

The following facts pertinent to the statutory subject matter issue are either undisputed or represent the version alleged by the nonmovant. See *Anderson v. Liberty Lobby,* **[*1371]** *Inc., 477 U.S. 242, 255, 91 L. Ed. 2d 202, 106 S. Ct. 2505 (1986)*. The patented invention relates generally to a system that allows an administrator to monitor and record the financial information flow and make all calculations necessary for maintaining a partner fund financial services configuration. As previously mentioned, a partner fund financial services configuration essentially allows several mutual funds, or "Spokes," to pool their investment funds into a single portfolio, or "Hub," allowing for

149 F.3d 1368, *; 1998 U.S. App. LEXIS 16869, **;
47 U.S.P.Q.2D (BNA) 1596

consolidation of, inter alia, the costs of administering the fund combined with the tax advantages of a partnership. In particular, this system provides means for a daily allocation of assets for two or more Spokes that are invested in the same Hub. The system determines the percentage share that each Spoke maintains in the Hub, while taking into consideration daily changes both in the value of the Hub's investment securities and in the concomitant amount of each Spoke's assets.

In determining [**6] daily changes, the system also allows for the allocation among the Spokes of the Hub's daily income, expenses, and net realized and unrealized gain or loss, calculating each day's total investments based on the concept of a book capital account. This enables the determination of a true asset value of each Spoke and accurate calculation of allocation ratios between or among the Spokes. The system additionally tracks all the relevant data determined on a daily basis for the Hub and each Spoke, so that aggregate year end income, expenses, and capital gain or loss can be determined for accounting and for tax purposes for the Hub and, as a result, for each publicly traded Spoke.

It is essential that these calculations are quickly and accurately performed. In large part this is required because each Spoke sells shares to the public and the price of those shares is substantially based on the Spoke's percentage interest in the portfolio. In some instances, a mutual fund administrator is required to calculate the value of the shares to the nearest penny within as little as an hour and a half after the market closes. Given the complexity of the calculations, a computer or equivalent device [**7] is a virtual necessity to perform the task.

The '056 patent application was filed 11 March 1991. It initially contained six "machine" claims, which incorporated means-plus-function clauses, and six method claims. According to Signature, during prosecution the examiner contemplated a § 101 rejection for failure to claim statutory subject matter. However, upon cancellation of the six method claims, the examiner issued a notice of allowance for the remaining present six claims on appeal. Only claim 1 is an independent claim.

The district court began its analysis by construing the claims to be directed to a process, with each "means" clause merely representing a step in that process. However, "machine" claims having "means" clauses may only be reasonably viewed as process claims if there is no supporting structure in the written description that corresponds to the claimed "means" elements. See *In re Alappat, 33 F.3d 1526, 1540-41, 31 U.S.P.Q.2D (BNA) 1545, 1554 (Fed. Cir. 1994)* (in banc). This is not the case now before us.

When independent claim 1 is properly construed in accordance with § 112, P 6, it is directed to a machine,

as demonstrated below, where representative claim 1 is [**8] set forth, the subject matter in brackets stating the structure the written description discloses as corresponding to the respective "means" recited in the claims.

1. A data processing system for managing a financial services configuration of a portfolio established as a partnership, each partner being one of a plurality of funds, comprising:

(a) computer processor means [a personal computer including a CPU] for processing data;

(b) storage means [a data disk] for storing data on a storage medium;

(c) first means [an arithmetic logic circuit configured to prepare the data disk to magnetically store selected data] for initializing the storage medium;

(d) second means [an arithmetic logic circuit configured to retrieve information from a specific file, calculate incremental increases or decreases based on specific input, allocate the results on a percentage basis, and store the output in a [*1372] separate file] for processing data regarding assets in the portfolio and each of the funds from a previous day and data regarding increases or decreases in each of the funds, [sic, funds'] assets and for allocating the percentage share that each fund holds in the [**9] portfolio;

(e) third means [an arithmetic logic circuit configured to retrieve information from a specific file, calculate incremental increases and decreases based on specific input, allocate the results on a percentage basis and store the output in a separate file] for processing data regarding daily incremental income, expenses, and net realized gain or loss for the portfolio and for allocating such data among each fund;

(f) fourth means [an arithmetic logic circuit configured to retrieve information from a specific file, calculate incremental increases and decreases based on specific input, allocate the results on a percentage basis and store the output in a separate file] for processing data regarding daily net unrealized gain or loss for the portfolio and for allocating such data among each fund; and

(g) fifth means [an arithmetic logic circuit configured to retrieve information from specific files, calculate that information on an aggregate basis and store the output in a separate file] for processing data regarding aggregate

149 F.3d 1368, *; 1998 U.S. App. LEXIS 16869, **;
47 U.S.P.Q.2D (BNA) 1596

year-end income, expenses, and capital gain or loss for the portfolio and each of the funds.

Each claim component, recited [**10] as a "means" plus its function, is to be read, of course, pursuant to § 112, P 6, as inclusive of the "equivalents" of the structures disclosed in the written description portion of the specification. Thus, claim 1, properly construed, claims a machine, namely, a data processing system for managing a financial services configuration of a portfolio established as a partnership, which machine is made up of, at the very least, the specific structures disclosed in the written description and corresponding to the means-plus-function elements (a)-(g) recited in the claim. [HN3] A "machine" is proper statutory subject matter under § 101. We note that, [HN4] for the purposes of a § 101 analysis, it is of little relevance whether claim 1 is directed to a "machine" or a "process," as long as it falls within at least one of the four enumerated categories of patentable subject matter, "machine" and "process" being such categories.

This does not end our analysis, however, because the court concluded that the claimed subject matter fell into one of two alternative judicially-created exceptions to statutory subject matter. n1 The court refers to the first exception as the "mathematical algorithm" exception [**11] and the second exception as the "business method" exception. Section 101 reads:
[HN5]
Whoever invents or discovers any new and useful process, machine, manufacture, or composition of matter, or any new and useful improvement thereof, may obtain a patent therefor, subject to the conditions and requirements of this title.

[HN6] The plain and unambiguous meaning of § 101 is that any invention falling within one of the four stated categories of statutory subject matter may be patented, provided it meets the other requirements for patentability set forth in Title 35, i.e., those found in § § 102, 103, and 112, P2. n2

n1 Indeed, although we do not make this determination here, the judicially created exceptions, i.e., abstract ideas, laws of nature, etc., should be applicable to all categories of statutory subject matter, as our own precedent suggests. See *Alappat, 33 F.3d at 1542, 31 U.S.P.Q.2D (BNA) at 1556;* see also *In re Johnston, 502 F.2d 765, 183 U.S.P.Q. (BNA) 172 (CCPA 1974)* (Rich, J., dissenting).

n2 As explained in *In re Bergy, 596 F.2d 952, 960, 201 U.S.P.Q. (BNA) 352, 360 (CCPA 1979)* (emphases and footnote omitted):

The first door which must be opened on the difficult path to patentability is § 101....The person approaching that door is an inventor, whether his invention is patentable or not....Being an inventor or having an invention, however, is no guarantee of opening even the first door. What kind of an invention or discovery is it? In dealing with the question of kind, as distinguished from the qualitative conditions which make the invention patentable, § 101 is broad and general; its language is: "any *** process, machine, manufacture, or composition of matter, or any *** improvement thereof." Section 100(b) further expands "process" to include "art or method, and *** a new use of a known process, machine, manufacture, composition of matter, or material." If the invention, as the inventor defines it in his claims (pursuant to § 112, second paragraph), falls into any one of the named categories, he is allowed to pass through to the second door, which is § 102; "novelty and loss of right to patent" is the sign on it. Notwithstanding the words "new and useful" in § 101, the invention is not examined under that statute for novelty because that is not the statutory scheme of things or the long-established administrative practice.

[**12]

[*1373] The repetitive use of the expansive term "any" in § 101 shows Congress's intent not to place any restrictions on the subject matter for which a patent may be obtained beyond those specifically recited in § 101. Indeed, the Supreme Court has acknowledged that [HN7] Congress intended § 101 to extend to "anything under the sun that is made by man." *Diamond v. Chakrabarty, 447 U.S. 303, 309, 65 L. Ed. 2d 144, 100 S. Ct. 2204 (1980);* see also *Diamond v. Diehr, 450 U.S. 175, 182, 67 L. Ed. 2d 155, 101 S. Ct. 1048 (1981).* n3 Thus, it is improper to read limitations into § 101 on the subject matter that may be patented where the legislative history indicates that Congress clearly did not intend such limitations. See *Chakrabarty, 447 U.S. at 308* ("We have also cautioned that courts 'should not read into the patent laws limitations and conditions which the legislature has not expressed.'" (citations omitted)).

n3 The Committee Reports accompanying the 1952 Act inform us that Congress intended statutory subject matter to "include anything under the sun that is made by man." S. Rep. No. 82-1979 at 5 (1952); H.R. Rep. No. 82-1923 at 6 (1952).

Page 6

149 F.3d 1368, *; 1998 U.S. App. LEXIS 16869, **;
47 U.S.P.Q.2D (BNA) 1596

[**13]

The "Mathematical Algorithm" Exception

[HN8] The Supreme Court has identified three categories of subject matter that are unpatentable, namely "laws of nature, natural phenomena, and abstract ideas." *Diehr, 450 U.S. at 185.* Of particular relevance to this case, the Court has held that mathematical algorithms are not patentable subject matter to the extent that they are merely abstract ideas. See *Diehr, 450 U.S. 175, 67 L. Ed. 2d 155, 101 S. Ct. 1048,* passim; *Parker v. Flook, 437 U.S. 584, 57 L. Ed. 2d 451, 98 S. Ct. 2522 (1978); Gottschalk v. Benson, 409 U.S. 63, 34 L. Ed. 2d 273, 93 S. Ct. 253 (1972).* In Diehr, the Court explained that certain types of mathematical subject matter, standing alone, represent nothing more than abstract ideas until reduced to some type of practical application, i.e., "a useful, concrete and tangible result." *Alappat, 33 F.3d at 1544, 31 U.S.P.Q.2D (BNA) at 1557.* n4

> n4 This has come to be known as the mathematical algorithm exception. This designation has led to some confusion, especially given the Freeman-Walter-Abele analysis. By keeping in mind that the mathematical algorithm is unpatentable only to the extent that it represents an abstract idea, this confusion may be ameliorated.

[**14] [HN9]

Unpatentable mathematical algorithms are identifiable by showing they are merely abstract ideas constituting disembodied concepts or truths that are not "useful." From a practical standpoint, this means that to be patentable an algorithm must be applied in a "useful" way. In Alappat, we held that data, transformed by a machine through a series of mathematical calculations to produce a smooth waveform display on a rasterizer monitor, constituted a practical application of an abstract idea (a mathematical algorithm, formula, or calculation), because it produced "a useful, concrete and tangible result"--the smooth waveform.

Similarly, in *Arrhythmia Research Technology Inc. v. Corazonix Corp., 958 F.2d 1053, 22 U.S.P.Q.2D (BNA) 1033 (Fed. Cir. 1992),* we held that the transformation of electrocardiograph signals from a patient's heartbeat by a machine through a series of mathematical calculations constituted a practical application of an abstract idea (a mathematical algorithm, formula, or calculation), because it corresponded to a useful, concrete or tangible thing--the condition of a patient's heart.

Today, we hold that [HN10] the transformation of data, representing discrete dollar amounts, [**15] by a machine through a series of mathematical calculations into a final share price, constitutes a practical application of a mathematical algorithm, formula, or calculation, because it produces "a useful, concrete and tangible result"--a final share price momentarily fixed for recording and reporting purposes and even accepted and relied upon by regulatory authorities and in subsequent trades.

The district court erred by applying the Freeman-Walter-Abele test to determine whether the claimed subject matter was an unpatentable abstract idea. The Freeman-Walter-Abele test was designed by the Court [*1374] of Customs and Patent Appeals, and subsequently adopted by this court, to extract and identify unpatentable mathematical algorithms in the aftermath of Benson and Flook. See *In re Freeman, 573 F.2d 1237, 197 U.S.P.Q. (BNA) 464 (CCPA 1978)* as modified by *In re Walter, 618 F.2d 758, 205 U.S.P.Q. (BNA) 397 (CCPA 1980).* The test has been thus articulated:

First, the claim is analyzed to determine whether a mathematical algorithm is directly or indirectly recited. Next, if a mathematical algorithm is found, the claim as a whole is further analyzed to determine whether the algorithm is "applied [**16] in any manner to physical elements or process steps," and, if it is, it "passes muster under § 101."

In re Pardo, 684 F.2d 912, 915, 214 U.S.P.Q. (BNA) 673, 675-76 (CCPA 1982) (citing *In re Abele, 684 F.2d 902, 214 U.S.P.Q. (BNA) 682 (CCPA 1982)).* n5

> n5 The test has been the source of much confusion. In *In re Abele, 684 F.2d 902, 214 U.S.P.Q. (BNA) 682 (CCPA 1982),* the CCPA upheld claims applying "a mathematical formula within the context of a process which encompasses significantly more than the algorithm alone." *Id. at 909.* Thus, the CCPA apparently inserted an additional consideration-- the significance of additions to the algorithm. The CCPA appeared to abandon the application of the test in *In re Taner, 681 F.2d 787, 214 U.S.P.Q. (BNA) 678 (CCPA 1982),* only to subsequently "clarify" that the Freeman-Walter-Abele test was simply not the exclusive test for detecting unpatentable subject matter. *In re Meyer, 688 F.2d 789, 796, 215 U.S.P.Q. (BNA) 193, 199 (CCPA 1982).*

After Diehr and Chakrabarty, the Freeman-Walter-Abele **[**17]** test has little, if any, applicability to determining the presence of statutory subject matter. As we pointed out in *Alappat, 33 F.3d at 1543, 31 U.S.P.Q.2D (BNA) at 1557,* application of the test could be misleading, because a process, machine, manufacture, or composition of matter employing a law of nature, natural phenomenon, or abstract idea is patentable subject matter even though a law of nature, natural phenomenon, or abstract idea would not, by itself, be entitled to such protection. n6 The test determines the presence of, for example, an algorithm. Under Benson, this may have been a sufficient indicium of nonstatutory subject matter. However, after Diehr and Alappat, **[HN11]** the mere fact that a claimed invention involves inputting numbers, calculating numbers, outputting numbers, and storing numbers, in and of itself, would not render it nonstatutory subject matter, unless, of course, its operation does not produce a "useful, concrete and tangible result." *Alappat, 33 F.3d at 1544, 31 U.S.P.Q.2D (BNA) at 1557.* n7 After all, as we have repeatedly stated,

every step-by-step process, be it electronic or chemical or mechanical, involves an algorithm in the broad sense of the term. **[**18]** Since § 101 expressly includes processes as a category of inventions which may be patented and § 100(b) further defines the word "process" as meaning "process, art or **[*1375]** method, and includes a new use of a known process, machine, manufacture, composition of matter, or material," it follows that it is no ground for holding a claim is directed to nonstatutory subject matter to say it includes or is directed to an algorithm. This is why the proscription against patenting has been limited to mathematical algorithms ....

In re Iwahashi, 888 F.2d 1370, 1374, 12 U.S.P.Q.2D (BNA) 1908, 1911 (Fed. Cir. 1989) (emphasis in the original). n8

n6 See e.g. *Parker v. Flook, 437 U.S. 584, 590, 57 L. Ed. 2d 451, 98 S. Ct. 2522 (1978)* **[HN12]** ("[A] process is not unpatentable simply because it contains a law of nature or a mathematical algorithm."); *Funk Bros. Seed Co. v. Kalo Inoculant Co., 333 U.S. 127, 130, 92 L. Ed. 588, 68 S. Ct. 440 (1948)* ("He who discovers a hitherto unknown phenomenon of nature has no claim to a monopoly of it which the law recognizes. If there is to be invention from such a discovery, it must come from the application of the law to a new and useful end."); *Mackay Radio & Tel. Co. v. Radio Corp. of Am., 306 U.S. 86,*

94, 83 L. Ed. 506, 59 S. Ct. 427 (1939) ("While a scientific truth, or the mathematical expression of it, is not a patentable invention, a novel and useful structure created with the aid of knowledge of scientific truth may be.").

When a claim containing a mathematical formula implements or applies that formula in a structure or process which, when considered as a whole, is performing a function which the patent laws were designed to protect (e.g., transforming or reducing an article to a different state or thing), then the claim satisfies the requirements of § 101.

Diehr, 450 U.S. at 192; see also *In re Iwahashi, 888 F.2d 1370, 1375, 12 U.S.P.Q.2D (BNA) 1908, 1911 (Fed. Cir. 1989); Taner, 681 F.2d at 789, 214 U.S.P.Q. (BNA) at 680.* The dispositive inquiry is whether the claim as a whole is directed to statutory subject matter. It is irrelevant that a claim may contain, as part of the whole, subject matter which would not be patentable by itself. "A claim drawn to subject matter otherwise statutory does not become nonstatutory simply because it uses a mathematical formula, computer program or digital computer." *Diehr, 450 U.S. at 187.* **[**19]**

n7 As the Supreme Court expressly stated in Diehr, its own holdings in Benson and Flook "stand for no more than these long-established principles" that abstract ideas and natural phenomena are not patentable. *Diehr, 450 U.S. at 185* (citing *Chakrabarty, 447 U.S. at 309* and *Funk Bros., 333 U.S. at 130.*).

n8 In *In re Pardo, 684 F.2d 912 (CCPA 1982),* the CCPA narrowly limited "mathematical algorithm" to the execution of formulas with given data. In the same year, in *In re Meyer, 688 F.2d 789, 215 U.S.P.Q. (BNA) 193 (CCPA 1982),* the CCPA interpreted the same term to include any mental process that can be represented by a mathematical algorithm. This is also the position taken by the PTO in its Examination Guidelines, *61 Fed. Reg. 7478, 7483 (1996).*

[HN13] The question of whether a claim encompasses statutory subject matter should not focus on which of the four categories of subject matter a claim is directed to n9 --process, machine, manufacture, or composition of matter--but rather on the essential characteristics of the subject matter, in particular, its practical utility. **[**20]** Section 101 specifies that statutory subject matter must also satisfy the other "conditions and requirements" of Title 35, including novelty, nonobviousness, and adequacy of disclosure and notice. See *In re Warmerdam, 33 F.3d 1354, 1359, 31 U.S.P.Q.2D (BNA) 1754, 1757-58 (Fed. Cir. 1994)*. For purpose of our analysis, as noted above, claim 1 is directed to a machine programmed with the Hub and Spoke software and admittedly produces a "useful, concrete, and tangible result." *Alappat, 33 F.3d at 1544, 31 U.S.P.Q.2D (BNA) at 1557*. This renders it statutory subject matter, even if the useful result is expressed in numbers, such as price, profit, percentage, cost, or loss.

n9 Of course, the subject matter must fall into at least one category of statutory subject matter.

◆ INVENTORS AND INVENTIONS ◆

Hedy Lamarr

SPREAD SPECTRUM TECHNOLOGY

Once upon a time (in 1913 to be precise), a lady named Hedwig Eva Maria Kiesler was born in Vienna, Austria. At a young age, she dropped out of school in 1930 and studied acting under theater director Max Reinhardt in Berlin. When she was only 19-years old, she made worldwide cinema history because of a ten-minute appearance in a few nude swimming scenes in the Czech film *Ecstacy* in 1932. Needless to say, this brought fame to Ms. Kiesler. Why is this story here? Read on.

At age 19, Hedwig Kiesler's parents accepted her marriage to a wealthy Austrian munitions dealer, Fritz Mandl. They lived in a luxurious apartment in the heart of Vienna. As Mandl's wife, she accompanied him on many trips to meet high ranking officers of Hitler's German and Mussolini's Italian armies, where Mandl engaged in selling munitions, even if such sales were in violation of the Versailles Treaty. To assist him in the success of his arms deals, Mandl often took Hedwig and her dazzling beauty and charm with him to help entertain his prospective customers. She also attended meetings between Mandl and his munitions engineers. Having a curious mind, she did not just idly stand by and smile at these meetings. She learned a great deal by listening carefully to the conversations about weaponry and weapons systems. She also learned of problems Mandl and his engineers were trying to solve with radio controlled torpedoes.

Hedwig felt herself cast more in a role as a trophy wife to Mandl, who was a very possessive control freak. He even attempted to buy back all of the prints of *Ecstacy* he could find. Mussolini had a copy, but would not sell it to Mandl. Prints are still out there today.

Intellectual Property Law for Engineers and Scientists, by Howard B. Rockman
ISBN 0-471-44998-9 © 2004 The Institute of Electrical and Electronics Engineers

At about the same time, she became disenchanted with the Nazis. After four years of marriage to Mandl, she made the decision to leave him.

In 1937, she drugged the maid responsible for watching her, and donning a maid's uniform, snuck out through the service entrance. She made it to London, where she worked in several stage productions. She was introduced to MGM's Louis B. Mayer, who signed her to a contract in 1939, but with mixed emotions because of *Ecstacy*. Her nude performance had brought about an international scandal of sorts (it *was* 1932 and the U.S. Government operated a film censorship office in those days), but her notoriety and fame added up to dollars. Mayer said her name had to be changed, and she would make only wholesome movies from then on out. While traveling together to New York on the Normandy, Mrs. Mayer came up with the name Lamarr, as in Barbara Lamarr. The name means "the ocean," which Hedwig thought appropriate. "Kiesler" was changed to "Lamarr" and her former name "Hedwig" was shortened to "Hedy," which she had been called by her family and friends in Austria.

She immediately became one of the sultry glamour stars in the MGM world, making her American debut in the 1939 film, *Algiers,* and appearing in many films such as *White Cargo* (1942) and *Samson and Delilah* (1949). Are you still asking why this matters? Read on.

She left the castle, but Mandl followed her. She eventually moved into an establishment that had rooms upstairs where sordid things took place. Hedwig, as the story is told, bribed the establishment's doorkeeper to deny her whereabouts, but Mandl outbribed her and entered the club. Hedwig hid in one of the rooms, and while there a male customer of the establishment entered, thinking she was the woman he had just paid for. As the tale goes, Hedwig was forced to become intimate with this man in the room to avoid being given over to her husband. Hedwig later claimed that Mandl was banging on the door at this time. This first attempt to escape failed, and she was forced back to Salzburg Castle.

Prior to the U.S. entry into World War II, Ms. Lamarr became involved with a composer named George Antheil. As the story is told, she was listening to a concert where Antheil used 16 player pianos. At the same time she was thinking of how to make an anti-jamming radio control for naval torpedoes. I will bet you always wondered what movie stars think of in their spare time?

The constantly varying notes on the piano gave Ms. Lamarr an idea. Rather than transmitting radio control signals to a torpedo over a single transmit and receive frequency, which can be readily jammed or intercepted, the signals could be sent over continually changing frequencies in a pre-established pattern, similar to the continually changing notes of a piano composition. By synchronizing the transmitter and the receiver to the same pattern of frequency changes, the transmitter and receiver could communicate, and an enemy who did not know the frequency change pattern could not locate or jam the signal.

This was 1941, and Mr. Antheil designed a device using many player piano mechanisms that would create the frequency change pattern ("frequency hopping") for the transmitter and the receiver. On June 10, 1941, Ms. Lamarr and Mr. Antheil filed a patent application covering their device and system, which issued as U.S. Patent No. 2,292,387, and is titled "Secret Communication System." A copy of the cover page of the '387 patent follows. In filing the patent application, Ms. Lamarr used her married name at that time, Hedy Kiesler Markey. The Navy scoffed at the idea of player piano rolls in torpedoes and shelved the idea to Hedy's disappointment. However, she gave the patent to the U.S. government as gratitude for being in America. It was subsequently held in secrecy by the wartime government and not made public until 1981.

Their "frequency hopping" idea involved two paper player piano rolls perforated with identical patterns, one roll in the airplane overhead to guide the torpedo to its target, and the other in the torpedo receiver. Signals emitted by the transmitter, over rapidly changing frequencies, are recognized by the receiver in the torpedo. The objective was to prevent an enemy from deflecting the torpedo by false transmissions, or by jamming a single frequency.

Due to the size of the device George Antheil designed to embody the invention, the navy never adopted the system, which was 20 years ahead of its time. Lamarr helped the war effort in another front—she sold war bonds. During one promotion, a purchase of $25,000 worth of bonds earned a kiss from Hedy Lamarr. In one night, she sold $7 million worth of bonds.

After the war, the idea behind the Lamarr–Antheil invention virtually disappeared. However, in 1957, engineers at Sylvania Electronics Systems Division resurrected the "frequency hopping" idea and used a transistor circuit to make the concept work. Ships deployed to quarantine Cuba in 1962 were the first to use the Lamarr–Antheil system. The patent had expired by then.

Today, the concept disclosed in Hedy Lamarr's 1942 patent is known as "spread spectrum" technology. Systems which presently use this technology include Qualcomm's code-division multiple access (CDMA) cell phone technology, high-speed 802.11 wireless internet access systems, videoconferencing, and the U.S. military's Milstar satellite communications network, wireless heart monitoring in hospitals, wireless PDA's and internet, high-end cordless phones, and bluetooth, to name a few. In excess of 1,000 issued U.S. patents directed to spread spectrum technology have the Lamarr–Antheil patent cited as a prior art reference.

Hedy Lamarr's idea is considered by many as the foundation for the modern wireless technologies used today, allowing a large number of signal transmitter and receiver devices to operate in the same radio spectrum, with no interference among each other's signals. Thus, a multiplicity of cell phones can operate simultaneously in a similar radio spectrum without bumping into one another, because each signal is broadcast over differing patterns of microsecond frequency changes. Today, interlocking cells of radio signal coverage and spread spectrum technology often work together in wireless communication systems.

Hedy Lamarr passed away in 2000, having never made a dime on her patent or invention. However, she was pleased that her idea led to a massive change in the way people throughout the world communicate. In the year 2002, IEEE honored women who "distinguished themselves as engineers." Hedy Lamarr was one of them—and now you know why her story appears in this book.

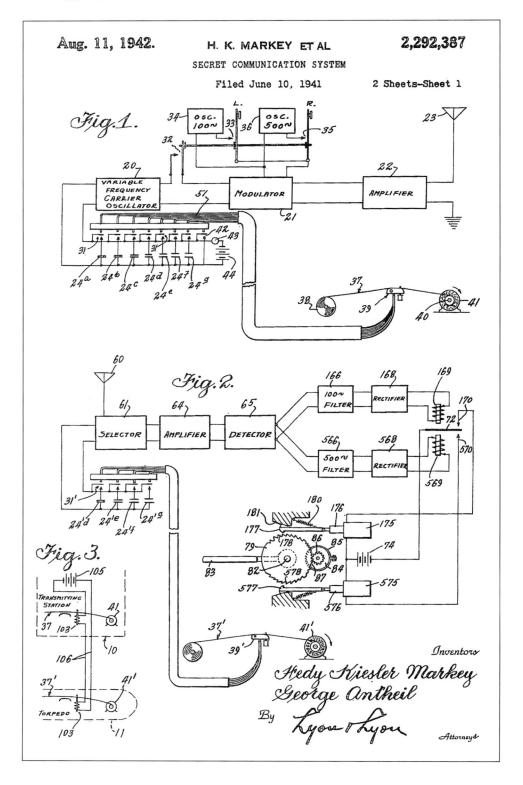

Aug. 11, 1942.   H. K. MARKEY ET AL   2,292,387

SECRET COMMUNICATION SYSTEM

Filed June 10, 1941   2 Sheets—Sheet 1

Fig.1.

Fig.2.

Fig.3.

Inventors

Hedy Kiesler Markey
George Antheil

By

Attorneys

15 Patentability of Biotechnology Inventions

15.1 DEVELOPMENT OF BIOTECHNOLOGY

"Biotechnology" is a term first created by the Hungarian engineer Karl Erkey in 1919. At that time, the term biotechnology encompassed the production of products from raw materials with the aid of living organisms. Biotechnology, in fact, can be traced back to approximately 6000 B.C.E. when the Sumerians and Babylonians first used yeast to make beer. Around 4000 B.C.E. fermentation processes were discovered in China for preserving milk by lactic acid bacteria to make yogurt, and molds were used to produce cheeses. More modern biotechnology can be traced back to the 1700s, during which time inoculation with smallpox was practiced to invoke an immune response and prevent development of more serious cases later in life, cross-fertilization in corn was discovered, crop rotation was employed by farmers in Europe to increase the yield in land use of leguminous crops, and heat sterilization was discovered. During the 1800's, epidemiological observations were used to develop the hypothesis of cross-infection by spread of child-bed fever from mother to mother by physicians, which led to the hypothesis that physicians wash their hands after examining each patient. Also, during this time period, Louis Pasteur proved that microbes were responsible for fermentation and received a patent on a process of beer fermentation in 1873, Darwin published his landmark book "On the Origin of Species", and Pasteur invented the pasteurization process by heating wine sufficiently to inactivate microbes. In addition, Gregor Mendel's presentation of the laws of heredity, the discovery of mitosis, the isolation of DNA (deoxyribonucleic acid) from trout sperm found in the Rhine River, the investigation of anthrax, the discovery of chromosomes, the development of Pasteur's rabies vaccine, and the discovery of the protozoan plasmodium as a cause of malaria all were precursors to the modern technology spectrum of biotechnology.

Modern biotechnology, therefore, is the natural extension of many thousands of years of scientific research, discoveries and invention. As encompassed today, modern biotechnology is largely based on recombinant DNA technology and the uses of recombinant organisms in the production of foods, medicines and in the solution of environmental problems. Biotechnology may be divided into four general areas: agricultural biotechnology, pharmaceutical biotechnology, environmental biotechnology and industrial biotechnology. The areas of pharmaceutical biotechnology and agricultural biotechnology are the ripest for patenting activity.

Modern biotechnology traces its roots to the early 1980s, when recombinant human insulin was first commercialized in the United States. The commercialization of recombinant human insulin was the result of research begun in the early 1970s to construct vectors of DNA fragments pieced together to create a new piece of DNA called "recombinant DNA." This recombinant DNA was inserted into the bacterium *Escherichia coli* by a process known as transformation. If the new recombinant DNA included the genetic code for production of a protein enzyme that breaks down a particular antibiotic, that bacterium will be resistant to the antibiotic. The human gene for producing insulin was added to the recombinant DNA that conferred antibiotic resistance of *E. coli*, and this recombinant DNA containing the human insulin gene was then used to transform *E. coli*. The transformed *E. coli* was found to grow in the presence of the antibiotic and also contained not only the antibiotic resistant gene but also the insulin gene. An expression of the human insulin gene was accomplished by adding additional pieces of DNA to the original recombinant DNA to promote the expression of the human insulin gene so that the new recombinant DNA, know as an expression vector, could be used to transform *E. coli*. In this matter large quantities of human insulin messenger RNA were formed which translated into the production of large quantities of the human insulin protein. The foregoing represents an example of a research component of modern biotechnology.

Process engineering or process development is the next stage of modern biotechnology and involves methods of protein production. During process development, the scale of the process necessary to produce sufficient quantities of the biotechnology product needed for pre-clinical or clinical trials and for commercial manufacture is undertaken. Process development includes development of media, buffers, reagents, solutions, assays, and tools of choice such as bioreactors or liquid chromatography equipment, for growing recombinant cells or for the isolation and purification of recombinant proteins and for quality control tests.

Manufacturing occurs after process development and entails cellular growth and testing in order to achieve commercially viable product volumes. Patentable subject matter may arise at any of the foregoing stages including the research, process development or manufacture stages of the modern biotechnology process.

The vast majority of biotechnology patents are issued for inventions stemming from the research component of biotechnology. As it relates to biotechnology, patentable subject matter has been held to include novel, useful and non-obvious microbes, plants, animals, natural and synthetic compounds, genes, proteins, DNA, RNA, recombinant cells, proteins expressed by genes in recombinant cell lines, methods of expressing protein in animals and mammals, methods of preparing proteins, processes for recovery of proteins, processes for medically delivering recombinant proteins, and methods of altering natural properties of plants such as stress, disease or pest resistance.

15.2   THE SUPREME COURT, THE U.S. PATENT OFFICE, AND BIOTECHNOLOGY INVENTIONS

In the United States, with the 1930 Plant Protection Act, Congress extended patent protection for the first time to living organisms. This statute related to plant breeders who were concerned that reproducing asexual plant varieties should be protected. In 1970, Congress enacted the Plant Variety Protection Act, extending protection to sexually reproduced plants. In 1985, the Patent and Trademark Office Board of Appeals in the case of *Ex parte Hibberd,* 227 USPQ 443 (1985), reversed a patent examiner's denial of a utility patent for a maize plant that produced seeds with increased levels of amino acids. The Board held that there was no need for additional legislation to enable patenting of living organisms, and that nothing in the Patent Act excluded the granting of utility patents for new varieties of plants.

Patenting of modern biotechnology inventions was solidified by the United States Supreme Court when it decided the case of *Diamond v. Chakrabarty,* 100 U.S. 696 (1980), and held that a living, genetically altered (recombinant) microorganism constituted patentable subject matter.

The Supreme Court found that patent claims directed to a man-made *Pseudomonas* bacterium containing at least two stable energy-generating plasmids, each plasmid providing a separate hydrocarbon degradative pathway was, as claimed, a "manufacture" or a "composition of matter" and therefore patentable subject matter within the meaning of 35 U.S.C. §101. In support of this finding, the Supreme Court found that the patentable organism "is not nature's handiwork, but his (the inventor's) own; accordingly it is patentable subject matter under §101." The Court stated that a modified microorganism was not a product found in nature, and therefore was patentable. The Chakrabarty microorganism was man-made, which is the basis for its patentability. Microorganisms that are naturally found in nature are not subject to patent protection, but if purified and isolated can be considered as patentable subject matter.

The Chakrabarty invention comprised live, human-made, genetically altered *Pseudomonas* bacterium capable of eating oil, and was useful in breaking down multiple components of crude oil in cleaning oil spills. The Court in the Chakrabarty case relied upon a statement made during the Congressional hearings which lead to the enactment of the 1952 Patent Act that: "the subject matter of patents includes anything under the sun that is made by man." An example is a permutation or modification of a naturally occurring protein, even though it exists in nature in a different form. Laws of nature, physical phenomenon and abstract ideas remain on the list of unpatentable subject matter since they are manifestations of nature, free to all men and reserved exclusively to none.

In 1987, the Board of Patent Appeals of the U.S. Patent & Trademark Office, in the case of *Ex parte Allen,* 2 USPQ 2d 1425 (Bd. Pat. App. & Int. 1987), was faced with the question of the patentability of a multicellular animal, in particularly a man-made oyster. This patent application was initially rejected by the patent examiner on the basis that the man-made oyster would have been obvious to one skilled in the art. The Board of Appeals and Interferences upheld the rejection on obviousness grounds, but did note that the question of whether the claimed subject matter was patentable under the patent statutes is simply whether the subject matter is made by man. Thus, the Board reaffirmed the concept that the threshold for patentability is not whether the invention is alive, but whether it has been created by man. The standards of novelty and non-obviousness still have to be satisfied, and here the Board felt this was an obvious oyster.

Following the *Allen* decision, the Patent Commissioner felt compelled to clarify the Patent & Trademark Office position on patents relating to live animals. This pronouncement appeared as a publication in the Official Gazette of the U.S. Patent & Trademark Office of April 21, 1987, above the signature of the Commissioner of Patents. Following are excerpts from that pronouncement, eliminating the recitation of cases relied upon by the Commissioner in support of his position:

"A decision by the Board of Patent Appeals and Interferences in *Ex parte Allen* held that claimed polyploid oysters are non-naturally occurring manufactures or compositions of matter within the meaning of the patent statute. The Board in reaching its decision relied upon the Supreme Court case of *Diamond v. Chakrabarty,* and the *Ex parte Hibberd* decision of the Patent Office Board of Appeals and Interferences. Congress intended statutory subject matter under the patent laws to "include anything under the sun that is made by man." The Patent and Trademark Office now considers non-naturally occurring non-human, multi-cellular living organisms, including animals, to be patentable subject matter within the scope of 35 U.S.C. §101 (the patent statute provision that defines patentable subject matter).

The Board's decision does not affect the principle and practice that products found in nature will not be considered to be patentable subject matter under the patent statutes. An article of manufacture or composition of matter occurring in nature will not be considered patentable unless given a new form, quality, properties or combination not present in the article existing in nature in accordance with existing law.

A [patent] claim directed to or included within its scope a human being will not be considered to be patentable subject matter under the patent statutes. The grant of a limited, but exclusive property right in a human being is prohibited by the Constitution. Accordingly, it is suggested that any claim directed to a non-plant, multi-cellular organism which would include a human being within its scope include the limitation "non-human" to avoid this ground of rejection."

Accordingly, the U.S. Patent and Trademark Office now examines claims directed to multi-cellular living organisms, including animals, to the extent that the claimed subject matter is directed to a non-human, non-naturally occurring manufacture or composition of matter—a product of human ingenuity. Such patent claims will not be rejected as being directed to non-patentable subject matter.

After pondering this subject matter, I was speaking to one of my clients who asked whether or not a patent could be obtained on a device for re-attaching one's hand to an arm after the hand had been inadvertently severed from the arm. Would that constitute obtaining a patent on a human being which is forbidden under the Constitutional mandate which abolished slavery? I told my client that I honestly didn't know, but that would be one of the issues that eventually may be decided by the courts when determining the patentability of biotechnology inventions. The device *per se* would be patentable; rejoining the arm may not be.

The courts, the Patent & Trademark Office and the legal commentators have substantially reached the conclusion that inventions in technology areas that were not foreseen by Congress when the patent laws were enacted are not to be held unpatentable as not meeting the statutory requirement for patentable subject matter. As stated in one Federal Circuit Court decision in 1985: "It is the public interest in the progress of the useful arts that is benefited as new technologies evolve. An interpretation of the statute to deny patent rights in micro-biological inventions would be contrary to law. The Patent & Trademark Office must continue to adapt its procedures to facilitate the advance of science and technology." Thus, the law has evolved to the point where whether an invention is living or not is of no consequence in determining its patentable subject matter status.

It is also clear now that patent protection is available for novel one-celled organisms such as bacteria or fungi, and for cell cultures derived from either plant or animal tissue. The commentators also state that patent protection for new multi-cellular organisms is also available. Prior to the *Allen* decision in 1987 by the U.S. Patent & Trademark Office, multi-cellular animals were not regarded as patentable subject matter. However, in the *Allen* decision, involving the man-made oyster, the Patent & Trademark Office acknowledged that the patent statutes did allow the granting of patents on multi-cellular plants and on animals.

Since the *Chakrabarty* decision, biotechnology patenting has literally exploded. In response to the increase in biotechnology patent filings, the U.S. Patent & Trademark Office increased its core of examiners in the biotechnology areas by almost 300 percent between 1982 and 1990. This trend for increased demand on the biotechnology examining groups at the U.S. Patent & Trademark Office continues to this date.

The significance of biotechnology and the demands the industry makes on the biotechnology examining core at the U.S. Patent & Trademark Office was specifically addressed in the 21st Century Strategic Plan of the United States Patent and Trademark Office, which may be found at: `www.uspto.gov/web/offices/com/strat2001`. In the strategic plan, the peculiar demands of the chemistry and biotechnology fields were recognized and in particular the plan found that "applications in biotechnology frequently claim tens, hundreds, or thousands of nucleotide and/or amino acid sequences in a single application and many times in a single claim. Each and every nucleotide and/or amino acid sequence, even if they are all isolated from the same source, are independent and distinct. . . ." Thus, biotechnology inventions impose a high burden on the resources at the U.S. Patent & Trademark Office, and given the broad latitude of patent claiming in the biotechnology area, the U.S. Patent & Trademark Office is taking concerted measures to meet the increased demand being placed upon it.

A major event in biotechnology occurred when the first "new" animal patent was issued in 1988 to Harvard University for an animal whose cells carry onco genes. This patent, No. 4,736,866, contained a claim that read "a transgenic non-human mammal all of whose germ cells and somatic cells contain a recombinant activated onco gene sequence introduced into said mammal, or an ancestor of said mammal, at an embryonic stage." The "Harvard mouse," as this invention became known, was characterized by abnormal susceptibility to the development of cancer in the female of the species, due to the fact that the germ cells and somatic cells of the mice contain an activated oncogene sequence that was introduced at an embryonic stage. This mouse was expected to, and subsequently has, in fact, proven to be an important research tool both for identifying carcinogens and for investigating the mechanics by which cancer develops.

Prior to issuance of the patent on the Harvard mouse, several Congressmen and Senators attempted to enact legislation calling for a moratorium on animal patents. However, no such legislation then, or since the preparation of this text, has been enacted. Thus, the U.S. Patent & Trademark Office has accepted the position that patenting of non-human animals is covered within the patent statute. As discussed previously, the inventor of patentable subject matter must disclose the invention in sufficient detail to the Patent & Trademark Office to enable adequate review during the examination process by the patent examiner. However, due to the inherent nature of biotechnology inventions, problems arise as to what should be disclosed. Where an adequate capability to disclose the details of the invention do not exist, a procedure has been established in the form of a deposit requirement in lieu of the written disclosure. A deposit of the micro-organism, cell line, hybridoma or other biological material must necessarily accompany the patent application. The deposit requirement is discussed further in Section 15.6.

15.3 DNA

Among the subject matter of biotechnology materials that are now considered as patentable subject matter are genes not as they are found in nature, such as isolated sequences of DNA that encode for the production of therapeutically useful proteins such as insulin. A patent application would not properly claim invention in the gene as it appeared in nature, but in its isolated form or as part of a vector or transformed cell. The gene can only be patented to the extent that it is "man-made," such as in a purified and isolated DNA sequence. The DNA variant could be produced by some human controlled microbiological process where the invention produces a new microorganism which has improved or altered useful properties because of the DNA.

All living organisms contain the same genetic code and the same genetic material, which is DNA or RNA (ribonucleic acid). Among different organisms, DNA varies only in its sequence of nitrogen bases. Foreign DNA that is inserted into an organism can become part of the organism's own genetic material. Molecular biologists can use DNA for transferring desired characteristics from one organism to another, in a process of transferring DNA know as "genetic engineering." Genetic engineering produces a new, non-natural piece of DNA that contains a desired gene. This new piece of DNA is called "recombinant DNA," which is a novel DNA sequence found *in vitro* through the joining of two or more non-homologous DNA molecules. This new genetically engineered DNA sequence that the U.S. Patent & Trademark Office has deemed to be patentable subject matter. However, political and social controversy around this practice still exists, since some feel that patenting such health related subject matter may eventually restrict doctors and scientists from treating many genetic diseases by repairing defective DNA.

15.4   SCIENCE, RELIGION, AND LIVING ORGANISM PATENTS

During hearings before the U.S. Congress relating to the efforts to enact legislation calling for a moratorium on animal patents, the critics of the U.S. Patent & Trademark Office position argued that the allowance of animal patents might encourage further development of transgenic animals, which would result in additional suffering by the animals. They also argued that the granting of animal patents would have an adverse effect on beliefs in the worth and dignity of life, and that such patents would disrupt the traditional production methods used on family farms. These are arguments that will continue in the spotlight as the field of biotechnology and animal development increases. Witness, for example, the arguments pro and con regarding cloning.

Theological arguments were also presented to Congress in 1987 during the consideration of proposed legislation regarding transgenic animals. The testimony of one member of the clergy in the Congressional Record reads as follows:

> "When the National Counsel of Churches has issued this statement of concern, it comes from the background of Judeo-Christian thinking about how we relate to the natural environment. In a nutshell, that background says that we have a responsibility for preserving the integrity of that creation, and for working with it to preserve its intrinsic values. The Doctrine of Trust in legal parlance is synonymous about the relation of creation to humanity. The Judeo-Christian view says that the creation is, in essence, held in trust; there are limitations on what we can do. We have a responsibility to see that its integrity is preserved. This background has lead to legislation such as endangered species laws, animal welfare laws, and laws regarding environmental quality."

Given the many and deep seated theologic foundations in our world's cultures, and the history of the United States and other countries in the advancement of science and technology involving medicine and food development, this apparent conflict will most likely continue. My purpose is not to expand or comment upon the varying opinions I have encountered between moral and theological thinking, and the advancement of science. However, this may be a good subject for additional discussion, dissecting the "patenting life" controversy as it is known, which continues to cast a shadow over the fruits of biotechnology research that are, in the minds of some, of arguably greater technological and commercial importance than moral standards. The author is, and shall remain, a mere observer of this debate.

15.5   EXAMPLES OF BIOTECHNOLOGY PATENT CLAIMS

To illustrate the breadth and flexibility of biotechnology patent claiming, the following patent claims are representative of the different types of subject matter that are eligible for patent protection:

- U.S. Patent No. 5,621,080: An isolated erythropoietin glycoprotein having the in vivo biological activity causing bone marrow to increase production of verticulacytes and red blood cells, wherein said erythropoietin glycoprotein comprises the mature erythropoietin amino acid sequence of Figure 6 and has glycosylation which differs from that of human urinary erythropoietin.

- U.S. Patent No. 6,048,971: A secretable mutant human erythropoietin having an amino acid residue which differs from the amino acid residue present in the corresponding position in wild type human erythropoietin, the amino acid residue of said wild type erythropoietin selected from the group consisting of amino acid residue 103, amino acid residue 104 and amino acid residue 108.

- U.S. Patent No. 5,618,698: A process for the preparation of an in vivo biologically active erythropoietin product comprising the steps of:

   (a) growing, under suitable nutrient conditions, host cells transformed or transfected with an isolated DNA sequence selected from the group consisting of (1) the DNA sequences set out in FIGS. 5 and 6, (2) the protein coding sequences set out in FIGS. 5 and 6, and (3) DNA sequences which hybridize under stringent conditions to the DNA sequences defined in (1) and (2) or their complementary strands; and

   (b) isolating said erythropoietin product therefrom.

- U.S. Patent No. 5,641,670: A homologously recombinant cell having incorporated therein a new transcription unit, wherein the new transcription unit comprises an exogenous regulatory sequence, an exogenous exxon and a splice-donor site, operatively linked to the second exxon of an endogenous gene, wherein the homologously recombinant cell comprises an exogenous exxon in an addition to exxons present in said endogenous gene.

- U.S. Patent No. 6,048,524: A method of expressing erythropoietin in a mammal comprising the steps of:

   (a) obtaining a source of primary cells from a mammal;

   (b) transfecting primary cells obtained in (a) with a DNA construct comprising exogenous DNA encoding erythropoietin and additional DNA sequences sufficient for expression of the exogenous DNA in the primary cells, thereby producing transfected primary cells with express exogenous DNA encoding erythropoietin;

   (c) culturing a transfected primary cell produced in (b), which expresses the exogenous DNA encoding erythropoietin, under conditions appropriate for propagating the transfected primary cell which expresses the exogenous DNA encoding erythropoietin, thereby producing a clonal cell strain of transfected secondary cells from the transfected primary cell;

(d) culturing the clonal cell strain of transfected secondary cells produced in (c) under conditions appropriate for and sufficient time for the clonal cell strain of transfected secondary cells to undergo a sufficient number of doublings to provide a significant number of transfected secondary cells to produce erythropoietin; and

(e) introducing transfected secondary cells produced in (d) into a mammal of the same species as the mammal from which the primary cells were obtained in sufficient number to express erythropoietin in the mammal.

- U.S. Patent No. 4,397,840: A method for the preparation of an erythropoietin product having no inhibitory effect against erythropoiesis which comprises the steps of:

  (a) absorbing a crude erythropoietin product obtained from the urine of healthy human onto a weakly basic anion exchanger from a neutral or weakly acidic aqueous solution in the presence of an inorganic neutral salt concentration in the range of 0.1 to 0.2 mole per liter, and

  (b) eluding the thus absorbed erythropoietin product with an aqueous eluant solution containing an inorganic neutral salt in a concentration in the range of 0.5 to 0.7 mole per liter.

- U.S. Patent No. 5,629,175: A method for producing a mammalian peptide which comprises:

  growing tobacco plant cells containing an integrated sequence comprising, a first expression cassette having the direction of transcription (1) a transcriptional and a translational initiation region functional inset plant cells, (2) a structural gene coding for said mammalian peptide, and (3) a termination region, whereby said structural gene is expressed to produce said mammalian peptide.

- U.S. Patent No. 5,780,709: A method to increase water stress resistance or tolerance in a monocot plant comprising:

  (a) introducing into cells of a monocot plant an expression cassette comprising a pre-selected DNA segment comprising an mtlD gene, operably linked to a promoter function in the monocot plant cells to yield transformed monocot plant cells; and

  (b) regenerating a differentiated fertile plant from said transformed cells, wherein the mtlD gene is expressed in the cells of the plant so as to render the transformed monocot plants substantially tolerant or resistant to reduction in water availability that inhibits the growth of an untransformed monocot plant.

- U.S. Patent No. 5,662,813: A method for enriching a whole blood sample for rare nucleated blood cells comprising the step of passing the whole blood sample through a counter flow stabilized charge-flow separator apparatus, in which the mobility of each cellular component in the whole blood sample in the presence of an applied electrical field is opposed by a buffer counter flow, thereby causing at least one nucleated blood cell fraction to concentrate from enucleated blood cell fractions present in the whole blood sample.

- U.S. Patent No. 6,194,146: A hybridization method for hybridizing labeled nucleic acid probes to nucleic acid sequences to form labeled hybridized complexes, comprising the steps of:

(a) de-naturing nucleic acid sequences within an isolated population of biological matter;

(b) hybridizing labeled, nucleic acid probes having less than or equal to 75 bases with specific portions of the de-natured nucleic acid sequences in the presence of a carbinol-based formamide-free hybridization buffer to form labeled hybridized complexes, the hybridization being carried out at a temperature between 42°C and about 85°C; and

(c) washing the labeled hybridized complexes, the washing being carried out at a temperature between about 47°C and 55°C.

Each of the above patents may be viewed at `www.uspto.gov`.

From the foregoing examples it, is apparent that there is a considerable breadth and latitude granted in patenting different subject matter pertaining to biotechnology. Such strong intellectual property protection is generally considered to be essential to the viability and continued survival of the over 1,200 biotechnology companies in the United States. The biotechnology industry organization has gone so far as to say "for these companies, the patent system serves to encourage development of new medicines and diagnostics for treatment and monitoring intractable diseases, and agricultural products to meet global needs."

15.6 ENABLEMENT AND WRITTEN DESCRIPTION REQUIREMENTS IN BIOTECHNOLOGY PATENT APPLICATIONS

There have been difficulties in obtaining broad effective patent protection for biotechnology inventions, because the statutory requirement of enablement under 35 U.S.C. §112, second paragraph, has been stringently applied to biotechnology inventions, as compared to technology areas such as mechanical inventions or electronic inventions. While many view the apparent stringency of the enablement requirement for biotechnology inventions as being unfair, when viewed in light of public policy underlying the enablement requirement, others hold the view that the strictness is quite understandable and appropriate.

The enablement requirement under 35 U.S.C §112, first paragraph, as discussed earlier, requires that the description of the invention contained in a patent application specification be sufficient to allow one of ordinary skill in the art to practice the invention. The fact that some experimentation may be necessary to practice the invention does not preclude statutory enablement, but the amount of experimentation required must not be unduly extensive. See: *Atlas Powder Co. v. E.I. Dupont De Nemours & Co.,* 224 U.S.P.Q. 409 (Fed. Cir. 1984).

The biotechnology field presents potential difficulty in complying with the written description and enablement requirements of 35 U.S.C. §112. For example, where the invention is a new cell line, or a specific monoclonal antibody, biological material must be deposited with a recognized patent depository, such as the American-type culture collection in Rockville, Maryland if it cannot be described in words. In other cases, broad patent protection may be obtainable without the need for making a deposit of biological material with a recognized patent depository. Whether or not a deposit is required, or even advisable, is determined by the level of specificity of the written description and enablement for the scope of patent claims sought. Where it may be necessary to make a deposit because insufficient information is known about the biological material, clearly it will be very difficult to sufficiently describe the biological material in order to comply with the written description and enablement requirements, and a deposit is advisable. However, where an event of biological material may be obtained or may be described by its method of obtaining the biological material, claims to the biological material along with a description of how to obtain the biological material, such as a screening assay to identify affinity characteristics of a monoclonal antibody, have been found to overcome the need for a deposit. See: *Hybritech Inc. v. Monclonal Antibodies Inc.,* 231 U.S.P.Q. 81 (Fed. Cir. 1986). Thus, the advisability of making a deposit to comport with the description and enablement requirements hinges on the level of experimentation necessary to obtain or practice the claimed invention given the guidance in the specification of the patent application.

Regardless of whether a deposit is made or not made for purposes of compliance with the written description and enablement requirements, it may, in fact, be advisable to make a deposit of the biological material in order to comply with the best mode requirement. It is important to remember that the written description, enablement and best mode requirements are separate statutory requirements, each of which must be met by the patent application in order to have a validly issued patent claim. Thus, when the subject of a patent application is, for example, a monoclonal antibody, a cell line, a transfected plant, proteins, or virtually any type of genetically engineered biological material, such material is susceptible of deposit with a recognized patent depository under the Budapest Treaty, such as the American-type culture collection, and may assist in complying with the patentability requirements of sufficient written description, enablement and best mode.

15.7 BIOTECHNOLOGY INDUSTRY AND PATENTS

While many biotechnology patents have been the subject of political controversy, patenting of biotechnology inventions has been directly responsible for the growth of an industry in which the total value of publicly traded biotechnology companies, at then existing market prices, was $224 billion as of early May 2002. The biotechnology industry tripled in size in the ten years from 1992 to 2001, with revenues increasing from $8 billion to $27.6 billion in 2001. The U.S. biotechnology industry employs 179,000 people, providing jobs for more than all the people employed by the toy and sporting goods industries in the United States. Biotechnology is also representative of a tremendous vehicle for research and development and is the most research-intensive industry in the world. $15.6 billion was spent on biotechnology research and development in the United States in the year 2001 alone. The top five biotechnology companies spent an average of over $89,000 per employment on research and development in 2002. All of these revenues and expenditures and jobs are created in about 1,457 biotechnology companies in the United States, of which approximately 340 are publicly traded.

These expenditures and revenues have all been generated by biotechnology research, which has had a tremendous impact on the lives of millions of people worldwide. The Biotechnology Industry Organization estimates that more than 325 million people worldwide have been helped by more than 130 drugs and vaccines derived from biotechnology which have been approved by the U.S. Food and Drug Administration. Of the biotechnology drug medications on the market, approximately 70% of these have been approved in the last six years. Currently there are more than 350 biotechnology drug products and vaccines in clinical trials which target more than 200 diseases, including Alzheimer's Disease, various cancers, diabetes, multiple sclerosis, AIDS, arthritis, and heart disease. Biotechnology is also directly responsible for the development of hundreds of medical diagnostic tests that detect the presence of the AIDS virus, Hepatitis-C virus and other blood-borne bacterial or viral infections in the nation's blood supply, and that can detect many other conditions early enough to result in successful treatment. Home pregnancy and AIDS tests have also found their way from the biotechnology lab into our daily use.

In the agricultural area, industry spokespersons note that foods have been improved by the use of biotechnology, such as papayas, tomatoes, soybeans and corn. Many bio-pesticides and other agricultural products are currently being used to improve our food supply and reduce our dependence on conventional chemical pesticides.

Environmental hazardous waste spills have been cleaned up far more efficiently by harnessing pollution-eating microbes derived from environmental biotechnology products without the need to use conventionally caustic chemicals. Biotechnology has found its way into industrial applications that have led to cleaner processes that produce less waste and use less energy and water in the chemical, pulp and paper, textiles, food, energy, metals and minerals industries. Most laundry detergents now produced in the United States, and in common use, no longer contain phosphates but contain biotechnology-originated enzymes. Even criminal investigations and forensic medicines have been significantly advanced by DNA fingerprinting which has allowed inmates on death row convicted of crimes to be set free and the responsible criminals located, indicted and jailed.

The growth of the biotechnology industry is directly proportional to the total number of biotechnology patents granted each year by the U.S. Patent & Trademark Office. In 1985 approximately 1,500 U.S. patents for biotechnology inventions were issued. A mere 15 years later in the year 2000 almost 14,000 U.S. patents for biotechnology inventions were issued, with the major growth occurring in the years between 1994 and 2000. The projections and actual data for continued growth of the issuance of biotechnology patents predict, and have shown, a similar annual growth as that recognized for the past six years. During this same period of time, market capitalization for biotechnology companies increased from $45 billion to over $350 billion, with a resulting increase in the number of biotech drug and vaccine approvals by the U.S. Food and Drug Administration from approximately seven in 1994 to thirty-two in the year 2000.

Few industries in our country's history can trace their very existence to a system of laws governing and protecting intellectual property and inventions. The biotechnology business, both domestically and worldwide, uniquely is driven by, and attributes it growth to, the patent rights granted in the inventions derived from the efforts of the many thousands of research and development scientists working in the biotechnology field.

15.8 MEDICAL PROCEDURES

The "Trade-Related Aspects of Intellectual Property" (TRIPS), part of the GATT Agreement, was ratified by the United States several years ago. This is the treaty that established the World Trade Organization (WTO). Article 27(3)(a) of TRIPS allows member nations to exclude from patentable subject matter "diagnostic, therapeutic and surgical methods for the treatment of humans or animals." The TRIPS Agreement does not compel a member nation to enact such legislation, however the European Patent Office does forbid patents to be granted on such diagnostic, therapeutic and surgical methods, on the grounds that exclusive rights should not prevent patients from having access to the finest medical treatment available. For the same reasons, for many years, the patenting of pharmaceutical products in many countries was forbidden. Today, the TRIPS Agreement allows countries to issue patents on pharmaceutical products.

In 1996, the United States Congress enacted legislation that, while allowing the granting of patents covering medical procedures and techniques, severely limited the remedies an inventor or owner of such patents could recover for infringement. In January 1992, a Dr. Pallin obtained U.S. Patent No. 5,080,111, entitled "Method of Making Self-Sealing Episcleral Incision," directed to a method of making incisions during surgery on the eye. An infringement suit was filed, *Pallin v. Singer,* 36 U.S.P.Q. 2d 1050 (D. Vt 1995), where the District Court denied summary judgment without deciding whether or not the surgical method was patentable or not. The lawsuit was terminated when each party agreed to the patent's invalidity based upon prior art. The litigation, however, was the subject of much controversy in the medical profession, primarily because it raised awareness of the fact that the U.S. Patent & Trademark Office had a practice of granting patents on surgical procedures.

As a result, Section 287(c) was added to the U.S. Patent Act in 1996, the primary provision which states:

> "(c)(1) With respect to a medical practitioner's performance of a medical activity that constitutes an infringement under Section 271(a) or (b) of this title, the provisions of Sections 281, 283, 284 and 285 of this title shall not apply against the medical practitioner or against a related healthcare entity with respect to such medical activity."

The statute defines "medical activity" as "the performance of a medical or surgical procedure on a body." The statute also expressly states that the use of patented machines, compositions of matter, the practice of a patented use of a composition of matter, and the practice of a patented biotechnology process do not comprise "medical activity." The exemption for processes covered under a "biotechnology patent" were inserted into the legislation at the behest of the biotechnology industry. However, the term "biotechnology patent" is not defined in the statute.

The effect of the statute is that the performance of a surgical procedure may still constitute an infringement of a patent. However, the medical professionals, and the organizations for which they work, are not liable for monetary damages or attorneys fees, and no injunctive relief may be obtained by a patent owner against the use of the method by a medical professional or a related healthcare entity. The statute defines "related healthcare entities" as clinics, HMO's, hospitals and any entity "with which a medical practitioner has a professional affiliation." Note that the statute does not exempt the patient who receives the procedure. Subparagraph (3) of Section 287(c) sets forth an "anti-research" exemption. Researchers "engaged in the commercial development...of a machine, manufacture or composition of matter" are not afforded protection under the statute. This may be considered an anomoly, since this provision specifically works against encouraging research and development by failing to protect researchers against patent infringement.

It is interesting to note that this statute only covers "medical practitioners," and not a lay person who offers medical help in an emergency. I personally doubt whether a case will actually arise regarding enforcement of a medical procedure patent against a citizen offering emergency medical help to someone in need. However, these are the kinds of issues that ultimately end up providing fodder for discussion and debate between doctors and attorneys. Therefore, when a patent is sought on a method constituting a medical procedure, you will probably be advised by your patent professional that claims should be directed to the apparatus, machine or device by which the procedure is carried out, and possibly eliminate claims in the patent application directed to the steps of the medical procedure itself. Note that the European Patent Office does not even allow method claims directed to a surgical procedure to remain in a patent application.

Therefore, it is important that if your medical device and procedure patent application is to be filed in several countries, including Europe, claims be included in the patent application that your patent professional knows will be accepted in those foreign countries.

A short word on pharmaceutical patents. Before the TRIPS Agreement was concluded, a large group of developing nations excluded from their patent laws the ability not only to obtain patents on medical therapies and devices, but also pharmaceutical products. Several major nations did not grant pharmaceutical patents until recently. For example, such patents were authorized in Japan only as of 1976, Switzerland in 1977, and Italy in 1978. Other countries such as Greece, Norway, Portugal and Spain did not allow the issuance of pharmaceutical patents until 1988. One of the goals of the TRIPS Agreement is to end such exclusions, and to forbid developing and other countries from excluding pharmaceuticals from the realm of patent protection. Article 27 of the TRIPS Agreement requires nations to provide patents for pharmaceuticals, although "developing" countries have until January 2005 to pass legislation to grant such patents, if such patent grants have been previously excluded.

◆ INVENTORS AND INVENTIONS ◆

Rosalind Franklin
James Watson
Francis Crick
Maurice Wilkins

DISCOVERY OF THE MOLECULAR STRUCTURE OF DNA

The discovery of the molecular structure of deoxyribonucleic acid (DNA), which makes up the chromosomes in every human cell, is a story of intense competition, intrigue, questions of betrayal and duplicity and of professional and scientific ethics, the Nobel Prize for Medicine and Physiology, charges of sexism, and, above all, continued debate after 50 years as to who should receive proper credit for the discovery. I will present the facts according to my research, and let you be the judge and jury regarding the propriety of the conduct of the participants in this story.

DNA was originally discovered in 1869, but scientists considered that it only had a small part to play in genetics. At that time, scientists were convinced that proteins, which perform most of the essential tasks in the human body, were probably responsible for passing on hereditary traits. The DNA molecule that was discovered in 1869 seemed too simple a molecule to perform this function.

DNA contains the patterns for constructing proteins in the body, including the various enzymes. For years, scientists tried to uncover the structure of the DNA molecule that led to heredity and to hereditary disease. As is known today, DNA consists of two chains twisted around each other in the form of a double helix of alternating phosphate and sugar groups on the outside of the helix "ladder". The two chains are held together by hydrogen bonds between pairs of organic bases. These bases are adenine (A) with thymine (T), and guanine (G) with cytosine (C). The discovery of the structure of DNA created the science of modern biotechnology, which includes the ability to modify the DNA of host cells that will then produce a desired product, for example, insulin.

In 1950, biologists were still concerned with whether protein or DNA held the secret to genetic inheritance. Even after 80 years, most researchers felt that proteins were the answer, and only a few scientists were involved with DNA research. One of these handful of scientists pushing DNA was Linus Pauling, of the California Institute of Technology, who preferred constructing Tinkertoy-like models of molecules, and rearranging the pieces until they fit together. In approximately 1950, Pauling used this procedure to discover that certain proteins had a corkscrew, or helical, shape. This led other scientists to speculate that possibly DNA might also be helix shaped. In the fall of 1951, it was known that Pauling was looking for good photographs of DNA to confirm the structure of his DNA molecule. However, Pauling's model yielded a fundamentally flawed three-chained helix with its backbone in the center, as was later determined.

The groundwork that was a precursor leading to an understanding of the DNA molecule structure and its appearance comprised several benchmark events:

1. DNA was already known for its exclusive role as genetic material—the only molecule that stored all of the information required to naturally create a living being.
2. The advances in X-ray crystallography in studying macromolecules.
3. Increasing evidence from geneticists that heredity stemmed from DNA, not protein, in chromosomes.
4. Erwin Chargaff's discovery that DNA includes equal numbers of A and T bases and of G and C bases.
5. Pauling's discovery of the helical shape of some proteins.

Before continuing the story, a brief biography of the four individuals mentioned at the top of this essay is in order. Rosalind Franklin was a British scientist who was born in England in 1920, decided to become a scientist at the age of 15, and enrolled in the Newnham College at Cambridge, England in 1938, studying chemistry and physics and graduating in 1941. In 1942, in the middle of the war, she took a position at the British Coal Utilization Research Association, making fundamental studies of carbon and graphite microstructures, and earning a Doctorate degree based on her studies from Cambridge in 1945.

She spent 1947 to 1950 in Paris at the Laboratoire Central des Services Chimiques de l'Etat, where she became highly regarded as an expert in X-ray diffraction photographic techniques. While in Paris, Rosalind Franklin was introduced to the technique of X-ray crystallography, which was used in studying organic macromolecules. She became a respected authority in industrial physicochemistry. In 1951, Rosalind Franklin returned to England as a biophysics research associate in John Randall's laboratory at King's College, London. Her responsibility there was to upgrade the X-ray crystallographic laboratory at King's College for work on DNA, and to investigate the crystal structure of DNA. Her work was guided by her feelings that science, as was life, was based upon fact, experience, and experiment.

Maurice Wilkins was already working for Randall at King's College London, and it was his idea to study DNA by biophysical and biochemical molecular analysis, which he had already begun to implement when Franklin was appointed to the laboratory by Randall. However, the relationship between Wilkins and Franklin was, unfortunately, very bad, and the two hardly ever talked to each other. This is due to the fact that when Rosalind Franklin was appointed by Randall, it was her understanding that she was to head her own project on DNA research. This occurred while Wilkins was on vacation, and when he returned, it was his understanding that Rosalind Franklin was only a research assistant, and was subject to his authority. As a result, during the entire time they worked "together," they hardly spoke, and did not enjoy the comaraderie, cooperation, and exchange of ideas that is the hallmark of quality scientific research.

Crystallography in 1950 was a new process for studying biological molecules. It involved shining X-rays on a molecule, and as the beams ricocheted off the atoms, the result was captured on film. This was found to be an excellent tool to comprehend the structure of complex molecules such as DNA. Using this technique, the location of atoms in any crystal can be mapped by viewing the image of a crystal under an X-ray beam. Many of the photographs were fuzzy and difficult to interpret. However, at King's

College Laboratory in London, Wilkins and Franklin were taking the world's finest portraits of DNA.

Notwithstanding the friction with Wilkins, Rosalind Franklin applied her substantial talents to the DNA molecule. After making a complicated analysis, she discovered, and was the first to promulgate, that the sugar–phosphate pairs of the bases of DNA were on the outside of the molecules. She also photographed the basic helix construction of the DNA molecule. She discovered the B form of DNA, recognized that there were two states of the DNA molecule, and defined the conditions for the transition. Her work was the foundation for the quantitative analysis of diffraction patterns.

Meanwhile, in 1951, James Watson, from Chicago in the United States, arrived at the Cavendish Laboratory in Cambridge, England with a degree in zoology and a Doctorate from the University of Indiana, also in zoology, where he became interested in genetics. At the Cavendish Laboratory, there were several important X-ray crystallographic projects in progress under W. L. Bragg's leadership, including Max Perutz's investigation of hemoglobin. Working under Perutz was Francis Crick, who was a physicist from University College, London. When Watson arrived at the Cavendish Laboratory, he recruited Crick to assist him in working with molecular models. The two rapidly put together several models of DNA using all the information they could obtain at the time.

In November of 1951, Watson was invited by Wilkins to hear Franklin speak in London, and Watson expected that Franklin would show him her DNA photographs, which did not happen. Watson did not take notes at that lecture, but tried to memorize most of Franklin's comments. Franklin, in her comments, stated that DNA was probably a helix with the sugar–phosphate backbone on the outside. Upon returning to Cambridge, Crick and Watson built a model based on Watson's recollection of Franklin's seminar talk. This model consisted of a three-stranded helix with the A, T, G, and C bases poking inward.

Watson and Crick subsequently invited Franklin and Wilkins to observe the model they had constructed. Franklin and Wilkins advised them that the model was wrong, stating that it contained several errors of basic chemistry, a subject which neither Cambridge scientist was familiar with. For example, the three-chain model of DNA was wrong, and the phosphates were likely hydrated and on the outside of the molecule. Following this, Sir Lawrence Bragg, leader of the Cavendish Laboratory, ordered Crick and Watson to forget about DNA, and to work on other projects. Bragg felt that it would not be fair to compete with King's College's scientists who had previously begun working on the DNA molecule.

In May 1952, while keeping up her pace of generating X-ray photos of DNA, Franklin took one she labeled Photograph 51. In December that year, Watson found that Pauling had figured out DNA's structure and would soon publish an article on the structure of the DNA molecule. Watson and Crick obtained an early draft of Pauling's article, and were happy to note that Pauling's DNA model was built of three strands, and was therefore wrong, just as they had been advised by Franklin and Wilkins that their own model was wrong.

On January 28, 1953, Watson went to London again, to hear Franklin present a seminar on the unpublished results of her latest DNA experiments. Wilkins, who at that time was not on speaking terms with Franklin, quietly pulled Watson aside and showed Watson Franklin's unpublished Photograph 51. The disclosure of Photograph 51 to Watson by Wilkins was without the knowledge of Franklin, and Franklin was never told that he had surreptitiously shown the information to Watson. Watson stated in a later publication that the instant he saw the picture, his mouth fell open and his heart began to race. When he saw Franklin's crisp, high-resolution photograph of DNA, he immediately recognized the black cross of reflections could only arise from a helix structure, and it provided him with several of the vital helical parameters. Watson then asked Wilkins for information on the measurements from the photographs, such as the distance between each corkscrew turn of the helix and the density of the atoms in the pack. Wilkins divulged the details.

On his way back to Cambridge, Watson sketched the DNA molecule with the corkscrew-like helical strands, and a few days later he and Crick secretly started building a new model of the DNA molecule. In an effort to gain more information, Wilkins was invited to lunch by Crick, and during the lunch Wilkins stated that Franklin had prepared a report on her latest measurements of the DNA molecule for the British Medical Research Council, a government agency. Franklin's unpublished report was not confidential nor was it in wide circulation. Crick later obtained a copy of the report from a member of the Council, Max Perutz. Upon seeing Franklin's information, Crick concluded that the DNA molecule was indeed made of two strands—a double helix—and that the strands ran in opposite directions. Commentators have proposed that Watson and Crick were model builders who required the collaboration of the experimentalists Franklin and Wilkins, since only the latter were capable of providing the necessary X-ray evidence of the helical configuration of DNA.

Watson was the one who put the final piece into the puzzle. He pondered the cardboard replicas he and Crick had constructed of the four bases that constitute DNA's alphabet: adenine, thymine, guanine, and cytosine, or A, T, G, and C. He realized that an adenine–thymine (A–T) pair held together by two hydrogen bonds was identical in shape to a guanine–cytosine (G–C) pair. These pairs of bases could then serve as the rungs on the twisting ladder of the DNA molecule. The "complementarity" between A and T and between C and G was the key to replication. In the double helix, a single strand of genetic alphabet, say, CAT, is paired, rung by rung, with its complimentary strand, GTA. Upon the unzipping of the helix, the complimentary strand becomes a template; its G, T, and A bases naturally attract bases that amount to a precise copy of the original strand, CAT. In this way, a new double helix is constructed. On the night of February 28, 1953, Crick walked into the Eagle Pub in Cambridge, England and announced that "we had found the secret of life." Thus, this date is now recognized as the discovery of the structure of the DNA molecule.

Rosalind Franklin died of ovarian cancer in 1958 at the age of 37. Up to the time she died, she was never advised that Watson had viewed her Photograph 51, shown to him by Wilkins. In 1962, Watson, Crick, and Wilkins were jointly awarded the Nobel Prize in Medicine and Physiology. Rosalind Franklin was not mentioned, because the Nobel Prize is not given posthumously. Crick later stated that in his view, if Franklin had lived, "it would have been impossible to give the prize to Wilkins and not to her, because she did the key experimental work." Franklin's supporters urge that her involvement in the development work that resulted in Watson, Crick, and Wilkins receiving the Nobel Prize, and in advising Watson and Crick that their earlier three-helix model was wrong, which sent them back to the drawing board, and her notebook entries, all show that she was working toward the solution until Watson saw her Photograph 51 and figured out the rest. Her notebook showed that she had narrowed the DNA molecule structure down to a sort of double helix, but she did not use the type of three-dimensional molecular models that Watson and Crick were building at Cambridge. John Bernal, the eminent physics professor at Birkbeck College, who worked with Rosalind Franklin during the last five years of her life, was quoted in the London Times as stating that Rosalind Franklin's ingenious experimental and mathematical techniques of X-ray analysis enabled her to verify the hypothesis of Watson and Crick regarding the double spiral structure of DNA. She positively established that the main sugar–phosphate chain of nucleic acid lay on the outside, and demonstrated that a double helix structure was compatible with the X-ray patterns of both the A and B forms of DNA. She also contributed the technique of preparing X-ray photographs of the two hydrated forms of DNA, and applied Patterson function analysis to demonstrate that the structure was best accounted for by a double spiral of nucleotides, in which the phosphorus atoms lay on the outside.

As stated above, the relationship between Franklin and Wilkins was such that the two scientists rarely spoke to each other, and, therefore, did not share their findings. Meanwhile, Crick and Watson worked famously together, and shared information between them that probably lead them to win the race to the discovery of the structure of the DNA molecule. For example, it was Crick who had knowledge of a theoretical hunch of a natural attraction between A and T, and C and G. He then urged that Watson accept the complimentarity hypothesis as a possible explanation of "Chargaff's rules," which hold that DNA contains like amounts of adenine and thymine, and of guanine and cytosine. It was later stated by authorities that it was this type of synergy that Rosalind Franklin lacked in her work with Wilkins. Also, working in a largely male scientific field at a time when women were not even allowed in the faculty dining room, Franklin had no one to bond with; no support of someone like Crick, whose knowledge matched her gaps or whose gaps her knowledge matched.

Crick and Watson wrote up their findings and had them published in the journal *Nature* on April 25, 1953 in an article titled "A Structure for Deoxyribose Nucleic Acid." Wilkins and Franklin also prepared accompanying corroborating articles that were printed simultaneously in *Nature*. Franklin was pleased, not bitter, that her work was used in the discovery of the DNA molecule structure.

Today, it is clear that the DNA molecule appears as a spiral staircase, having a twisted double strand of alternating phosphate and sugar molecules on the outer rails, while hydrogen bonds between pairs of groupings of the four "bases" (A, C, T, and G) form the steps of the staircase and hold the two twisted strands together. It is also clear that the base pairing is critical to the hereditary function of DNA. The discovery by Franklin, Wilkins, Watson, and Crick led future scientists to learn not only how the DNA molecule duplicated itself, but also how it stored information and turned it into a usable form. Many have stated the view that Rosalind Franklin's contribution to the discovery of the structure of the DNA molecule was equal to those who were awarded the Nobel Prize. One historian noted that although Franklin was a bold experimentalist, she was critical of speculation and leaned towards inductive reasoning, which worked to her benefit in her work with coal, but which allowed others to pass her on DNA.

At the request of The Royal Society (London), Franklin prepared an exhibit at the 1958 Brussels World's Fair on the structure of DNA and the structure of small viruses. In 2002, the British Trade and Industry Secretary created a Franklin Medal in honor of Rosalind Franklin, to raise the profile of other women scientists, carrying a £30,000 annual prize awarded by the Royal Society for exceptional innovation by men and women scientists.

16 Business Method Protection

16.1 BUSINESS METHODS CONSTITUTE PATENTABLE SUBJECT MATTER

On January 8, 1889, the era of automated financial/management business data processing method patents was born. United States Patents Nos. 395,781; 395,782; and 395,783 were granted to inventor Herman Hollerith. Mr. Hollerith's method and apparatus patents automated the tabulating and compiling of statistical information for businesses and enterprises. The protection afforded by his patents allowed his fledgling Tabulating Machine Company to succeed. In 1924, Thomas J. Watson, Sr. changed the company name to International Business Machine Corporation (IBM). Hollerith's manual punch cards (IBM punch cards) and his methods for processing business data were still being used up until the birth of the personal computer.

Many automatic business data processing methods were invented over the past 100 plus years, however the bulk of that time was spent perfecting the automated business data processing machines upon which the methods were run. Only recently, have data processing systems become sufficiently developed to allow the economy to begin to fully tap the ingenuity and value in the business method itself.

The arrival of electricity as a component in business data processing systems was a major historical watershed event. Electrical-mechanical devices included switches that were ultimately replaced by individual transistors. Individual transistors were ultimately replaced by small-scale integrated circuits, which, in turn, were replaced by large-scale integrated circuits. Each new generation of technology resulted in increased business data processing power and new inventions. However, one key element was not significantly improved by these advances. Each data processing system had to be individually designed at the transistor level and hard wired to perform the correct business data functions. The replacement of specific-function large-scale integrated circuits by software-controlled microprocessors became the latest evolutionary step to bring the economy to the use of business data processing systems and the methods they incorporate throughout industry and business today.

Prior to the 1998 *State Street* decision, the pertinent portion of which is reprinted at the end of this chapter, many court decisions assumed, and held, that methods or processes of doing business did not qualify as patentable subject matter under the patent laws. However, these prior cases also found the method claimed in the patents before the courts at that time unpatentable for other reasons, such as lack of novelty of the claimed process, the claims merely presenting an abstract idea in the form of a mathematical algorithm, or the claims were too broad to be patentable. In its *State Street* decision, the CAFC cleared the air and firmly held that process claims in a patent directed to a method of doing business, whether implemented in a computer-related system or not, were to be treated as any other process claims, and not turned down on the sole grounds of being directed to a business method. Such patent application claims may still be rejected as defining an old and/or ob-

Intellectual Property Law for Engineers and Scientists, by Howard B. Rockman
ISBN 0-471-44998-9 © 2004 The Institute of Electrical and Electronics Engineers

vious method, or as being too broad or too vague, but not for the singular reason that the patent is directed to a business method.

Prior to the *State Street* decision, several courts tackled the question of whether borderline "business method" patents should be allowed. In the case of *Paine Webber, Jackson and Curtis, Inc. v. Merrill Lynch, Pierce, Fenner and Smith, Inc.,* 564 F. Sup. 1358 (Del. 1983), the patent claims involved an innovative cash management system developed by Merrill Lynch. The District Court refused to invalidate the claims as constituting a "business method." The Court stated that the patent claims described a highly useful business method that would be unpatentable if done by hand, however, the Court did uphold the patent stating:

> "The CCPA, however, has made clear that if no Benson algorithm exists, the product of the computer program is irrelevant, and the focus of analysis should be on the operation of the program on the computer. The Court finds that the '442 patent claims statutory (patentable) subject matter because the claims allegedly teach a method of operation on a computer to effectuate a business activity. Accordingly, the '442 patent passes the threshold requirement of Section 101."

It is apparent that the U.S. Patent and Trademark Office and the Courts recognize that new technology was bringing software and new business methods to the point of having enhanced value in the world economy. Most new business techniques, particularly in the financial industry, were implemented by computer software, and could be characterized as computer-related inventions. Prior to *State Street,* the U.S. Patent and Trademark Office was issuing patents on computer-related financial and business inventions, where these patents appear to rely upon their computer dependence for their validity. However, the *State Street* case expanded the trend of the U.S. Patent and Trademark Office to grant patents on computer software, on computer-related business techniques, and to all business methods, whether computer-related or not.

A year after the *State Street* decision was decided by the CAFC, the Patent Act was amended by adding a new Section 273, which provides "prior user rights." Section 273 establishes an absolute defense available to the accused infringer of a "business method" patent if the accused infringer had, acting in good faith, actually reduced the patented subject matter to practice at least one year before the effective filing date of the allegedly infringed patent, and the accused infringer had commercially used the subject matter before the effective filing date of the patent. Note that this defense is limited solely to patent claims directed to "a method of doing or conducting business." The purpose of this statute was to protect individuals or businesses who achieve the relevant invention before the patent owner did, but who did not apply for, or may not be entitled to, a patent on the invention.

Under Section 273, it would be possible for a person who "invents" the business method after the invention date of the patent holder to successfully assert a defense, if that person had used the invention commercially one year before the effective filing date of the patent. Therefore, if you are contemplating the filing of a business method patent, it would be prudent to file the application at the earliest possible time, before the business method is made public, to prevent a subsequent user of the business method from asserting this defense. Also, under Section 273, courts in the future will be faced with the problem of defining whether a method is a method of "doing business" or whether the patent defines the means of carrying out the method of doing business.

16.2 FOREIGN BUSINESS METHOD AND SOFTWARE PATENTS

As of the writing of this text, Rule 52(2) of the European Patent Convention (EPC) stated that business methods (and computer programs) shall not be regarded as "inventions" within the EPC definition of patentable subject matter. Although this may appear as an airtight prohibition against obtaining business method patents and computer program protection in Europe, two decisions in 1998 and 1999 by the European Patent Office (EPO) Board of Appeals hold that although "computer programs *as such*" could not be considered as patentable subject matter, computer programs that are *not* "computer programs *as such*" but have a "technical character" are patentable. In both cases, the EPO Board of Appeals permitted the granting of a European patent for a computer system that claimed the method embodied in the system, the apparatus adapted to carry out the same method, and the software or computer program product, the latter which includes all of the features enabling operation of the method when loaded in a computer. See T 1173/97 Computer Program Product/IBM (1998), and T 0935/97 Computer Program Product II/IBM (1999). See also *Business Method Patents: Adapting to a New Concept,"* paper presented by Steven S. Boyd at the 14th Annual Intellectual Property Law Course, Dallas, TX, March 1–3, 2001.

The above reasoning is incrementally being applied to allow the granting of European patents directed to business methods. The EPO Guidelines, Part C, Chapter IV (2) (the EPO equivalent of the MPEP of the USPTO), state that business methods are not patentable since they are "items of an abstract or intellectual character," and do not lead to a direct technical result. Therefore, to determine whether your novel business method will support a patent in Europe, consider the following:

1. Claims in your patent application for an abstract business method, which do not recite any physical elements or apparatus to carry out the method, are not patentable under current EPO standards.

2. Claims which recite computer elements, computer networks, or digital devices for performing the method, or certain steps of the business method, are patentable subject matter when considered as, and meeting the standards of, other computer-related inventions, that is, have a "technical character."

3. Claims for business methods that recite noncomputer equipment or devices to carry out the process, such as mobile voice communication devices, mechanical apparatus, or the like, are also considered for patentability applying the same standards used to examine computer-based business methods.

See *Trilateral Project on Business Methods,* App. 6, Examination of Business Method Applications (EPO), p. 3 (2000) (www.uspto.gov/web/tws/appendix 6. pdf).

Therefore, if your business method invention can support a claim, or claims, including a computer-related or noncomputer-related device in the performance of the method, European patent protection is probably available.

However, in the above analysis, keep in mind that the "technical means" must be claimed as producing a solution to the technical problem that the business method claim addresses, and cannot claim merely a "method of doing business as such." See T 0931/95 Pension Benefit Systems Partnership, re: Improved Pension Benefits System (EPO Board of Appeals 2000, at p. 7).

Keeping in line with the trend in Europe, the Japanese Patent Office (JPO) in November 2000 published for comment revised "Examination Guidelines" covering computer and software-based inventions, which include business method inventions. See Revised Examination Guidelines, JPO (`www.jpomiti.go.jp/ikene/pdf/feedback_121102_2.pdf`).

The JPO proposed guidelines state, however, that where the software or business method invention can be readily obtained by combining prior art apparatus and methods known by one having ordinary technical skill in the related field, patentability will *not* be found.

In Japan, computer software has been realized as patentable subject matter since at least July 1, 1993, when the JPO promulgated guidelines for the examination of software patent applications. These guidelines state that the following comprise statutory invention:

1. Inventions in which natural laws are utilized in the information processing by software, for example:
    a. Execution of control of hardware resources or processing accompanying the control
    b. Execution of information processing based on the physical or technical nature or properties of an object
2. Inventions utilizing hardware resources

See: *Q&A's on Japanese Patent Practice 26,* p. 62, paper by the Japanese Patent Attorney Association (JPAA) (November 1983) distributed at the Seminar on Japanese Patent Practice and Prosecution, AIPLA/JPAA, June 15 and 18, 1992; Gregory A. Stobbs, *Software Patents, 2nd Edition,* Aspen Publishers, Inc., 2000, pp. 509–510.

Likewise, inventions in information processing are not patentable if based on mathematical process, schemes, rules, or methods for doing business or performing mental acts. Also, when the limitations imposed by hardware resources in a claim correspond to an inevitable restriction (mere use of hardware resources) resulting from the use of a computer, ". . . the claimed invention is not considered to use natural laws, and is not patentable under Japanese law," *ibid.*

Presently, in Japan, inventions may be deemed patentable as being based on the physical or technical nature of an object that include, but are not limited to, data formatting, word processing, protocol and signal architectures, and signal/noise properties. Inventions that are *not* considered as based on the physical or technical nature of an object, and thus not patentable, include methods based on economic rules, methods of doing business, man-made rules, mathematical algorithms or formulas, programming languages, computer programs per se, and computer programs recorded on a storage medium (*ibid.* Stobbs at p. 512). The latter, novel programs recorded on a storage medium, can be considered as patentable subject matter in the United States. My prediction is that eventually the JPO will also adopt this same policy and grant patents routinely on computer software, and even on methods of doing business.

Also, Australia seems to be allowing business method patents at present. Of note, the Australian Court relied upon the language in the Australian Patent Act that defines a "patentable invention" as including "any manner of new manufactures," which is language first found in the 1623 English Statute of Monopolies. In the decision of *Welcome*

Real-Time S.A. v. Catuity, Inc., FCA 445 (2001), the Federal Court of Australia commented upon the *State Street* decision in the United States, and then went on to say:

> "But the social needs the law has to serve in that country (USA) is the same as in ours. In both countries, in similar commercial and technological environments, the law has to strike a balance between, on the one hand, the encouragement of true invention by the grant of monopoly and, on the other hand, freedom of competition."

This decision emphasizes the need of the patent laws to continually push the envelope to encompass new technologies as they are developed.

The primary business method patents that have issued from the U.S. Patent and Trademark Office prior to and since the *State Street* decision relate primarily to financial methods on the internet. However, I have recently filed a patent application for a client directed to a method of doing business that pertains to literary structures, and has nothing to do with computers.

Much commentary has arisen regarding the "mundane" and "obvious" business methods that are being awarded patent protection. One such case involved U.S. Patent No. 5,960,411, owned by Amazon.com, entitled "Method and System for Placing a Purchase Order via a Communications Network." This patent issued in 1999 and the business method permits customers to purchase online with one click of the computer mouse, avoiding delay encountered with inputting address and credit card information. This patent has been criticized due to its "apparent obviousness" when viewed with hindsight. Some have argued that this is an obvious adaptation of an old method to new technology. Note that Amazon.com filed a lawsuit against Barnes&Noble.com, and obtained a preliminary injunction preventing Barnes&Noble.com from using the method described in Amazon.com's patent. However, on appeal, the CAFC found that there were substantial questions regarding whether the subject matter of the patent was anticipated or rendered obvious by the prior art, and the preliminary injunction against Barnes&Noble.com was vacated. See *Amazon.com v. Barnes&Noble.com,* 239 Fed. 3d, 1343 (Fed. Cir. 2001).

One of the questions that arose is whether or not business methods are encompassed by the term "technology" to be protected by the patent system. The CAFC in the *State Street* decision has clearly come down on the side that even business methods can be included within the definition of "technology."

16.3 PREPARING A PROPER BUSINESS METHOD PATENT APPLICATION

When reviewing your patent application directed to a business method, whether computer-related or not, ensure that the patent application defines the invention as a whole as accomplishing a practical application, that is a "useful, concrete and tangible result," and that the invention possesses a level of "real world" value, as opposed to subject matter that represents nothing more than an idea or concept or simply a starting point for future investigation or research. These are the primary statements that the patent examiner will look for during the prosecution of your patent application before the U.S. Patent and Trademark Office. Thus, it is vitally important that the specification is detailed, complete and clearly identifies any and all practical applications for the claimed invention.

It is recommended that the specification of the patent application include the following:

1. A clear description of the invention, and a description of the problem the invention is aimed at solving.
2. A discussion of the most relevant known prior art that pertains to the invention, including a description of how others have tried previously to solve the problem and have failed.
3. A description of the best mode of the invention.
4. A clear identification of all practical applications asserted for the invention, describing how the claimed invention produces a useful, concrete and tangible result.

The patent application description should convey with reasonable clarity to one skilled in the art that the inventor had possession of the claimed invention at the time the application was filed. This should be shown by a clear depiction in detailed drawings in the application, and a written description describing suffcient relative identifying characteristics of the business method sought to be patented. Note that what is conventional or well-known to one skilled in the art need not be disclosed in the application in detail, but should be referred to when describing the prior art.

STATE STREET BANK & TRUST CO., Plaintiff-Appellee, v. SIGNATURE
FINANCIAL GROUP, INC., Defendant-Appellant.

96-1327

UNITED STATES COURT OF APPEALS FOR THE FEDERAL CIRCUIT

149 F.3d 1368; 1998 U.S. App. LEXIS 16869; 47 U.S.P.Q.2D (BNA) 1596

July 23, 1998. Decided
[**22]

The business method exception has never been invoked by this court, or the CCPA, to deem an invention unpatentable. n11 Application of this particular exception has always been preceded by a ruling based on some clearer concept of Title 35 or, more commonly, application of the abstract idea exception based on finding a mathematical algorithm. Illustrative is the CCPA's analysis in *In re Howard, 55 C.C.P.A. 1121, 394 F.2d 869, 157 U.S.P.Q. (BNA) 615 (CCPA 1968)*, wherein the court affirmed the Board of Appeals' rejection of the claims for lack of novelty and found it unnecessary to reach the Board's section 101 ground that a method of doing business is "inherently unpatentable." *394 F.2d at 872, 157 U.S.P.Q. (BNA) at 617.* n12

The Business Method Exception

As an alternative ground for invalidating the *'056* patent under § 101, the court relied on the judicially-created, so-called "business method" exception to statutory subject matter. We take this opportunity to lay this ill-conceived [**21] exception to rest. Since its inception, the "business method" exception has merely represented the application of some general, but no longer applicable legal principle, perhaps arising out of the "requirement for invention"--which was eliminated by § 103. Since the 1952 Patent Act, [HN14] business methods have been, and should have been, subject to the same legal requirements for patentability as applied to any other process or method. n10

n10 As Judge Newman has previously stated,

[The business method exception] is ... an unwarranted encumbrance to the definition of statutory subject matter in section 101, that [should] be discarded as error-prone, redundant, and obsolete. It merits retirement from the glossary of section 101. ... All of the "doing business" cases could have been decided using the clearer concepts of Title 35. Patentability does not turn on whether the claimed method does "business" instead of something else, but on whether the method, viewed as a whole, meets the requirements of patentability as set forth in Sections 102, 103, and 112 of the Patent Act.

In re Schrader, 22 F.3d 290, 298, 30 U.S.P.Q.2D (BNA) 1455, 1462 (Fed. Cir. 1994) (Newman, J., dissenting).

n11 See Rinaldo Del Gallo, III, *Are 'Methods of Doing Business' Finally out of Business as a Statutory Rejection?*, 38 IDEA 403, 435 (1998).

n12 See also *Dann v. Johnston, 425 U.S. 219, 47 L. Ed. 2d 692, 96 S. Ct. 1393 (1976)* (the Supreme Court declined to discuss the section 101 argument concerning the computerized financial record-keeping system, in view of the Court's holding of patent invalidity under section 103); *In re Chatfield, 545 F.2d 152, 157, 191 U.S.P.Q. (BNA) 730, 735 (CCPA 1976)*; *Ex parte Murray, 9 U.S.P.Q.2D (BNA) 1819, 1820 (Bd. Pat. App. & Interf. 1988)* ("The claimed accounting method [requires] no more than the entering, sorting, debiting and totaling of expenditures as necessary preliminary steps to issuing an expense analysis statement. ...") states grounds of obviousness or lack of novelty, not of non-statutory subject matter.

[**23]

[*1376] Similarly, *In re Schrader, 22 F.3d 290, 30 U.S.P.Q.2D (BNA) 1455 (Fed. Cir. 1994)*, while making reference to the business method exception, turned on the fact that the claims implicitly recited an abstract idea in the form of a mathematical algorithm and there was no "transformation or conversion of subject matter representative of or constituting physical activity or objects." *22 F.3d at 294, 30 U.S.P.Q.2D (BNA) at 1459* (emphasis omitted). n13

n13 Any historical distinctions between a method of "doing" business and the means of carrying it out blur in the complexity of modern business systems. See *Paine, Webber, Jackson & Curtis v. Merrill Lynch, 564 F. Supp. 1358, 218 U.S.P.Q. (BNA) 212 (D. Del. 1983)*, (holding a computerized system of cash management was held to be statutory subject matter.)

State Street argues that we acknowledged the validity of the business method exception in Alappat when we discussed Maucorps and Meyer:

Maucorps dealt with a business methodology for deciding how salesmen should best [**24] handle respective customers and Meyer involved a 'system' for aiding a neurologist in diagnosing patients. Clearly, neither of the alleged 'inventions' in those cases falls within any § 101 category.

Alappat, 33 F.3d at 1541, 31 U.S.P.Q.2D (BNA) at 1555. However, closer scrutiny of these cases reveals that the claimed inventions in both Maucorps and Meyer were rejected as abstract ideas under the mathematical algorithm exception, not the business method exception. See *In re Maucorps, 609 F.2d 481, 484, 203 U.S.P.Q. (BNA) 812, 816 (CCPA 1979); In re Meyer, 688 F.2d 789, 796, 215 U.S.P.Q. (BNA) 193, 199 (CCPA 1982)*. n14

> n14 Moreover, these cases were subject to the Benson era Freeman-Walter-Abele test--in other words, analysis as it existed before Diehr and Alappat.

Even the case frequently cited as establishing the business method exception to statutory subject matter, *Hotel Security Checking Co. v. Lorraine Co., 160 F. 467 (2d Cir. 1908)*, did not rely on the exception to strike the patent. [**25] n15 In that case, the patent was found invalid for lack of novelty and "invention," not because it was improper subject matter for a patent. The court stated "the fundamental principle of the system is as old as the art of bookkeeping, i.e., charging the goods of the employer to the agent who takes them." *Id. at 469.* "If at the time of [the patent] application, there had been no system of bookkeeping of any kind in restaurants, we would be confronted with the question whether a new and useful system of cash registering and account checking is such an art as is patentable under the statute." *Id. at 472.*

> n15 See also *Loew's Drive-In Theatres v. Park-In Theatres, 174 F.2d 547, 552 (1st Cir.*

1949) (holding that the means for carrying out the system of transacting business lacked "an exercise of the faculty of invention"); *In re Patton, 29 C.C.P.A. 982, 127 F.2d 324, 327-38 (CCPA 1942)* (finding claims invalid as failing to define patentable subject matter over the references of record.); *Berardini v. Tocci, 190 F. 329, 332 (C.C.S.D.N.Y. 1911); In re Wait, 22 C.C.P.A. 822, 73 F.2d 982, 983 (CCPA 1934)* ("Surely these are, and always have been, essential steps in all dealings of this nature, and even conceding, without holding, that some methods of doing business might present patentable novelty, we think such novelty is lacking here."); *In re Howard, 55 C.C.P.A. 1121, 157 U.S.P.Q. (BNA) 615, 617, 394 F.2d 869 (CCPA 1968)* ("We therefore affirm the decision of the Board of Appeals on the ground that the claims do not define a novel process...[so we find it] unnecessary to consider the issue of whether a method of doing business is inherently unpatentable."). Although a clearer statement was made in *In re Patton, 29 C.C.P.A. 982, 127 F.2d 324, 327, 53 U.S.P.Q. (BNA) 376, 379 (CCPA 1942)* that a system for transacting business, separate from the means for carrying out the system, is not patentable subject matter, the jurisprudence does not require the creation of a distinct business class of unpatentable subject matter.

[**26]

This case is no exception. The district court announced the precepts of the business method exception as set forth in several treatises, but noted as its primary reason for finding the patent invalid under the business method exception as follows:

If Signature's invention were patentable, any financial institution desirous of implementing a multi-tiered funding complex modelled (sic) on a Hub and Spoke configuration would be required to seek Signature's permission before embarking on [*1377] such a project. This is so because the '056 Patent is claimed [sic] sufficiently broadly to foreclose virtually any computer-implemented accounting method necessary to manage this type of financial structure.

927 F. Supp. 502, 516, 38 U.S.P.Q.2D (BNA) 1530, 1542 (emphasis added). Whether the patent's claims are too broad to be patentable is not to be judged under § 101, but rather under § § 102, 103 and 112. Assuming the above statement to be correct, it has nothing to do with whether what is claimed is statutory subject matter.

149 F.3d 1368, *; 1998 U.S. App. LEXIS 16869, **;
47 U.S.P.Q.2D (BNA) 1596

In view of this background, it comes as no surprise that in the most recent edition of the Manual of Patent Examining Procedures (MPEP) (1996), a paragraph of § [**27] 706.03(a) was deleted. In past editions it read:

Though seemingly within the category of process or method, a method of doing business can be rejected as not being within the statutory classes. See *Hotel Security Checking Co. v. Lorraine Co., 160 F. 467 (2nd Cir. 1908)* and *In re Wait, 73 F.2d 982, 24 U.S.P.Q. (BNA) 88, 22 C.C.P.A. 822 (1934).*

MPEP § 706.03(a) (1994). This acknowledgment is buttressed by the U.S. Patent and Trademark 1996 Examination Guidelines for Computer Related Inventions which now read:

Office personnel have had difficulty in properly treating claims directed to methods of doing business. [HN15] Claims should not be categorized as methods of doing business. Instead such claims should be treated like any other process claims.

Examination Guidelines, *61 Fed. Reg. 7478, 7479 (1996).* We agree that this is precisely the manner in which this type of claim should be treated. Whether the claims are directed to subject matter within § 101 should not turn on whether the claimed subject matter does "business" instead of something else.

CONCLUSION

The appealed decision is reversed and the case is remanded to the district court for further proceedings [**28] consistent with this opinion.

REVERSED and REMANDED.

Wilbur and Orville Wright

CONTROLLED POWERED FLIGHT

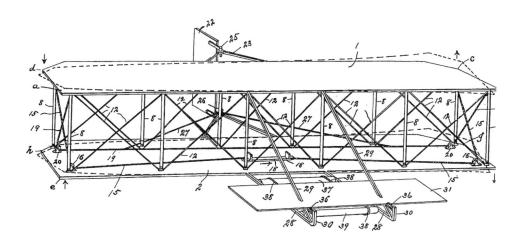

For those of us who are beyond middle age, it is practically impossible to listen to Rossini's "William Tell Overture" without thinking of our Western hero, The Lone Ranger. Likewise, most of the world today cannot hear the word "inventor" or "flight" without immediately thinking of the Wright brothers. The Wright brothers are credited with achieving the first powered, sustained, and controlled flight of a heavier than air airplane.

Wilbur and Orville Wright were the sons of Milton Wright, a bishop in the United Brethren Church. Wilbur was born on April 16, 1867 on a farm near New Castle, Indiana. Orville Wright was born in Dayton, Ohio on August 19, 1871. Both went through high school in Dayton, but never received their diplomas. After Orville initiated a printing business, the brothers later launched a weekly newspaper, the *West Side News,* edited by Wilbur. They then began to sell and lease bicycles, and by 1896 migrated to manufacturing and assembling bicycles in a room above their shop.

The Wright brothers reportedly became interested in flight after reading about the death in 1896 of Otto Lilienthal who was a glider pioneer. They began studying the construction of gliders and, based upon the Weather Bureau's recommendation, picked Kill Devil Hills, a small strip of sand near Kitty Hawk, North Carolina, to conduct their experiments. Kitty Hawk provided the high-velocity winds necessary to launch the gliders off the ground, and the soft sand to cushion the impact when a glider flight was not successful.

The Wright brothers observed that all of the newspaper accounts of earlier aircraft reported that such aircraft lacked controls. They felt that a pilot in an aircraft should be able

Intellectual Property Law for Engineers and Scientists, by Howard B. Rockman
ISBN 0-471-44998-9 © 2004 The Institute of Electrical and Electronics Engineers

to balance the aircraft in the air, somewhat as bicyclists balance their bicycles while riding them, banking or leaning into their turns. Wilbur also saw that buzzards, when turning, twisted one wing tip up while the other twisted down. Then, Wilbur was playing with a narrow, long cardboard box, which he twisted over and over again—one edge up, one edge down. The box retained its rigidity and did not break. The brothers then installed a series of pulleys and wire ropes that allowed them to "warp" the glider wings up and down. They first tested this theory in a biplane kite constructed in 1899 in their Dayton shop, with a wing that mechanically twisted (warping). They continued these tests in two additional gliders they constructed.

The Wrights constructed their glider wings based on an idea of Octave Chanute, an American aviation pioneer of French origin, which comprised biplane wings stiffened with a Pratt truss. The Pratt truss had been patented in 1844 by Thomas and Caleb Pratt, not for flying craft, but for an earthbound railroad bridge.

In 1900, the Wright brothers tested their first glider that could carry a person; it measured 16 feet from wing tip to wing tip. In 1901, they returned to Kitty Hawk with an even larger glider. Although these two gliders demonstrated control of sideways balance by tipping the ends of the right and left wings at different angles to the wind, neither the 1900 nor 1901 gliders had the power to produce the lift they had anticipated. Also, these gliders were not fully controllable.

During the winter of 1901–1902, the Wright brothers constructed a 6 foot wind tunnel in their shop to conduct an analysis of the optimum wing shape for an airplane. They reportedly tested more than 200 wing models in the tunnel. As a result of these tests, the Wright brothers produced the first reliable tables of air pressures on curved surfaces. They also found that air pressure tables produced previously by Otto Lilienthal were wrong. By using their own analytical tables, the Wright brothers designed a wing surface and controls for the wing surface that ultimately led to successful flight. By the end of the 1902 flying season, the third Wright glider is credited with being the first fully controllable aircraft, with roll, pitch, and yaw controls.

With their 1902 glider, the Wright brothers made almost 100 glides covering distances of more than 600 feet on some of the flights. In 1903, the Wright brothers applied for a U.S. patent with the help of an experienced patent attorney; the patent discloses the 1902 glider. The patent, which is reprinted following this essay, can be noted to include no mention of power or of a motor.

During the winter of 1902–1903, the Wright brothers' mechanic, Charles Taylor, assisted the Wrights in constructing a light gasoline combustion engine that was powerful enough to drive a propeller for an aircraft. They also used the time to design the first true airplane propellers, and constructed a new powered aircraft. This became known as the 1903 Wright Flyer I. Their new aircraft, which cost less than $1,000 to build, had a wing span of 40.5 feet, and weighed approximately 750 pounds. This included the weight of the pilot.

In the summer of 1903, the Wright brothers found themselves under severe pressure. Samuel P. Langley, the secretary of the Smithsonian Institution in Washington, had also constructed a powered aircraft, modeled after his previous unmanned "Aerodrome," which had flown successfully in 1896. The Wright brothers were also encountering problems with their propeller shafts and the weather, which gave Langley time to test his aircraft two times in late 1903. However, both attempts by Langley failed, and on December 17, 1903, Wilbur and Orville Wright prepared to test their powered aircraft at Kill Devil Hills in North Carolina.

The Wright brother's theoretical work predicated on their wind tunnel experience is credited with allowing them to create the first successful controllable powered aircraft. The Wright brother's gliders were typically unstable, and the success of the Wright brothers is largely due to their ability to balance their craft in the air. For example, Octave Chanute was in Europe in 1902 and, while passing through France, addressed a group of aeronautical engineers, experimenters, and enthusiasts who had been concentrating their efforts on lighter-than-air aircraft, such as balloons and dirigibles. He described to the French his own work in heavier-than-air aircraft and the gliding experience of the Wright brothers that successfully took place in 1902. Although the French aeronautical enthusiasts constructed many variations of the Wright glider design over the next three years, none paid attention to the theoretical and analytical work of the Wright brothers. The French concentrated on creating an inherently stable aircraft, one that would remain pointed in a single direction with the right side up, with little input from the pilot. The French failed to understand the importance of control, which was the Wright brothers' ultimate reason for success. Much later than the Wright brothers, the French finally came around to understanding that the Wright brothers' theory of control is the most important aspect in successful controlled powered flight.

December 17, 1903 is the day that marks the beginning of controlled powered flight. Considering all of the different types of aircraft flying today, it is hard to believe that this event happened only 100 years ago. The Wright brothers arrived in Kitty Hawk in September 1903 to test out their new powered and controlled aircraft. However, defects and storms on the coast prevented them from conducting their experiments until December 17.

The Wright brothers had a certain modicum of anticipation that their flights at Kill Devil Hills in December 1903 would be successful. Their previous glider flights in 1902 had proven the reliability of their aircraft's control system. The brothers had also become skilled pilots, and their research work with the wind tunnel had given them a sense of aerodynamics that allowed them to use technical analysis to arrive at the design of their aircraft.

On the evening of December 16, 1903, a northeast storm hit the Wright brothers' camp at Kitty Hawk. By morning, the rain had stopped, but the winds continued to blow in from the ocean, gusting at approximately 30 miles an hour. The wind chill factor was 4 degrees Fahrenheit. However, the Wright brothers decided to go ahead and attempt their flight, and it is reported that one of the main reasons was that if they were unable to leave Kitty Hawk shortly, they would not be back in Dayton, Ohio in time for Christmas.

Shortly past 10:00 AM, the Wright brothers hoisted a red blanket on the side of their hanger, which was a signal advising the Kitty Hawk Lifesaving Crew that they needed additional manpower to prepare their aircraft for flight. The Wright brothers began preparing the wooden track extending 200 feet from the hanger while waiting for the lifesaving crew to arrive.

Then, five men—John Daniels, Adam Etheridge, Will Dough, W. C. Brinkley and John Moore—arrived and helped the Wright brothers drag their 600-pound-plus aircraft across the frozen sands of Kill Devil Hills. These gentlemen offered their services out of the warmth of their own hearts, and were not compensated by the Wright brothers.

By 10:30, the Wright brothers' crew had the Wright Flyer I on its launching rail, the brothers cranked the propellers, and the engine groaned into operation. It was Orville's turn to fly in their rotation, and he mounted the flyer in the middle of the lower wing. He warped the wings, rotated the rudder, operated the elevators, and checked the controls. At that point, history was rewarded when Wilbur asked John Daniels of the lifesaving crew to take a photograph just as the Wright Flyer I reached the end of its launching rail. Orville also asked the rest of the crew to clap, be joyful, and make a lot of noise to cheer Orville on his way.

At 10:35, Orville Wright released the wire restraining the aircraft, and the craft moved along the rail into a 27 mile an hour headwind. Wilbur ran alongside the aircraft, something that you probably could not do today during take-off. Approximately two-thirds along the length of the rail, the Wright Flyer I lifted into the air. Orville had not accurately predicted the elevators' effectiveness, and the craft rose rather quickly. To compensate, Orville moved the elevator down and the aircraft dived. For 12 seconds, the aircraft went up and down, up and down, and then landed, both the pilot and the airplane in one piece except for a cracked skid. The plane had traveled 120 feet from the end of the launching rail. But, for the first time in history, a flying aircraft under power had taken off from level ground, flown through the air under the control of its pilot, and also landed under the control of its pilot. The trip was a nerve-wracking one, the controls were unsteady, and the craft wavered during flight, but it was under control.

Not satisfied with just a single flight that day, at approximately 11:30, the Wright brothers made a second flight, this time with Wilbur acting as pilot, and flew 175 feet. Shortly thereafter, Orville took the controls and the craft flew for a third time, arriving approximately 200 feet from its starting point. And then, at approximately noon, Wilbur returned to the controls for the fourth flight. The beginning of this flight was as rocky as the first three flights, with the aircraft pitching in the wind as Wilbur struggled to control the elevator. It is reported that approximately 100 feet out, the aircraft was moving up and down like a bull at a rodeo. The bucking got worse at 200 feet, but after approximately 300 feet, Wilbur obtained a feel for the elevator and the craft's path smoothed out. Wilbur flew past the 800 foot mark, when a gust of wind caused the airplane to begin its wild, bumpy ride again. Wilbur tried to regain control, but the Flyer suddenly darted for the ground, as Orville later described it. The plane finally landed approximately 850 feet from its starting point and 59 seconds later. Other than damaging the support for the elevator, the pilot and the craft were both in one piece.

However, as the crew was in the process of carrying the craft back to the launching point for a possible fifth flight, a sudden gust of wind picked up one wing. Daniels, the photographer, grabbed one of the wing struts and ended up being caught in the bracing wires while the machine was rolled over several times by the wind. When the craft stopped rolling with Daniels attached to it, nothing was left but shards of wood, ripped cloth fabric, and an unharmed Daniels. Due to this damage, the world's first true powered and practical airplane would never fly again.

Almost a hundred years later, analysts and aeronautical engineers used computers to reconstruct the flight characteristics of the Wright Flyer I. They discovered that the elevator was extremely sensitive, making the craft nearly uncontrollable. According to the computer simulation, the pilot needed the strength of a professional athlete to control the plane while in the air.

Following their fourth flight on December 17, the Wright brothers sent a telegram back to their father, Bishop Milton Wright in Dayton, Ohio, marking their success. Milton Wright immediately telegraphed the news to Octave Chanute, who was Orville's high school chum and who had been collaborating with the Wright brothers. From this time on, man was not limited to two-dimensional travel along the earth's surface. Human life from that time on became three dimensional.

Prior to their December 1903 flights, the Wright brothers decided to obtain additional resources to continue their aeronautical experiments. To accomplish this purpose, they concluded that they needed a patent to protect their invention. The brothers had previously filed a patent application themselves, which had been rejected by the United States Patent Office. This time, they made a decision to hire an accredited patent attorney, Henry A. Toulmin, of Springfield, Ohio, who initially advised the brothers to continue their work on a practical flying machine, but not to publicly disclose their invention until the patent was granted. Thus, the Wright brothers continued their experimentation in secret, making no public flights, including the flights in December 1903. They even went to the extent of attempting to sell aircraft to the United States and other governments, under the condition that the purchase contracts be signed before any demonstration flight was made to the prospective purchaser. As a result of that proviso, and the fact that the Wright brothers had difficulty making additional long, sustained flights during the next two years, the various governments refused to enter into contracts with them for the construction of powered aircraft. For example, in 1904, 40 efforts at flight were made by the Wright brothers, the longest being only 600 feet. The problem, they later discovered, was that the aircraft itself had to move at 27 to 28 miles per hour relative to the wind for a successful take-off. If the wind was moving slower, the airplane had to go down the launch rail at a much faster speed. For example, the winds at Kitty Hawk on December 17 were so high that forward motion of the aircraft of only three miles per hour was required to lift the Wright Flyer I off the launching rail that day.

The Wright brothers filed their patent application through Mr. Toulmin on March 23, 1903, almost nine months prior to their first successful flight. This patent application, one of many obtained by the Wright brothers, disclosed the control structure and mechanisms of the 1902 glider, and makes no mention of, nor any disclosure of, an engine or any means for powered flight.

The Wright brother's patent application issued as U.S. Patent No. 821,393 on May 22, 1906. Once the patent was noted as allowed, the Wright brothers decided to make public flights of their aircraft. The first public flight by the Wright brothers was in France on August 8, 1908, and was followed by others. These public flights finally resulted in the Wright brothers obtaining fame for their aeronautical feats. They set up a factory to manufacture aircraft and opened flight schools in both the United States and Europe.

Once their aircraft had flown in public, it was easy for others to copy the Wright brothers' designs, which resulted in the Wright brothers being involved in lengthy and expensive patent law suits in both America and Europe. The most bitter of these, and one that had a profound and lasting effect on both of the brothers, was the patent fight with Glenn Curtiss. In the patent litigation instituted by the Wright brothers, Curtiss, in an effort to prove his defense of patent invalidity, borrowed Langley's previously unsuccessful aircraft from the Smithsonian Institution and rebuilt and modified it in an effort to prove that the "Aerodrome" could have flown before the Wright Flyer I. However, Curtiss had to make extensive alterations to the Aerodrome to get Langley's aircraft in the air, and the court ruled in favor of the Wright brothers. However, the actions by the Smithsonian in supporting Curtiss' argument resulted in a long-lasting antagonism of the Wrights toward the Smithsonian Institution.

Additionally, money in the aircraft business in those days was to be made in exhibition flying, where audiences were looking for death-defying feats of aeronautical daredevilship. The Wright brothers employed pilots who were compelled to fly increasingly more recklessly to satisfy their audiences. As pilots began to die in accidents, the stress of this plus the legal battles distracted the brothers from their work of invention and innovation. Thus, by 1911, aircraft manufactured by others were considered better than the Wright brothers' flying machines.

In 1912, Wilbur Wright became exhausted from both the legal and business problems, and died from typhoid. In 1916, Orville Wright sold the Wright Company and began working on other projects that interested him.

One of Wilbur's projects was a long, continuing battle with the Smithsonian Institution, that continued after the First World War, when the Smithsonian promoted Langley's contributions to the history of flight, while seeming to make little of the Wright brothers' contribution. The battle to rewrite history continued over many years. As retaliation, in 1928 Orville sent the repaired 1903 Wright Flyer I, in which he and Orville had made the first powered flights, to the Science Museum of London in England. In the 1930's, even Charles Lindbergh attempted to arbitrate the battle between the two, but to no avail. In 1942, Orville Wright's biographer, Fred Kelly, encouraged the Smithsonian to back down from its statements and provide the public with the truth. When this was done, Orville instructed the Science Museum to return the Wright Flyer I to America. However, the Second World War intervened, and the Wright Flyer I was finally returned to the Smithsonian in 1948, where it is displayed to this day.

Orville Wright died on January 30, 1948 of a heart attack. The invention and innovation of the Wright brothers lives on in modern society. The basic principles of their aircraft, on display at the Smithsonian, are used in every airplane manufactured today.

No. 821,393.

PATENTED MAY 22, 1906.

O. & W. WRIGHT.
FLYING MACHINE.
APPLICATION FILED MAR. 23, 1903.

3 SHEETS—SHEET 1.

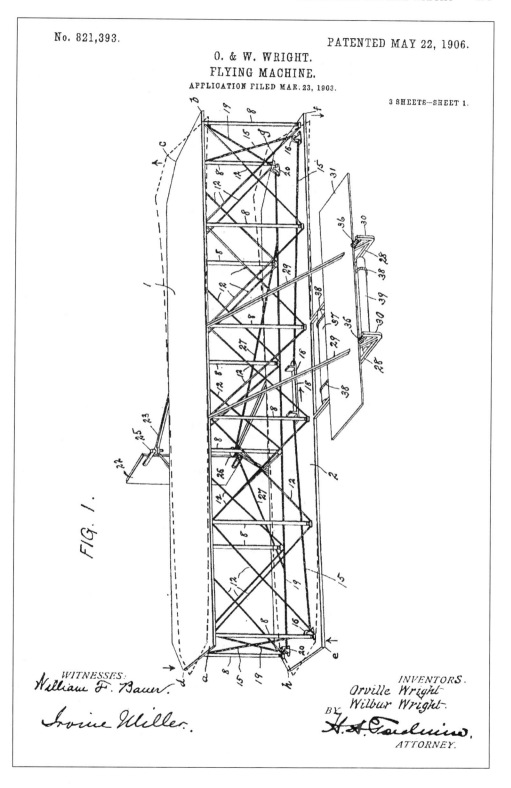

FIG. 1.

WITNESSES:
William F. Bauer.
Irvine Miller.

INVENTORS.
Orville Wright
Wilbur Wright
BY
H. A. Toulmin,
ATTORNEY.

17 Foreign Patent Protection

17.1 INTRODUCTION

With the advent of market "globalization," your inventions will most likely be valuable in many countries outside your home country. Obtaining a patent in your home country does not provide patent protection in any other country, and unlike copyright protection which is covered in Chapter 22, there is no "world patent." A patent right is enforceable against an infringer only in the country which issues the patent. Thus, patents must be obtained from the Patent Office, or equivalent government agency, in each of the countries where protection is sought. If a product or process is being marketed or used in a foreign country, you must have obtained a patent in that country to stop such infringement, and to collect damages resulting from the infringement.

Although the standards for obtaining patent protection in most of the countries of the world are generally the same, there are several important differences. For example, under U.S. patent law, an inventor has one year in which to file a patent application following a "public disclosure" of the invention. "Public disclosure" is a flexibly defined term, whereby a public disclosure of an experimental version or prototype of your invention normally will not prevent the issuance of a valid patent in the U.S. However, in many foreign countries where you may be seeking patent protection, there is no one year "grace period" between public disclosure and filing a patent application. In those countries which adhere to the "absolute novelty" rule in their patent statutes, the patent application must be filed with the Patent Office of that country before there is any public disclosure or public knowledge of the invention anywhere in the world. There are limited exceptions to this rule in some countries, such as a public disclosure prior to filing the patent application at a "recognized trade show" in the country in point, which may allow the inventor three months or so from the date of the trade show to file a patent application without losing patent rights.

In an effort to prevent a public disclosure from having an adverse affect on patent rights anywhere on the planet, I encourage my inventor clients to refrain from any public showing of their invention before we can prepare and file a patent application. For reasons I shall explain, this one step, if adhered to, will protect the inventor's ability to obtain foreign patent rights in their invention, while doing the opposite will most likely destroy the possibility of obtaining patent rights in many important countries.

Remember however, that refraining from disclosing your invention may not be easy. Most inventors I have met consider their invention as their own "babies" which they conceived and gave birth to. How many mothers will agree to hold back showing off their newborn child? But, if you desire to gain maximum advantage from the intellectual effort that went into creating your invention, you will have to keep the cover over the baby buggy until your patent attorney gives you the OK to lift it.

Over 100 years ago, the nations of the world recognized problems in protecting foreign patent rights in what was fast becoming an industrialized world, and enacted a treaty that

Intellectual Property Law for Engineers and Scientists, by Howard B. Rockman
ISBN 0-471-44998-9 © 2004 The Institute of Electrical and Electronics Engineers

would assist inventors in their efforts against losing foreign patent rights in an invention conceived and reduced to practice in their home countries. Subsequent to that time, two other additional important treaties have come into being that also dovetail with the earlier treaty to protect the loss of foreign patent rights. These three treaties are: the Paris Union Convention of 1883, the Patent Cooperation Treaty (PCT), which became operational in 1978, and the European Patent Convention (EPC), which also became operational in 1978. All of these three treaties are compatible, and work with each other. The Paris Union Convention and the PCT are worldwide patent treaties, while the European Patent Convention covers only adherent European countries.

17.2 TRADITIONAL SYSTEM OF OBTAINING FOREIGN PATENTS

Until 1978, obtaining foreign patents was controlled solely by the Paris Union Convention of 1883, which is commonly known among patent attorneys as the "Paris Convention." This treaty remains in force today in most of the major industrialized nations of the world, covering approximately 190 countries. Prior to enactment and enforcement of the Patent Cooperation Treaty in 1978, obtaining patent protection under the Paris Convention involved filing first a patent application in the inventor's country of origin, and within one year of the filing of the home or first patent application, directly filing a separate patent application corresponding to the first patent application in each distinct country where patent protection was sought. A copy of the originally prepared and filed patent application, which for United States' inventors is drafted in English, is then transmitted to a patent attorney or agent in the foreign country. The application is filed without translation if the foreign country is English speaking, or the patent application is translated before filing in non-English speaking countries. Therefore, it is important to note at this juncture that the patent application originally crafted by your patent attorney and filed in your home country is not rewritten for foreign filing, but translation may be required. Under the provisions of the Paris Convention, the separate patent applications must be drafted or translated into the language of each selected country and filed according to the applicable laws and rules of the Patent Office of each selected country.

A primary feature of the Paris Convention is that patent applications filed in the foreign countries within the prescribed twelve month period from the home country filing date provided under the treaty, are considered as though they had been filed in the foreign country on the original filing date in the home country. This is defined as a "right of priority." As a result of the Paris Convention, the effective filing date of your foreign patent application is the same as the home country filing date. It follows that if your home country filing date is prior to any public disclosure, public knowledge or publication of your invention, then your rights in foreign countries are protected vis-a-vis the rules of absolute novelty of those foreign countries. Thus it is important to remember that obtaining a home country filing date before any public disclosure of your invention saves your valuable foreign patent rights. As a corollary, a public disclosure of your invention one day after your home country filing date will not destroy foreign patent rights, as long as the Paris Convention rules are adhered to and foreign patent applications are filed within the 12 month period from the initial home country filing date. It is extremely important to remember this provision, since most of the inventions that you will work on during your career, I am sure, will have potential use in countries throughout the world.

17.3   PATENT COOPERATION TREATY (PCT)

In 1978, the Patent Cooperation Treaty (PCT) went into effect, which works with and utilizes the provisions of the Paris Convention of 1883. Thus, subsequent to 1978, applicants for foreign patents can also claim the benefit of the right of priority (their home country filing date) under the PCT as will be explained. Under the Patent Cooperation Treaty, the priority period for filing an application in a foreign country is also 12 months, the same as the Paris Convention. Also, claiming the right of priority is available under the PCT to applications filed in any member country of the Paris Convention.

The PCT came into affect in 1978 to cure one of the major drawbacks of the Paris Convention. Under the Paris Convention, filing several separate patent applications in various different countries involves considerable duplication with multiple filings and searches in each of the countries, and in the languages of each of those countries which can be rather expensive. Under the Paris Convention, the several global patents that are granted based upon your first filed home country patent application typically have different claims resulting from the varying and separate examination procedures in different countries. Additionally, annuity fees must also be paid in the currency of each country in which your patent application was filed under the Paris Convention.

Therefore, one of the major goals of the Patent Cooperation Treaty is to reduce the costs in time and money involved in obtaining worldwide patent protection under the Paris Convention, depending on the number of countries in which patent protection is sought. Another factor was to provide additional time beyond the 12 month period of the Paris Convention in which an inventor, or the inventor's employer, could decide whether significant sums of money should be spent to obtain foreign patent protection on a particular invention. The period has been increased to up to 30 or 31 months, and sometimes more.

Keep in mind, however, that none of the treaties that I've mentioned so far provide that single "world patent" that would be enforceable in every country. That result may be achieved someday, but not now. Every so often, various countries of the world try to get together to harmonize their patent statutes, but each country recommends that all the other countries adopt their procedures. On that issue, the most recent harmonization efforts came to naught. One of the major drawbacks is the provision that is standard in many countries that the first inventor to file a patent application will ultimately be granted the patent, and not necessarily the first inventor. In the United States, however, those involved in harmonization discussions were adamant about retaining the provision in the U.S. patent law that patent rights are granted to the first to invent, and not the one who has engaged the services of a speedier patent attorney.

17.4   BROAD PROVISIONS OF THE PATENT COOPERATION TREATY

The first economic simplification provided by the PCT is that the form and content of an international patent application filed under the PCT is the same for all signatory countries. Thus, an application that complies with the PCT rules also meets the requirements of your home country Patent Office, and all other signatory national Patent Offices. Once your original patent application has been prepared by your patent attorney and reviewed by you as the inventor and filed, the procedure for filing a PCT application comprises identifying your home country patent application in a document filled out by your patent attorney, setting forth all the details of the patent application, such as the inventor's name, address, home country, title of the application, original home country filing date and serial number, and additional information.

Under the PCT rules, this PCT patent application document must be filed within one year from the original home country filing date. Several major Patent Offices around the world are designated as central receiving offices (the United States Patent & Trademark Office is a central receiving office) where your PCT application can be filed, along with the appropriate filing fee. The form to be submitted with the application sets forth a country listing, allowing the inventor to designate all of the signatory countries in which patent protection is desired, or may be desired. It is possible to designate one or several countries in which you presently believe you will want to obtain patent protection, however you are not compelled later to actually seek patent protection in all of those countries previously designated. Again, to obtain the benefits of the Paris Convention, the PCT application must be filed on or before the first year anniversary of the original home filing date, which is now known as the "priority date."

During the first phase of prosecution, or Chapter I, of the PCT procedure, a prior art search is conducted automatically and compulsorily by a patent examiner in the central receiving office and sent to your patent attorney, after which the application and the search report are published. For example, if you have filed a United States patent application first, and have then timely filed a PCT application within the 12-month period, the PCT prior art search will most likely be conducted by the same patent examiner handling your United States patent application. Upon receipt of the search report by your patent attorney and you as the inventor, the prior art patents are reviewed to determine the degree to which they are relevant to your invention. No response to the search report is required.

In the second phase of procedure under the PCT, or Chapter II, a preliminary examination is conducted at the inventor's or patent attorney's request. During this examination, the prior art uncovered by the search is applied to the claimed invention. The patent examiner will then provide your patent attorney with an International Preliminary Examination Report directed to the patentability of the claims in the patent application. Under Chapter II, the applicant is then allowed a total of approximately 30 months from the initial filing date of the home patent application (the priority date) before the applicant must decide whether or not to proceed with filing national applications to obtain patent protection in some or all of the individual member countries of the PCT that were designated in the originally filed PCT application document. The inventor and the inventor's attorney have the right to amend the PCT application if the results of the search and examination indicate that such alterations are desirable to obtain allowance of the PCT application. For U.S. applicants, these amendments can be made in the English language. Also note that in many countries, a request for preliminary examination is no longer required to obtain the full 30 (or 31) months to file national applications. However, requesting examination provides advantages in expediting and reducing the cost of national patent prosecution.

Timing is important at all stages of the PCT procedure. If no demand for examination is made under Chapter II of the PCT, the time in which the several national applications must be filed may be limited to 19 months from the original filing or priority date. Therefore, requesting such examination extends the time at which the decision has to be made in which country applications should be filed from 19 months to approximately 30 or 31 months. Thus, one of the major advantages of the PCT over the Paris Convention is that you have approximately 2½ years from the original filing date of your home country patent application to decide among those countries in which you deem that you will achieve commercial success in marketing your invention. If no PCT application is filed, the Paris Convention requires that the decision as to foreign national filings must be made within 12 months, or in the first year, from the date of filing the home patent application. Therefore, the Patent Cooperation Treaty can be looked at as providing an extension of time to make that important decision regarding the filing of foreign patent applications.

At the end of the 30- or 31-month period, assuming a Chapter II examination has been requested, the applicant must designate those national countries in which it desires to obtain patent protection based upon the PCT application. Note that the European Patent Convention, discussed in Section 17.6, provides that most of Western Europe at this point is considered as one nation. After the PCT search and examination procedure is completed, the search report, copies of the prior art and the application are sent to the national Patent Offices of each of the countries designated by the applicant to initiate the process of separate examinations for patentability in each designated country. At this point, the patent application must be translated into the appropriate national language, and a patent agent engaged in each country to prosecute your application before the designated national Patent Office. Since this is an additional expense, the applicant under the PCT has been given substantial time to determine in which countries it is economically viable to proceed with obtaining patent protection.

The national Patent Offices which receive your patent application are not bound by the preliminary examination report, and in most cases the national patent examiners conduct their own search. Each national Patent Office is responsible for issuing its own patents in accordance with its own laws and regulations.

17.5   NATIONAL PATENT LAWS AND THE PCT: DIFFERENCES AND ALTERATIONS

Several countries, including the United States, have altered their patent procedures to conform with PCT requirements. However, as indicated previously, one procedure that the United States has not changed is that the inventor who can prove that he or she was the first to invent, rather than the first to file, must be allowed to claim rights to the invention. Thus, a patent applicant for a similar invention in a foreign country, which applicant has filed their application in that foreign country before your initial filing date in the United States, may obtain patent protection covering your invention in that foreign country, while not in the United States. To best avoid this type of situation from occurring, it is highly desirable for U.S. patent applicants to file their patent applications as early as possible to establish a priority date at the earliest possible time.

Under the PCT, patent applications are published 18 months after their home country, or priority, filing date. This provision has been matched in the United States just recently, whereby U.S. patent applications filed today are published within 18 months after filing, unless the U.S. applicant notifies the U.S. Patent & Trademark Office that the applicant has no desire whatsoever of filing a foreign patent application. One advantage of publication of the patent application is that of providing notice to potential infringers in this country and abroad of the existence of your patent application.

The single most important advantage provided by the PCT is the ability to obtain at the outset, with a single standardized application, the equivalent of preserving the right to file patent applications in many foreign countries. Translation costs and application filing costs are deferred to a later stage of the proceedings, usually after the inventor or the inventor's company has determined that the invention has commercial possibilities and that such expenses are now warranted. Since the single application that complies with the PCT requirement also complies with the national requirements of all signatory nations of the PCT, no or minimal alterations to the application to meet national requirements are necessary. Thus, it can be expected that fewer objections will arise, if any, from the foreign patent examiners, and a quicker and more sustained resolution of the patent granting procedure in the foreign countries can be expected.

17.6 EUROPEAN PATENT CONVENTION (EPC)

The European Patent Convention became operational in 1978, and the European Patent Office (EPO) began operation in Munich, Germany. Most, but not all European nations are signatory to the EPC. Norway, for example, is not a member. Each member state has a Patent Office to receive EPC patent applications, and only one set of documents is required at the initial stage of filing in one of three official languages: English, French and German.

Following the award of a filing date for your patent application with the EPC, a preliminary search of the invention claimed in the patent application is performed and the results published. The application is then examined by the European Patent Office, and if found patentable, is again published for possible opposition by third parties. Some nations, if designated, may require the entire application to be translated into their native language before a patent is issued in those countries.

The European Patent Office grants a single patent and publishes only one patent specification which acts as a national patent in each country designated by the applicant, and where specifically registered by the applicant. Therefore, once the European Patent Office allows your patent application, you must then designate those EPC member countries in which you desire to obtain patent protection. A fee, which is not insubstantial, must be paid to each of the countries' Patent Offices in which registration of your European patent is effected. It is not necessary to designate your patent to be enforceable in all of the countries of the EPC. In addition, annual annuities must be paid during the life of the patent application and patent in each separate country under the EPC.

Here is an additional fact to remember that is quite important for applicants having filed a United States patent application. It is possible that your U.S. patent application may still be pending before the U.S. Patent & Trademark Office at the time your foreign patent application is undergoing searching and examination. International search reports are being developed under the PCT and/or the EPC, and additional prior art developed in those searches will be furnished to your patent attorney. Under U.S. Patent & Trademark Office Rule 56, all prior art which you and your attorney become aware of during the pendency of your U.S. patent application must be brought to the attention of the United States patent examiner. Therefore, it is important to remember that any new prior art developed in the PCT, EPC or any other patent searches must be brought to the attention of the United States patent examiner, if such foreign prior art is received during the pendency of your United States patent application, which is any time up to the day of issuance of your U.S. patent. Failure to do so could invalidate your patent if an action is brought in the United States to enforce your patent against an infringer.

17.7 COMMUNICATIONS TO FOREIGN NON-ATTORNEY PATENT AGENT

In the United States, the practice of patent law and prosecution of patents before the U.S. Patent & Trademark Office is primarily performed by registered patent attorneys, who are licensed attorneys as well as members of the separate bar of the U.S. Patent & Trademark Office. However, in most countries outside the United States, the practice of patent prosecution is conducted mainly by patent agents, who are not legally trained, and who are not licensed lawyers. Under the U.S legal system, any communication between a lawyer and that lawyer's client is privileged, and under normal circumstances cannot be disclosed by the lawyer to a third party, even in litigation in court.

The question arises whether or not the communications between your U.S. patent lawyer and a non-lawyer foreign patent agent are also privileged from disclosure. This becomes important in litigation, where your patent attorney in the U.S. may have discussed several negative aspects of prosecution of your patent application in a foreign country with a foreign patent agent. If patent enforcement or other litigation ensues, it is not prudent to have such negative statements entered into the record of the lawsuit. Thus, there is a universal rule that if the communication between a non-attorney patent agent and his or her client, in the foreign country in question, is subject to a privilege against disclosure in that country, the same privilege will apply to discussions between your patent attorney and that non-attorney patent agent in that country. This is a point that I recommend you clarify with your patent attorney when it comes time for you to consider and file patent applications in foreign countries.

Robert Goddard

ROCKET PROPULSION AND CONTROL

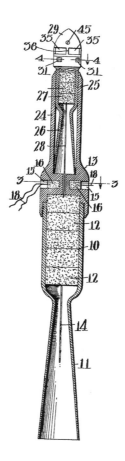

His name is synonymous with rocketry, and his work resulted in sending people into space. Robert H. Goddard is recognized as the father of modern rocket propulsion and he held 214 patents related to rocketry.

Goddard was born on October 5, 1882 in Worcester, Massachusetts. Even as a young boy, Goddard was interested in rocketry. At the age of 5, he watched electricity being produced from a Leclanche battery in his uncle's workshop. He also observed that he could make sparks by scuffing his feet along the carpet. He decided that if he combined the two, he could create a large enough spark to propel him to the moon. So he took a zinc rod, rubbed it on his shoes and scuffed his feet on the sidewalk in front of his house. During

Intellectual Property Law for Engineers and Scientists, by Howard B. Rockman
ISBN 0-471-44998-9 © 2004 The Institute of Electrical and Electronics Engineers

his experiment, his mother came out and told him to be careful and that it might work and send him sailing away with no way to bring him back. Because of this, he hid the zinc rod and decided to give up on the study of space flight for the time being.

Goddard attended Worcester Polytechnic Institute from 1904 to 1908. In 1907, he obtained his first public attention. This was the result of a large cloud of smoke created by a powder rocket he "launched" in the basement of the physics building at Worcester Polytechnic Institute. Instead of expelling Goddard, the school took interest in its student's work.

In 1912, Goddard first mathematically investigated the use of rocket power to reach a high altitude and escape gravity. In July, 1914 he received two U.S. patents. One was for a gun rocket using liquid fuel, and the other covered a two- or three-stage solid-fuel rocket. These patents are reprinted following this biography.

In 1918, Goddard developed and demonstrated several types of solid-fuel rockets that could be fired from a tripod or hand-held launching tubes. His launching platform was a music stand. This, of course, was the basis of the American "bazooka."

At his own expense, Goddard conducted studies of the propulsion force produced by various types of gunpowder. In 1916, he documented his studies in a request for funds to continue his research from the Smithsonian Institution. This study was published, along with additional research he and the Navy conducted, in a "Smithsonian Miscellaneous Publication" No. 2540, in January 1920. The study was entitled "A Method of Reaching Extreme Altitudes." Near the end of his treatise, Goddard referred to the possibility of a rocket reaching the moon and exploding a quantity of flash powder to visibly prove its arrival. This was too much for the *New York Times,* which, on January 13, 1920 published an editorial pronouncing that space travel was impossible, since the lack of an atmosphere in space would not provide a resistance which a rocket force could push against. The *Times* commented that Professor Goddard (of Clark University) lacked "the knowledge ladled out daily in high schools." Goddard, from that time on, had a cool, and sometimes nonexistent relationship with the press. After Apollo II blasted off in 1969 to land the first human on the moon, almost 25 years after Goddard's death, the *New York Times* took a rearward look at its 1920 editorial. The paper, in 1969, commented that: "Further investigation and experimentation have confirmed the findings of Isaac Newton in the 17th century, and it is now definitely established that a rocket can function in a vacuum as well as in an atmosphere. The Times regrets the error."

The derision he received from the press did not stop Goddard's experiments. In 1923, he tested the very first liquid-fuel rockets, and on March 16, 1926 he launched the first liquid-fuel rocket at Auburn, Massachusetts. The fuel was made of gasoline and liquid oxygen. The rocket, named "Nell," was ten feet long, flew 41 feet up and reached a speed of 60 miles per hour, landing 2½ seconds later, 184 feet away in a frozen cabbage patch. The Smithsonian Institution, which had given Goddard a subsidy, was not too impressed with the report of the flight. They wanted larger rockets that could perform as well as smaller ones.

Goddard's Nell rockets became increasingly large and harder to hide from his critics. In 1929, an 11 foot missile launch resulted in an intervention by the Worcester police, followed by the press. The local headline the next day laughingly touted: "Moon Rocket Misses Target by 238,799½ Miles." Soon after, on July 17, 1929, Goddard sent up a rocket carrying scientific instruments, a barometer, thermometer, and a small camera. He continued theses studies from 1930 to 1942 in Roswell, New Mexico with the aid of a Guggenheim Foundation grant. His research was greatly expanded and his new rockets could reach heights of one-and-a-half miles and speeds of up to 550 miles per hour.

NASA named a space flight center in Greenbelt, Maryland after him on May 1, 1959. On September 16, 1959 the 86th Congress authorized the insurance of a gold metal in honor of Professor Robert H. Goddard.

Goddard made most of his engineering advances in rocketry in the 1920s and 1930s. He calculated the energy-to-weight ratio of several potential fuels; he discovered that a rocket could fly in a vacuum (see Newton's laws of action and reaction); he did away with powder fuels by using liquid propulsives, such as kerosene or liquid hydrogen mixed with liquid oxygen, to allow combustion to occur in airless space. He also developed rockets that climbed to 9,000 feet, exceeded the sound barrier, and incorporated fin-stabilized steering. He also obtained patents covering gyroscopic guidance systems, multistage rockets, and a multitude of other inventions.

Goddard's 1920 Smithsonian report was distributed in Europe, where the German Rocket Society was founded in 1927 and the German Army initiated a rocket program in 1931. German scientists began contacting Goddard with technical questions on rocketry, and he would informally send responses. In 1939, the inquiries from Germany abruptly stopped. Being disturbed by this, Goddard approached the U.S. Army in Washington, and showed films of his various Nell rocket launches. The Army thanked him for the information, and dismissed him and his ideas. Five years later, the first German V-2 rocket headed for London, and by 1945, Germany had launched over 1,100 V-2's. At the end of World War II, Goddard inspected a German V-2 and determined that it appeared to utilize his technology. An anecdote holds that when a captured German scientist was debriefed about the V-2 rocket development, he was heard to respond: "Why don't you ask Dr. Goddard? He knows better than any of us." U.S. scientists then worked alongside "imported" German scientists after the war to develop Goddard's improvements into the Redstone rocket, which launched the first Americans into space, and was the precursor of almost every other rocket used by the United States.

Robert Goddard died on August 10, 1945. During his long career dedicated to rocket propulsion theories and the practicalities needed to enable the rocket to begin the "space age" he was a creative scientist who also had the engineering skills to bring his theories to fruition. Although his work in rocketry was mostly disregarded in the United States during his lifetime, the dawn of the space age has caused the scientific, engineering, and government communities to recognize all that this man accomplished.

R. H. GODDARD.

ROCKET APPARATUS.

APPLICATION FILED OCT. 1, 1913.

1,102,653.

Patented July 7, 1914.

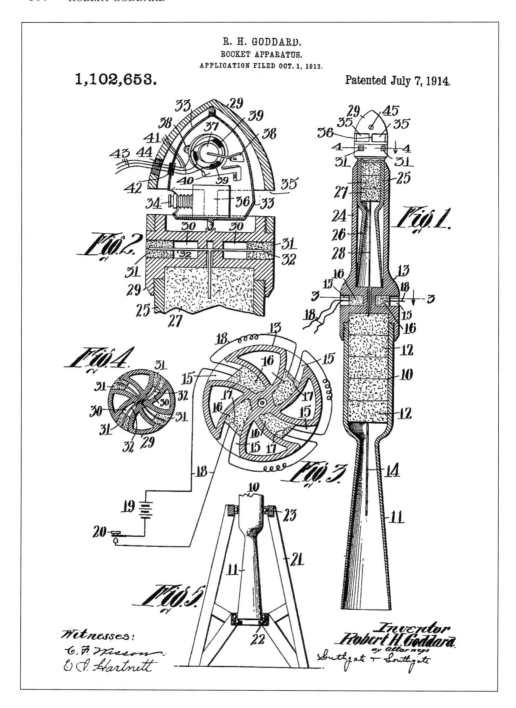

Witnesses:
C. F. Nisson.
C. S. Hartnett.

Inventor
Robert H. Goddard
by attorneys
Southgate + Southgate

R. H. GODDARD.
ROCKET APPARATUS.
APPLICATION FILED MAY 15, 1914.

1,103,503.

Patented July 14, 1914.

2 SHEETS—SHEET 1.

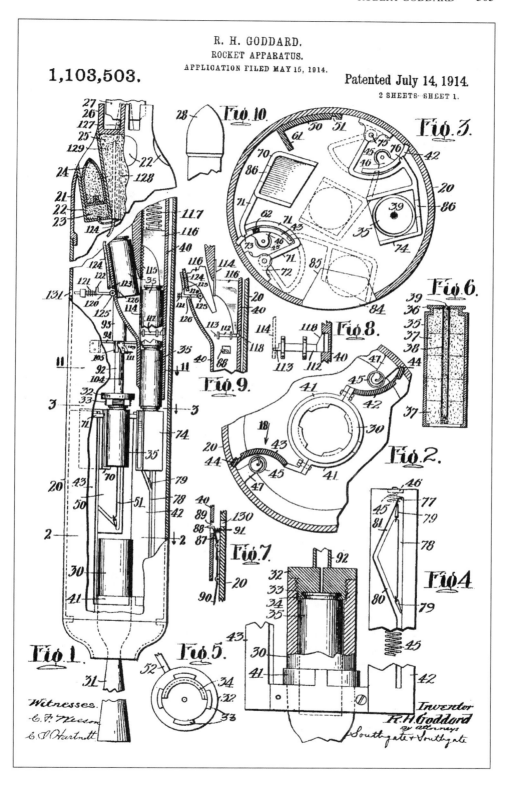

Witnesses.
C. F. Kieson
C. J. Hartnett

Inventor
R. H. Goddard
by attorneys
Southgate & Southgate

18 Enforcement of the Patent Right

18.1 PATENT CLEARANCE PROCESS

Previously in this text, we have reviewed the procedures for obtaining a patent covering your invention. Now the patent has issued with all claims found allowable, and the issued patent is available to the public, including your competitors. A savvy competitor will obtain a copy of your patent to determine the scope of coverage (metes and bounds) of your patent claims for the purposes of:

1. Ensuring that no present product of the competitor infringes the patent; and
2. Ensuring that development projects the competitor has in progress do not lead to products that potentially infringe your patent.

At this point, I am shifting the discussion focus from you as the inventor, and placing you in the shoes of the competitor. What steps do you take to avoid infringing someone else's patent? The following recommended procedures apply even to a product or process for which you may have obtained a patent, because your patented item or method may still infringe an earlier or later issued patent. Avoiding patent infringement is important because defending your product in a patent infringement lawsuit is very expensive in terms of cost and expenditure of time of personnel who could well be working on more productive matters.

18.1.1 Infringement Search and the Non-Infringement Opinion Letter

In my intellectual property law practice, when a client presents me with its invention on a new product or process for patenting, we initially conduct a novelty search, as discussed at Chapter 9, Section 9.1. In many instances, I recommend that the search also include a "preliminary infringement search." This authorizes the searcher not only to be aware of prior art bearing on the issue of novelty, but also to be on the lookout for issued patents that potentially may cause infringement problems if the development project for the new product continues along its present design direction.

Normally, novelty searches are conducted at the beginning of a product's development, and the finished product is still months, or even years away. It is not practical to conduct a full patent infringement search until the final design has been signed off, since most, if not all, products and processes change radically through the development process. From the results of a "preliminary infringement search," I have been able to advise clients to make "mid-course corrections" during the product development stage to avoid potential infringement problems.

Once the patent attorney receives the results of the novelty and "preliminary infringement" search, he or she will advise you, as part of his/her confidential opinion letter, which unexpired patents uncovered by the search may raise potential infringement prob-

Intellectual Property Law for Engineers and Scientists, by Howard B. Rockman
ISBN 0-471-44998-9 © 2004 The Institute of Electrical and Electronics Engineers

lems. Of course, an expired patent cannot be infringed. Once you receive this advice, you may find it practical to meet with your patent attorney to discuss potential patent infringement problems and formulate a course of action leading to an avoidance of these problems at the early stage of your development program.

Certain companies, and inventors, take an additional step in ensuring they become aware of potentially infringed patents as such patents issue by establishing a patent "watch" procedure. As mentioned previously, U.S. patents issue every Tuesday of the year, holiday or not, and an abstract and one figure of the patent are published in the *Official Gazette* of the U.S. Patent and Trademark Office. The patents are organized in the *Official Gazette* in numerical order of class and subclass of issuance. Prudent product development managers have their patent attorney review the particular classes and subclasses of inventions that relate to their business each week in the *Official Gazette*, and to furnish the product manager with information about those newly issued patents that should be reviewed for potential infringement issues. Since the *Official Gazette* is organized by subject matter, a review of relevant issued patent abstracts by the patent attorney can be accomplished relatively quickly and inexpensively on a weekly basis.

Near the point of completion of the development project, after the final design has been approved, a full infringement search should be conducted to determine what unexpired patents there are that would lead their owners to think about charging you with patent infringement. This search is also best conducted at the public search facilities of the U.S. Patent and Trademark Office, where the searcher has access to paper copies of relevant patents, as well as the electronic searching tools available in the search facility. The infringement search is slightly more expensive than the novelty search, since the searcher must read the claims of those patents which appear relevant from the drawings. Upon completion of the infringement search, the results comprising those patents of some relevance to your device or process are forwarded to your patent attorney for analysis of the claim coverage of each patent. Note also that expired patents may also be included in the search results, if the unexpired patents disclose that some elements or features of your invention are in the public domain, and are freely available to include in your development project.

Your patent attorney will review each of the claims of the relevant unexpired patents uncovered by the search, since infringement of one claim of a patent constitutes infringement to the same degree as infringing several claims of the same patent. It is also possible that your new development may potentially infringe claims in more than one patent.

All claims that recite an element that your development product or process does not have is cast aside as not infringed, unless your product or process includes an equivalent to the missing element or step. Under the legal doctrine known as the "Doctrine of Equivalents," if your development product or process does not include all of the elements or steps of an article or method claim, respectively, of a patent, there still may be infringement. Application of the Doctrine of Equivalents is discussed just ahead. If a patent appears to give rise to potential infringement problems, your patent attorney will probably read the documented history of that patent during prosecution before the U.S. Patent & Trademark Office to determine if the claims have been limited in interpretation and scope by the application of prior art by the patent examiner and responsive limiting amendments to the claims made by the inventor's patent attorney.

The results of the infringement search are set forth in a carefully crafted opinion letter directed to you or your company's legal counsel. However, prior to furnishing the infringement opinion letter, do not be surprised if your attorney calls you or meets with you face to face to discuss potential infringement problems uncovered by the search, and explores ways to alter your design direction to avoid infringement. I have spent considerable hours working with inventors assisting them in making changes to their designs so that a path towards infringement is avoided. The patent attorney will most likely not put in writing that your design infringes another's patent. As will be explained, the infringement opinion letter may be admitted as evidence in future patent litigation, and a document stating that your device or process infringes the asserted patent is not helpful to your defense of non-infringement. After you and your patent attorney have modified the design to avoid all apparent potential infringement problems, the patent attorney prepares a non-infringement opinion directed to a comparison between your modified design and the claims in the relevant prior issued patents. If infringement cannot be avoided, possible alternative actions include changing the design parameters completely, or beginning negotiations with the owner of the potentially infringed patent to obtain a license at a reasonable royalty, or possibly acquiring the patent. Licensing and assignment of patent rights are covered later in the text.

The patent attorney's non-infringement opinion letter that you receive is very valuable if and when the owner of one of the patents discussed in the opinion decides to charge you and/or your company with patent infringement. Here's why. Normally, a charge of patent infringement is initiated by one party sending a letter to the potential infringing party, notifying the latter of the existence of the patent, and demanding that the infringing activities cease and desist immediately. A copy of the asserted patent is usually attached to the letter. The recipient of that letter, and patent, is henceforth "on notice" of the existence of the patent, and any infringing activities carried out after the day of receipt of the letter may be characterized as "willful and wanton." In patent litigation, if you are found to have "willfully and wantonly" infringed a patent, the judge has the discretion to penalize you by increasing, by up to three times, the damages you are required to pay to the patent owner.

In defending against a charge of "willful and wanton" infringement by a patent holder/plaintiff in a patent infringement lawsuit, the accused infringer/defendant normally contends that it's continued activities after notice of the patent are not "willful and wanton" because they were acting upon "advice of counsel" that the patent in question was not infringed, was not valid, and/or was not enforceable. The "advice of counsel" is set forth in the non-infringement opinion letter received from the defendant's patent attorney. When this defense is raised, the opinion letter, and any exhibits and/or attachments, are entered as evidence in the litigation. The patent attorney who authored the opinion is also subject to having his/her deposition taken, while the patent owner's attorney attempts to uncover flaws in the opinion and show that the opinion is erroneous. The author of the opinion, that is, your patent attorney, may also be compelled to testify at trial about the thoroughness and accuracy of the opinion letter. However, the "advise of counsel" opinion letter does not have to be correct to protect the client from a charge of willful infringement. It must, however, be artfully researched and reasoned, so that a reasonable businessperson could rely on the opinion.

Where does this lead us? Back to the infringement search and preparation of the non-infringement opinion letter. Whenever I prepare a non-infringement opinion, I ensure that the information in the letter is sufficiently detailed in technical comparisons and legal support to withstand attack by the opposing lawyer. I prepare these opinions knowing that someday I may have to defend each step of my analysis while undergoing close cross examination by an opposing lawyer. I highly recommend that you, as the possible developer of a potentially infringing product, or process, carefully review the technical facts and conclusions reached by your patent attorney in a non-infringement opinion letter to insure that all technical conclusions about your product and about the patent claims are correct. Better you than a patent owner's attorney find mistakes in the opinion. If you do find flaws, your patent attorney can prepare a supplemental opinion letter, stating why the first opinion was in error, but still concluding there is no infringement, if such is the case. However, if you do discern technical errors in your patent attorney's opinion letter, and the revised conclusion is that the potential risk for infringement is high, go to "plan B," which is discussed immediately in the next section.

18.1.2   "Right-to-Use" or "Knock-Out" Search

If your infringement search and patent attorney's analysis conclude that there is one, or more than one, patent claim which is potentially infringed and a) you cannot work around the patent claim(s) and b) your chances of obtaining a license from the patent owner are slim to none, a "right-to-use" or "knockout" search is commissioned. This search is directed to seeking out relevant prior art not previously cited by the patent examiner during prosecution of the potentially infringed patent before the U.S. Patent & Trademark Office. If such prior art is found, your patent attorney will advise you whether the newly found prior art constitutes a strong enough technical disclosure to support a defense that the patent is invalid in view of the newly discovered prior art. Even though the patent in question, and for that matter any issued patent, has undergone rigorous examination by the patent examiner, a U.S. Federal Court has the power to declare the patent invalid and unenforceable based on prior art not seen and cited by the patent examiner during prosecution of the patent.

As an alternative to a patent invalidity opinion, it is possible to initiate an inter-parties re-examination proceeding in the U.S. Patent & Trademark Office in an effort to invalidate a potentially blocking patent. This procedure, described *infra* at §12.11, is especially useful where one is contemplating a new product or business venture, and desires to invalidate a patent before investing resources in the new project.

18.2   ATTEMPT TO DESIGN AROUND A PATENT; MOST INFRINGERS DO NOT SLAVISHLY COPY THE PATENTED INVENTION

The purpose of printing and publishing issued patents is to make them available to potential competitors so that competing non-infringing products and processes may be developed outside of the fence of exclusivity awarded to the inventor by the patent grant. The grand scheme is that by designing around another's patent claims, the competitor will develop a new and even better product, and advance technology and the "progress of the useful arts" as our Founding Fathers mandated in the U.S. Constitution.

Upon being made aware of the scope of claim coverage in relevant unexpired patents uncovered by your search, and as advised by your patent attorney, you begin to develop or modify your proposed competing product or process by using elements, functions or steps that are not covered by the claims of any of these patents. You are also careful to avoid substituting elements, functions or steps which may be deemed "equivalent" to an element of the patent claim(s) you are trying to avoid.

The prior art comes in handy during this process. If the novel feature of a patent claim under analysis is, say, element A, and you find that you can replace element A and its function with element B and its function, which are both shown in the prior art in existence before the potentially infringed patent under analysis, you may take the position that infringement has been avoided because your competing product follows the teachings of the prior art, and not the patent claim. Put another way, if the patent claim under analysis is interpreted to read on your newly developed competing product, that patent claim also will read on the prior art which you incorporated in our example, since your competing device follows the prior art. However, such an interpretation of the claim under analysis cannot be made. Each issued patent is presumed by statute (35 U.S.C. §282) to be valid, and by law, a patent claim cannot be given an interpretation that would cause the claim to read on the prior art and become invalid. Thus, the claim cannot be interpreted to read on your product or process.

Remember also that if you see a competing product on the market which you consider may infringe a patent of yours, the chances are that the competing product was designed with input from the competitor's patent attorney, who advised the competitor that its product does not infringe your patent. However, your patent attorney may compare the competing product to your patent claims, and conclude that there is infringement. How can two competent patent attorneys come to divergent opinions on patent infringement regarding the same patent and same product? Don't get me started, but believe me, it happens. This is the nature of the law. Sometimes these different opinions are what lead to the filing of lawsuits to expensively determine who is right. Where millions of dollars are at stake in product sales, the expense may be worth it.

18.3   LITERAL INFRINGEMENT OF A PATENT CLAIM

This next discussion goes into detail as to how a determination is made whether or not a patent claim is being infringed by a device or process. This analysis applies both (a) to those situations where your patent is being compared to the potentially infringing device of a competitor to determine whether infringement exists, and (b) to the opposite situation where your product or process is being compared to a competitor's patent to determine whether or not your product or process avoids patent infringement. The same principles apply to both types of analyses.

Thus an infringement analysis normally begins in one of two ways. The first is, when you are the owner of an issued patent, or you have a pending patent application going through examination, and you determine that a competitive product has appeared on the market which may fall within the scope of protection of the claims of your patent or pending patent application. In such situations, you will most likely require the opinion of a patent attorney to determine whether or not infringement exists. If your patent application is still pending, it may be possible to amend your application during prosecution to add broader claims to cover the potentially infringing device. Second, you may be part of an organization that desires to bring a new product to market, and the question becomes whether your new product or process would infringe someone else's patent, such as a competitor's patent. Again, a detailed study must be made of any patents that may possibly be infringed, and compare those patents to the potentially infringing product or process you intend to bring to market.

It is important to remember that in a patent infringement analysis, it is the claims of the patent or the patent application under consideration that are compared to the structure or process of the accused or prospectively accused device or method. Keep in mind that this is unlike the novelty investigation discussed previously, where the invention that you are attempting to obtain patent protection for is compared to the entire disclosure of a prior art reference patent publication, public disclosure, or publicly sold device.

The initial step in conducting an infringement analysis is to determine whether or not the patent contains a claim or several claims which literally read on the accused device. This means that each of the elements of the patent claim are found in the accused device. Literal patent infringement occurs where the device or process under investigation incorporates each and every one of the claimed elements literally set forth in the patent claim. If the device or process does not incorporate all of the elements of the claim, there still may be infringement under the Doctrine of Equivalents, discussed shortly, where the only difference between the patent claim and the device or process under analysis constitutes a substitution of equivalent elements.

In certain patents, the claims are written in "means plus function" language, wherein the element of the claim is described as a means for accomplishing a certain function. For example, your computer screen normally would be described as a cathode-ray tube, or a plasma display unit. However, a patent attorney would probably describe the same screen as a "means for displaying electronically formed images," which language would not only cover a cathode ray or plasma type of screen, it would also cover a billboard made of light bulbs or any other electronic display device. As another example, a table can also be described as a means for keeping documents from falling on the floor. Of course, a hammock full of papers would also meet that requirement, while the hammock would not qualify as a table or desk. For many many years, means plus function language has been recited by patent attorneys in patent claims in an effort to broaden the scope of protection afforded by the patent. However, today means plus function language in patent claims is limited to those elements described in the patent specification, and any equivalents to those elements described in the specification. Therefore, if the claim under interpretation does contain means plus function language, it would be prudent to obtain the services of a qualified patent attorney to provide you with a clear understanding of the true scope of the claim.

If it is determined that viable questions of literal infringement exist after comparing the patent claims to your device or process, it is next advisable to have your patent attorney review the prosecution history of the competitor's patent application before the U.S. Patent and Trademark Office to determine if the scope of any element in the patent claims has been limited by amendments and/or comments in the prosecution of the patent. This rule applies whether you are comparing a competitor's device to your patent or comparing your device to a competitor's patent.

18.4 "DOCTRINE OF EQUIVALENTS," WHERE THE CLAIM IS NOT LITERALLY INFRINGED

18.4.1 How the Doctrine of Equivalents Works

In applying the test set forth above to determine whether literal infringement of a patent claim exists, it may be determined that one or more of the elements in the patent claim are not found in the potentially infringing device. However, the test for patent infringement does not end at this point, since the Supreme Court has established the "Doctrine of Equivalents." Infringement of a patent under the Doctrine of Equivalents occurs (1) where the accused device or process, although not literally the same as the elements of the patent claims, accomplishes substantially the same purpose in substantially the same way and with substantially the same elements as are recited in the patent claim or claims, and (2) the differences between the elements in the patent claim and the elements in the accused device or process are "insubstantial." Thus, where the patent claim differs from the accused device or process in only small or equivalent ways, patent infringement is still a possibility.

The purpose of this doctrine, which was established by the U.S. Supreme Court, was to prevent an infringer from getting away with patent infringement by merely substituting known equivalent elements for the elements in the patent claims. Thus, if my patent claim calls for a coil spring as one of the elements, and you have substituted a torsion spring to accomplish the same purpose in the same way, and the torsion spring is determined to be substantially the same element as the coil spring, patent infringement still exists. The most recent pronouncements by the Supreme Court regarding the Doctrine of Equivalents can be found in the cases of *Hilton-Davis Chemical Company v. Warner-Jenkinson, Co.,* 117 S. Ct. 1040, 41 USPQ 2nd 1865 (1997), and *Festo Corp. v. Shoketsu Kinzoku Kogyo Kabushiki Co., Ltd.,* 122 S.Ct. 1831, 62 USPQ 2d. 1705 (2002)

In making an infringement determination under the Doctrine of Equivalents, look for the element that is missing from the literal infringement analysis, and determine if there is anything in the device or process under analysis which is technically equivalent to the missing element. Then apply the previously stated thought process. Your patent attorney will be of significant assistance in conducting this highly complex analysis.

18.4.2 Limits on the Doctrine of Equivalents

When applying the Doctrine of Equivalents, you are essentially determining whether or not an element set forth in a patent claim can be given an interpretation beyond its literal meaning to cover potentially equivalent structure or steps in the potentially infringing device or process under analysis. However, the prosecution of the patent before the U.S. Patent and Trademark Office may have placed certain limitations on the Doctrine of Equivalents. In my above example regarding the coil spring and the torsion bar, assume there was a prior art patent reference applied by the patent examiner during the prosecution of the patent in question, which reference showed a torsion bar, and to obtain allowance of the patent claim the patentee and his or her attorney amended the claim to particularly distinguish the coil spring from the torsion bar. Under this situation, there is no infringement under the Doctrine of Equivalents, because during the prosecution of that patent, a sharp distinction was made between a coil spring and the torsion bar to obtain allowance of the claim. In such instances, that patent claim would be limited to the coil spring, and the torsion bar would not constitute an equivalent element covered by the claim. Thus, when applying the Doctrine of Equivalents, it is important to have your patent attorney review the prosecution history of the subject patent, and determine what amendments were made to the claims, and what remarks the patent attorney prosecuting that patent made to the patent examiner by way of arguments and changes to the claims to obtain allowance over the prior art. Comments and/or amendments may have been made that limit the scope of the claims such as they cannot be applied to the device or process being reviewed under the Doctrine of Equivalents.

Also, it is important to have the patent attorney review the prior art cited and applied by the patent examiner during examination of the subject patent, to determine whether the potentially infringing device or process follows the structure and function of the prior art, thereby precluding the application of the claims of the patent to the accused device or process under the Doctrine of Equivalents. As stated previously, a common precept of patent law is that the accused infringer never slavishly copies the patented product. Therefore, the application of the Doctrine of Equivalents is very important in determining if infringement exists, whether it is your device or process, or that of a competitor's that is under analysis. Also remember that under the Doctrine of Equivalents, the claim cannot be construed to have a meaning such that the claim will ultimately read on the prior art. This would give the claim an invalid meaning, and this cannot be done due to the statutory presumption of validity of a patent claim. Also, you cannot stretch the meaning of an element in a patent claim to read on, or apply to, an element that has been excluded or distinguished in responding to the patent examiner. This is known as the "Doctrine of Prosecution History Estoppel."

In sum and substance, the point to remember is that even though a patent claim does not literally read on a device or process under comparative review, the application of the Doctrine of Equivalents could result in a holding of infringement. Therefore, it is highly recommended that a complete and thorough analysis of infringement be conducted prior to bringing a product to market so that all possible avenues of infringement allegations are closed off. Also, ensure that your patent attorney provides you with a competent and thorough non-infringement opinion.

18.5 DEFENSES TO A CHARGE OF INFRINGEMENT

18.5.1 Non-Infringement

Let us look at the situation where your product or process is accused of infringing someone else's patent. We use this scenario for purposes of analysis, however remember that the same analysis would occur if you accused another device of infringing your patent, and your competitor set about to determine defenses to that charge.

One of the primary defenses against a charge of patent infringement is, of course, that the device or process in question does not infringe the claims of the patent, either literally or under the Doctrine of Equivalents. When asserting this potential defense, the owner or producer of the accused device will most likely set forth arguments and provide charts and other technical data showing why the potentially accused device does not fall within the scope of the patent claims. This analysis involves interpretation of the claims, and a review of the specification and the patent's examination history before the U.S. Patent and Trademark Office to determine the precise meaning of the claims. Prior to filing a lawsuit, it is normal that the patent owner, or the patent owner's attorney, causes a letter to be sent to an accused infringer, and the accused infringer or its attorney also responds by letter. Quite possibly, several additional letters of infringement accusations and denials will go back and forth between the two parties. Ultimately, if no agreement, or license or assignment, or other accomodation can be reached on the issue of infringement, it is quite possible that the owner of the patent may file a lawsuit in Federal Court to obtain an injunction and damages for patent infringement.

18.5.2 Patent Invalidity

Another defense that is asserted on behalf of the potential infringer of a patent is that for one or several reasons, the patent may be invalid, and should never have issued in the first place. Since an invalid patent cannot be infringed, the invalidity defense is raised in most, if not all, patent litigation. There are several grounds that are normally asserted by an accused infringer in asserting that the patent is invalid. These include, among others:

1. The subject matter of the patent claims is shown or taught in prior art not previously seen by the patent examiner.

2. The patent owner and inventor and/or the inventor's attorney were guilty of "inequitable conduct" in that they were aware of prior art that was not disclosed to the patent examiner during the prosecution of the patent application before the U.S. Patent and Trademark Office.

3. The inventors named in the patent are not the true inventors of the patented subject matter.

4. The patent does not describe the best mode of the invention known to the inventor at the time of filing the patent application.

5. The description of the invention in the specification does not enable one skilled in the art to practice the invention without undue experimentation.

6. The device shown and claimed in the patent is inoperative for its intended purposes.

7. The inventor publicly disclosed the invention to another more than one year before filing the application for the patent.

8. The claimed subject matter was invented by another inventor prior to the invention by the named inventor(s) in the patent.

Any one of these defenses or others, when proven by competent evidence, could result in the patent being held invalid. During a recent conversation with a Federal Judge during a break in settlement discussions of a patent infringement lawsuit, the Judge, who is a particularly congenial individual, asked me why patent attorneys in litigation always attack the work of other patent attorneys. He thought that this practice was rather unusual. I thought for a moment and responded that the patent statute provides defenses to one who is charged with patent infringement that require the "beating up" of the inventor and the patent attorney who obtained the patent to establish the defense of patent invalidity. He thought this was rather strange, and so did I, however at present, this is way the patent laws are written.

18.5.3 Unenforceability of the Patent

Aside from the defenses named above, a patent can be held unenforceable against a particular defendant for several reasons. One of these defenses is called the "Doctrine of Laches," which means that the patentee knew about the infringing activity, but waited too long to file its lawsuit. In other words, the patent owner sat on his/her rights while the infringing activity continued. During the long wait, the defendant/potential infringer formed the opinion that the patent owner was not going to charge his or her device with infringement, and therefore the potential infringer continued to produce and sell the product in question.

Another grounds for holding a patent to be unenforceable is the "Doctrine of Equitable Estoppel," where the patent owner has made some positive steps, including silence where a response was due, that led the potential infringer to reasonably understand that no charge of patent infringement would be lodged. Relying upon this action or silence, the potential infringer continued to produce and sell the product. The two Doctrines of Laches and Equitable Estoppel are somewhat related, and their differences lie in the application of specific legal principles which it is not necessary for me to bore you with.

Another reason for holding a patent to be unenforceable against a potential infringer is that the potential infringer has obtained a license or an implied license from the patent owner, which allows the patent infringer to continue manufacturing the product or using the process. As an example of an implied license situation, I recall a patent lawsuit that I was involved in many years ago while part of the staff of the Patent Litigation Section of the United States Department of Justice in Washington. A patent owner had licensed the supplier of a particular crimping tool to the government under a first patent owned by that company. That company then purchased a second broader patent that also covered the same crimping tool. The company, now holding both patents, then sued the U.S. Government for infringing the second, broader patent. In defending the Government, I raised the argument that this was unfair, since the Government was licensed under the more limited patent, and they should also be considered to have an implied license under any other patent, broader or otherwise, that the same company owned, so that the Government was able to practice the license obtained under the more limited patent. The court accepted my argument, and held that the license granted under the more limited patent also implied that the Government would have a license under any other dominating patent owned by that same company. This was another situation where the good guys won. Also, lawyers rarely discuss a case where they didn't win.

18.6 PENALTIES AND DAMAGES FOR PATENT INFRINGEMENT

The patent laws award to a prevailing plaintiff in a patent infringement action an injunction against any further infringement of the patent. Thus, the losing defendant in a patent infringement case may be ordered by the court to stop the manufacture, sale, marketing, advertising, use, etc. of the alleged infringing device. This may include a recall by a manufacturer of infringing devices previously sold to its customers.

The patent owner, when prevailing in a patent infringement case, is also entitled to monetary damages, such as a reasonable royalty covering all past infringement involved in the litigation, or the patent owner's lost profits. One of the rules of patent infringement litigation, however, is that the patent owner cannot collect royalties moving backwards beyond six years from the date of filing the complaint starting the lawsuit. A reasonable royalty is usually established by the prevailing royalty standard in the industry, and/or other licenses that may have been granted by the Plaintiff and/or the Defendant, or other competitors in the same industry. Royalties apply to the past sales of the infringing product by the Defendant. If the infringer takes a license covering future production, the royalty rate applies to future sales. In those cases where the infringing device is a small part of a larger machine, the royalty percentage is normally applied only to the value of the small part, and not to the whole machine. Therefore, if the infringing device is a lug nut on a tire of an automobile, the reasonable royalty rate is usually not applied to the cost of the entire automobile.

Where a patent owner can show that no one else in the industry for the patented product or process, except the infringing defendant and the patent owning plaintiff, are producing and selling the patented product or process, the patent owner may convince the court or jury that it is entitled to its lost profits rather than a reasonable royalty, which are usually higher. The reasoning is that but for the defendant's infringement of the plaintiff's patent, the patent owner would have made the sales and profits of the infringer. Thus, if you are in a situation where your product infringes the patent of another, investigate to determine whether or not the patent owner and you are the only ones in the market. If so, you face the potential loss of higher damages in the form of lost profits.

As stated previously, if infringement can be shown to be willful, where the infringer knew of the existence of the patent, the court may increase damages by multiplying them by up to three to compensate the patent owner and punish the defendant for such willful infringement. Therefore, as we discussed earlier, it is important to obtain a competent opinion from your patent attorney prior to engaging in potentially infringing activities, so that there is no viable charge of willful infringement lodged against you and/or your company.

18.7   MARKING THE PATENTED PRODUCT WITH THE PATENT NUMBER

Section 287 of the Patent Law (35 U.S.C. §287), states that patentees and persons making, offering for sale, or selling a patented article or importing an article may give notice to the public that the same is patented by placing the patent number on the product, or where the character of the article prohibits this, by fixing the patent number to the package or a label. When the patented product is so marked, damages for all infringement may be recovered, by the patentee, dating back six years from the date of filing a lawsuit. In the event of a failure to mark the product with the patent number, no damages for patent infringement can be recovered by the patentee except from the date that the infringer was actually notified of the patent and of its infringement, where the one on notice continued to infringe thereafter. Thus, infringement damages may be recovered only for infringement occurring after notice if the product is not marked with the patent number.

Therefore, it is good advice to mark each patented product, or its container, label or point of purchase literature with the patent number to ensure that if an infringer appears on the horizon, the full measure of damages can be recovered from that infringer.

Charles Kettering

AUTOMOTIVE SELF-STARTER

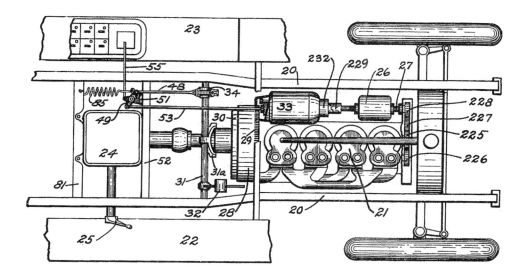

If you are over the age of 16, and not a total environmentalist, you have probably used his invention. No, not the car but the electrical ignition system. The inventor's name is Charles Franklin Kettering.

Charles Kettering invented the first electrical ignition system, the self-starter for automobile engines, and the first practical engine-driven generator. He was born on a farm near Loudenville, Ohio on August 29, 1876. He earned an engineering degree from Ohio State University in 1904, and joined the engineering staff of National Cash Register Company (NCR). At NCR, he oversaw the development of several products, including the electrically operated cash register and accounting machines. One source states that he invented the automobile ignition system while moonlighting in Edward Deeds' barn in Dayton, Ohio.

In 1909, Kettering left NCR, and he and Deeds formed the Dayton Engineering Laboratories Company, now known as Delco. Before Delco was acquired by General Motors in 1916, Kettering invented his most significant engine devices, including the Delco engine-driven generator that furnished electricity to millions of people in rural areas.

By 1910, automobiles had developed enough to be considered practical. They had speedometers, lights, almost workable brakes, and somewhat of a suspension system. One problem stood out—each car had a handle, or crank, at the front that was attached to the engine crankshaft. Using both hands, and sufficient muscle, on the crank, the engine could be turned through several revolutions. By retarding the ignition, advancing the throttle, and enriching the air/fuel mixture, the engine could start. If not, the driver cranked until the engine started, or his arms gave out. Most women at the time did not have the upper body strength to operate the crank. At times, an engine would backfire and kick the crank back with excessive force, causing injury to a driver who was still holding on. At least one driver of a Cadillac was killed in 1910 when a crank hit him in the face.

The first attempt at building a self-starter for automobiles was patented by Clyde Coleman in 1903, as U.S. Patent No. 745,157, reprinted following this biography. Coleman's solution failed to satisfactorily meet the requirements of torque and starter disengagement. He applied a clutch in the flywheel to try to take care of the disengagement issue after ignition, and added a governor to the starter to prevent the starter from drawing down excessive current. Neither of these solutions proved practical.

Charles Kettering developed the first practical self-starter at Delco in 1911, when he learned that Cadillac was not pleased with their starting system. Delco was invited to solve the problem. Delco then licensed Coleman's patent, and Kettering drew on his own electrical and mechanical knowledge to approach the problem.

A starter today is a "fattened" electric motor with a small pinion gear at the end of the drive shaft. An electromagnet causes the gear to slide on the shaft to engage the flywheel teeth when the motor turns in one direction, and to move the gear on the shaft out of engagement with the flywheel when power to the starter is cut off. The starter has thick wires connected to a solenoid since it draws several hundred amperes of current when operating.

Kettering, in 1911, did not solve the disengagement problem. His electric motor was permanently engaged with the flywheel. When the engine started, the engine flywheel rotated the starter shaft, and the starter was transformed into a generator, charging the battery. This was a practical solution, since the rpm's of automobile engines in 1911 were relatively low. Torque requirements were met by engaging the pinion gear with a flywheel having 25 times the number of teeth on the pinion gear. Consider the problem this would cause in today's automobiles operating at 3,000 rpm. Kettering's early starter shaft, if directly driven by the flywheel, would rotate at 75,000 rpm, leading to the real possibility that pieces of starter motor would be scattered throughout the parking lot.

Two years after Kettering developed his self-starter in 1911, Victor Bendix created a starter design that disconnected the starter gear from the flywheel after ignition. However, Kettering's starter was tested and accepted in 1911 by Cadillac, and Delco was given an order for several thousand starters, which were installed in 1912 Cadillacs. Delco licensed its starter technology to other manufacturers, and practically all cars offered an optional electric starter by 1920. Consider also that Kettering's self-starter invention allowed motoring to be accepted by women, which doubled the size of the potential automobile purchasing market.

Kettering went on to have an illustrious and rewarding technology career, with over 140 patents to his name.

When Kettering and Deeds sold Delco to General Motors for nine million dollars in 1916; they started a factory to produce Kettering's farm lighting system. Kettering also helped establish the Dayton Airplane Company, which enlisted the skill of Orville Wright as a consulting engineer. One of the company's main goals was to perfect Orville's automatic flight system, and produce planes for private use.

After the United States entered World War I, the Dayton Airplane Company received a contract to produce 5000 DeHavilland warplanes with the new "Liberty" engine and a new, more reliable ignition system for the "Liberty" engine. During the war, Kettering developed the first synthetic aviation fuel and was asked to produce a "flying bomb" that would carry explosives to their target 50 miles away. Kettering selected Dayton Wright as the contractor and Orville Wright as the aeronautical consultant. World War I ended before the flying bomb, or "Kettering Bug" as it was commonly called, could be put to use. The bug was patented, however, and kept as a military secret until World War II when the Germans produced the V-1 rocket, employing the same concept.

In 1920, General Motors took over many other business interests of Kettering's and created the General Motors Research Corporation with Kettering appointed as president. Soon after that, he was made vice-president of General Motors and named to its board of directors.

Kettering proceeded to find a practical gasoline additive to eliminate engine "knock." With the help of Tom Midgley, he discovered that tetraethyl lead was the most effective substance. Kettering's ethyl gasoline added more horsepower, greater safety, reliability, and speed not only to cars but to airplanes. Today, leaded gasolines are banned in the United States as environmentally dangerous.

Today, Charles Kettering is probably best known for the Sloan-Kettering Institute for Cancer Research in New York City. He and Alfred Sloan, president of General Motors, created the institute with an endowment in 1945. Charles Kettering died on November 25, 1958.

C. F. KETTERING.
ENGINE STARTING DEVICE.
APPLICATION FILED JUNE 15, 1911.

1,150,523.

Patented Aug. 17, 1915.
3 SHEETS—SHEET 1.

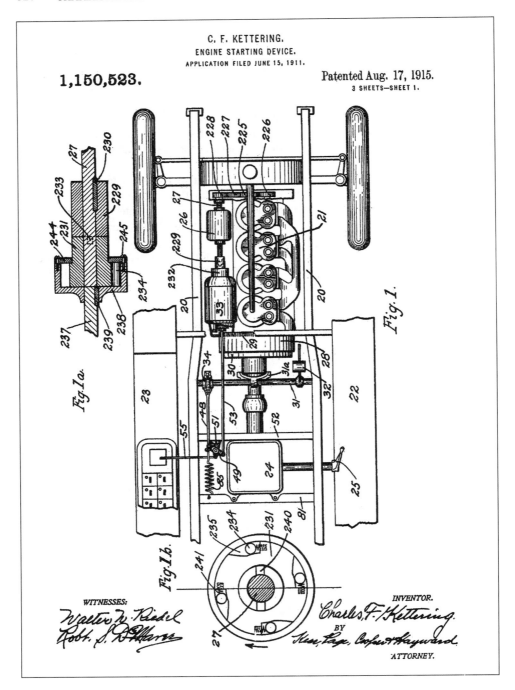

Fig.1a.

Fig.1.

Fig.1b.

No. 745,157.

PATENTED NOV. 24, 1903.

C. J. COLEMAN.
MEANS FOR OPERATING MOTOR VEHICLES.
APPLICATION FILED FEB. 11, 1901.

NO MODEL.

2 SHEETS—SHEET 1.

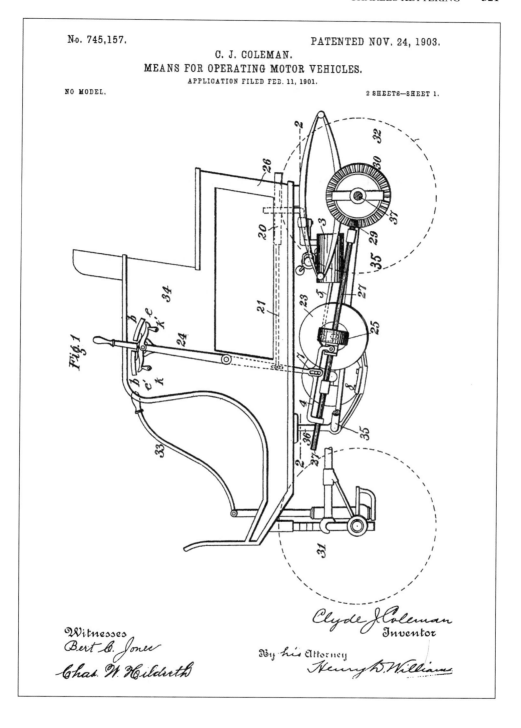

Fig. 1

Witnesses
Bert C. Jones
Chas. W. Hildreth

Clyde J. Coleman
Inventor

By his Attorney
Henry D. Williams

19 Ownership and Transfer of Patent Rights

19.1 INVENTORSHIP, OWNERSHIP, AND ASSIGNMENT OF PATENT RIGHTS

Once a patent on your invention is granted, you may treat the exclusive rights provided by the grant as an asset. Your exclusive rights may be sold to another party, or licensed to another party. Under certain circumstances, your employer may obtain a legal, non-exclusive right to use your invention, even though you did not intend to grant this right to your employer. Assignments and licenses are effected by written contracts, in most cases, after you have decided to have someone else exploit your invention on your behalf. Thought must be given to whether (1) you are going to manufacture, market, sell and distribute your invention yourself, (2) you are going to sell all rights in your invention to someone else for a sum of money, or (3) you will license someone else to produce and bring your product to market under specified terms that must be met for the licensee to keep the license. If you decide on the license route, terms satisfactory to you and your licensee must be mutually agreed to and placed in a license agreement. This chapter discusses how you, either as the inventor or one seeking to obtain rights under another's invention, can accomplish your goals.

19.1.1 Patent Right as an Asset

As discussed previously, the rights given to an inventor or inventors under the patent laws are intangible rights. You cannot see or touch these rights, such as you can with cash, a stock certificate, or a bank account statement. However, once the inventor has show the Patent & Trademark Office that a novel and unobvious invention has been created, a certificate of Letters Patent is awarded, and those intangible rights are now memorialized in a written document, bearing a U.S. Government seal. The Letters Patent define with precision the extent of and limitations on the awarded patent rights. By reading the Letters Patent, the rest of the world is made aware of, and is on notice of, the rights secured to the inventor.

The intangible patent rights defined by the tangible Letters Patent, which can be seen and touched, have also now been transmogrified into an "asset" of its owner. This asset can now be dealt with by the owner in the same manner as any other asset. The "patent asset" may be transferred by assignment, license or any other applicable legal vehicle, in whole or in part. The term "Assignment" defines a sale of the patent rights to another, where the inventor relinquishes ownership of the patent rights. A "License" grants another party the right to make, use, import, offer for sale, and/or sell the patented article or method under the authority of the patent owner, and the patent owner retains the ownership of the patent. When a patent is assigned, the prior owner primarily bows out of the

Intellectual Property Law for Engineers and Scientists, by Howard B. Rockman
ISBN 0-471-44998-9 © 2004 The Institute of Electrical and Electronics Engineers

picture. When a patent right is licensed, the owner of the patent normally includes provisions in the license agreement which gives the patent owner considerable say in the exploitation of the patented product or process by the licensee.

The owner of the Letters Patent is entitled to receive a negotiated compensation for the transfer of the patent rights to someone else, just as a seller of any asset receives value in return for the transfer of the asset. Thus, the patent system has changed what once was merely an intellectual image in the mind of an inventor, or group of inventors, into a tangible "thing," that is, intellectual property, that can be sold or otherwise transferred for sometimes large sums of money, similar to any other valuable asset, such as your house, car, boat, and so on. Compensation for assigning patent rights can be in the form of a one time payment, or a royalty based on future sales of the patented invention, or a combination of both.

19.1.2 Initial Ownership of the Patent Right

The role and definition of the "inventor(s)" in the creation of the invention, and ultimately the patent rights in that invention were described previously in Chapter 8, Section 8.1. Recall that in the U.S., all patent applications must be filed with the U.S. Patent & Trademark Office in the name(s) of the true inventor(s). At that moment, the inventor(s) own all of the patent rights applied for, except where they have previously agreed, in writing, to assign the invention and the patent rights in that invention to another, such as an employer.

If you are hired by a company, firm, partnership or other business entity to develop new products or processes, you may be required as a condition of your employment to agree beforehand to transfer ownership of all of your inventions or proprietary developments that relate to the employer's business which you come up with while in the company's employ. This agreement normally covers even those inventions or ideas you derive while at home, on your own time and with your own tools and materials, that may have value to your employer's business. However, I have been involved in several situations where an inventor developed a novel device at home and on his own time, which had no relation to his employer's business. According to the employment agreements these inventors signed, there was no obligation to assign these inventions to their employers, since the agreement to assign only pertained to inventions related to the company's business. Therefore, when you enter a new employment situation, or are asked to sign an "invention rights" contract, read the document carefully to determine whether you have an obligation to assign "all" inventions you come up with while an employee, or only those inventions which relate to the business of the employer. It could make a difference as to how you spend your spare time.

Also, even though your invention may relate to the company's business, management may express that it has no interest in using your invention. Your next step is to ask management to sign a release or waiver of their invention assignment right, and grant you the right to exploit the invention on your own, so long as your exploitation does not conflict with the employer's business interests.

If you have not signed an invention rights assignment agreement, and a patent application is filed covering your invention, you as the inventor own all rights to the invention, the patent application, and any patent that issues from the application. You may assign your patent rights to anyone at any time during this period, up to the time the issued patent expires. You may also assign your patent rights to one of your co-inventors, or assign a portion of your patent rights to someone else while retaining a portion of the rights yourself. Remember though, that any person, company or entity which owns even a small fraction of a patent right can exploit that patent right without accounting to the other owners as to financial or other benefits received for such exploitation. However, the default provision that no accounting is owed to the other owners can be modified by a contract between the inventors or co-owners of the patent.

19.1.3 Shop Rights

Some inventors conceive of an invention that has nothing to do with their employer's business, or under other situations where there is no obligation to assign the invention to the employer. However, to reduce the concept to practice, the inventor used his or her employer's time and/or materials and/or equipment, as a matter of necessity or not. This fact circumstance gives rise to a "shop right" in the employer, who automatically and under the operation of law, obtains a royalty free, non-exclusive non-transferable license to use or otherwise exploit the invention, and whether or not the inventor desires to grant his employer such rights. Therefore, before you develop an invention at work, using your employer's time, material and/or machinery, consider whether you would be better off conducting your development work at home, using your own or borrowed equipment.

The shop rights obtained by an employer, however, may have certain limitations. For example, the shop right generally does not give the employer the right to grant sub-licenses under the patent. Some states have laws preventing the employer from using the inventions beyond the employer's normal course of business.

19.2 PATENT LICENSING

A patent license allows the licensor, usually the inventor, to grant permission to someone else to exploit the patented invention (the licensee). A decision to grant a license is normally weighed against the advantages, or disadvantages, of producing the product embodying the invention yourself, or assigning your patent rights outright to another party, such as an established manufacturing company. If your ultimate decision is to grant a license, an acceptable licensee must first be sought. Once an acceptable "license partner" is found, the license agreement must be negotiated and set forth in a written agreement. While patent attorneys normally are not involved in your search for an appropriate licensee, the attorney is normally involved in negotiating and preparing the license agreement. The same is normally true regarding assignment agreements.

19.2.1 Difference Between a Patent Assignment and License

When an inventor, or subsequent owner of a patent, assigns or sells the intangible rights embodied in the Letters Patent, the inventor or owner divests himself of all rights he had in the patent prior to the sale. The former owner, even if he is the inventor, has no right to control who may make, use or sell the patented invention, cannot sue infringers of the patent, and cannot collect royalties for another's use of the invention. Just like the sale of a house, you can't move back in without repurchasing the house.

In most astute patent assignment agreements, the former owner, also described as the seller or assignor, receives a one-time payment, or time scheduled payments, of a fixed amount as consideration for relinquishing the patent rights. Alternatively, the assignor may receive a royalty-based payment for the assignment, where compensation is based on a royalty or percentage of the sale price of each product sold, or process used, which includes the invention covered by the patent. In this latter situation, the inventor or assignor can anchor his/her compensation to the success of the product.

One other point bears mentioning. In most patent assignment agreements I have been responsible for preparing, the inventor agrees that if an infringement lawsuit is brought by the new owner, or if other litigation flares up questioning the validity of the patent, the inventor agrees to assist the assignee in defending the patent against attacks on the patent. These defensive attacks are normally asserted by an accused infringing defendant in patent lawsuits. The inventor also agrees to provide deposition and trial testimony, if necessary and if requested to do so by the new owner of the patent rights.

A patent license is, for our purposes, a completely different creature compared to an assignment of your patent rights. Assume the following facts: You are the inventor of a new form of hybrid internal combustion/electrical powered automobile power system that showed enormous potential during two years of testing. You are an automotive power expert working on this project for a major engineering institution of higher learning in the U.S. You and your school have an agreement to share in any income obtained from exploiting your invention. You recognize that (1) your invention could have considerable importance in the near future, particularly during the 20 years of exclusive rights of exploitation afforded by a patent grant, and (2) there are several truck, automobile, boat and engine producing companies that are interested in further developing and commercializing your invention. You and your school decide that for an invention of such potential importance, you want several, if not all of these companies to adopt and work with your invention, and not provide any single company with an exclusive right to make, use and sell your invention. You also decide that you and your school desire to retain a degree of control over the future development and commercialization of your invention.

Therefore, instead of assigning your invention to a single company, which would relieve you entirely of your patent rights, your patent attorney suggests that you initiate a program offering non-exclusive licenses under the patent to those interested companies. If your invention is as important as expected, this procedure will result in several licensees paying royalties to you and your school, rather than just a single source of income were the patent assigned to a sole entity.

A license, as distinguished from an assignment, provides many benefits. When granting a license under your patent rights, you maintain ownership and control over the patent right, but are granting someone else the right to make, use and/or sell the patented invention pursuant to mutually agreed upon terms which are normally set forth in a written License Agreement, which is a legally binding contract between the Licensor (owner of the patent right) and the Licensee (the party desiring to make, use and/or sell the invention). Thus, the licensee can use the inventive technology, without infringing the patent.

19.2.2 When to Think "License"

In the movie *The Candidate,* after successfully being elected a U.S. Senator as an "outsider" reformist against the "entrenched" incumbent candidate in a bitter campaign, Robert Redford utters the famous last lines of the movie: "What do we do now?" No one answers, and the story ends. As an inventor, you ultimately reach the point where the development of your invention is complete, and your patent application has been filed with the U.S. Patent & Trademark Office. You then ask the question: "What do we do now?" Unlike the Robert Redford movie, I will answer that question.

Once your patent application has been filed, and before it issues as a patent several years later, you are free to begin commercializing and/or exploiting your invention to obtain the benefit of all of your hard work in bringing the invention to fruition. Under U.S. Patent Law, you could have begun publicly exploiting your invention no earlier than one year before your patent application filing date. However, as mentioned previously, such activities would lead to adverse effects on obtaining patent protection in certain other major industrialized nations. So, for purposes of explanation, we shall consider that you did not make your invention publicly known prior to the filing date of your patent application in the United States.

You have now perfected an "official filing date" for your patent application. When the rules of the International treaties governing patents are followed by your patent attorney, your U.S. filing date, or "priority date" is the effective filing date in those countries that are part of the treaties, which is almost every country. Therefore, you can now publicly disclose your invention without fear of losing foreign patent rights in treaty bound countries. In addition, since your invention is now of record as a filed patent application with an official U.S. government office, no one else can steal your invention and file a patent application on that invention prior to your filing date. As a result, it is generally considered safe to make your invention publicly known, and take steps leading towards the entry of a product or products, or process, into the marketplace so that the world will have the benefit of your invention, and you will reap the rewards for the advance in technology represented by your invention.

It is highly recommended, however, that even after your patent application has been filed, the invention should be disclosed to others only after a confidential, non-disclosure agreement has been signed by the recipient. This should continue at least until a public disclosure occurs, such as a public sale, offer for sale, or public use of the invention, or the patent is published or issued. This affords added protection for the invention, since the interaction between patents and trade secrets in the early stages of patent application filing complement one another, and are not mutually exclusive.

Consider the following true example: Company A filed a patent application covering its invention, and also had disclosed the invention to Company B under a non-disclosure agreement. A patent issued on the invention, and Company A eventually claimed Company B infringed the patent and that the non-disclosure agreement was breached. Damages of over $50 million were awarded to Company A. On appeal, the appeals court held the patent invalid, but let the damages award stand because of the breach of the nondisclosure agreement. Therefore, had Company A not had the non-disclosure agreement in place, it would have not recovered anything.

We are now also considering the situation where you, as the inventor, are under no obligation to assign your invention to another, such as your employer. The invention and the patent rights you have applied for are yours to deal with as you please. If you have access to manufacturing, marketing, distribution, sales, financial, accounting and advertising capabilities, you may be able to place your invention on the market yourself. However, most of the inventors I have dealt with, who have not previously assigned their patent rights to their employers, were not in an economic position to successfully bring a product to market without considerable help. Consider my client the bank manager who developed a new automotive accessory product, or the college student who developed a technical advance in in-line skates. The list goes on. It is these inventors who should "think license" as a way to make their invention publicly known and used.

I have represented several inventors who have attempted to form a business, such as a company, partnership or other entity, to produce and sell their inventions. These inventors usually have no prior experience in the market for their invention, or have not previously attempted to start a business from the ground up. The initial problem each of these inventors face is raising enough money, usually in the one-half million to several million-dollar range, to finance a new company's ability to get started. Most of these efforts either take a long time to produce results, or fail altogether. The proper way to raise financial backing for a new venture is beyond the scope of this course, so I shall immediately fast forward to the subject of licensing, which I perceive as the more expedient, less stressful way to gain the benefits of the work you put into your invention, and to place your invention in the hands of the waiting purchasing public.

Efforts toward licensing your patent rights can and should begin as soon as possible after the patent application has been filed. There is no need to wait until the patent issues. Most license agreements are written granting license rights under a pending patent application, and under any patent or patents ultimately issuing from your application. Since the search conducted prior to preparation and filing of your patent application indicated that your invention or elements of your invention, were novel and non-obvious in view of the prior art, you operate under the assumption that ultimately a patent will be awarded covering your invention. Therefore, your efforts at obtaining someone to license your invention can justifiably proceed on a positive note regarding ultimately obtaining an issued patent.

19.2.3 Developing a Relationship With a Licensee

In some technology areas and industries, a trade association or other industry source may maintain a list of established businesses that are looking for new inventions and products to add to their existing lines, or to improve their present products. If you can locate such a list, your first step should be to contact those on the list that meet your criteria for a successful licensing partner. I shall cover these criteria shortly. This is accomplished by sending a letter to the prospective licensee, broadly defining your invention and what your invention accomplishes, and inquire if they have any interest. Of course, if you obtained the name of the prospective licensee from a list defining the technology they were interested in, you extol the advantages of your invention toward the technology the prospective licensee is looking for. Also, you state in your letter that you have a patent application pending covering your invention.

In most instances, you will receive a response letter indicating that the recipient has a policy of not considering unsolicited or outside ideas, unless the inventor agrees that the invention is being submitted on a non-confidential basis, and that if the inventor ever makes an accusation that the prospective licensee acted unlawfully with respect to the invention, the inventor will only resort to its patent or copyright rights, and will not accuse the prospective licensee of misappropriation of trade secrets. This form of agreement protects the recipient of your letter in the event, for example, they reply that they have examined your invention and have no interest in it, and several years later, you discover they are selling your invention without your approval. It is difficult for the recipient of your invention disclosure to defend itself against a theft of trade secret case, so the prospective licensee protects itself against a possible trade secret misappropriation lawsuit in the future.

However, the prospective licensee is agreeing to honor your patent rights and/or copyright rights.

When you receive a non-confidential disclosure letter such as described above, my advice is first have your patent attorney review the letter to ensure it doesn't include any additional adverse provisions. If the letter is approved by your attorney, sign it and send it back. Why? You already have a patent application pending covering your invention, which in all probability will ultimately issue as a patent. If the prospective licensee does unlawfully adopt your invention, you will be able to use your patent to stop such conduct.

19.2.4   Selection of an Appropriate Licensee

Assume you desire to have someone else develop and introduce your invention to the market, and to pay you handsomely for the right to do so. Beside seeking one interested in your invention from those seeking new technology, another avenue is to seek out prospective licensees who may not necessarily be looking for new technology, but may be interested in your invention once they see it.

The first step is to determine who manufactures products, or uses processes, in areas of technology related to your invention. This may be easy to determine, or you may have to ask a retail store manager to give you the name of a distributor of a related product. You then can ask the distributor who manufactures products that would be enhanced by your invention. Once you have the names of several manufacturers in hand, contact the marketing department of one or more of those companies, not the engineering or technical departments. Why? It's called the NIH syndrome—"not invented here." The postulate goes that when you present your invention to other engineers, they may initially conclude that if your idea were a good one, they would have thought of it. Since the idea came from an outside source, these internal engineers then may decide that your idea is not very good. However, by approaching the marketing department first, you are talking to business and project oriented personnel, not technicians. If you can convince the marketing department that your invention would be a profit making addition, extension or improvement to their existing product line, those marketing types will provide an opening for serious consideration of your invention by the target company.

A word on selecting your target company(s). Your invention most probably requires further development work to engineer its most expedient production, and to bring the manufacturing cost down to a minimum. Then the product incorporating the invention has to be manufactured by your target company, which can most economically be accomplished by using the existing production machinery and electronics of your target, without major new capital outlays. Therefore, you should investigate to determine if one or more target companies satisfy, or come close to satisfying these criteria.

After manufacture, the product embodying your invention will have to enter a distribution channel that moves the products to distributors, wholesalers, and the like, each of whom have marketing, advertising and sales capability to place your product in the hands of the type of retail store where your inventive product can be purchased by a consumer. It follows that your investigation should lead you to conclude that your target company(s) have distribution, sales, marketing and advertising capability, as well as manufacturing potential. For example, if your invention is a new hardware item, a company with distribution in place to appliance stores will not do you any good. Your target company should have a distribution network already in place that sends its salespeople to every hardware store or buying consortium in the country, and in other countries as well.

Once you select one or more target companies, contact each of them with a letter explaining your invention, stating that you have initiated the process for obtaining patent protection, and where possible, include a sample of your invention in an attractive form or display, to appeal to the recipient's aesthetic senses. The better your product looks, the easier it is to interest someone else. If you receive back a non-confidential invention submittal form, have your patent attorney review it, and if approved, sign the form and send it back. If your target is interested, negotiations towards a license agreement come next.

License negotiations most effectively begin with one of the parties preparing a Letter of Intent, and forwarding same to the other party. The Letter of Intent follows an initial discussion between you and your potential licensee of the broader terms and objectives of the desired licensing arrangement. The Letter of Intent, which is not a binding agreement, sets forth those general terms which the parties desire to include in the final agreement after successful negotiations. For example, the Letter of Intent is merely an expression of the initial understanding reached between you and your target, which generally indicates whether an exclusive or non-exclusive license under the patent rights is contemplated, the identification of the parties to the agreement, the extent of the technology to be licensed, whether the license is for certain countries, parts of countries, or worldwide, and a brief statement of the financial arrangement contemplated by the parties, for example, royalty payments, lump sum payment, advance against royalties, etc.

You have most likely selected your target company without assistance from your patent attorney, because it is not wise to pay legal fees for such a non-legal function. However, after you have selected and initially discussed interest in your invention by the target company, I recommend that you seek assistance from your patent attorney in preparing or reviewing the Letter of Intent, and in negotiating the terms of the License Agreement.

19.2.5   Primary License Negotiation and Agreement Considerations

After the Letter of Intent has exchanged hands, and the parties agree to move forward and execute a formal license agreement, the patent attorney for one of the parties, usually the inventor or licensing party (Licensor), is requested to prepare the first draft of the license agreement, which is forwarded to you, the inventor, for approval, before it is transmitted to the lawyer for the other party (Licensee).

To give you an idea of the principal terms that are usually incorporated in a Patent License Agreement, I have listed and discussed below some of these points. Remember, however, these points are not all inclusive, and where special conditions apply, such as receipt of FDA approval before the term of the license begins in a medical device Patent License Agreement, these additional considerations will also be added to the agreement.

Exclusivity or Non-Exclusivity in the Covered Territory   In all probability, your licensee will request an exclusive license under your patent rights which means that you will not be able to grant any other licenses during the term of your license agreement. This is to enable the licensee to gain a foothold in the market with your new product, without fear that competition will erode its position. This is contrasted to the situation where you grant non-exclusive licenses to many manufacturers in a given industry. Here, in order to get your invention off the ground, your licensee is requiring exclusivity in the territory covered by your license agreement. If you have filed a patent application only in the United States, your territory is limited to the United States and its possessions. However, if you have protected your ability to file foreign patent applications, the license that you grant may be worldwide, or cover only those segments of the world in which your exclusive licensee has marketing capability. Therefore, in negotiating a license, make sure you do not grant worldwide rights to a manufacturer or licensee that does not have the capability to sell your invention worldwide.

Most license arrangements are conducted and finalized during that time period in which the inventor still has the choice in which countries he/she will file foreign patent applications. Since your licensee is obtaining an exclusive license, and you are substantially locked into the arrangement, certain other provisions which I will discuss shortly are inserted in the license agreement, which ensure maximum performance by your licensee in all territories. If certain requirements are not met, either the license agreement is cancelled, or the exclusive license reverts to a non-exclusive license.

Advance Against Royalties at Signing   By the time you begin negotiations with the licensee concerning your patent rights, you have expended time, effort and your own resources to bring the invention and the patent rights to the point at which they now exist. One of the theories of patent licensing is that the licensor, or the inventor, receive an advance against royalties at the signing of the license agreement which will at least repay the inventor for expenditures relating to development work and obtaining the patent up to the time of the signing of the license agreement. Besides determining your out of pocket expenses, it is prudent to calculate the amount of hours spent in bringing the invention and patent rights to the present point, and to assign an hourly rate to your work. This amount should be added to your out of pocket expenses, such as sums paid to your patent attorney and payment for materials and other costs you incurred in perfecting your invention. The advance against royalties amount negotiated in the contract should be equal to or more than the calculated amount spent by the inventor prior to entering into the licensing agreement. Another reason supporting the advance royalty amount is that this is the cost the licensee would have incurred had the licensee developed the same invention, secured patent rights, and developed the invention to the point where it could be commercialized. Thus, the licensee is merely paying you back for your work on their behalf up to the time the license agreement is signed.

Royalty Rate as Quid Pro Quo for the Grant of the License   Your license agreement could provide that you receive a one-time, lump sum payment for the grant of the license. However, most license agreements tie the compensation to the inventor to the success of the licensed product. The normal procedure is to provide that the inventor is compensated by a royalty rate applied to the net sale price of products sold. The calculation of the royalty rate, in theory, is based upon splitting the profits from the sale of the invention, or the products containing the invention. For example, if you determine that the licensee will earn a 10% net profit on the sale of goods comprising your invention, a reasonable royalty rate may be 5% of net sales. In this example, you and your licensee are equally dividing the profit grained from sales of the invention. Of course, this calculation is not precise, since the licensee will incorporate the cost of your royalty payments into the cost of manufacturing, and then predicate profit from that point. However, it is usually considered good practice to compensate an inventor at approximately half of the what net profit would be from sales of the invention.

If necessary, the royalty rate can be negotiated between the parties based upon other royalty rates that the licensee is paying on licenses under other patents. Also, a given industry may have a standard recognized royalty rate that is paid amongst its members, and the royalty rate you negotiate can be 1 or 2 points above or below that particular figure, as arrived at during an arms-length negotiation. If, however, your invention is a pioneer invention that will create a totally new industry or a new series of product lines, the negotiated royalty rate can be higher. Further, if the licensee indicates that because of the newness of the product and the industry, massive advertising expenditures must take place to introduce the public to the new product on the market, the licensee may ask for a lower royalty rate in order to take into account the additional early advertising expense. There are also license agreements where the royalty rate is reduced after certain increased levels of sales are made of the product, to provide an incentive for the licensee to aggressively market the product.

To What Is the Royalty Rate Applied The negotiated royalty rate is usually applied as a percentage of net sales of the product embodying the invention. Net sales is normally defined as the price charged by the licensee to its customers, less pass-through items such as taxes, insurance, advertising and shipping costs. Most license agreements contain a formula for the determination of net sales to which the royalty rate is applied. The licensee is usually required to provide the licensor with quarterly reports of net sales, and to submit this report along with a royalty check payable to the inventor.

Where the license relates to a process rather than a product, the royalty rate may be applied to a certain quantitative value, such as tons or square feet of product produced by the licensed process. If the process relates to the production of a gaseous material, the total cubic feet of production, for example, could be used as a basis for applying the royalty.

Minimum Royalty Payments As stated previously, you are willing to grant your licensee an exclusive license under your patent rights. Since you are prevented from granting additional licenses, additional provisions must be included in the agreement to keep the licensee's feet to the fire in terms of aggressively promoting your invention. One provision to accomplish this purpose is to require the licensee to make minimum annual royalty payments to maintain the exclusivity of the license. This minimum royalty payment requirement may increase each year into the term of the license agreement, which reflects the fact that you expect your licensee to continually increase its sales from year to year. The minimum royalty payment is a negotiated amount that the licensee must pay each year to retain exclusivity under the agreement. If the minimum royalty payments are not met, the license reverts to a non-exclusive agreement, giving you the right to seek additional licensees.

In those instances where the actual royalty paid by your licensee over a year period falls slightly short, the licensee has the option of making up the difference by paying the additional amount to meet the minimum royalty payment requirement, and thus retain the exclusive license. However, if this practice continues during the term of the license, you as the inventor lose your advantage of maximizing the full economic potential of your patent rights. You did not enter into the license agreement to have your licensee sell only enough licensed products to meet the minimum royalty requirements of the agreement. The pre-agreement negotiations to establish the minimum royalty payments are based upon expected reasonable sales of products over the term of the license agreement. As the inventor, you naturally expect those sales and royalty payments to increase.

Sales Goals or Minimum Production Goals In addition to the requirement of minimum royalty payments, the license agreements I negotiate include sales goals which must be met by the licensee each year, or the licensor, which is you the inventor, have the right to terminate the agreement and seek a new licensee. Where a process is involved, minimum production or output goals are established which, if not met, also provide the inventor with the right to terminate the agreement. Therefore, the combination of minimum royalty payments and sales goals or minimum production goals are effective in providing the licensee with the incentive to aggressively market the product embodying your invention, or lose exclusivity, or the license agreement altogether. Negotiated sales goals are arrived at by determining the level of reasonable sales per year during the term of the agreement.

Territorial Extent of the License   Most license agreements are negotiated at that point in time where the inventor/licensor has filed PCT and/or Foreign National Phase Patent applications that are still pending, whereby the process is moving forward to protect your invention in many foreign countries. Thus, you have the ability to grant your exclusive licensee, or a non-exclusive licensee, rights under any one or more of your international patent rights. It is important, therefore, to investigate the marketing extent of your potential licensee, and determine those countries in which your licensee has marketing and sales organizations. If there are certain parts of the world where your licensee does not have sufficient sales capability, you do not want to grant your licensee an exclusive right in those countries. Therefore, the license agreement should state that your licensee has exclusive rights under your patent rights in only certain countries. This will provide you with the ability to establish other exclusive licenses with additional licensees in those countries not covered by your original license.

Also, if necessary, you may grant an exclusive license for only portions of one country, such as the United States. For example, you may give one party an exclusive license to sell your product east of the Mississippi, while another party has an exclusive right to sell your product west of the Mississippi. You may also grant one party the exclusive right to sell your invention to one trade or industry, and grant another licensee the exclusive right to sell your invention to another trade or industry. For example, if your invention relates to internal combustion engines, you could grant one licensee the right to manufacture and sell the inventive product in the automotive field, while giving someone else the right to license the product for use in small internal combustion engines, such as lawn mower engines. Yet another exclusive license could be granted to manufacture the product for use in engines for driving electrical generators.

19.2.6   Additional License Considerations

In addition to those recommended license provisions discussed previously, there are additional matters to be considered to properly construct a license arrangement with your potential licensee.

The Time and Form of Payment   The license agreement should indicate when the licensee is to tender payment to the licensor. This provision should be tied into the existing accounting practices of the licensee. Normally, the licensee is required to perform an accounting after every three-month period of sales of the licensed product, preparing a report of total amounts of licensed products sold, the net sales in dollars of the licensed products sold, and a calculation of the amount due to the licensor when the royalty rate is applied to the total net sales. This report is normally furnished to the inventor/licensor, along with a check in the amount of the royalty payment due as shown by the accounting. The inventor/licensor is normally given the right to have an independent accountant inspect the books of the licensee at least once a year to determine that the reports and royalty payments are honest.

While the quarterly payment program is used in many industries, it may be more prudent for your licensee to pay you either monthly or yearly or any other term. Also, if the licensee is in another country, it may be prudent to indicate that the royalty payment is to be made in U.S. dollars, Euros, or some other convenient currency. There are certain countries that deduct taxes before your licensee in that country remits payment under your license agreement. In such cases, provisions for handling and deducting tax amounts and how they effect the amount you receive should be negotiated into the contract.

Who Enforces the Patent Against Infringers   The license agreement normally takes into consideration the prospect that infringers of your patent rights may try to enter the market in competition with your licensee. Taking action to halt such infringing conduct is an expensive proposition, and the decision who will be responsible for enforcing the patent rights must be carefully negotiated. For example, you, as the inventor, may not have the financial resources to support a patent infringement action against a potential infringer. Therefore, the license agreement could prudently state that the licensee, who may be a major corporation, would be responsible for enforcing the patent against potential infringers. The agreement may also lower the amount of royalty payments you receive during the pendency of the infringement action to enable the licensee to expend its resources toward successfully enforcing the patent.

On the other hand, if you as the inventor are sufficiently reimbursed from the royalty payments under the agreement, you may agree to enforce the patent rights when requested to do so by the licensee. The patent rights enforcement provision must be carefully negotiated to ensure that the combination of the inventor and the licensee have the ability to successfully enforce the patent. In some cases, both the licensee and the licensor share equally in the expense and responsibility for enforcing the patent against infringers, and in any award of damages awarded against the infringer.

Defense of the Licensed Product Against a Charge of Infringement Under a Third Party Patent   As discussed previously, the fact that you have a patent on your product does not necessarily mean that the licensed product manufactured under your patent rights will not infringe a patent of a third party. The patent license agreement takes this into consideration by including a clause that gives one party or the other, or both parties, the responsibility of defending the licensed product against charges of infringement of another patent owned by a third party.

A prudent measure prior to entering into the license agreement and bringing the product to market is to conduct a full infringement search to ensure, as best you can, that there are no unexpired patents that may be infringed by sale of the licensed product. However, there may be issued patents that were pending when your search was conducted, and were not revealed by your search, and issued after your licensed product hit the market. It is normally prudent to insert a clause in the agreement that if a patent infringement lawsuit is filed against the licensed product, both parties will share in the cost of defending the licensed product against the charge of infringement. Alternatively, the licensee alone may take on the laboring oar of defending the infringement suit brought by the third party, with a reduction in royalty payments during the pendency of such litigation. Again, these provisions are subject to arms-length negotiations between you, the licensor, and your licensee.

Term of the License   The term of the license agreement may extend to the time of expiration of the last of the patents that are licensed under the license agreement. If there is only one patent being licensed, the license agreement would end at the expiration of that licensed patent. It is unlawful for a license to extend beyond the expiration of the licensed patent, since consideration for the license no longer exists. Where you grant a license for the life of the patent, it is important to include in your agreement the minimum royalty payment and minimum sales goal or production goal default provisions discussed previously. It would not be in your best interests to exclusively tie up your patent rights for the life of the patent with a licensee that does not aggressively market the product and maximize your royalty payments.

Many license agreements are written for a term of 5 or 10 years, where the licensee has a right to renew the contract upon equal terms, or lesser terms such as on a year to year basis. This allows the licensee to continue the license agreement as long as sales of licensed products are profitable, and to terminate the agreement if the product becomes non-profitable. In the same vein, most license agreements do not provide the licensor with the right to yank the license from the licensee after the licensee has invested its resources in tooling up, creating a production capability, and advertising and marketing the invention embodied in the licensed products. The one thing I have always strived to accomplish when I represent a licensee in a patent license negotiation is to prevent the licensor from having the ability to terminate my license if a competitor offers a higher percentage royalty to the licensor if the licensor would terminate the agreement with my licensee client.

The term of the license could also reflect the expected marketable life of the licensed product. For example, if your invention lies in an industry where normally a product is successful for three or four years, and then is overcome by new advances in technology, establishing the first term of the license for three years, with renewal rights after that, may be the way to go.

Indemnification   A license agreement, by itself, does not immunize the licensee from the possibility that another's intellectual property rights will be infringed, or from the possibility that the patented product will injure someone, giving rise to tort liability facing both the patent owner and the licensee. Indemnification clauses are inserted in license agreements to enable the patent owner and the licensee to balance the risks and rewards of the business venture embodied in the license agreement. As an example, the extent of the patent owner's indemnification may be capped at a sum equal to royalty payments received under the agreement.

In many negotiations, failure to agree on indemnification leads to a failure to conclude a contract. Patent owners should be particularly aware of this issue, since many patent owners mistakenly conclude that if they indemnify the licensee, their total liability cannot exceed the royalties they receive. This is incorrect, and an ill-considered indemnity clause can potentially cost the patent owner an excessive amount of money, and possible bankruptcy.

Agreement on indemnification should take into consideration who will profit more from the deal, and which party is in the best financial position to bear the risk. Consider also that tort liability is normally the subject of insurance coverage, while coverage against liability for patent infringement may be obtained.

19.2.7 Acts Causing Termination of the License

Breach of Contract   Most license agreements, and as a matter of fact most legal agreements, contain a provision that the contract can be terminated by either party where the other party has breached any of the material terms of the agreement. The contract will also set forth those types of conduct which may be considered a material breach, giving the other party the option to terminate the contract immediately, or to terminate the agreement if the breach is not cured within a short time period, such as 30 days. Normally, the failure to make a royalty payment within thirty days of its due date constitutes a material breach of the contract, giving the inventor/licensor the right to terminate the contract immediately or after the cure period. Other breaches, which may not be that serious, give rise to the right of the breaching party to overcome the breach and continue the agreement.

Insolvency   Many license agreements include a provision that if the licensee becomes insolvent or files for bankruptcy, the license agreement is terminated. However, the bankruptcy courts are now ignoring that clause, and holding that the license agreement is an asset of the bankrupt licensee that can be sold to someone else for revenue that would bring money into the bankruptcy estate, which can be distributed to the bankrupt's creditors. Therefore, the situation exists whereby if your licensee declares bankruptcy, the license agreement instead of being terminated, can be sold to one of your major competitors, and your major competitor now has a license under your patent. This may not be in your best interests, since the competitor may be one that you would not want to license under your patent rights in the first place. The issues raised by the possibility of insolvency or bankruptcy are important, and should be discussed with your patent attorney when negotiating your license.

Confidentiality   A well crafted license agreement will also include a provision stating that any information of a confidential nature that you furnish to the licensee which enables them to perform efficiently under the agreement will be held in confidence by the licensee, not used on other products that the licensee may be manufacturing without your permission, and not disclosed to any other party who is not involved in the production or marketing of the licensed product. The confidential information should also be returned to you upon termination of the license.

19.2.8 Grant Back Clauses

A grant back clause covers the situation where the licensee, during the development and production of your licensed product, makes patentable improvements or enhancements to the product.

A grant back clause states that any such improvement or enhancement to the licensed product made by the licensee shall be owned by you, the original inventor and licensor, and any patent rights arising from such improvement inventions will be owned by you as the licensor. The grant back clause also grants the licensee a license under such improvement patents without any additional cost. The clause usually indicates that any confidential information regarding the improvement furnished by the licensee to the licensor shall be held confidential by the licensor.

19.3   CONCLUSION

As is apparent from the above discussion, a license agreement contains many provisions that are intertwined and dependant upon each other. My recommendation is that when the time arrives when it is prudent for you to begin license negotiations with a potential licensee relating to your patent rights, you engage the services of a competent patent attorney to negotiate the terms of the agreement on your behalf. In addition to the terms that go into a typical patent license agreement that I've mentioned above, there are additional terms that may be applicable to your particular industry or particular product. For example, if your are licensing a telecommunications transmitting product that must be compatible with receiving equipment, the license agreement should include provisions whereby the licensee is required to inform you of it's quality control measures to ensure the compatibility of the licensed product with receiving devices in the market.

Remember that your license agreements are consensual, and call for mutual agreement by both parties to enter into a final, executed agreement. Therefore, during the negotiations you may be asked to give up certain provisions you want in exchange for the other party giving up certain provisions that it wants. Also, remember that a license agreement is drafted at a time when you and your licensee are working towards a common goal. However, the license is also crafted to take care of situations that arise in the future where the licensee and you may have major disagreements over one or several aspects of the manufacturing, marketing, or sales of the licensed product. The license agreement should include provisions that enable both parties to mutually discuss any foreseeable problems that may arise, and to attempt to work out a satisfactory resolution of such problems. Once signed by both parties, the license agreement becomes a legal contract, binding both sides, which may be enforced in a court of law. Also, please remember not to sign any agreement until you understand and agree with all of the terms in the agreement.

◆ INVENTORS AND INVENTIONS ◆

Philo Farnsworth

THE INVENTION OF TELEVISION

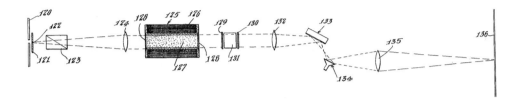

The story of the invention of television is still shrouded in controversy, characterized by many as the classic battle between the sole inventor and the large corporation, between individual creativity and corporate strength. Although the Radio Corporation of America (RCA) is usually given credit for bringing television to the forefront, the name of Philo Taylor Farnsworth has been relegated to the background. However, researchers of late have dug into the details of the stories and have begun to promote Farnsworth as the true father of television. As usual, in contests over inventorship between inventors, the United States Patent Office became involved and, in this case, produced decisions that gave solace to the Farnsworth supporters.

The story of Philo T. Farnsworth and his development of television begins as he was plowing a field while attending Rigby, Idaho High School in 1921. As he himself related during subsequent lawsuits regarding the inventorship of television, at that time he had a dream to send pictures over the air, as sound was sent over the radio. At age 14, he was plowing a field with his horse-drawn disc harrow and visualized that the tracks in the field would be the same as tiny electrons creating a beam that could scan an image line by line. Beginning with this inspiration, Farnsworth eventually developed the first working electronic television, in contrast to the mechanical televisions that predated it. Believe it or not, in his later years, Farnsworth stated that he felt he had created some kind of monstrous device, that provided people with a means to waste their time. He complained about the programming. Does this sound familiar?

Philo Taylor Farnsworth was born in a log cabin in Indian Creek, Utah in 1906, and lived his early life in rather remote areas, devoid of the nuances of modern technology facilities. When he was 12 years old, the family moved to a ranch home in Snake River Valley, Idaho, where Farnsworth found hidden in the attic of the house a large quantity of magazines devoted to science and radio. In the magazines, Farnsworth read about a favorite topic of science and science fiction writers at the time: television, the concept of transmitting pictures through the air. Farnsworth also read about the almost-fictional particle that was invisible to the eye, the electron. He considered that the electron, with its relative freedom from inertia, filled all the necessary requirements for his considerations of a workable all-electronic television transmitter and receiver system. The ranch in Idaho

Intellectual Property Law for Engineers and Scientists, by Howard B. Rockman
ISBN 0-471-44998-9 © 2004 The Institute of Electrical and Electronics Engineers

was the first place that he had lived in where there was electricity, and he began creating devices that he attached to the power generator. For example, since he had the household chore of operating the crank handle for his mother's hand-operated washing machine, he created a motor by rewinding an armature, and attached the motor to his mother's washing machine.

In the early 1900's, transmitting messages along wires via telegraph, and transmitting sound across wires or the airwaves by telephone and radio, were already in an advanced stage of development and were generally known to most people. Farnsworth, however, thought about the next advance in technology, changing images into electric impulses or signals and transmitting those signals to a receiving unit where they would produce a viewable image. At that time, other partly electrical, partly mechanical television devices had been created, most employing rotating disks. However, he strove for the use of electrons in television transmission to produce improved images without moving or mechanical parts.

Farnsworth was fascinated with electricity and electron movement, and persuaded his high school chemistry teacher, Justin Tolman, to provide him with special instruction and also allow him to audit a senior course in electronics. One day in 1921, Farnsworth decided to present his "television" idea to Justin Tolman. Going to the blackboard, Farnsworth drew a series of diagrams that were rough sketches of a vacuum tube containing a cathode and an anode with an external lens and a static machine, according to Tolman's recollection. Farnsworth also indicated to Mr. Tolman that he had been reading about mechanical television systems then being developed on the east coast, and that electron systems would eventually replace spinning-wheel systems.

According to young Farnsworth's concept, light from an optical image would be projected upon a photosensitive cathode where each elementary area of the cathode emitted electrons at a rate proportional to the intensity of light falling upon that area. The electrons would flow to the anode and return to the cathode by means of external circuits and a battery that Farnsworth developed, thus creating a current flow between the cathode and anode, and through the external circuits. Electrons emitted from the elementary areas of the cathode would travel toward the anode plates in substantially parallel lines due to the high potential between the cathode and the anode. The electron flow would create an electron beam and the various elementary areas of any transverse cross section of the beam would produce an electron or current density proportional to the intensity of light falling on the corresponding elementary area of the cathode at the instant of emission of the electrons in the cross section. Therefore, the cross section of the electron beam constituted a current pattern corresponding to the light pattern of the optical image that originated the current flow. This defined the "electrical image" as described in Farnsworth's United States Patent No. 1,773,980, which he obtained on his television system on August 26, 1930 upon an application filed January 7, 1927.

Only the electrons directly in line with an aperture and a plate passed through the aperture and impinged on the target anode in Farnsworth's device. Thus, the current from only a single elementary area of the electron beam or "electrical image" passed through a resistance. Sawtooth voltages, however, applied to deflecting plates caused the electron beam to continually move across the face of each plate such that each of the elementary areas of the beam were successively directed toward the aperture, and the electrons in the areas impinged upon the anode. Thus, the aperture scanned each elementary current of the electron beam, and scanned the electrical image. The electrons impinging upon the target anode constituted the current flowing through the resistance, and the potential drop across the resistance enhanced the output signal proportional at successive instances to the electron or current density of the elementary area of the electron beam being scanned. Thus, Farnsworth's device divided a picture into lines of light and shade, and a quickly changing electromagnetic field scanned the picture line by line. The electrons were collected at the far end of the camera tube and formed a stream of electric pulses that were transmitted to an antenna. In the receiver, the electronic pulses were converted back into a series of lines, and the image was reconstituted on the receiving screen.

At that time, there were other inventors unknown to Philo Farnsworth who were also working on the development of electronic television. Vladimir Zworykin, who had immigrated to the United States from Russia in 1919 and had taken a job with Westinghouse Corporation in Pittsburgh, Pennsylvania, was considered by some to be ahead of Farnsworth in the development of television during the 1920s. Zworykin was highly educated, holding a PhD in electrical engineering from Petrograd Institute of Technology in Russia, where he studied before coming to the United States under scientist Boris Rosing, who was already working on cathode ray tubes for mechanical-scan television. Rosing was attempting to transmit pictures by wire in his physics laboratory in Petrograd. He and Zworykin experimented with a cathode ray tube that had been previously developed by the German Carl Ferdinand Braun. In 1910, Rosing had demonstrated a television system employing a mechanical scanner in the transmitter, and using the electronic Braun tube as the receiver.

In 1923, Zworykin applied for a patent for an approach to television he first encountered while working in Russia with Boris Rosing. The 1923 patent application of Zworykin predated the 1927 patent application filed by Farnsworth for electronic television. More on these patent battles later.

Prior to the mid-1920s, television employed spinning disks and mirrors in attempts to scan, transmit, and reassemble a moving image. Inventors such as Jenkins, Ives, Alexanderson, and Baird, among others, based their work on spiral-perforated spinning disks that were first proposed in the 1880s by the German scientist Paul Nipkow. These concepts did not involve electronic imaging, and today nothing is left of the technology developed by these inventors in the television systems used around the world.

Prior to Farnsworth's developments, other companies such as RCA had created wireless facsimile transmission systems by the end of the 1920s. However, the wireless transmission and reproduction of moving images proved more difficult for those inventors working on electromechanical television systems. Eventually, all-electronic television systems won out worldwide.

Zworykin enrolled as a graduate student at the University of Pittsburgh and received his PhD in 1926. While at Westinghouse, he conducted research on photoelectric vacuum tubes as well as television. Philo Farnsworth began college in Utah, but dropped out of school at the age of 18 when his father passed away and he was required to support his family. In 1925, when Farnsworth was 19 years old, he decided to move forward with his idea for electronic television. He described his idea to two California businessmen, Les Gorrell and George Everson. They agreed to a $6,000 investment, allowing Farnsworth to construct a prototype of his television concept. At that time, the two investors were putting up their life's savings. William W. Crocker, President of Crocker National Bank in San Francisco, and Roy Bishop, a respected San Francisco capitalist, also backed Farnsworth's efforts.

With this seed money, Farnsworth and his wife Pem moved to Los Angeles from Salt Lake City and set up a makeshift laboratory in the dining room of their small house in

Hollywood. The two investors were also there, winding magnetic coils, putting other components together, and going around town scrounging up materials to help Farnsworth continue his experiments. At that time, Farnsworth could not find existing optical or electrical components, and everything he needed had to be assembled from the beginning. After three months, Farnsworth was ready to test his first electronic television camera tube. With everything in place, Farnsworth pushed the button, and the entire contraption exploded. The power surge from the generator had blown up the total experiment, television tube and all.

After picking themselves up and dusting themselves off, Farnsworth and his investors obtained additional funding from bankers. Farnsworth promised to build a camera tube that would turn an image into a stream of electrons, and a television receiving tube that could convert the string of electrons back into a visual image, in one year. Realizing that he had substantial work to do to overcome his early failure, the circuitry of Farnsworth's devices became more and more complicated. He found it difficult to provide an image in the first prototypes of his camera tubes. Fortunately, each day the particulars of Farnsworth's progress were recorded in his notebooks. These were very important to him when the patent battles began.

At the same time, Zworykin's early efforts to produce electronic television were not received with favor by the Westinghouse research staff. When Zworykin performed his first demonstrations in the 1920s, several of the Westinghouse people who saw the demonstrations were not enthusiastic, and research on the mechanical system of television continued. The mechanical television program moved beyond the research stage in the late 1920s, when the first television drama, "The Queen's Messenger," was broadcast. It is reported that the actors in this performance had no need to fear recognition when they walked in the streets because the images that appeared on the receiving screen were fuzzy.

Also, at the BBC in England, inventor John Logie Baird was successfully using spinning disks in a television system. His devices were shown to the Royal Institution on January 27, 1926, showing two television images in light and shade for the first time. It was an image, although it was barely visible.

Receiving news of the mechanical television systems, Farnsworth's financial backers began to worry. This worry was relayed back to Farnsworth by urging him to progress more rapidly with his all-electronic television development.

On September 7, 1927, Farnsworth successfully demonstrated the principle of his electronic television invention in his San Francisco laboratory at 202 Green Street, where he had moved from Los Angeles. This was the first demonstration of the transmission of an electrical image without mechanical devices. Thus, it is said that Farnsworth replaced the spinning disks and mirrors of the mechanical televisions with the electron, a particle so small and light that it could be deflected back and forth in a vacuum tube tens of thousands of times per second. Farnsworth was the first to form and manipulate an electron beam, which is the quantum leap in knowledge that is used in all televisions and electronic monitors today.

At his demonstration on September 7, 1927, Farnsworth coated a square of glass brick with dark paint, and etched a line in the center of the coated glass. In another room, his brother-in-law, Cliff Gardner, placed the glass between the "Image Dissector," the camera tube that Farnsworth had developed previously that same year, and a very bright carbon arc lamp. Farnsworth, his wife, and one investor, George Everson, saw the straight line image on the receiver, and as Cliff Gardner rotated the image, the viewers saw the receiver image move. Thus, these three people were the first to see an all-electronic television picture. Later that evening, Farnsworth wrote in his laboratory journal: "The received line picture was evident at this time." However, the telegram that George Everson sent to another investor states it more succinctly: "The damned thing works!" The image was only the size of a postage stamp, but it brought Farnsworth a modicum of fleeting fame.

Farnsworth, who was only 22 years old in 1927, wanted to take his fragile prototype to the next step. However, this would require significant additional funding. Farnsworth was concerned that his investors were looking to sell the company, and Farnsworth with it, unless he produced something workable in a short period of time.

An article in the September 3, 1928 *San Francisco Chronicle,* second section, announced Farnsworth's work. It described his invention as follows:

> In any method of transmitting any moving images at a distance, some means must be evolved of breaking the image into pin-points of light. These points are translated into electrical impulses, the electrical impulses are collected at the receiving end and translated back into light, and the image results.

The article went on to state that the television systems then in use employed a revolving disk, two feet in diameter, to break up or "scan" the image. A similar disk was at the receiving end, and the two disks had to revolve at precisely the same instant and the same speed, or blurred vision resulted. Farnsworth's system was reported as using no moving parts. Instead, his system varied electric current that played over the image and thus obtained the necessary scanning.

Farnsworth also created a second major advance, that being cutting in half the waveband length necessary to prevent television broadcasts from interfering with each other. This was important since television requires approximately four times the waveband length than ordinary radio sound broadcasting. The article continued by stating that Farnsworth's system transmitted 20 pictures per second with 8,000 elements or pin-points of light to ensure detail in every picture. The laboratory model Farnsworth built transmitted the image on a screen 1¼ inch square. The article stated that perfection of Farnsworth's invention was now a matter of engineering.

Meanwhile, David Sarnoff had risen to the top of RCA, which was also part owner of Westinghouse Corporation. At that time, RCA controlled the entire spectrum of radio by owning the transmitters, studios, and the rights to build radios. Sarnoff appeared ready to adapt his vertical integration business techniques to television. Zworykin had demonstrated his invention of the iconoscope in 1923, which was the subject of the patent application he filed that same year. The quality of the iconoscope picture was rather poor, although it was an improvement over the mechanical scanning television devices of the day. Westinghouse withheld funding until Zworykin obtained an audience with David Sarnoff, which meeting took place in 1929. Sarnoff, who himself was a Russian immigrant, when told by Zworykin that it would cost $100,000 to design and build his television invention, approved the beginning of a development program. Ultimately, it turned out that the estimate of $100,000 was off only by an amount of $49,900,000.

Zworykin and other Westinghouse engineers were transferred to the RCA research plant at Camden, New Jersey, and Sarnoff also purchased the Jenkins Television Company in order to obtain their patents on mechanical television systems. Zworykin and Sarnoff realized that they were behind Farnsworth, who had already developed an electronic television camera. In 1929, Zworykin's prototype television could not produce images if the light was too low, and as soon as Sarnoff and Zworykin heard about

Farnsworth, they wanted to find out what he was doing, and also figure out how to avoid his patents.

Thus, in the spring of 1930, Zworykin contacted Farnsworth to schedule a meeting at Farnsworth's laboratory in San Francisco to investigate Farnsworth's progress. Farnsworth, it is reported, was pleased to demonstrate his camera to Zworykin, since Farnsworth had depleted his financial resources and was interested in having RCA finance his work. Zworykin visited Farnsworth's laboratory pretending to be a colleague interested in Farnsworth's work. Farnsworth, who was known to be generous with his knowledge and information, showed Zworykin how his image dissector worked. At the meeting, Zworykin looked around closely at all of Farnsworth's equipment, and is reported to have said, "That's a beautiful tube. I wish I had invented it." Then Zworykin advised Farnsworth that he did not think that there was any equipment that he saw that would be useful to RCA's development. However, Zworykin, after going to his hotel room that day, sent a telegram back to RCA describing in detail Farnsworth's image dissector tube.

It is reported that when Zworykin came back east, a prototype of Farnsworth's camera tube had already been built by RCA, and Zworykin set about to see if he could produce a television camera without infringing Farnsworth's patents. It has also been reported that Zworykin was still struggling for a viable solution when he visited Farnsworth's Lab in 1930. He then duplicated Farnsworth's equipment in the Westinghouse laboratory in Pittsburgh, and built his working iconoscope based upon Farnsworth's work. The iconoscope that Zworykin developed after returning to RCA has been characterized as being strikingly similar in function to Farnsworth's image dissector.

On August 26, 1930, Farnsworth's first patent, No. 1,773,980, was issued by the United States Patent Office. Sarnoff was aware of the importance of patents, but he also was firmly against the idea of RCA making royalty payments to anyone. He decided first to buy Farnsworth out by offering him $100,000 for his patents, services, and entire business. However, Farnsworth rejected the idea since he thought of himself as an inventor who should be compensated by receiving a royalty on sales of products embodying his invention.

History then records that upon Farnsworth's rejection of the offer, Sarnoff began a program to promote the idea that Zworykin demonstrated electronic television before Farnsworth, and to defeat Farnsworth by using the patent and legal systems. However, in 1931, Farnsworth obtained a licensee for his television technology, and signed a secret deal in Philadelphia with a company called Philco that was seeking to obtain a jump start in the television field. Part of the agreement between Farnsworth and Philco was that Farnsworth had to move his laboratories to Philadelphia, the home of Philco. In order to hide his plans from RCA, the entire Philco deal was arranged and carried out in secret. For example, when the Farnsworth employees arrived in Philadelphia they were compelled to eat in the executive dining room. They thought this was a wonderful idea, but they did not realize it was to prevent the employees from talking to anybody else about Farnsworth's deal with Philco.

However, when Philco began test transmissions of television, the signals were picked up by RCA in its nearby Camden, New Jersey plant. Actually, both RCA and Philco were tuning in to each others' experimental television broadcasts, and the pace to develop commercial television advanced exponentially. Sarnoff added financial resources to RCA's commitment to television, and in the early 1930s had a significant team of engineers and patent lawyers ready to go.

Farnsworth ultimately left Philco and set up his own research facility in Philadelphia.

More than a year later, in 1934, he made the first successful public demonstration of electronic television at the Franklin Institute in Philadelphia. The demonstration required a viewing screen approximately one foot in diameter, and substantial light since the cameras were not very sensitive at that time.

A year after his public demonstration, Farnsworth won his first patent victory against RCA. But Sarnoff told the newspapers that useful television was still years away, and he instructed his attorneys to appeal the patent decision. In the 1935 appeal decision based upon an April 24, 1934 hearing, the United States Patent Office in Patent Interference No. 64027, "Farnsworth v. Zworykin," decided that priority of invention of electronic television belonged to Farnsworth and not to Zworykin. An interference is a proceeding in the Patent Office to resolve conflicting claims of first inventorship of an invention, since the patent is awarded to the first inventor. This decision held that the then-pending patent application filed by Zworykin in 1923 did not disclose the concept of an "electrical image" that was specifically stated in the claims and the specification of the Farnsworth patent that had issued in 1930. In other words, the decision held that Zworykin's application did not contain sufficient information to meet the requirement that an "electrical image" could be formed, either demonstrably or inherently, in the structure disclosed in the Zworykin patent application.

Ultimately, the 1923-filed patent application of Zworykin issued (No. 2,141,059) after much modification, and over the objection of the U.S. Patent Office, and not until the Patent Office was overruled by a Court of Appeals. RCA then used the earlier application filing date of 1923 to advertise to the public that Zworykin had invented television before Farnsworth's first successful transmission on September 7, 1927. Sarnoff and RCA appealed the 1934 decision of the United States Patent Office awarding priority of invention to Farnsworth through the courts, but after seven years of litigation, Sarnoff was compelled to admit that he could not defeat the Farnsworth patents. In October 1939, for the first time in RCA's history, RCA began paying royalties to an outside inventor. As the anecdote goes, the RCA lawyer had tears in his eyes upon signing the document agreeing to pay Farnsworth the money for the cross-license agreement.

The question of whether Zworykin's originally disclosed invention in his 1923-filed patent application would work remains open. Some have stated that the idea was on the right track, but the disclosure in that application did not disclose the device that paved the way toward electronic television. For example, the Patent Office decision of 1935 in the interference between Zworykin and Farnsworth concluded that the Zworykin invention, which was given two different interpretations, did not produce an "electrical image" as was disclosed in the Farnsworth patent application. The Farnsworth application defined the term "electrical image" as follows:

> Light from all portions of the object who's image is to be transmitted is focused at one time upon a light-sensitive plate of a photoelectric cell to develop an electronic discharge from the plate. Each portion of the cross-section of the electronic discharge corresponds in electrical intensity with the intensity of light imposed on that portion of the sensitive plate from which the electrical discharge originated. Such discharge is termed an electrical image.

The Patent Office held that the electric pattern formed by the electron or current density in the electron beam of Farnsworth's device did not describe any form of an electrical pattern that corresponded to an optical image. Thus, the term "electrical image" had a restricted meaning set forth in Farnsworth's application, and the Zworykin device which used photosensitive material in the form of discrete globules, did not fall within the meaning of "electrical image" as set forth in the Farnsworth patent. Therefore, Zworykin could not copy the broad electrical image claim from the Farnsworth patent and insert it into his own patent application.

There is very little evidence that Zworykin ever constructed the system disclosed in the 1923 patent application. The patent interference record is totally void of evidence that the Zworykin 1923 device was successfully constructed and tested. The actual device itself, if it existed, was not introduced in evidence during the taking of testimony in the interference proceedings. Zworykin could not make the count of the interference because the image in his application was not scanned to produce the television signal. There is one reported story, however, about Zworykin's attempt to demonstrate his 1923 concept to executives of Westinghouse. The report indicates that the demonstration failed, and instead of providing him with further encouragement or funding, Zworykin's managers instructed him to find something "more useful" on which to spend his time.

In 1931 and 1932, Zworykin conducted tests that are disclosed in a December 1933 Institute of Radio Engineers (IRE) paper. This paper indicates that he was still using a mechanical scanning transmitter along with a cathode tube as a picture tube at that time.

Under the Farnsworth system, when an optical image is focused on a photoelectric surface, the light-sensitive chemicals admit an array of electrons—the "electrical image"—which is then scanned to form a fluctuating current. This is the essence of electronic television, and is the subject matter encompassed in claim 15 of Farnsworth's patent. In an attempt to initiate the patent interference, Zworykin attempted to copy Farnsworth's claim 15 into Zworykin's patent application, argue that his application supported that claim, and that he (Zworykin) was the first inventor. The Patent Office disagreed. RCA attempted to show that the 1923 Zworykin application disclosure would have created the same electrical image as disclosed by Farnsworth. The Patent Office ruled in the 1935 interference decision that "Zworykin has no right to make the count because it is not apparent that the device (of Zworykin) would operate to produce a scanned electrical image unless it has discrete globules capable of producing discrete space charges, and the Zworykin application as filed does not disclose such a device."

In the mid-1930s, Farnsworth had also met Englishman John Logie Baird, the inventor of a mechanical television system, with the objective of selling a license to Baird to save Farnsworth's company from bankruptcy because of the patent litigation with RCA. Baird was a Scottish scientist who had been working with cathode ray tubes. By 1926, Baird's machine could produce the discernable image of a face. Farnsworth demonstrated his electronic television system to Baird, and the following day Farnsworth and Baird entered into a contract. Upon his return home, in 1936, Farnsworth launched his own experimental television station in the suburbs of Philadelphia, W3XPF.

However, in the middle and late 1930s, the public was not buying television sets because each manufacturing company was producing incompatible television sets. Thus, each brand of television was only able to receive images from its own broadcast station. This led to the introduction of federal broadcast standards that eliminated the problem. These standards, however, were not instituted until after World War II. Farnsworth also purchased a company to start manufacturing television sets, but until his patent dispute with RCA was resolved, he put everything on hold.

This series of events put substantial stress on Farnsworth in the late 1930s, and he was not getting the sleep he needed. He left Philadelphia, and he and his wife bought a home in Maine and left his managers in charge of his television company in Philadelphia. While in Maine, he was hospitalized several times, reportedly because of alcohol-related problems. While Farnsworth was attempting to recover in Maine, David Sarnoff unveiled RCA's television to America at the New York World's Fair in 1939. At that time, Farnsworth's first public demonstration in Philadelphia in 1934 was practically forgotten by the public. Also, when RCA was asked about the invention of television, the spokesperson dwelled upon the work of Sarnoff and Zworykin, but never mentioned Farnsworth.

In 1939, Farnsworth was in an envious position to become very wealthy because of his patent license with RCA. However, fate extended its fickle hand. In 1941, the United States entered the Second World War and created a four-year blackout for commercial television. Television technology was required for defense needs, and although Farnsworth's company contributed to the war effort, the fact that his principal patents would expire in 1947 destroyed any hopes he might have had of making money from royalties on his television invention.

By the war's end, Farnsworth's key patents were close to expiring, RCA quickly increased the production and sales of television sets, and a vigorous public relations campaign promoted both Zworykin and Sarnoff as the fathers of television, while Farnsworth withdrew to his house in Maine. Embodying the concept that no good deed goes unpunished, Farnsworth's Maine house burned to the ground in 1947.

For the remainder of his life, Farnsworth devoted his time to studying nuclear fusion, which to this day has not been brought to practical fruition.

Much credit for refining all the aspects of early television correctly goes to the engineers of RCA. Many, many research engineers and scientists contributed to the further development of electronic television prior to television broadcasting becoming available to the general public in the late 1940s and early 1950s. However, the role of Philo Farnsworth in creating television is now coming to the surface, and he is beginning to receive the recognition he deserves. Statues in his honor have been erected in the Capitol buildings in Utah and in Washington, D.C., and in September, 1983, the U.S. Postal Service issued a stamp in commemoration of Farnsworth's achievements. Farnsworth held the basic television patents covering scanning, focusing, synchronizing contrasts, controls, and power. Farnsworth died on March 11, 1971, but his work lives on as a realization of the spirit and ingenuity of the single inventor.

Why is this story important? Because a large company attempted to convince the public that scientific progress and advancement of the useful arts was the result of the work of corporate institutions, not individuals with the spark of ingenuity. This train of thought would lead each citizen of the general population to place their faith in these corporate institutions, rather than in individual inventors, or even themselves. Invention and creativity are the unique and compelling aspects of the human experience. As stated by Szent-Gyorgi, "Discovery is seeing what everybody has seen, and thinking what nobody else has thought." Farnsworth, rather than one who could see what others were doing and improve upon it, was a true visionary who could see the obvious and think up something entirely different. If the stories of these types of inventors were suppressed, we the public would not be able to understand this important factor of the human character. It is important for all of us to know that a medium such as television was the consequence of individual inventorship and ideas, rather than corporate engineering. Farnsworth saw how the 19th century visionaries were attempting to send pictures through the air with spinning disks and mirrors. However, he alone had the concept of replacing all the moving parts with invisible electrons, and he kept working until that concept was realized.

In the development of both mechanical and electrical television, the independent inventors are represented by John Logie Baird, Paul Nipkow, C. Francis Jenkins, and Philo Farnsworth, who were compelled to bring their discoveries forward against the power of large corporations. The large corporations are represented by Vladimir Zworykin, David Sarnoff, and Earnst Alexanderson. For more on this, see *Tube: The Invention of Television,* by David E. Fisher and Marshall John Fisher, Washington, DC: Counterpoint, 1996, xvii at 427.

Aug. 26, 1930.   P. T. FARNSWORTH   1,773,980

TELEVISION SYSTEM

Filed Jan. 7, 1927   4 Sheets—Sheet 1

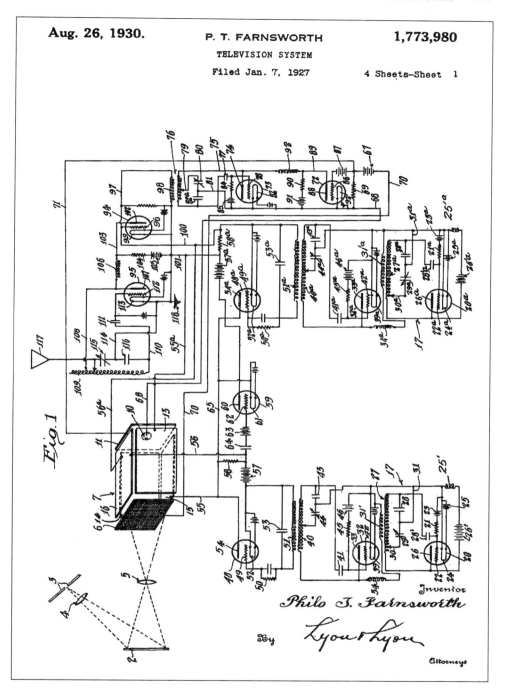

Fig.1

Inventor

Philo T. Farnsworth

By Lyon+Lyon

Attorneys

Aug. 26, 1930.   P. T. FARNSWORTH   1,773,981

TELEVISION RECEIVING SYSTEM

Original Filed Jan. 7, 1927

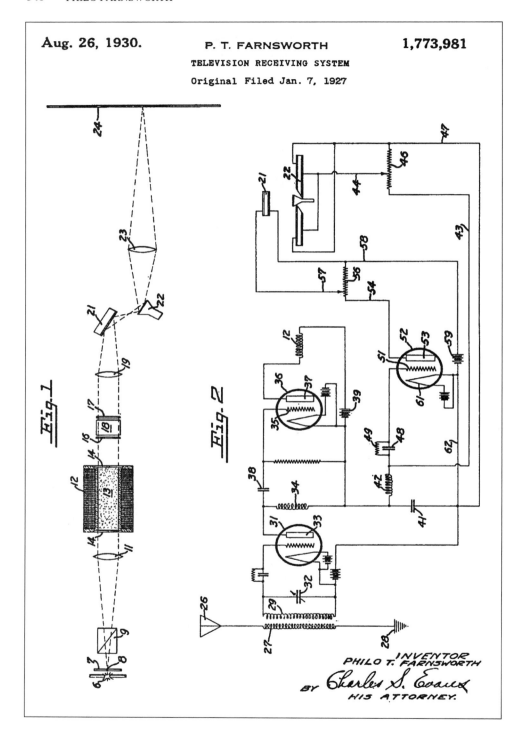

Fig. 1

Fig. 2

INVENTOR

PHILO T. FARNSWORTH

BY Charles S. Evans

HIS ATTORNEY.

Dec. 20, 1938.

V. K. ZWORYKIN

2,141,059

TELEVISION SYSTEM

Filed Dec. 29, 1923

3 Sheets—Sheet 1

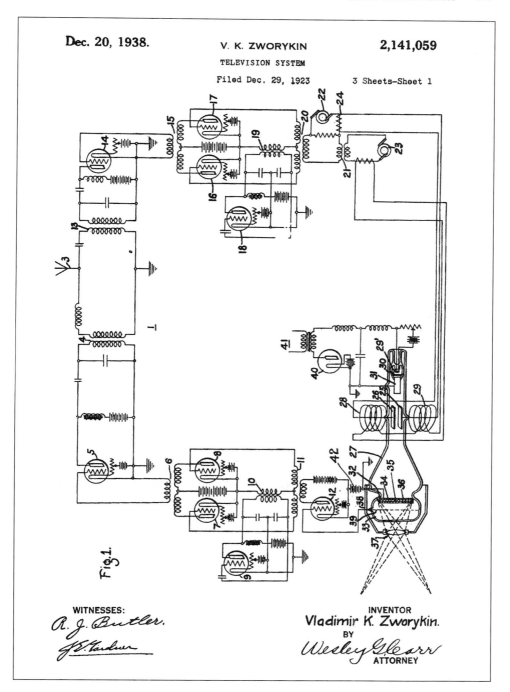

Fig.1.

WITNESSES:

R. J. Butler.

JE Gardner

INVENTOR

Vladimir K. Zworykin.

BY

Wesley G Carr

ATTORNEY

20 Employment Contracts and Non-Compete Restrictions

20.1 EMPLOYMENT CONTRACT PROVISIONS RELATING TO INTELLECTUAL PROPERTY

As a technology professional, your initial contact with intellectual property development and protection may occur while pursuing undergraduate or graduate studies, and most assuredly will be evident when entering the engineering or scientific communities at the end of your studies. In school, one may be working under a foundation, industry or government grant, and after graduation will normally be working for an established organization, such as a corporation or other entity, engaged in research and development leading to new technology. In any of these situations, a common thread exists. You are being engaged by someone who is relying on your knowledge, skills and training to develop new technologies for exploitation and profit. You will be compensated for creative thinking, developing novel ideas, and the incorporation of those intangible ideas into tangible products, processes or services for the benefit of your employer, or your own enterprise.

As discussed in the chapters devoted to Patents and Copyrights, the initial owner of patentable inventions and/or copyrightable works of authorship is you, the inventor or creator. See Chapters 8 and 22. However, since an employer is compensating you for use of your technical skills, the employer normally demands assurances that:

a. Any new technology or works of authorship that you develop during your employment, that relate to the business of your employer, becomes the property of the employer;

b. Any confidential or trade secret information you develop or are made privy to during your employment will be maintained in confidence; and

c. You are restricted from working for a competitor, under reasonable terms and conditions, for a period of time following your employment.

Each of these circumstances is discussed below in more detail. Keep in mind, however, that as an engineer or scientist entering a new employment opportunity, you may be faced with considering and being asked to agree to clauses in an employment contract that you may want to review and possibly amend before signing on. For example, before signing the agreement to produce this book, I suggested changes in the agreement regarding the relationship between this copyrightable work and a previous text I authored for purposes of a law school textbook. The point is that you should carefully review the papers you are signing, and ensure yourself that you haven't given away rights to technology developments you may have made in the past.

On the flip side, you may be an employer or the managing director of a technology driven enterprise that relies on the creative juices of your engineers and scientists to keep

Intellectual Property Law for Engineers and Scientists, by Howard B. Rockman
ISBN 0-471-44998-9 © 2004 The Institute of Electrical and Electronics Engineers

your products and services on the leading edge of technology. Therefore, it is important that all of your employees and consultants have agreed from their first day of engagement to transfer ownership of any business-related invention or creative work of authorship to your company, that your company's trade secrets will not be divulged to a competitor, and that your employees cannot be easily enticed away to work for a competitor. The following sections are directed to you in either the position of employee or employer.

20.2   OWNERSHIP OF INTELLECTUAL PROPERTY

20.2.1   Inventions

A typical clause in an employment invention rights contract states that in consideration for your present and future employment by the employer, and use of the employer's time, materials, facilities, equipment and funds, including your compensation, (1) any inventions or improvements conceived or developed by the employee during the term of their employment, and possibly for one year thereafter, (2) which pertain to the business of the employer, or to related fields, shall be the property of the employer. The primary consideration is that the employee is being paid to invent, and such inventions belong to the employer. Employment agreements normally include provisions that the employee will sign all formal papers required to assign all rights to intellectual property to the employer. The agreement may also provide that the employee will have opportunities to share in any royalties or other remuneration when the intellectual property developed by the employee is marketed and/or licensed by the employer.

Another typical provision in an employment agreement requires that the employee is under an obligation to disclose to the employer all tangible results of the research that the employee develops, which results relate to the business of the employer, that are conceived, reduced to practice, invented or otherwise created, either solely or jointly with others, during the course of employment. This provision ensures that the employer has knowledge of and access to any development made by an employee, and the employer is able to decide which technology should be protected. This provides the entire engineering management team with the opportunity to evaluate all projects for their potential importance. The employee also normally agrees to execute all documents necessary to assist the employer, both during and after the term of employment, to enable the employer to obtain and enforce any patent application filed and any issued patent covering the intellectual property rights developed by the employee.

The inventor is also normally obligated to maintain records of all research and development work performed during employment, and to document and date such records in an accessible format, such as in lab notebooks, that can be readily evaluated by the employer. The employee is also normally required to turn over such records to the employer when leaving employment. This latter provision is equally applicable to confidential and trade secret documents and materials in the possession of a departing employee.

If the inventor owns patents of his or her own, or is a named inventor in patents from a previous employer, it is highly recommended that these facts be brought to the attention of the new employer, so that notations can be made in the employment contract indicating that the obligation to assign invention rights does not extend to previous inventions, pending patent applications, or patents.

Note that the above typical provisions pertain to your inventions, which relate to the business of the employer. This is an important factor, and an employee should ensure himself or herself that such language does appear in the agreement. I have seen agreements that state that any invention developed by an inventor during the course of employment, whether or not the invention relates to the business of the employer, may become the property of the employer. Only those inventions that relate to the business of the employer should be covered by the agreement. This will enable you to tinker in your kitchen or garage at night and develop a totally unrelated invention that may be worthy of patent protection for your own benefit.

I have also experienced situations where although the inventor developed a new technology that was related to the business of the employer, the employer was not particularly interested in that technology when presented to the employer for evaluation, and the employer granted a waiver to the employee to patent and exploit the particular invention on his own. Thus, keep in mind that even though you have signed an agreement which provides that all inventions you develop during the course of your employment that relate to the business of the employer become the property of the employer, the employer may, if you ask, grant a waiver of that provision, and allow you to exploit your invention on your own.

To further protect the intellectual property of the employer, a provision may be included in the employment agreement prohibiting the employee from publishing information about any invention or new technology without the written approval of the employer. For example, if an employee attends a technical conference, and publishes material regarding work the employee is presently conducting relating to product development, such publication may end up being a bar to future patentability. Employees are also normally obligated to devote his or her best efforts to promote the business and professional interests of the company while employed by the company.

20.2.2 Copyrightable Works of Creative Authorship

In addition to compelling the employee to assign all rights to inventions and improvements to the employer, a typical employment agreement usually contains similar provisions relating to works of authorship and copyrightable subject matter created by the employee during the term of employment. Again, ownership of any such works of authorship and copyrightable subject matter, in the typical employment agreement, are assigned over to the employer, so long as the subject matter pertains to the business of the employer, or related fields. This clause is particularly important regarding the development of software, and also relates to technical drawings, illustrations and computer assisted drawings that are developed during the conception and reduction to practice of a computer-related invention by an engineer or scientist.

Normally, all of the above provisions relating to inventions apply to works of authorship and copyrightable subject matter in a typical employment agreement. However, there is one additional clause relating to copyrightable material that should be inserted into the agreement. This clause will state that any work developed by the employee engineer or scientist shall be considered a "work for hire" pursuant to the agreement, it being recognized between the parties that the work is intended to be owned by and used by the employer during the performance of the employee's duties on behalf of the employer.

Further provisions may indicate that notwithstanding the declaration that the copyrightable work will be a work for hire, in the event that there is any finding by any tribunal or court that the work is not a work for hire, the author agrees to assign to the employer all copyrights in the work worldwide. As you will discover in Chapter 22 of this book, the term "work for hire" has a particular meaning in the copyright law, and these clauses are usually included in employment contracts to cover the situation where a dispute may arise as to whether or not the work was a "work for hire" within the meaning of the copyright statute. As a general rule, any work of authorship or other copyrightable subject material created by an employee who is being compensated for such work by his or her employer will automatically be a work for hire, and that work is owned by the employer. See Chapter 22, Section 22.9.

20.3 CONFIDENTIALITY AGREEMENTS AND PROVISIONS

During the course of your employment, you will develop and will be provided with information and know-how which has increased value to your employer by the mere fact that this information is not known by others, particularly competitors. This information and know-how are considered as "trade secrets" which are the property of your employer, and which your employment agreement normally includes provisions to protect. Such trade secrets are also normally referred to as "confidential information" or "proprietary information," and the three terms are used interchangeably. Sometimes there is a thin line between trade secret or confidential information, and the normal skills and knowledge that are known to an engineer or scientist that are learned during employment. If an issue ever rises as to whether trade secrets or confidential information have been misappropriated, the lawyers will assist you in trying to draw this ephemeral line.

Note also that provisions maintaining the confidentiality of trade secret and proprietary information normally extend beyond the term of employment. Therefore, once you are informed that information is confidential, it would be prudent to make notations of what general categories of information are considered confidential by your present employer, so that upon entering a new employment position, you know not to disclose the details of these general areas of technology to your new employer. Also, you will know not to use such confidential information yourself.

In addition to confidential information developed by you as an employee, you will be made familiar with additional trade secret information that has been developed by others during the course of their employment with your employer. The prudent employer will clearly identify such material as confidential, and will make such information available to its employees only on a need to know basis. Therefore, you will know what is confidential and what is not, according to the company's policies.

Typical non-disclosure agreements, or non-disclosure clauses of an employment agreement, provide that the employee agrees to keep confidential all trade secrets and proprietary information relating to the employer's business which are developed or received by the employee during the course of employment. In addition, the employee also agrees not to use, publish or disclose confidential information to anyone outside the company without the written approval of the company. Such proprietary information could include, but is not limited to, technology under development, design practices and procedures, engineering practices and procedures, marketing and business plans, programs, data, formulas, customer and vendor lists, compilations of information, business information such as profit, cost and other financial data, and any other information that the company deems and identifies as confidential. The employee normally will also agree not to take any confidential materials upon the termination of employment, and will return all such materials to the employer.

There are normally exclusions in the confidentiality agreement or clauses stating that no information may be considered confidential if: (1) the information is in the public domain through no fault of the employee, (2) the information becomes public knowledge during the term of the agreement, (3) the information is not part of the employee's obligation of confidentiality, (4) the information was previously obtained from a third party under lawful circumstances allowing the disclosure and use of such information, or (5) the information was developed by someone else without reference to and totally independent of the employer. The agreement may also provide that confidential information may be disclosed if ordered by a court of law, such as in a patent infringement or breach of confidentiality lawsuit. Such disclosures can be made under a "Protective Order," which maintains the confidentiality of the information during the court proceedings, and after the proceedings end.

Particular care should be taken in working with vendors who are furnishing the employee with information about parts, services or processes that can be purchased from the vendor. It is important to realize that any confidential information furnished to the vendor during your course of discussions should be covered by a signed confidentiality agreement, where the vendor agrees in writing not to disclose the confidential information to others, and not to use the confidential information for the vendor's own benefit. Also, if you are disclosing a prototype of a new product to a customer or a vendor, marking that particular prototype with the notation "Confidential" or similar language prevents a "public disclosure" bar from arising, as discussed previously in the Patent chapter of this text, as well as identifying the prototype as a "trade secret."

Well-prepared confidentiality agreements should provide that information to be protected will be marked as "Confidential," to distinguish such information from that which is not confidential. Also, typical agreements usually indicate that the confidentiality provision applies to both written and oral disclosures of information, and requires that all oral disclosures of confidential information be followed up in writing, to make such oral transmission tangibly available. It is also prudent to provide that the confidentiality provisions remain in force for a reasonable period beyond termination of employment. It is also recommended that confidentiality agreements clearly advise an employee not to disclose to the employer any proprietary information belonging to any prior employer, or any third party, including trade secrets or confidential information related to the business of the prior employer or third party. The confidentiality agreement should also generally compel the employee not to disclose any ideas, writings, or intellectual property to the new employer, which was owned by the employee and/or a former employer, and were developed while the employee was previously employed. The employment agreement may provide that any invention conceived prior to employment with the new employer is the property of the new employer, even where a patent application has previously been filed, but the invention was reduced to practice during the new employment. Careful consideration has to be given to these situations to avoid possible conflict and avoidable litigation.

It is important that a new employee be obligated to disclose to the new employer any previous contracts, such as confidentiality or trade secret agreements, that the employee entered into with prior employers, and also disclose the general nature of the work they were performing for such prior employers. This will prevent the employer from placing the employee in a position where the employee may be prone to violate trade secret provisions contained in contracts with prior employees.

20.4   OUTSIDE INFORMATION RECEIVED BY THE EMPLOYEE OR EMPLOYER

In the normal course of conducting one's business, unsolicited ideas from outsiders may be received by the business for consideration. My recommendation is for such business enterprises to initiate a policy that no unsolicited ideas will be considered or reviewed, unless the submitter signs a written agreement that the submitter will never bring an action against the company for misappropriating the submitted idea, and will only enforce any rights the submitter may have under the appropriate patent or copyright laws. The submitter will also agree that they are not submitting the information in confidence, but reserve their rights only under the patent and copyright laws.

The reason behind this recommendation is that a majority of unsolicited ideas received by a company are reviewed, rejected and returned to the submitter with an indication that the company is not interested in that particular idea at that time. Assume, however, that subsequently an employee of the company independently comes up with the same idea, totally on his/her own, having forgotten about or never being made aware of the earlier submittal. The company at that later time gains interest in the idea and proceeds to produce a product embodying that idea. In my hypothetical scenario, the previous submitter of the unsolicited idea then files a lawsuit accusing the company of stealing the submitter's trade secrets. At this later point in time, without adequate records, it would be difficult for the company to prove that its employees did not use the ideas that were submitted years previously.

Therefore, to insulate a company from a possible legal action by the submitter, the unsolicited idea is initially taken by the company only on a nonconfidential basis, which eliminates a theft of trade secret lawsuit from being filed several years later. However, the submitter is also allowed to protect the idea under the patent or copyright laws, and pursue an action against the company if such laws are violated in the future. It also has been my experience that if the developer of an unsolicited idea has patent or copyright protection, that makes the idea more sellable to the company, since not only is the idea being offered, but the intellectual property protection on the idea also forms part of the proposal.

When an unsolicited idea is properly submitted, before review of the idea is embarked upon by the recipient company, a due diligence should be conducted inside the company to determine whether similar development work is already in progress within your own R&D or other departments. If your R&D department is working on the same or a similar idea, it may be desirable to return the unsolicited submittal without a technical review to avoid even the appearance of adoption of the unsolicited idea.

Also, while working with vendors, ensure that no confidential material is given to the vendor without protecting the secrecy of the information. It is prudent to have a broad confidentiality agreement in place with all of your regular vendors to prevent them from divulging any confidential information within the vendor's organization, or to other customers of the vendor. It is also prudent to add to the confidentiality contracts with vendors, that any work of authorship that they develop during the course of your mutual dealings is a "work for hire," and therefore any copyrights belong to your company.

In addition to confidentiality agreements which obligate one party not to disclose confidential information to another, there are many forms of mutual disclosure agreements and provisions which allow two companies or entities to exchange confidential technology or other information, without being in a position later of defending an accusation of theft of trade secrets. Such mutual confidentiality agreements normally contain the same provisions as above, but are equally applicable to both parties.

As previously noted, the provisions signed by an employee regarding maintaining the confidentiality of trade secret and confidential material that comes into the employee's purview during employment may extend beyond the term of employment. Therefore, when the engineer or scientist enters into a new employment relationship, it is important to disclose to the new employer that you have signed confidentiality agreements with your previous employer, and define in broad and general terms the field of technology that you were engaged in at your prior position. This is important in allowing the new employer to place you in a position in the company where you will not be tempted to disclose or use trade secret information learned from a prior employer. Of course, you are free to use the skills you learned at your prior position.

20.5   NON-COMPETE PROVISIONS

A brief comment is in order regarding typical non-compete clauses in employment contracts. My first suggestion is that before signing any non-compete clause, any engineer or scientist should first obtain advice, possibly from a qualified employment law specialist, to determine what the state laws are regarding the scope and enforceability of non-compete clauses in the jurisdiction where the employment agreement is effective. Non-compete provisions usually require the employee to agree that for a certain period of time following the termination of his or her employment, the employee will not seek or enter into employment with a competitor of the business of the employer. However, since the legal system looks harshly at provisions that would deprive a skilled professional of the ability to earn a living, non-compete restrictive clauses must be reasonable in time, scope and geographical extent before they are deemed enforceable. For example, certain states limit the effectiveness of non-compete clauses to a term of just one year. Thus, if a non-compete clause in your employment contract states that you cannot be employed by a competitor for three years following termination, if the applicable state law indicates that three years is unreasonable, either that provision will be held invalid altogether, or a court may interpret that provision as just being applicable for one year, and no more.

Also, non-compete provisions may prevent you from being employed by a competitor in the same line of business as your current employer, and within a certain geographical area. Again, the individual state laws must be reviewed to determine what the applicability of these provisions are and the extent to which they are enforceable. Also note that if a new employee is placed in a position where it is inevitable that he or she will disclose or use trade secrets of a former employer, a court may enjoin that employee from working in that new position.

20.6   ENFORCEABILITY OF A NON-COMPETE AGREEMENT

Generally speaking, the legitimacy of a non-compete or restrictive covenant in the various jurisdictions depends upon (1) whether the terms of the agreement are reasonable and necessary as to time, territory and activities, and (2) are the restrictions necessary to protect a legitimate business interest of the employer. What is "reasonable" necessarily turns on the facts and circumstances of each case. Most courts in the U.S. will generally enforce one and two year restrictive employment agreements. Some courts, in my experience, have held that three years was reasonable under the circumstances, but I suggest that restrictive agreements beyond three years have a poor chance of being upheld. Courts are generally against enforcing restrictive employment agreements that are overly broad in geographic scope, however, as with time restrictions, each situation is decided on its own facts. Courts generally look to see if the geographic area of exclusion is co-extensive with the territory in which the employer is conducting its business. For example, where the employer was doing business nationwide, a restrictive covenant having no geographical limitation was upheld.

Restrictions against a former employee which are merely an attempt by the employer to prevent competition are per se unenforceable. For example, a restriction that prohibited the employee from contacting any potential customers of the employer was stricken as being unenforceable. Likewise unenforceable was a restrictive covenant that forbade the employee from associating with any company that engaged in the same type of activity as the employer. However, a court is likely to uphold a restrictive employment agreement that is reasonable as to time and territory, where the employer provided valuable training to its employees and/or substantial time and resources in cultivating its clients. Also, a restrictive covenant was found to be valid where the purpose of the restriction was to protect the employer from losing customers to a former employee who, by virtue of his employment for the employer, gained special knowledge and familiarity with the customer's product lines and requirements.

The Illinois courts, for example, have recognized two situations in which an employer has a legitimate business interest to justify enforcement of a covenant not to compete: (1) where the customer relationships are near-permanent and but for the employee's association with the employer, the employee would not have had contact with the customers; and (2) where the former employee acquired trade secrets or other confidential or proprietary information through his employment and subsequently tried to use such information for his or her own benefit, or divulged such information to third parties.

Several factors are considered in determining whether the relationship between an employer and its customer is "near permanent" for purposes of analyzing the reasonableness of a restrictive employment agreement. These factors include:

a. The time, cost and difficulty in developing and maintaining the customer relationship;

b. The intention of the employer and customer to remain affiliated for a long period of time; and

c. The continuity and duration of the relationship.

The nature of the business itself is also considered. Professional relationships such as doctors, veterinarians, and the like are mostly treated as near permanent relationships. Courts will also look at the source of the customer relationship, for example, was the customer a company or institutional customer, or was the customer developed by the employee? It is clear from a review of the court decisions on the enforceability of restrictive employment contracts that businesses that do not create customer loyalty with a unique product or specialized personal service, or where businesses are one of several suppliers to a customer for a given product or service, that customer-business relationship is unlikely to meet the "near-permanency" test.

Courts are more likely to find information a "trade secret" or "confidential" if the information has been developed by the employer over a given span of time, at considerable expense, maintained under tight security, and is not generally known to the public. In situations involving former employees charged with usurping the trade secrets of their former employer, information that is readily available to all employees or others in the trade, or can be found in phone books or trade directories, or where customers can be identified by others outside of the company, will not be found to be confidential.

For a restrictive covenant to be reasonable, it must not be greater than necessary to protect the employer, must not be oppressive to the employee, and must not be injurious to the general public. For example, generally speaking, a contractual obligation in an employment agreement to maintain the secrecy of proprietary information will not be considered to be void or unenforceable solely for lack of geographical limitation.

Where the services to be performed under an employment contract are unique and special, such as those of an entertainer, athlete or the like, you usually find terms that express that the personal services are irreplaceable, and such contracts may be enforced to compel the employee to perform.

If a non-compete clause does not set forth territorial and time limit restrictions, a court, when asked to enforce an agreement, may insert such provisions. Also, it is generally deemed unreasonable to expect the parties to intend that a non-compete restriction goes on forever, or that the non-compete provision would cover geographical territories in which the employer does not do business. Certain courts have indicated that the absence of limitations as to time and geographic scope in a non-compete agreement will result in invalidation of the provision. In other cases, covenants containing no geographic limitation have been upheld as reasonable when the purpose of the restriction was to protect the employer from losing customers to a former employee who, by virtue of his employment, gained special knowledge and familiarity with the customer's requirements. In this case, the employee was only restrained from contacting former customers, and a geographic limitation would not serve any purpose.

Courts are hesitant to enforce non-competition agreements that prohibit employees from soliciting customers they never solicited or had contact with while employed. The courts usually uphold only those non-competition agreements that protect the employer's legitimate proprietary interests, and not those agreements whose effect is to prevent competition per se. Thus, an activity restraint, such as a covenant not to solicit other customers which lacks both a geographic limitation and any qualifying language concerning the particular customers to which it applies, generally will be struck down as unreasonable.

As an example of the wide range of state laws regarding restrictive covenants, note that with certain limited exceptions, California presently renders non-competition clauses void, while Maryland law permits them so long as they are reasonable in scope and duration. The California law invalidates employment contracts that prohibit an employee from working for a competitor when the employment has terminated, unless necessary to protect the employer's trade secrets.

Under Illinois law, for example, it is generally recognized that upon the termination of employment, an employee may not take with him or her confidential, particularized plans or processes developed by his or her employer and disclosed to him or her during the employer/employee relationship. This applies to trade secrets which are unknown to others in the industry and which give the employer an advantage over its competitors. On the other hand, an employee is free to take with him or her general skills and knowledge acquired during employment with the former employer. The courts have emphasized that the right of an individual to follow and pursue the particular occupation for which he or she is best trained is a most fundamental right of our extremely mobile and competition-based free economy. One who has worked in a particular field cannot be compelled to erase from his or her mind all of the general skills, knowledge and expertise acquired through experience while employed. These skills are valuable to the employee in the marketplace for his or her services. Restraints cannot be lightly placed upon the right of the employee to compete in the area of his or her greatest worth. In the case of *Colson Co. v. Wittell,* 210 Ill.App. 1030, 1039, 569 N.E.2d 1082, 1087; app'l denied, 141 Ill. 2d. 537, 580 N.E.2d 110 (1991), the court said:

> ". . . any other rule would force a departing employee to perform a prefrontal lobotomy on himself or herself. It would disserve the free market goal of maximizing available resources to foster competition . . . it would not strike a proper balance between the purposes of trade secret law and the strong policy in favor of fair and vigorous business competition."

20.7   INEVITABLE DISCLOSURE

If you embark upon a new employment that will "inevitably" lead you to rely on a former employer's trade secrets, you may be stopped by your former employer from taking that position. In such cases, the former employer has the burden of proving that in your new employment, you could not perform your duties or meet your responsibilities without using the former employer's trade secrets.

20.8   FORM AGREEMENTS

At the end of this chapter are a sample employee intellectual property agreement and sample mutual and individual confidentiality agreements. However, the inclusion of these sample agreements in this text does not indicate that these forms of agreement should be used without the consultation and advice of a qualified employment and/or intellectual property attorney. There are no two employment situations that are alike, and each agreement should be tailored to meet the specific needs of both the employer and the employee for their mutual benefit. Thus, these are merely suggestions, and not the end point of any agreement that may be applicable to your situation.

Certain employers may have a written intellectual property, confidentiality and non-compete policy statement that the employee must read, and which terms are incorporated by reference into the terms of the employment agreement.

20.9   CONSULTANTS

When dealing with consultants, it is extremely important that the consultant contract include a provision compelling the consultant to assign all inventions and other intellectual property developed in the course of:

1. Performance under the consultant's contract; and/or
2. Performance under a sponsored research project of the employer,

to the employer, in consideration for the consultant's compensation. All such agreements should be in writing, and cover contributions to patentable inventions, trade secret generation, and copyrightable subject matter created by the consultant relating to work performed pursuant to the consulting agreement.

If a proper consulting agreement is not in place, there is no way to obtain an assignment of patent rights to you from the consultant in a situation where the consultant is one of, or the sole, contributor to the intellectual property development. As a result, the consultant may be the legitimate owner, or part owner of rights to the technology you employed the consultant to assist with you. Take my word for it—this has caused problems for some of my clients several times over the course of my practice, but only where these clients have consulted with me after they made an oral or improper written agreement with the consultant.

SAMPLE EMPLOYEE INTELLECTUAL PROPERTY AGREEMENT

I, the below named EMPLOYEE, in consideration of my employment by [Employer], an _____ corporation, or if such employment has already commenced, in consideration of my continued employment with [Employer], which I acknowledge would be terminated but for my execution of this Agreement and my willingness to be bound by the terms of this Agreement, and in further consideration of subsequent salaries and wages which are to be paid to me, agree as follows:

1.   All inventions, improvements, works of authorship, and copyrightable subject matter authored, conceived or developed by me during the term of my employment by [Employer], and for one year thereafter, which pertain to the business of [Employer], or to related fields, shall be disclosed promptly by me to [Employer], and shall be assigned by me to [Employer]. I agree to execute, upon request, such formal papers as may be required to assign and transfer my entire right, title and interest in and to such inventions, improvements and copyrights, including applications for and/or letters patent of the United States and all other countries, and copyrights to [Employer], and at its expense, to do all things necessary to perfect [Employer's] ownership therein, except those inventions, improvements, works of authorship, and copyrightable subject matter which [Employer] has agreed in writing are to be owned by me.

2.   To keep secret and confidential any confidential or proprietary information or any other information relating to [Employer's] business, not generally known to the trade or to the public, received by me from [Employer], or developed by me on [Employer's] behalf, and I agree that no such information shall be published or disclosed to others without the written authority of [Employer]. Such information shall include, but not be limited to, design practices and procedures, engineering practices and procedures, marketing plans and programs, trade secrets, data, formulas, compilations of information, business and financial information, customer lists and any other information of [Employer], or its customers or vendors, whether or not authored, invented, developed or discovered by me during the course of my employment with [Employer]. I further agree not to disclose to [Employer] any information which is confidential or proprietary to others.
  These obligations shall apply to any information which is considered confidential or to otherwise be trade secrets of either [Employer] or its customers or vendors.

3.   To devote my best efforts to the interests of [Employer].

4.   Upon termination of my employment by [Employer], for any reason, I will promptly deliver to [Employer] all files, sketches, drawings, blueprints, manuals, letters, notebooks, reports and all other materials which relate to [Employer] or its customer's or vendor's businesses that are in my possession or control.

5.   I represent and warrant that there are no agreements between myself and others that would in any way impede my full performance under this Agreement and I agree not to enter into any agreement which would conflict with this Agreement. I further represent and warrant that I am not now actively pursuing, prosecuting, developing or licensing any intellectual property owned by me or a business owned or controlled by me. [Note: If this is not true, discuss with your employer.]

6.   If I am transferred to, or perform work for any successor, division, subsidiary or affiliated concern of [Employer], this Agreement shall remain in force and effect and shall define my relationship to [Employer] and its successor, division, subsidiary or affiliated concern.

7.   [Employer's] remedy in the form of monetary damages for any breach by me of any provision of this Agreement is likely to be inadequate to adequately compensate [Employer] for such breach, and, in addition to any such remedy for breach, [Employer] shall be entitled to institute and maintain any appropriate proceeding or proceedings, including suit for specific performance and/or injunction against me and any company which employs me in violation of the terms of this Agreement.

8.   This Agreement shall be binding upon my heirs, executors, administrators, legal representatives, nominees and assigns and shall inure to the benefit of the successors of [Employer]. Should any part of this Agreement be held to be void or voidable or unenforceable in whole or in part by any court, the remainder of this Agreement shall remain in full force and effect. This Agreement shall be deemed to be made in the State of _____, and all of its provisions shall be governed by the laws of the State of _____ and enforceable in the courts of _____.

EMPLOYER   EMPLOYEE

Date: Date:
Name: _____   Name: _____
Title: _____

SAMPLE MUTUAL CONFIDENTIALITY AND NONDISCLOSURE AGREEMENT

This Agreement is made this ____ day of _____ by and between ABC Co. and XYZ Co.

WHEREAS, the undersigned parties recognize that each others business involves specialized and proprietary knowledge, information, methods, processes, techniques and skills peculiar to their security and growth;

WHEREAS, the parties acknowledge that any disclosure of such knowledge, information, methods, processes, techniques and skills or other confidential or proprietary information would substantially injure the parties' businesses, impair the parties' investments and goodwill and jeopardize the parties' relationship with the parties' clients and customers,

WHEREAS, the parties presently desire to mutually discuss and pursue certain potential business opportunities;

WHEREAS, in the course of such mutual discussions and pursuit of such business opportunities, the parties anticipate disclosing to each other certain information of a novel, proprietary or confidential nature and desire that such information be subject to all of the terms and conditions set forth below.

NOW THEREFORE, in consideration of the obligations herein contained and for other good and valuable consideration, the receipt and sufficiency of which is acknowledged, the parties agree as follows:

1. Definition. Confidential, proprietary or novel information ("Information") shall mean and include, but not be limited to, any written Information in the form of financial and statistical data, sales data, client information, trade secrets, inventions, copyrights, methods, techniques, prototypes, drawings, technical data, know-how and business plans pertaining to the above parties' businesses that is identified in writing as confidential at the time of disclosure and marked "Confidential" or "Proprietary." Information which is orally or visually disclosed to the recipient shall not be deemed confidential unless at the time of oral disclosure, the disclosing party indicates the information is confidential or proprietary and such party then reduces the information to a writing within five days of the initial disclosure. The Information shall not include material which the recipient party can by reasonable proof:

    (a) show that such Information, in its disclosed combinations, is in the public domain through no fault of recipient;

    (b) show that such Information becomes public knowledge during the term of this Agreement without breach of this Agreement;

(c)   show that such Information is contained in a written record in the recipient's files without an obligation of confidentiality prior to the date of its receipt from the proprietor;

(d)   show that the recipient had at any time lawfully obtained said Information from a third party under circumstances permitting its disclosure and use;

(e)   show that such Information was developed by the receiving party without reference to, and totally independent from, the Information.

2.   Dissemination of Information. Neither party shall use the Information of the other party in any manner which may be detrimental to that other party. The parties agree that they will not publish, disclose, communicate or reveal any Information to any person, corporation or third party or to any of their own employees who do not need to know the information in the performance of their duties. Proprietary information or data marked with a restrictive notice shall be delivered only to the following individuals authorized to receive such data-

ABC Co.   XYZ Co.
123 Fourth Street   567 8th Blvd.
Any City, USA   Anyplace, Worldwide

3.   Protection of Information. The standard of care for protecting Information, imposed on the party receiving the Information, will be that degree of care the receiving party uses to prevent disclosure, publication, or dissemination of its own proprietary or confidential information, but in no event less than reasonable care.

4.   Ownership of Information. The parties agree that any Information revealed to the other by them remains the exclusive property of the proprietor. The parties agree that, upon the termination of their relationship and upon written request, they will either surrender to each other any Information transmitted to them by the other party or certify that such Information has been destroyed.

5.   Term. This Agreement shall remain in effect for one year from the date set forth above, except for the obligations of the receiving party with respect to Information received prior to the termination of this Agreement, which shall survive such termination for three (3) years after the date of disclosure.

6.   Termination. Either party hereto, upon written notice to the other, may terminate this Agreement. Such termination shall be effective thirty (30) days after receipt of such notice to the address specified in Paragraph 2 above. All obligations arising under this Agreement shall survive any termination of this Agreement for three (3) years after the date of disclosure.

7.   Severability of Provisions. Should any part of this Agreement be declared invalid by a court of law, such decision shall not affect the validity of any remaining

portion which shall remain in full force and effect as if the invalid portion was never a part of this Agreement when it was executed. As it is the parties' intent that this Agreement be enforced to the fullest extent permitted by law, such invalidated section shall be deemed amended so as to avoid the reasons for its invalidity.

Should the severance or amendment of any such part of this Agreement materially affect any other rights and obligations of the parties, the parties will negotiate in good faith to amend this Agreement in a manner satisfactory to the parties.

8. <u>Non-Assignability</u>. Neither party hereto shall, directly or indirectly, assign or purport to assign this Agreement or any of its rights and obligations in whole or part to any third party without the prior written consent of the other party.

9. <u>Amendment</u>. This Agreement shall not be amended, modified or altered, except as set out in Paragraph 7 above, except in writing, duly accepted and executed by both parties.

10. <u>Governing Law</u>. This Agreement shall be governed by, and construed in accordance with the laws of the State of _____, without regard to its conflict of law provisions.

11. <u>Entire Agreement</u>. This Agreement constitutes the entire, agreement and understanding of the parties hereto, and no representations or promises have been made that are not fully set forth herein.

IN WITNESS WHEREOF the parties hereto have caused this Agreement to be executed by a duly authorized officer.

By: By:
Title: Title:
Date: Date:

SAMPLE CONFIDENTIAL DISCLOSURE AND NON-USE AGREEMENT
(LONG FORM)

_____ (hereinafter "DISCLOSER") is the owner of certain confidential information, for a _____ as described on the product description, a copy of which is attached hereto (hereinafter "INFORMATION").

_____ (hereinafter "RECIPIENT") currently makes and offers numerous _____ products and has been requested to review the INFORMATION for possible use in developing RECIPIENT'S own products for _____. For their mutual benefit, RECIPIENT accepts and DISCLOSER is willing to furnish such INFORMATION to RECIPIENT upon the following terms and conditions:

The parties agree that:

1. The precise INFORMATION disclosed to RECIPIENT under this Agreement and marked as CONFIDENTIAL will be received and held in confidence by RECIPIENT, and RECIPIENT will take such steps as may be reasonably necessary to prevent disclosure of said information to others, and will not disclose the same to others without the prior consent of DISCLOSER, said standard not requiring greater security steps than RECIPIENT uses for its own information.

2. RECIPIENT will not use or allow others to use said INFORMATION, except for _____ without the written consent of DISCLOSER.

3. The commitments set forth in the preceding paragraphs shall not extend to any portion of the disclosed INFORMATION which:

   a. is in the public domain at the time of receipt by RECIPIENT;

   b. was known to RECIPIENT prior to the receipt of same from DISCLOSER;

   c. is now or hereafter through no fault on the part of RECIPIENT becomes generally available to the public;

   d. is an application of commonly known principles of _____ manufacturing;

   e. which is published or furnished to RECIPIENT by any third party not under a duty of nondisclosure;

   f. is discovered by independent development;

g.   is discovered starting with a known product and working backward to find the method by which it was developed (reverse engineering);

h.   observation of the item in public use or on public display; or

i.   obtaining the INFORMATION from published literature.

4.   This Agreement shall remain in effect for one year from the date hereof.

5.   This Agreement shall be governed by the laws of the State of _____, and any enforcement action must be brought in Federal court for the _____, or a state court in _____.

(RECIPIENT)   (DISCLOSER)

By:_____   By:_____
Title:_____   Title:_____

SAMPLE CONFIDENTIAL DISCLOSURE AND NON-USE AGREEMENT
(SHORT FORM)

_____ (hereinafter Discloser) owns confidential information, trade secrets and inventions for a _____ (hereinafter "Confidential Information");

_____ (hereinafter Recipient) has expressed a desire to learn certain aspects of said Confidential Information for evaluation. For their mutual benefit, Recipient accepts and Discloser is willing to furnish such Confidential Information to Recipient upon the terms and conditions set forth below. The parties recognize that the Confidential Information has or may have commercial value;

Recipient agrees that: (1) all Confidential Information disclosed to Recipient under this Agreement will be received and held in confidence by Recipient, and Recipient will take such steps as may be reasonably necessary to prevent disclosure of said information to others and will not disclose the same to others without the prior written consent of Discloser; and (2) Recipient will not use said information, except for said evaluation without the written consent of Discloser.

The commitments set forth in the preceding paragraphs shall not extend to any portion of the disclosed Confidential Information which: (1) was known to the Recipient prior to the receipt thereof from Discloser; or (2) is now or hereafter through no act on the part of the Recipient becomes generally available to the public; or (3) which is furnished to Recipients by any third party having a bona fide right to do so.

This Agreement shall be governed by the laws of the State of _____.

ACCEPTED:

_____   _____

By:_____   By:_____

Title:_____   Title:_____

Date:_____   Date:_____

◆ INVENTORS AND INVENTIONS ◆

William Lear

AUTOMOBILE RADIO

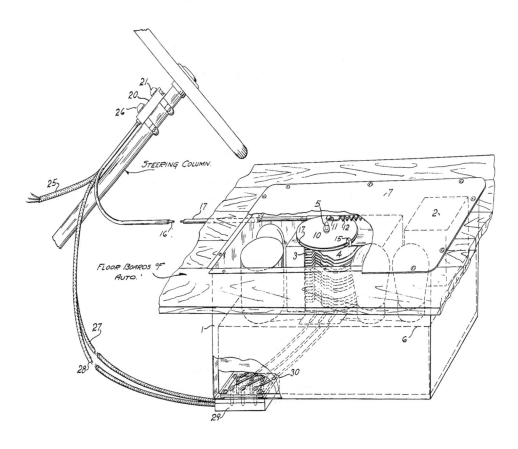

When you think of William Lear what comes to mind? The answer should be planes, trains, and automobiles, or at least planes and automobile radios. Although his name is most often associated with corporate jet planes, William Lear earlier made his mark in car radios and by inventing the now-deceased eight-track player.

William P. Lear was born in Hannibal, Missouri on June 26, 1902. He attended school in Chicago, Illinois. Although Lear never continued his formal education past the eighth grade, he continued learning on his own.

In 1920, Lear decided to go west and made it to Denver, Colorado. Out of money and wanting to see the world, he decided to join the Navy, which sent him back to the Great Lakes Naval Base near Chicago. While in the Navy, he studied radio electronics.

After World War I, the Navy decided to reduce its number of recruits and offered an early honorable discharge. Lear decided that the Navy was too constricting, so he was one of the first people to take the offer for an early discharge.

From 1922 to 1924 Lear established and ran Quincy Radio Laboratories in Quincy, Illinois. In 1924, he moved to Tulsa to live with his grandmother. There he created another company, Lear Radio Laboratories. He also attempted to finish four years of high school in only one semester, but this did not work because he had a quarrel with one of his teachers and, consequently, never received his diploma.

In 1927, he moved back to Chicago to work as a consultant for Grigby Grunrow. During this era, Lear redeveloped the "B" battery to get rid of the hum that was produced by other "B" batteries.

In 1930, Lear teamed with Paul Galvin Manufacturing Company and created the first functioning automobile radio. This endeavor was a success, although Lear decided to sell his radio and coil company to Paul Galvin. This company later became known as Motorola Corporation.

Lear decided to move on after this and create yet another company, this one called Lear Developments, that also produced car radios. Lear then moved to New York in 1934, where he invented the all-wave radio receiver, which aids in the navigation of airplanes by using the signals from radio beacons. RCA decided to buy this invention from Lear for $50,000. Lear later invented another airplane guidance system called the Lear-o-Scope automatic direction finder, and an autopilot system called F-S Autopilot.

Lear then decided that he needed a new and bigger challenge. He dreamt of a small businessman's aircraft. This dream came true on October 7, 1963 in Wichita, Kansas when the first Lear Jet took to the skies.

After selling Lear Jet Industries, the makers of the Lear Jet, to Gates Rubber Company in 1967, Lear moved his interests to a deserted Air Force base in Reno, Nevada. Here he started working with steam to create efficient pollution-free vehicles. He worked on the Lear Vapordyne race car, a steam bus, and a steam car. After working on these projects for many months and spending millions of dollars of his own money he realized that the steam engine worked, but it just was not as efficient as a conventional fossil-fuel engine.

Lear's final project was another airplane built entirely of composite materials, called the Lear Fan. But Lear had problems with his health; he had advanced leukemia and only two months to live. In his last two months he told his wife Moya to finish the Lear Fan, and he died on May 14th, 1978. She and many dedicated employees debuted this final project for William Lear two and a half years after his death in December 1980. However, the Lear Fan was never put into production.

Jan. 16, 1934.   W. P. LEAR   **1,944,139**

RADIO APPARATUS

Filed Aug. 3, 1931

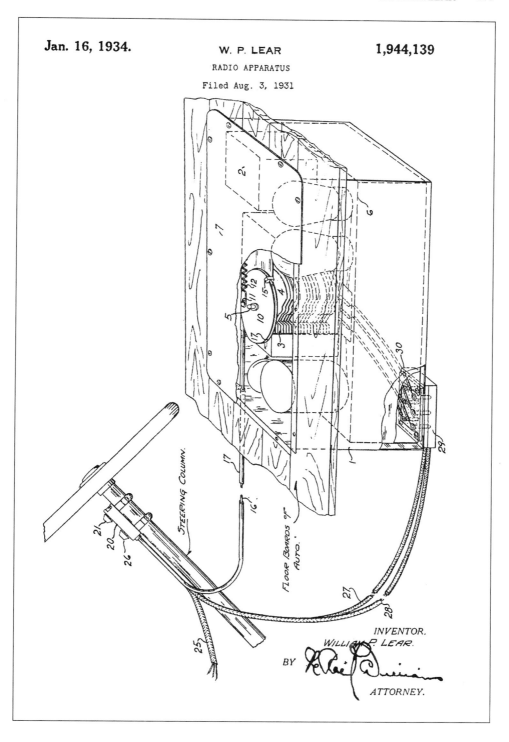

INVENTOR.

WILLIAM P. LEAR.

BY

ATTORNEY.

21 The Engineer and Scientist as Expert Witness; and Ethics

21.1 THE ENGINEER AND SCIENTIST AS EXPERT WITNESS

At a trial where complex scientific or technical matters are raised, and are in dispute, the court will allow one side, or usually both sides, to offer testimony from an expert in the relevant field of science or technology. These expert witnesses are permitted to testify as to their expert qualifications, to lay a foundation for their testimony by establishing the experiments, tests, analysis or research they conducted pertinent to their testimony, and then state their opinion based upon the investigative work they conducted.

Opinion testimony from ordinary non-expert witnesses in a trial is inadmissible. Opinion testimony is predicted upon the conjecture or supposition of the witness, based upon the analysis by the expert. Such conjecture is not a pure fact, and can be termed an "indeterminate conclusion," which the law courts look upon with disfavor in the case of ordinary fact testimony. However, in many, if not most legal situations, making a close as possible determination of these "indeterminate conclusions" will assist the judge or jury to understand the cause of the problem, and fault which led to the lawsuit.

For example, a factory worker is injured when a machine he or she was operating malfunctioned. The operator may not have the technical skills to know what went wrong, but an expert, or experts, in the design, function and operation of the specific machine can analyze the machine after the accident, and can usually pinpoint what caused the problem and where the fault lies. If the expert witnesses convince the judge or jury that there is a design, manufacturing or failure to warn defect in the production or sale of the machine, the manufacturer of the machine may be liable for the operator's injury. However, if the expert testimony shows that the machine was in perfect operating condition, and that the accident most likely occurred due to the operator failing to heed warnings or instructions, the operator may be found to be the cause of his or her own injury.

In similar fashion, the design and manufacturing criteria of a structural member that failed would be the proper subject of expert testimony. Also, the "similarity" between a copyrighted work and an allegedly "pirated" work would be the subject of a literary or music expert. In patent cases, testimony about the comparisons between the prior art and the patent claims, and the comparisons between the patent claims and the allegedly infringing product or method, are presented by technical expert testimony. An expert witness also normally presents estimates of damages incurred by an injured party in a court of law.

Those of you who have witnessed films of the Galloping Gertie Bridge failure at Takoma Narrows can understand and appreciate that testimony regarding the design stages of a span to be constructed across a windy chasm, after the span has collapsed, can be developed through opinion testimony of bridge and harmonic experts who have studied the situation. Usually the studies take place after the accident has occurred,

Intellectual Property Law for Engineers and Scientists, by Howard B. Rockman
ISBN 0-471-44998-9 © 2004 The Institute of Electrical and Electronics Engineers

where the experts also look at the adequacy of the studies made during the design and construction phases.

21.1.1 Need for Experts

Lawyers are not qualified to testify in courts of law about facts, nor give opinions as to facts, since they do not have the requisite personal, first hand knowledge of the facts. They are just guiding the testimony of the fact witnesses for the benefit of the court. There is also a presumption that the court and the jury are incapable of drawing intelligent conclusions based on complicated scientific or technical questions. For such purposes, an expert witness is needed. An "expert" is one who has specific skill, knowledge or experience in a given technology or other field that an ordinary person would not have. The expert must be qualified in the given technology or field through education, on the job experience, training, or observation.

Before an expert witness testifies, that witness presents evidence to the court setting forth his or her qualifications to provide expert testimony in a specified area. The expert qualifies him or herself as a credible witness by testifying about his or her education, experience in projects in which he or she has been involved, specialized training, whether he or she is registered, and other similar attributes. Upon cross-examination, normally the opposing counsel challenges the witness' qualifications, and the witness must be so well qualified, and prepared, as to withstand any such challenge. Based on this type of evidence presentation, the court and jury then determines whether the witness is qualified or not to present expert testimony on the qualifying subject.

Consider also that either side will present experts to provide their opinions based on a certain factual matter, each expert coming to a different conclusion, based sometimes on the same set of facts. Therefore, which expert is to be believed sometimes depends on the quality of the qualifications of the particular expert. Obviously, the more detailed the examination, testing, analysis and research conducted by the expert witness prior to testifying, and the clarity of the presentation based on that examination, the more that witness's testimony is apt to be believed over the conflicting testimony of the opposition's expert witnesses.

Remember, that just because you offer expert testimony, there is no guarantee that a judge or jury will ultimately believe that testimony, whether such testimony is the best opinion or not.

21.1.2 Expert Assistance by Engineers and Scientists in Complex Litigation

There are three ways that you may be engaged to provide expert assistance in a legal matter. You may be engaged to participate in one, two or all three of these capacities. You may be asked to provide consulting advice, where you assist the lawyers in the preparation of the presentation of the technical issues in the case. You may also be asked to assist at counsel's table at trial, and be present during the examination and cross-examination of the opposing expert witnesses in the area of your scientific or technical expertise. You may also be asked to present expert testimony at the trial, and to prepare yourself for rigorous cross-examination.

Advice and Consultation As in most matters in life, it is often necessary for a person such as an engineer or a scientist who is thoroughly familiar with a technical or scientific concept to explain that concept to ordinary people, such as a lawyer preparing for trial, or ultimately a judge or jury. A jury is composed of a sampling of a given community, and is not a panel of experts on some particular scientific or technical viewpoint. Therefore, part of an engineer's or scientist's function when providing advice and consultation in preparation for trial is to present to their attorney the technical facts in the case such that an ordinary person can understand the complexities inherent in the facts. In patent litigation, at least one of the lawyers usually has an engineering or science degree or background, for this is a requirement of becoming a licensed patent attorney. However, most patent attorneys are involved in many technical disciplines, and are the master of no particular technology. Thus, the engineer expert advisor must not only have the technical proficiency, but also the ability to effectively express his or her knowledge. Even the patent attorney must be able to understand the expert's expression of the relevant facts.

In preparation for acting effectively as an advising consultant or as an expert testifying witness, you must be so thoroughly familiar with the facts of the case that no opposition attack will come as a surprise. Drawings, sketches or specifications may have to be thoroughly reviewed, substances and material thoroughly tested, building codes or other laws fully examined, and/or prior art technical material may have to be analyzed. As an expert, you will then be asked to advise the attorney on your side of the case about every step you took in conducting your research, analysis, testing and examination. Also, assistance in the preparation of a legal brief requires that your technical analysis be complete and strong enough to repel the opposing side's attack from its expert.

An engineer providing assistance to an attorney in the preparation of a trial, or at the trial of a case, must have an open and objective approach to the technical facts. The engineer must present to the lawyer facts to support a client's claim, as well as all opposing facts known to the engineer that may rebut or go against the client's position. There are two sides to any legal issue, and the engineer as an expert consultant must be willing to show the attorney and the client both sides of important issues bearing on the factual and legal questions in the case. This enables the attorney to prepare an effective rebuttal to expected adverse testimony from the opposing expert(s).

Trial Assistance   The engineer expert acting as a trial assistant prepares questions that the attorney should ask the opposing expert witnesses, and the opposing fact witnesses, to convince the jury that your presentation of the testimony is the correct one. The expert engineer offering trial assistance also helps the attorney prepare cross-examination questions of the opposing expert, and some of these questions arise unplanned as the trial progresses.

For example, your party's attorney might not catch a mistake in the technical argument by an opposition expert witness, but it probably would not escape your notice as a technical expert. The expert witness giving trial assistance will be able to prepare the attorney to ask the appropriate questions on cross-examination that may show that the opposing expert did not do his or her homework properly. Also, such assistance may be used to prepare questions to be presented to your own testifying expert when placed on the stand to counter the opposition's expert testimony.

Opinion Testimony   Again, expert technological and scientific testimony must be presented in a court of law in a simple way that can be readily understood by individuals with no technical background, such as the judge and members of the jury. This is accomplished by the expert witness providing a basic, easily understood foundation for his or her testimony, and then relating all of the more complex facts and opinions to that basic foundation. It usually takes the cooperation of the expert and the attorney to get the expert's testimony to this point of a lay person's comprehension.

The expert witness is usually called upon to testify regarding technical or scientific principles and comparing them to events that happen every day, or with science principles the average judge or juror may recall from high school or college. Charts, pictures, electronic presentations, models and drawings can be used by the expert witness to establish a clear meaning of the technology. The expert usually dedicates several hours to preparing such demonstrative evidence, and cannot rely upon the work of others, with the exception of "learned treatises." Also, each part of the evidence must be presented with such accuracy and clarity that it is incapable of successfully being adversely rebutted by opposing counsel.

The testifying expert must be completely honest in presenting his or her testimony, even if it means making a statement that does not fully support the client's allegations. The opposing attorney will look for any point you make on the witness stand that is not fully truthful in an effort to destroy your credibility. Any small gap in the fabric of truth of the evidence can destroy the total effect of the testimony. Thus, the truth and presenting honest opinions are imperatives.

In presenting expert testimony, if an engineer witness does not know the answer to a particular question on cross-examination by opposing counsel, a perfectly proper answer is "I don't know." If the question relates to testimony you gave previously, such as on direct examination, you as an expert witness may request the reading of the previous testimony before responding to the question. If a question requires mathematical analysis or other calculations, or a consultation with other witnesses or your attorney, time for such calculation or consultation may be requested from the court, and may or may not be granted.

One of the most important facets of giving expert testimony is the presence, attitude and demeanor of the expert on the witness stand. He or she must come across to the judge and jury as inspiring confidence in the truth and honesty of his or her abilities and testimony. If you equivocate, the judge and jury may not accept anything you say. The expert witness' conduct and attitude throughout the entire proceeding must be favorably received by those who are evaluating the credibility of the technical or scientific testimony. During cross-examination, opposing counsel will attempt to discredit you, or demean you, or pick apart testimony damaging to your opponent's case. The more damaging your expert testimony is to the opposing attorney's case, the more the effort the opposing attorney will make to destroy your credibility and weaken the effect of your expert testimony. If this fails, the opposing attorney may attempt to harass the expert witness and have the witness become angry on the stand. Attorneys commonly use this tactic in an attempt to transfer the witness' anger amongst the jurors, who will then direct their anger to the witness. Therefore, it is most important that the witness remains calm and provide thought-out responses. Courtesy, assuredness in your answers, and self control must be exercised at all times. A simple "yes sir," "no sir," "yes ma'am," "no ma'am" in your cross-examination responses is greatly appreciated by your attorney.

Your expert opinion testimony may include reference to texts, materials and writings by acknowledged authorities in technical fields relating to your testimony. Sometimes a quotation from a "learned treatise" or textbook is more meaningful than oral testimony by the author of the text.

21.1.3 Expert Depositions

If you are designated by the trial counsel who retained you to appear and present expert testimony at the trial of a technically complex case, after you have prepared your testimony and prepared a written "expert report," and prior to trial, you will be presented for a discovery deposition to be taken by the opposing counsel, who may examine you as to the experimentations, tests, examinations, and/or analysis you've made, and the conclusions you've drawn from your work relating to the issues in the lawsuit. You will also be required to bring with you all of the documents and other materials you relied upon in preparing your testimony. The deposition affords opposing counsel the ability to know what your testimony is going to be before you testify. This is part of the American judicial system, and not only your expert testimony but the testimony of all witnesses on both sides will be known prior to trial through the use of discovery depositions taken by counsel for both parties.

21.1.4 Deciding Whether You Can Provide the Requisite Expert Assistance

It is very important that scientists and engineers who are requested to testify or work as expert witnesses, either as a testifying or consultant expert, first come to the conclusion that they truly believe they can honestly testify towards the prospective client's position. You must firmly believe in the case of your client, and in the testimony you are to give, or else you should decline to act as an expert witness. First of all, you should not be compelled or even asked to testify as to matters that you yourself do not believe are accurate or soundly founded in fact. Secondly, if you testify having anything less than full conviction in the substance of your testimony, your lack of conviction will be apparent in the manner in which you will be testifying before the court and jury, and your testimony will not be worth very much when subjected to vigorous cross-examination.

21.1.5 Expert Witness Fees

All expert witnesses in litigation are paid for their services, unless they choose not to. Engineers and scientists testifying as expert witnesses in highly complex matters are thus paid fees for the presentation of their testimony.

Your expert witness fee must not be contingent on the outcome or result of the case. Normally at deposition and during trial, the expert witness will be asked if he or she is being paid for their testimony, and will also be asked how much. These are legitimate questions and you should not hesitate to answer truthfully and positively. If you are being paid only on the contingency that your client wins the case, then the jury can conclude that your testimony is biased. However, if you are getting paid straight time or on a flat fee basis for your testimony, the jury can assume that you were just paid for your services, and that your testimony should be taken as credible.

By way of example, many years ago I was representing a chemical formulation company in a case my client brought against two former employees of the company, alleging that the two former employees had stolen trade secret formulas of my client, which the defendants then used to start a competing company. We engaged the services of a chemist who owned a competing chemical formulation company to provide expert testimony comparing the defendants' formulae to our client's original formulae. The expert witness did not request a fee, and received none for his testimony. During cross-examination of our expert witness by the defendants' attorney, the expert was asked if he was receiving a fee for his testimony, which is a legitimate and regularly asked question of expert witnesses on cross-examination. Our witness replied "No." At this point, a good lawyer knows not to ask a question on cross-examination where he or she does not know the answer. However, the defendants' lawyer than asked "Why?" Our witness stated "Because the scum that you represent have to be eradicated from our industry."

21.2   ETHICS

Over the past hundred years, the science and engineering disciplines have reached the level of professionalism often accorded the fields of medicine, law and theology. While engineering as a technology-oriented discipline has existed for nearly two centuries, only in recent times is it considered a profession. Also, with the advance of technology, many new and different areas of interest inside the professions of engineering and science have been created. The current technology explosion is causing new scientific and engineering areas to be created regularly.

The dictionary meaning of the term "profession" is: "A vocation or occupation requiring advanced training in some liberal art or science, and usually involving mental rather than manual work." It is an endeavor where the labor and skill involved is predominantly mental or intellectual, as compared to physical or manual, per *Black's Law Dictionary*. For example, the United States Labor Management Relations Act defines the term "professional employee" as follows:

> "An employee engaged in work predominantly intellectual and varied in character as opposed to routine mental, manual, mechanical or physical work, or involving consistent exercise of discretion and judgment in his performance."

To some extent, the states have varying requirements for members of a profession. For example, doctors, lawyers and engineers are obligated to obtain a state registration or license before they can practice their profession in that state. Professionals are normally organized into professional societies, which provide substantial peer self-regulation of the profession's members and conduct. The professions are normally those vocations that have a large component of public interest and public service built into their way of earning a living, and whose conduct is guided by a Professional Code of Ethics.

Today, in the profession of engineering, civil engineers and public works engineers, among others, are required to register with the state in which they work. Under normal circumstances, engineers working for corporations or as consultants are usually exempt from registration requirements. Many states require professional engineers to be registered before they are allowed to practice, and many states have reciprocal agreements allowing an engineer registered in one state to work in another state. The purpose of the registration laws is to protect the public from unacceptable and improper engineering work product. To become registered, an engineer must establish to the satisfaction of the Board of Examiners that he or she possesses the requisite abilities established by state standards. Registration normally involves a review of the candidate's past engineering work experience, training, and an examination must be successfully completed. It is also quite true that the acceptance of an occupation as a profession requires continuing efforts to maintain high standards of service to the public.

21.2.1   Professional Societies

Many of today's established engineering disciplines have at least one society of its members such as IEEE, ASME, AIChE and others. Likewise, societies of scientists abound, each one dedicated to providing professional stature to their members, and a conduit for the exchange and validation of new ideas. The Accreditation Board of Engineering and Technology, among other things, examines accredited engineering and technology curriculum in schools of higher education at least once every six years.

The American Association of Engineering Societies was formed in 1979 to advance the development and practice of the public interest involvement in engineering. The association also acts as an information exchange agency for its member's interests and activities.

The National Society of Professional Engineers (NSPE), formed in 1934, is largely responsible for the passage of engineering registration laws in the various states, and in promoting public recognition of engineering as a profession.

21.2.2   Code of Ethics

"Ethics" is defined as "a system or code of morals of a particular group, profession, etc." Ethics are the rules and regulations we each impose on ourselves to govern our day-to-day conduct, in accordance with what we individually believe is right or wrong. Our desire is to have others trust in our abilities, and we perform our professions so as to earn and receive this trust from others. Honesty and integrity are two important ingredients making up one's character that are visible to others, and which result in loyalty from those whom you desire to engage in a business/professional relationship. For example, no Constitution, Federal or State law requires an engineer or scientist to provide a totally honest, unbiased report of the results of his or her analyses. However, engineers and scientists are guided on the straight track of truth and honesty by two important factors of conscience. One is the moral code guiding that person in expressing the results of his or her work. The other is the peer review that will test the integrity of their work when made public. One's life experiences, observations, and teachers contribute to the make-up of an individual's moral platform. These are added to the engineering and science experiences one gains during development as a professional, which evolves into the moral standards one applies to themselves at any given time.

A Code of Ethics does not stand as a body of rigid, unchangeable regulations or standards. Ethics exist as a guiding light to direct an engineer's or scientist's own moral standards, and to assist in altering the engineer's conduct to satisfy those standards. Any standard of ethics has great value to an individual in communicating and dealing with others, and provides the path towards professionalism in the work of the engineer and scientist.

21.2.3   Brief Comments Regarding the National Society of Professional Engineers (NSPE) Code of Ethics for Engineers

This code requires that engineers exhibit the highest standards of honesty and integrity, that the services provided by engineers be performed impartially, fairly and equitably, and must be directed towards the protection of public health, safety and welfare. This latter provision is of utmost importance, since the average person who observes or uses the work of an engineer cannot tell what degree of expertise went into that work, but just assumes that the bridge they are crossing or the television they are turning on is safe for their use.

Some of the fundamental cannons of the NSPE Code of Ethics are:

- Holding high the health, safety, and welfare of the public;
- Performing only in one's areas of competence, experience and education;
- Being objective and truthful in issuing public statements;
- Providing services for each employer or client as faithful agents or trustees;
- Avoiding deceptive acts; and
- Conducting oneself honorably, responsibly, ethically and lawfully to enhance the honor, reputation and usefulness of the engineering profession.

The NSPE code also provides guidelines to assist an engineer in exercising his or her own judgment, for example, where his or her judgment may be overruled under circumstances that could endanger life or property. Under such circumstances, the engineer is ethically required to advise an employer, client, or such other authority as may be appropriate of their opinion or conclusions. Also, engineers shall not permit the use of their names in endeavors which they have reason to believe involve fraudulent and dishonest enterprises. Further, if engineers have knowledge of any violation of the code of ethics by others, they are morally obligated to report such violation of another to an appropriate professional body, and when deemed relevant, to public authorities.

Engineers are also obligated under the NSPE Code of Ethics to disclose all or known potential conflicts of interest that could influence, or appear to influence, their judgment or the quality of their services. Also, if an engineer is compelled by a client or employer to conduct him or herself in an unprofessional or illegal manner, the engineer is obligated under the Code to notify the proper authorities, and withdraw from further service on the project.

The Code also includes a very important provision restricting engineers from disclosing, without consent, confidential information or trade secrets concerning the business affairs or technical processes of any present or former client, employer, or public body on which they serve. Such disclosure could result in a trade secret misappropriation legal action against both the new employer and the miscreant engineer, which becomes costly and could interfere with the engineer's new position. A further provision regarding confidentially provides that engineers should not participate in or represent an adversary interest in connection with a project in which the engineer has gained particular specialized confidential knowledge on behalf of a former client. This provision requires an engineer, upon taking a new position, to fully disclose to the new employer all previous positions and generally describe projects he or she has worked on, to avoid the appearance of a conflict of interest. Also, any previous non-compete agreements that the engineer has signed should be made fully available to the new employer.

Under the Code, engineers are also obligated to give credit and attribution for engineering work to those to whom credit is due, and to recognize the proprietary interests of others. This requires engineers to honestly name the person or persons who may be individually responsible for designs, inventions, writings and other accomplishments. For example, the true inventors of an invention must be named in a U.S. patent application, or the patent ultimately issued may be held invalid and unenforceable. Therefore, there is no advantage in naming uninvolved individuals as inventors in patent applications. Also, my experience has shown that acknowledging the fine work of others can create a high level of morale in an organization or project team. Everyone wants to be told that the work they are doing is appreciated.

Engineers using designs supplied by a client must recognize that the designs are the property of the client and remain so, and may not be used or duplicated by the engineer for other projects without express permission of the client for whom the designs were first made.

The Code also provides that before undertaking work for others in connection with which the engineer may make improvements to existing works, plans, designs, inventions or other works that may justify copyrights or patents, the engineer should enter into a written agreement regarding ownership of such improvements, etc. In most situations, if the engineer is being paid to develop such improvements or inventions, the ownership will be in the person making payment to the engineer. This is discussed in more detail in Chapter 19.

An engineer's designs, data, records and notes referring exclusively to an employer's work are the employer's property, and cannot be taken with the engineer once employment is terminated. The employer also should indemnify the engineer for use of the information for any purpose other than the original purpose.

21.2.4   Comparing the Law and Ethics

An unethical action is not necessarily "illegal." Thus neither the examining boards nor the courts regulate or are involved in the ethical practices of engineers. Negligence of engineers is another story, and the courts become directly involved with negligence in engineering design and manufacturing practices. Thus, the redress for moral misconduct of an engineer comes from engineering societies. For example, the American Medical Association and the local state bar associations have the ability to deprive a doctor or lawyer of the right to practice his or her profession in a given state. However, there has not yet been a society developed with equivalent powers in the engineering profession. It is quite possible that procedures for holding hearings on unethical engineering practices may be developed at some future date. Today, if an engineer is guilty of performing an unethical practice, that engineer may be removed from membership in an engineering society. Other penalties would include the loss of a job or project. Public knowledge of such censure is a severe factor curtailing the miscreant's ability to earn a living.

The various codes of professional ethics that are in existence lead to the conclusion that those who are honest and loyal and adhere to a standard of moral and professional ethics in dealing with others often find that, as a result, others are honest and loyal in reciprocal dealings with them.

To maintain the impartiality and integrity of engineers and scientists, many corporations and governmental agencies which hire engineers have adopted policies restricting or eliminating receipt of gifts by engineers from vendors, where the engineer is in a position to specify the purchase of products from among a plurality of vendors. Those in the engineering profession correctly understand that an engineer's integrity cannot and should not be purchased by those whom the engineer deals with on the employer's behalf.

21.2.5   Recruiting Practices

The market for qualified engineering and science professionals ebbs and flows. In years of rapidly advancing technology in a viable economy, qualified engineers and scientists have been in short supply. Industry sources have reported that this can lead to odd, and even objectionable, recruiting activities. In a situation where there is a shortage of engineers, one company will usually contact another company's engineers in an effort to lure them away. This is considered by some to be unethical, however, it is a common practice. Of course, if the engineer makes the first move to seek a new position, the resulting job change usually is considered to be proper.

The blame for a company's loss of engineers sometimes is it own myopic fault. For example, management of a company may have a policy of ignoring contributions made by their engineers, such as where an engineer's design change results in substantial savings to the employer. Engineers and scientists normally feel that good work should result in recognition, for example in the way of monetary or other reward for saving the company money. The company, on the other hand, may take the position that engineers are paid both for periods in which their contributions are outstanding and for other periods in which their achievements are quite lackluster. Because of these conflicting points of view, engineers may become disillusioned, and they begin to seek out offers of new employment. Therefore, one huge way to maintain the integrity of your workforce is to give praise where praise is due for outstanding jobs. Everyone needs to be valued.

An engineer's ethics will be tested many times on the job. For example, consider the hypothetical situation where an engineer knows of a design problem with the speaker system of a new cellular phone regarding radiation emissions. The engineer is told that management has decided that the $0.75 per unit required for repair of the design is too huge of a cost factor. What should the engineer do? Send an e-mail questioning the decision? Discuss the matter with a supervisor, mentioning that the old design could be a health hazard? Advise the press of the potential health hazard? Send a memorandum questioning the decision and emphasizing that lives may be at risk? Provide the press with information about the chosen design and the cost of alternatives? The ultimate decision becomes: when has the engineer done enough to satisfy his or her ethical obligation. This has to be decided by each engineer on a case by case basis, and calls into play the engineer's own moral convictions.

An example of an engineer's ethical dilemma can be found in classic literature. Suppose an engineer becomes aware of a discharge of a carcinogenic chemical into a river used as a source for drinking water. Does the engineer have a duty to report the discharge? If so, to whom: the engineer's supervisor, the Environmental Protection Agency, the local authorities using the river for drinking water, or the press? No clear answers exist; hence the engineer must base such decisions on personal ethics and values. Over a hundred years ago, the Danish author, Henrik Ibsen, wrote a play titled *Enemy of the People,* in which an engineer for a city's water works did exactly this—he tried to shut down the water supply of a city known for its warming spas and healthful waters because of an unacceptable high level of bacteria in the water. Everyone ultimately chastised him for his work. Thus, the title of the play, *Enemy of the People.* Under today's standards, the "hero" of Mr. Ibsen's play would be praised and not condemned.

Luther Burbank

PLANT BREEDING

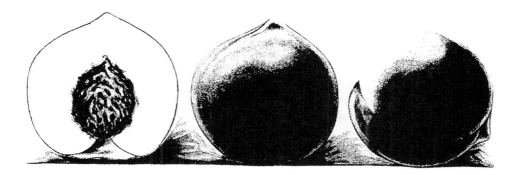

Luther Burbank was a horticulturist who devoted his life to breeding plants. He is credited with developing over 800 strains or varieties of plants, including 113 varieties of plums and prunes, 10 varieties of berries, 50 varieties of lilies, the freestone peach, and the Idaho potato.

Luther Burbank was born on March 7, 1849 on a farm near Lancaster, Massachusetts. He showed an interest in nature and mechanics at an early age, although he received little more than a high school education. He obtained much of his encouragement and enthusiasm for nature from his uncle, who was a department head at a Boston museum, and his uncle's friend, the Swiss/American naturalist, Louis Agassiz.

Upon his father's death, Burbank and his family moved to a small farm in Groten, Connecticut. At the age of 21, he purchased 17 acres of land close to Lunenburg, Massachusetts, and began a career of plant breeding and growing that lasted the remaining 55 years of his life. Drawing inspiration from Charles Darwin's *Variations of Animals and Plants Under Domestication,* Burbank decided that better plants could be developed through natural selection, and new plant varieties could be created through cross-breeding or hybridization. In 1871, he planted 23 seeds from a potato seed ball in a special plot, which resulted in many large firm potatoes. He then replanted these and reaped the small harvest of fine potatoes, called the Burbank potato, that was ultimately introduced into Ireland to help combat the potato famine. He then sold the rights to his potato for $150, which money he used to travel to California, where he established a nursery garden, greenhouse and experimental farms in Santa Rosa.

The Santa Rosa Farm became famous throughout the world. Burbank worked primarily by obtaining multiple crosses of foreign and native strains of fruits, vegetables, and flowers to obtain seedlings. He grafted those seedlings onto fully developed plants and was able to rapidly assess their hybrid characteristics. His work at natural selection and hybridization techniques in developing new plants was by no means small. At any one

Intellectual Property Law for Engineers and Scientists, by Howard B. Rockman
ISBN 0-471-44998-9 © 2004 The Institute of Electrical and Electronics Engineers

time, he was working on three experiments at the same time, involving millions of plants on his farm. Regarding plums alone, he tested about 30,000 new varieties. Much of his experimental data is not available, but he did write several books. In 1914–1915, his twelve-volume work, *Luther Burbank, His Methods and Discoveries and Their Practical Applications,* was published. Burbank is credited with developing many of California's plums and prunes, the Shasta daisy, and novelty fruits such as plum cots, furless blackberries, and the spineless cactus.

In 1930, the Congress of the United Sates passed the "Plant Patent Act of 1930," providing protection for new and distinct varieties of asexually reproduced plants, except for tuber-propagated plants. This law resulted from the fact that plant breeders were aware that they had no financial incentive to breed plants because they could not exercise control over their discoveries. Although Luther Burbank died four years before the enactment of the Plant Patent Act, sixteen plant patents were issued to Burbank posthumously.

Just before his death at the age of 77 in 1926, Luther Burbank found himself compelled to voice his opinions supporting his philosophy as a naturalist, in both the scientific and philosophical arenas. Up until 1926, Burbank is not known for expressing his thoughts on the universal contest between science and religion. However, the Scopes "monkey trial" of 1925 had pushed the concepts of Darwin's evolution onto the national stage, and Henry Ford, Luther Burbank's close friend, had published his own views in favor of reincarnation. A reporter for the *San Francisco Bulletin,* Edgar Waite, conducted an interview with Burbank and obtained his reaction to Ford's ideas. The resulting article which appeared on January 22, 1926 ran the headline "I am an infidel, declares Burbank, casting doubt on the soul immortality theory." During the interview, Burbank doubted that there was an afterlife, and later repeated and reinforced his comments that he was an infidel. Burbank considered himself a scientist, who believed in the truth as developed by science, and felt that religions were on a tottering foundation. In 1926, this story created shockwaves around the world, and Burbank was the object of hatred within 24 hours. He was inundated with thousands of letters, and he assumed the obligation to respond to as many as possible. This controversy proved to be Burbank's last battle. Because of the physical task in responding to the volume of letters he received, using mild but fearless comments in response to those who were attacking him, and amplifying his original statements for those who supported him, he fell ill in attempting to keep up with the task. Luther Burbank died in April 11, 1926. Ten thousand people attended his funeral.

April 5, 1932.   L. BURBANK   Plant Pat.   15

PEACH

Filed Dec. 23, 1930

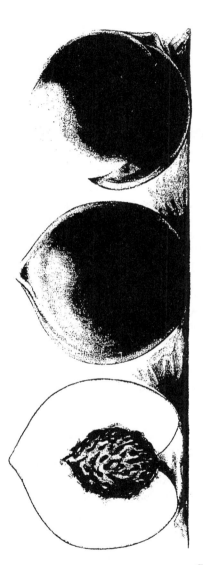

E. W. BURBANK
Executrix of
LUTHER BURBANK, Deceased

By *Robb&Robb*

ATTORNEYS

22 Copyrights as a Vehicle for Technology Protection

22.1 BRIEF HISTORY OF COPYRIGHT LAW

22.1.1 Pre-U.S. Constitution English Law

As the name of this aspect of intellectual property law implies, we are now dealing with the effect of "copying" the original, creative work of another. At this point, I'd like to pose a rhetorical question: When, in the scheme of civilized history, did the need for a copyright law arise? You each have a few moments to ponder this question. Now that the few moments are up, if you were thinking about the "copy" window on your computer, or the use of xerographic copying machines, or an audio tape deck having two decks in tandem, or photography, your answers would have been close, but not quite on the mark. The answer is: The invention of the printing press with moveable type that could produce and reproduce massive amounts of printed material, by German inventor Johannes Gutenberg about the year 1454. This single invention is credited with the beginning of the dissemination of learning throughout the world.

Imagine that prior to the invention of the printing press, if you caught someone copying your secret, unpublished work, and tried to imprison them, the court would probably be faced with the problem of imprisoning a monk who was part of a religious order, and was copying your manuscript by hand. Also, prior to the invention of the printing press, how many duplicates of your manuscript could that monk make? Gutenberg's printing press, a hallmark invention in the progress of civilization and information technology, made works available to be copied and furnished to a wide audience. Copying on the new Gutenberg press could also be done relatively inexpensively, therefore providing a profit to whoever performed the copying. Consider also that under the common law in England prior to 1709, the author's rights in his/her manuscript were depleted once the manuscript was published, and there was no legal way to prevent the mass production of the work after it had been initially published and disseminated.

In 1556, the English Crown under Mary I placed all printing in the realm under its control. A group of publishers known as the Stationers' Company was granted exclusive rights to conduct printing. Those desiring to publish a work were necessarily required to approach the Stationers' Company, and no one else, who then granted the right to exclusively publish that work forever.

However, these restrictions in England on printing ended at the end of the 17th century, and the members of the Stationers' Company found that this had cost them their exclusive publication rights. In response, they sought legislation from Parliament, and in 1709 Parliament enacted the Statute of Anne, 8 Anne c.19, "An act for the encouragement of learning by vesting the copies of printed books in the authors or purchasers of

Intellectual Property Law for Engineers and Scientists, by Howard B. Rockman
ISBN 0-471-44998-9 © 2004 The Institute of Electrical and Electronics Engineers

such copies, during the times therein mentioned." The purpose of the Act was to control the printing, reprinting and publishing of books and other writings with the consent of their authors or their owners, and to encourage learned men to compose and write useful books.

The Statute of Anne provided writers of new works the exclusive right to publish their works for 14 years, measured from the date of first publication. A second 14-year term would also vest in the author, if alive. Before enforcing these rights, the work was required to be registered and copies deposited at official libraries. Penalties were imposed upon those who unlawfully printed covered works without the authors' permission, and fines were assessed and books were destroyed. Research shows that no one was beheaded.

At the advent of the American Revolution, the state of Copyright Law in England was as described above. As mentioned previously, the framers of the American Constitution adopted a provision to protect inventors and authors, which is the foundation for American Intellectual Property law covering both copyrights and patents.

22.1.2   U.S. Constitution and Statutes

U.S. Copyright law stems from the portion of the U.S. Constitutional provision relating to authors and their writings. Article I, Section 8. In Federalist Paper 43, James Madison set forth the aims of this particular clause of the Constitution as follows:

> "The utility of this power will scarcely be questioned. The copyright of authors has been solemnly judged in Great Britain, to be a right of common law. The right to useful invention seems with equal reason to belong to inventors. The public good fully coincides in both cases with the claims of individuals. The States cannot separately make effectual provision for either of these cases, and most of them have anticipated the decision of this point, by laws passed at the instance of Congress."

In 1790, the Congress of the United States passed the first Federal Copyright Statute. That statute granted protection to charts, books and maps for a term of 14 years. The term was non-renewable. As the industrial revolution steamed forward, and new technology was continually being brought to the forefront, Congress over a period of time extended the effective life of a copyright, and also brought additional subject matter under the jurisdiction of copyright protection. For example, new covered subject matter included prints (1802); musical compositions (1831); dramatic works (1856); photography works (1865); and the fine arts (1870).

In 1909, a comprehensive new copyright act was enacted, and this statute remained in effect until 1976. The 1909 statute covered "all the writings of an author," in an effort to encompass any material that can be considered the work product of one who is an "author." However, since the law was enacted in 1909, and technology moved rapidly after that time with the advent of radio, television, computer, VCR, CD, DVD, and other electronic devices, it became apparent that the 1909 act had to be revised.

Between the years 1955 to 1976, twenty-one years, Congress wrestled with creating a new copyright act, which eventually became effective in 1976. It is interesting to note that in the year following enactment of that statute, VCRs hit the United States market, enabling anybody to tape a signal off of their television transmission, which was not directly covered in the 1976 law. It is also important to note that the Copyright Act of 1976 resulted from compromises between many diverse groups who lobbied their positions between the authors and the users of copyrighted works. For example, should a doctor who is treating a rare disease be compelled to buy one or more volumes of books that relate to that disease, or merely call the National Institutes of Health Library in Bethesda, Maryland, and have NIH copy only the relevant pages of these texts? The copyright law established compromises for that type of duplication, as well as compromises relating to the use of copyrighted works in classroom study material.

Moving backwards in time for a moment, following the American Revolution in 1776, many of the newly constituted states enacted copyright statutes, most resembling the Statute of Anne. Some of the state statutes based the grant of limited monopolies to authors under their statutory power, while other states saw copyright as a "natural right" of the creator or author of the work. There was a lack of uniformity in these laws, and works that were disseminated across state lines at that time were not easily protected. This dilemma was solved when the Constitution placed copyright enactment and enforcement provisions exclusively in the hands of the newly formed Federal Government, to eliminate the diversity among the state laws.

As the copyright law evolved from 1790 in the United States, subsequent enactments have expanded the scope and protection of the copyright law by broadening the type of subject matter included under the law, and this usually came about in response to technological advancement. Subsequent laws have also lengthened the term of copyright protection, which is now under attack as I shall explain, as well as broadening the array of exclusive rights that the copyright law encompasses.

Most important, the copyright law progression has reduced the formalities and other barriers to protection that were involved in earlier copyright laws, and today the adherence by the U.S. to the Berne Convention provides a truly internationalization of copyright protection. Whereas patent and trademark protection must be obtained in each of the countries in which you desire protection, your copyright is now provided automatically, and your copyright is enforceable in many other countries under the Berne Convention. My prediction is that following the lead of the Berne Convention, ultimately there may be an international patent and trademark. However, as previously noted, that is still a work in process.

The adherence of the United States to the Berne Convention began on March 1, 1989, and made significant changes in U.S. copyright law. The most significant of these changes was the elimination of the requirement that a notice be placed on all copyrighted works to secure copyright. Therefore, prior to 1989, everyone was accustomed to seeing the copyright notice with a familiar (c) and the year, and sometimes the word "Copyright," or the words "All Rights Reserved." However, such notice is no longer required under United States law. The 1976 Copyright Act also eliminated the renewal term in favor of a single term for copyrights measured then in the life of the author plus 50 years for works created by individuals.

In 1980, Congress also amended the definition of "literary works" to ensure that the copyright law included computer programs, to address the problem of copying of software. In 1990 Congress protected the commercial rental of computer software. In 1992, Congress clarified that audio taping strictly for home use was legal, while a royalty had to be imposed on the sale of digital recording media and devices. Congress also required such devices to embody controls against copying to prevent serial copying of digital works. In 1995, Congress enacted a public performance right for a limited purpose for sound recordings played by digital subscription services. Congress has also enacted other changes to the copyright laws, which are rather extensive and complicated, and I will leave it to other professional resources to furnish you with information about such changes as the need arises in your careers.

22.2 NATURE OF COPYRIGHTS

22.2.1 What a Copyright Is, and Is Not

Understanding what a copyright is, and is not, is a difficult concept to grasp. However, we will move forward and I will try to enlighten you on this very arcane subject. Of all the intellectual property rights, however, copyright is the one that is more "in your face" than any of the other laws. Every time you pick up a book, read a newspaper, see a billboard, listen to music, watch television or a movie, VHS tape, or DVD, you are involved in the vast scheme of copyright law protection.

In its most simplistic of terms, the copyright is the right of an author to control the reproduction of the expression embodied in his or her intellectual creation. Intellectual creations can take many forms, as I will discuss shortly. It is quite apparent that whenever a work of an author is disclosed to the public, it then becomes possible for the public to reproduce that work. Every one of you know how easy it is to duplicate a program from a software disk or online. Copying machines have been around for approximately 40–50 years that enable you to copy almost any document. The copyright law is a legal device granting the author or creator of the work the right to control reproduction of his/her work after the work has been fixed in a tangible medium.

An important precept to remember is that copyright does not preclude others from using the information or ideas that are embodied in the author's work. Copyright protection pertains only to the form in which the author expresses the creative and intellectual concepts. Thus, the copyright law is designed to prevent the public from copying the author's expression, while anyone is free to evolve their own expression of the same concepts, or to use the expressions of the author, so long as there are no copies made. For example, if I wanted to write a story about an obsessive sea captain chasing a great white whale, I could do so, so long as I did not copy any or all of the passages from Herman Melville's classic *Moby Dick.*

22.2.2 Intangible Rights in a Work Embodied in a Tangible Medium

Copyright, as the patent right, is a unique type of intangible right. Thus, to be effectively protected, the author's intellectual and creative work must be embodied in a tangible medium, such as a manuscript, a book, a painting or sculpture, a record, a film or even a digital disk or tape. These tangible articles containing and embodying the work may ultimately be distributed to many persons other than the copyright owner, and these persons may use the work for their own enjoyment. However, the copyright law restrains the one in possession of that work from reproducing that work without the owner's consent.

To provide you with a better understanding of this concept of the nature of copyrights, visualize if you would the original physical tangible copy of an authors work, such as a written work, software, music, painting, sculpture, words to a song, a dance or any other material that fits within the realm of covered copyrightable works. Imagine also, hovering over that tangible work are several intangible rights of copyright provided by the Federal Copyright system. The mere act of creation of a completed copyrightable work in a tangible medium instantly creates these intangible rights of copyright that are owned by the author of the work. As I will discuss, the "author" could be the creator him or herself, or it could also be the employer of the creator.

As soon as the work is fixed in a tangible medium of expression, the copyright laws automatically come into play. For example, fixing an electronic program on a CD, disk or hard drive is considered as fixing that program in a tangible medium of expression. Thus, once the work is reduced to writing or recorded on a tape or canvas or block of granite or film or a phonograph or on a CD or a hard drive, the Federal Copyright Law automatically applies and the intangible rights of copyright are created in the author.

22.2.3 Moral Rights

A quick word on "moral rights." In the United States, the legal commentators generally agree that the United States Copyright Law is founded on property rights. However, in some European countries, commentators have characterized the copyright as the personal right of the author, or even as a combination of personal and property rights. An author's intellectual creation, such commentators say, has the stamp of his or her personality and is identified with that author. But these rights also can be assigned to other persons and survive after the author's death. Thus, they are a unique kind of personal rights, since personal rights usually expire as the author expires.

You usually find in the copyright laws of European and other countries provisions for protecting the "moral rights" of authors. These are intended to protect the author against certain acts that may injure their personal identity or reputation. In some countries, the author has the right under the moral right provisions to have his or her name appear on all copies of the work, to prevent the attribution of him or her to another persons work, and to prevent reproduction of his work in a distorted or degrading form. In some countries the moral rights survive the authors' death and may be enforced by his/her heirs.

In the United States, the moral rights of authors have never been treated as an attribute of copyright. However, authors in this country have been given much the same protection of their personal rights under general principles of the common law, such as those relating to unfair competition, misrepresentation and defamation. California has a specific statute that prevents one from using the name of a deceased movie star for profitable uses without permission from the decedent's estate.

22.2.4 Protecting the Balance Between the Public and the Author

It must be kept in mind that one of the primary purposes of the copyright law is to engender the creation and dissemination of intellectual works for the public welfare. The opposing balancing factor in the copyright law is to provide authors the reward due to them for their contributions to society, and to encourage authors to create more works of benefit to society. Authors, like all of us, could not devote themselves to their creative efforts without knowing that they may be remunerated for such efforts. By providing authors with a vehicle for securing the economic reward afforded by the marketplace, the copyright law stimulates the creation and dissemination of intellectual works. Also, copyright protection allows publishers and other distributors to invest their resources in making the works of the creators available to the public.

One of the important aspects of copyright law is to allow certain material to remain in the public domain, such as ideas, facts and generic forms of expression that may be required for authors in the future to create their own new and intelligent works. Thus, new authors must be able to rely upon pre-existing forms of expression in creating their new works. When developing a new work, an author usually refers to certain works that preceded his/her new work to incorporate, and to some extent, the ideas and facts set forth in the pre-existing work. For example, the writer of a play may base their characters on characters drawn from real human beings, or on other playwrights' characters, as the recent controversy over the *Gone With the Wind* characters appearing in a subsequent book proved. Authors of novels usually draw their information from their own experiences, or from plots and facts within other materials. Also, software authors use the logic in programming in previous software programs. This is not considered piracy today; this is considered creatorship. Thus, the copyright law as enacted by Congress must draw a balance between providing incentives to create from material already in the public domain and provide the widest access to such material, and on the other hand provide a system that will reward authors so they may extend their efforts towards creating new copyrightable works to advance knowledge.

You may often hear the argument that the copyright law may intrude into the exercise of free speech and free press under the Constitution. However, the copyright law does not stop one from copying or making use of another's ideas, it merely prohibits the unauthorized copying of the expression of those ideas by the first author. Additionally, fair use defenses (covered below) set forth in the copyright law, and other specific exemptions to liability, give the public wide latitude to use an author's expression when the First Amendment may be in conflict.

22.2.5 Requirements of Copyrightable Subject Matter

To be copyrightable, the law requires that the subject matter be original, and that it be fixed in a tangible medium of expression. These standards for copyrightability are much lower than the standards for obtaining a patent. Also, note that to obtain a patent, you must file a patent application with the United States Patent and Trademark Office, and that application goes through vigorous examination. However, under the federal Copyright Law, your copyright is effective automatically, as a matter of law, as soon as your work of authorship is fixed in a tangible medium of expression, such as a book manuscript, a canvas for a painting, or a digital disk containing a program, movie, sound or other material. Your copyright exists whether or not you have applied for a copyright registration. However, in the United States you must have at least applied for a copyright registration before you can enforce your copyright in court. In those situations in the United States where you do apply for a copyright registration, the application is examined for compliance with registration requirements, but the work referenced in the application is not compared to other works to verify originality.

Also, the protection afforded by copyright is lower than that afforded by a patent. As the first four letters of the word copyright indicate, your copyright only protects against copying. If someone else independently creates your same work, there is no infringement. In other words, the copyright law prevents someone else from copying your particular method of expression of your ideas or facts, while giving no protection to the ideas or facts themselves.

The requirement of "originality" is met by most works, so long as they embody some creative effort, and are not merely copies or plagiarism. There are some instances where works that are created by an author or creator fail to meet the originality requirement, especially if the work consists of factual, historical information or previously published material. However, compilations of factual or historical information, even the telephone directory, are susceptible to copyright protection as new "compilations" of material.

The "originality" requirement is exemplified in one of my own personal life experiences. Many years ago I conceived of printing coffee mugs with a tart quotation from the immortal bard, William Shakespeare. The quote: "The first thing we do, let's kill all the lawyers!" from the play *2 Henry VI,* Act IV, Scene II. The expression was used in a conversation relating to the characters' plot to overthrow the Crown, and they expressed their feeling that lawyers could interfere with their evil plot. Thus, the expression is a compliment to the lawyers of Shakespeare's time.

I filed an application to register my coffee mug/expression combination for copyright protection. The application was refused since the expression was not original to me, and neither were my coffee mugs. I continued to sell the mugs, however, without protection.

Ownership and transfer of the original physical copy of a copyrightable work are covered by state concepts of contract law. However, the federal Copyright Laws govern the ownership, transfer and protection of the intangible rights of copyright that flow from the creation and fixation of the original work in a tangible medium of expression. For example, the federal Copyright Law controls who may inherit rights of renewal in certain copyrightable works created prior to 1976. When music previously written by a deceased person is subject to copyright renewal, arguments arise as to who has the right of renewal. I have personally been through such matters, and they are extremely complex.

22.3 EXCLUSIVE RIGHTS

When someone purchases an original physical copy of an authors work, such as an original painting, or a lithograph, or a book, the purchaser will have the right to look at, privately display, and enjoy the painting or lithograph, or to read the book. If the work is a piece of music, the purchaser will be able to play and listen to the music for his or her own enjoyment. However, unless the purchaser also purchased at the time the intangible rights of copyright in that work, the purchaser does not have the right to make copies of the work, to reproduce the work or to use the work to prepare derivative works, or to distribute copies of the work to the public. The purchaser does not even have the right to publicly display the work except under certain conditions, such as at home.

The rights obtained under copyright are exclusionary in nature; they allow the copyright owner certain exclusive rights with respect to the work and the right to prevent others from engaging in those activities. The Federal Copyright Law, at Section 106, gives the owner of the copyright five intangible exclusive rights:

1. The exclusive right to copy or reproduce the work;
2. The exclusive right to prepare derivative works based upon the original work;
3. The exclusive right to distribute copies of the work to the public by sale or other transfer of ownership, or by rent, lease, lending or license;
4. The exclusive right to perform the work publicly if the work is a literary, musical, dramatic, choreographic, audio visual work, a pantomime or motion picture; and
5. The exclusive right to display the work publicly.

This bundle of rights can be licensed to others in one fell swoop, or can be broken up and each right can be sold or licensed independently of the others. For example, the owner of the copyright in a literary work, such as a novel, can license a publishing house to publish the book, and then issue a second license to a movie studio to make the movie. A third license can be granted to present the book in segments over the internet, and a fourth to create a stage drama or musical adaptation of the novel.

Once the copyright owner has sold a copy of a work, unless specifically provided otherwise in the contract of sale, there is no limitation on certain of the buyer's rights to "use" the work. For example, when a copyrighted novel or software is sold to a buyer, the buyer can use the work by reading it as many times as he or she wishes, or the buyer can sell, lease or rent that copy of the work to another, or the owner may even mutilate and destroy the work. However, the user cannot copy the work. The same is true of copyrighted drawings, manuals, or the product literature of a company which is sold to third parties without any specific limitations on how the third parties may use the works. However, a competitor of a company producing product literature cannot copy the product literature of another in advertising its own products.

22.4 FAIR USE

There is one important limitation on the exclusive rights granted to the copyright owner. This is known as the doctrine of "fair use," which are acts of copying that are not considered an infringement of the copyright of the creator or copyright owner. The "fair use" moniker is somewhat confusing since the doctrine allows fair "copying." One who legally obtains a copyrighted work can "use" that work in any legitimate way, but can make copies only if such copying is "fair."

The "fair use" doctrine was long a part of court-developed law, and was codified by Congress in Section 107 of the Copyright Act of 1976 (17 U.S.C. §107). The Copyright Act sets forth certain examples of copying that can take place without constituting an infringing act. These examples can be extrapolated by courts to other equivalent situations in determining fair use on a case-by-case basis.

Section 107 of the Copyright Act states that making a copy of a protected work for purposes such as criticism, comment, news reporting, teaching (including multiple copies for classroom use), scholarship or research does not constitute an infringement of the copyright. The law also sets out certain factors to be considered when the fair use doctrine is applied. The factors given by way of example in the statute are as follows:

1. Consideration of the purpose and character of the use, such as whether the use is commercial, or is it for a non-profit educational purpose;
2. The nature of the copyrighted work;
3. The amount and substantially of the portion used in relation to the copyrighted work as a whole; and
4. The effect of the use upon the potential market for, or value of, the copyrighted work.

Note that these factors are only examples. For instance, making one copy of a video tape of a movie for your home use is considered fair use. If you try to sell that copy or other copies you made from the original work or from your copy, that would constitute an infringement of the copyright.

In one famous case, the U.S. Supreme Court noted that the question of when, where and how a work was to be initially published were important decisions reserved to the author of a protected work. As a result, the court held that the publication of excepts of President Gerald Ford's memoirs in the *Nation* magazine, prior to their scheduled publication in *Time* magazine, constituted copyright infringement, and was not a fair use.

The determination of what constitutes fair use varies from case to case. The most important factor is the effect of the use of the work on the commercial market for the original work. Since the purpose of the Copyright Law is to provide incentives for authors to create, usages which adversely impact the commercial market for the author's work are viewed as frustrating the intent of the Copyright Law and are not considered fair use. Thus the parameters of fair use are narrowed when the use of a copyrighted work is commercial.

For the application of principles akin to fair use, see Chapter 23 covering the Digital Millennium Copyright Art of 1998.

22.5   INFRINGEMENT

It is often difficult to prove the act of copying, since the copying by the alleged infringer may have taken place in a darkened room with no one else around but the copier. However, circumstantial or non-direct evidence can be relied upon to prove the act of copying. Under present court decisions, the evidence required to support a finding of infringement is: a) that the alleged infringer had access to the copyrighted work, and b) the infringing work is substantially similar to the copyrighted work. Normally, detailed expert testimony is presented to establish the substantial similarity of works involved in a copyright infringement lawsuit.

22.6   NOTICE

For many, many years up until March 1, 1989, the U.S. Copyright Law required the placement of a statutory notice, such as the letter C in a circle, on all publicly distributed works to advise the public of the existence of the copyright owner's rights. Normally you would see "All Rights Reserved" on a work to satisfy the requirements of a treaty known as the Buenos Aires Convention, which is a treaty to which the United States and several Latin American countries belong. However, most countries, such as the European countries and other English speaking countries belonged to other treaty arrangements, which did not require this additional phrase or any copyright notice at all. One such treaty is the Berne Convention to which the United States became an adherent in 1989. The Berne Convention dates back to 1886, and includes approximately 80 countries within its bounds. To conform to the Berne Convention, the U.S. Congress passed a law that as of March 1, 1989, the long-standing U.S. requirement of the copyright notice for works published after March 1, 1989 was abolished. The act defines the term "publication" as the distribution of copies of the work to the public by sale, rental, lease, lending or license. However, there are many, many copyrighted works that presently exist that were published before March 1, 1989, and the prior laws regarding notice as to works published before that date are still in effect.

The author recommends that applying a notice to your copyrightable work is still a good idea. Sections 401-406 of the Copyright Law provide that authors who place a notice of copyright on their works obtain advantages when enforcing their copyrights. For example, if the defendant in a copyright infringement lawsuit had access to your work with notice applied, no weight is given to a defence of innocent infringement in mitigation of actual or statutory damages, except in limited non-profit and public broadest "fair use" instances.

22.7   REGISTRATION AND ITS IMPORTANCE

The U.S. Federal Copyright Act provides that at any time during the existence of a copyright, the owner of the copyright in the work may obtain a federal registration of its copyright claim by applying to the Copyright Office, paying the requisite fee, and making the required deposit of the work to be protected along with the application. No legal action in the courts for infringement of a work created in the United States can be taken until the owner of the copyright has at least applied for copyright registration. However, as to works originated outside of the United States, no registration is required to bring an action for infringement of the copyright in that work.

The Copyright Act provides "statutory damages" for infringement. This is applied where actual damages are minimal; statutory damages usually are sufficient to prevent an infringer from getting away with a minor slap on the wrist. The Copyright Act also provides that an infringer is liable for either the copyright owner's actual damages and any additional profits of the infringer, or statutory damages. Thus, the copyright laws are strict, in that an infringer could pay the copyright owner's actual damages and, in addition to that, the actual profits of the infringer. Statutory damages are defined as not less than $500 or more than $20,000 as the court considers just for each infringing work. If the court finds that the infringement was willful or purposeful, the court may increase the award of statutory damages to the sum of not more than $100,000 for each infringing work.

It is important that registration under the federal copyright law be sought within three months after first publication of the work, since no award of statutory damages or of attorney's fees may be made for infringement of copyrighted works commenced after the first publication date and before the effective date of the registration, unless the registration is made within three months of the first publication.

22.8   THE DURATION OF INTANGIBLE RIGHTS OF COPYRIGHT

Since copyrights cannot be granted in perpetuity, the Copyright Law grants rights which expire after a certain time period. On October 27, 1998, the Sonny Bono Copyright Term Extension Act was signed into law in the U.S. effectively extending the life of copyright for an additional 20 years compared to the terms established in the previous 1976 act. Specific provisions are:

1. For works created after January 1, 1978, copyright protection endures for the life of the author plus an additional 70 years. For a joint work, the term is 70 years after the last survivor's death. For anonymous and pseudonymous works, and works for

hire such as where the owner of a copyright is a corporation or entity other than a natural person, the term is 95 years from the year of first publication or 120 years from the year of creation, whichever expires first.

2. For works created but not published or registered before January 1, 1978, the term is the life of the author plus 70 years, but in no case will such copyright expire earlier than December 31, 2002. If the work is published before December 31, 2002, the term of copyright will not expire before December 31, 2047.

3. For works created prior to 1978 which are still in their original or renewal term of copyright, the total term is extended to 95 years from the date that copyright was originally obtained.

Take, for example, the first "publication" of the Mickey Mouse character in the cartoon film *Steamboat Willie* in 1928, which was a take-off of an earlier Buster Keaton movie *Steamboat Bob*. Without copyright extension as enacted in 1998, Mickey's copyright would have entered the public domain in 2004. However, he is now protected until 2024.

The 1998 copyright term extension law was originally opposed by public domain advocates, such as internet publishers and certain academics, and resulted in a lawsuit challenging the authority of Congress to grant "limited" rights in copyright that now extend for generations in some circumstances. However, on January 15, 2003, the U.S. Supreme Court, in the case of *Eldred v. Ashcroft*, No. 01-618, held in a 7-2 decision that Congress had not exceeded its authority under the patent/copyright clause of the U.S. Constitution. The Court held that it was not deciding whether extending copyrights for so long a time was or was not a good idea when balancing the rights of authors and creators against the public's unfettered right to eventually use such writings and creations. The Court instead decided the case on the grounds that the wisdom of Congress' action was not within the province of the Supreme Court to second guess, and that: "It is Congress that has been assigned the task [under the Constitution] of defining the scope of the limited monopoly that should be granted to authors to give the public appropriate access to their work product."

Additional provisions in the Sonny Bono law cover specific situations, such as sound recordings made prior to February 15, 1972, presumption of an author's death, and the like. Note however, that this law does not restore copyright protection to any works that have previously fallen into the public domain, except certain foreign created works.

After the copyright expires, anyone can slavishly copy the work. For example, if one could lawfully obtain access to an original Rembrandt painting in the museum, since the rights of copyright have expired, one could photograph the painting, creating a derivative work, and then sell the photographic copies. For this reason, many museums are very careful to whom they loan their paintings, and prohibit their patrons from photographing the works.

22.9 WORKS FOR HIRE

The individual who creates a work is deemed to be the "author" of the work and is the initial owner of all copyrights. There are two situations where another entity is the author of the work, both exceptions being referred to as "works made for hire."

The first exception is where the work was created in the course and scope of employment of the creator. In that situation, the employer is deemed to be "the author" of the work and is the owner of all rights of copyright. Note however, that the various federal courts have reached somewhat different results recently as to when certain persons are to be considered an "employee" for purposes of the copyright laws. For example, if the author has an independent contractual relationship with the person who commissioned the work, that may affect the outcome of copyright ownership.

The second exception occurs when the individual who creates the work was commissioned to create the work on an independent contractor basis for one of nine specified purposes, and a written contract is signed by the independent contractor stating that the work is made for hire. The nine specified purposes are:

1. A contribution to a collective work;
2. A part of a motion picture or other audio/visual work;
3. A translation;
4. A supplementary work;
5. A compilation;
6. An instructional text;
7. A test;
8. Answer material for a test; and
9. An atlas.

The present version of the Copyright Law provides that the sale or transfer of the physical object upon which copyrights are based does not in and of itself transfer any of the intangible rights of copyright. The only way to effect a valid transfer of the copyright is by a written document signed by the owner of the rights conveyed, or his or her duly authorized agent.

By way of example, if an individual employed by a company creates a copyrightable work during employment, the company is deemed to be the author of the work and is the owner of the physical work as well as the exclusive rights of copyright in that work. Thus, the company would have the right to prepare derivative works, to make copies of the work, to distribute those copies and otherwise license the work. The employee retains none of those rights. However, where the employee creates a work outside the scope and course of his or her employment, the employee is deemed to be the author and the initial owner of all the exclusive rights of copyright. If the individual used the company's time, facilities and/or materials to create his or her unrelated copyrightable work, the company has a right to use the ideas embodied in the work. However, the company will not have the right to reproduce or market the form of expression embodied in the copyrighted work owned by the employee.

A common situation occurs where a corporation commissions or hires a professional photographer to photograph the corporation's goods for use in a catalog. The photographer provides the corporation with the negatives. If the contract included the magic words "work for hire," the company would own all rights in the negatives and the photographs. However, if those magic words were not utilized in the contract, and the photographs did not fall within any of the nine specified uses provided in the Copyright Act under the work for hire definition, since the photographer is not an employee of the corporation, and the photographer is deemed to be the "author" of the works, the corporation will not have the right to reproduce the works or use the negatives to create additional works without the approval of the photographer. Believe it or not, this happens over and over again in the trade. During my career as a practicing attorney, I have run into this situation several times. This problem can be solved by placing language in the agreement with the photographer that all works he creates during his engagement are "works for hire."

22.10   COPYRIGHT REGISTRATION FOR COMPUTER PROGRAMS

The Copyright Act defines a computer program as a set of statements or instructions to be used directly or indirectly in a computer to bring about a certain result. Copyright protection extends to all of the original copyrightable expression embodied in a computer program. However, keep in mind that your protection extends to all copyrightable expression embodied in a tangible form in the computer program, but does not cover the ideas, program logic, algorithms, systems, methods, concepts or layouts in the program.

The author of a computer program is the one who creates the computer program itself, the entire text of the program, the entire program code, the text of the user's manual, etc. If your computer program contains a substantial amount of previously published, registered or public domain material, such as sub-routines, modules, text or images, or if the work was developed using an underlying computer program or authorized tool, your work is known in copyright parlance as a "derivative work" or a "compilation." Derivative works and compilations are copyrightable under the U.S. Copyright Act.

To obtain the full benefits of registration, each individually published version of a computer program must be separately registered, provided each contains a sufficient amount of new or revised authorship to sustain a claim to copyright. If the deposit material accompanying the application for the computer program does not provide a printed title and/or version indicator, the title and any indicia that appropriately identifies the particular program must be added.

22.10.1   Protecting Computer Programs That Do Not Contain Trade Secrets

If the computer program you are attempting to protect under a copyright registration does not contain any trade secret material, the copyright application filed with the Copyright Office will be accompanied by transmitting a "deposit" of one copy of identifying portions of the program. This is accomplished by furnishing the first 25 and last 25 pages of the source code, reproduced in a form visually perceptible without the aid of a machine or device, either on paper or in microform, together with the page or equivalent unit containing the copyright notice, if a copyright notice has been applied. For programs less than 50 pages in length, the application must be accompanied by a visually perceptible copy of the entire source code. If the program is so structured that it has no identifiable beginning or end, the copyright applicant makes a determination as to which pages of the source code reasonably represent the first 25 and last 25 pages.

By now, several of you may have undergone a case of apoplexy when I mentioned that the source code had to be furnished to the Copyright Office, because materials furnished to the Copyright Office become publicly available, and many, if not all programmers have no desire to reveal their source code. Therefore, the Copyright Office provides that where an applicant for registration is unable or unwilling to deposit the source code, the object code may be furnished instead. However, the applicant must state in writing that the work as deposited in object code contains copyrightable authorship. The Copyright Office will then send a letter to the applicant stating that registration has been made under its rule of doubt, and warning that the existence of copyrightable authorship has not been determined.

If a published user's manual or other printed documentation accompanies a computer program copyright application, one copy of the user's manual is also deposited with the copyright application, along with one copy of the identifying material for the program, which comprises either the requisite pages of the source code or the object code.

For programs written in HyperCard® and other scripted languages, the script is considered the equivalent of source code. Thus, the same number of pages of script would be required as are required when submitting a source code. Note that reproductions of on-screen text, buttons and commands are not an appropriate substitute for the source code deposit.

22.10.2   Computer Programs Containing Trade Secrets

The Copyright Office has also provided for the registration and deposit of copyrightable material in software programs that contain trade secret material which the applicant desires to maintain in secret. Thus, where a computer program contains trade secret material, the copyright applicant is instructed to include a cover letter with the application stating that the copyrightable work contains trade secrets, along with the page containing the copyright notice if any, plus one of the following:

Entirely New Computer Programs   Submit the first 25 and last 25 pages of source code with portions containing trade secrets blocked out, or the first 10 and last 10 pages of the source code alone with no blocked-out portions, or the first 25 and last 25 pages of object code plus any 10 or more consecutive pages of source code, with no blocked out portions. For programs 50 pages or less in length, the entire source code with trade secret portions blocked out must be submitted.

Revised Computer Programs   If revisions to a revised computer program are present in the first 25 and last 25 pages, any one of the four options above is appropriate for the deposit requirement with the copyright application. If the revisions are not present in the first 25 and the last 25 pages, the applicant must submit either 20 pages of source code containing the revisions with no blocked-out portions, or any 50 pages of source code containing the revisions with portions blocked out.

The Copyright Office requires that when filing such applications, the blocked out portions must be proportionally less than the material remaining, and the visible portion must represent an appreciable amount of original computer code.

22.10.3   Screen Displays

The Copyright Office has consistently held a position that a single registration is sufficient to protect the copyright in a computer program and the related screen displays, including video games, without a separate registration for the screen displays or a specific reference to them in the application to register the computer program. By defining the description of the nature of authorship in the application as an "entire work," or as a "computer program," such description will cover any copyrightable authorship contained in the computer program and screen displays, regardless of whether identifying material for the screen is deposited. A specific copyright claim in the screen displays may be asserted in the application, and in such case, identifying materials for the screens must then be deposited with the application.

22.10.4 Patent, Copyright, and Trade Secret Protection in Computer Software

As gleaned from the material in this text, both patents and copyright registrations are available to protect the unlawful duplication and copying of computer software. Although patents usually provide stronger intellectual property rights, patents are normally more costly and possibly more difficult to obtain than copyright registrations. The patent law requires a full disclosure of the best mode of carrying out the steps in the computer program invention as they were contemplated by the inventor. In contrast, as stated above, copyright registration is available for software where the owner prefers aspects of the software to remain secret.

Keep in mind that unlike patents, copyrights only provide protection from copying, and not independent creation of a same or similar work. Also, in most countries throughout the world, copyright protection is automatically available whenever a work is created in a tangible form. This contrasts with the patent law, where protection does not arise until the examination process in the U.S. or foreign Patent and Trademark Office has been completed and the patent has been issued by a governmental body. Also, copyright registration must take place within three months after the first publication of the work to provide the full range of remedies under the copyright law. By using the methods described above where trade secret material is blocked out, the owner of a computer program can obtain meaningful copyright protection without revealing any trade secrets that are embedded in the program.

Deposit material is sent to the Copyright Office as a means of later identifying the work covered by the copyright certificate if the copyright registration is being enforced in litigation. When you obtain a certificate of registration from the Copyright Office, the work that was deposited with the Copyright Office does not accompany that registration, and certain deposits of works are ultimately destroyed. Therefore, the registration certificate must contain sufficient information to allow the proper identification of the work covered by the certificate.

22.10.5 Contracts and "Shrink-Wrap" Licenses

Software copying can also be prevented through the use of an arm's length agreement entered into between the producer and purchaser of software. The agreement can clearly state the limits on use and prohibitions against disclosure and reverse engineering of the software by the purchaser, that making copies except for backup is prohibited, and proscribe the penalties, monetary and injunctive, if the terms of the agreement are breached. This type of arrangement is particularly useful for the sale of custom software for use on sizable computer networks.

In the case of mass-marketed software, a written signed agreement between producer and buyer is not practical. Many software publishers sell or license their software through a so-called "shrink-wrap" license. A typical shrink-wrap license provides that by opening the cellophane packaging surrounding the program and removing the contents, the customer accepts the terms of the software provider written on or in the package. Typical shrink-wrap licenses specify that uses otherwise permissible under copyright law, or at least considered a "fair use," are not allowed by the purchaser under the contract, such as using the same software on a second computer owned by the same purchaser.

Recently, several state courts have held shrink-wrap licenses enforceable. In similar fashion, on-screen agreements are normally embedded in software programs that are displayed during installation. The user must "accept" these terms in order to proceed with the installation. Legend has it that no one bothers to read these terms when they appear, however, if you are a frequent user of new software programs, and you occasionally "manipulate" a program or two, it may be wise to stop and read one of the agreement terms the next time one pops into view. I have no doubt that you will be held to these terms if an issue of misuse arises, even though you may not have bothered to read them.

22.11   COPYRIGHT REGISTRATION FOR AUTOMATED DATABASES

The Copyright Office defines an automated database as a body of facts, data, or other information assembled into an organized format suitable for use in a computer and comprising one or more files. The copyright law does not specifically enumerate databases as copyrightable subject matter, however the Copyright Office has determined that the legislative history of the Copyright Act indicates that Congress considered computer databases and compilations of data as "literary works" that were subject to copyright protection. Thus, databases may be considered copyrightable as a form of compilation, which is a work formed by the collection and assembling of pre-existing materials or of data that is selected, coordinated, or arranged in such a way that the resulting work as a whole constitutes an original work of authorship. Thus, a compilation of pre-existing data is eligible for copyright protection, where the compilation represents original authorship.

The Copyright Law distinguishes between "published" and "unpublished" works. Here is one of those situations where the Copyright Law and its definitions may be outdone by the very nature of cyberspace. The Copyright Law defines publication as "the distribution of copies or photorecords of a work to the public by sale or other transfer of ownership, or by rental, lease or lending." Also, the offering to distribute copies of a work to a group of persons for purposes of further distribution, public performance or public display constitutes publication. The Copyright Office has made a positive determination that it is "unclear" whether online availability, with or without printers for the user, constitutes publication of a work under the Copyright Law. Thus it is left up to the copyright owner to determine whether their particular database is "published" or not.

Registration for copyright protection covering an automated database is accomplished using a single copyright application, making a deposit with the Copyright Office, and paying the appropriate filing fee. Automated databases may be registered in either one of two ways:

1. As a single basic registration covering the database as published on a given date, or if unpublished, as created on a given date; or

2. As a group registration for a database with its updates or revisions (or for only its updates/revisions) added over a period of time, whether or not they are published, but only if certain conditions are met. These conditions are available from the Copyright Office, or a copyright professional.

22.12 COPYRIGHT REGISTRATION FOR ONLINE WORKS

Online works made available over a communications network such as the internet are subject to copyright protection. This also applies to works accessed via a network, such as World Wide Web sites and home pages, FTP sites and Gopher sites, and files and documents transmitted and/or downloaded by a network. For works transmitted online, the copyrightable authorship may consist of text, artwork, music, audio-visual material (including any sounds), sound recordings, etc. Note that copyright does not protect ideas, procedures, systems or methods of operation of online works.

For all online works other than computer programs and databases, the copyright registration extends only to the copyrightable content of the work as received in the Copyright Office and identified as the subject of the claim for copyright protection. For published works, the registration will be limited to the content of the work asserted to be published on the date set forth in the copyright application.

22.12.1 Revisions and Updates

Many works transmitted online are revised or updated frequently. For individual works, however, there is no blanket registration available to cover revisions published on multiple dates. A revised version for each periodic revision may be registered separately, provided the revisions constitute copyrightable authorship. Thus, a separate application, and the present $30 filing fee would be required for each separately published update.

22.12.2 Databases

In some cases, a frequently updated online work may constitute an automated database. A group of updates to a database, published or unpublished, covering up to a three-month period within the same calendar year may be combined in a single copyright registration.

22.12.3 Serials and Newsletters

Group registration (a single registration covering multiple issues published on different dates) is available for serials (published weekly or less often) and daily newsletters (published more often than weekly), including those published online.

To obtain copyright registration for works transmitted online, there are two types of deposit requirements that define the material to be submitted with the application to identify the work to the Copyright Office. The first option is submitting a computer disk, clearly labeled with the title and the author's name, containing the entire work, and in addition, representative portions of the authorship being registered in a format that could be examined by the Copyright Office, such as a printout, and audio cassette or a video tape. The second option is a reproduction of the entire work, regardless of length. If the second option is used, no computer disk is required to accompany the application.

22.13 ARCHITECTURAL WORKS

Congress passed the Architectural Works Copyright Protection Act in 1990. Prior to that time, the copyright laws protected architectural blueprints and plans; however, this protection did not extend to the design features of the building itself when the building was created. When the United States decided to join the Berne Convention in 1989, the U.S. was required to protect architectural works, including the building itself, as well as the architectural plans and the drawings.

Of course, sometimes it is difficult to determine what constitutes the design or overall form of a building, excluding individual standard features which, of course, are not protected by copyright.

The owner of a copyright in an architectural work has the exclusive right to make and distribute copies and to prepare derivative works. However, these rights are subject to "fair use" by others. Congress also adopted new laws specifying that the making, distributing or displaying of pictures, paintings or photographs of a building that has been constructed is not an infringement of the copyright in the design of that building. For similar practical reasons, Congress also adopted a provision to allow the owner of a building to make or authorize alterations, or even the destruction of the building. Since this law is new, the total implication of this Act is far from clear, and as court cases are decided in the future, a clarification of the scope of protection for architectural works will evolve.

John Bardeen
Walter Brattain
William Shockley

THE TRANSISTOR

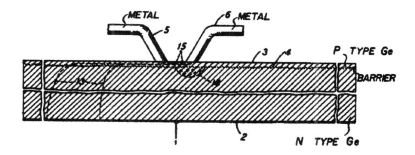

In November–December 1947, John Bardeen and Walter Brattain invented the transistor while working at Bell Labs in Murray Hill, New Jersey. The transistor was a major breakthrough in the field of solid state electronics, which dates back to the invention of the solid-state rectifier in 1874 by Ferdinand Braun. Braun's rectifier used a point contact based on lead sulfide, which resulted in a rather unstable device. Later in the 1800s, the vacuum tube was invented, which rapidly made the Braun solid-state point contact rectifier obsolete. Subsequently, scientists working at very high frequencies found that vacuum tubes would not work at the desired frequencies, and the idea of a point contact rectifier was rethought. In the 1920s, the theoretical development of quantum mechanics became an important driving force in solid-state electronics, and a comprehensive understanding of solid materials and their conductivity was developed.

In 1936, Mervin Kelly, President of Bell Labs, the research arm of AT&T, decided to start a solid-state device group. He employed people such as Bill Shockley, Russell Ohl, Jack Scaff, and others to commence work in the new group. Kelly felt that vacuum tubes were reaching the limits of their potential as voice signal amplifiers, and were not going to be the ultimate answer in electronics, particularly in telephone systems and for military use. The objective of Bell Labs' solid-state physics group was to provide a new, sturdy, and more efficient amplifier to replace the vacuum tube in AT&T's telephone system.

By 1940, the members of the solid-state team at Bell Labs had completed a great deal of work in understanding silicon crystals. For example, they learned that depending upon how single crystals of silicon were prepared, either N- or P-type silicon resulted. In those days, this indicated whether the rectifier was positive or negative. Russell Ohl made a sample in which the top part was a P-type region and the bottom was N-type; when light was impinged on the device, a voltage developed. Bell Labs management gave Ohl's sample to Walter Brattain for remeasurement and verification. Brattain was able to confirm Ohl's effect.

The solid-state group of engineers and physicists at Bell Labs was disbanded during the Second World War. When the war ended, Kelly restarted the group for the purpose of continuing their work in solid-state electronics. In 1946, Kelly appointed Bill Shockley and Stanley Morgan as heads of the team, which included Walter Brattain, John Bardeen, and several others. At the outset, this group decided that it would begin work with the simplest of semiconductors, silicon and germanium.

Shockley revived the idea of developing a field-effect device. This involved applying a voltage to a semiconductor that would result in a change in the conductivity. Bardeen found through simple calculations that a relatively low concentration of surface states would screen any voltage from the interior of the semiconductor. Bardeen suggested that they might clean the surface to reduce the effects of the surface states and make a useful device. The group of engineers and scientists worked very synergistically with each other. Each researcher had a specific area of expertise, and if one got stuck on an experiment, there was always another person to turn to for help. Their research was based on the quantum mechanics theories about semiconductors that had been developed during the 1930s.

On November 17, 1947, Walter Brattain dumped an entire experiment into a thermos of water. The silicon device he was experimenting with was designed to help him analyze how electrons behaved on the surface of a semiconductor, and why these electrons were behaving such that it was impossible to build an amplifier. In his previous experiments, condensation kept forming on the silicon and ruined each experiment. Brattain conducted this whole experiment under water, which was effective in getting rid of the condensation. He was surprised to find that the wet device created the most significant amplification he had achieved to date. He and one of the other scientists, Robert Gibney, found that by turning up a positive voltage, the effect was increased even more. Turning the voltage to negative would get rid of the effect completely. Apparently, whatever the electrons were doing on the semiconductor surface to block amplification was somehow cancelled out by the water. Thus, the obstacle to building an amplifier had been overcome.

Walter Brattain then told John Bardeen of his results, and Bardeen suggested pushing a metal point into the silicon, surrounded by distilled water. His thought was that the water would eliminate the electron problem just under the point as it had in Walter Brattain's thermos of water. The contact point could not touch the water; it could only touch the silicon. Ultimately, Walter Brattain built the proposed amplifier and it worked, producing only a tiny bit of amplification. However, it did work.

The engineers and scientists at Bell Labs had obtained a small amount of amplification using a tiny drop of water, but Bardeen and Brattain deduced that by using different materials, setups, and electrolytes in place of the water, even larger increases in current could be obtained. On December 8, 1947, Bardeen suggested that the silicon be replaced with germanium, which resulted in a current jump or amplification of 330 times. However, the jump was in the exact opposite direction they expected. Instead of moving the electrons (the negatively charged elements in the silicon), the electrolyte was moving the holes (the positively charged elements in the silicon).

It was determined that the increase in amplification only worked for certain types of current, ones with very low frequencies. This was unacceptable for use in a phone line that handled the complex frequencies of a person's voice. So the work continued to try to obtain amplification at various frequencies.

Bardeen and Brattain replaced the liquid with germanium oxide, which is equivalent to a little bit of germanium rust. On December 12, Brattain inserted the point contacts, but nothing happened. As Brattain repeatedly poked the gold contacts into the germanium, he realized there was no oxide layer on the germanium. It had been washed off by accident. Brattain continued to manipulate the point contact and to his surprise, voltage amplification was produced at all frequencies, but at a low level. The gold contact made holes in the germanium, and these positively charged holes cancelled out the effect of the negatively charged electrons at the surface in the same manner that the water had done previously. This was considered an improvement because the device was now increasing the current at all frequencies.

Therefore, at this juncture, Bardeen and Brattain were obtaining large amplification at some frequencies, and small amplification for all frequencies. The objective now was to combine the two to produce a workable device. The key components of their experiment at that time were a piece of germanium and two gold point contacts, just fractions of a millimeter apart. Walter Brattain then placed a ribbon of gold foil around a plastic triangle, and sliced through the gold at the tip of the triangle with a razor blade, resulting in two gold contacts approximately .002 inches apart. The entire triangle was then held over a crystal of germanium using a spring, and the contacts lightly touched the surface of the germanium. The germanium sat on a metal plate attached to a voltage source. By placing the point of the triangle on the germanium, a signal came in through one gold contact and increased as it raced out the other. This small amount of gold, germanium, and plastic resulted in the first working solid-state amplifier.

This first transistor was gigantic in dimension, being approximately half an inch high. Consider that, by today's standards, 7 million transistors fit on a single computer chip. The reason the transistor worked was that germanium is a semiconductor and, if properly treated, allows a significant amount of current through it, or none at all. The germanium had an excess of electrons, but when an electric signal traveled in through the gold foil, it injected holes into the surface. This created a thin layer along the top of the germanium with too few electrons.

N-type semiconductors are those with too many electrons. P-type semiconductors are those with too few electrons. The boundary between these two kinds of semiconductors is known as a P–N junction. At this junction, current flows from one side to the other, and in Brattain's first transistor, current flowed toward the second gold contact. Thus, a small current passing through one contact changed the nature of the semiconductor, resulting in a separate current flowing across the germanium and out the second contact. As a result, a small current flow could alter the flow of a much larger one, thus amplifying the current. When the input signal creates additional holes in the germanium, the way current flows across the crystal is altered and the output current gets larger and smaller, duplicating the input.

Germanium is a grayish-white element with brilliant metallic luster and a crystalline structure having a diamond pattern. A semiconductor is a crystalline solid material having electrical properties that may be varied over wide ranges by the addition of small quantities of other elements. Electrons having a negative charge, and that are within the semiconductor materials, carry the electric current. Current is also carried by the positively charged holes. The reason germanium was used as a semiconductor material in the early experiments of Bardeen and Brattain was that shortly after World War II, methods of purifying germanium to the requisite degree had already been developed. The electrical properties of semiconductors are sensitive to traces of other elements, such that only one part per billion of other elements can be tolerated in material to be used for making semiconductor devices. During the late 1950s, the purification of silicon succeeded, and this new material was used for semiconductor devices, as it is today.

A transistor (short for "transfer resistance") is basically a switch or an electronic gate that opens and closes to allow the passage of current. They are solid-state and based on semiconductor materials such as silicon. Crystals of these elements have properties that are between those of conductors and insulators, hence the name ``semiconductors." A semiconductor crystal can be produced to act as a conductor for electrical current passing through the material in one direction by adding impurities, such as small amounts of boron or phosphors.

In the first transistor, the bottom electrode was the base of a germanium crystal. The other two leads were formed on the tip of a block above the germanium crystal. The tip had a first coat of metal, then a wax layer over the top, and another metal layer. The bottom was sheared off, leaving essentially an inside metal layer, a layer of insulating wax, and a layer of metal. This assembly was pressed onto the germanium surface, and the inside metal became the collector and the outside metal became the emitter. In the initial experiment, the outside metal made contact with an electrolyte. Thus, the first time gain was realized, the device was conducting current through the electrolyte, and the gain configuration was such that the emitter-to-collector current was modulated by the base current.

In those days, a point contact device was the only configuration under study. However, Brattain rapidly realized that painting two metal stripes close together on the surface of the germanium produced a much better device. This improved device was built and presented to the management of Bell Labs on Christmas Eve, 1947.

Public announcement of the discovery of the first transistor was delayed for several months until June 1948, to allow the inventors time to obtain an understanding of the device, and to prepare their patent position. The public reaction to the announcement appeared to be "oh well." It has been stated that it was very difficult in 1948 to understand the full implication of something such as the transistor invention, unless you were a scientist or an engineer. Because Bell Labs was operating under various consent decrees in those days, it had no choice but to license the invention. Thus, the transistor was offered to all responsible parties at an advance license fee of $25,000, which was applied against royalties.

William Shockley had been away in Europe on a short sabbatical during late 1947 and early 1948, and was aware when he returned that he was not part of the invention of the transistor. However, Shockley subsequently made very important contributions to the further development of the transistor. At that time, Bardeen felt that the conductivity on the surface layer of the transistor was being changed, and the change in conductivity was causing the amplification. Shockley had a different opinion. He felt that the bulk of the crystal was somehow involved in the amplification. During the next two months, in the beginning of 1948, Shockley proceeded to expand on his theory of the bipolar junction transistor, which theory depended on the introduction of minority carriers. Thus, Shockley was the first person to both clearly see and discuss minority carrier injection into the semiconductor. However, Shockley kept this idea secret for some time. In February of 1948, John Shive conducted an experiment that verified Shockley's idea that minority carrier injection was indeed involved in the amplification of the transistor.

Although transistors today are at the heart of computer science and technology, they were actually used before the digital explosion, and were the basis of important improvements in existing analog systems, such as radios and stereo music amplifiers. Solid-state technology has allowed the mass production of transistors by the millions on a sliver of a silicon semiconductor chip. In 1956, Bardeen, Brattain, and Shockley were awarded the Nobel Prize in Physics for their invention of the transistor.

The first computer, the ENIAC, built in 1946 at the University of Pennsylvania, comprised more than 1,800 vacuum tubes, weighed 30 tons, filled an entire room, and consumed 150 kilowatts of electricity per hour. This computer must be compared with the laptops of today, which weigh about 5 kilograms, are driven by batteries, and run 100,000 times faster than the ENIAC.

By the 1960s, computers were being developed that employed hundreds of thousands of transistors. This, coupled with the need for lightweight electronic missile guidance systems, resulted in the invention of the integrated circuit independently by Jack Kilby of Texas Instruments in 1958, and by Jean Hoerni and Robert Noyce of Fairchild Semiconductor in 1959. Kilby is credited with developing the concept of integrating device and circuit elements into a single silicon chip, whereas Noyce conceived the method for integrating the separate elements. Thus, the integrated circuit was a further development begun by the invention of the transistor. In late 1970, the first microprocessor was introduced, which contained the arithmetic, logic, and control circuitry necessary to perform the functions of a computer's central processing unit. This type of large-scale integrated circuit was developed by a team at Intel Corporation.

April 4, 1950

W. SHOCKLEY

2,502,488

SEMICONDUCTOR AMPLIFIER

Filed Sept. 24, 1948

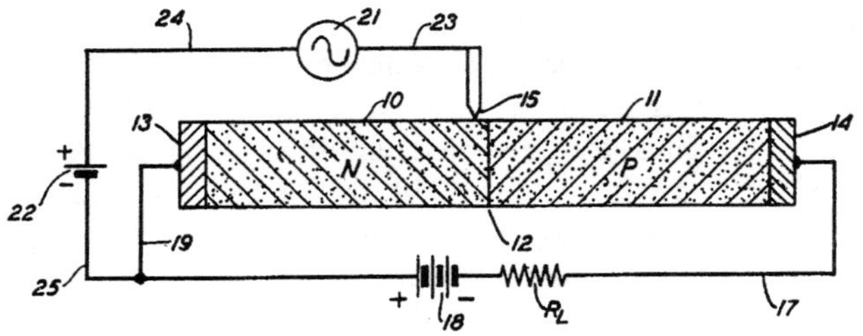

INVENTOR
W. SHOCKLEY

BY

ATTORNEY

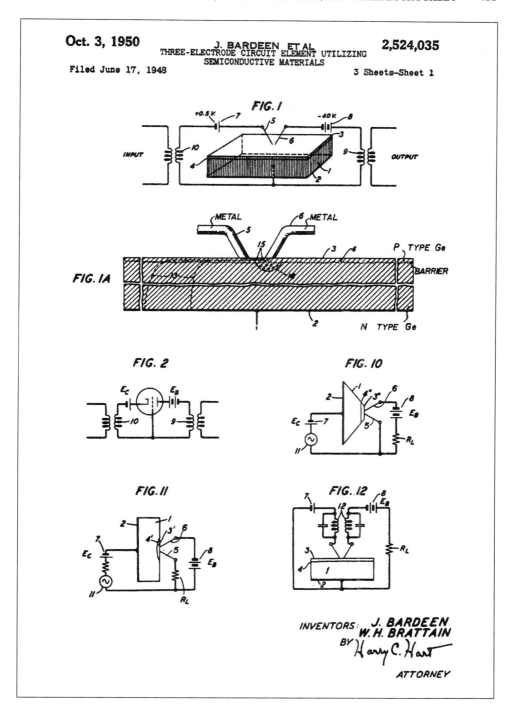

Oct. 3, 1950   J. BARDEEN ET AL.   2,524,035
                      THREE-ELECTRODE CIRCUIT ELEMENT UTILIZING
                              SEMICONDUCTIVE MATERIALS

Filed June 17, 1948   3 Sheets—Sheet 1

FIG. 1

INPUT   OUTPUT

FIG. 1A

METAL   METAL   P TYPE Ge
                                                    BARRIER
                                                    N TYPE Ge

FIG. 2   *FIG. 10*

FIG. 11   *FIG. 12*

INVENTORS: *J. BARDEEN*
           W. H. BRATTAIN
        BY *Harry C. Hart*

           ATTORNEY

23 The Digital Millennium Copyright Act of 1998 (DMCA)— An Overview

23.1 PURPOSE OF THE DMCA

The course of history has shown that as technology advances, at whatever speed, new laws of intellectual property protection are enacted or old laws are given a new interpretation to keep pace. In 1980, the U.S. Supreme Court held that new and non-obvious living creatures (human-made, genetically engineered bacterium) were patentable in *Diamond v. Chakrabarty,* 447 U.S. 303 (1980), providing a significant boost to the biotechnology industry. In 1998, the Court of Appeals for the Federal Circuit held that new and nonobvious methods of doing business that produce a useful, concrete and tangible result fell within the definition of "patentable subject matter" (35 U.S.C. §101). *State Street Bank & Trust Co. v. Signature Financial Group, Inc.,* 149 F.3rd 1368 (Fed. Cir. 1998). In 1996, the U.S. Patent and Trademark Office published guidelines to assist patent examiners (and inventors) in reviewing computer software patent applications, which a few years earlier were considered as covering non-patentable subject matter. See: 61 Fed. Reg. 7478 (1996).

Since the 1980s the transmission and use of data on digital-based platforms and interconnecting systems has transformed how information is stored, delivered and made available worldwide to anyone with access to a computer. Along with the "digital revolution" has come readily available means to copy almost anything that can be digitally transmitted, including works of authorship that are protected against copying by national copyright laws, and international treaties that bind the national copyright laws together, such as the Berne Convention (see page 388, *supra*). This ease of copying, including textual material, music and video works has caused concern amongst copyright owners, particularly those in the entertainment industry, who began to use digital encryption codes in their products that prohibited duplication. However, others began to develop technology that would avoid or nullify the encryption codes, thus enabling the duplication of the encrypted and protected works. Copyright owners responded by seeking ways to prevent others from breaking their encryptions, and disseminating unlawful copies of their works.

In 1996, the World Intellectual Property Organization (WIPO) developed two treaties: The WIPO Copyright Treaty and the WIPO Performances and Phonograms Treaty. These treaties compelled signatory member nations to enact laws that prohibited the circumvention of technology embedded in works for the purpose of inhibiting access to copyrighted works. The treaties also required members to provide legal measures to prohibit tampering with copyright management information (CMI) encoded into copyrighted works. The U.S. Congress followed by enacting legislation which implemented these two WIPO treaties into U.S. law, and also several additional provisions not in the WIPO treaties, to strengthen the ability of an owner of a digital work to prevent unlawful duplication. For example,

Intellectual Property Law for Engineers and Scientists, by Howard B. Rockman
ISBN 0-471-44998-9 © 2004 The Institute of Electrical and Electronics Engineers

the U.S. law prohibits the dissemination of devices and products which enable one to circumvent encoded anti-copying measures, and includes criminal penalties for those who violate the law. The legislation, when still before the U.S. Congress, was commented upon by those who felt the new law would impede legitimate academic research into, and development of, encryption techniques. Several exemptions were added to the law, which are discussed below. On October 28, 1998, President Clinton signed the Digital Millennium Copyright Act (DMCA) into law as part of the U.S. Copyright Law, 17 U.S.C. §1, *et seq.*

What follows is a brief overview of the DMCA, which taken as a whole is a complex piece of legislation that will probably take several court interpretations, and possible further amendments by Congress, to deal with the competing interests which were considered during the pre-enactment discussion before congressional committees, such as claims that the DMCA would prevent research into encryption techniques, stop reverse engineering in the development of software, and chill the dissemination of education and research.

Further, as technology advances and new digital techniques are developed to transmit and access digital works, the use of legal remedies to protect copyright owners may have to be repeatedly examined.

23.2 CIRCUMVENTION OF TECHNOLOGICAL PROTECTION MEASURES

23.2.1 General Approach

Pursuant to each of the WIPO treaties, each member state of the WIPO, which includes the United States, is obligated to enact laws that (1) prevent circumvention of technological measures that are adopted by a copyright owner to protect copyrighted works, and (2) prevent tampering with the integrity of copyright management information (CMI) embedded in a copyrighted work, such as the owner of the copyright, the author and other licensing information. Under the treaties, these are considered as technological adjuncts to the exclusive rights granted by Copyright Law.

In the words of the WIPO treaty, contracting parties are obligated to provide effective legal remedies "against the circumvention of effective technological measures that are used by authors in connection with the exercise of their rights . . ." to protect their copyrightable works. New §1201 of the U.S. Copyright law, Title 17 of the U.S. Code, divides technological measures into two categories. The first are those that prevent unauthorized access to a copyrighted work, and the second are measures that prevent unauthorized copying of a copyrighted work. The production or selling of devices or services that are used to circumvent either category of technological measures is prohibited in certain circumstances. The prohibition against acts of circumvention took effect two years after the effective date of the DMCA, however the prohibition on the manufacture and distribution of circumvention devices took effect on October 28, 1998.

The law prohibits one from circumventing measures used to prevent access to a copyrighted work, but does not prohibit the circumvention of measures that prohibit copying of the work. This distinction was employed in the act to ensure that the public has the continued ability to make fair use of copyrighted works, under circumstances previously discussed in this text. However, since the doctrine of fair use is not a defense to the act of gaining unauthorized access to a work, the act of circumventing a technological measure to gain access is prohibited in its entirety.

Section 1201 of the new DMCA clarifies that the prohibition on circumvention devices does not obligate manufactures of consumer electronics, computer equipment or telecommunications devices to design their products to respond to any particular technological measure. Despite this general "no mandate" rule, the law does mandate one affirmative response. Eighteen months after enactment, all analog video cassette recorders must be designed to conform to certain defined technologies, commonly known as Macrovision. At the time of enactment of the statute, this system was in use for preventing unauthorized copying of analog video cassettes and certain analog signals.

The provision of the DMCA prohibiting the production or selling of products or services used to defeat technological measures controlling access to copyrighted works includes those "black boxes" that are created for the purpose of circumventing protection measures, and which have no other commercial value. These black boxes normally are marketed solely for the purpose of circumventing digital encoding measures, and are therefore unlawful.

23.2.2   Exceptions to the Prohibitions

In an effort to meet the requirements of the competing interests who lobbied against the enactment of stringent provisions of the DMCA, §1201 of Title 17 of the U.S. Code includes several exceptions to the operation of that section of the law.

The broadest exception in the statute establishes an ongoing administrative rulemaking proceeding within the Library of Congress, with the recommendations of the Register of Copyrights, to evaluate the impact of the prohibition against the act of circumventing access-control measures. This prohibition did not take effect until the year 2000, and once in effect, the prohibition against circumventing is subject to an exception for users of a work which is in a particular class of works if the user is, or is likely to be, adversely affected by virtue of the prohibition against making non-infringing uses.

The Library of Congress will make periodic rules to ensure that one has access to encrypted works, specifically for the purpose of non-infringing uses. The Library of Congress, and the Register of Copyrights are compelled to consider various factors during the two year transition period that ended October 28, 2000, and for succeeding three year periods, in determining who would be adversely affected by the prohibition against their ability to make non-infringing uses of a class of works. Various factors to be considered are: the use of a work for non-profit, archival preservation and educational purposes; any impact that the law has on criticism, news reporting, comment, scholarship, teaching or research; and any effect the law may have on the marketability or value of copyrighted works.

The exceptions are as follows:

1. Law enforcement, intelligence and other governmental activities.

2. Non-profit libraries, archives and educational institutions are permitted to circumvent encrypted digital works solely for the purpose of making a good-faith determination as to whether they desire to obtain authorized access to the work.

3. To allow reverse engineering of a copyrighted digital work, an exception permits circumvention, and the development of technological means for such circumvention, by a person who has lawfully obtained a right to use a copy of the computer program, for the sole purpose of identifying and analyzing elements of the program necessary to achieve interoperability with other programs.

4. The law also contains an exception for encryption research, which permits circumvention of access control measures, and the development of technological means to do so, for the purpose of identifying flaws and vulnerabilities of encryption technologies.

5. The protection of minors exception allows a court, applying the prohibition to a component or part, to consider the necessity for its incorporation in technology that prevents access of minors to material on the internet.

6. The personal privacy exception permits circumvention when the technological measure, or the work it protects, is capable of collecting or disseminating personally identifying information about the online activities of a natural person.

7. The security testing exception permits circumvention of access control measures and the development of technological means for such circumvention for the purpose of testing the security of a computer, computer system or computer network with the authorization of its owner or operator.

Each of the above exceptions has its own applicability provisions which are set forth in the statute.

23.3 COPYRIGHT MANAGEMENT INFORMATION

The DMCA also comprises a new §1202 of the Copyright Act to protect the integrity of copyright management information (CMI). The statute defines CMI as identifying information about the work, the author, the copyright owner, and in certain cases, the performer, writer or director of the work, as well as the terms and conditions for use of the work such as licensing, and other information that the Register of Copyrights may prescribe by regulation. The purpose of embedding this information in the digital work is to allow ease of finding the copyright owner so that a license agreement can be reached for use of the protected work. The DMCA prohibits the knowing provision or distribution of false CMI, if accomplished with the intent to induce, enable, facilitate or conceal infringement. The statute also bars the intentional removal or alternation of CMI without authority, as well as the dissemination of CMI or copies of works, knowing that the CMI has been removed or altered without authority. Liability under the act requires that such conduct be done with knowledge, or with respect to civil remedies, with reasonable grounds to know that such conduct will induce, enable, facilitate or conceal an infringement.

The DMCA also includes limitations on the liability of broadcast stations and cable systems for removal or alteration of CMI in certain circumstances where there is no intent to induce, enable, facilitate or conceal infringement.

23.4 REMEDIES

The DMCA is quite stringent, and includes both criminal and civil liability for violation of the act. For example, a willful violation of either §§1201 or 1202 of the act, and for purposes of commercial advantage or private financial gain, is a criminal act. Penalties for criminal violations range up to $500,000 fines or up to five years imprisonment for a first offense, and up to a one million dollar fine or up to ten years in prison for subsequent offenses. However, nonprofit libraries, archives and educational institutions are entirely exempted from criminal liability.

Any copyright owner injured by a violation of §§1201 or 1202 may bring a civil action in a federal court, and the courts are given the power to grant a range of equitable and monetary remedies similar to those under the Copyright Act, including statutory damages. Special protection is given to non-profit libraries, archives and educational institutions which are entitled to a complete remission of damages in circumstances where they can prove that they were not aware, and had no reason to believe, that their acts constituted a violation of the DMCA.

23.5 ADDITIONAL PROVISIONS OF THE DMCA

The DMCA also adds a new section to the Copyright Act to create four new limitations on liability on copyright infringement by online service providers. Thus, such online service providers would be limited in their liability resulting from transitory communications, systems caching, storage of information on systems or networks at the direction of users, and information location tools. A party seeking the benefit of these limitations, of course, must first qualify as a "service provider," which is defined as "an entity offering the transmission, routing, or providing of connections for digital online communications, between or among points specified by the user, of material of the users choosing, without modification to the content of the material as sent or received."

The DMCA also expands the existing exemption relating to computer programs in §117 of the Copyright Act, which allows the owner of a copy of a program to make reproductions or adaptations when necessary to use the program in conjunction with a computer. The amendment in the DMCA permits the owner or lessee of the computer to make, or authorize the making of, a copy of a computer program in the course of maintaining or repairing the computer. The exemption only permits a copy that is made automatically when a computer is activated, and only if the computer already lawfully contains an authorized copy of the program. The new copy cannot be used in any other manner and must be destroyed immediately after the maintenance or repair is completed.

The DMCA contains many more complex provisions. The author recommends that if you find yourself working in the area of digital reproduction or analysis, that you consult a professional with familiarity with the DMCA to determine your rights and liabilities.

23.6 EXAMPLE OF POTENTIAL CONFLICT

Consider the following true facts. On September 6, 2000, the Secured Digital Music Initiative Foundation (SDMI), a consortium of almost 200 companies in the recording, consumer electronics, information technology, security technology, and internet service provider industries, invited the public to attack digital security measures and other technologies that protect copyrighted digital materials, for the purpose of allowing SDMI to determine which security system it should recommend for adoption by its members. The challenge invited the public to defeat the security measures, by altering or removing such measures, but not adversely effecting the quality of a digital music performance. Also, the digital performance must be available to be downloaded. Those challengers who were successful could either receive a monetary compensation and assign their patent and copyright rights to SDMI, or they could retain ownership rights to the circumventing intellectual property with encouragement to submit the results of their successful challenges to SDMI. The entrants to the challenge were only authorized to attack the encoded digital music samples and files, where SDMI and their copyright owners retained all their rights, and the challengers were prohibited from reproducing, modifying, performing, distributing or making any use of the samples derived during the challenge.

One team of challengers successfully attacked five of the six technologies offered by SDMI. This team wrote a technical paper setting forth the research and successful attacks, and desired to submit this paper to a peer review scientific conference for subsequent publication. The paper was originally accepted for publication, and communications began between the challenger and one of the companies which produced one of the technologies used in the challenge. The company expressed concern about dissemination of the detailed information provided in the paper describing the challenger's research. The challenger then received a letter from the Recording Industry Association of America (RIAA), stating that the company's security measures were being used commercially, and the publication of the challenger's research paper could seriously jeopardize the security technology. The RIAA letter also indicated that if the research were published, the DMCA would subject the research team to liability.

On June 6, 2001, the head of the challenging research team filed a lawsuit against RIAA, stating in its complaint that the DMCA goes against the Constitution of the United States by restricting freedom of speech and of the press, as well as academic freedom. The research team leader was asking the court to declare that full and open access to research in areas potentially covered by the DMCA was required, because otherwise scientists and programmers working on digital works could not exchange ideas and fully develop their own research. The allegation was made that the DMCA would thus harm the advance of science. In this particular litigation, the court ultimately dismissed the complaint of the challenge research team's leader, on the basis that the leader and other team members did not have standing to pursue their claim.

In this case, the research team was allowed under the DMCA to conduct its research to circumvent the security measures embedded in the digital work, however they were not allowed to disseminate the results of that research in published form. The question for debate is whether or not the encryption defeating research would be distributed in a manner that advances the state of knowledge, or in a way that allows ease of infringement. The research team was seeking the right to advance the right to publish information obtained through individual research, a practice common throughout the entire engineering and scientific community. Thus, although the research that was conducted fell under the protection of an exemption of the DMCA, subsequent publication of that research may be considered a violation of the law if such distribution is interpreted as allowing copyright infringement to be facilitated.

This case illustrates the conflicting rights between the interests of the entertainment industry to ensure protection for its copyright holders' rights, and the technological, engineering and scientific communities' need to advance technology through the use of publication, peer review and commentary, and to openly discuss weaknesses in encryption technology. It is the judgement of the author that future court decisions, and possibly amendment of the DMCA by Congress, may set forth more specific provisions defining what research is considered as leading to infringement, and what is pure scientific, peer review research, and allow the publication of the latter. Possibly the entertainment industry and the academic and scientific communities can come together to propose guidelines upon which a consensus can be reached on this issue.

◆ INVENTORS AND INVENTIONS ◆

Jack Kilby
Robert Noyce

MINIATURIZED INTEGRATED CIRCUITS

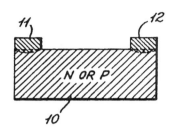

Jack Kilby and Robert Noyce are credited with the invention and development of the semiconductor integrated circuit, and the interconnection techniques used to make the circuits (ICs) practical. Semiconductor integrated circuits are also known as monolithic integrated circuits, or microchips. An integrated circuit combines transistors, resistors, and capacitors on a single semiconductor chip, which is a monolithic IC. The work of these two gentlemen comprised the conceptual and technical basis for the field of modern microelectronics, providing the breakthrough that resulted in the sophisticated high-speed computers and large-capacity semiconductor memories used today. The development of the microchip transformed yesterday's house-size computers into today's array of mini-computers, personal computers, and mainframes that are available to everyone.

Jack St. Clair Kilby was born on November 8, 1923 in Jefferson City, Missouri, and obtained a BS degree in Electrical Engineering from the University of Illinois in 1947 and his Masters of Science degree in Electrical Engineering from the University of Wisconsin in 1950. From 1947 to 1958, he was employed by Centralab Division of Globe Union, Inc., where he was engaged in the design and development of semiconductor devices with ceramic-based, silk-screened circuits. In June, 1958, Kilby began working for Texas Instruments, Inc. (TI) at TI's semiconductor lab in Texas. However, to complete the story of Jack Kilby and Robert Noyce's work, the proper historical perspective must first be laid.

The thinking that led Kilby to eventually develop the integrated circuit began in the way most inventors begin their projects: he attempted to find the solution to a specific problem. The specific problem was called the "the tyranny of numbers." For practically the first 50 years of the 20th century, the electronics industry used vacuum tube technology. These vacuum tubes, for those of us who can remember them, were fragile, unreliable devices that used lots of power and produced a considerable amount of heat. In 1947, the invention of the transistor by Bell Telephone Laboratories developed technology that replaced vacuum tubes. Transistors were much smaller compared to vacuum tubes, had a high degree of reliability, produced less heat, used less power, and lasted much longer. With the advent of the transistor in 1947, engineers began to design and create more complex electronic circuits and equipment that contained hundreds or even thousands of small components such as transistors, diodes, rectifiers, resistors, and capacitors. This led to another problem: all of these components had to be connected to each other to form electrical circuits. The hand-soldering technique that had to be used in the beginning to connect thousands of components to thousands of bits of wire was expensive and time-consuming, and was also unreliable. Those of you who have constructed your own electronic circuits realize that every soldered joint was a source of potential problems. Thus, the problem facing Kilby in 1958 was to find low-cost, efficient, and reliable ways to produce electronic components and interconnect them.

Prior to 1958, an attempted solution to the "tyranny of numbers" problem was known as the Micro-Module Program of the United States Army Signal Corps. The impetus behind this program was to create all electrical components in a uniform size and shape, with wiring built into the components. The modules could then be snapped together to make circuits, which eliminated wiring the connections together.

When Kilby began working at TI in 1958, TI was already working on the Micro-Module Program. Kilby began working in the semiconductor building of TI, and quickly concluded that the Micro-Module was not the answer to the problem, since it did not address the situation caused by large quantities of components in complex electronic circuits. He decided that the only thing a semiconductor house such as TI could make cost-effectively was a semiconductor. As Kilby wrote in a 1976 article titled "Invention of the IC," he concluded in 1958 that semiconductors were all that were really required. Resistors and capacitors (passive devices), could be made from the same material as the active devices (transistors). He also realized that since all the components could be made of a single material, they could also be made in place and interconnected to form a complete circuit.

In July 1958, Kilby began to work on his ideas, and recorded and illustrated his thoughts as his development project progressed. During the summer of 1958, most TI employees had left for the traditional two-week vacation period, except Kilby. As a new employee with no vacation time earned, he had to stay to man the shop. Kilby worked with borrowed and improvised equipment to conceive and construct the first electronic circuit in which all of the components, both active and passive, were fabricated in a single piece of semiconductor material half the size of a paper clip. By September 1958, he was ready to demonstrate his working integrated circuit, which he constructed on a piece of semiconductor material. This demonstration took place on September 12, 1958, in front of several executives of Texas Instruments. Kilby showed them a slice of germanium with protruding wires, and a transistor and other components glued to a glass slide. It was an extremely crude device, but when Kilby turned on the current, an unending sine curve undulated across an oscilloscope screen. Kilby's invention, on a 7/16 inch by 1/16 inch substrate, was called an integrated circuit, and marked the beginning of the revolution in the electronics industry that is still going on today.

The United States Air Force showed interest in Kilby's integrated circuit, but skepticism defined industry's reaction. However, the integrated circuit gained acceptance when the Air Force adopted the silicon chips for its first computers in 1961, and for the Minute Man missile in 1962. At that time, the chairman of TI, Patrick E. Haggerty, wanted Kilby to come up with a "demonstration product" that would show the wide uses that the integrated circuit chip could be put to. Haggerty challenged Kilby to design a calculator that would be as powerful as the large electro-mechanical desktop calculators used at that time, but small enough to fit into a coat pocket. Kilby met the challenge, produced a small electronic hand-held calculator that is credited with the beginning of the successful commercialization of the integrated circuit.

Kilby's work was the breakthrough that made possible the sophisticated high-speed computers and large-capacity semiconductor memories of today's information age. He later was also a coinventor of the thermal printer that is used in portable data terminals. From 1978 to 1984, he held the position of distinguished professor of electrical engineering at Texas A & M University.

In 2000, Jack Kilby was awarded the Nobel Prize in Physics for his part in the invention and development of the integrated circuit.

The second inventor in the integrated circuit equation is Robert N. Noyce, who was born in Burlington, Iowa on December 12, 1927. Noyce received a B.A. degree, and gained Phi Beta Kappa, at Grinnell (Iowa) College in 1949. He then obtained a PhD degree in physical electronics at MIT in 1953. Upon completion of his schooling, he was employed by the research division of Philco Corporation, working in developing high performance germanium surface-barrier transistors. He later joined the Shockley Semiconductor Laboratory of Beckmann Instruments in Palo Alto, California, shortly after its formation in 1956. There he worked on diffused silicon devices.

Shortly thereafter, in 1957, Noyce was one of the founders of Fairchild Semiconductor Company, where he was Director of Research. He was responsible for the commercial realization of the double-diffused masa and planar silicon transistors. During this period of time, he contributed heavily to the practical integrated circuit.

Soon after Fairchild Semiconductor was formed, Noyce began constructing silicon transistors, which were wired together by hand after manufacture. Fairchild's principals soon came to the realization that if they were to be successful, an improved production method had to be found. Noyce and Fairchild cofounder Gordon Moore began studying methods of joining transistors that would do away with after-production wiring. They developed the theory that transistors could be combined in a solid block of silicon. Noyce began making notes in his lab notebook, totally unaware that a somewhat similar theory had been developed the summer before in the Texas Instruments semiconductor laboratories by Jack Kilby.

After Kilby announced his discovery of the integrated circuit on September 12, 1958, development work at Fairchild Semiconductor accelerated; the Fairchild research and development engineers were focused on making the connections between the small transistors and the other components an integral part of the manufacturing process itself. Jean Hoerni, another of Fairchild's original founders, developed the "planar" process, using oxidation and heat diffusion to create a smooth insulating layer on the surface of a silicon chip. This allowed the embedding of insulated layers of transistors and other electronic components in silicon. The planar process provided insulation between layers, so that each layer could be isolated electrically, thus eliminating the requirement to cut apart the layers and wire them back together again.

On July 30, 1959, Fairchild Semiconductor filed for a patent covering a semiconductor integrated circuit based on the planar process. This began a ten-year-long legal battle between Texas Instruments and Fairchild. TI had previously filed a similar patent based on Kilby's technology. Years later, the U.S. Court of Customs and Patent Appeals decided that Noyce's claims on interconnection techniques had priority, but Kilby and Texas Instruments were given credit for constructing the first working integrated circuit. Thus, without knowing each other, through two independent paths, both Kilby and Noyce invented, almost at the same time, the integrated circuit, which today is commonly known as "the chip."

In July 1968, Robert Noyce continued his entrepreneurial bent when he and Gordon Moore cofounded Intel Corporation. Noyce was president of Intel until 1975, and Chairman of the Board of Intel from 1975 to 1979. Robert Noyce passed away on June 3, 1990.

June 23, 1964   J. S. KILBY   3,138,743

MINIATURIZED ELECTRONIC CIRCUITS

Filed Feb. 6, 1959   4 Sheets—Sheet 1

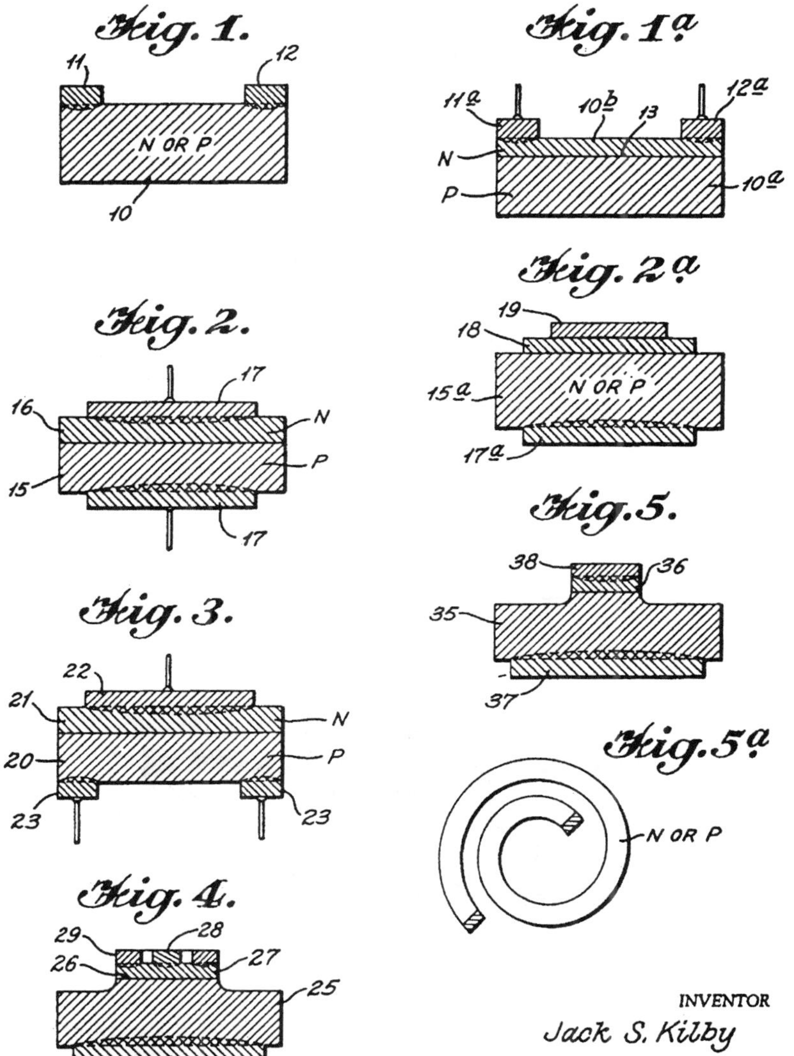

Fig. 1.

Fig. 1ª

Fig. 2.

Fig. 2ª

Fig. 5.

Fig. 3.

Fig. 5ª

Fig. 4.

INVENTOR

Jack S. Kilby

BY

Stevens, Davis, Miller & Mosher
ATTORNEYS

April 25, 1961   R. N. NOYCE   2,981,877

SEMICONDUCTOR DEVICE–AND–LEAD STRUCTURE

Filed July 30, 1959   3 Sheets–Sheet 1

FIG-1

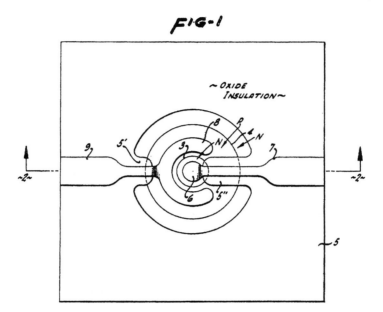

~ OXIDE INSULATION ~

FIG-2

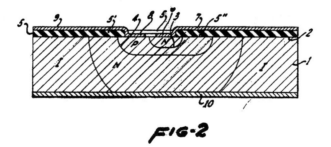

INVENTOR.
ROBERT N. NOYCE

BY

ATTORNEYS

24 Mask Work Protection

24.1 INTRODUCTION

This chapter is directed to a discussion of the protection afforded to semiconductor chips under the U.S. Copyright Law, in an amendment enacted in 1984. The subject law is discussed, as well as the definition of "mask works" subject to the law's protection, the rights acquired by the creator of a mask work, the ownership, transfer and licensing of mask works, and the limitations on the exclusive rights obtained by the creator of a mask work.

24.2 THE SEMICONDUCTOR CHIP PROTECTION ACT OF 1984

In 1984, the United States Congress passed the Semiconductor Chip Protection Act of 1984, 17 U.S.C. §902 *et seq.* (the "Chip Act"). Although the Chip Act is part of the Copyright Law and is administered by the Copyright Office, the law embodies both copyright and patent law concepts to provide protection for the physical "chips" upon which computer technology presently depends. Because of the nature of the covered technology, the Chip Act protects computer code as circuitry, including code fixed in ROM chips. Before the enactment of the Chip Act in 1984, this type of code was not universally protected under copyright law.

Mask works protected under the Chip Act are defined as follows:

"A series of related images, however fixed or encoded (1) having or representing the predetermined three dimensional pattern of metallic, insulating or semiconductor material present or removed from the layers of a semiconductor chip product; and (2) in which series the relation of the images to one another is that each image has the pattern of the surface of one form of the semiconductor chip product."

The integrated circuits, better known as "semiconductor chips," are defined in the Chip Act as:

"The final or intermediate form of any product (1) having two or more layers of metallic, insulating, or semiconductor material, deposited or otherwise placed on or etched away or otherwise removed from a piece of semiconductor material in accordance with a pre-determined pattern; and (2) intended to perform electronic circuitry functions."

Protection under the Chip Act extends to the three dimensional images or patterns formed on or in the layers of metallic insulating or semiconductor material, and fixed in a semiconductor chip product. This is also defined as the "topography" of the chip. These patterns are purely functional, and normally would not be covered under the standard copyright law. However, under the Chip Act, they are protected, provided that the mask work configuration is not dictated by a particular electronic function, and is not one of only a few available design choices that will accomplish that function. Protection of a mask work is initiated upon registration according to the law, or commercial exploitation, whichever occurs first. Commercial exploitation consists of distributing a semiconductor chip comprising the mask work to the public for commercial purposes, or a written offer to sell a chip already in existence. The Chip Act also requires that the mask work be original, and mere ideas are not protected, which is in keeping with the overall provisions of the copyright law.

Because certain semiconductor computer chip designs were not considered as copyrightable subject matter, as being "useful articles" under the copyright laws, Congress passed the Semiconductor Chip Protection Act of 1984. The law is based on Congress' powers under the Constitution to protect "writings" under the intellectual property clause found in Article I, Section 8 of the Constitution. Also, as in the case of patents or copyright infringement, the federal court system has exclusive jurisdiction over infringement actions relating to mask work protection.

24.3 MASK WORKS GENERALLY

As mentioned previously, the Chip Act defines semiconductors and the mask works used to create the semiconductors. The law also defines what constitutes fixing of a mask work on a chip product. The owner of a protectable right under the Chip Act is the creator, or the one to whom the rights in the mask work have been transferred. If the mask work is made by an employee, the employer is automatically considered the owner of rights in the mask work.

The owner of the mask work can register a claim of protection under Section 908 of the Copyright Statute with the U.S. Copyright Office of the Library of Congress to protect the mask work. The application must be filed within two years of the first commercial exploitation of the work anywhere in the world, and identifying material for the mask work must be submitted with the application. Protection is effective from the application filing date, when the identifying material and filing fee have been submitted with the application. If a registration certificate is refused by the Copyright Office, this refusal can be appealed to the United States District Court.

24.4 SUBJECT MATTER OF MASK WORK PROTECTION

The law protects a mask work fixed in a semiconductor chip product. There is no protection if the mask work is not original. Also, there is no protection if the mask work consists of designs which are staple, commonplace or familiar in the semiconductor industry, or variations combined whereby when considered as a whole, the combination is not original. In no case does protection for mask works extend to any idea, procedure, process, system, method of operation, concept, principle or discovery regardless of the form in which it is described, explained, illustrated or embodied in such work. This follows the general theme of the copyright law that only expressions of ideas fixed in a tangible medium are protectable, not the ideas themselves.

24.5 OWNERSHIP, TRANSFER, AND LICENSING OF THE MASK WORK

The exclusive rights in the mask work belong to the owner of the mask work. The owner may transfer or license those exclusive rights, or less than all of those rights, by a written document. Also, these rights may be bequeathed by will and be passed as personal property upon the death of the owner. Documents relating to ownership or transfer of a mask work may be recorded in the Copyright Office to establish and prove transfer and ownership at a later date. The recordation provides all persons with constructive notice of the facts stated in the document regarding the transfer.

Mask works prepared by an officer or employee of the U.S. government are not subject to protection of the copyright law, but the United States government may receive and hold exclusive rights in mask works transferred to the government.

24.6 DURATION OF PROTECTION

Protection begins on the date a mask work is registered, or on the date the mask work is first commercially exploited anywhere in the world, whichever occurs first. Mask work protection lasts for ten years from the date upon which the protection commences, and the term of protection runs until the end of the calendar year in which the registration would otherwise expire.

24.7 RIGHTS OF OWNERSHIP IN A MASK WORK

The owner of a mask work has the exclusive right to do, or to authorize others to do, the following:

1. To reproduce the mask work by optical, electronic or any other means; or
2. To import or distribute a semiconductor chip product in which the mask work is embodied; or
3. To induce or knowingly to cause another person to do any of the first two acts.

24.8 LIMITATIONS ON EXCLUSIVE RIGHTS, REVERSE ENGINEERING, AND FIRST SALE

The exclusive rights of the owner of a mask work are not infringed where one reproduces the mask work solely for the purpose of teaching, analyzing or evaluating the concepts or techniques embodied in the mask work, or in the circuitry, logic flow or organization of components used in the mask work. Also, there is no infringement where a person performs analyzes or evaluations by reverse engineering to incorporate the results in a new original mask work which is made to be distributed. Further, the purchaser of a semiconductor chip product made by the owner of the mask work or one authorized by the owner may import, distribute or otherwise dispose of or use, but not reproduce, that particular semiconductor chip product without the authority of the owner of the mask work.

An innocent purchaser of an infringing semiconductor chip product bears no liability for infringement prior to the time the innocent purchaser has notice of the protection, and is liable for a reasonable royalty only after having notice of such protection.

24.9   MASK WORK NOTICE

There is no absolute requirement, however the owner of a mask work protection may affx a notice to the mask work and to the semiconductor chip products embodying the mask work to provide reasonable notice of such protection. As stated above, this provision is not obligatory. Placing notice of protection on the product is not a condition of protection under the Chip Act, but does constitute prima facie evidence of the fact that you have given notice to others of your protection. If you do apply the notice, it shall consist of the word "Mask Work," the symbol "M" or the symbol "M" in a circle, followed by the name of the owner or owners of the mask work, or an abbreviation by which the owner can be recognized or identified.

24.10   INFRINGEMENT OF MASK WORK PROTECTION RIGHTS

Actions may be brought in the Federal courts to enforce mask work protection rights. Exclusionary orders for infringing imported products may be issued pursuant to provisions of the Secretary of Treasury and the U.S. Postal Service, and the infringing chips will not be allowed into the country.

   In an infringement action, one found liable for violating another's mask work protection rights may be compelled to pay the owner of those rights the infringer's profits, plus the amount of damages caused to the owner of those rights. The law also provides for the impounding of semiconductor chips subject to a lawsuit under the Chip Act.

24.11   GENERAL COMMENTS ABOUT MASK WORK PROTECTION

The Chip Act provides the owner of mask work protection the exclusive right to reproduce the mask work by any method, as well as to import and distribute a semiconductor chip that embodies the protected mask work. Remember however, that it is not infringement to "reverse engineer" the mask work for most purposes. You may also incorporate the results of your reverse engineering analysis into a new mask work, so long as the new mask work meets the originality requirement. Under the law, if you sell a chip embodying a mask work, the right to copy that mask work is not conveyed with the sale. This is the same as the copyright law that provides that you do not purchase the right to copy a book when you purchase the book. You may only read the book or use it in other legitimate ways.

◆ INVENTORS AND INVENTIONS ◆

Federico Faggin
Marcian Hoff
Stanley Mazor

SINGLE-CHIP CPU

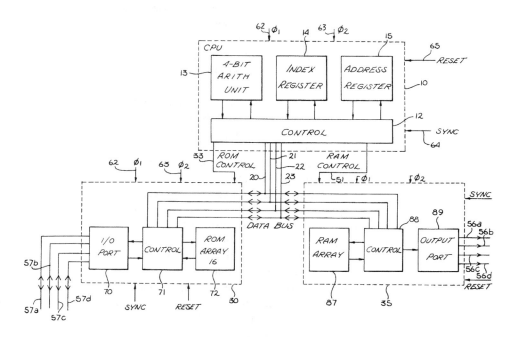

Dr. Federico Faggin was born in Vicenza, Italy in December 1941. He graduated from the Institute Industriale at Vicenza in 1960, and obtained his Doctorate in Physics from the University of Padua in 1965. He was employed by Fairchild Semiconductor Corp., where he developed the original silicon gate technology. In 1970, he joined the 4004 Project at Intel Corp. He has produced new chip designs for the personal computer industry since 1974, and has founded several technology companies.

Dr. Marcian Edward (Ted) Hoff, Jr. was born in Rochester, New York in October, 1937. He earned his BEE degree in 1958 from Rensselaer Polytechnic Institute in Troy, New York. He attended Stanford as a National Science Foundation Fellow, and received his MS (1959) and Ph.D. (1962), both in electrical engineering. He joined Intel as a Fellow, the highest technical position in the company. He has also worked for Atari and Teklicon, Inc.

Stanley Mazor was born in Chicago, Illinois in October 1941, and went on to study mathematics and computer programming at San Francisco State University. He eventually joined Fairchild Semiconductor in 1964 as a programmer, and then worked as a computer designer in the digital research department. In 1969, he joined Intel. He began his teaching career in Intel's technical training group, and later taught at Stanford, the University of Santa Clara, KTH in Stockholm, and Stellenbosch, S.A. In 1984, he worked at Silicon Compiler Systems. He coauthored a book on chip design language while at Synopsis from 1988 to 1994. He presented "The History of the Micro Computer" at the 1995 IEEE proceeding, and currently is the training director at BEA Systems.

In the late 1960s, there was much discussion in the computer industry about the possibility of a computer embedded on a semiconductor chip. A semiconductor is a material that conducts electricity better than insulators, such as a ceramic or glass, but does not provide the conductivity of well-known electrical conductors such as copper, iron, and the like. However, it was the consensus of the industry that integrated circuit technology was not quite ready for on-chip computers. In the late 1960s, Federico Faggin had invented a MOS (metal-on-silicon) process called silicon gate technology. This became the dominant semiconductor process for advanced integrated circuits. Eventually, it was recognized that silicon-gated MOS technology might evolve into a single-chip computer if a sufficiently simple chip architecture could be developed. Ted Hoff developed such an architecture with just over 2,000 transistors.

In 1969, a Japanese calculator manufacturer requested Intel to design and produce a new set of chips, and Ted Hoff was assigned to work with the Japanese company's engineers. Hoff realized at that time that the twelve-chip design used by the Japanese calculator could not meet the project's cost objectives. He proposed an alternate architecture in which a single-chip general-purpose computer central processor unit (CPU) could be programmed to perform most of the calculator functions.

Further modifications in the architecture and logic design were made by Stanley Mazor and Federico Faggin. Faggin was the one who brought the silicon chip to reality. The first working CPU was delivered to the Japanese customer in February, 1971. The single chip had as much computer power as the first electronic computer, the 1946 ENIAC, which used vacuum tubes and filled an entire room at the University of Pennsylvania.

Hoff, Mazor, and Faggin eventually convinced Intel to sell single-chip CPUs to the entire industry. The Intel "4004" CPU was formally introduced in November 1971. Since the 4004 was designed under contract for the Japanese customer, the Japanese company owned the rights to it. However, Intel bought back the rights to the 4004 by returning the $60,000 development costs, and agreed to produce the chip at a lower cost for the Japanese customer. This was followed by the modern computer revolution, and it now appears that the $60,000 paid back to the Japanese customer was the best investment Intel ever made.

Hoff, Mazor, and Faggin were also involved in developing Intel's second- and third-generation CPUs, the 8008 and the 8080.

The chip is now commonly known as a microprocessor.

United States Patent [19]

Hoff, Jr. et al.

[11] **3,821,715**

[45] **June 28, 1974**

[54] **MEMORY SYSTEM FOR A MULTI-CHIP DIGITAL COMPUTER**

[75] Inventors: **Marcian Edward Hoff, Jr.,** Santa Clara; **Stanley Mazor,** Sunnyvale; **Federico Faggin,** Cupertino, all of Calif.

[73] Assignee: **Intel Corporation,** Santa Clara, Calif.

[22] Filed: **Jan. 22, 1973**

[21] Appl. No.: **325,511**

[52] U.S. Cl. .... **340/172.5,** 340/173 R, 340/173 SP, 307/238

[51] **Int. Cl.** G06f 13/00, G11c 11/44

[58] **Field of Search** .... 340/172.5, 173 SP, 173 R; 307/238, 279

[56] **References Cited**

UNITED STATES PATENTS

3,460,094	8/1969	Pryor	340/172.5
3,641,511	2/1972	Cricchi et al.	307/238 X
3,680,061	7/1972	Arbab et al.	340/173 R
3,681,763	8/1972	Meade et al.	340/173 R
3,685,020	8/1972	Meade	340/172.5
3,702,988	11/1972	Haney et al.	340/172.5
3,719,932	3/1973	Cappon	340/173 R
3,731,285	5/1973	Bell	340/172.5
3,735,368	5/1973	Beausoleil	340/173 R
3,737,866	6/1953	Gruner	340/172.5
3,740,723	6/1973	Beausoleil et al.	340/172.5

OTHER PUBLICATIONS

Schuenemann, "Computer Control" in IBM Technical Disclosure Bulletin, Vol. 14, No. 12, May 1972; pp. 3794–3795.

Primary Examiner—Paul J. Henon
Assistant Examiner—Melvin B. Chapnick
Attorney, Agent, or Firm—Spensley, Horn & Lubitz

[57] **ABSTRACT**

A general purpose digital computer which comprises a plurality of metal-oxide-semiconductor (MOS) chips. Random-access-memories (RAM) and read-only-memories (ROM) used as part of the computer are coupled to common bi-directional data buses to a central processing unit (CPU) with each memory including decoding circuitry to determine which of the plurality of memory chips is being addressed by the CPU. The computer is fabricated using chips mounted on standard 16 pin dual in-line packages allowing additional memory chips to be added to the computer.

17 Claims, 5 Drawing Figures

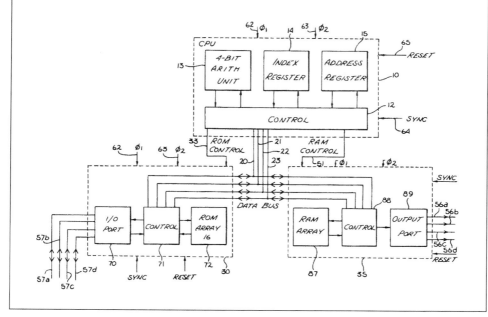

25 Trade Secrets

25.1 INTRODUCTION TO TRADE SECRETS

In addition to the exclusivity of intellectual property rights afforded by the patent, trademark and copyright laws, one may maintain exclusive rights in a development by keeping the development as a trade secret, both under common law and state statutes. There is no federal, or even state, registration system for trade secrets. The key is the secrecy of the development. Discussed in this chapter are the origins of trade secret law, the nature of trade secrets, how to establish and enforce your trade secret rights, and how to create a proper trade secret protection program in your technology business.

25.2 DEVELOPMENT OF TRADE SECRET LAW

Trade secret law developed from the common law, and not from statutory or legislative origins. This area of the law encompasses two broad policies: first, to provide an enforceable standard of commercial ethics, and second, to encourage innovation by providing protection that is supplemental to that offered by the Federal Patent and Copyright Laws. Also, unlike a patent or a copyright, a trade secret has no limited life, and may last forever under certain conditions, since trade secret law does not derive from the Constitutional provision which mentions inventors and authors. Moreover, trade secret protection extends to practically all types of information, new or not, and protection is acquired without any need to file any applications for registration or without any other formalities, except that efforts must be made to successfully maintain the confidentiality and secrecy of the information. Once the information legally becomes public knowledge, the secrecy is lost, and protection is also lost.

Since 1939, trade secret law has been substantially influenced by Sections 757 and 758 of the First Restatement of Torts. The Restatement is a compilation of laws by legal scholars published by the American Law Institute, in an attempt to summarize the existing court developed common law on several important subjects. Since the misappropriation of one's trade secret is considered a tort, the Restatement of Torts, at Sections 757 and 758, set forth the law, as it has been known and has evolved, governing many of the court decisions on trade secret law.

Section 757 of the First Restatement of Torts states:

"One who discloses or uses another's trade secret, without a privilege to do so, is liable to the other if:

1. He discovered the secret by improper means, or
2. His disclosure or use constitutes a breach of confidence reposed in him by the other in disclosing the secret to him, or
3. He learned the secret from a third person with notice of the fact that it was a secret and

Intellectual Property Law for Engineers and Scientists, by Howard B. Rockman
ISBN 0-471-44998-9 © 2004 The Institute of Electrical and Electronics Engineers

that the third person discovered it by improper means or that the third person's disclosure of it was otherwise a breach of his duty to the other, or

4. He learned the secret with notice of the fact that it was a secret and that its disclosure was made to him by mistake."

Restatement Section 758 provides:

"One who learns another's trade secret from a third person without notice that it is a secret and that the third person's disclosure is a breach of his duty to the other, or who learns the secret through a mistake without notice of the secrecy and the mistake,

1. Is not liable to the other for disclosure or use of the secret prior to receipt of such notice, and
2. Is liable to the other for a disclosure or use of the secret after the receipt of such notice, unless prior thereto he has in good faith paid value for the secret or has so changed his position that to subject him to liability would be inequitable."*

In 1979, the National Conference of Commissioners on Uniform State Laws published the Uniform Trade Secrets Act. This act was not a national or state law, but was promulgated to encourage state legislators to adopt the law. As of the present, most of the states of the Union have adopted the 1979 version, or a revised version that was promulgated in 1985. The Uniform Trade Secrets Act and the Restatement of Torts are quite similar in many respects, and the Restatement provisions continue to be influential in interpretations of the various state Uniform Trade Secrets Acts.

25.3 NATURE OF A TRADE SECRET

When analyzing trade secret misappropriation claims, two basic questions are analyzed. First, does the information or idea at issue qualify as a trade secret? And second, if it is a trade secret, is the defendant's acquisition, disclosure or use of the trade secret prohibited under one or more of the concepts set forth in either the Restatement of Torts, or the Trade Secrets Act in effect in the state where the misappropriation took place. It must be kept in mind that state trade secret law prohibits the disclosure of confidential industrial technology developed by its developer, even though that technology is not patented or even patentable. Thus, trade secret law addresses different, noninventive subject matter, where the focus is directed on the unlawful conduct utilized to obtain the secret information, as compared to technology which was independently developed by the one acquiring the information.

Trade secret laws of the states and the federal patent and copyright laws co-exist. Thus, the concept of trade secret misappropriation is handled at the state court level, and under state laws, either statutory or common law. The Federal Doctrine of Preemption applies to the patent and copyright laws, which under this doctrine makes the copyright law and the patent law entirely a federal jurisdictional matter. In contrast, trade secret law is entirely within the purview of the states. In Chapter 26, trademark law is discussed, which presents a mixed bag of both federal and state law jurisdiction.

Trade secret protection is obtained by not publicly disclosing the secret, which is in direct contrast to the purpose of a patent which provides the inventor a definite period of exclusive rights in exchange for the inventor's public disclosure of the invention. Under the Uniform Trade Secrets Act, and under the common law relating to trade secrets, one who discloses or uses another's trade secret is generally liable if he or she discovered or obtained the secret by improper means, or if the disclosure or use constitutes a breach of confidence between the one who is charged with liability and the owner of the trade secret.

25.4 DEFINITION OF A "TRADE SECRET"

The applicable law normally defines a trade secret as consisting of any formula, pattern, device or compilation of information that gives the owner an opportunity to obtain an advantage over competitors who do not know or use the particular secret. The definition includes chemical formulas, computer programs, manufacturing processes, compositions of articles, machine patterns, actual and potential customer lists, pricing information, future business plans, vendor lists, technical or non-technical data, compilations, techniques, drawings, devices, financial information and the like. A trade secret is normally considered a process or device for continuous use in the operation of a business, and not merely a secret bit of information that just has usefulness for a very short period of time or instantaneously.

By way of example, the Illinois Trade Secrets Act, found at Illinois Revised Statutes 1991, Chapter 140, Paragraph 352, Section 2(d), defines a trade secret as follows:

> "Trade secret" means information, including but not limited to, technical or non-technical data, a formula, pattern, compilation, program, device, method, technique, drawing, process, financial data, or list of actual or potential customers or suppliers that:
>
> 1. Is sufficiently secret to derive economic value, actual or potential, from not being generally known to other persons who can obtain economic value from its disclosure or use; and
> 2. Is the subject of efforts that are reasonable under the circumstances to maintain its secrecy or confidentiality.

The above provision of the Illinois Trade Secret Statute, and court decisions defining common law rights in the owner of a trade secret, normally define the existence of the trade secret in quite the same way from state to state. Thus, the above definitions are generally universal, and comprise any information that has long term usefulness for a corporation or other entity that is maintained in secrecy, and that gives the owner of the trade secret information a competitive advantage.

25.5 ESTABLISHMENT OF AN ENFORCEABLE TRADE SECRET RIGHT

To establish an enforceable trade secret right, the owner of the alleged trade secret must show that steps were taken to maintain the secrecy of the information. Thus, if the information sought to be protected as a trade secret is obvious and totally apparent upon viewing an object or device embodying the secret, or if the information is merely a base of experimental knowledge that is readily available to others in the same industry, it is highly unlikely that a court would protect the information as a trade secret. However, and this is important, the availability of information through publicly accessible sources is irrelevant, and a violation of one's trade secret rights can be proven if the information is shown to have been maintained in a secret status by the owner, and the one accused of misappropriating and using or disseminating the secret information has acquired the secret information through a breach of a confidential relationship, or through the use of other unlawful and improper means, and has not availed himself of the publicly accessible sources to obtain the subject information.

Several factors are considered in determining whether or not a certain body of information is confidential enough to support a claim of trade secrecy:

1. Is the information known outside of the trade secret owner's business?
2. How extensive is the information made known to employees and others involved in the business of the owner of the alleged trade secret?
3. What specific steps have been taken by the owner of the trade secret to guard the secrecy of the information, and to restrict its access to others, including employees not involved in use of the secret information?
4. What is the value of the alleged secret information to the trade secret owner and to his competition?
5. How much in terms of resources and effort has the owner of the alleged trade secret spent in protecting the secret information? and
6. How easy is it for the information to be properly acquired, duplicated or reverse engineered by others, such as competitors?

If the information attempted to be maintained as a trade secret can be obtained through reverse engineering of a product embodying the trade secret, such as using chemical analysis equipment, and the alleged misappropriator of the trade secret has used such reverse engineering to obtain knowledge of the trade secret, the alleged misappropriator faces no liability, for they have done nothing wrong. However, the essence of trade secret law is that if one used improper means, such as theft of the trade secret formula, or a bribe to an employee of the owner of the trade secret to unlawfully divulge the secret information, this constitutes the tort of theft of a trade secret, and the one perpetrating the theft will be held liable to the owner for misappropriation of the trade secret.

Even though the trade secret may be susceptible of becoming public knowledge through legal reverse engineering, if the alleged thief did not resort to such lawful means as reverse engineering, but instead unlawfully misappropriated the trade secret through unlawful or underhanded measures, the tort of misappropriation of the trade secret can be established. In every trade secret litigation in which I have been involved, the defendant who has had his hand caught in the cookie jar comes into court arguing that the alleged secret information is available to the public, and therefore is not a trade secret. We consistently counter this argument by enumerating the steps taken to maintain the trade secret, and proving to the court that the actions taken by the defendant to secure possession of the secret information were not the lawful route, but rather the unlawful route. Thus, the availability of information through public sources is not an adequate defense in a trade secret misappropriation case, unless the accused thief can show that he actually used the particular public source to acquire the information.

It is apparent that only certain information can be maintained in secret. If the information is available to anyone once a machine, article or process is used in public, that information obviously cannot be maintained as a secret. Certain items, such as chemical formulas, chip architecture and operation, coatings and the like can be maintained in secret, so long as the actual use or sale of the product does not divulge the secret.

Since the heart of trade secret misappropriation is the use of unlawful steps to obtain the secret information from its owner, independent development by another of the same information is a proper way of acquiring the secret information, even though its owner has maintained the secrecy of the information. Courts have held that one who obtains knowledge of a process or secret without spending the time, money and effort to discover the information independently has improperly obtained such information, unless the holder of the secret voluntarily discloses the information, or if the holder of the secret information fails to take reasonable precautions to ensure the secrecy of the information. The rationale behind the body of trade secret law is to establish and maintain standards of commercial ethics and morality.

The requirement that a trade secret be kept in secret by its owner is not an absolute requirement. For example, if others know of the same information through independent sources, but are also keeping the information secret, the first owner of the same information also has a trade secret that can be protected. The standard of secrecy requires that a sufficient element of secrecy must exist so that except by the use of improper means, it would be difficult or impossible to acquire the information from its owner.

Computer programs are initially created in a source code, which is a mathematical and word language that those trained in the art can understand. Upon completion, a source code is converted to an object code to guide and deliver the electrical impulses that operate the associated computer. Normally, the object code cannot be read, and it is this object code that is imbedded on the chips, disks or the medium distributed to the user of the program. What would happen if a software company mass produced and distributed CD's containing its program to the public, but kept the source code in confidence, and maintained it in secrecy? Would the program be deemed sufficiently secret to merit trade secret protection? In the case of Q-Co. *Industries, Inc. v. Hoffman,* 625 F.Supp.608; 228 USPQ 554 (SDNY 1985), the court held that the program was still sufficiently secret to permit trade secret protection.

Obviously, if one creates a trade secret in the course of their business, others connected with the business, such as employees, must be able to access and use the secret information in order to manufacture the goods or services which the company produces to generate income. Thus, it is quite common that secret information is disclosed to a select group of the owner's employees, licensees, distributors, vendors and others working in close relationship with the owner of the secret information. This practice is permissible without destroying the trade secret status of the information, as long as the information is restricted to those who actually have a requirement to use the information, and the owner takes reasonable precautions, such as confidentiality agreements, to ensure that the information is kept confidential among the small group to which the information is disseminated.

25.6   EVEN THREATENED TRADE SECRET THEFT CAN BE STOPPED

Once a trade secret is out, it cannot be returned to its secret status—you can't unpop a balloon. As a result, threatened or inevitable misappropriation of a trade secret may be stopped by a court before it happens. Suppose, for example, an employee has taken a new position working for a direct competitor, and that employee had knowledge of your company's trade secrets. In the new position, the employee will be placed in a job with identical or similar tasks compared to his employment for your company. In this situation, even though no secrets have been misappropriated, a court may prevent the employee from entering into employment with your competitor for a reasonable time period after leaving your employ. One court, in such a situation, stated that unless an employee possesses an uncanny ability to compartmentalize information in his or her head, he/she of necessity will be using and relying upon the former employer's trade secrets. The rationale for this "inevitable" potential use of the former employer's trade secrets was stated as: "When an employee is placed in a position where he is called upon to solve problems similar to or the same as those solved for his past employer, the employee, consciously or unconsciously, will inevitably draw upon the knowledge, including trade secret information, obtained while working for his past employer." See: *C&F Packing Co. v. IBP, Inc.,* 1998 U.S. Dist. Lexis 3221 (N.D. Ill. 1998), slip opinion at 23, 25; *PepsiCo, Inc. v. Redmond,* 54 F. 3d 1262, 1268 (7th Cir. 1995). The "inevitable disclosure" rule is not applied in all cases. For example, the wood and building products business was considered comparatively "low-tech," and a former employee's tasks for his former employer were considered to be driven by general expertise he learned on the job, rather than by highly technical, proprietary or secret information. Thus the employee was allowed to accept his new job. See: *International Paper Co. v. Suwyn,* 996 F. Supp. 246 (S.D.N.Y. 1997). The concept of protecting trade secrets from unlawful disclosure is also an important consideration in crafting confidentiality and non-competition agreements between employees and their employers. As stated previously in §§20.3–20.7 of this text, an employee leaving one position to begin working for a competitor of the former employer is allowed to use the normal skills and knowledge that are learned during the prior employment at his or her new employment. However, a line is drawn in the sand preventing the employee from using or disclosing trade secret, proprietary or confidential information (they all mean the same thing) that was made known to, or developed by, the employee at the former position. I therefore recommend that whether you are an employee about to embark on a new employment, or if you are the manager or owner of a business that has a portfolio of trade secret information, be sure that you enter into trade secret agreements with full knowledge of what is expected of you if and when your employment picture changes. Your skilled intellectual property and/or employment legal professional can assist you.

25.7   CREATING A MEANINGFUL TRADE SECRET PROTECTION PROGRAM

As you continue through your careers, it will be important for you to identify the protectable trade secrets and confidential business information you are working with on a regular, ongoing basis. You will probably be asked to establish, or may be working with, a trade secret protection protocol that is designed to protect such information. The identification and protection of trade secret information is a continuing dynamic process, and does not stay still. Your and your company's portfolio of trade secrets will constantly change, as certain information becomes obsolete and is no longer commercially valuable, and new information is created which may be extremely valuable, and must be properly protected.

A recommended starting point for the development of a trade secret protection program comprises an audit of relevant intellectual property to identify the company's protectable trade secrets. This audit should be conducted in conjunction with your intellectual property attorney, so that the results of the audit can be protected from discovery if litigation involving the trade secrets arises. The audit should be conducted often enough to establish a viable trade secret program, possibly once every year or every other year.

The first aspect of the audit is to identify each element of proprietary information used in your organization that may concern research and development, production or production processes, and/or quality control procedures. The audit should also identify proprietary business information relating to sales, marketing, customers, financial information including pricing and purchasing, and administrative information that is intended to be kept secret. After this categorization is completed, and if practiced, identify the present steps or levels of security necessary to maintain secrecy of the information. The more confidential the information is, the higher the steps of secrecy that should be maintained, for obvious reasons. However, keep in mind that any information that you ultimately desire to hold as confidential must be subject to some degree of security.

The following are examples of suggested steps that can be taken to protect trade secrets. Not all are required to establish an effective secrecy program; those that are practical to implement in your organization should be adopted:

1. Most importantly, each recipient of your trade secrets must be notified, preferably in writing, that the transmitted information is confidential and/or proprietary, and that the information is not to be disclosed to others, or used by the recipient for the recipient's benefit, without the express written approval of the owner of the trade secret. This is usually accomplished by placing a confidentiality notice on all proprietary drawings, documents and media that are submitted to the recipient of the trade secrets, as well as the word "Confidential" placed on each page or item that is divulged. The recipient should also sign a confidentiality or non-disclosure agreement, which can be a short document that merely states that the recipient shall not disclose the confidential information to others, or use the information for the recipient's own benefit without the written authorization of the trade secret owner.

2. Confidentiality and non-disclosure agreements should be signed by each employee of your company on the day they are hired, including management.

3. Create a confidential and trade secret maintenance policy which sets forth procedures to be used inside the company to maintain the confidentiality of your proprietary information. This policy statement should be given to each employee, and each employee should sign a document acknowledging receipt of the confidentiality policy.

4. The trade secret policy information given to the employees should include procedures preventing the inadvertent disclosure of trade secrets in written publications, speaking engagements, at trade shows or other organizations where trade secrets may be divulged while one is trying to sell the company's products. This procedure should be particularly applicable to your sales force.

5. Access to your plant or research and development facility should be made available only to your employees upon identification, and to all others who sign in at a front desk, loading dock, or other entrance. Also, your facility should have doors that can be locked when the facility is not in use, as well as alarm systems on the doors and windows, and, if necessary, after hour security personnel. A physical se-

curity system can be created based upon the specific needs of your company, and the specific nature of its proprietary information.

6. The trade secret documents inside your facility should only be disseminated to those on a "need to know" basis. These employees who need to use such information should sign a log indicating when they have the proprietary information in their possession, and when they have returned it, preferably to a vault or other secure place.

7. If possible, you should apply codes, preferably secret, to identify data or ingredients in your proprietary information.

8. Where possible or practical, the components of a trade secret can be segregated amongst the different departments or company personnel so that each has only a "piece of the puzzle." This is particularly applicable in the development of software.

9. Keep all confidential drawings and documents in locked drawers or areas when not in use.

10. Enter agreements with each of your vendors regarding their obligation to maintain your confidential information in secret. It is also wise to enter into agreements with your vendors that if they are part of a group that develops patentable or proprietary subject matter while working on your projects, that you and your company become the owner of such new technology.

11. Erect physical barriers inside your facility to prevent the unauthorized viewing of proprietary process technology. Install "Keep Out" or "Authorized Personnel Only" signage at the entrance points to sensitive areas of the plant, and have a written policy regarding who may enter the authorized areas.

12. Ensure that each of your employees know that they are prohibited from remaining in the plant after hours without express permission from authorized personnel, and inform your security staff to rigidly enforce these rules and regulations.

13. Make sure your employees know which areas they are allowed to access freely, and which areas require special access permits.

14. Require employees to wear identification badges or carry identification cards. This is something that is more and more common these days, and your employees should not object to such identification criteria.

15. Reproduce only a limited number of sensitive documents and maintain procedures for retrieving and collecting all copies used by your employees. This includes a written procedure for ensuring that all copies that were disseminated have been returned after use.

16. Use authorized access codes or passwords for copying machines and computers. Also, use key and encrypted computer data access to control theft of secret computer-stored information. Do not electronically transmit sensitive materials through unsecured electronic paths.

17. Have written and established policies and procedures controlling the destruction of documents, and monitor compliance with this policy.

18. Establish a program to regularly advise your company's employees regarding the maintenance of trade secrets and confidential business information.

19. Conduct "exit interviews" to obtain the return of all company documents that are

confidential, and to remind ex-employees of their obligation not to use or disclose confidential information of the company to future employers or others, or to use such confidential information for their own benefit or the benefit of their new employer.

I fully realize that it would be impractical for you or your company to incorporate all of the above suggestions into a confidentiality program. However, to maintain the secrecy of your confidential information, those above measures that are reasonable under the circumstances to maintain secrecy should be implemented. Remember, if you are compelled to charge a former employee with theft of trade secrets, you must first establish to the satisfaction of the court and/or jury that you took reasonable precautions to ensure that your confidential information was adequately protected under the circumstances. Note that unduly expensive or extreme procedures are not required by the courts to be implemented to protect trade secrets.

25.8 DAMAGES AND INJUNCTIONS

Where the trade secret owner has taken action against one who has misappropriated its trade secrets, the Uniform Trade Secrets Act provides for injunctive relief, monetary damages, and under certain circumstances the recovery of attorneys fees. Appropriate injunctive relief prohibits the defendant from further use or dissemination of the secret information, and from further use or sale of any product or process that incorporates the secret information. It is also possible for the owner of a trade secret to obtain relief against a future threatened misappropriation of trade secrets, as well as actual misappropriation.

Monetary damages could include both the actual loss in terms of dollars caused by the misappropriation, and the value of the unjust enrichment caused by the misappropriation that is not taken into account in computing actual loss. If neither of these factors can be proved by a preponderance of the evidence, it is possible for the court or jury to award damages measured in terms of a reasonable royalty for the misappropriator's unauthorized disclosure or use of a trade secret. Keep in mind that if willful and malicious misappropriation exists, the court may award reasonable attorneys fees to the prevailing party. In my experience, it has always been that the one who misappropriates another's trade secrets does it willfully and with malicious intent. It is very hard to steal one's trade secrets without fully intending to do so.

25.9 CONFIDENCE

The unlawful taking of one's trade secret rights may arise from a breach of confidence or breach of confidentiality, such as a situation arising from a technical relationship in which confidentiality is expected for one or more reasons inherent in the relationship. Examples are the attorney/client relationship, partner and partner relationship, and those relationships arising informally, from moral, social, domestic or purely personal interaction. For example, several courts have found that confidential relationships exist when the parties' relationship is that of partners, joint venturers, licensor and licensee, and employer and employee.

Generally, not all employment relationships involve a degree of confidentiality. However where an employee acquires an intimate knowledge of the employer's business, and the nature of that business is to maintain its knowledge and technology in secret, the relationship can be deemed a confidential one. In such situations the law implies, as a part of the employment relationship, an agreement not to use or disclose confidential information that an employee receives incident to the employment, when the employee knows or should have known that the employer desires such information to be kept secret. Any unauthorized use or disclosure of trade secret information learned through a confidential relationship constitutes a misappropriation of that trade secret information. This confidentially extends even beyond the term of employment.

The courts have developed a rule that a former employee is free to use the general knowledge, skills and experience gained during prior employment. This is true even when the employee has increased his or her skills or has received complex training during the former employment. However, a line is attempted to be drawn in the sand where the employee, in his or her next employment uses information that constitutes the trade secrets or confidential information of the first employer. Therefore, as you move from one employment position to another during your career, you must remember that any information that was given to you in confidence by your prior employer cannot be used for your benefit or for the benefit of your new employer.

◆ INVENTORS AND INVENTIONS ◆

Stephen Wozniak

PERSONAL COMPUTERS

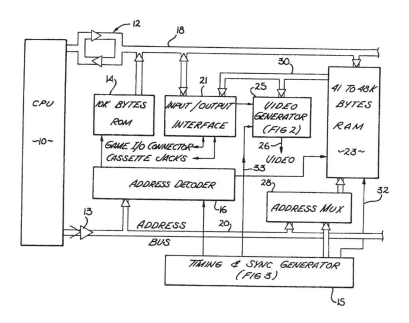

Stephen Wozniak developed the Apple II computer, which was one of the first personal computers to be used by medium- to large-size businesses and, ultimately, by home users. Wozniak, along with Steve Jobs, created Apple Computers, Inc., the first in the market with personal computers. They are credited with beginning the computer industry, which is still on an exponential rise.

Stephen G. Wozniak was born in 1950, and as a child was extremely interested in mathematics and computers. He was the son of a Lockheed engineer, who first incubated his technology interests. Wozniak's father assisted him in science fair projects devoted to electronic themes. By fifth grade, Wozniak was building large computer-like science fair projects, and in sixth grade he built a computer that played tic-tac-toe. He also built his own amateur radio station and received his ham radio license in the sixth grade. He designed complete computers and constructed them all through high school and college. He built his first computer at age 13, and was president of the Electronics Club in high school. This drive led him on a path to becoming an engineer; however in the mid 1970s, Wozniak decided to drop out of his engineering studies at the University of California at Berkeley. He went to work for Hewlett-Packard designing calculator chips, and there he met a fellow worker, John Draper, who was working in his spare time on a "blue box," an illegal phone attachment permitting users to make free long distance telephone calls.

Intellectual Property Law for Engineers and Scientists, by Howard B. Rockman
ISBN 0-471-44998-9 © 2004 The Institute of Electrical and Electronics Engineers

Wozniak also met a summer employee, Steve Jobs, and Jobs soon was helping Wozniak sell the blue boxes.

While still working at Hewlett-Packard, Wozniak joined, and then became the "spiritual" leader of a group of computer "wonks" in Palo Alto, California, known as the Home Brew Computer Club. In 1975, Steve Jobs also began attending meetings of the club. Working in Steve Jobs' bedroom, Wozniak and Jobs designed what would later become the Apple I computer. The prototype was constructed in Job's garage. Jobs then convinced a local electronic retailer to order 25 Apple Is. To obtain the capital necessary to manufacture these 25 machines, Jobs sold his Volkswagen Microbus, and Wozniak sold his HP scientific calculator, enabling them to raise $1,300. They also obtained credit from local electronic suppliers, and began producing the Apple I. Wozniak later resigned from Hewlett-Packard and became Vice President in charge of R&D of this new company, which was called Apple Computers.

Urban legend holds that the name "Apple" came from a summer job that Jobs had picking apples in Oregon. The company logo, an Apple with a bite missing from it, is a reference to the computer term "byte," which is defined as a sequence of binary digits acted upon by a computer.

Steve Wozniak is credited with single-handedly designing and constructing the Apple I computer, which initially sold for $666 and was the first single-circuit-board computer with read-only memory (ROM). The ROM instructed the computer how to load additional programs from external sources. The computer also had a built-in video interface. During the time of Wozniak's development, the prices of microprocessors and memory chips had gotten so low that he could afford, from his Hewlett-Packard salary, enough to design and build his own computer. Wozniak owned a TV set and a typewriter and that got him to thinking that a computer should be designed as a typewriter with a video screen. His high school electronics courses taught him enough about circuitry to understand how to drive a TV monitor and to get it to draw shapes of characters and other things. With the Apple I, Wozniak had constructed a computer that could place words on a screen using a keyboard, and operate a programming language for playing games. He was proud of the fact that he did this all himself. After he had developed his Apple I, he brought it to work at Hewlett-Packard and solved some engineering and design problems he was working on for HP. He also assisted others to construct their own computers by passing out schematics and going over to friend's houses and soldering wires together. Then Steve Jobs saw what Wozniak was doing and suggested that they make a PC board that could be sold for $40 and would cost only $20 to make. This was the beginning of Apple Computer. Neither of them gave up their daytime jobs. Steve Jobs lived at home with his parents, and Wozniak continued working for Hewlett-Packard. Six hundred Apple I computers were sold by Apple, generating revenues of $775,000.

Among Wozniak's early achievements was the development of a computer in which the disk drive, which had up to then been built with 50 chips, was built with five chips. This resulted from his successful effort to build a small circuit that could output a signal on a disk or tape, and somehow, when it was played back, figure out what it is. The development of these new chips also assisted Wozniak in the development of his computers.

Wozniak then set about to design and introduce the Apple II computer, which he also single-handedly designed. The Apple II began when Wozniak designed, in hardware form, the game "Breakout" for Atari. Wozniak desired to create "Breakout" in software for Apple II, which he found easy to do since he had written the Basic program that translated instructions to machine language. After obtaining a ball bouncing around on the screen, he added sound by adding speakers. Then he developed a minimum-slip paddle circuit to provide paddles to move the ball. In collaboration with Randy Wigginton, Wozniak developed a disk operating system that would load files from fixed locations on the disks in response to one-letter commands. However, this Basic control program did not provide the flexibility for efficient use of the disk drive.

Further effort was required to create a disk operating system (DOS), because one side of the RAM memory in the Apple II comprised the floppy disk and the disk drive hardware. These components are adapted to accept a program to be loaded and executed on the other side of an electronic chasm constituting the interface card and the connecting cable. The control program that Wozniak wrote has been compared to a rope bridge crossing a chasm. Wozniak's development became a foundation for the operating system, and after further development, Apple came out with DOS 3.1. The Apple II circuitry allowed the computer to operate directly with a color video monitor.

The Apple II first appeared at the West Coast Computer Faire in 1977, and included a central processing unit (CPU), a keyboard, and a floppy disk drive. To promote use of the Apple II, Jobs challenged programmers to develop applications for the machine, which resulted in the generation of several programs, including VisiCalc, which was a budget analyzer, and myriads of games. In a span of three years, the Apple II created earnings of approximately $140 million, and was the best-selling computer for five years straight, with a growth rate of 700 percent. Wozniak and Jobs came to represent the free-spirited, open minded "nerd" ingenuity that could succeed when applied to commercial enterprises. The later developed Apple II Plus and Apple III did not reach the same sales popularity as the Apple II, and the Apple III was recalled in 1981 due to design flaws. At the same time, IBM developed and introduced its new PC, garnering a major share of the office computer business from Apple.

In February, 1981, Wozniak was involved in a private plane crash, and received a concussion that temporarily prevented him from remembering things. For example, he could not recall that he was in an accident, he could not recall playing games with his computer, and he could not recall who visited him earlier in the day. When he recovered from the concussion, he took a sabbatical from Apple, married, returned to college at Berkeley, and, in 1982, received his degrees in electrical engineering and computer science. He participated in other companies involving computer technology until June, 1983, when he decided to return to Apple and provide his assistance to the company once again. Steve Wozniak helped Apple develop the Macintosh computer upon his return. In 1985, both Steve Wozniak and Steve Jobs received the National Technology Medal from President Regan at the White House. Wozniak decided then it was time to leave Apple (again) and Steve Jobs left shortly thereafter.

It is undisputed that Steve Wozniak was one of the major players in creating the computer industry that today reaches the lives of almost everyone in the world in one way or another. Steve Wozniak has credited his high school electronics teacher as greatly encouraging his development work. He recalled that his high school teacher wrote his own courses and assignments. Today, Wozniak is teaching computer classes using the same technique.

Steve Wozniak is presently involved in various philanthropic and business ventures. He created an initiative in 1990 to place computers in schools in the former Soviet Union. He has also donated computers and even entire computer labs to schools, and has worked on providing servers and internet access to students, providing laptops for students and computer training for teachers and students.

United States Patent [19]

Wozniak

[11] **4,136,359**

[45] **Jan. 23, 1979**

[54] **MICROCOMPUTER FOR USE WITH VIDEO DISPLAY**

[75] Inventor: **Stephen G. Wozniak,** Cupertino, Calif.

[73] Assignee: **Apple Computer, Inc.,** Cupertino, Calif.

[21] Appl. No.: **786,197**

[22] Filed: **Apr. 11, 1977**

[51] Int. Cl.² H04N 9/44
[52] U.S. Cl. 358/17
[58] Field of Search 358/17, 148, 150

[56] **References Cited**

U.S. PATENT DOCUMENTS

3,581,011   5/1971   Ward et al. 358/17

Primary Examiner—Richard Murray

Attorney, Agent, or Firm—Blakely, Sokoloff, Taylor & Zafman

[57]   **ABSTRACT**

A microcomputer including a video generator and timing means which provides color and high resolution graphics on a standard, raster scanned, cathode ray tube is disclosed. A horizontal synchronization counter is synchronized at an odd-submultiple of the color subcarrier reference frequency. A "delayed" count is employed in the horizontal synchronization counter to compensate for color subcarrier phase reversals between lines for the non-interlaced fields. This permits vertically aligned color graphics without substantially altering the standard horizontal synchronization frequency. Video color signals are generated directly from digital signals by employing a recirculating shift register.

8 Claims, 4 Drawing Figures

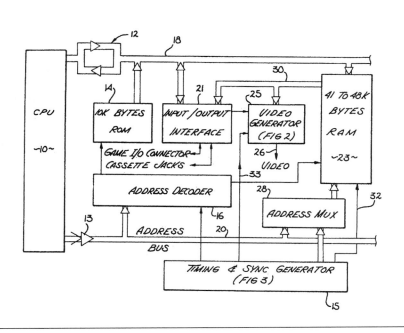

26 Trademarks

26.1 ORIGIN OF THE PROTECTION OF TRADEMARKS AND SERVICE MARKS

The area of trademark law has developed over many centuries to protect the good-will and reputation of a manufacturer or distributor of a product, or the provider of a service, from being unlawfully usurped by a competitor or others in an attempt to confuse the public into believing that the quality of the competing producer's products or services, are somehow the same as the first users products or services. This goodwill is primarily embodied in the brand names, logos, or product configuration designs used by manufacturers and service providers in association with their products, or in the delivery of their services to the consuming public. You can think of many brand names, such as Coca-Cola, Ford, Xerox, and IBM, where it can be argued that the most valuable corporate asset of the owner of the mark is the trademark itself. Thus, a major purpose underlying the trademark laws is to protect the public so that a consumer may be confident that when purchasing a product bearing a particular trademark, logo, or configuration with which the consumer has familiarity, and is favorably inclined toward, the consumer will receive the product and the quality which it asks for and wants to obtain.

A second purpose of the trademark laws applies where the owner of a trademark has spent energy, time and resources in advertising its product to the public. The manufacturer's investment is protected from misappropriation by "tyrants and cheats." Thus trademark laws were designed to protect the consumer as well as the manufacturer or service provider.

Most writers today on the subject of trademarks attribute the origins of trademark laws to the medieval era, when skilled craftsmen and artisans formed guilds. The symbols of those guilds and/or of the individual craftsmen were applied to products to indicate the source or identity of the makers of those products. The time reference of this history is undergoing some revision as of late, since archeologists are uncovering artifacts from times predating the medieval years which show the use of symbols on products to identify their makers.

The English common law, which predated the establishment of the United States, protected trademarks through actions for deceit. At about the beginning of the 19th Century, English and American common law advanced the tort of fraud and deceit into an action called "passing off" or "palming off." This unlawful act was committed when a producer passed off or palmed off his goods as the goods of another. Approximately 200 years later, this practice is still in vogue today.

Trademark rights, and the enforcement of those rights still exist in the common law today primarily in those countries which base their legal systems on the English common law system. However, the federal Congress in the U.S. has periodically taken steps toward federalizing the protection of trademarks, and the U.S. law today exists in parallel with the state common law systems, while not replacing the state systems. Congress enacted the first federal trademark statute in 1870, which law was ultimately held unconstitutional by the U.S. Supreme Court on the grounds that Congress did not have the power to enact such a law. Remember that Article 1, Section 8 of the Constitution provides a Constitutional framework for the establishment of patent and copyright laws. However, the entire Constitution is silent as to trademark protection.

To overcome this rebuke by the Supreme Court, Congress reenacted new trademark legislation, and based its foundation on the Commerce Clause of the Constitution by indicating that the federal protection of trademarks would only apply to those trademarks that are used in interstate commerce, or in foreign trade. This is still the law today. If your trademark is used on goods or services which pass only within the borders of your state, the mark cannot be protected under the federal trademark law, but can be protected by your state trademark laws. For example, a name of a single restaurant is considered an interstate use, since patrons from other states may eat at the restaurant. Each state has its own trademark law that adequately protects the users of purely intrastate marks. The current version of Federal Trademark Law is the Lanham Act, enacted in 1946, and updated many times since then. The Lanham Act today acts in parallel with the state common laws and state trademark statutes to provide extensive protection for trademark owners.

One of the features of the federal trademark statute is that by applying for and obtaining a federal registration for your trademark after examination by the U.S. Patent and Trademark Office, you have established that you have a prima-facie right to exclusively use the mark on the products or services which are listed in your registration in interstate commerce. Thus, if you deem it necessary to file a lawsuit against an infringer of your mark, you do not have to spend time or effort in court proving that you have used the mark extensively, proving how much you have spent in advertising the mark, and what your total sales have been to establish that you have a right in your mark. The federal registration provides notice to the world that you are the owner of that trademark registration, and that you have the exclusive right to use that mark in commerce on the goods or services recited in your registration. The burden then shifts to the alleged infringer to attempt to invalidate that trademark registration on one of several grounds, or to prove that the accused mark is not the same as or confusingly similar to your registered mark.

An equally important reason for the trademark registration system is that upon filing an application to register a trademark, that trademark, along with information describing the goods or services with which the mark is used or intended to be used, is listed in the federal trademark search database. Thus, you can easily conduct a search to determine whether a trademark that you propose to adopt and use would be the same as or confusingly similar to someone else's mark. The search will indicate to you, before you adopt your mark, whether or not it would be prudent to move forward and use that particular trademark. If someone else is using a same or similar mark for similar goods or services, you can avoid very expensive litigation by changing to another non-infringing mark. One of the major legal services that I have been furnishing to clients over the years provides clearance of their proposed trademarks or service marks before they begin to use them, to avoid problems in the future.

When a trademark is applied to a product or a service mark is used in conjunction with a service, the mark's primary purpose is to identify the "origin" or "source" of the product or services. A trademark or service mark serves its function even though it may differ from the name of the company which offers the product. For example, many people know of Scotch tape, but not necessarily that the product is made by 3M Company.

26.2 TRADEMARK ADOPTION AND SELECTION PROCESS

Earlier chapters in this text have been directed towards your inventive and creative efforts in producing new or improved products or process, or expressions of ideas and concepts, that can be protected under the patent and/or copyright laws. Once these products or processes are introduced to the market, they usually bear a trademark or service mark by which each product or service is identified as having originated with you or your company. The field of trademark law is dedicated towards protecting your rights in that trademark to prevent someone else from adopting and using your mark, or a confusingly similar mark, that might confuse purchasers in buying other products when they think they are buying yours. An equally important premise in trademark law is the protection against the consumer being deceived into purchasing a product or service which bears a confusingly similar trademark or service mark compared to a well advertised or well known brand. Therefore, when a producer or service provider selects a mark, a mark should be chosen that is not confusingly similar to someone else's mark and is not likely to cause consumer confusion. Also, a mark should be selected that is not too descriptive of goods or services such that the mark may not be registerable. By the way, when I use the term trademark, I will be using it generically to encompass trademarks, service marks and even collective membership marks, such as the Good Housekeeping seal.

Over the years, trademarks have empirically been divided into four types: 1) arbitrary; 2) suggestive; 3) descriptive; and 4) generic. Arbitrary and suggestive marks are registerable and useable without further proof that the marks are distinctive, that is, distinguish your goods from those of a competitor. This, of course, presumes that the mark does not conflict with another earlier mark. An arbitrary mark is one that is made-up and has no meaning in the relevant market, such as KODAK, which has no defined meaning in any language. A suggestive mark is one that would require an observer of the mark to go through several mental steps before associating the mark with its related goods or services. EVEREADY for a reliable flashlight battery comes to mind, for example.

A descriptive mark, however, is one that describes a quality, characteristic or other feature of the product or service with which the mark is associated. These are usually weak marks, but they can be registered with proof of eventual distinctiveness or "secondary meaning" after years of use. The term "secondary meaning" in trademark law equals "distinctiveness." This means that a term used as a trademark distinguishes the products or services of the mark's user from those of its competitors, and the mark has been accepted by the public as a source identifier. Such "secondary meaning" can be shown for a descriptive mark by extensive advertising of a mark, and sales of the product associated with the mark, over a long period of time, whereby consumers begin to recognize the mark as having two meanings: 1) recognizing you as a source of products or services associated with the mark, and 2) the normal everyday meaning of the same mark. I mention the mark BEST BUY for your consideration.

Generic terms are the accepted common meaning of goods and/or services, and can never be registered as trademarks, since once a trademark is registered, that word is removed from the public domain and cannot be used by others in association with the listed products or services. It is against public policy in the United States and most every other jurisdiction to remove a generic term from the realm of the public and deprive competitors of the right to use the same generic term to describe and offer their goods. For example, the terms "escalator," "aspirin," and "cellophane" are former trademarks which became generic of their respective products to the extent that competitors could not sell their products without using these terms to define or describe the nature of their competing products. Eventually, the registrations for these trademarks were cancelled. Within recent memory, the mark "thermos" also lost its registerability and became available for competitors to use as a generic term. In case you are wondering, the generic name for a thermos bottle, without using the name thermos, would be "vacuum bottle." How many people go into a store and order a "vacuum bottle?" Thus, the competitors of King Sealy, the former owner of the "thermos" trademark, argued that they could not sell their competing products unless they were also permitted to call them "thermos bottles" because of the public's generic use of that term.

Keep in mind that a trademark never stands by itself. It is always used as an adjective followed by the descriptive term or generic term for the goods or services with which the mark is associated. Thus, Scotch is followed by the word "tape." Xerox is followed by the term "copying machine."

26.2.1   Creating a Trademark

The creation of a trademark normally begins in a brainstorming session where the technical and marketing people have defined the "point of difference" between your new product (or service) and that of a competitor, and have decided where they want to position the new product in the marketplace vis à vis competing products already on the market. Next, prospective trademarks, symbols, logos, or other source identifying devices are tossed onto the table in an effort to find a brand name that will extol the "point of difference" of the product, yet not be generic or descriptive of the different qualities or capabilities of the product. For example, consider the number of brands incorporating the prefix or suffix "max" to imply the "maximum" strength, ability or value of a product compared to the competition. Normally, at these sessions, several prospective marks or brands are initially chosen, to hedge against the possibility that one or more of the marks may not be available for use.

Care must also be taken when creating a mark or brand to avoid foreign translations that may have a negative slant when applied to your product. For example, "Nova," a mark used for a car, in Spanish means "no go." Also, the mark must not be misleading, such as "Metl-Wax" for a polishing product that contains no wax. The marks that you propose should be capable of becoming strongly identified with your product, while at the same time not being descriptive of a component, quality or characteristic of the product.

26.2.2   Screening Or Narrowing Step

Once a list of prospective trademarks has been created, the next step is to narrow the list to four or five good candidates. First, those marks which may be descriptive or may be negatively viewed in other countries should be eliminated. Next, a preliminary computer database search is conducted to identify, and avoid, those prospective marks which may be the same as, or similar to, marks already used by others for similar or related products. This "screening" search can be conducted inexpensively using the database of U.S. Federal trademark registrations and applications (www.uspto.gov), and other databases of state and international registrations and applications. Note that these preliminary screening searches are inadequate to be used for a final determination whether a mark you adopt may conflict with a prior mark. The full clearance process, described in the next section, is mandatory before making a final decision on adopting a mark or brand name for your product.

26.2.3   Clearance Process for Determining the Availability of a Trademark for Your Use

The list of trademarks surviving the preliminary screening process are furnished to your marketing people or trademark attorney to have a comprehensive search conducted to determine the availability of the selected trademarks. The person conducting the analysis is furnished with two things: first the trademark or service mark that you propose to adopt, and second, the goods and/or services with which the mark is intended to be used, including the relevant channels of commerce through which the goods will pass or services will be provided.

The above information is then furnished to the person responsible for conducting the search. A full search is conducted on a database comprising corporate names, trade directory or journal information, website domain names, telephone directories, and other sources of information about products and services. There are several sources available through electronic databases with the ability to furnish this information. The typical intellectual property law office usually includes one or several individuals who are trained in conducting such trademark searches. The search develops a list of trademarks that both the computer program and the individual conducting the search deem relevant for your perusal to determine whether or not there exist any potentially conflicting marks. The primary function of this search is to determine a) whether any marks identical to your proposed marks for similar or related goods have been uncovered, and b) whether or not a likelihood of confusion will arise between any of the trademarks or service marks uncovered by the search, which are in use, and the mark that you are interested in adopting.

Factors used in comparing your mark to existing marks to determine if a likelihood of confusion between source or origin may occur are: the degree of similarity of the trademarks in appearance, pronunciation and suggested meaning; the relationship between the goods or services themselves; the respective channels of distribution and/or marketing of the goods or services in question; and the possible expansion of the first user of a relevant mark into your line of products. There are other factors to be considered, however your trademark professional can comment to you upon these factors when the time comes for you to conduct the trademark search.

It is apparent that certain marks taken directly from the English language can be used by a variety of concerns in selling their products or services, so long as there is no conflict. A prime example is the trademark "United" which identifies an airline, a national moving company, and a soccer team, amongst others. These entities can all use the same marks because their goods or services do not travel in the same channels of commerce, and no confusion as to source or origin is likely to occur.

If a potentially conflicting mark is found from the comprehensive search, an additional investigation is conducted to determine if the conflicting mark is still being used by its indicated owner. If the mark has not been used by its owner for several years, the registration for that mark may be considered invalid, and thus not a bar to your adoption and use of the same or similar mark. Consider Packard and Hudson for automobiles.

If the search results indicate that your mark does not conflict with any other mark, you may begin to use the mark immediately, and apply for federal registration, which has a high degree of certainty of ultimately being granted. However, if your prospective trademark is deemed to be confusingly similar to someone else's mark on goods or services that pass in the same or similar channels of commerce, conventional wisdom dictates that you would be wise to choose another mark, and not adopt your first mark. If you are the second user of a confusingly similar trademark, most certainly the first user of that trademark will threaten you with a lawsuit and an immediate injunction unless you stop using the mark. Your trademark attorney may advise you that you do not stand a very good chance of winning such a lawsuit, which would be expensive to fight, and the wise path would be to choose another mark. Thus the primary function of the search is to provide you with information that you can use to avoid walking into expensive litigation.

Another reason for conducting a trademark search is that the U.S. Patent & Trademark Office will examine the application for registration of your trademark by comparing it for similarity to other registered and pending marks. If a previously registered mark is found to be the same as, or confusingly similar, to yours, and the goods or services are related, the trademark examiner will refuse registration. Therefore, there appears to be no good reason to adopt a mark that is found to be in distress as a result of the search.

The U.S. Patent & Trademark Office uses the International Trademark Classification system to categorize the different types of goods or services for which marks are registered. If a registered mark is found during your search in the same class that the mark you are intending to use is potentially to be classified, there is a high probability that if the marks are confusingly similar, the goods are also traded in the same channels of commerce. It is also possible that the search skipped over a relevant mark in a totally different class, which mark could cause a likelihood of confusion if the goods are still related. For example, you may be searching the availability a mark for tires and find that the same or a similar mark is being used for automobiles. This could cause a likelihood of confusion, due to the relationship between automobiles and tires. By way of contradicting myself, note that the Jeep Wrangler vehicle and Wrangler tires are made by two different companies, however, Wrangler tires are sometimes used on Jeep Wrangler vehicles. I am sure that this is through agreement between the two companies that manufacture the respective products. However, this indicates that trademark decisions are made with many, many factors in mind.

It also must be remembered that because the basis of trademark law in the U.S. is the common law system, and the same is true in many other English speaking countries around the world, enforceable trademark rights can be gained by merely using a trademark in a certain trading channel for a period of time, without bothering to obtain a state or federal registration of that mark. Under the common law, you may secure rights in your trademark through prior use that would defeat a second users' right to use the mark, even if the second user obtained registration. However, to establish your right to enforce the mark, it is easier and less expensive to obtain a registration for your mark.

26.3   FILING FOR REGISTRATION OF YOUR TRADEMARK

A trademark application covering your finally selected and properly cleared mark is then filed with the U.S. Patent & Trademark Office. Your trademark professional will assist you in properly completing the application, which identifies the mark to be registered, the owner of the mark (which can be a corporation, partnership, individual, organization, or any other entity), the identification of the goods or services associated with the mark, the classification of the goods or services, and the dates of first use anywhere and first use in interstate commerce, if use of the mark has commenced at the time of filing the application. This application, along with a specimen of how the mark is being used on the product or service, such as a label, name plate, hang tag, advertisement in the case of a service mark, etc., is filed with the appropriate fee with the U.S. Patent & Trademark Office.

Under today's U.S. trademark laws, you may also file an application to register a trademark without having started actual use of the mark on your products or with your services. An application may be filed based upon your "bona fide intent" to use the mark in the near future. Your intent-to-use application will be examined, and possibly approved. However, before your trademark will be registered in the U.S., evidence of the commencement of actual use of the mark must be submitted to the U.S. trademark examining attorney.

Upon filing, an examining attorney researches the proposed mark to determine whether any other identical or confusingly similar marks have been previously registered or applied for. The application is also examined to ensure that the goods associated with the work are properly identified. If no conflicting marks for similar or related goods are discovered, your application is approved for publication in the *Official Gazette* of the U.S. Patent & Trademark Office, a public document. Anyone who believes they or their business will be adversely affected by registration of your mark can file an opposition, and present evidence to the U.S. Patent & Trademark Office showing why your mark should not be registered. You then respond stating why your mark should be registered, and a tribunal in the USPTO (the Trademark Trial & Appeal Board) then decides whether your mark should be registered in view of the opposition.

If no opposition is filed, or you successfully rebuff the opposer, your trademark application will proceed to registration. Upon receipt of registration, and not before, you are entitled to apply the familiar registration symbol ® next to your mark each time it is used, either on the product, or in advertising for the product. Prior to obtaining registration, it is customary to sue the symbols TM (trademark) or SM (service mark) adjacent the mark to alert the public that you consider the mark as identifying your company as the source or origin of your products.

If your trademark application encounters delay during examination, it may be advantageous to obtain several state trademark registrations for your mark. This will provide trademark protection while you are establishing the distinctiveness of your mark through sales and advertising. Each state has its own trademark registration system, which is primarily used for those products and services that do not enter into interstate commerce, such as a local plumbing or roofing business. State trademark registrations are usually easier and quicker to obtain than federal registrations.

26.4 PROTECTING AND MAINTAINING YOUR TRADEMARK REGISTRATION

To adequately protect your trademark rights, vigilance is required to uncover the use by another of the same or confusingly similar mark on or in association with similar or related goods or services, such as FJORD for a Norwegian brand of automobile. Trademark "watch" services are available to monitor trademarks entering the market that may infringe upon, or dilute the uniqueness of, your registered mark. In addition, your sales force is a good source of uncovering competing products with confusingly similar brand names.

Each week, the *Official Gazette* of the USPTO publishes a list of approved marks, with their goods and services, which may identify potentially conflicting new marks. Also, trade and industry journals provide fertile grounds for discovering what new brand names your competitors have begun to use, or are planning to use.

Protection of your mark also involves furnishing your employees with instructions and guidelines on proper use of your company's trademarks, such as always placing the generic product identification after the trademark each time the mark is used, whether on the products themselves, or in advertising and promotions for the product. For example, "XEROX copying machine" is proper. A "XEROX" is totally improper. Failure to adequately protect trademarks caused aspirin, cellophane, escalator, and thermos to become generic names and enter the public domain. The purpose of protecting your mark is to ensure that it maintains its unique and distinctive status as identifying you as the source of your product in the eye and mind of the consumer.

Maintenance of your trademark registration is also an ongoing concern. Between the fifth and sixth year following U.S. registration of your trademark, an affidavit or declaration must be filed with the U.S. Patent & Trademark Office, attesting to continual use of the trademark, or setting forth a good reason why use of the mark has stopped, and also stating that you intend to resume use of the mark in the foreseeable future. If this declaration or affidavit is not properly filed, the registration will be cancelled and purged from the Trademark Register.

26.5   TRADEMARK PROTECTION OUTSIDE OF THE UNITED STATES

If you are a U.S. producer, it is more than likely that any product you introduce to the market will ultimately be sold in countries outside the United States. To protect your trademark in other countries, several approaches are available. One way is to file an application and obtain registration of that mark in each selected country. In many nations throughout the world, particularly those that are based on the civil code legal system rather than the common law of the English origin countries, the trademark rights that you obtain in those countries are strictly granted by the government, and rights are not obtained by use of the mark. Therefore, in a foreign country, someone can register a trademark without ever having used it. Also, in many foreign countries, when your trademark application is filed, it is not examined for confusing similarity with someone else's registered trademark. Therefore, two exact trademarks can be issued by the Trademark Offices in certain countries covering the same or similar goods. The foreign Trademark Office takes the position that if there is a conflict between two trademarks, let the parties duke it out in court, rather than have the government spend money to determine any likelihood of confusion. As you can see from my previous comments, the situation in the United States is just the opposite.

Because of the fact that trademarks can be registered in many foreign countries without actually having used those trademarks, the problems that have arisen are probably quite evident to you. For example, if a trade journal announces that your company is introducing a new product line under a new brand name, individuals in foreign countries can read that trade journal, and then spend a few hundred dollars to register that trademark for the same goods in their home country. Later, when your product is successful and you proceed to introduce your product in foreign countries, someone knocks on your door and advises you that you are infringing their trademark rights. Their object is to sell the trademark back to you at a handsome price. This practice is much more prevalent throughout the world than you would think. For one of my clients, I was involved in a transaction where the client was compelled to pay U.S.$100,000.00 to buy its primary trademark back from a "pirate" in Argentina. I have anecdotal information that Holiday Inn paid a substantial amount to buy their trademark back from someone who had hung a sign on several hotels in Mexico with the same mark before Holiday Inn started doing business in Mexico. Thus, if you ever get to the point where your products are going to be marketed internationally, and you want to use your U.S. trademark in those foreign countries, talk to your trademark attorney early on, and be sure that you have taken adequate steps to protect your mark and prevent piracy.

Another foreign trademark system was created by the European Union, which established a single trademark registration designated the Community Trademark or CTM, which covers 15 member states with one trademark application and registration. Elsewhere throughout the world, registrations presently must be obtained individually in each country to obtain trademark protection. However, in 2003, the United States and several other countries joined the Madrid Protocol, which provides trademark and service mark protection in many countries by filing a single trademark application in your home country and designating those member countries in which you desire to obtain registration of your mark. I suggest you contact your trademark attorney for more details about the Madrid Protocol, since at the time of preparation of this text, the use of this system was not defined by laws, rules or regulations in the United States, and a few other newly adherent countries.

There are several other aspects of trademark law that are quite complicated. For example, the resolution of many trademark issues center around attempting to predict the impression on consumers made by the use of one or a few words, symbols or logos. I cannot overemphasize the importance of seeking the advice of a trademark law professional before beginning to use a new mark, to adequately ensure that you protect yourself, and that you do not interfere with the trademarks rights of others.

26.6 OVERVIEW OF THE MADRID PROTOCOL—THE "INTERNATIONAL" TRADEMARK

At the end of 2003, the United States implemented the "Protocol Relating to the Madrid Agreement Concerning the International Registration of Marks". The "Madrid Protocol," as the treaty is commonly called, is an international treaty originally dating back to 1891, that allows individual, corporate or other owners of trademark registrations or applications in their home country to obtain enforceable trademark rights in other member countries. For a current list of contracting countries, refer to `http://www.wipo.org/treaties/registration/madrid/index.html`.

In accordance with the Madrid Protocol, one who is using or intends to use a trademark files an application to register that mark in his or her home country. The application can be filed in the English or French language. It is not necessary to obtain the services of a trademark "agent" in other countries. Fees are paid in a single currency, such as dollars for U.S. applicants. By using the Madrid Protocol, it is about fifty percent less expensive to extend your trademark rights to six or eight countries compared to filing individual applications in each country, which is still an option.

To extend trademark rights to additional countries based on the home application, steps are taken to obtain registration of the mark in the register of the International Bureau of the World Intellectual Property Organization (WIPO) by filing an international application with the home country trademark registration office.

The national trademark registration office checks the international application for conformity to the rules, and then forwards the application to a WIPO examiner. The WIPO examiner reviews the application for formalities (fees, goods, proper class), and the mark is published in "Marques," the WIPO official listing of applied-for marks. Notice of the application is then forwarded to the trademark registration office of those countries the applicant designates for protection. The application is then examined within 18 months by each national trademark registration office receiving a copy of the application from WIPO. If the application passes examination, the mark is published for opposition by others. Upon issue, each national registration is valid for 10 years from the date of filing of the international application. Each registration may be renewed for additional ten year periods upon the payment of a fee.

The Madrid Protocol provides trademark owners with a relatively inexpensive procedure to obtain trademark protection in many countries, through the filing of a single application in one language. It is anticipated that for a short period of time after the U.S. became signatory to the Madrid Protocol, search and clearance procedures may be complicated. However, it is also expected that competent search engines will enable marks filed with WIPO from any member country to be properly searched. The Madrid Protocol provides that the International Bureau may undertake searches for anticipation (likelihood of confusion) among marks that are the subject of international registrations.

◆ INVENTORS AND INVENTIONS ◆

Percy Julian

THE SYNTHESIS OF CORTISONE

Percy Lavon Julian, a prominent chemist, was born in Montgomery, Alabama on April 11, 1899, the oldest of six children born to James Julian, a railroad mail clerk, and his wife, who was a school teacher. Julian's parents both emphasized the importance of education. Percy Julian spent his life in chemical research, often making use of soya bean products, which led to inventions and discoveries in the manufacture of inexpensive drugs, hormones, vitamins, amino acids, and paint and paper products. Julian's research resulted in over 100 patents being awarded in his name, as well as many honors being bestowed upon him by professional and communal organizations.

Percy Julian attended high school at the State Normal School for Negroes in Montgomery Alabama, and, in 1916, he entered by DePauw University in Green Castle, Indiana. He began as a "subfreshman" student, and was compelled to take upper level high school courses along with his freshman and sophomore class load. He earned his way through undergraduate school at DePauw by digging ditches and waiting on fraternity house tables. As a result of his innate brightness, he became a member of Sigma Xi honorary society, as well as Phi Beta Kappa. He was the class valedictorian at his graduation from DePauw in 1920. However, he was discouraged from applying to graduate school at that time because of the possibility of adverse racial sentiment. Instead, he became a chemistry teacher at Fisk University, an African-American college in Nashville, Tennessee.

Two years later, Julian earned the Austin Fellowship in Chemistry at Fisk, and then attended Harvard University in Cambridge, Massachusetts, where he finally had the opportunity to engage in graduate level studies, in which he excelled. Julian finished at the top of his Harvard class, and received a Masters degree in chemistry in 1923. However, because of his race, he was unable to obtain a position at a major university as a teaching assistant, reportedly due to the perception that white students would refuse to learn under an African-American instructor. Therefore, Julian took a position at the West Virginia State College for Negroes, and after that became associate professor of chemistry at Howard University in Washington, D.C. for two years.

In 1929, Julian received a fellowship from the General Education Board, and in 1931 he obtained a PhD degree in chemistry in Vienna, Austria. It was in Vienna that he developed an interest in the soya bean, and he focused on organic chemistry.

Upon returning to the United States, Julian served at Howard University as the head of the chemistry department, but he soon left Howard and moved back to DePauw, where he was appointed as an instructor in organic chemistry. While at DePauw, he and an associate from Vienna, Dr. Josef Pikl, developed the synthesis of physostigmine, a pharmaceutical product used to treat glaucoma by reducing the pressure inside the eyeball. This work brought Julian international acclaim, and he *almost* became the chair of the chemistry department at DePauw. However, the Dean of the university was compelled to change his mind by others in the department, reportedly due to concerns over Julian's race.

Upon returning to DePauw, Julian became interested in drug synthesis, including investigating traditional medicinal plants, such as the African calabar bean, from which physostigmine was first synthesized. On December 24, 1935, Julian married Anna Johnson.

During the 1935–1936 period, Julian learned that chemists in Germany were discovering that the steroid stigmasterol, which Julian had recovered as a by-product of the physostigmine synthesis process but knew was also obtainable from soy beans, could be used in the preparation of sex hormones. Julian followed up this lead, and in 1936 wrote to the Glidden Company in Chicago, requesting sample soybean oil. Glidden's Vice President, W. J. O'Brien heard about Julian's accomplishments, and offered him a position as Director of Research of the Glidden Soya Products Division. The Glidden Company was a leading manufacturer of vanishes and paints, and wanted Julian to research and develop compounds from soy-based products for use in paints and other products. Julian accepted the job, and remained at Glidden until 1954, at which time he founded his own company, Julian Laboratories.

While at Glidden, Julian noticed one day in 1939 that a water leak in a tank of purified soybean oil produced a unique by-product: the soy sterol created by this leak could be used to manufacture female and male hormones, progesterone and testosterone, respectively. Progesterone later proved efficient in treating cancer and problem pregnancies. He synthesized the hormones progesterone and testosterone from soybean oil, and also obtained a patent on an early liquid crystal. Julian also developed many commercial processes, including the isolation and preparation of soya bean protein, which is used to coat and size paper, create cold-water paints, and size textiles.

During the Second World War, Percy Julian created a foam product, Aero-Foam, from soy protein that was useful in smothering oil and gas fires. This fire-extinguishing material was rapidly adopted by the military, and it is reported that countless sailors' lives were saved during the war by Julian's Aero-Foam product.

The Mayo Clinic, in 1948, discovered cortisone, a compound that was effective in relieving rheumatoid arthritis. However, natural cortisone was very difficult and expensive to obtain, since it had to be extracted from the adrenal glands of oxen, and cost hundreds of dollars per drop. However, Percy Julian attacked the problem, and in October 1949, his team had completed the process of synthesizing a cortisone substitute that cost only pennies per ounce, rather than hundreds of dollars per drop for the natural substance. Julian located a wild sweet potato in Guatemala, and discovered how to synthesize cortisone from it for just pennies a gram. As a result of his work on cortisone, the City of Chicago in 1950 named Julian Chicagoan of the Year.

In 1949, Julian published a paper directed to a synthesis for Reichstein's Substance, which is also present in the adrenal cortex, and differs from cortisone by lacking a single oxygen atom at a specific molecular position. Hydrocortisone is today produced from the substance. It enables those suffering from rheumatoid arthritis to regain the use of their limbs.

In 1950, Julian, his wife, and his two children moved to the Chicago suburb of Oak Park, famous for its Frank Lloyd Wright homes. Soon after purchasing his home, an arsonist set fire to their house on Thanksgiving Day of 1950. A year later, dynamite was thrown at the house from a passing car, exploding beneath the bedroom window of Julian's children. As a result of these atrocities, a community group in Oak Park rose to the defense of the Julian's rights as the first African-Americans to live in Oak Park, and the community offered support to the family. Julian remained in Oak Park and became a life-long resident of the community, as well as a symbol for racial integration in the village. In 1985, Hawthorne School in Oak Park was renamed to honor Percy Julian. Today, Julian's birthday is celebrated as a holiday in Oak Park.

Julian left the Glidden Company in 1954, and established his own company, Julian Laboratories, producing his synthetic cortisone. Upon discovering that the yams in Mexico could be used to produce synthetic cortisone and some of his other products, he opened Laboratorios Julian de Mexico, which farmed the yams and sent them back to Oak Park for synthesis. In 1961, he sold his Oak Park and Mexico plants to Smith, Kline and French, a pharmaceutical company, for the sum of 2.3 million dollars. He also sold another chemical plant in Guatemala to Upjohn Company in 1961.

During his lifetime of research, Julian received numerous awards and honors, including the prestigious Spingarn Medal from the NAACP, 19 honorary doctorate degrees, nine universities naming schools and buildings in his honor, induction into the National Inventors Hall of Fame, and election to the National Academy of Sciences. Percy Julian also assisted in founding the Legal Defense and Educational Fund of Chicago, an organization whose purpose is to enhance the living conditions of African-Americans. In 1956, he was the first African-American and first layman to lead the Counsel for Social Action of the Congregational Christian Churches. An additional school on the south side of Chicago was also named after Percy Julian.

Percy Julian succumbed to liver cancer in 1975, leaving behind a life and a career that stands as a beacon both in the world of chemistry, and for future generations of African-American scientists.

United States Patent Office

2,752,339

Patented June 26, 1956

1

2,752,339

PREPARATION OF CORTISONE

Percy L. Julian, Maywood, John Wayne Cole, Oak Park, and Edwin W. Meyer and William J. Karpel, Chicago, Ill., assignors to The Glidden Company, Cleveland, Ohio, a corporation of Ohio

No Drawing. Application September 9, 1950, Serial No. 184,124

29 Claims. (Cl. 260—239.55)

The present invention relates to the preparation of 4-pregnene-17α,21-diol-3,11,20-trione and its 21-monoacetate, generally known as cortisone and cortisone acetate, respectively.

The name "cortisone" has been given to the compound previously known as "Kendall's Compound E," which is 4-pregnene-17α,21-diol-3,11,20-trione. The discovery by Kendall and his coworkers that cortisone is beneficial in the relief of the symptoms of rheumatoid arthritis greatly stimulated research on the partial synthesis of this material from other steroid raw materials. These partial syntheses involve degradation of the side chain of sterols, bile acids and steroid saponins to an acetyl group, introduction of a 17α-hydroxy group, introduction of a 21-hydroxy or acyloxy group, introduction of an 11-keto group, conversion of a 3-hydroxy group to a keto group, and formation of a 4,5 double bond where this is not already present. Processes are known whereby each of these results may be achieved. However, there is a multiplicity of steps involved, the overall yield is, of course, low, and in all cases consideration must be given to the particular reactions being carried out in the light of the various functional groups present.

The present invention is not concerned with the introduction of the 11-keto group, nor with the formation of the acetyl group in the 17-position of the molecule, but is concerned with the other conversions and reactions mentioned.

It is accordingly an object of the present invention to provide a novel process for the manufacture of cortisone.

Another object of the invention is to provide a process for producing cortisone from 10,13-dimethyl-3-hydroxy-11,20 - diketocyclopentanopolyhydrophenanthrene compounds of the C-21 series.

A further object of the invention is to provide a series of reactions useful in the production of cortisone.

An additional object of the invention is to produce new compounds useful for producing cortisone.

Other objects will be apparent to those skilled in the art from the following description:

A fundamental aspect of the invention is the use of 16,17-oxido-pregnan-3α-ol-11,20-dione for the manufacture of cortisone. This oxido compound may conveniently be made by treatment of 16-pregnene-3α-ol-11,20-dione with a suitable epoxidizing agent such as perbenzoic acid, or more conveniently with alkaline hydrogen peroxide.

The conversion of the 16,17-oxido-pregnan-3α-ol-11,20-dione into cortisone involves the following reactions: (1) the conversion of the 16,17-oxido group to a 17α-hydroxy group by treatment with HBr, followed by removal of the 16-bromo group thus introduced by treatment with Raney nickel; (2) introduction of a 21-acyloxy group by first brominating to introduce a 21-bromo group, followed by treatment with a metal salt of a carboxylic acid, such as sodium or potassium acetate, formate, benzoate, etc., to replace the 21-bromo

2

group with an acyloxy group; (3) oxidation of the 3α-hydroxy group to a keto group; and (4) introduction of a 4,5-double bond by first brominating a 3-keto compound at the 4-position, followed by removal of HBr. It is not essential that the various reactions or steps be carried out in the order recited, but in some cases certain of the reactions must take place subsequent to others. Thus considerable flexibility is inherent in the overall procedure, as is shown by the flow sheet and as will be more fully explained.

PREPARATION OF 17α-HYDROXY COMPOUNDS

The 16,17-oxidopregnan-3α-ol-11,20-dione may be prepared from 16-pregnen-3α-ol-11,20-dione, which may in turn be prepared as described in co-pending application Serial No. 152,752, filed March 29, 1950, by treatment of the pregnene with epoxidizing agents such as perbenzoic acid; or, preferably, by treatment with alkaline hydrogen peroxide, as is more fully disclosed in co-pending application Serial No. 165,120, filed May 9, 1950.

The first step in the conversion of the oxido group is the treatment of the oxido compound with HBr, which results in the production of a 16-bromo-17α-hydroxy-bromhydrin. The treatment with HBr may take place at any stage of the process at which the oxido group is present. The oxido group is restored when the α-bromhydrin structure is subjected to an alkaline treatment. Thus, treatment of the 21-bromo compound with the metal salt to introduce the 21-acyloxy group will inherently restore the oxido group where the bromhydrin grouping is also present. Also in some instances it may be desirable to deliberately restore the oxido group by a mild alkaline treatment, since the oxido compounds are generally high-melting materials and readily crystallized. Also, since the presence of a 17α-hydroxy group is preferred for introduction of the 21-bromo group, as will more fully appear, it will be apparent that the opening up of the oxido group and its restoration may in some cases be advantageous. Of course, ultimately the conversion of the oxide to the bromhydrin and removal of the 16-bromo group must be brought about.

The 16-bromo group may be removed at any stage in the process up to and including the last step in the formation of the cortisone acetate. The treatment with Raney nickel, however, would remove a 21-bromo group, if present, and as no useful purpose would be served by such removal, the treatment with Raney nickel of a 21-bromo compound is ordinarily to be avoided.

INTRODUCTION OF THE 21-ACYLOXY GROUP

The first step in the introduction of the 21-acyloxy group is the treatment with bromine. The presence of the 17α-hydroxy group is essential to the introduction of the 21-bromo group. If an oxido compound is treated with bromine, some HBr will be formed which will open up the oxide ring, and introduction of a 21-bromo group will follow. However, such a procedure leads to difficultly separable mixtures and low yields and is to be avoided for best practice.

The bromination may be carried out in a variety of solvents. When a solvent such as acetic acid, or other acylating mixture, is used, the 3-OH group will, of course, be acylated, and when the use of such a solvent is contemplated for the bromination, it is preferred to first acylate the 3-OH group before brominating. However, non-acylating solvents such as carbon tetrachloride, chloroform, and the like, may be employed.

The replacement of the 21-bromo group by an acyloxy group is effected by treatment with a metallic salt of a carboxylic acid, such as potassium or sodium acetate,

27 Cybersquatting

27.1 TRADEMARK VENTURI CAUSED BY THE INTERNET

I assume that most of you have much more of a familiarity with the internet phenomenon than myself, who grew up in the age of crayons, pencils and slide rules. It is not easy being a certified dinosaur. However, the advent of the internet has presented a new problem to trademark lawyers, and one that has cost many individuals and companies a large sum of money due to a lack of diligence. The good news is that solutions to most of those problems are now in place.

Internet domain names are familiar, easy to remember names or addresses, for each of the multitude of computers connected throughout the internet. Domain names correspond to a series of numbers (the Internet Protocol numbers) which serve as routing addresses on the internet network. Rather than trying to access a website through a series of numbers, domain names are used as a convenient way of reaching a posting, such as a website, or contacting others through email on the internet. Thus, from a trademark standpoint, the internet network can be thought of as a single channel or one lane road on which all businesses, entities and individual computers travel and communicate. Anyone desiring to contact another one of these computers on an internet site must travel across the same internet highway. Thus, on the internet, there are no multiple or parallel " channels of commerce."

A directory, organized hierarchically of domain names and their corresponding computers, has been organized whereby each computer address is registered to a particular individual or entity attached to the internet. When you register a domain name, that domain name is associated with the computer on the internet channel that you designate during the effective period of the registration.

The present system allows domain names ending with the top level designators .com, .net, or .org, and recently several others, to be registered through several various registering entities, defined as "registrars," that actually compete with one another for your registration business. You can choose among any one of the listed registrars to list your domain name. The registry provides all the computers on the internet the required information necessary to send you an email or to find your website. For the purpose of enforcing consumer protection laws, trademark laws, anti-pornography laws, and other laws, the registrar of your domain name will make your address information available to the public on a "Whois" site.

The .com, .net, .org and other domain names are available for registration by internet users anywhere in the world. Credited registrars are located in various countries throughout the world. As you probably realize by now, a series of country code (cc) top level domain names has been added to the internet registry system, as well as new top level domain names such as .biz, .coop, .museum and others. These additional top level domain names have been added due to the vast increase in users of the internet around the world.

Intellectual Property Law for Engineers and Scientists, by Howard B. Rockman
ISBN 0-471-44998-9 © 2004 The Institute of Electrical and Electronics Engineers

27.2 INTERNET CORPORATION FOR ASSIGNED NAMES AND NUMBERS (ICANN)

The Internet Corporation for Assigned Names and Numbers, known by its acronym ICANN, and available on the internet at www.icann.org, was created in October, 1998 as a technical coordination body for keeping the millions of internet domain names organized and functional. ICANN was created by a broad coalition of the internet's business, technical, academic and user communities, as well as the U.S. Government which, as we know, created the internet in the first place. The functions performed now by ICANN were previously performed by the U.S. Government, or under U.S. Government contract by organizations such as NSI. The function of ICANN is to coordinate the assignment of identifiers used along the internet highway, where each identifier must be specifically and globally unique, or else the internet will not function.

For obvious reasons, no two designation points on the internet can have the same address. Therefore, ICANN controls the assignment of identifiers such as internet domain names, internet protocol address numbers, and protocol perimeter and port numbers. ICANN is a non-profit, private sector corporation and is responsible for the operational stability of the internet, and also for promoting competition to achieve broad representation of global internet communities. ICANN has also been given the responsibility of developing policies to keep the traffic on the internet highway freely flowing.

ICANN has been recognized by not only the U.S., but by other governments throughout the world as the global entity responsible for managing the internet's domain name system, among other responsibilities. All of you who have established your own websites have done so under the authority of ICANN's responsibility for the assignment of the internet unique name and number identifiers. In considering the interface between the internet's required unique name/number identifiers and the trademark laws, ICANN is the one responsible for keeping accidents from happening along the internet roadway system.

Regarding competition, at present ICANN envisions that along with NSI, at least 52 other companies around the world will also be eligible to offer registration services for internet domain names. Standing alone, ICANN has no power to force any individual or entity to do anything: its authority is nothing more than the reflection of the willingness of the members of the internet community to use ICANN as a consensus development vehicle.

As you browse the internet today, you will find that many of the domain names end with a "cc" followed by a country designation, such as UK, FR, or the like, or merely followed by a country designation code without the cc. I found this aspect of ICANN's responsibilities rather interesting from a political standpoint. The term "country code top level domain" is a bit of a misnomer since several of the top level domains in that category are not actually countries. The country code top level designations comprise domain names created on the basis of a table created previously by the International Standards Organization, which compiled a list of countries and geographically distinct territories along with the unique two and three character abbreviations assigned to each by ISO. A more accurate term than "country code" would be "geographical" top level domain names, since this class of TLD's is defined by their association with defined geographic units, which are not necessarily countries. The ISO table used by ICANN in its country code top level domain name designations is widely used throughout the world for a variety of purposes, from currency abbreviations in the world banking systems and financial markets, to the national origin stickers on the backs of automobiles. For example, when you see the initials CH in an oval on the back bumper of an automobile, do you know that that car comes from Switzerland? By relying upon the ISO standards, ICANN keeps itself out of the business of determining what is and is not a country, or a geographically distinct territory, and leaves those issues to a politically recognized expert authority. I thought this was one of the better decisions made in the establishment of ICANN.

27.3 ICANN'S UNIFORM DISPUTE RESOLUTION POLICY

A primary responsibility of ICANN is the administration of the Uniform Dispute Resolution Policy (UDRP), which is a written policy that provides a mandatory, non-binding, non-judicial and relatively inexpensive system for the resolution of claims of abusive, bad faith cybersquatting. If a dispute in cyberspace erupts over a domain name, ICANN engages the dispute resolution providers. ICANN also maintains a master database of all proceedings regarding the resolution and handling of such disputes.

Since the internet is a single channel or highway leading to all of the various addressed computers connected to the internet, and considering that each computer must have a unique name or address, those companies or entities that operate their businesses under the same names, such as United Airlines, United Van Lines and the United soccer team, cannot all use their primary source identifier, or trademark, as their domain name or website address. At present, the first entity who legitimately registers a domain name, including their trademark, will have the right to use that website address, and others will have to slightly alter their names to provide a unique address for their website.

As a way of preventing cybersquatters from purposefully registering someone else's trademark or service mark as a domain name, and then using bad faith tactics to sell that domain name registration to the trademark owner or its competition at a vastly inflated price, the UDRP has compelled those who register their domain name to also incorporate by reference into the registration agreement specific terms and conditions by which disputes can be appropriately resolved between the entity registering the domain name, and any party who believes they will be injured by such registration. Proceedings are governed by the rules for uniform domain name dispute resolution which are available on the ICANN website.

By applying to register a domain name, as part of the registration process you are representing and warranting to ICANN the following:

1. That the statements made in your registration agreement are complete and accurate;
2. That to your knowledge, the registration of the domain name will not infringe upon or otherwise violate the rights, such as trademark rights, of any other party;
3. You are not registering the domain name for any unlawful purpose; and
4. You will not knowingly use the domain name in violation of any applicable laws or regulations.

Under ICANN's policy, it is the registering party's responsibility to determine whether its domain name registration infringes or violates someone else's rights, for example, trademark rights.

In proceedings conducted under the UDRP, ICANN will cancel, transfer or otherwise change domain name registrations under several circumstances. Two of these circumstances are receipt by ICANN of an order from a court or arbitral tribunal requiring them to take such action, and/or receipt of a decision of an administrative panel requiring such action in any administrative proceeding to which the domain name registrant was a party and which was conducted under either the UDRP or a later version of this policy adopted by ICANN.

If a dispute is filed by a trademark owner against a domain name registration, proceedings are conducted before one of the administrative dispute resolution service providers established by ICANN. The registration agreement requires the registering party to submit to a mandatory administrative proceeding in the event that another party asserts the following:

1. The registered domain name is identical or confusingly similar to a trademark or service mark in which the complainant has rights; and
2. The registering party has no rights or legitimate interests in the domain name; and
3. The domain name has been registered and is being used in bad faith.

In such administrative proceedings, the person filing the Complaint must prove that each of these three elements are present.

ICANN has established several factors which they consider beforehand to be evidence of bad faith registration and use, as follows:

1. The cybersquatter has registered or acquired the domain name primarily for the purpose of selling, renting or otherwise transferring the domain name registration to the complaining party who is the owner of the trademark or service mark forming part of the domain name, or to a competitor of that complainant for valuable consideration in excess of the documented out-of-pocket expenses related to the domain name registration process; or
2. One has registered the domain name for the purpose of preventing the owner of the trademark or service mark from reflecting the mark in a corresponding domain name, provided that the registrant has engaged in a pattern of such conduct; or
3. The domain name has been registered primarily for the purpose of disrupting the business of a competitor; or
4. By using the domain name, the cybersquatter has intentionally attempted to attract, for commercial gain, internet users to its website, or other online location, by creating a likelihood of confusion with the complainant's mark as to source, sponsorship, affiliation or endorsement of its website location or of a product or service on your website or location.

However, if one registers a domain name which includes a trademark of another, it is possible that the registrant may have legitimate rights in the use of that mark in his or her website address. If one receives a complaint relating to his or her website address, the following circumstances, if found by the dispute resolution authority to be proved based on its evaluation of all the evidence, go towards demonstrating the first registrant's rights or legitimate interests to the domain name:

1. Before receiving any notification of a dispute, the registrant's use of or preparations for use of a domain name, or a name corresponding to the domain name, occurred in connection with a bona fide offering of goods or services; or

2. The first registrant, as an individual, business or other entity, is commonly known throughout the relevant trade by the domain name, even if no trademark or service mark rights have been acquired in that portion of the domain name; or

3. The registrant is making a legitimate non-commercial use, or a fair use, of the domain name for commercial gain, without intentionally misleadingly or diverting consumers, or tarnishing the trademark or service mark rights of the complaining party.

When a complaint is filed under the UDRP, all fees charged by the provider of the dispute resolution panel are paid by the complainant, except where the domain name registrant elects to expand the administrative panel from one to three members. Your agreement with ICANN specifically states that ICANN will not be liable as the result of any decisions rendered by the dispute resolution panel.

The remedies available to a complainant pursuant to any proceeding before an administrative panel established by ICANN are limited to requiring the cancellation of the domain name, or the transfer of the domain name registration to the complaining party; the panel cannot award monetary damages. All decisions under the UDRP are published in full over the internet, except in exceptional cases as decided by the administrative panel. Once the panel has made its decision, either party to a domain name dispute can submit the dispute to a court of competent jurisdiction for independent resolution.

To prevent deceptive practices during the conduct of a domain name dispute, the agreement you signed upon registering your domain name states that you may not transfer your domain name registration to another party during a pending administrative proceeding or for a period of 15 business days after the proceeding is concluded, or during a pending court proceeding or arbitration commenced regarding your domain name, unless the party to whom the domain name registration is being transferred agrees in writing to be bound by the decision of the court or arbitrator. Also, you may not transfer your domain name registration to another registrar during a pending administrative proceeding or for a period of 15 business days after the conclusion of such proceeding.

My recommendation is that before you attempt to register a domain name, have a search conducted to determine whether or not your domain name will interfere with the trademark or service mark rights of another. If your search indicates that your domain name registration may cause problems, it is very simple to switch to another domain name. This procedure is vastly less costly than registering your domain name, and then facing the expense of fending off a challenge by a registered or non-registered trademark or service mark owner. There is no legitimate reason for walking head first into a legal dispute.

Current Events

AC VERSUS DC

One of the most bizarre battles between competing technologies, and U.S. corporate moguls, took place in the late 1800s, and as a result practically every electric power system in the world today uses alternating current (AC) rather than direct current (DC). The story of this intense struggle includes tales of lighting the "White City" at the Chicago Colombian Exposition in 1893, animals purposely sacrificed for electrocution, and the invention of the electric chair.

As chronicled earlier in this work, after Thomas A. Edison successfully developed a practical incandescent light bulb in 1880 that could safely illuminate the indoors with electricity, he also has his research and development team create complete systems for generating electricity, including networks for transmitting and distributing the current to the homes and buildings that were customers for his light bulbs. Edison concluded (mistakenly) that only DC at 110 volts could be used to power his bulbs. As we shall see, he stubbornly held to this idea for over 20 years, which led him and his cohorts to engage in a battle that cost animal and human lives before he was convinced that AC could also light his bulbs. However, let us not get ahead of our story.

Nikola Tesla, in 1887, formed the Tesla Electric Company in New York City, a few short blocks from Edison's work facilities. A. K. Brown, the manager of Western Union Telegraph Company, gave Tesla the financial help he needed to use this new company to develop an AC system for providing and using electricity. Tesla started immediately to develop, engineer, and file patents for his complete AC polyphase systems for single-phase, two-phase, and three-phase AC. For each system, he created dynamos, transformers, and controls.

At this point in time, AC, DC, and gas were already in use for various forms of electrical power and illumination. High-voltage electric carbon-arc illumination was used in street lighting, with wires carrying approximately 1,000 volts strung precariously on poles along and above city streets; each light produced about 4,000 candlepower. Since the carbon-arc light could not be subdivided (broken down into smaller units that would not blind people), this form of lighting was not suitable for indoor use. Gas lights and lamps were still the light source of choice for homes and buildings, the gas being supplied through a network of gas mains meandering beneath the city streets.

Prior to 1887, and following Edison's introduction of his DC illumination system anchored at Pearl Street in New York City, many central stations producing and delivering AC had been established in America, using many different circuits and equipment. Thomson-Houston had installed a small transformer and alternators in 1886 to light its factory. William Stanley, chief engineer for Westinghouse Electric Company, had designed a transformer system in 1886, based on the U.S. Gauland-Gibbs patent rights acquired by Westinghouse. Transformers were required to decrease and increase voltages in power

Intellectual Property Law for Engineers and Scientists, by Howard B. Rockman
ISBN 0-471-44998-9 © 2004 The Institute of Electrical and Electronics Engineers

transmission over short and long distances. By 1887, Westinghouse had over 30 AC power generating plants operating.

When Tesla began developing his AC systems in 1887, there was no workable AC motor in existence. Six months after starting his new business, Tesla had constructed, tested, and filed patent applications for the commutator-less AC induction motor he had sketched in the dust in Budapest several years earlier, which had practically no moving parts to wear out. Between 1887 and 1891, Tesla obtained 40 patents covering his AC motor and systems. Tesla received wide acclaim for his new motor, and lectured about his systems before the American Institute of Electrical Engineers on May 16, 1888. Using Tesla's AC systems, higher voltages could be transmitted over greater distances compared to DC, and Edison's light bulb could be lit using AC or DC. Also, AC generating systems did not require a substation every several miles.

George Westinghouse decided that Tesla's AC patents were the missing link in Westinghouse's AC systems and, in 1888, after making a personal inspection of the new, quiet AC motors humming in Tesla's shop, he convinced Tesla to sell Westinghouse the patents Tesla had been accumulating. The agreement between Tesla and Westinghouse dated July 7, 1888, granted Tesla $60,000, comprising $5,000 in cash and 150 shares in Westinghouse Electric Company. Of more importance, however, Tesla was also to receive $2.50 for each horsepower of electrical power sold by Westinghouse using Tesla's systems. Tesla was obliged to share this income with A. K. Brown and his other investors, so although Tesla became comfortable (for a while) and socially acceptable in New York, he never became one of the ultra-rich.

Tesla decided that the ideal AC cycle for his induction motor was 60 cycles per second. Westinghouse's engineers had previously developed a 133 cycle system, and it took many months of expensive experiments and arguments before Tesla convinced the other engineers that he was right. Ever since then, 60 cycles has been the standard upon which AC is generated and used.

When Edison found out about the Westinghouse–Tesla agreement, and since he was stubbornly committed to his DC system, he decided to launch a public relations battle to establish the superiority of DC over AC. This battle eventually made today's political fights seem like child's play by comparison. Previously, Edison was involved in a campaign to prove the desirability of his electric incandescent lamps compared to gas lamps, with tactics that today might be called into question. Edison, upon publicly announcing his light bulb, was met with extra-strength resistance from the gas monopolies of the day. Edison responded by reporting and publishing commentary exposing, with joy, the extreme hazards of gas main explosions, incidents in which employees in gas-lit plants and buildings experienced health problems due to gas, and damage to vision caused by gas lights. With this background and experience, Edison launched his response to the incursion of Westinghouse and Tesla's AC into his DC domain. Edison's propagandists began barraging the public and industry in an alarming fashion about the dangers of AC. Not only did Edison take advantage of AC electrical accidents that did occur, several additional "accidents" were created just for the purpose of Edison's campaign bent on proving that AC would ruin the entire electric light and power industry.

Edison's West Orange, New Jersey R&D laboratory became the epicenter for "scientific" information used in a vitriolic press battle, with Edison's point being the dangers of AC. In 1887, several "experiments" were carried out, such as the electrocution of stray cats and dogs, before the press and "guests," by placing the animals on a tin sheet and passing 1,000 volts AC through the tin and animal. In one such display, one of Edison's key assistants, Charles Batchelor, was badly throttled when he received an electric shock himself while holding a puppy on the plate. Batchelor recovered in a few days; not the dog, however.

Soon, the neighbors around Edison's West Orange facility became fearful of losing their pets when Harold Brown, a self-appointed crusader for Edison's anti-AC holy war, began paying a reward of 25 cents for each canine and feline brought in for electrocution by local children. These "experiments" were augmented in February 1888 with press releases by Edison's forces, warning the public of electrical fatalities in factories, theaters, and along high-voltage arc-light power lines, and to be wary of Westinghouse and others who were attempting to plug AC into their very homes. Westinghouse replied by issuing statements that Edison was wrong; that Stanely's transformers were located outside of the buildings, stepping down the high-tension voltage and delivering AC current to the building at a low voltage, comparable to that of the DC system.

Harold Brown was a former Edison laboratory assistant in West Orange, and by that time an engineering and electrical consultant. He launched his campaign against AC after a 15-year-old New York peddler boy and new immigrant was electrocuted when he grabbed a fallen live telegraph wire, which wire had been dangling free in the street for months following a severe blizzard and ice storm that hit New York on March 12, 1888, dumping 22 inches of snow in its wake. Brown wrote a letter to the June 5, 1888 edition of the *New York Evening Post,* in which part of his comments were directed to branding AC and its potential dangers as "damnable," and subjecting the public to "constant danger from sudden death." His letter demanded passing a law to prohibit AC transmission above 300 volts, which would make AC useless. Note that the *Evening Post* was published by an Edison investor, Henry Villard, who later became president of Edison's company. Brown himself apparently had no direct ties to the Edison camp, and no one knows why he carried out his campaign against AC. However, he became a man of action in support of DC, and carried Edison's written and oral slings against AC to a higher, or perhaps lower, latitude.

In July, 1888, Westinghouse's pro-AC forces began to fight back. On June 8, 1888, Brown had proposed new safety rules for electricity to the New York City Board of Electrical Control, insisting that his published letter to the newspaper be made of record. His comments were sent to several electric companies, including Westinghouse, for a response. Westinghouse responded by pointing to fires that had caused three DC central electrical generating stations to be destroyed, including the Boston station, and the destruction by fire of a large theater in Philadelphia supplied with DC, as well as many other fires caused by DC.

Harold Brown allegedly was supported by Edison and his DC forces, decided to create and deliver the "scientific" evidence his critics were demanding on the all-important safety issue. On July 30, 1888, Brown conducted a "demonstration" at the School of Mines of Columbia College (now Columbia University) attended by over 70 invitees, including reporters. Brown's combatitiveness was already a given, and the room was filled with expectation. Brown began by extolling DC over AC, stating that his prior testing had shown that animals could withstand electrical shocks from continuous DC better than AC. Brown then proceeded to place a 76 pound black retriever dog into a cage, the dog's legs attached to wires. He applied first 300 volts DC, than 400, 700, and 1,000 volts DC to the wires. Those in the audience watched the dog struggle, cry, and thrash in the cage. Many left, others yelled to Brown to cease the torturous exhibition. Brown stopped at 1,000 volts DC, then attached an alternator to the wires, applied 330 volts

AC, and the dog died. Both a reporter for the *New York World* and a representative of the American Society for the Prevention of Cruelty to Animals (ASPCA) approached Brown and demanded that he not electrocute any more dogs. Observing the hostile audience in front of him, Brown agreed.

Many in the audience felt that Brown had not presented scientific evidence of the dangers of AC, since they concluded that the DC jolts had sufficiently weakened the dog to the point where 330 volts AC would prove fatal. Brown retaliated by announcing to the spectators as they left the hall that he had previously experimented on a sufficient amount of dogs to assure them of AC's dangers to the entire mammal kingdom.

Undaunted, four days later, Brown returned to Columbia College, where, before a smaller crowd of reporters, health administrators for the city, and his helpers, he electrocuted a 61 pound dog using less than 300 volts AC, a 91 pound Newfoundland in 8 seconds, and a 53 pound Setter–Newfoundland mixed breed in 4 painful minutes, all with AC current. The warm and humid heat of the night wafted the aroma of the dissection of one of the deceased animals over those leaving the audience, leaving them with a vivid and lasting impression of the events of the evening. Brown felt he had proved his point: any current that could kill a healthy dog would do the same to a human. He used the term "Westinghoused" to refer to the electrocution processes he applied to the dogs.

After returning from a brief rest in the mountains, Brown began an even more horrendous episode in the AC–DC war. The New York State assembly in the Fall of 1888 passed a law substituting electrocution instead of hanging as the means of carrying out capital punishment in the state, as a result of lobbying efforts by both the AC and DC camps. The lawmakers were convinced that electrocutions would be fast, humane, and painless, leaving no marks on the body. A state committee was formed to obtain advice from the Medical-Legal Society of New York on the best use of electricity to kill humans. The committee chairman, Dr. Peterson, happened to be Harold Brown's aide in the two dog electrocution "shows" at Columbia College. Brown, although a DC advocate, was obsessed with having the rival AC used as the preferred form of electrocution. This, apparently, would help in his campaign to expound on the dangers of AC to human life.

Brown and Dr. Peterson conducted heinous experiments in Edison's West Orange laboratory on how to efficiently kill mammals larger than dogs using electricity. On December 5, 1888, before a group of reporters and others at the West Orange laboratory, and also graced by the presence of Thomas Alva Edison himself, who up to then was content to stay in the background, more experiments took place. First, 700 volts AC were applied to a 124 pound calf. The calf was dispatched in about 30 seconds. A second 145 pound calf was electrocuted in 5 seconds. Then, a 1,230 pound healthy horse was killed using 700 volts AC. The Medical-Legal Society adopted a resolution recommending to the state that the official means of criminal electrocution be by alternating current, on a table or sitting in a chair.

George Westinghouse responded in published newspaper articles espousing on the number of people who had survived 1,000 volt AC jolts and lived to tell about it, and that his companies were illuminating approximately 12 times the number of lights as Edison's companies. He claimed that his company would not have had such success if AC were unsafe.

Edison's DC forces had, at this time, successfully framed the AC versus DC debate on the issue of safety, pushing aside the need for thicker copper wires, the higher expense of DC, and the fact that DC was only suitable for use in crowded cities. Brown was also chosen to design the apparatus for electrocution to be used by New York. His aim was to have Westinghouse AC electricity permanently associated with human mortality.

The first man scheduled to be electrocuted in New York's electric chair was one William Kemmler of Buffalo, who had axed Tillie Ziegler, his female partner in March, 1889. Harold Brown had been referring to AC as "the executioner's current," and this was his chance to prove it. Brown, who was seeking Edison's help in purchasing a Westinghouse AC dynamo to perform the electrocution at Auburn prison, was initially unsuccessful in doing so. Then, Charles Coffin, J. P. Morgan's man running Thomson-Houston Company, stepped up. At that time, Thomson-Houston and Edison Electric Co. were on the verge of a merger, and Coffin aided Brown in obtaining used Westinghouse Electric AC generators for Auburn and two other prisons. Thus, Westinghouse's AC dynamos were poised to kill humans, one of Brown's marketing goals. In August, 1889, someone broke into Brown's office and took over 40 pieces of correspondence showing that he had been advised and paid by the Edison Electric Company, and by Thomson-Houston, both Westinghouse competitors. The *New York Sun* obtained the letters, and ran the story under the headline "FOR SHAME, BROWN!"

Prior to Kemmler's execution, a Western Union Telegraph lineman, while working 40 feet over the street near New York City's City Hall, was electrocuted while cutting a wire he thought was inert. He was burned, sparks were flying, and he actually seemed to be on fire. He fell across several other wires that kept him suspended 40 feet over the street, his corpse held in mid-air for 45 minutes as crowds gathered and watched to their horror. It was not until the current was turned off that he was brought to the ground.

Public outcries compelled the New York electric companies to cease operating their high-voltage electric arc street lights, and to upgrade the maze of wires suspended above the streets. After this event, Edison himself came to the forefront of the War of the Currents, personally calling for the demise of high-voltage AC entirely. He continually urged politicians and the public that only low-voltage DC moving along buried cables was safe. His campaign was predicated upon instilling a fear of AC among the citizens, and William Kemmler was slated to become the "poster boy" for the DC forces.

After Kemmler had run the appeal process to its end, the "experimental" execution was scheduled for August 6, 1890 at Auburn Prison. Executives of Edison's company were ready to convince the public that Mr. Kemmler had been "Westinghoused," since Westinghouse's dynamos were to be used to carry out the electrocution.

The AC dynamos at Auburn prison were located several hundred yards from the electric chair, and bells were used to communicate between the operators and the electrocutioneer. As Kemmler was strapped into and "connected to" the chair, the Buffalo District Attorney left the room of 24 official witnesses, went into the corridor, and reportedly fainted.

The switch in the room with the AC generators was thrown at approximately 6:40 AM Kemmler's face went white as ash, and the prison physician pronounced Kemmler dead. The switch was turned off less than 20 seconds after the first jolt. But blood was coming from a small cut on Kemmler's finger, signifying that his heart was still beating. His chest was still throbbing and he appeared to be trying to breathe. The scalp electrode was re-attached, and the switch was thrown a second time. Kemmler became rigid, his skin and hair notably burned. His clothes were on fire and the odor was awful. The current remained turned on for several minutes, after which the doctors present declared him dead again. For the witnesses, it was not a pleasant sight.

Kemmler's autopsy showed that his body had been rigidly formed into a sitting position by rigor mortis, and scorch marks identified where metal pieces had contacted his body. Some concluded that Kemmler may have been cooked to death in a rather inhumane way. Indeed, the newspaper reports described the execution in every morbid detail. The public's first impression of electrocution was not a favorable one, although the problems were ultimately solved, and the electric chair has been widely used to inflict capital punishment for many years, replaced of late by injections of lethal chemicals.

For unknown reasons, Harold Brown made no comment after the botched Kemmler electrocution. In point of fact, Harold Brown was never heard from publically again.

* * * *

One footnote to this story is worthy of mention. Westinghouse, in 1890, saw his AC electric business increase, despite the Kemmler execution. But all of the large electric power generating companies were on slippery financial footing due to the capital investment required. The debt of both Edison Electric and Westinghouse Electric grew, and financiers such as J. P. Morgan gained increasingly more power over the electric companies. On February 17, 1892 it was announced that the Edison Electric Company had merged with the Thomson-Houston Company, under the presidency of Charles Coffin, who worked for the House of Morgan. From that day to the present, the merged company would be known as General Electric Company.

Rumors also circulated that Westinghouse Electric would soon be absorbed into General Electric. If this latter takeover would take place, Morgan would be able to control the future of electrifying America, both AC and DC. To make this monopoly into a reality, Morgan would need control over the Tesla AC patents, owned by Westinghouse. But, Westinghouse was obsessed with proving that his AC system was superior and should replace DC systems. Westinghouse refused to play Morgan's game, and Morgan started rumors of mismanagement at Westinghouse, driving Westinghouse stock downward. Westinghouse fought back by merging with smaller companies, such as Consolidated Electric Light Company and U.S. Electric Company.

The patent royalties owed to Tesla by Westinghouse, due to the success of AC power generation, were enormous. While no records were kept, Tesla was on the brink of becoming one of the world's richest man. Westinghouse's investors insisted that the Tesla royalty contract be terminated. George Westinghouse resisted, but the banks insisted. An embarrassed George Westinghouse met with Tesla and told him that if the AC system royalty contract were not modified in some way, Westinghouse Electric would cease to be under his control. Westinghouse also told Tesla that if Tesla agreed to forgo royalties, he would continue to move forward with plans to electrify America with AC systems and current.

Tesla, not being an astute businessman or financial wizard, but trusting in George Westinghouse's judgment, tore up the royalty contract and reportedly accepted the total sum of $216,600 for the full assignment of his AC patent rights to Westinghouse, forgoing the receipt of any future royalties.

Westinghouse remained true to his promise to Tesla, and worked to bring AC electrification to the dominant position it enjoys worldwide today. In 1892–1893, Westinghouse successfully outbid General Electric Company for the right to provide the electric incandescent light system for Chicago's Columbian Exposition. George Westinghouse and Nikola Tesla appeared at the Exposition, showing off the wonders of AC electricity in what became known as the "White City." The Westinghouse Electric and Manufacturing

Company grew and prospered. Tesla never wavered in his admiration for George Westing-house.

When Tesla gave up his claim to past and future royalties from his AC patents, he probably did himself, and the world, a great disservice. He managed to live comfortably for another 10 years or so, working on additional inventions. However, Tesla ultimately encountered a shortage of money for additional research and development lasting over the remainder of his life. Therefore, the question must be asked: how many potential future beneficial inventions and discoveries were denied to the populace due to the financial stiffling of Tesla's immense capacity for creativity.

In this essay, I have only scratched the surface of the lives and accomplishments of those inventors and industrialists who brought electricity out of the fictional arms of the mythical god Thor, and developed the machinery and processes that deliver it in useful abundance to every corner of the globe. For additional information about the extraordinary, and many times ordinary, lives of these creative individuals, I highly recommend further reading of the fine books and other sources of biographical material in the Bibliography.

Bibliography

ELI WHITNEY

United States Patent No. 72x (March 14, 1794).

Digital Classroom, *Teaching With Documents: Eli Whitney's Patent for the Cotton Gin,* U.S. National Archives & Records Administration, Washington, D.C. (1986), http://www.archives.gov/digital-classroom/lessons/cotton-gin-patent/cotton-gin-patent.html (2002).

Mirsky, Jeanette and Nevins, Allan, *The World of Eli Whitney,* Macmillan Co. (1952).

American Innovators, *Eli Whitney, Pioneer of Modern Manufacturing,* http://technology.ksc.nasa.gov/ETEAM/whitney.html (2002).

Eli Whitney, http://www.troop100.org/whitney.htm (2002).

Wilson, Mitchell, *American Science and Inventions: A Pictorial History,* Simon & Schuster, N.Y. (1954) pp. 78–83, Eli Whitney Museum, *The Inventor,* http://www.eliwhitney/org/inventor.htm (2002).

CHAPTER 1

United States Constitution, Article I, Section 8, Clause 8 (1787).

United States Patent Statutes, 35 U.S.C. § 1-376.

Francis, William H. and Collins, Robert C, *Cases and Materials on Patent Law,* 4th Ed. West Publishing Co., St. Paul, MN., 1995, pp. 1–3.

Barrett, M., *Intellectual Property Cases and Materials,* West Group, St. Paul, MN, 2001, pp. 2–3.

United States Patent No. 4,736,866 (April 12, 1988).

United States Patent No. 4,259,444 (March 31, 1981).

Diamond v. Chakrabarty, 447 U.S. 303, 306 USPQ 193 (Supreme Court 1980).

State Street Bank & Trust Co. v. Signature Financial Group, Inc., 149 F. 3d 1368 (Fed. Cir. 1998), *cert denied,* 525 U.S. 1093 (Supreme Court 1999).

United States Trademark Act, 15 U.S.C. §§ 1051-1129.

United States Copyright Act, 17 U.S.C. §§ 101-1332.

Uniform Trade Secrets Act, 1985 revised form, National Conference of Commissioners on Uniform State Laws (1985).

The Semiconductor Chip Protection Act of 1984, 17 U.S.C. §§ 901-914.

CYRUS MCCORMICK

United States Patent No. 8277x (June 21, 1834).

Wisconsin Historical Society Archives, *Cyrus Hall McCormick,* http://www.wisconsinhistory.org/archives/ihc/cyrus.html (2002).

Public Broadcasting System, *American Experience, Chicago: City of the Century, People and Events,* http://www.pbs.org/wgbh/amex/chicago/peopleevents/p_mccormick.html (2003).

Virginia Polytechnic Institute, *Biography of Cyrus McCormick,* http://www.vaes.vt.edu/steeles/mccormick/bio.htm (2003).

The World Book Encyclopedia, *McCormick, Cyrus Hall,* World Book, Inc., Chicago, 1994, vol. 13, p. 336.

CHAPTER 2

Adelman, M. J.; Rader, R. R; Thomas, J. R. and Wegner, H. C., *Cases & Materials on Patent Law,* 2nd. Ed., Thomson West, St. Paul, MN. 2003, pp. 26–38.

Berman, Bruce, *From Ideas to Assets,* John Wiley & Sons, New York, 2002, pp. 4–5, 10–17.

Chisum, D. S.; Nard, C. A.; Schwartz, H. F.; Newman, P. and Kieff, F. S.; *Principles of Patent Law,* Foundation Press, New York, 1998, pp. 50–72.

Weisburd, S. I., *Strategies in Creation of Intellectual Property Technology Assets,* Seminar: Handling Intellectual Property Issues in Business Transactions, Practicing Law Institute, New York, 2003, pp. 141–173.

Barrett, M., *Intellectual Property,* 2d Ed., West Group, St. Paul, MN., 2001, pp. 2–3.

Rivette, K. G. and Kline, D., *Rembrandts in the Attic,* Harvard Business School Press, Boston, MA., 2002, 1–106.

Rockman, H. B., Author's personal files and notes, *Establishing an Effective Corporate Intellectual Property Development and Enforcement Program,* 2002.

CHARLES GOODYEAR

United States Patent No. 3,633 (June 15, 1844).

The World Book Encyclopedia, *Goodyear, Charles,* World Book, Inc., Chicago, 1994, vol. 8, p. 270.

Goodyear Corporate, *The Strange Story of Rubber,* reprinted from Readers Digest, Jan. 1958 ed., http://www.goodyear.com/corporate/strange.html (2002).

Goodyear, Charles, *Columbia Encyclopedia, Encyclopedia.com,* 6th ed. 2003, http://www.encyclopedia.com/htm/G/goodyear.asp (2003).

CHAPTER 3

United States Patent & Trademark Office, *Manual of Patent Examining Procedure ("MPEP"),* Edition 8, August 2001, Revised February 2003, Section 600.

United States Patent Statutes, 35 U.S.C. § 112 (1952).

Rockman, H.B., *The Practice of Intellectual Property Law,* Law Bulletin Publishing Company, Chicago, 1998, pp. 8–11.

Merges, R.P. and Duffy, J.F., *Patent Law and Policy: Cases and Materials,* 3rd Edition, Matthew Bender & Co., Inc., Newark, N.J., 2002, pp. 13–26.

GEORGE WESTINGHOUSE

United States Patent No. 5,504 (Reissued July 29, 1873).

Jonnes, Jill, *Empires of Light,* Random House, New York, 2003, pp. 118–119, 121–122.

Larson, Erik, *The Devil in the White City,* Crown Publishers, New York, 2003, pp. 5, 131, 141.

Cheney, Margaret, *Tesla, Man Out of Time,* Dorset Press, New York, 1989.

Pennsylvania Biographies, George Westinghouse, www.geocities.com/heartland/4547/westinghouse (2003).

George Westinghouse—His Original Internet Site, www.georgewestinghouse.com/george (2003).

The Life of George Westinghouse—Succeed through Biographies, www.school-for-champions.com/biographies/westinghouse (2003).

IEEE History Center—Legacies: George Westinghouse, www.ieee.org/organizations/history-center/legacies/westinghouse (2003).

Levine, I. E., *Inventive Wizard—George Westinghouse,* Julian Messner, Inc., New York, 1962; http://ivory.lm.com/~rs7717/book.html (2003).

George Westinghouse—Westinghouse Air Brake and the Little Town of Wilmerding, www.pittsburgh-diary.com/aug/GWest/givesting.html (2003).

Westinghouse Electric Company—Our Company, www.westinghouse.com/A1b.asp (2003).

Westinghouse Works, 1904-About George Westinghouse, www.loc.gov/annem/papr/west/westgorg (2003).

CHAPTER 4

Francsis, W. H. and Collins, R. C., *Cases and Materials on Patent Law,* 4th Edition, West Publishing Co., St. Paul, MN., 1995, pp. 64–73.

Adelman, M. J., Rader, R. R., Thomas, J. R. and Wegner, H. C., *Cases and Materials on Patent Law,* 2nd Edition, Thomson—West, 2003, pp. 8–17.

Rockman, H. B., *The Practice of Intellectual Property Law,* Law Bulletin Publishing Company, Chicago, 1998, pp. 7–8.

Walterscheid, E. C., *To Promote the Progress of Useful Arts,* Fred B. Rothman & Co., Littleton, CO., 1998, pp. 23–80.

Constitution of the United States, Article I, Section 8, Clause 8 (1787).

The United States Patent Act, 35 U.S.C. §§1 et seq.

Chisum, D. S., Nard, C. A., Schwartz, H. F., Newman, P., and Kieff, F. S., *Principles of Patent Law,* Foundation Press, New York, 1998, pp. 7–23.

Merges, R. P. and Duffy, J. F., *Patent Law and Policy: Cases and Materials,* 3rd Edition, Matthew Bender & Co., Inc., 2002, pp. 1–13.

Goldstein, P., *Copyright, Patent, Trademark and Related State Doctrines,* 5th Edition, Foundation Press, New York, 2002, pp. 386–387.

JOHN DEERE

United States Patent No. 46,454 (February 21, 1865).

Deere and Company, *John Deere History and Information About the Company,* www.johndeere.com/en_us/compinfo/history/index.html?sidenavstate=0000001 (2003).

John Deere Pioneers the Prairie Plow, www.field-reporter.com/The_Green_Girl/gg_11-20-00 (2003).

MIT Inventor of the Week Archive, *John Deere, Self-Polishing Cart Steel Plow,* http://web.mit.edu.invent/iow/deere.html (2003).

CHAPTER 5

United States Patent Act, 35 U.S.C. §§101, 102, 103.

Diamond v. Chakrabarty, 447 U.S. 303, 306 USPQ 193 (Supreme Court 1980).

State Street Bank & Trust Co. v. Signature Financial Group, Inc., 149 F. 3d 1368 (Fed. Cir. 1998), *cert denied,* 525 U.S. 1093 (Supreme Court 1999).

United States Constitution, Article I, Section 8, Clause 8 (1787).

ALFRED NOBEL

United States Patent No. 57,175 (August 14, 1866).

United States Patent No. 78,317 (May 26, 1868).

Nobel e-Museum, *Alfred Nobel—His Life and Work,* The Nobel Foundation, 2003, www.nobel.se/nobel/alfred-nobel/biographical/life-work/index (2003).

Nobel e-Museum, *Life and Philosophy of Alfred Nobel,* The Nobel Foundation, 2003, www. nobel.se/nobel/alfred-nobel/biographical/frangsmyr/index (2003).

Alfred Nobel Biography, http://wawa.essortment.com/alfrednobel_rbki.htm (2003).

Alfred Nobel Invents Dynamite—1866, 1999, campus.northpark.edu/history/Web Chron/Technology/Nobel.CP (2003).

The Norwegian Nobel Institute—Alfred Nobel, Biography, 2001, www.nobel.no/eng_com_will1 (2003).

The World Book Encyclopedia, *Nobel, Alfred Bernhard,* World Book, Inc., Chicago, 1994, vol. 14, pp. 439–440.

CHAPTER 6

United States Patent Statutes, 35 U.S.C. §§ 102, 351–376.

Rockman, H. B., *The Practice of Intellectual Property Law,* Law Bulletin Publishing Company, Chicago, 1998, pp. 27–36.

Merges, R. P. and Duffy, J. F., *Patent Law & Policy: Cases and Materials,* 3rd Edition, Matthew Bender, Newark, N.J., 2002, pp. 361–642.

Adelman, M. J., Rader, R. R., Thomas, J. R. and Wegner, H. C., *Cases and Materials on Patent Law,* 2nd Edition, Thomas-West, St. Paul, MN, 2003, pp. 159–307.

LOUIS PASTEUR

United States Patent No. 135,245 (January 28, 1873).

Cohn, D. V., *The Life and Times of Louis Pasteur,* Lecture, February 11, 1996, www.louisville.edu/library/ekstrom/special/pasteur.cohn (2003).

Hyperlab, Famous French Scientists, *Louis Pasteur,* http://ambafrance-ca.org/HYPERLAB/PEOPLE/_pasteur (2003).

Walsh, J. J., *Louis Pasteur,* New Advent, Catholic Encyclopedia, 1911, 2003, www. newadvent.org/cathen/11536a (2003).

Rhee, Y.R., National Health Museum, About Biotech, *Louis Pasteur (1822–1895),* www.accessexcellence.org/AB/BC/Louis-Pasteur (2003).

BBC Education, Medicine Through Time, *The Industrial Revolution, Disease and Its Treatment, Louis Pasteur (1822–1895),* www.bbc.co.uk/education/medicine/noniut/dt/indtbi4 (2003).

Bartleby.com, *Louis Pasteur (1822–95) Scientific Papers. The Harvard Classics 1909–14,* www.bartleby.com/38/7/1003 (2003).

The World Book Encyclopedia, *Pasteur, Louis,* World Book, Inc. Chicago, 1994, vol. 15, p. 193.

CHAPTER 7

United States Patent Statutes, 35 U.S.C. §103 (1952).

Hotchkiss v. Greenwood, 52 U.S. (11 HOW.) 248 (1850).

Atlantic Works v. Brady, 107 U.S. 192 (1882).

Goodyear Rubber and Tire Company v. Ray-O-Vac Company, 321 U.S. 275 (1944).

Cuno Engineering Corp. v. Automatic Devices Corp., 314 U.S. 84 (1941).

The Great Atlantic & Pacific Tea Company v. Supermarket Equipment Corporation, 340 U.S. 147 (1950).

Graham v. John Deere Company, 383 U.S. 1 (1966).

Francis, W. H. and Collins, R. C. *Cases and Materials on Patent Law,* 4th Ed., West Publishing Co., St. Paul, MN, 1995, pp. 315–336.

ALEXANDER GRAHAM BELL

United States Patent No. 174,465 (March 7, 1876).

Bruce, R. V., *Bell: Alexander Graham Bell and the Conquest of Solitude,* Little, Brown and Company, Boston, 1973, pp. 157–187, 258–280.

United States v. The American Bell Telephone Company, 128 U.S. 315 (Supreme Court 1888).

IEEE Virtual Muesum, IEEE History Center, *Alexander Graham Bell, 1847–1922,* 2003, www.ieee.org/organizations/history-center/legacies/bell (2003).

The World Book Encyclopedia, *Bell, Alexander Graham,* World Book, Inc., Chicago 1994, vol. 2, pp. 240–241.

Fitzgerald Studio, *Alexander Graham Bell, The Inventor,* 2003, www.fitzgerald.ca/html/bell/inventor (2003).

Gorman, M. E., University of Virginia, *Alexander Graham Bell's Path to the Telephone* and references cited therein, 1994, jefferson.village.virginia.edu/albell/introduction (2003).

U.S. House of Representatives, *Text of House Resolution 269 Honoring the Achievements of Antonio Meucci,* June 11, 2002, www.alexcell.org/HR269 (2003).

Fossella, Congressman V. J., *Representative Fossella's Resolution Honoring True Inventor of Telephone to Pass House Tonight,* June 11, 2002, www.house.gov/fossella/pr020611 (2003).

Grosvenor, Edwin S., *News Flash: U.S. House of Representatives Says Alexander Graham Bell Did Not Invent the Telephone,* September 17, 2002, http://hnn.us.comments/2642.html (2003).

Meucci and Bell: The Facts, www.alecbell.org/BellvGlobe.

Complete text of the ruling in the Antonio Meucci case, American Bell Telephone Co. v. Globe Telephone Co. and others, 31 Fed. 728 (S.D.N.Y. 1887), www.alecbell.org/BellvGlobe.

Zanuck, Darryl F., *The Story of Alexander Graham Bell,* 20th Century Fox Film Corporation, released 1939 with Don Ameche and Loretta Young, 20th Century Fox Studio Classic.

CHAPTER 8

United States Patent Statutes, 35 U.S.C. §§ 100, 101, 102(a), (b), (e) & (g), 103, 111, 112, 115, 116, 119, 135, 151, 152, 261 and 262.

Zanuck, Darryl F., *The Story of Alexander Graham Bell,* 20th Century Fox Film Corporation, released 1939 with Don Ameche and Loretta Young, 20th Century Fox Studio Classic.

THOMAS EDISON

United States Patent No. 223,898 (January 27, 1880).

Jonnes, J., *Empires of Light,* Random House, New York, 2003, pp. 55–71.

Josephson, M., *Edison—A Biography,* Francis Parkman Prize Edition, History Book Club, New York, 1959, reprinted 2003, pp. 175–279.

Larson, E., *The Devil in the White City,* Crown Publishers, New York, 2003, pp. 5, 131, 155, 247, 285.

Cheney, M., *Tesla—Man Out of Time,* Dorset Press, New York, 1981, p. 28, 33.

Friedel, R., *New Light on Edison's Light,* Great Inventions That Changed the World, American Heritage Division of Forbes, Inc., 1994, Des Moines, IA, pp. 26–31.

Sahlam, R., *Thomas Alva Edison,* Spectrum Home and School Magazine, C.B. Shaw www.incwell.com/Spectrum (2003) .

U.S. National Park Service, *Edison Biography,* http://www.nps.gov/edis/edbiography.htm (2003).

Rutgers, the State University of New Jersey, A Shorter Chronology of Edison's Life, http://edison.rutgers.edu/brfchron.htm (2003).

Bellis, M., *Inventors—The Inventions of Thomas Edison,* About Network, About, Inc., http://inventors.about.com/library/inventors/bledison.htm (2003).

United States Library of Congress, American Memory, *The Life of Thomas Alva Edison (1847–1931),* http://memory.loc.gov/ammem/edhtml/edbio.html (2003).

CHAPTER 9

United States Patent Statutes, 35 U.S.C. §§ 102, 302–318.

Rockman, H. B., *The Practice of Intellectual Property Law,* Law Bulletin Publishing Company, Chicago, 1998, pp. 27–31.

U.S. Patent and Trademark Office, *Manual of Classification,* available at www.uspto.gov (2003).

GEORGE EASTMAN

United States Patent No. 226,503 (April 13, 1880).

United States Patent No. 388,850 (September 4, 1888).

The World Book Encyclopedia, *Eastman, George,* World Book, Inc., Chicago, 1994, vol. 6, p. 47.

KODAK: *History of Kodak: George Eastman—The Man,* http://www.kodak.com/US/en/corp/aboutkodak/kodakhistory/eastman.shtml (2003).

Bellis, M., *Inventors—George Eastman—The History of Kodak—Rolled Photographic Film,* About Network, About, Inc., http://inventors.about.com/library/inventors/bleastman.htm (2002).

Rose, M. and McLead, H., *George Eastman and His Development of Kodak Equipment,* University of Rochester, http://www.history.rochester.edu/class/Kodak/Kodak.htm (2003).

Kelsey, *George Eastman, Inventor of the Kodak Camera,* School, Chores and Jobs, http://www.kidsnewsroom.com/elmer/InfoCentral/frameset/inventors/eastman/index.html (2003).

The Great Idea Finder, *George Eastman,* http://www.ideafinder.com/history/inventors/eastman.htm (2002).

CHAPTER 10

United States Patent & Trademark Office, MPEP, Chapter 600, Sections 601, 608.01 (a) to (h) (2001, 2003).

Francis, William H. and Collins, Robert C., *Cases and Materials on Patent Law,* 4th Ed., West Publishing Co., St. Paul, MN., 1995, pp. 1–3.

Rockman, H. B., *The Practice of Intellectual Property Law,* Law Bulletin Publishing Company, Chicago, 1998, pp 8–11, 83–98.

United States Patent Statutes, 35 U.S.C. §§ 111–115, 116–118.

OTTMAR MERGENTHALER

United States Patent No. 317,828 (May 12, 1885) .

The World Book Encyclopedia, *Mergenthaler, Ottmar,* World Book, Inc., Chicago 1994, vol. 13, p. 418.

Roberson, *Mergenthaler, Ottmar (11 May 1854–28 Oct. 1899),* University of Central Oklahoma, http://www.libarts.ucok.edu/history/faculty/roberson/course/1493/supplements/chp18/18.%2... (2003).

The Linotype Machine: Thomas Edison Called It the "Eighth Wonder of the World," University of Richmond, 1996, http://oncampus.richmond.edu/academics/journalism/limo.html (2003).

Kahan, B., *Ottmar Mergenthaler—The Man and His Machine,* Oak Knoll Press, New Castle, Del., 1999.

Cazoo Library, *Ottmar Mergenthaler,* German Information Center, New York, 1976, http://www.cazoo.org/library/Ottmar Merganthaler.html (2003).

Infoplease.com, *Mergenthaler, Ottmar,* Columbia Electronic Encyclopedia, Columbia University, New York 1994, 2000, http://www.inforplease.com/ce6/people/A0832771.html (2003).

Shea, *Mergenthaler on U.S. Postage Stamp,* http://www.serve.com/shea/germusa/mergenth.htm (2003).

CHAPTER 11

United States Patent & Trademark Office, MPEP Chapter 600, Sections 608.01 (i) to (n) (2001, 2003).

Rockman, H. B., *The Practice of Intellectual Property Law,* Law Bulletin Publishing Company, Chicago, 1998, pp. 10, 11, 45–82.

Adelman, M. J., Rader, R. R., Thomas, J. R. and Wegner, H. C., *Cases and Materials on Patent Law,* 2nd Ed., Thomson-West, St. Paul, MN, 1998, 2002, p. 12.

NICOLAUS OTTO AND RUDOLF DIESEL

United States Patent No. 365,701 (June 28, 1887).

United States Patent No. 608,845 (August 9, 1898).

Bellis, M., *The History of the Automobile,* About Network, About, Inc., http://inventors.about.com/library/weekly/aacarsgosa.htm (2003).

Moros, R., *Four-Strokecycle-Ottocycle,* University of Leipzig, ITC, 1998, http://techni.tachemie.uni-leipzig.de/otto/otto_g0_eng.html (2003).

European Automotive Hall of Fame, *The Foundation of the Modern Engine,* 2003, http://www.autonews.com/files/euroauto/inductees/otto2002.htm (2003).

Nicolaus Otto, Winnipeg Free Press, Winnipeg, Alberta, Canada, May 2, 2003, http://www.winnipegfreepress.com/autos/articles/profiles/v-printerfriendly/story/1044084 p…(2003).

Bellis, M., *Nicolaus Otto,* About Network, About, Inc., 2003, http://inventors.about.com/library/inventors/blotto.htm (2003).

Nikolaus August Otto: Inventor of the Internal Combustion Engine, Pagewise, Inc., 2001, http://ia.essortment.com/nikolausaugust_rcoe.htm (2003).

Robinson, Rowan, *The Great Book of Hemp,* Park Street Press, Rochester Vermont, 1996, pp. 27–32, 139, 149–151.

Kaiser, Prof. Dr. Walter, *Rudolf Diesel and the Second Law of Thermodynamics,* German News, German Embassy of India, June/July 1997, http://www.germanembassy-india.org/news/june97/76gn16.htm (2003).

Rudolf Diesel: 1858–1913, Hempcar Trans-America, Hemp Car, http://www.hempcar.org/diesel.shtml (2003).

Rödl, Ernst, *The First Diesel Engine,* Deutsches Museum, Munich, Power Machinery Dept., http://www.deutsches-museum.de/ausstell/meister/e_diesel.htm (2003).

Lienhard, J. H., *Engines of Our Ingenuity, No. 1435: Rudolf Diesel,* University of Houston, 1988–2001, http://www.uh.edu/engines/epi1435.htm (2003).

Auer, Georg, European Automotive Hall of Fame, *Renaissance Man Set the Automobile Industry on Fire,* 2002, http://www.autonews.com/files/euroauto/inductees/diesel.htm (2003).

Bellis, M., *Rudolf Diesel (1858–1913),* About Network, About, Inc., 2003, http://inventors.about.com/library/inventors/bldiesel.htm (2003).

CHAPTER 12

United States Patent & Trademark Office, MPEP Chapter 700, Sections 701-724.06, 1300, 1401 et seq., 2200, August 2001, rev. February 2003.

United States Patent Statutes, 35 U.S.C. §§ 101, 102, 103, 112.

Rockman, H. B., *The Practice of Intellectual Property Law,* Law Bulletin Publishing Company, Chicago, 1998, pp. 99–138.

NIKOLA TESLA

United States Patent No. 381,968 (May 1, 1988).

United States Patent No. 645,576 (March 20, 1900).

United States Patent No. 586,193 (July 13, 1897).

Popvić, V., Horat, R., and Nikolić, N., *Nikola Tesla, Lectures, Patents, Articles,* Nikola Tesla Museum, Belgrade, Yugoslavia, 1956.

Cheney, M. *Tesla—Man Out of Time,* Dorset Press, New York, 1981, pp. 1–41, 62–75, 176–184.

Marconi Wireless Telegraph Company of America v. United States, 320 U.S. 1, 87 L. Ed. 1731 (Supreme Court 1943).

IEEE History Center, IEEE Virtual Museum, *Nikola Tesla, 1856–1943,* Rutgers University of New Jersey, http://www.ieee.org/organizations/history_center/legacies/tesla.html (2003).

Tesla and the Exploration of Cosmos, Tesla Memorial Society of New York, New York, http://www.teslasociety.com/radio.htm (2003).

Papadopoulos, P. J., *Nikola Tesla, The Guglielmo Marconi Case—Who is the True Inventor of Radio,* Mercury Research Systems, Greece, http://www.mercury.gr/tesla/marcen.html (2003).

Beaty, W. J., *Tesla Invented Radio?,* 1997, Science Hobbyist, http://www.amasci.com/tesla/tradio.txt (2003).

Tesla—Life and Legacy, *Who Invented Radio?,* Public Broadcasting System, http://www/pbs.org/tesla/11/11_whoradio.html (2003).

Anderson, Leland, *Priority in the Invention of Radio—Tesla vs. Marconi,* Antique Wireless Association, MONOGRAPH (New Series) No. 4, March 1980, pp. 1–9.

CHAPTER 13

United States Patent Statutes, 35 U.S.C. §§ 171–173.

United States Copyright Statues, 17 U.S.C. § 102(a).

HERMAN HOLLERITH

United States Patent No. 395,781 (January 8, 1889).

United States Patent No. 395,782 (January 8, 1889).

O'Connor, J. J. and Robertson, E. F., *Herman Hollerith,* School of Mathematics and Statistics, University of St. Andrews, Scotland, http://www.gap/dcs.st_and.ac.uk/Nhistory/Mathematicians/Hollerith.html (2003).

Russo, M., University of Rochester, *Herman Hollerith, The World's First Statistical Engineer,* http://www.history.rochester.edu/steam/hollerith (2003).

Bellis, Mary, *Herman Hollerith Invented Computer Punch Cards,* About Network, About, Inc. http://inventors.about.com/library/inventors/blhollerith.htm (2003).

NIST Virtual Museum, *Herman Hollerith,* National Institute of Standards and Technology, U.S. Commerce Department, http://museum.nist.gov/panels/conveyor/hollerithbio.htm (2003).

CHAPTER 14

United States Patent Statutes, 35 U.S.C. § 101.

United States Patent and Trademark Office, *Examination Guidelines for Computer-Related Inventions,* February 18, 1996, 61 Fed. Reg. 7478, http://www.uspto.gov/web/offices/com/hearings/software/analysis/files/guides.doc (2003).

Chisum, D. S., Nard, C. A., Schwartz, H. F., Newman, P. and Kieff, F. S., *Principles of Patent Law,* Foundation Press, New York, 1998, pp. 754–764, 788–893.

Adelman, M. J., Rader, R. R., Thomas, J. R., and Wegner, H. C., *Cases and Materials on Patent Law,* 2nd. ed. West Group, St. Paul, MN, 2003, pp. 60–100.

Merges, R. P. and Duffy, J. F., *Patent Law and Policy: Cases and Materials,* 3rd. ed., Matthew Bender & Co., Newark, NJ, 2002, pp. 131–165.

Stobbs, G. A., *Software Patents,* 2nd ed., Aspen Publishers, Inc., New York, 2000, pp. 134–138, 147–159, 172–185, 667–673.

Francis, William H. and Collins, Robert C., *Cases and Materials on Patent Law,* 4th ed., West Publishing Co., St. Paul, MN. 1995, pp. 484–503.

IEEE, *Standard Dictionary of Electrical and Electronics Terms,* 5th ed., 1993, p. 308.

State Street Bank & Trust Co. v. Signature Financial Group, Inc., 149 F.3d 1368 to 1375 (Fed. Cir. 1998).

HEDY LAMARR

Photograph obtained with permission from http://silverscreensirens.com/galleries/hedy.28.htm.

United States Patent No. 2,292,387 (Aug. 11, 1942).

IEEE The Virtual Museum, IEEE History Center, Women's History Month Feature, *Hedy Lamarr,* Rutgers University, N.J., http://www.ieee.org/organizations/history_center/lamarr.html(2003).

Maney, K., USA Today, Money, Technology, *Remember When Movie Stars Invented Stuff to Save the World?,* 2002, http://www.usatoday.com/money/industries/technology/money/2002-09-03-money_x.htm(2003).

Martin, L., IMD6, Internet Movie Database, Inc., *Hedy Lamarr,* 1994, 2002, http://www.Imdb.com/name/nm0001443/(2003).

Boehm, V. and Jackson, D., IMDb Internet Movie Database, Inc., *Biography for Hedy Lamarr,* 1994, http://www.Imdb.com/name/nm0001443/bio (2003).

Introduction, Hedy Lamarr Inventor/Film Star, http://www.britneyspears.ac/physics/intro/hedy.htm (2003).

Baalman, C and Reitcheck, A., *Not Just Another Pretty Face Starring: Hedy Lamarr,* 1999, History Day, http://www.hoxie.org/news99/senior99/hedy/.html (2003).

Bernstein, R.B., 07/07/1999: *Footnote in Movie History: Hedy Lamarr, Brilliant Inventor and Film Star,* http://www.mrcranky.com/movies/fullmonty/108/575.html (2003).

CHAPTER 15

Darwin, C., *On the Origin of Species By Means of Natural Selection, On the Preservation of Favoured Races in the Struggle for Life,* Publisher: John Murray, Albemarle St., London, 1859 .

United States Patent Statutes, 35 U.S.C. §§112, 161–164, 287(c).

United States Patent and Trademark Office, MPEP, Chapter 2400, Sections 2401, 2402, 2411, 2420, 2422.

General Agreement on Tariffs and Trade (GATT), *Trade-Related Aspects of Intellectual Property (TRIPS),* Article 27(3)(a), Uruguay Round Agreements Act, 108 Stat. 4809, 4973,-4990 (1994); See also: www.wto.org/english/docs_e/legal_e/27-trips.pdf.

Chisum, D. S., Nard, C. A., Schwartz, H. F., Newman, P., and Kieff, F. S., *Principles of Patent Law,* Foundation Press, New York, 1998, pp. 286–334.

Merges, R. P. and Duffy, J. F., *Patent Law & Policy: Cases and Materials,* 3rd ed., Matthew Bender & Company, Newark, NJ, 2002, pp. 97–131.

Adelman, M. J., Rader, R. R., Thomas, J. R., and Wegner, H. C., *Cases and Materials on Patent Law,* 2nd. ed., West Group, St. Paul, MN, 2003, pp. 100–132.

Francis, W. H. and Collins, R. C., *Cases and Materials on Patent Law,* 4th ed., West Publishing Company, St. Paul, MN, 1995, pp. 516–526.

Slaughter, D., *From Ideas to Assets,* Berman, B., Editor, John Wiley & Sons, Inc., 2002, pp. 316–321.

ROSALIND FRANKLIN, JAMES WATSON, FRANCIS CRICK, AND MAURICE WILKINS

Maddox, B., Rosalind Franklin, *The Dark Lady of DNA,* Harper Collins, New York, 2002.

Watson, James D. and Berry, A., *DNA, The Secret of Life,* Alfred A. Knopf, New York, 2003, pp. 35–61.

Strak, M., *Race to the Double Helix Took Many Twists, Turns,* The Sunday Sun Newspaper, Baltimore, MD, February 23, 2003, pp. 1A, 14A.

Nelson, B., *Watson On: The Discovery, The Controversy, The Legacy,* Newsday.com, 2003, http://www.newsday.com/news/health/ny_hscov0128,0,4862117.story? call=ny-health-utility (2003).

Stueland, J., Urbano, L., Dell'Orto, G. and Berler, A., *Rosalind Franklin, History of Science 3333H,* December 8, 1997, http://www1.umn.edu/scitech/franklin.htm(2003).

Rosalind Elsie Franklin: Pioneer Molecular Biologist, http://www.sdsc.edu/ScienceWomen/franklin.html(2003).

Ardell, D., *About Biotech-Rosalind Franklin (1920–1958),* http://www.accessexcellence.org/A/B/BC/Rosalind_Franklin.html (2003).

Public Broadcasting System, A Science Odyssey, People and Discoveries, *Rosalind Franklin, 1920–1958,* http://www.pbs.org/wgbh/aso/databank/entries/bofran.html (2003).

CHAPTER 16

United States Patents Nos. 395,781; 395,782; and 395,783 (January 8, 1889).

State Street Bank & Trust Co. v. Signature Financial Group, Inc., 149F.3d 1368, 1375-7 (Fed. Cir. 1998).

United States Patent Statutes, 35 U.S.C. §§101, 273.

European Patent Convention, Rule 52(2), www.european-patent-office.org/legal/epc/e/ma1.htm (2003).

Love, J. J. and Coggins, W. W., *Successfully Preparing and Prosecuting a Business Method Patent Application,* Speech presented at American Intellectual Property Law Association meeting, Spring 2001, http://www.uspto.gov/web/menu/pbmethod/aiplapaper.rtf(2003).

United States Patent and Trademark Office, White Paper, *Automated Financial or Management Data Processing Methods (Business Methods),* http://www.uspto.gov/web/menu/busmethp/index/html (2003).

WILBUR AND ORVILLE WRIGHT

United States Patent No. 821,393 (May 22, 1906).

Crouch, T., *The Bishop's Boys—A Life of Wilbur and Orville Wright,* W. W. Norton, New York, 1989.

The Published Writings of Wilbur and Orville Wright, edited by Jakabar, P. L. and Young, R., Smithsonian Institution Press, Washington, D.C., 2000.

Young, R. C., *Controversy at Kitty Hawk—Who Were the Real Fathers of Powered Flight?,* unpublished paper, Blue Island, IL, 2003.

Wright Brothers Aeroplane Company Museum, *The Wright Story,* http://www.first-to-fly.com/History/Wright%20Story/wright%20story.htm(2003).

CHAPTER 17

United States Patent Statutes, 35 U.S.C. §102.

The Paris Convention for the Protection of Industrial Property, Stockholm revision, 35 U.S.C. §1119, 21 U.S.T. 1583, T.I.A.S. 6295 (rev. 1967), www.wipo.int/treaties/ip/paris/paris/pdf(2003).

The Patent Cooperation Treaty (PCT) of 1978, 28 U.S.T. 7645, TIAS No. 8733 (opened for acceptance June 1970; in force January 1978) www.uspto.gov.int/pct/en/texts/pdf/pct.pdf(2003).

The European Patent Convention (EPC) of 1978, www.european-patent-office.org/legal/epc/e/ma1.html(2003).

Merges, R. P. and Duffy, J. F., *Patent Law and Policy: Cases and Materials,* 3rd ed., Matthew Bender & Company, Newark, N.J., 2002, pp. 54–64, 508–515.

Lange, D., LaFrance, M. and Myers, G., *Intellectual Property, Cases and Materials,* West Group, St. Paul, MN., 1998, pp. 1098–1112.

Adelman, M. J., Rader, R. R., Thomas, J. R. and Wegner, H. C., *Cases and Materials on Patent Law,* 2nd ed., West Group 2003, pp. 699–743.

Stobbs, G. A., *Software Patents,* 2nd ed., Aspen Publishers, Inc., 2000, pp. 491–519.

ROBERT GODDARD

United States Patent No. 1,102,653 (July 7, 1914).

United States Patent No. 2,397,657 (April 2, 1946).

The World Book Encyclopedia, Goddard, Robert Hutchings, World Book, Inc., Chicago, 1994, vol. 8, pg. 244-5.

National Aeronautics and Space Administration, NASA Facts, *Robert H. Goddard: American Rocket Pioneer,* Goddard Space Flight Center, Greenbelt, MD., http://pao.gsfc.nasa.gov/gsfc/service/gallery/fact_sheets/general/goddard/goddard.htm (2003).

Clark University, *Dr. Robert H. Goddard Web Pages,* Clark University, Worcester, MA, 2003, http://www.clarku.edu/offices/library/archives/ExhibitionRoom.htm; and http://www.clarku.edu/offices/library/archives/GoddardBio.htm (2003).

Kluger, J., *Rocket Scientist Robert Goddard,* TIME 100: Scientists & Thinkers, http://www.time.com/time/time100/scientist/profile/goddard.html (2003).

Goddard Biography, http://www.northstar.k12.ak.us/schools/ryn/spacerace/people/goddard.htm (2003).

CHAPTER 18

United States Patent Statutes, 35 U.S.C. §§ 271–273, 281–297.

Rockman, H. B., *The Practice of Intellectual Property Law,* Law Bulletin Publishing Company, Chicago, 1998, pp. 29–30, 139–148.

United States Patent and Trademark Office, *Official Gazette,* published on Tuesday of every week throughout the year.

Stobbs, G. A., *Software Patents,* 2nd Ed., Aspen Publishers, Inc., 2000, pp. 648–662.

Merges, P. R. and Duffy, J. F., *Patent Law and Policy: Cases and Materials,* 3rd Ed. Matthew Bender and Company, Newark, NJ, 2002, pp. 871–1038.

Chisum, D. S., Nard, C. A., Schwartz, H. F., Newman, P. and Kieff, F. S., *Principles of Patent Law,* Foundation Press, New York, 1998, pp. 1030–1271.

Adelman, M. J., Rader, R. R., Thomas J. R., and Wegner, H. C., *Cases and Materials on Patent Law,* 2nd Ed., West Group, St. Paul, MN., 2003, pp. 744–929.

CHARLES KETTERING

United States Patent No. 1,150,523 (August 17, 1915).

United States Patent No. 745,157 (November 24, 1903).

The World Book Encyclopedia, *Kettering, Charles Franklin,* World Book, Inc., Chicago, 1994, vol. 11, p. 307.

van der Linden, P., *Gentlemen! Start Your Engines!,* Rolls-Royce Starter Motors Origin Invention, 2002, http://afu.com/rolls/starter.html (2003).

National Aviation Hall of Fame, WWI, *Charles Kettering—Innovator,* http://www.nationalaviation.org/museum.asp? eraid=2&section=museum (2003).

Bellis, M., *Charles Kettering (1876–1958),* About Network, About, Inc., 2003, http://inventors.about.com/library/inventors/blignition.htm (2003).

Hall, Dr. Arlie, *The Industrial Foundation,* The Lane Report—Manufacturing March 2001, http://www.kybiz.com/lanereport/departments/industry/manufacturing301.html (2003).

CHAPTER 19

United States Patent Statutes, 35 U.S.C. §§ 101, 102, 115, 116, 151, 152, 261, and 262.

Arrow, K.A., *Managing IP Financial Assets -Principles from the Securities Markets,* From Ideas to Assets, edited by Berman, B., John Wiley & Sons, Inc., New York, 2002, pp. 111–116.

Merges, R. P. and Duffy, J. F., *Patent Law and Policy: Cases and Materials,* 3rd Ed., Matthew Bender and Company, Newark, NJ, 2002, pp. 1255–1317.

Stobbs, G. A., *Software Patents,* Aspen Publishers, Inc., New York, 2000, *The Beta Testing License Agreement,* pp. 628–630.

Adelman, M. J., Rader, R. R., Thomas, J. R., and Wegner, H. C., *Cases and Materials on Patent Law,* 2nd Ed. West Group, St. Paul, MN, 2003, pp. 1000–1007, 1056–1074.

PHILO FARNSWORTH

United States Patent No. 1,773,980 (August 26, 1930).

United States Patent No. 1,773,981 (August 26, 1930).

National Inventor's Hall of Fame, Inventor Profile, *Philo Taylor Farnsworth—Television System, Cathode-Ray Tube,* http://www.invent.org/hall_of_fame/56.html (2003).

WhoWasHe, *Philo Taylor Farnsworth,* http://philotfarnsworth.com/whoIsHe.html (2003).

Schatzkin, P., *Reconciling the Historical Origins of Electronic Video,* The Farnsworth Chronicles, 1977, 2001, http://www.farnovision.com/chronicles/tfc-who_invented_what.html (2003).

McCullough, D., *Big Dream, Small Screen (Transcript),* The American Experience, Public Broadcasting System, http://www.pbs.org/wgbh/annex/technology/bigdream/bigdreamts.html (2003).

Postman, Neil, *Electrical Engineer—Philo Farnsworth,* TIME 100: Scientists & Thinkers, http://www.time.com/time/time100/scientist/profile/farnsworth.html (2003).

Patiris, P. D., *A Pilgrimage to the Birthplace of Electronic Television,* Modern Television, 1997, http://www.moderntv.com/modtvweb/media/birthplace1.htm (2003).

San Francisco Chronicle, Second Section, September 3, 1928, *Inventors Online Museum Presents*

Philo Farnsworth Inventor of Television 1928 Article, http://www.inventorssmuseum.com/farnsworth.htm (2003).

Dave, *Science Hero: Philo T. Farnsworth,* Scientist Heroes, 2002, http://www.myhero.com/hero.asp?hero=philoTFarnsworth (2003).

United States Patent and Trademark Office, Decision of Board of Patent Interferences, Patent Interference No. 64027, *Farnsworth v. Zworykin,* Decision date: July 22, 1934; Final hearing: April 24, 1934, obtained by author from Paul Schatzkin, who advised that be obtained the copy from Mrs. Philo T. Farnsworth.

IEEE Virtual Museum, *Vladimir K. Zworykin,* IEEE History Center, 2003, http://www.ieee.org/organizations/history_center/legacies/zworykin.htm (2003).

CHAPTER 20

Ball, F.R., Silverman, M. and Daley, P., Seminar, *Protect Your Client: Non-Competition Agreement Enforcement,* National Business Institute, Duane Morris Law Firm, Chicago, 2003.

Kenyon, R., *Intellectual Property Provisions in Employment Contracts and Policies,* The European Legal Alliance, Paper, Field Fisher Waterhouse, 2002.

Balough, R. C., *Covenants Not To Compete or Trade Secret: Which Is Better When a Key Employee Walks Out the Door?,* Presentation to Intellectual Property Law Association of Chicago, December 1, 1998, http://www.balough.com/writings/covenant.asp (2001).

Vaughn, R. C., *Legal Aspects of Engineering,* 6th Ed., Kendall/Hunt Publishing Company, Dubuque, IA, 1999, pp. 258–9.

WILLIAM LEAR

United States Patent No. 1,944,139 (January 16, 1934).

National Inventors Hall of Fame, Inventor Profile, *William P. Lear,* 2002, http://www.invent.org/hall_of_fame/94.html (2002).

San Diego Aerospace Museum, *William P. Lear, These We Honor,* International Hall of Fame, 1984, http://www.allstar.fiu.edu/aero/lear.htm (2003).

The Lear Archives, *Bill Lear Biography,* http://lear-archives.com/learbiography02.htm.

Michigan Aviation Hall of Fame, William P. Lear, http://www.michiganaviation.org/enshrinees/Bios/lear.html (2003).

CHAPTER 21

Vaughn, R. C., *Legal Aspects of Engineering,* 6th Ed., Kendall/Hunt Publishing Company, Dubuque, IA, 1999, pp. 10–18, 38–40.

Ibsen, Henrik, *Enemy of the People,* Penguin, New York, 1882, 1977.

Federal Rules of Civil Procedure, as amended to May, 2002, Rule 26(a)(2)(B); 26(b)(4); 43.

LUTHER BURBANK

United States Plant Patent No. 15 (April 5, 1932).

Barker, D., *The Forgotten Story of Luther Burbank,* Freethought Today, August 1993, http://www.ffrf.org/fttoday/back/burbankbio.html (2003).

City of Santa Rosa, California, Luther Burbank Home & Gardens, *History,* http://ci.santa-rosa.ca.us/lbhg/history.asp (2003).

Gold Ridge, *Luther Burbank's Experiment Farm, Est. 1885,* Burbank Farm, http://www.wschsgrf.pon.net/bef.htm (2003).

San Jose State University, *Luther Burbank,* SJSU Virtual Museum, http://www.sjsu.edu/depts/Museum/bur.html (2003).

Discovering Books, *Luther Burbank,* http://www.discoveryingbooks.com/burbank (2003).

CHAPTER 22

United States Copyright Statute, 17 U.S.C.:

  Architectural Works—§§ 101, 102(a)(8), 120.

  Copyrightable Works—§§ 102, 103, 104.

  Enforcement—§§ 501, 505, 507(b), 508, 511, 512, 513.

  Exclusive Rights—§§ 106, 107.

  Fair Use—§ 107.

  Fixed in a Tangible Medium—§ 102.

  Literary Works—§ 101.

  Notice—§§ 401–406.

  Registration—§§ 408–412.

  Term of Copyright—§§ 301–305.

  Works for Hire—§§ 101, 201(b).

Library of Congress, Copyright Office, *Copyright Registration for Computer Programs,* Circular 61, 2003, http://www.copyright.gov/circs/circ61.html (2003).

Library of Congress, Copyright Office, *Copyright Registration for Automated Databases, Circular 65, 2003, http://www.copyright.gov/circs/circ65.html (2003).*

Library of Congress, Copyright Office, Copyright Registration for Online Works, Circular 66, 2003, http://www.copyright.gov/circs/circ66.html (2003).

English Statute of Anne, *An Act for the Encouragement of Learning by Vesting the Copies of Printed Books in the Authors or Purchasers of Such Copies, During the Times Therein Mentioned,* 8 Anne c.19 (1709).

Constitution of the United States, Article I, Section 8, Clause 8 (1787).

Convention for the Protection of Literary and Artistic Works, (Berne Convention) signed at Berne, Switzerland, September 9, 1886, accession by United States March 1, 1989, Treaty Document 99-27, 828 U.N.T.S. 221 (Paris rev. 1971).

Halpern, S. W., Shipley, D. E., and Abrams, H. B., *Copyright Cases and Materials,* West Publishing Company, St. Paul, MN, 1992, pp. 1–13, 38–42.

Vaughn, R. C., *Legal Aspects of Engineering,* 6th ed., Kendall/Hunt Publishing Company, Dubuque, IA, 1999, pp. 268–273.

Goldstein, P., *Copyright, Patent, Trademark and Related State Doctrines,* 5th Ed., Foundation Press, New York, 2002, pp. 568–569, 805–893 (Computer Programs).

Lange, D., La France, M., and Myers, G., *Intellectual Property, Cases and Materials,* West Group, St. Paul, MN., 1998, pp. 644–651.

Barrett, M., *Intellectual Property, Cases and Materials,* 2nd Ed., West Group, St. Paul, MN. 2001, pp. 394–402.

Harper & Row Publishers, Inc. v. Nation Enterprises, 471 U.S. 539 (U.S. Supreme Court 1985) (The Gerald Ford Autobiography case).

JOHN BARDEEN, WALTER BRATTAIN, AND WILLIAM SHOCKLEY

United States Patent No. 2,502,488 (April 4, 1950).

United States Patent No. 2,524,035 (October 3, 1950).

Brinkman, W. F., Haggan, D. E. and Troutman, W. W., *A History of the Invention of the Transistor and Where It Will Lead Us,* IEEE Journal of Solid State Circuits, December 1997, vol. 32, No. 12, pp. 1858–65.

American Institute of Physics and SciencCentral, Inc., *Solid State Science Takes Root at Bell,* Public Broadcasting System, 1999, http://www.pbs.org/transistor/background/events…(2003).

Encyclopedia Britannica, *Electronics—Invention of the Transistor: The Solid-State Revolution,* Encyclopedia Britannica, Inc., 1996, http://home.ewha.ac.kr/~ewhaelec/easyie/chapter5/tr.htm (2003).

National Inventors Hall of Fame, *Inventor Profile—John Bardeen,* http://www.invent.org/hall_of_fame/8.html (2003).

National Inventors Hall of Fame, *Inventor Profile—Walter H. Brattain,* http://www.invent.org/hall_of_fame/19.html (2003).

National Inventors Hall of Fame, *Inventor Profile—William Bradford Shockley,* http://www.invent.org/hall_of_fame/134.html (2003).

University of Illinois at Urbana Champagne, *John Bardeen,* http://www.physics.uiuc.edu/People/jbarden.html (2003).

Nobel e-Museum, *John Bardeen—Biography,* The Nobel Prize in Physics 1956, http://www.nobel.se/physics/laweater/1956/bardeen-bio.html (2003).

The Great Idea Finder, *Invention of the Transistor, 2002,* http://www.ideafinder.com/history/inventions/transistor/htm (2003).

Groeger, M., *Invention of the Transistor,* http://www.silicon-valley-story.de/sv/transistor/html (2003).

Macaulay, D., *The Way Things Work,* Houghton Mifflin Company, Boston, 1988, pp. 342–343.

Trefil, J., *Encyclopedia of Science and Technology,* Routledge, New York–London, 2001, pp. 484–485.

The World Book Encyclopedia of Science, Vol. 2, *Physics Today,* World Book, Inc., Chicago, 1994, pp. 126–129.

CHAPTER 23

United States Copyright Statutes, 17 U.S.C. §§ 117, 1201, 1202.

Convention for the Protection of Literary and Artistic Works (Berne Convention), signed at Berne, Switzerland, September 8, 1886, accession by United States March 1, 1989, Treaty Document 99-27, 828 U.N.T.S. 221 (Paris rev. 1971).

WIPO (World Intellectual Property Organization) Copyright Treaty, Adopted by the Diplomatic Conference on December 20, 1996.

WIPO Performance and Phonograms Treaty, Adopted by the Diplomatic Conference on December 20, 1996.

The Digital Millennium Copyright Act of 1998, Public Law No. 105–304, 111 Stat. 2860 (1998).

Library of Congress, Copyright Office, The Digital Millennium Copyright Act of 1998, U.S. Copyright Office Summary, December 1998, pp. 1–14.

Harper, Tieffa, *Does the Digital Millennium Copyright Act Impede Scientific Expression?* Entertainment and Sports Lawyer, American Bar Association Forum on the Entertainment and Sports Industries, vol. 19, no. 4, pp. 1–6.

Goldstein, P., *Copyright, Patent, Trademark and Related State Doctrines,* 5th ed., Foundation Press, New York, 2002, pp. 732–735 .

Barrett, M., *Intellectual Property, Cases and Materials,* 2nd ed., West Group, St. Paul, MN., 2001, pp. 400, 615–618.

United States Copyright Office, *Rulemaking on Exemptions from Prohibition on Circumvention of*

Technological Measures That Control Access to Copyrighted Works, http://www.copyright. gov/1201/ (2003).

JACK KILBY AND ROBERT NOYCE

United States Patent No. 2,981,877 (April 25, 1961).

United States Patent No. 3,138,743 (June 23, 1964).

IEEE History Center, *Jack St. Clair Kilby, 1923– ,* IEEE Virtual Museum, 1986 IEEE Annual Awards Presentation Booklet, 2003, http://www.ieee.org/organization/history_center.legacies/ kilby.html (2003).

IEEE History Center, *Robert N. Noyce, 1927–1990,* IEEE Virtual Museum, 1978 IEEE Annual Awards Presentation Booklet, 2003, http://www.ieee.org/organization/history_center/legacies/ noyce.html (2003).

Texas Instruments, Inc., *About Jack, The Chip that Jack Built Changed the World,* Company Info, 1995–2003, http://www.ti.com/corp/docs/kilbyctr/jackbuilt.shtml (2003).

National Inventors Hall of Fame, *Jack S. Kilby,* Inventor Profile, 2002, http://www.invent. org/hall_of_fame/87.html (2003).

National Inventors Hall of Fame, *Robert N. Noyce,* Inventor Profile, 2002, http://www.invent.org/ hall_of_fame/113.html (2003).

The Great Idea Finder, *Integrated Circuit,* 2002, http://www.ideafinder.com/history/inventions/integratedcircuit.htm (2003).

Pubilc Broadcasting System, *Robert Noyce,* Transistorized, 1999, http://www.pbs.org/transistor/album1/add1bios/noyce.html (2003).

Bellis, M., *Inventors of the Modern Computer,* About, Inc., 2003, http://inventors.about.com/library/weekly/aa080498.htm (2003).

The Robert Noyce Institute of Technology, *Robert Noyce,* Grinnell College, IA, http://www.grinnelliowa.com/noyce/noyce.html (2003).

CHAPTER 24

Semiconductor Chip Protection Act of 1984, 17 U.S.C. §§ 902–914.

United States Copyright Office, *Federal Statutory Protection for Mask Works,* Circular 100, 2003, http://www.copyright.gov/circs/circ100.html (2003).

United States Copyright Office, *Part 211—Mask Work Protection,* a257.g.akamaitech. net/7/257/2422/14mar20010800/edocket.access.gpo.gov/cfr_2002/julqtr/pdf/37cfr211.2.pdf (2003).

Cornell University, Legal Information Institute, U.S. Code Collection, *Notes on Sec. 914,* http://www4.law.cornell.edu/uscode/17/914.notes.html (2003).

FEDERICO FAGGIN, MARCIAN HOFF, AND STANLEY MAZOR

United States Patent No. 3,821,715 (June 28, 1974).

National Inventors Hall of Fame, *Federico Faggin, Inventor Profile, 2002, http://www. invent.org/hall_of_fame/55.html (2003).*

National Inventors Hall of Fame, *Marcian E. (Ted) Hoff,* 2002, http://www.invent.org/hall_ of_fame/79.html (2003).

National Inventors Hall of Fame, *Stanley Mazor,* 2002, http://www.invent.org/hall_of_ fame/100.html (2003).

The Great Idea Finder, *Invention of the Microprocessor,* Ideafinder, http://www.ideafinder.com/history,inventions/microprocessor.htm (2003).

The Great Idea Finder, *M.E. "Ted" Hoff,* Ideafinder, http://www.ideafinder.com/history/inventors/hoff.htm (2003).

Davidson, M. W., *Molecular Expressions: The Silicon Zoo-Federico Faggin,* University of Florida, 1995–2003, http://micro.magnet.fsu.edu/creatures.pages/faggin.html (2003).

CHAPTER 25

American Law Institute, First Restatement of Torts, Sections 757, 758, Copyright 1939, Reprinted with the permission of the American Law Institute.

National Conference of Commissioners on Uniform State Laws, Uniform Trade Secrets Act, Chicago, 1979, rev. 1985.

Illinois Trade Secrets Act, Illinois Revised Statutes 1991, Chapter 140, par. 352, section 2(d).

Lange, D., LaFrance, M. and Myers, G., *Intellectual Property, Cases and Materials,* West Group, St. Paul, MN, 1998, pp. 392–443.

Barrett, M., *Intellectual Property, Cases and Materials,* 2nd ed., West Group, St. Paul, MN., 2001, pp. 36–110.

Goldstein, P., *Copyright, Patent, Trademark and Related State Doctrines,* 5th ed., Foundation Press, New York, 2002, pp. 108–166.

STEPHEN WOZNIAK

United States Patent No. 4,136,359 (January 23, 1979).

Srivastava, M., *Steve Wozniak,* 1996, http://ei.cs.vt.edu/~history/WOZNIAK.htm (2003).

Wolfson, J. and Leyba, J., *An Interview with Steve Wozniak,* San Jose Mercury News, 1996, http://www.thetech.org/revolutionaries/wozniak/i_a.html (2003).

Zeiler, D., *A Conversation with Steve Wozniak,* Sunspot.net-plugged in June 5, 2003, http://www.sunspot.net/technology/custom/pluggedin/bal-mac060503,0,7125240.column?.. (2003).

Zeiler, D. *Wozniak Looks Back,* Sunspot.net-plugged in, June 12, 2003, http://www.sunspot.net/technology/custom/pluggedin/bal-mac061203,0,6666486.column (2003).

National Inventors Hall of Fame, *Steve Wozniak,* Inventor Profile, 2002, http://www.invent.org/hall_of_fame/155.html (2003).

CHAPTER 26

United States Constitution, Article 1, Section 8, Clause 8 (1787).

The Lanham Act Trademark Statute, 15 U.S.C. §§ 1051–1129 (1946):

Applications for Registration, Use Based and Intent to Use §§ 1051, 1057, 1072.

Cancellation Proceedings § 1064.

Declaration of Continued Use § 1065.

Descriptive Marks § 1052(e).

Distinctiveness; Secondary Meaning § 1052(f).

Federal Search Data Base § 1112.

Generic Marks § 1052(e).

Infringement § 1114.

Searching; The International Classification System § 1112.

Opposition Proceedings § 1063.

Publication of Marks § 1062.

Registration Symbol ® § 1111.

Renewal of Registration § 1059.

Rights Obtained by Registration; Exclusive Rights § 1115.

Supplemental Register § 1091.

Barrett, M., *Intellectual Property, Cases and Materials,* 2nd ed., West Group, St. Paul, MN., 2001, pp. 674–963.

Lange, D., LaFrance, M., and Myers, G., *Intellectual Property, Cases and Materials,* West Group, St. Paul, MN., 1998, pp. 88–169.

Rockman, H., *The Practice of Intellectual Property Law,* Law Bulletin Publishing Company, Chicago, 1998, pp. 157–180.

Cotrone, C., *The United States and the Madrid Protocol: A Time to Decline, A Time to Accede,* Marquett Intellecutal Property Law Review, 4 Marq. Intell. Prop. L. Rev. 75 (2000).

World Intellectual Property Organization (WIPO), Protocol Relating to the Madrid Agreement Concerning the International Registration of Marks (as signed at Madrid on June 27, 1989), WIPO Publication No. 204(E), http://www.wipo.org/madrid/en/legal_texts/madrid_protocol.htm (2003).

McGrath, K., Elias, S. and Shena, S., *FAQ: Registering a Trademark,* Nolo Press, Legal Encyclopedia, 1998, http://nolo.com/ChunkPCT/PCT30.html (1998).

PERCY JULIAN

United States Patent No. 2,752,339 (June 26, 1956).

Public Broadcasting System, *Percy Julian 1899–1975,* A Science Odyssey: People and Discoveries, 1998, http://www.pbs.org/wgbh/aso/databank/entries/bmjuli.html (2003).

National Inventors Hall of Fame, *Percy Lavon Julian,* Inventor Profile, 2002, http://www.invent.org/hall_of_fame/84.html (2003).

Percy Julian, http://www.blackinventor.com/pages/percyjulian.html (2003).

Lienhard, J. H., *No. 659: Percy Julian,* Engines of Our Ingenuity, 1988–97, http://www.uh.edu/engines/epi659.htm (2003).

The Chemical Heritage Foundation, *Chemical Achievers, Percy Lavon Julian and Carl Djerassi,* 2000, http://www.chemheritage.org/Educationalservices/chemach/ppb/ld.html (2003).

Hurder, S., *Meeting the Challenges,* A Brief History of Oak Park, Historical Society of Oak Park and River Forest, 1996–2001, http://www.oprf.com/history/challenges.html (2003).

The Historical Society of Oak Park and River Forest, *Dr. Percy L. Julian,* 2003, http://www.oprf.com/oprfhist/julianp.htm (2003).

Pristone Entertainment Ltd., *Percy Julian, A. Man of Great Medical Discoveries,* Black History Daily, 1999, 2000, http://blackseek.com/bh/2001/02_PercyJulian.htm (2003).

CHAPTER 27

The Internet Corporation for Assigned Names and Numbers, http://www.icann.org (1993).

The Anticybersquatting Consumer Protection Act, Public Law No. 106-113, 113 Stat. 1501; 15 U.S.C. 1125(d), 1129 (1999).

CURRENT EVENTS

Josephson, Matthew, *Edison—A Biography,* History Book Club, New York, 1959, 2003, pp. 343–350.

Jonnes, Jill, *Empires of Light,* Random House, New York, 2003, pp. 141–229, 247–275.

Larson, Erik, *The Devil in the White City,* Crown Publishers, New York, 2003, pp. 131, 247, 373.

Cheney, Margaret, *Tesla, Man Out of Time,* Dorset Press, New York, 1981, pp. 38–50, 70, 88.

Tesla, Nikola, *On Electricity,* Speech, The Ellicott Club, Buffalo, New York, January 12, 1897, Nikola Tesla, Lectures, Patents Articles, Nikola Tesla Museum, Belgrade, 1956, pp. A-101 to A-108.

Index